D0679625

WAR FROM THE TOP

WAR FROM THE TOP

*German and British Military Decision Making
during World War II*

ALAN F. WILT

INDIANA UNIVERSITY PRESS
Bloomington and Indianapolis

© 1990 by Alan F. Wilt

All rights reserved

No part of this book may be reproduced or utilized in any form or by
any means, electronic or mechanical, including photocopying and
recording, or by any information storage and retrieval system, without
permission in writing from the publisher. The Association of American
University Presses' Resolution on Permissions constitutes the only
exception to this prohibition.

The paper used in this publication meets the minimum requirements
of American National Standard for Information Sciences—Permanence of Paper
for Printed Library Materials, ANSI Z39.48-1984.

⊗™

Manufactured in the United States of America

Library of Congress Cataloging-in-Publication Data

Wilt, Alan F.
    War from the top : German and British military decision making
during World War II / Alan F. Wilt.
        p.   cm.
    Includes bibliographical references.
    ISBN 0-253-36455-8 (alk. paper)
        1. World War, 1939–1945—Campaigns.   2. World War, 1939–1945—
Germany.   3. World War, 1939–1945—Great Britain.   4. Strategy.
I. Title.
D757.W545   1990
940.54'01—dc20   89-45566
                                                            CIP

1 2 3 4 5   94 93 92 91 90

Contents

Preface   vii

Acknowledgments   x

ONE. Directing the War   1

TWO. Running the War: The Organization   24

THREE. Running the War: The Personalities   42

FOUR. Planning the War: The Early Years   62

FIVE. Planning the War: The Middle and
Later Phases   86

SIX. Fighting the War, 1939–1940   120

SEVEN. The Russian Front, 1941–1943   154

EIGHT. North Africa and Sicily, 1941–1943   177

NINE. The Battle of the Atlantic   207

TEN. Strategic Bombing vs. Air Defense   226

ELEVEN. Burma and Western Europe, 1944–1945   246

Conclusion   286

Appendix: Code Names   295

Notes   299

Bibliography   350

Index   378

LIST OF MAPS, FIGURES, AND TABLES

MAPS

6-1:	Polish Campaign, 1939	123
6-2:	Battle of France	138
7-1:	Russo-German Front, 1941–43	159
8-1:	North African and Sicily Campaigns, November 1941–May 1943	184
11-1:	Burma Campaigns, 1944	251
11-2:	Western Front, 1944–45	268

FIGURES

2-1:	British Chiefs of Staff	26
2-2:	German High Command, 1939–42	26
2-3:	German High Command, 1942–45	32

TABLES

4-1:	Aircraft and Tank Production, 1939–41	84
5-1:	Tank Production, 1942–44	101
5-2:	Aircraft Production, 1942–44	102
5-3:	Aircraft Production (By Type)	103
5-4:	Armed Forces (In Millions)	104
6-1:	Opposing Forces for the Polish Campaign, September 1939	122
6-2:	Opposing Forces for the Battle of France, May 1940	136
7-1:	Opposing Forces at the Onset of Barbarossa, June 1941	157
8-1:	Opposing Forces at El Alamein, October 1942	194
9-1:	Allied Merchant Ship Losses, 1942	209
9-2:	German Submarines, 1942	210
9-3:	German Submarine Characteristics	211
9-4:	Total Allied Merchant Ship Losses and North Atlantic Losses, January–May 1943	218
9-5:	German Submarine Losses and North Atlantic Losses, January–May 1943	219
9-6:	Coastal Command Actions, April–May 1943	221
9-7:	Submarine Kills, April–May 1943	223
9-8:	Allied Gains in Merchant Shipping	225
10-1:	Bomber Command, 1942	235
10-2:	Bomber Command, 1943	241
10-3:	8th Air Force Heavy Bomber Missions, 1943	242
11-1:	Opposing Forces on the Eve of Overlord, June 1944	267

Preface

Despite the veritable flood of books and articles on World War II, various dimensions of that immense conflict still remain relatively neglected. Not only do the economic, political, and social contexts of the war as part of the "new" military history need to be examined in much greater depth, but even certain military aspects have not received the attention they deserve. This is especially the case when one looks for comparative studies of the war.[1]

Why has there been so little comparative research on the war's major developments? Why virtually no comparisons even of the major belligerents? One reason, no doubt, stems from the vastness of the conflict. It affected all corners of the globe, was an integral part of this century's technological revolution, and was truly a total war fought at home as well as at the battle fronts. In fact, it has been considered too multidimensional to be comprehended in its entirety. Another reason is that the war is too recent—at least for historians—to have been assimilated into the mainstream of historical periodization. The Middle Ages in Europe conjures up certain notions—no matter how erroneous—as do the Renaissance, the Reformation, and the Industrial Revolution. But World War II has only begun to be fitted into the historical mosaic, and it will be some time before its place in history can be put into proper perspective. A further reason for the dearth of comparative research on the war is historians' seeming inability to find an adequate model. Perhaps social scientists or the growing number of quantitative historians have proper models, but I have not found one that can be adapted for our purposes. I therefore decided to use the traditional approach of looking at the war from the top down. This is not an attempt to study the origins of the military decisions reached by the various combatants, enlightening as that process may be, but rather primarily an examination of the decisions once they have been formulated. The scheme I have worked out is straightforward: first, to assess the roles of the national war leaders—or, if one prefers, that of the warlords or war directors; second, to discuss the mechanism the military used for running the war, namely, the high-command systems; third, to describe the strategies worked out by the military decision makers; and then, fourth, to give a number of examples of the carrying out of their various strategies, indicating where they were right and where they went wrong. In this way it will be possible to look at the effects of decision making from the leadership at the top, down to the actual operations themselves.

Rather than attempting to cover all the major combatants—a task better left to a team of historians—this investigation is limited to two nations—Great Britain and Germany. Both countries obviously form excellent examples of comparison and contrast. Not only was one a democracy and the other an authoritarian state, but they also exemplify two contrasting societies with two quite different leaders during the war. Yet both were the only European powers directly involved from beginning to end. They were constantly fighting each other, and their combat encompassed warfare in all of its then possible land, sea, and air dimensions. And now, with increased access to archival intelligence materials, documentation on Great Britain's and Germany's military forces is relatively comprehensive as well as readily available. These two systems therefore lend themselves to an extended comparison.

The framework used is first an examination of Hitler and Churchill (and to a limited extent Neville Chamberlain during the first eight months of the war) and their considerable influence on the military decision-making process. This is followed by a comparison of Britain's chief-of-staff system with Germany's less streamlined version, an assessment of both nations' military strategies as they changed throughout the conflict, and then a description of the transformation of their strategies into actual operations. In the last instance, eleven different campaigns are discussed, a number that makes it possible to evaluate the variety of commitments undertaken by each side. Those to be emphasized are as follows:

Germany	*Great Britain*
Poland (1939)	Blockade (1939)
France (1940)	France (1940)
Britain (1940)	Britain (1940)
Barbarossa (1941)	Crusader (1941)
Brunswick (1942)	El Alamein (1942)
Kursk (1943)	Sicily (1943)
Atlantic (1943)	Atlantic (1943)
Air Defense of Reich (1943–45)	Strategic Bombing (1942–43)
Gazala (1942)	Burma (1944)
Normandy (1944)	Normandy (1944)
Ardennes (1944)	Veritable-Grenade (1945)

As is evident, many operations involved head-to-head combat between Germany and Britain, but others do not. The focus, however, is not so much on the confrontations between the two combatants as it is on how and why they conducted the war as they did.

The comparative approach allows us to analyze a number of issues from fresh perspectives. For example, the military traditions of both nations—Britain as the foremost sea power, Germany as a dominant land power—provide the necessary backdrop for understanding the early stages of the war, from an offense-oriented Germany to a defense-minded Britain (even though Churchill seldom, if ever, thought in defensive terms). Likewise, the governmental systems of Britain's democracy and Germany's dictatorship generally shaped the political and administrative structures with which these countries prosecuted the war. With regard to the economy, although material factors largely determined the war's outcome, the methods and extent to which the British and German war machines marshaled resources for the conflict differed markedly.[2] Along similar lines, despite the driving force of technology, the tactics by which the armed forces fought the war differed according to the strategies each side adopted.[3] Thus, the comparative approach, by giving us a different perspective on political, economic, and especially military issues, can thereby contribute to a better understanding of the war in all its aspects.

Acknowledgments

Over the years of doing research and writing this book, I have incurred many debts. Iowa State University provided me with faculty leaves at critical stages. The staffs of the United States National Archives, the Public Record Office, the Bundasarchiv-Militärarchiv, the Imperial War Museum, the British Museum Library, the USAF Historical Research Center, and the Liddell Hart Centre for Military Archives gave me untold assistance in my research. Fellow historians Donald McKale, Marc Milner, Earl Ziemke, Robin Higham, and Charles Burdick graciously read portions of the manuscript and saved me from errors of fact and interpretation. Colleagues who form the Vigilantes group at Iowa State University also criticized a number of chapters. Errors which remain are, of course, my responsibility. Audrey Burton typed and retyped the manuscript with her usual efficiency, and Karen S. Craig of Indiana University Press was especially helpful in editing the manuscript for publication. To the above individuals my heartfelt thanks. I would finally like to thank again my wife, Maureen, for her love and encouragement that have sustained me for more than a quarter of a century.

ONE

Directing the War

In war, as in other endeavors, decision making is most often concentrated at the top. This has been the case in the twentieth century as in the past, and it certainly applies to Germany and Great Britain during World War II. These two countries, like the others, depended on civilian leaders to direct the war, and whatever one thinks of Adolf Hitler and Winston Churchill, there is no doubt of their conspicuous, one is tempted to say overwhelming, presence as war leaders. They directed their countries' war efforts up close, not only in the political sense as chancellor and as prime minister, but in the military sense as well. Churchill, when he took office on May 10, 1940, also became minister of defence. From these two positions he oversaw Britain's grand strategy along with the military part of that strategy. As Harry Hopkins, President Franklin Roosevelt's trusted adviser, reported to Roosevelt after visiting the British Isles in early 1941: "Churchill is the government in every sense of the word—he controls the grand strategy and often the details."[1]

Hitler's position as it evolved within the German military hierarchy became even more dominant. When he became president as well as chancellor in August 1934, officers and enlisted personnel took an oath to serve him instead of the "nation and fatherland" as before. In 1938, he became head of the armed forces following drummed-up scandals against Field Marshal Werner von Blomberg, the minister of war, and General Werner von Fritsch, the commander-in-chief of the army. In December 1941, Hitler assumed command of the army itself. As he became more and more enmeshed in the ever broadening war, he began to devote all of his efforts to it, often at the expense of other governmental matters. In August 1944, Hitler described his single-minded concern with the war in the following terms: "For the past five years I have cut myself off from the other [civilian] world. . . . I live only for the single task of leading this struggle."[2] In conducting the struggle, Hitler—and Churchill—were the dominant forces for their respective nations.

Historically, both leaders seemed to represent their countries' glorious military pasts. In Britain, Churchill was cast as the latest in a long line of great wartime prime ministers, from the Elder and Younger Pitt in the eighteenth century to Lloyd George in World War I. In Germany, Hitler saw himself as a warlord in the mold of Frederick Barbarossa and Frederick the Great.

Nevertheless, despite their influential roles, their war leadership has not been compared on any extended basis.[3] The reason is not difficult to ascertain. Churchill is seen, at least in the West, as one of the great figures of the twentieth century, the defender of freedom, a person of charm and wit, and the embodiment of good. Hitler is viewed as one of the most tyrannical figures of our time, the perpetrator of Nazi aggression, a man of crude and vulgar tastes, the incarnation of evil. The Führer, in short, is a repulsive individual when compared to the British prime minister. Yet their differences— even if overdrawn—should not dissuade us, more than forty years later, from evaluating in some depth their leadership in the war effort.

How can these two quite different individuals be characterized? With regard to Hitler (1889–1945), even though he lacked the stature of Churchill (or of Schweitzer or Gandhi, for that matter), he continues to be a person of never-ending fascination.[4] Despite prodigious efforts by historians, we know comparatively little about his early life except that he was the son of a minor Austrian official, received no extensive formal education, lived for a time in Vienna, and served in the German army during World War I, eventually rising to the rank of lance corporal. Yet his commonplace beginnings did not deter him from becoming a prominent political figure during the 1920s and the chancellor of Germany in January 1933 at the age of forty-three.

Hitler's personality is difficult to plumb.[5] In a sense he changed a good deal, especially during the war. Between 1939 and 1941, he became ever more self-confident as he learned about the military process and as Germany moved from success to success. But once reverses began to set in, he became more intractable and "fanatical" in outlook and would brook no interference in his desire to conduct the war only according to his dictates. Yet in another sense he did not change. As Sebastian Haffner has pointed out, there was "no development, no maturing in Hitler's character and personality." It was an "arrested," if consistent, character to which nothing was added over the years. It comprised a number of negative traits—a diabolical ruthlessness, an iron will, excessive aggressiveness and opportunism. But these traits also have a positive, if "hard," connotation to them. Ruthlessness cannot always be divorced from necessity. The will to power need not be negative. Aggression at times is closely related to boldness and daring. Opportunism can bring about positive results. Hitler's conduct exhibited such positive aspects as well.

Hitler's other dominant characteristics also display a certain dichotomy. He was bright—so bright, in fact, that he often put the generals and bureaucrats to shame, especially when it came to detailed knowledge on particular subjects. Yet his intelligence had its limitations. Albert Speer, his close associate, writes of Hitler's dilettantism:

> Amateurishness was one of Hitler's dominant traits. He had never learned a profession and basically had always remained an outsider to all fields of endeavor. Like many self-taught people, he had no idea what real specialized knowledge

meant. Without any sense of the complexities of any great task, he boldly assumed one function after another. . . .

He seemed to be constantly endeavoring to show himself the equal of or even the superior of the experts. The real expert sensibly does not burden his mind with details that he can look up or leave to an assistant. Hitler, however, felt it necessary for his own self-esteem to parade his knowledge. But he also enjoyed doing it.[6]

Another trait, Hitler's charisma, has been commented upon many times. One need only watch Leni Riefenstal's *The Triumph of the Will* or one of Hitler's filmed speeches to appreciate his love of spectacle, his magnetism, and his ability to inspire the German populace. Although he stood only 5'9" and weighed barely 150 pounds, he seemed to be born for the podium. But even his ability to inspire his audience has to be qualified. His public addresses often displayed attributes of acting, striking a pose rather than dealing with matters of real substance. In fact, he prided himself on wearing a mask, on never showing his true self. Though a brilliant orator, his conversations in more intimate settings brought out the other side of his nature. While he could be charming, even witty, in the company of women and with friends and foreign dignitaries, he could also be extremely brutal, vulgar, and given to fits of rage, especially during the war, when his speech increasingly reflected his barracks-like existence. If his conversations could be crude, his writing was even worse. *Mein Kampf* is so turgid and poorly conceived that one suspects it was much more praised than read even in the homes of the faithful. His artistic tastes were more commendable, however; he was greatly interested in the music of Wagner and in architecture, which he discussed with Speer at great length.

Also, Hitler had a *petit bourgeois* quality, a type of ordinariness which endeared him to males and females alike. He lived simply, loved children, enjoyed flowers. Unmarried (until the last day of his life), he was, as his propagandists put it, married to the German people.

Hitler did not, however, reciprocate the adulation of his subjects. As Eberhard Jäckel points out:

In general, the relationship of the Germans to Hitler rested on deception, conscious deception on his part and self-deception on their part. He concealed his plans from them, although he knew exactly what he wanted, and they failed to recognize in him a causal agent even when he translated his intentions into actions. They rewarded his deception with trust and, even under the worst circumstances, did not believe that they were being deceived but rather that he was being deceived.[7]

While the people were engaging in "if the Führer only knew" fantasies, his ultimate deception was that he neither loved nor respected them except for the power they could give him. When the Wehrmacht began to suffer defeats, he contended that the German people were unworthy of him. When the defeats led to disaster, their unworthiness generated utter disdain on his part. If he lost, Germany and its people should also lose, to the point of destruction if necessary. He thus equated Germany's fate with his own.

If Hitler's view of the population at large was based on deceit, his treatment of his associates was more varied. Toward his personal staff he was correct, respectful, at times even concerned about their welfare. Toward close associates, especially those who had shared in the mythological "years of struggle," he displayed a fondness and loyalty which often made him reluctant to remove many of them, though incompetent, from party or government positions. As for civil servants and business leaders, he generally left them alone, thereby gaining their support.[8]

Regarding the two other elements so necessary for waging war, the diplomatic and the military, Hitler has been pictured as treating them with contempt. This view is largely correct, though it does need some modification. He determined the broad outlines of foreign policy and tied them closely to his war program—campaigns to the east and west which would in turn prepare for the defeat of the Soviet Union and an eventual war against the United States.[9] During 1938, he rid himself of the conservative and traditional Konstantin von Neurath as foreign minister and replaced him with someone more to his liking, Joachim von Ribbentrop. While he was willing to listen to some of his diplomats' ideas, including those of Anglophobe von Ribbentrop, in the end the Führer never abandoned his basic concepts. By late 1940, he had pushed aside von Ribbentrop's schemes for a "continental bloc," which was to include the Soviet Union, and the officials of the foreign office were thereafter definitely relegated to subordinate roles. They exercised some latitude in minor projects, but the major decisions had to conform to Hitler's preconceived notions.

As for the military, Hitler detested many of the generals, such as Ludwig Beck, Franz Halder, and even Erich von Manstein, but admired others, such as Walter Model, Heinz Guderian, and for a time Erwin Rommel. While holding the generals up to ridicule, he realized he needed them.[10] Not only did he "learn a lot from them, studying their methods and adopting their vocabulary," but he also required their expertise for running the war, from the deployment of reserves to the training of troops to logistical considerations. Nevertheless, during the course of the war, he stripped the army not only of its privileged position, but of its dignity and conscience as well. Toward the navy, he was more favorably disposed.[11] He got along well with Grand Admiral Erich Raeder until the end of 1942. His relationship with Raeder's successor, Karl Dönitz, was sincere and frank, and he allowed Dönitz to deal with naval matters much as he saw fit. Hitler's view of the air force changed during the course of the war. As long as Reichsmarschall Hermann Göring and his Luftwaffe were gaining victories, the Führer was very positive toward them, holding up their attitude and reliability as traits the army could well emulate.[12] But when the victories gave way to defeats, Hitler's respect for Göring and his staff (some contend as early as the Battle of Britain) diminished to the point that by 1944 "his aversion against the Luftwaffe and the Luftwaffe general staff . . . reached its high point."[13] In fact, Hitler became so disgruntled with General Werner Kreipe, one of his last air force chiefs of staff, that he forbade him from setting foot inside the Führer's headquarters and had him replaced.

An additional aspect of Hitler's makeup that requires comment is his rationality. Popular belief after the war has held that he was indeed a madman, particularly toward the end of his life. With regard to military as well as other issues, however, the notion of Hitler's being a raving psychotic is difficult to support.[14] He was, no doubt, indecisive, obstinate, arrogant to the point perhaps of considering himself irreplaceable. He also committed numerous blunders both large and small—so many, in fact, that psychohistorian Robert Waite suggests his mistakes were probably "the result of a strong, unconscious impulse for self-destruction."[15] Hitler has further been accused of making his military decisions on an intuitive rather than factual basis. But while his "intuitive genius" may have played a role in his decisions before 1939, it was only evident to a limited extent, if at all, once the war began. That in many cases his decisions were wrong does not mean that they were irrational or unsupported. As the Israeli historian Martin van Creveld has noted, ". . . it is necessary to stress that Hitler's decisions, whether right or wrong, were not just the ravings of a deranged dictator. In almost all cases they were based on some kind of reason. . . . To say this is not to vindicate him; rather, it is to indict him more strongly. For a maniac is not responsible for his actions. Hitler was."[16]

Before examining Hitler's normal daily routine, it is instructive to note where he actually was during the war years.[17] During the conflict, he had fourteen headquarters built for him and occupied six of them. From September 1939 until the onset of the Russian campaign in June 1941, he resided mainly in Berlin, though he moved about more early in the conflict than later on. He was at headquarters or near the fronts a good deal during the Polish and French campaigns, spent considerable time at his mountain retreat, the Berghof, especially during the last half of 1940, and visited allied and neutral leaders at various locations in Europe. But once the war began on the Russian Front, he spent almost all of his time at the Wolf's Lair, a dreary headquarters he had built near Rastenberg in East Prussia, or at his Werewolf headquarters near Vinnitsa in the Ukraine. In March 1943, on the insistence of his doctors, he started spending less time at his eastern "monasteries." During the spring in both 1943 and 1944, he stayed primarily at the Berghof, though in the summer and autumn months he went back to his eastern headquarters to oversee the war from there. On July 14, 1944, he left his beloved residence in the Bavarian Alps, never to return, and in November of that year, as the front in the east contracted, he departed the Wolf's Lair for the last time. During the final months of the war, except for five weeks at his Eagles'

Nest headquarters near Bad Nauheim, where he directed the ups and downs of the Ardennes offensive, he lived in the Reich Chancellery in Berlin, fittingly spending his last days in an underground bunker beneath the Chancellery garden before committing suicide on April 30. Overall, during the 2,069 days in which Hitler was involved in the war, he spent approximately 945 of them in the east at headquarters (and occasionally at the front), 492 in Berlin, and 366 at the Berghof (or at nearby Klessheim Castle, where he often met foreign dignitaries).

His daily work schedule varied, depending on where he was at any given time, but it followed a general pattern.[18] Each morning, Hitler studied the latest reports from the war fronts, including, as the war went on, enemy night-bombing attacks. Between nine and ten, he took a walk, often in a woods, with his dog and possibly some assistants. Then he read morning newspapers and worked on government papers until the main military conference of the day.

At these formal meetings, which began at noon and usually lasted two to three hours, Hitler initiated most of his important military decisions. The conferences consisted of a number of briefings, which covered the war theaters and other events of the past twenty-four hours as well as special topics, such as new weapons research or war-production statistics. The Führer usually listened attentively and interjected his thoughts on occasion, but also allowed others to add their opinions. Contrary to popular belief, General Alfred Jodl, his main briefing officer, and others contend that Hitler seldom made strategic decisions on the spur of the moment. For such decisions he often relied on materials he had received days ahead of time and used these, plus advice from service representatives attending the meetings, as the basis for issuing initial instructions. His *Oberkommando der Wehrmacht* (OKW) staff then fashioned his instructions into a draft directive, and after input from the services involved, a detailed plan was worked out for further discussion and the Führer's eventual approval. Once his decision had been made, OKW prepared a final directive subject only to last minute changes he might desire. In addition to such general directives, Hitler issued more specific orders to commands at lower levels, increasingly so after fall 1941.

After the midday conference, Hitler ate a light meal and filled the rest of his afternoon with dictation, reception of guests, and discussions with military, party, and government representatives. At six o'clock he would hear the latest reports from the fronts, and at eight would sit down to the main meal of the day. The atmosphere around the dinner table changed considerably as the war dragged on. At first as many as fifteen guests might be invited, often including Himmler, Goebbels, Robert Ley, or other party leaders, the Reich press chief, Otto Dietrich, and one of Hitler's doctors, Theo Morell. To the Führer's left sat Jodl, opposite him Martin Bormann and Field Marshal Wilhelm Keitel, and at the end of the table government liaison officials and military adjutants. The conversation, though dominated by Hitler's monologues, was often fresh, spirited, sometimes even lighthearted. After Stalingrad, however, the number of people invited was severely restricted, and Hitler usually preferred to dine only with secretaries, who were subjected to his increasingly long-winded diatribes.[19]

After dinner, the Führer went to his quarters, sometimes with guests to critique the most recent newsreel or perhaps to relax. During this time he often made a telephone call to Eva Braun. At midnight was a less formal briefing, in which younger staff officers reported the latest developments. This was followed by tea and cakes before the Führer retired to bed, sometimes not until four in the morning.

This rigorous routine, in which as Hitler himself stated military decisions alone consumed roughly ten hours each day, took its toll.[20] Not only did it put enormous strains on Hitler's military advisers, but as one of his biographers, Joachim Fest, has noted, it actually "did violence to his nature and was in deliberate opposition to his inveterate yearning for passivity and indolence." Nevertheless, it accorded with Hitler's desire to direct the war in all of its aspects.

The British leader, Winston Churchill (1874–1965), presents an interesting contrast to the National Socialist dictator. Churchill's life before he became prime minister is well known.[21] A descendant of the Duke of Marlborough, he was born in Blenheim Palace and attended public school at Harrow and military college at Sandhurst before serving as a subaltern in India and a war correspondent during the Boer War. He was initially elected to Parliament as a Conservative in 1899, switched parties for a variety of reasons, though mainly over free trade, and first became a minister as a Liberal in 1905. The most notable event in his early career occurred during World War I when he resigned as first lord of the admiralty for his part in the Gallipoli disaster. He went on to serve a tour on the Western Front and, because of his great abilities, was once again named to governmental positions, first as a Liberal and then as a Conservative in the late teens and twenties. In 1929 the Labor Party returned to power, and Churchill left office. At this point he began his years in the "wilderness," brought on largely by his unwavering opposition to the Conservative Party's more "liberal" policy toward India as well as to Neville Chamberlain's appeasement policies. Yet when the war broke out, Chamberlain called on Churchill to become an integral part of his wartime government, again as first lord. At age sixty-five, Churchill was serving in this capacity when the King, on May 10, 1940, asked him to become prime minister.

Like Hitler, Churchill is an exceedingly interesting individual.[22] And like the Führer, he exhibited numerous seemingly contradictory qualities. On the one hand, one of Churchill's most noteworthy characteristics was his ability to separate the important from the unimportant, to get quickly to the heart of a matter, to simplify complex issues. On the other hand, he was constantly concerned about minutiae, from examining daily reports of the number of tons of goods Axis ships unloaded at North African ports in early 1943 to asking "whether wax could be supplied to troops to put in their ears in order to deaden the noise of warfare."[23] While his desire to oversee the war in detail was in part a result of Churchill's boundless energy, it also proved frustrating to advisers and subordinates.

The war also brought to the fore a number of Churchill's other attributes. His pugnacity and insistence on fighting back were at times offset by his impetuous, changeable nature. His vitality and drive gave way on occasion to restlessness and impatience. His vivid imagination and willingness to entertain new ideas sometimes led him to advocate impractical, even impossible, undertakings. Once he had formed an opinion, it was only with great difficulty and persistence that advisers could persuade him to abandon it. Still, overall he displayed an amazingly flexible mind which went hand in hand with his inflexible purpose to do everything within his power "to win a complete and decisive victory over the forces of evil."[24]

An important negative aspect of Churchill's character was that he "suffered from prolonged and recurrent fits of depression."[25] For the most part, he was able to master this "dark dog" mentality with ceaseless activity. In fact, he was often depressed when not occupied, and a number of his achievements can be attributed to his success in overcoming his depressive temperament. Another aspect of Churchill's habits that deserves brief mention is his supposedly excessive drinking. Here, the evidence is not clear-cut. No one around him has denied that Churchill enjoyed a drink, or even quite a few in many instances, and some have contended that he was dependent on, but not addicted to, alcohol. Admiral Sir Andrew Cunningham, First Sea Lord toward the end of the war, goes so far as to describe a late-night meeting in the following terms: "There is no doubt that the P.M. was in no state to discuss anything. Very tired and too much alcohol."[26] But Sir John Colville, one of Churchill's private secretaries and a close associate, writes that he never saw him drunk "as the media and the less well-informed writers sometimes suggest that he frequently was." Nevertheless, the point is that whether or not Churchill on occasion had too much to drink, it did not seem to affect his conduct of the war.

As an orator and writer, Churchill had no peers. Although he stood only 5'6½" and was too heavy because of his love of food and drink, his speeches, which he composed himself, were generally inspiring, clear, and imaginative.[27] He had an "inspired instinct for the right word." His speeches are so memorable, in fact, that writers who attempt to characterize Churchill have to be on guard not to lapse into a series of Churchillian quotations. His rhetorical talents are mirrored in his writing. Although he was more interested in reading history than poetry or fiction, his many books reflect his artistic temperament— his love of broad strokes, color, show, magnificence.[28] His lengthy memoranda—and he wrote many of them—show a mastery of the English language which was particularly helpful in clarifying matters of strategy. In other artistic endeavors, his talents were more limited. He took up painting at age forty, and his landscapes showed ability, though not the introspective touch of many other artists. In music, his tastes remained at the level of Gilbert and Sullivan and music-hall songs.

Churchill's ability as a conversationalist is also open to some criticism.[29] No doubt his conversation could be forceful, brilliant, laced with wit, replete with quotations, often from poetry or songs, but as is often the case with those in power, it tended to be one-sided. He was not much interested in what others had to say, preferring to talk rather than to listen. Still, his informal conversations had a tone and substance about them that is praiseworthy. He did not indulge in profanity; he could talk knowledgeably of art, literature, drama, the role of government in society. In this sense, Churchill's conversations may merely have been a reflection of his aristocratic background and tastes, but it is a tone often missing in the conversations of other leaders, including Hitler's generally vulgar and rambling "table talk."

Churchill's aristocratic demeanor did not prevent him from showing deep feelings toward the British people.[30] His words were inspirational, and he inspired their confidence. There is the oft-told story of his inspecting the bombed-out London East End in September 1940, when the people mobbed him. As described by his defense secretary, General Sir Hastings Ismay, they cried: "'Good old Winnie. . . . We thought you'd come and see us. We can take it. Give it 'em back.' Churchill broke down, and as I was struggling to get him through the crowd, I heard an old woman say, 'You see, he really cares, he's crying.'"[31] Although Churchill's feelings were genuine, Desmond Morton, another of his close associates, especially during the 1930s and early in Churchill's tenure, contends that the prime minister's compassion was more passing sentiment than deep-seated concern. He simply lacked an awareness of what it was to live an ordinary life in an ordinary way.

Churchill's lack of empathy for average people carried over into the way he treated his personal staff.[32] He did things to suit his own convenience no matter how much he might inconvenience others. Sir John Colville records instances when Churchill kept typists up until three or four in the morning, even when there was no work to do, and at times servants were unable to clear the dinner table until after midnight. But he could also be considerate, finding "time to say or write a few words of appreciation which showed a quite exceptional generosity and kindness." There grew up between him and his staff, therefore, a type of affection despite his demanding nature.

While he loved his family dearly, Churchill had ambivalent relationships with close advisers, such as Sir Frederick Lindemann (Lord Cherwell), Lord Beaverbrook, Brendan Bracken, and Desmond Morton.[33] He enjoyed their company and gave them special tasks, but he was always his own person and never fell under their influence. As a result, he never developed complete friendships with them; his "friends" were thus individuals who were of use to him at the moment and changed accordingly.

Over his long and stormy career, Churchill attracted numerous opponents as well as many friends.[34] Some of his "enemies" were understandable. Many Labor Party leaders, while respecting Churchill's ability to conduct the war, were deeply suspicious of his policies, including his position on assistance to workers and his outdated view of empire. In this regard, Sir Stafford Cripps went so far as to propose having him replaced as prime minister. A good many of Churchill's Conservative Party colleagues also had reservations about him. Part of their concern reflected a devotion to Chamberlain. R. A. Butler, the longtime Conservative minister, for instance, characterized Churchill's ascension to power as a sudden coup in which "they [Chamberlain and other Conservative leaders] had weakly surrendered to a half breed American whose main support was that of inefficient but talkative people of a similar type. . . ." Even Colville, who came to respect and admire Churchill greatly, at first thought that "the country had fallen into the hands of an adventurer, brilliant no doubt, and an inspiring orator, but a man whose friends and supporters were unfit to be trusted with the conduct of affairs in a state of supreme emergency." Others had more lasting criticisms. Lady Robert Cecil was particularly outspoken in her condemnation of Churchill's love of war. In 1949 she wrote: "His passion for war and everything to do with it seems the only unchanging thing in his nature—it colours all his language and one supposes his thinking. He probably thinks of his watercolours as assaults upon the landscape." Still, those around him agree that he was never vindictive. He fought a foe with all of his considerable resources, but he never bore a lasting grudge.

Churchill could be difficult with his foreign policy and military advisers, too. He generally mistrusted Foreign Office officials (along with civil servants) because he considered many of them hidebound and socialist in outlook.[35] But for Sir Anthony Eden, who became foreign minister in December 1940, he had true affection. They argued at times, and Eden resisted some of Churchill's ideas, but they differed over details, not principles. As civil servant Sir William Strang noted: "In essentials the two were one."

Churchill's view of his military advisers was both simple and complex. It was simple in the sense that there were those he liked and those he disliked; those he could get along with and those he could not.[36] He finally settled on chiefs of staff he liked—Pound, Brooke, and Portal. He disliked or did not trust others, such as his army chief of staff during part of 1940 and most of 1941, General Sir John Dill, theater commander Field Marshal Lord Wavell, and fleet Admiral Sir Charles Forbes.

His attitude toward generals and admirals was more complicated than simple likes and dislikes, however.[37] Churchill considered war his metier. He knew it, or thought he knew about it, as well or better than the professionals who advised him. And at times his appraisal of strategic matters was superior to theirs. But he was also given to flights of fancy, to proposing impossible schemes. To combat his more impetuous notions he needed loyal but steadfast opposition from the chiefs of staff. This was not easy, for as the official historian, J. R. M. Butler, points out, "Mr. Churchill would not readily take no for an answer. Using all his great powers of argument he could bring extreme pressure to bear on his advisers. . . . in spite of his strong views and the force and tenacity with which he expressed them, he was loath to overrule his Service advisers on a military matter in which they stood firm in their opinion. But it was important that they should stand firm." This the chiefs of staff did, though some were better equipped to do so than others.

Churchill's thinking about military issues was further clouded by some of his appointments.[38] He was not the best "picker of men." This flaw on occasion led him—perhaps out of loyalty to old friends, perhaps because of a preference for mavericks or adventurers—to choose the wrong person for a job, such as when he early relied on Sir Roger Keyes as Chief of Combined Operations. Yet most of his military advisers came to appreciate and respect his judgments even when they disagreed with him.

At first glance, the prime minister's schedule does not do justice to his amazing energy.[39] During the 1,825 days he directed Britain's war effort until its end in Europe, he spent approximately 407 of them in other parts of the British Isles or abroad. His foreign excursions were demanding in that they took him to many parts of the world, including travel by sea and air to such places as Yalta in the Crimea, Quebec and Washington in North America, and the battle fronts in North Africa and Europe. At times Churchill used these occasions not only for meetings and visits to troops but also for vacations to Florida or Cairo or Marrakesh (in several instances to recuperate from illness), thus reflecting his wide interests and one of his methods for relieving the tensions of office.

While at 10 Downing Street, Churchill's daily regimen was just as demanding.[40] He awakened at eight, had breakfast, and usually stayed in bed throughout the morning, working through his black box of papers, dictating messages, and discussing with General Ismay recent developments and the schedule for the day. About twelve-thirty, he met with the chiefs of staff or the war cabinet. This was followed by lunch, an hour nap, further meetings late in the afternoon, dinner at eight, another meeting at ten or ten-thirty to explore a topic at some length, additional work, and finally to bed at two or three in the morning. It is little wonder that many around him were exhausted by his routine.

Several traits stand out in Churchill's conduct of business. In times of crisis, he dealt with issues methodically, allowing for discussion but settling them promptly and with dispatch. But according to one of his secretaries, Lord Bridges, when matters on the agenda were less important or pressing, "his love of argument and following a point that interested him would lead to long meetings." He also spent little time interviewing people, preferring to be addressed concisely in writing and to reply in kind. His notes were not always responses to memoranda from others, however. Often dictations initiated by himself and sent to advisers or even to cabinet colleagues, they set forth a question or a series of questions. As pointed out by Martin Gilbert, these "prayers," so-called because they often contained his injunctions "pray tell me" or "pray indicate to me," were intended not merely as statements of fact but as a means of entering into dialogue with the recipient. They were actually inquiries—to obtain information, to initiate discussion, or to propose ways for dealing with a matter—and they generally brought results.

For relaxation, Churchill spent almost every weekend at nearby Chequers, the British prime minister's retreat. He usually took along with him numerous personages as well as his family, and business was conducted from there, but with more time for informal talk and a nightly movie. The movies came to be dreaded especially by his staff. General Sir Leslie Hollis, one of his secretaries, remarked about them:

> If it was my duty weekend at Chequers I used to hope that I could take a back seat at the film and perhaps have a little doze before resuming the work which I knew would be required of me later in the evening. I was seldom able to achieve this respite because . . . Churchill would say "Come and sit beside me!" From time to time he would leave the room to see if there were any telegrams, and on his return he would expect an accurate recapitulation of what had occurred on the screen during his absence. Dire was the castigation one would receive if the report was not particularly accurate or informative. Churchill's favorite film was "Lady Hamilton," and I think I saw this no less than eight times.[41]

In comparing Churchill's daily routine with that of Hitler, one can see that the former's was more varied, but both men worked long hours and according to a similar pattern. They shared other characteristics also. Both had great endurance, were inspiring orators, and could be charming if inconsiderate toward others. Nonetheless, there were vast differences in tone and substance. Churchill was resolute but not vindictive, sentimental but not callow, aggressive but not ruthless. To Hitler's detriment, he was all of the above.

The similarities and dissimilarities of the two men carried over into the realm of ideas. Neither Churchill nor Hitler was particularly interested in philosophies or theoretical constructs, although the latter did have pretensions along these lines as evidenced in *Mein Kampf*. Despite the low intellectual level of his thinking, Hitler had three dominant ideas from which he never deviated: additional "living space" (*Lebensraum*), eventual world domination, and extermination of the Jews.[42] His virulent anti-Semitism was based on a crude sort of Darwinism, and except for a few misguided but vocal individuals, observers today generally accept it as a consistent, continuing, and significant part of Hitler's mental makeup. His belief in more living space and world domination are more controversial. No one doubts that Hitler desired more land and world power; the only question is how much land and how much power. Some historians contend that his primary goal was European hegemony, but others see worldwide aspirations in his thinking and actions.[43] While the idea that Hitler's territorial ambitions were unlimited is more persuasive, especially in light of the military buildup he advocated, the question is still not completely resolved.[44] Whatever one's view, there is widespread agreement that Hitler's foreign policy goals were far-reaching and would have resulted in radical changes in the world balance of power.

The Führer's thinking on foreign policy issues involves another historiographic controversy: that between the "intentionalists" and the "functionalists."[45] At the risk of overgeneralizing, one can say that the intentionalists assert that Hitler's will or intentions were consistent (at least as regards war) and decisive in Germany's taking the path that it did. The functionalists, basing their thinking on the domestic chaos that prevailed inside the Third Reich, see many of Hitler's decisions as attempts, which became increasingly radical, to escape the class conflicts and the "internal muddle" in which he and his associates found themselves. In other words, the "functioning" of the government and society (or their failure to function effectively) was as much a driving force in determining Germany's direction as was Hitler's arbitrary will.

Though instructive, the controversy seldom fits the views of the historians usually associated with it. With the possible exceptions of functionalist Timothy Mason and intentionalist Eberhard Jäckel, none seems to be exclusively on one side or the other. Even Jäckel at one point in his *Hitler in History* suggests that there were elements of both functionalism and intentionalism in Nazi Germany.[46] And from a different perspective—from a military standpoint—one can see that both elements were present. Hitler obviously tried to dominate all military developments down to the smallest detail, but after 1941 he was outstripped by events. He had unleashed or agreed to war on a worldwide scale, a war he could not control no matter how hard he tried. In this case, it was outside forces—the dimensions of the war—rather than internal ones which overwhelmed and wrested the initiative from him.

While Hitler was guided by delusions about race and space, Churchill seemed much more pragmatic. Certainly, Hitler often employed opportunistic and flexible means to achieve his goals, thus displaying a type of pragmatism in his own right. But the touchstones to Churchill's beliefs were more bound up with British traditions—love of freedom, defense of the Empire, balance of power—than with outlooks espousing a radical reordering of society and its structures. As the result of his upbringing and political background, he cherished Parliament and what it stood for and was devoted to the institution of monarchy and the retention of Britain's influence in world affairs.[47] This does not mean he did not enthusiastically support many new ideas, but he was more inclined to preserve than to overturn.

In one respect, however, the thinking of Churchill paralleled that of Hitler—an interest in war for its own sake. Hitler attempted to instill a martial mentality in the German people from the beginning, and rearmament was the key to everything else between 1933 and 1939.[48] Once the war started, he immersed himself in it. Churchill also enjoyed war and had thought deeply about it.[49] In part, his attachment to war reflected his romantic notions about gallantry in battle, but he also possessed a grasp of military and especially grand strategy that was often exceedingly perceptive. And his thinking about war contained an essential ingredient that Hitler's conception lacked: the prime minister wanted to retain rather than overthrow the existing world order.

But how consistent were Hitler's radicalism and Churchill's pragmatism when related to political, economic, and military matters? What were their views of allies? In these areas, as in others, they exhibited a number of likenesses and differences.

With regard to politics in the narrow sense, their party roles were quite different.[50] Hitler truly molded the National Socialist German Workers' Party in his image and used it as the main vehicle for dominating the state and its inhabitants. The party not only formed a basic part of Hitler's power structure but also provided an outlet for his organizing ability, a feature which explains a good deal of his success. Churchill, on the other hand, though nominal head of the Conservative Party, was not really a party person. He was not a Conservative by temperament or by conviction, and politically he remained a mixture of "radical and traditionalist" throughout the war. It is hardly surprising that he was despised as much by some Conservatives as by many of his Labor Party opponents.

Neither Churchill nor Hitler was greatly interested in administration.[51] Their lack of interest—despite Churchill's vast experience as a cabinet minister—led them to depend on others to run their governments. In the case of Hitler, the result has been described as "authoritarian anarchy," in which many of his associates attempted to accrue as much power for themselves as possible, setting up competing satrapies in the process. They then turned to Hitler as Führer to unravel the overlapping jurisdictions, thereby allowing him to increase his own power over them. Churchill never engaged in such machinations and preferred to let his ministers and the civil servants look after the government. He was concerned, especially about economic matters related to the war, but he seldom appears to have intervened with a heavy hand.

In the economic realm, any radical ideas the two war leaders may have held most often gave way to practical solutions.[52] This tendency is particularly evident in Hitler's handling of the German economy. Since he wanted to prepare the country for war, it might be expected that he would have favored centralized planning, but we find that he used both the public and the private sectors to a degree. If civilian industrialists were willing to undertake the measures he and his advisers wanted, they were encouraged to move ahead. If they were reluctant to become involved in what they conceived to be an unprofitable venture, as in the manufacture of low-grade iron ore from the Harz Mountains, the government stepped in. This dual approach allowed Hitler to develop the necessary economic infrastructure for war.

At first, the implementation of Hitler's thinking took the form of a series of short, one-front operations which did not require extensive reserves and permitted some butter at home (though severely cut) as well as guns at the front. However, the exigencies of the war—combined with Hitler's goals— forced him to make constant changes in economic priorities. After the Polish campaign, army weapons, ammunition, and equipment received top priority. In mid-July 1940, with the Battle of France won, the army was to be reduced and mechanized; naval and air forces, built up. The next month, Hitler revised his policy with respect to the army and decided to increase it to 180 divisions. At the end of 1941, the Wehrmacht's inability to bring the Russian campaign to a rapid conclusion induced him to step up the war economy, and during 1942 the Nazi regime instituted total war, in fact if not in name, for the duration of the conflict. This policy resulted in increased German war production into 1944, but at the cost of ever more drastic reductions in civilian consumption.

Great Britain was subjected to extensive civilian belt tightening from the start. Churchill appreciated this fact, and he tried to deal with such diverse problems as critical meat shortages in 1941, insufficient shipping in 1942, and inadequate housing throughout; but he generally permitted his ministers and the business leaders to deal with the economy so long as the war effort was pushed to the utmost without unduly restricting the civilian sector.

Churchill's willingness to let government officials and businessmen handle economic affairs did not, of course, apply to the military sphere.[53] He allowed his military advisers some input into broad political-strategic decisions, but he considered them too narrow and parochial to understand all aspects of grand strategy. Hitler went even further. He realized that many in the military prided themselves on being nonpolitical, and he used their lack of familiarity with political and foreign policy considerations to cement his control over them, contending that their limited, specialized outlooks prevented them from comprehending the myriad of issues affecting the formulation of national policy.

Hitler and Churchill held similar outlooks in other military matters as well.[54] Both had been greatly influenced by their World War I experiences, Hitler as a messenger on the Western Front, Churchill as First Lord of the Admiralty and later as a battalion commander in France. Both were risk takers. In fact, van Creveld has written that "Hitler waged war by a series of *coups* on a grand scale," from prewar surprises, such as his call for open remilitarization in 1935, to numerous wartime gambles, such as the Norwegian landings, the attack upon the USSR, and the two Ardennes undertakings in 1940 and late 1944. Churchill was constantly thinking along the same lines. Several of his audacious schemes included projected amphibious assaults into Norway and Sumatra, the plan for Sumatra being canceled only because of other commitments and insufficient equipment. Both leaders were obsessed with offensive operations. Churchill was advocating offensive measures even while Britain was on the defensive. Hitler's proclivities for the offensive were perhaps even more pronounced. He was always pushing German forces to take the offensive, and in a number of instances he refused to allow them to retreat. In the Red Army counteroffensive west of Moscow, this strategy worked; on other occasions, especially after mid-1942, his desire to hold on to territory at all cost often proved disastrous.

In addition, both men were meddlers. While some historians see Hitler as intervening less before 1942 than afterward, they all agree he interfered constantly. In May 1940, for instance, he personally briefed some of the soldiers and airmen before their attack on the critical Eben-Emael fortifications in Belgium. In December 1941, he was so dissatisfied with the Army High Command's conduct of the war that he took over the army himself. Prior to the 1944 Allied landings in Normandy, he assumed personal control over four of the ten panzer divisions stationed in the west. And on and on.

Churchill also intervened excessively. As Martin Gilbert put it, his "'sphere' was whatever he could see, sense or remember; it was everything he heard and everything that was on his mind. . . . every facet of war policy seemed to him a part of his legitimate concern, matters large and matters small." He was interested not only in the many commando raids off Norway and along the French coast, but also in why 108 searchlights were necessary for the naval base at Scapa Flow, and in whether German guns which were trophies in Britain could be reconditioned to assist in repelling a possible enemy landing. The desire of both Churchill and Hitler to direct the war down to the smallest detail obviously caused their subordinates much grief and many headaches.

In military technology, the two leaders' expertise was not so extensive as it might seem on the surface.[55] Both were fascinated with technical innovations, and both promoted a number of advances, as evidenced by Hitler's advocacy of the tank and its use in independent formations and Churchill's appreciation of the significance of radar. Despite their ability (especially Hitler's) to rattle off facts and figures, however, their actual understanding of the technology involved was relatively superficial. Albert Speer is particularly critical of what he calls Hitler's "anti-modernism," pointing to the latter's opposition to the tommy gun because, Hitler said, it made soldiers cowardly and prevented close combat and to Hitler's skepticism of jet fighters because their extreme speed was an obstacle to fighting. Speer contends that Hitler even distrusted German efforts to develop an atomic bomb and privately called "such efforts a spawn of Jewish pseudoscience." Churchill, to his credit, generally grasped the possibilities of the new technology although he did not always understand it. Yet even he at times was given to supporting rather fanciful projects, such as creating floating airfields out of ice mixed with wood pulp. He also continued to think of warfare in terms of years gone by—in the efficacy of "sabers and bayonets" and the power of battleships regardless of the circumstances. In this respect he, too, was antimodern.

Nevertheless, Churchill's and Hitler's views about things military did not always coincide.[56] Whereas both tended to dominate their military advisers, there was a crucial distinction: Hitler would not take no for an answer; Churchill would. Despite the fact that Hitler's generals and admirals served him well, they would soon find themselves on the retired list if they stood up to him or objected too strenuously once he had made up his mind. Consequently, although Hitler made few changes at the very top of the three services and OKW, he did insist on numerous changes at the chiefs of staff level as well as in the field. Churchill also vigorously—and eloquently—pursued matters he deemed of vital importance. But when his advisers put up a "brick wall," as they did increasingly once General Sir Alan Brooke became teamed with the air force and naval chiefs, Portal and Pound, after November 1941, the prime minister more often than not compromised or backed down. This does not mean he backed down graciously. General Hollis, one of Churchill's secretaries, relates one of the techniques Churchill used to try to deflect Brooke from his arguments. After listening to one of Brooke's suggestions that countered his own, Churchill would feign an inability to understand his rapid-speaking army head. The prime minister would then turn to General Ismay, cup his hand to his ear, and observe, "I cannot hear what he [Brooke] says," and have Ismay repeat Brooke's comments, only more slowly. If Churchill was especially upset with the viewpoint being expressed, he might change the subject. Or he might ask to have it repeated in an even louder voice a second time. "'Oh,' Churchill would say disconcertingly, 'Oh! so that's what he says. Oh! I see.'"

Whether the two leaders rejected, accepted, or reluctantly followed the military advice they received did not prevent them from making numerous strategic errors.[57] But there was a difference of degree. Ronald Lewin's *Hitler's Mistakes* chronicles the Führer's errors, from his failure to invade Britain immediately after the fall of France, to his attack on the Soviet Union, to his Ardennes "gamble" late in the war. On the other side, Sir Stephen Roskill has cataloged a number of what he considers Churchill's strategic blunders, including, among others, his blindness to the threat from Japan before the end of 1941, the disasters in Greece and Crete in midyear before North Africa had been cleared, the early bombing of Germany given precedence over securing the Atlantic sea lanes, and the fiasco in the Aegean after the 1943 Italian surrender. Still, Churchill's mistakes, though of consequence, were not fatal. Hitler's were.

Three other differences between the two in military matters can be linked to differences in their thinking.[58] For one thing, while both understood the value of, and eagerly sought, information about the enemy, Hitler used intelligence only to support his notions, not to alter them. Churchill, however, regarded intelligence, whether favorable or unfavorable, as one of the key elements in his conduct of the war. In fact, part of the reason for his impatience with field commanders, such as Wavell and General Sir Claude Auchinleck in 1941–42, was his knowledge, through Ultra, of what was happening. Second, although both enjoyed war for its own sake, Hitler did not mind the destruction it caused, whereas Churchill was always concerned about its effect on civilian populations. And third, the Nazi dictator did not really care about the welfare of his troops, as evidenced particularly during the war's later stages. This hard side of Hitler's personality was simply not part of Churchill's makeup.

There was also a vast difference in the two men's outlook toward allies. While this subject lends itself to book-length treatments if examined in depth, it can be said in general that whereas Churchill appreciated the value of allies, Hitler did not.[59] Despite recriminations afterward, the British leader did almost everything he could to keep France in the war. To be sure, he was acting on the basis of British self-interest, but his five trips to France during May and June 1940 attest to the sincerity of his views. He also showed great deference toward his Commonwealth and Grand Alliance partners, though in varying degrees depending on the situation. Hitler, perhaps because of his belief in Aryan superiority and economic dominance, never seemed to understand the necessity of allies in conducting war on such a vast scale. His relationship with Japan was a distant one both geographically and ideologically, although they probably got along well enough. His association with Italy was based on a lack of trust and reciprocity; with his European satellites it was often worse. Seeing his allies merely as conveniences rather than truly as partners was possibly one of Hitler's most telling failures.

In the final analysis, the ideas of Hitler and Churchill were neither totally radical nor totally pragmatic. The Führer's long-range goals would undoubtedly have meant a radical restructuring of the world order, but his means to accomplish these goals featured practical as well as revolutionary measures—practical in the economic and military sense and in the choice of allies, radical in his reorganization of the German state and society. It is ironic that his pursuit of eventual world domination accelerated a result he never would have countenanced—the decline of Europe and its replacement by the United States and the Soviet Union as the world's dominant powers. This result might have come about anyway, but Hitler certainly gave it a push.

At first glance, Churchill's ideas about politics, economics, military matters, and allies seem almost wholly pragmatic. His main goal was short range—to defeat the Axis, in particular Nazi Germany. His means was to form the Grand Alliance, a coalition in some ways even less compatible than that of the Axis. Yet practical though he was, there was also a strain of idealism in his thinking. The "sunlit uplands" that he envisaged may have been as much an attempt to rekindle past British greatness as it was to look ahead. But he often discussed the future shape of the world, and the alliance he forged represented the two foremost political and economic theories of the twentieth century: liberal democracy and communism. The thinking of both leaders thus contained idealistic and practical elements.

Obviously, the views of Britain's and Germany's two leaders toward the war changed as their fortunes changed. The most telling change occurred when the British Parliament went so far as to replace its prime minister and government at a seemingly inopportune moment—May 10, 1940—the day the battle for France and the Low Countries began. Yet the alteration did not adversely affect Britain's war effort and in fact helped rekindle it under Churchill's leadership. Caught in the middle was the first wartime prime minister, Sir Neville Chamberlain (1869–1940). Historians have not accorded Chamberlain especially high marks.[60] While acknowledging that his appeasement policy generally coincided with public opinion at the time, they are almost unanimous in their condemnation of his unwillingness to accept war as inevitable and to guide the country resolutely in that direction.

Is this a fair appraisal? Some historians, notably Sir Keith Feiling and, more recently, Gerhard Weinberg and David Dilks, have taken a more sympathetic view of the much-maligned prime minister.[61] Dilks in particular (though only the first volume of his Chamberlain biography, which takes the story to 1929, has been published) has emphasized a number of Chamberlain's more positive features: his outstanding command of the facts on a given issue, a capacity for hard work (despite becoming prime minister at age sixty-seven), an ability to speak effectively in and outside Parliament, a belief in helping the poor. He was also businesslike yet thoughtful, forceful yet considerate toward others. He rarely showed signs of anger, liked gentle humor, and was willing to admit a mistake.

Still, Chamberlain possessed some less endearing qualities. Like many other leaders, his public life belied a very private person at its core. He had few close friends outside his family. Even his Conservative Party colleagues, while admiring him, found him reserved and aloof. He preferred solitary pleasures—reading (especially Shakespeare), observing birds and flowers, fishing, puttering in a garden—to an active social life with its accompanying small talk. Colville, who was one of Chamberlain's private secretaries before serving under Churchill, describes one of the differences between the two men as follows:

> At weekends he [Chamberlain] retired to Chequers, where there was only one telephone (and that in the pantry). He disliked being disturbed, telephonically or otherwise, at weekends or after dinner at 10 Downing Street. He never took a Private Secretary with him to Chequers; nor did he ever invite the members of his staff to lunch or dine with Mrs. Chamberlain and himself. That was in marked contrast to Winston Churchill, who treated his Private Secretaries as part of the family.[62]

Chamberlain's traits were not necessarily negative, but they gave the impression, justified or not, that he was vain and arrogant. He resented criticism and took it personally. He did not like politics, with its compromises and intrigues, but accepted it as the price one had to pay to bring about improvements and progress.[63] Though willing to entertain contrary opinions, he liked people who knew what they were talking about, did their best, worked hard, and agreed with him. If persons whom he regarded as friends did not agree, it hardly mattered, for he did not render decisions to make himself popular but because he thought them right. If they were not right, he would bear his burdens alone, seldom confiding in others except in letters to his sisters and to other family members. In the end, these more negative aspects of his personality may have helped lead to his undoing.

But Chamberlain clung to another idea, which no matter how laudatory played a more important role in his demise: his genuine belief in peace. March 15, 1939, the day on which Hitler divided up what remained of Czecho-slovakia, is often given as the point when Chamberlain changed his thinking about war and peace. However, the explanation is not quite so simple.[64] Chamberlain by 1937 "had become at least intellectually convinced of the need for rearmament" in view of the German threat. What March 15 made clear was that Germany now definitely had to be stopped. He had finally realized that Hitler could not be trusted at all. Yet he was too peace-loving a person not to continue efforts to try to convince, if not Hitler, at least more moderate elements in Germany that war could be avoided. He gathered all of the means at his disposal—British and French rearmament, diplomatic guarantees, pressure on Italy, friendship with the United States, negotiations with the Soviets—to indicate to the Germans that Britain meant business.

But on September 1, if not before, the bankruptcy of Chamberlain's policy became evident. On September 3 he led Britain into the war. At 11:15 a.m. he broadcast to the nation:

> You can imagine what a bitter blow it is to me that all my long struggle to win peace has failed. Yet I cannot believe that there is anything more, or anything different that I could have done, and that would have been more success-ful. . . . We have a clear conscience, we have done all that any country could do to establish peace, but a situation in which no word given by Germany's ruler could be trusted, and no people or country could feel themselves safe, had become intolerable. . . . Now may God bless you all and may He defend the right. For it is evil things we shall be fighting against, brute force, bad faith, injustice, oppression, and persecution. And against them I am certain that the right will prevail.[65]

Despite the rhetoric, a wartime prime minister he was not, and he realized it. As early as September 10, he wrote: "While war was still averted, I felt I was indispensable, for no one else could carry out my policy. To-day the position has changed. Half a dozen people could take my place while war is in progress, and I do not see that I have any particular part to play until it comes to discussing peace terms,—and that may be a long way off."[66]

Chamberlain did his best to rally the British populace, but he was not an inspiring leader and did not immediately galvanize his colleagues into the special effort required of them.[67] He did, however, bring Churchill, one of his most vehement Conservative critics, into the war cabinet as first lord. (They had served together in the 1920s.) While exhibiting loyalty and support of Chamberlain, Churchill soon became the driving force of the cabinet as it attempted to accelerate the military buildup. With the debacle in Norway, it was time for a change. Although Chamberlain preferred Lord Halifax, his foreign minister, to succeed him, Churchill was acceptable, Halifax demurred anyway, and the now "Former Naval Person" took over.

Churchill's first months in office were not easy—defeat in France, a realization that Germany could not be brought to heel in the near future by blockade, an air war over Britain that increasingly devastated the country if not the people's morale. It was not a time to look ahead. When asked by Ivan Maisky, the Russian ambassador, on July 3, 1940, what his general strategy would be, Churchill replied, "to last out the next three months."[68] Nevertheless, it was probably the greatest period of his life. His extraordinary vitality and mental energy came to the fore. Britain did hold on, and the tone was set for the rest of his wartime prime ministership.

Once Churchill had brought the Soviet Union and the United States into an alliance, however, tensions began to arise—not only among the partners but also internally. While the problems were not insuperable, he went through one of his periods of depression, and his image started to tarnish, especially among those who advised him in conducting the war. His great gifts—his drive, his inspiration, his resourcefulness—were duly appreciated, but his impetuosity, his harebrained schemes, and his irritability were not. Possibly those around him had begun to realize that the prime minister was human after all. Brooke constantly fulminated in his diary about Churchill's overbearing, inconsiderate nature.[69] So on occasion did General Sir Henry Pownall, a longtime staff officer, who on June 10, 1944, wrote of Churchill's desire only to hear good news and of his increasing tendency to interest himself "in the tactical details of a current battle at the expense of longer term strategical planning which is his job." After a series of meetings on August 8, Admiral Andrew B. Cunningham, the naval representative to the Chiefs of Staff, wrote in his diary: "No decisions were reached; in fact, a thoroughly wasted day. What a drag on the wheel of war this man [Churchill] is. Everything is centralised in him with consequent indecision and waste of time before anything can be done."[70] The irony is that during the last half of the war, while the Allies were winning stunning victories and Churchill's popularity with the British people seemed to continue unabated, the gratitude of his military advisers, perhaps out of pique, perhaps because of fatigue,was less than might be thought.

Hitler's problems were of a different sort. While one might question the methods he used during the 1930s to overcome the Depression and to right the supposed territorial and military inequities imposed upon Germany by the Versailles Treaty, such steps were generally popular with the people. But actually going to war was another matter. Despite military successes during the early stages of the conflict, only after the victory over France did the German populace really become favorably disposed toward it.[71]

Also by mid-1940, and many historians would say two years earlier, opposition to Hitler's war thinking among the military had been largely silenced. While there were still times when the generals spoke out against his over-ambitious designs, their objections were neither unified nor consistent. Almost all of them by 1941 agreed that the defeat of the Soviet Union was not only plausible, but desirable. Of course, the anticipated quick victory did not occur, and this failure was in many ways a decisive turning point in the war.[72] Even Hitler temporarily indicated that the war might be lost. Later he went even further and stated that if he lost, the German people should go down with him. He held out the hope that if the Wehrmacht fought on with great determination, possibly the unnatural coalition against him might fall apart. When it did not, he was still willing to have his soldiers fight "until the bitter end."

Did Hitler's deteriorating health contribute to Germany's declining fortunes?[73] Although Werner Maser emphasizes this point, and it applies especially to the last weeks when those around Hitler noted his hunched posture, glazed eyes, and unkempt appearance, it is doubtful if his physical deterioration, brought on in part by drugs prescribed by his doctors, played much of a role in the war's outcome.

More significant is that even though Hitler "pursued the total destruction of Germany," his popularity with most Germans did not suffer accordingly.[74] Only a small proportion of the population understood (or admitted) what Hitler was about and wanted to overthrow the regime. He therefore in a perverse sense succeeded even while failing, for he concealed from the people his unrealistic as well as heinous goals. The idea of Hitler as a brilliant strategist and war leader continued until the final days.

As one might expect, Hitler and Churchill did not think highly of each other, and their views in this regard did not change throughout the conflict. At first after Churchill became prime minister, Hitler still hoped for some type of accommodation with the British. His public statements at the time were less shrill than later on. On September 4, 1940, he stated that Churchill's "chattering left the German people entirely cold, or moved them to great laughter," and on November 8 he went so far as to call Churchill a "general criminal."[75] But his remarks were framed primarily to show that Churchill was deluding himself and the British people by underestimating National Socialist Germany's strength and resolve. On May 4, 1941, however, in the midst of the Balkan campaign, Hitler threw off all restraint when in a Reichstag speech he referred to Churchill as a fool, a paralytic, a drunk, an insane person, "who as a soldier is a miserable politician and as a politician just as miserable a soldier."[76] Hitler continued in this vein both publicly and privately for the remainder of the war.[77] The British leader was an undisciplined swine, a crazy drunkard, and an idler of the first order. By February 4,

1945, he had become a "Jew-ridden, half-American drunkard." Even the British populace did not escape Hitler's wrath; it was their fate "to die of hunger and tuberculosis on their cursed island." The Führer's venom knew no bounds.

While Churchill was careful to separate "Hitler and his gang" from the German people, he made no secret of his hatred of Nazism.[78] On January 17, 1941, in a speech at Glasgow, he remarked: "My one aim is to extirpate Hitlerism from Europe." He later characterized Hitler as "this bad man" and "a squalid caucus boss and butcher." In a 1942 broadcast aimed at listeners on the Continent, he talked of the deficiencies of the Nazi system in the following terms: "What is he [Hitler] leaving behind him [in Europe]? He leaves behind him a Europe starving and in chains; a Europe in which execution squads are busy in a dozen countries every day; a Europe which has learned to hate the Nazi name as no name has ever been hated in the recorded history of mankind. . . ."[79] In a dinner speech after the war, Churchill summed up Hitler's main problem: "Hitler had only the Herrenvolk stuff and anti-Semitism. . . . That's all he had. He had no theme."

Was Churchill's evaluation accurate? As indicated earlier, Hitler did have themes—*Lebensraum*, world aggrandizement, hatred of Jews—and he consistently pursued their realization. Yet Churchill's assertion that Hitler "had no theme" is at least partially correct. The Führer's themes not only were unrealistic, they demonstrated the negative, primitive nature of his thinking as well.[80] While he had a human side, he saw the world in black and white terms. He treated allies, institutions, people, and individuals as conveniences, not as elements of true worth. He lacked the breadth of vision required of a wartime leader who expects ultimately to be successful.

Churchill, though perhaps overpraised, harbored a different vision. He believed in the defense of democracy, the balance of power, and Britain's worldwide interests, but his goals were more short term and featured "bringing the war to a victorious end in a reasonable period."[81] This for him meant defeating the Axis. It took until 1945 to do it instead of the end of 1943 or 1944 as he had hoped. But he did accomplish his more "limited" goal, and it is in this light that he is best remembered. As Clement Attlee, certainly not an unabashed admirer of Churchill, once remarked: ". . . history set him the job that he was the ideal man to do. . . . In this he was superbly lucky. And perhaps the most warming thing about him was that he never ceased to say so."[82] In its wartime leader, Britain could not have been better served.

TWO

Running the War

The Organization

Just as Hitler and Churchill dominated the military aspects of World War II in Germany and Great Britain, their personal preferences determined the systems each of them created for conducting the war. Nevertheless, their control over their respective systems was less than absolute.[1] In a war of such vast dimensions, neither possessed enough information—let alone insights—to oversee all of its many aspects. For political and economic concerns associated with the war, they required the assistance of civilian ministers. For strategic matters, they needed effective high-command structures, and the military chiefs and their staffs were to use their knowledge and expertise to prepare their countries' military forces, not only for the expected, but for the unexpected elements of war as well.

After receiving input from military staffs and civilian agencies, the high commands conducted the war on a day-to-day basis according to the dictates of modern communications, logistics, and weaponry.[2] The military organizations at the center became the crucial link between those who directed the war from home and those who fought it at the fronts. The chiefs of staff, whether in London or Berlin or accompanying their war leaders, worked out the strategy and logistical planning, subject, of course, to guidelines agreed upon in consultation with Hitler and Churchill. They then transmitted their orders to the operational commanders in the field. Although the commanders had input into the process during the planning stages, once the high commands had sent orders to them, their tasks and those of their staffs were normally limited to completing the detailed planning and assembling the forces prior to implementation. The field commanders then attempted to exercise control over their soldiers, sailors, and airmen during the ensuing campaign. At the same time, they remained in almost constant contact with the system at the center. In this way, the conduct of the war remained in the hands of the war leaders and their advisers and immediate staffs throughout. Although circumstances at times dictated that the field commanders make decisions on the spot and, conversely, "local" decisions at times had an impact on the high command, on the whole, centralized control was maintained.

This method of running a war upset a number of time-honored traditions, including the German notion of brooking little interference from the head of state while an operation was in progress and the shared British and German belief in allowing their theater commanders as much latitude as possible. Yet centralized control was inevitable so long as prosecuting the war depended on producing the necessary matériel at home and elsewhere rather than having troops live off the land. This elementary fact may seldom have been appreciated by commanders in the field (or by the public on the home front), but it was never far from the minds of the chiefs of staff. The overall responsibility, if not the glory, was theirs.

There were substantial differences between the two systems, not the least of which was that Hitler's dominance over his service chiefs was much greater than that exercised by Churchill. After the war, German staff officers were almost unanimous in the condemnation of their system as compared with that of Great Britain. As General Walter Warlimont, the deputy to Jodl at OKW, has written: ". . . the views and decisions of the [British] Chiefs of Staff generally prevailed when there was a difference of opinion [with Churchill]. In fact the advice of the British Chiefs of Staff and the US Joint Chiefs was a deciding factor in Allied strategy. At the comparable level in Germany there was nothing but a disastrous vacuum."[3] From a different perspective, General Kurt Zeitzler, the Army (OKH) chief of staff between 1942 and 1944, has pointed to Hitler's domination of the military and "how a flaw at the highest command level can penetrate down to the lowest echelons and directly affect all work; how a fanatical, unqualified, demonic person at the top can misuse and destroy a good organization and cause all practical work to come to nought."

Whether Warlimont and Zeitzler overstated their points or not, their thinking is obviously an important consideration in assessing the war machinery of both countries. But before drawing any conclusions, we first need to take an extended look at the nature of the British and German systems, their functions, and the personalities involved. Then, having examined the human and organizational components, along with the changes that took place during the conflict, we can place in perspective the roles played by each nation's high command in helping to direct their countries' war efforts.

When describing the high-command organizations of Germany and Great Britain, one distinction overshadows all others: the British had a unified system; the Germans did not. (At the risk of oversimplification, the basic relationship between the heads of the armed forces and their civilian leaders can be depicted as in figures 2-1 and 2-2.) In other words, the Germans had no true chiefs of staff. Although they supposedly had a high command in the form of the Armed Forces High Command, their organization never functioned as a true coordinating or overall decision-making body. All of the supreme commanders (*Oberbefehlshabern*) of the various branches had access to Hitler, and they did not speak with one voice. Nor did one service completely dominate, as the army had done in World War I. The commanders-in-chief represented their services' interests and advised the Führer, but individually, not together. The British chiefs of staff, on the other hand, met daily and attempted to sort out their differences before rendering advice to the prime minister. Like all strong-willed persons, they disagreed at times, and their differences might have required reconciliation in discussions with Churchill. But in most instances, they had agreed on the desired course of action beforehand and were able to present a united front. Whether they always agreed or not, they worked together and closely with Churchill in arriving at decisions.

This distinction should not lead one to conclude that the German system was as completely chaotic as many of its generals and staff officers have alleged. Though cumbersome, it was not so awkward as to prevent those involved from working through or around it when necessary. At its apex, of course, was Hitler. In most cases he was the initiator of strategy; but at times, as in arguments between the army and the navy over coastal-defense responsibilities, and between the army and air force over V-weapons, he acted more as an arbiter. Still, he always had the final decision.[4] And since military strategy is in part a matter of options, and Hitler's fertile mind never lacked for ideas, his advisers' roles were often restricted to restraining him from overambitious schemes for which Germany did not have adequate personnel or matériel at the time. Nevertheless, they generally did not disagree with him so much about his short-term goals as about his timing.

As mentioned above, Hitler preferred to work with his service heads separately rather than as a group. From September 1939 to the end of 1941, he brought them together only three times.[5] During the same period, his formal meetings with two of the service chiefs were limited to three occasions, and he met with their second in command—the actual chiefs of staff—only once. Was this part of a diabolical plot by Hitler to undercut the authority of the three services? Perhaps. More likely it was merely the way he preferred to conduct business. He treated party leaders and government officials in much the same way. He did not like making decisions by committee, for to do so ran counter to the *Führerprinzip* by which he dictated events, and so long as those in the party and state acceded to his thinking as the basis of governance, he was bound to remain the dominant force. The important

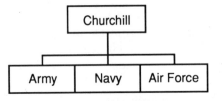

Fig. 2-1: British Chiefs of Staff

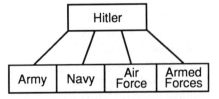

Fig. 2-2: German High Command, 1939-42

consideration from a military standpoint is that this method caused military planners great difficulties, and their attempts to formulate long-range, joint strategy often foundered as a result.[6]

Until December 1941, advice from the army (*Oberkommando des Heeres/ OKH*) to Hitler was rendered through its commander-in-chief, General Walther von Brauchitsch; his chief of staff, General Franz Halder; and their staffs and the field commanders. After Hitler took over total command, two things happened. One, the army's organizational structure changed. Prior to von Brauchitsch's enforced "retirement," the commander-in-chief and General Halder had divided the main duties of OKH between them. Besides advising Hitler, von Brauchitsch oversaw all aspects of the army, including the ever important area of personnel.[7] He was also ultimately responsible for the field army (*Feldheer*) and the replacement army (*Ersatzheer*). The replacement army under General Friedrich Fromm was exceedingly significant in the overall scheme, for it was responsible for all military administrative matters, such as inducting recruits, conducting basic training, procuring equipment, and sending reinforcements to the war theaters, as well as for handling units and troops within the Reich.[8]

Halder as chief of staff directed the field army. His organization consisted of the usual operations, intelligence, communications, transportation, and supply branches, but it also included ten other, more specialized branches.[9] The ten additional branches were organization, training, central (for general staff officers), deputy for operations, Luftwaffe General (for reconnaissance and antiaircraft coordination), mapping, weather, liaison officers, headquarters, and arms development (infantry, artillery, engineering, chemical warfare, and armor). Halder's primary functions were to use this extensive organization to plan the various land campaigns and to oversee their execution. This required him to be in constant contact with the commanders in the field and also with the branches under General Fromm at home. Close liaison was maintained with von Brauchitsch by having Halder's office at OKH field headquarters co-located with that of his commander. The only change in the structure early on occurred in the winter of 1939–40, when the Army Weather Service was dissolved in favor of using air force weather data.

After Hitler became supreme army commander, the structure underwent constant change.[10] During the next three years, of the fifteen branches under the chief of staff, two were abolished, one moved to another office, and one shifted within the OKH framework.[11] Moreover, two branches—Fortifications and Command Group—and a section to look after the increasing number of foreign soldiers were added in 1943 and 1944.

More important was what happened to the offices under von Brauchitsch.[12] After he retired, his control over personnel matters was transferred to OKW under Field Marshal Keitel, which meant, in effect, that army personnel came under Hitler's purview. This situation was made official in the fall of 1942, when the Army Personnel Office was placed directly under Hitler, and his adjutant, General Rudolf Schmundt, was named its head. While General Kurt Zeitzler, Halder's successor as chief of staff, resisted Schmundt's attempts to bring the army more under party control, Hitler, according to Zeitzler, "learned more unpleasant facts about the army—reports on court martials and desertions, for example—than he did about the other branches of the Wehrmacht, where these disagreeable matters were handled by the respective commanders-in-chief and never brought to his attention."[13] Such unsavory instances did nothing to endear the army to Hitler.

Hitler undercut the army in other ways. Not only personnel but also the replacement army came under Keitel's oversight after von Brauchitsch's departure. Moreover, in February 1943, Hitler removed the mobile forces section from the chief of staff, made it directly responsible to him, and put General Heinz Guderian in charge as inspector general.[14] Guderian and his staff were conveniently located near the Führer's headquarters. This proximity benefited Guderian in July 1944, for after the attempt on Hitler's life, the famous "panzer leader" became army chief of staff, replacing Zeitzler, who, though not involved, had long since lost favor with the Führer. The assassination attempt also led to the appointment of General Wilhelm Burgdorf as head of the Army Personnel Office. Burgdorf was an even more dedicated Nazi than Schmundt, who had been seriously wounded and eventually died from the bomb blast. And Heinrich Himmler, of all people, became head of the replacement army because of General Fromm's association with the plot. What all of the changes signified was that, by late July 1944, Hitler had *directly* under him OKW and thus ultimately the replacement army, the army chief of staff, the inspectorate for panzer forces, the Army Personnel Office, and the National Socialist Guidance Office along with the navy and the air force.[15]

Another change that occurred after Hitler became head of the army was that the army's influence over decision making continued to diminish. The diminution took several disparate forms. On a tangible level, by December 1941, OKH was already "dividing" control of the war theaters with the Armed Forces High Command (*Oberkommando der Wehrmacht*/OKW). The change had taken place in several stages. Between 1939 and early 1941 the army had put together the Polish, French, Balkan, and Russian campaigns with assistance from the other services and some interference from Hitler, but generally in accord with time-honored army procedures. However, in the case of Norway and Denmark, since the army was already heavily involved in planning the French campaign, Hitler circumvented normal OKH channels and made OKW responsible for the operation, though actual planning was entrusted to an army corps under General Nikolaus von Falkenhorst.

While the Danish-Norwegian undertaking provided the precedent, the Barbarossa campaign provided the occasion for Hitler to assume more control over the army.[16] During the spring and summer of 1941, all of the relatively quiet or minor combat theaters were placed under OKW. These so-called war theaters *(Kriegsschauplätze)* included, besides Denmark and Norway, northern Finland, the Balkans, western Europe, and North Africa (in conjunction with Italy). This meant, though not officially, that OKH was to confine its efforts to the Russian Front, and the war theaters were handled in this way thereafter. OKH directed the war in the east, and OKW oversaw the other theaters, a situation which caused considerable difficulties when OKW's *Kriegsschauplätze* became major combat zones themselves.

On an intangible level, von Brauchitsch's removal was equally devastating to the army. Regarding his dismissal, General Heinz von Gyldenfeldt, who had extensive experience at OKH headquarters, has written: "Worst of all was the feeling in the army that there no longer was a commander in chief whose heart beat for the army. Hitler had never been a friend of the army, and he never became one. Everywhere the absence of responsible representation through a commander in chief of the army made itself felt."[17] General Adolf Heusinger, the OKH operations officer throughout most of the war, describes the atmosphere at military meetings which Hitler dominated as follows:

> Hitler's acts of persuasion, his ferocious desire to win you over, were virtually limitless. I met with him six or seven hundred times at the daily conferences, and time and time again after I left the room I would allow myself an hour of relaxation and repose to clear my mind, to forget every word he said, and only then could I arrive at a rational and realistic decision.[18]

Even General Warlimont of OKW commented that, after December 1941, "the command organization of the Army fell apart. It lacked a man at the top who represented the Army exclusively."[19] The army had lost its dominant leadership role.[20]

Since the role of OKH was diminished, one might expect that that of OKW would be greatly enhanced, but this expectation is warranted only to an extent. To be sure, between 1938, when it was formed, and the spring of 1940, the Armed Forces High Command had little power and served primarily as Hitler's military working staff, but, as brought out earlier, OKW then began to acquire more responsibilities when additional war theaters were placed under its auspices.[21] Planning and coordination with commanders in the field was taken over by Keitel's chief of staff, General Jodl, and his operations branch. Since Keitel and Jodl met with Hitler almost daily throughout the war, they were well positioned to exercise considerable influence on him.

Nevertheless, OKW never did truly direct or coordinate the German war effort except at the very end, when the army general staff was finally placed under OKW as a consolidation move.[22] It did have legal, coordination, foreign and counterintelligence, and economics and armaments branches along with an operations component, but it lacked the clout and official recognition as well as the apparatus to provide the strategic and combat intelligence, training, transportation, communications, and equipment and supplies necessary for the soldiers at the front. These had to be provided by the army; consequently, the army branches responsible for supply, transportation, and other needs served OKH in the east as well as OKW in the other theaters. Despite the inconvenience, the system worked relatively well because the staff officers involved cooperated among themselves to ensure that most frictions were overcome.

Though satisfactory, the situation was far from optimal, and the leaders at both OKH and OKW made numerous attempts to overcome the lack of a unified command.[23] These attempts began even before the war. The minister of war, Werner von Blomberg, set up the Wehrmacht Office (*Wehrmachtamt*) in the 1930s to oversee the three services, a move especially upsetting to the army but resisted by the navy and air force as well. The Wehrmacht Office therefore exercised little power. At the outbreak of the war, the six-person Cabinet for the Defense of the Reich, which consisted of government, party, and military leaders, was created, but it seldom met and played no real role in the war. After the Polish campaign, Halder suggested that von Brauchitsch assume the additional title of chief of the army general staff to give him more prestige, and that he, Halder, harkening back to the World War I precedent, would become quartermaster general. But the army commander-in-chief would not agree to the change.

In December 1941, after von Brauchitsch was removed, Keitel proposed to Hitler that Jodl be made army chief of staff and that General Erich von Manstein replace Jodl as head of the OKW operations staff. Hitler, of course, had other ideas and soon placed himself as head of the army. After Zeitzler became army chief of staff in September 1942, conflicts between him and Jodl became commonplace, as each tried to persuade Hitler that his needs were paramount. Zeitzler contends he became so exasperated at one point that he went so far as to suggest that his rival, Jodl, be named army chief of staff. But Hitler replied: "No, I cannot do without you [Zeitzler]. Jodl has not had any experience in the East."[24] Even Guderian, beholden as he was to Hitler, proposed to the Führer while serving as army chief of staff in early 1945 that a general Hitler trusted be appointed head of OKW with the proviso that this person be allowed to truly coordinate the efforts of the three services.[25] Hitler, however, refused to replace Keitel, and by this time Guderian had to admit to himself that there was probably no high-ranking general whom Hitler would trust.

The end result of all these attempts to establish a more streamlined system thus came to nought. While OKW eventually had more of a say in military decisions, especially after 1941, Hitler remained the ultimate authority.

Hitler's power over the navy and the air force also increased as the war progressed, but under different circumstances. In the case of the navy (*Oberkommando der Kriegsmarine*/OKM), it was a matter of having to adjust to a more limited role. Although the surface fleet was soon eliminated as a major factor, so long as the U-boat was an important consideration in Germany's strategy, the navy, first under Grand Admiral Raeder and then after January 1943 under Grand Admiral Karl Dönitz, was bound to have a say in policy considerations and armaments priorities. After May 1943, however, when Dönitz had to call off his wolfpacks because of inordinate losses, the navy's active role was increasingly confined to coastal defense.[26] Even though improved submarines and other naval equipment continued to be built, the navy's goal, which it shared with Hitler, of achieving eventual world domination became more remote than ever before.

In addition, while OKM was relatively successful in keeping the Führer's interferences and those of the other services to a minimum, it remained a relatively minor component in Germany's war equation.[27] In September 1943, for instance, the navy's total personnel strength of 675,000 (although greatly expanded from its peacetime strength) pales markedly when compared with that of the army's 6,796,000, or even the air force's 2,002,000. Nor did the navy fare well in gaining control over aircraft for sea duties. In February 1939, the Luftwaffe agreed to provide the navy with aircraft and support for reconnaissance, mine laying, antishipping strikes, and other naval functions; after the war broke out, the air force began to circumvent the agreement. By the fall of 1941, Göring had convinced Hitler that the navy's air arm should be transferred to him. Thereafter, except for some seaplanes and smaller aircraft which remained under its control, the navy depended on the Luftwaffe to carry out its aerial activities, activities the air force generally did its best to avoid. Overall, then, despite Dönitz's continuing support from Hitler, Germany's limited resources, coupled with the deteriorating military situation, relegated the navy to a secondary position.

The situation for the air force (*Oberkommando der Luftwaffe*/OKL) was different in that its roles did not decrease but merely changed. The change, of course, came about because of the altered nature of German operations. During the Polish, French, and Barbarossa campaigns, the Wehrmacht emphasized its Blitzkrieg strategy, of which the Luftwaffe was an integral part. But once the long war of attrition set in, the Germans reluctantly started to move to a more defensive mode of thinking, which accelerated as the war dragged on. As the Allies' strategic bombing became increasingly effective, the Luftwaffe underwent a fundamental shift in priorities from tactical air support to air defense, and fighter aircraft, radar, and especially antiaircraft guns came to assume major functions. Overriding necessities therefore prevented the air force from developing a strategic air arm that could concentrate on offensive operations as at first tactical, then defensive air priorities prevailed.

Still, the Luftwaffe did suffer a diminution of power, and its main difficulty can be summarized in the phrase "failure at the top."[28] This failure took several forms.[29] Reichsmarschall Hermann Göring may have been an effective advocate for the Luftwaffe for a while, but his influence waned as Germany's military fortunes declined. He also did not understand the technological dimensions of war, and he went so far as to separate the air force's operational and technical branches, with the result that coordination between these two vital areas was often lacking. When questions of Allied numerical superiority arose, Göring took the "fanatical National Socialist approach" of stressing that German spirit and will would overcome the problem.

Equally devastating was that, with some exceptions, until late in the war, the Luftwaffe leadership echoed Göring's prejudices, emphasizing offensive, operational, and tactical features of aerial warfare and downplaying defensive, technological, and broad strategic aspects. These problems and others, including personal rivalries at the top, were finally resolved in 1944 when Hitler himself assumed more direct responsibility over the air war. He was the one who insisted on the production of V-2 rockets and other miracle weapons, and toward the end, only he could approve the movement of air units from one sector to another. By August 1944, Hitler had become so disillusioned with the Luftwaffe that he advocated disbanding the fighter arm and having its functions become part of a large, antiaircraft army. Göring was able to stave off such a drastic step, but the situation does indicate the extent of Hitler's disenchantment. By war's end, his "favorite" service had lost much of its independence as well as its presumably privileged status.

Besides the army, armed forces, navy, and air force high commands, two other elements in Germany's war machinery need to be mentioned—the Ministry for Armaments and War Production and the Waffen-SS, which played increasingly important roles in German decision making. (They eventually became so important that Hitler's command relationships might well be depicted as in figure 2-3.)

Power accrued to the armaments ministry and the Waffen-SS gradually. In 1940 Fritz Todt was put in charge of armament procurement and production, and his job was a particularly frustrating one because of the many conflicts among the military and civilian agencies associated with the war economy.[30] By December 1941, with a long, costly war now in prospect, he had become so disillusioned that he considered the war lost and recommended to Hitler that it be brought to an end. His recommendation may explain Todt's "unfortunate" death soon afterward in a February plane crash.[31]

Todt's successor, the ambitious and energetic Albert Speer, was the main

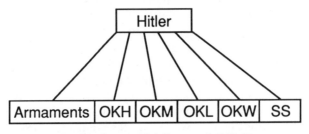

Fig. 2-3: German High Command, 1942-45

force behind the armaments ministry's rise in power. Eventually, Speer was able to overcome almost all of the competing authorities, and his position in many respects came to resemble that of an economic tsar. First the army by 1942, then the navy and other economic sectors by 1943, and finally the air force in 1944 were brought under his competence. In the meantime, he established what became known as "organized improvization," a system he acknowledged borrowing from Walter Rathenau, who had instituted it during World War I, and used to an extent by Todt earlier. "Organized improvization" involved bringing military and industrial personnel together into committees to plan and develop the various types of weapons needed by the services, to streamline production, and to speed up the allocation of finished matériel. Speer's ministry, whose name was changed to the more appropriate Ministry for Armaments and War Production (*Reichsministerium für Rüstungs und Kriegsproduktion*) in September 1943, did not run the economy with an especially heavy hand, preferring to "steer" it rather than directing it in detail. The well-known result was a dramatic increase in war production, an increase which continued into the fall of 1944 despite the growing might of Allied air power.

Speer's success can also be attributed to the backing he received from the Führer, who came to regard Speer, at least until toward the end, as an organizational genius. Speer describes the atmosphere in the ninety-five formal conferences between him and Hitler and their representatives as businesslike and cordial, a far cry from the sometimes heated and unproductive meetings between the Führer and his military advisers. Speer was of the opinion "that Hitler used these prolonged conferences on armaments and war production as an escape from his military responsibilities. He himself admitted to me that he found in them a relaxation similar to our former conferences on architecture."[32] Whatever the reason, the armaments ministry became a significant though late force in Germany's war effort.

The improved power position of the Waffen-SS also developed gradually.[33] Initially, the military arm of the SS was an elite force, mirroring the Aryan prejudices of Hitler, Himmler, and the party theoreticians, and numbering only 28,000 men at the war's outset. The growth of the Waffen-SS was also restricted because Hitler at this point agreed with the army that the size of the SS should be expanded only slightly. But the exigencies of the war changed the slow rise into a flood as the number of SS troops increased from 236,099 in September 1942 to 501,049 at the end of 1943 to a high of 594,443 in mid-1944.[34] In addition, Himmler gained more control over portions of the Wehrmacht in July 1944 when he assumed responsibility for the replacement army, most of the army's intelligence functions, and several other offices.[35]

Yet the Waffen-SS never became a "fourth service" as sometimes alleged by the generals. While there were frictions with the army, especially over procurement and recruitment, it remained under the army in combat and continued to depend on the latter for certain items, such as heavy weapons. It did reach a peak strength of thirty-eight divisions, but it never exercised independent command above the corps level. SS officers, such as Paul Hausser and Karl Wolff, rose to positions of prominence in the military hierarchy, yet the Waffen-SS had little influence in the upper echelons of the army and armed forces high commands except toward the end when Himmler's power became more pervasive. And while some of the SS divisions fought extremely well, particularly during the later stages of the war, their formations more and more came to be made up of ethnic Germans and other nationalities rather than Germans from the Reich. In the end, then, as Hans Buchheim has pointed out, the rivalry between the Waffen-SS and the Wehrmacht developed not so much between military units at the fronts as it did between political opponents in the rear.

Despite the diffusion of power and overlapping jurisdictions among Hitler's military agencies, the system was obviously not a total failure; German successes, especially in the early years, prevent us from concluding that it was. True, Hitler took advantage of the military leaders' lack of political acumen and sense of national loyalty as well as individual ambition to gain control over them in that sphere.[36] More difficult to explain, however, is the timidity of the generals and admirals in military matters. The primary reason seems to stem from their failure to understand Hitler's intentions. Though in a different sense, they, like him, venerated the Prusso-German military tradition and the modern industrial society of which they were a part. They further shared with him their disdain of what they considered Germany's horrible treatment after World War I. But whereas the military wanted the Reich to regain and enhance its influence as a world power, Hitler wanted more. He wanted eventual world domination, and when the first victims were occupied or defeated easily, he started to envisage his long-range goals as within his grasp. Thus, the differences between the ambitions of Hitler and the high command were of degree, not of substance, and this allowed him to undermine their position even before the war had begun.

Still, the system at the top was not as defective as it might have been.[37] The services at times disagreed violently over priorities and specifics, and the Führer's military conferences were not an effective instrument for directing the war, but the far-flung nature of the conflict dictated that the army, armed forces, navy, and air force commands engage in meaningful coordination outside Hitler's direct purview, a practice which continued with some exceptions until the very end. This coordination was a factor, though a subsidiary one, in explaining why the Wehrmacht fared as well as it did. In the long run, however, Germany's military successes are related more to its effective training and outstanding combat leaders than to its command system. It is to the credit of Germany's military leaders that they recognized and continued to emphasize these features at the tactical and operational levels, but at the highest, strategic level, the system proved deficient.

What the German high command lacked, the British system possessed: accountability, realism, flexibility, and systematic coordination. There was accountability in the German system, but it was accountability to a single person. In Britain, the military leadership was responsible to the war cabinet, which was, in turn, responsible to Parliament. Thus, a collective body rather than an individual exercised supreme authority. The British chiefs also exhibited a realistic approach to decision making. This was a result of their being given broadly defined powers and having excellent information on which to base their decisions. The Germans, too, had sufficient information, but their segmented system did not lend itself to a balanced outlook for dealing with problems. Furthermore, the British system was flexible; centralized control was maintained, but there was considerable give-and-take between the nerve center in England and the tentacles in the war theaters. While the Wehrmacht in theory also adhered to the principle of giving latitude to its field commanders, in practice those at the war fronts seem to have been more rigidly controlled than was the case with the British. Finally, the British chiefs of staff practiced better coordination than the Germans, as was apparent in all aspects of the decision-making process—among joint military committees and civilian and military agencies as well. Although there were exceptions, among the British the left hand generally knew what the right was doing.

It had not always been that way. During the early months of the war, the British military system did not function smoothly.[38] The key body was Chamberlain's eight-member, civilian war cabinet, which made the major decisions and assumed responsibility for the war. Under it was the smaller Ministerial Committee on Military Coordination and the chiefs of staff. The latter, assisted by the Joint Planning and Joint Intelligence committees, proposed the strategy to be followed, and their recommendations were then placed in the hands of the coordination committee of three civilian ministers and the minister of supply. Once the committee had completed its deliberations, its proposal was presented to the war cabinet for a decision. After reaching a decision, the chiefs of staff fashioned them into operations orders, sent them to the field, and oversaw their execution (except for the British Expeditionary Force in France, which was directly responsible to the war cabinet, not to the chiefs of staff.)

The problem with the system was that it did not make for rapid decision making. As General Ismay, military secretary to the war cabinet, has written:

. . . the system of supreme direction did not work satisfactorily. The Chiefs of Staff, after considerable discussion of a problem, would report their conclusions, or differences to the Ministerial Co-ordination Committee. There the whole ground would have to be gone over again, and perhaps a new set of conclusions or differences would be reached. The matter would then go to the War Cabinet, and once more the process of explanation and disputation would have to be repeated.[39]

General Sir Edmund Ironside, the new chief of the army, was even more outspoken in his criticism. His diary entry of November 5, 1939, is particularly interesting because it brings to light various problems in civil-military relations:

> Our military machinery of command is truly bad. . . . Our Army is under French command and must conform to the French general ideas. But the Air Force is not, and the [War] Cabinet dearly love directing its operations, discussing its most minute operations. . . . It is only in times of stress that civilian strategists are dangerous. They are impatient of delays due to administrative difficulties and they grasp at any mad idea in the hopes that they have discovered a golden road to victory. They may not be 'timid' or 'weak', but they are all acutely aware of the remarks of the Press, which often holds the power to dismiss them from office.[40]

While Ismay and Ironside obviously looked at the problems from a military standpoint, their opinions do show that even though civilian control is an essential part of the British system, during wartime it had to be brought in line with military realities.

Churchill put those realities into action. Despite the critical situation brought on by the French campaign, after he took over on May 10, 1940, he instituted a number of changes.[41] As prime minister, he created for himself also the position of minister of defence, through which he was directly linked with the chiefs of staff. Moreover, the Military Coordination Committee was renamed the Defence Committee. It now consisted of two sections, operations and supply, and the ten-member, civilian Defence Committee for Operations (with the chiefs of staff as advisers), was particularly important in the formulation of strategy. The war cabinet remained the supreme executive authority. Chamberlain continued to serve the new government as lord president, but Labor Party leaders were also brought in for the first time. Actual power soon shifted away from the war cabinet and into the hands of Churchill. He became the dominant element. As General Sir Leslie Hollis, a cabinet secretary recorded at the time: "The days of mere 'coordination' were out for good and all. We are now going to get direction, leadership, action—with a snap in it."[42]

The body that kept the instrument in tune was General Ismay's cabinet secretariat.[43] Its military head was General Ismay, and to his everlasting credit, he dissuaded Churchill from forming a group of unofficial advisers around him and persuaded him to put his trust in Ismay and his small staff. It was a fortunate decision. The secretariat was represented, not as decision makers, but as resource persons on all of the major committees—war cabinet, defence, and chiefs of staff. It also served as a conduit between Churchill and everyone in the governmental machinery concerned with military business. Consequently, as pointed out by Ronald Lewin, "all was brought within a unified and organic relationship . . . nobody relevant was out in the cold."

As the war progressed, Churchill and the chiefs assumed more and more actual power.[44] The prime minister continued to inform the war cabinet and Parliament of major developments, but the war cabinet's interventions in military operations became almost nonexistent after 1940. The number of cabinet meetings also declined from 312 in 1940 to 176 in 1944, and they were concerned increasingly with civil and diplomatic affairs instead of military strategy. Churchill continued to depend on the service departments for administrative concerns and utilized extensively a cabinet committee system—joint operational planning, intelligence, and administrative planning branches on the military side, and economic and statistical sections on the civilian side. There were, in addition, four other regular committees—manpower, principal military and administrative officers, and Allied supplies (mainly for Russia)— and seventeen subcommittees formed on an ad hoc basis to address special tasks, but all of them, regular or ad hoc, were to provide him and the chiefs with information and advice, not to exercise executive authority.[45] The same situation applied to the Defence Committee for Operations. Its number of meetings decreased from 52 in the last half of 1940 to 10 in 1944. In fact, by 1942 it had been superseded by what Churchill called "staff conferences," informal meetings between him and a few ministers with particular interests and with the chiefs of staff present.

The chiefs of staff, along with Churchill, ran the war.[46] Their relationship was never precisely defined, but it was close and constant. He met with the three of them (four if one counts Ismay) daily—441 times in 1941, 414 in 1944—and often on a less formal basis as well. At first Churchill had some difficulty getting service representatives he was comfortable with, but once Air Chief Marshal Sir Charles Portal had replaced Air Chief Marshal Sir Cyril Newall as chief of the air staff in October 1940, and General (later Field Marshal) Sir Alan Brooke had taken over for Field Marshal Sir John Dill as chief of the imperial general staff in late 1941, there were no changes at the top, except when Admiral Sir Dudley Pound died in September 1943 and was succeeded by Admiral Sir Andrew B. Cunningham as first sea lord. Another change, not in personnel, but in the composition of the committee, took place between March 1942 and September 1943, when Admiral Lord Louis Mountbatten, the chief of combined operations, was seated as an additional member when matters requiring his expertise were discussed. His inclusion reflected, of course, Churchill's predilection for offensive undertakings of all types.

In general, while Churchill and the chiefs worked together to forge Britain's war strategy, the day-to-day conduct of the war was relegated to the chiefs.[47] More specifically, as set forth by Brooke, the chiefs of staff checked into available resources for the war; allocated forces, shipping, and munitions to the many theaters; shuttled drafts of plans back and forth between London and the field; approved or rejected the plans themselves; issued orders and directives to the various war zones; and then oversaw the campaigns, rendering advice but seldom dictating their execution in detail. These duties, combined with developing strategy and "handling the political aspect of the military actions and their coordination with our Allies," left little time for anything but long hours and exhausting work. The actual running of the services was left to the vice chiefs, who, like their bosses, met together daily, the chiefs of staff in the morning, the vice chiefs in the afternoon. Sir Arthur Bryant has described the end result as "an expert precision-instrument for directing a vast, complex war machine."[48]

This positive view of the chiefs-of-staff system should not be construed to mean that the mechanism ran without friction and tensions. Churchill had numerous altercations with his service chiefs.[49] Sir Ian Jacob, one of the war cabinet secretaries, asserts that Admiral Pound "had many rough-and-tumbles with the Prime Minister, but held his own well." One of Pound's methods of putting off Churchill's wilder schemes was to have staff officers undertake a full-scale investigation of his proposal. The staff would then produce a detailed refutation of the project, and "this method . . . usually allowed the project to die quietly." General Brooke generally got along with Churchill by giving way on nonessentials. When a matter he considered vital arose, he would say to the prime minister, "I am your subordinate. I'll only carry out what you wish if you give it to me in writing and sign it." Lord Alanbrooke contends that on these occasions he never heard another word about the issue and that Churchill dropped it. The army chief also described a method used by Field Marshal Sir Harold Alexander for dealing with Churchill's interventions in the field. When Alexander was serving as head of the armies in Italy, he kept receiving telegrams from the minister of defence (Churchill), advocating that Alexander take certain actions. His method of replying was first to send the telegram to Brooke, who often knew nothing about it. Brooke would then fashion an answer and relay it back to Alexander, who, in turn, would send the reply to Churchill.

The prime minister did not always get along with subordinate committees either, especially the Joint Planning Staff, since its recommendations were often at odds with what Churchill wanted. Nevertheless, these committees and the chiefs of staff themselves benefited from his ceaseless probing. General Sir John Kennedy, head of the Joint Planning Staff, recalls that "his taunts and exhortations, and his criticism of every detail of our work, kept us continuously on our toes."[50]

Tensions also arose on occasion among the chiefs themselves.[51] There was constant friction between the navy and the air force over the allocation and use of aircraft, and conflicts between the air force and the army arose along the same lines. In these instances—as in matters of coastal defense, tactical air support, and strategic bombing—the Royal Air Force usually got its way, but not without some temporary hard feelings among the chiefs. Yet they were normally able to reconcile their differences. When they were unable to do so, Churchill had to step in. But since they fully accepted the principle of ultimate civilian control over the military, their problems never reached major proportions.

One other organizational feature of the British high-command system deserves special mention: the dependence on allies. Like all other proud peoples, the British did not relish the idea of dependence on other nations. But so long as it was a relationship based on mutual interests and cooperation, not one of inferiority-superiority, British leaders and the public at large accepted alliances and balance-of-power thinking as realistic approaches to help them solve their military problems.

Early on, the special relationship was with France. Although their alliance had been a troubled one during the interwar years, they had held numerous staff conferences prior to the war so that once the conflict had broken out, combined machinery was put into place almost immediately.[52] The main body was the Supreme War Council, made up of the respective prime ministers and one other cabinet minister from each country. They met at frequent intervals—eighteen conferences between September 1939 and June 1940—to discuss matters of common concern and to agree upon war strategy and policy. However, the council had no executive authority, final decisions being reserved to the British and French governments. The same situation applied to various economic agencies and military liaison commissions that were established on both sides of the Channel: they advised and coordinated but had no power of decision. In this case also, sovereign authority remained with the two governments acting on behalf of their parliaments. The development of Franco-British cooperation was subject to many frictions, particularly in the area of long-range planning, but undoubtedly part of the problem can be attributed to the difficulties both countries were experiencing in setting up their domestic war machinery. In fact, distrust among some elements of their own governments—as between the French general staff and their political leaders—was perhaps greater than between the representatives of the two nations. Yet in time a more closely integrated effort might well have been achieved had not the disastrous defeat of May–June 1940 intervened.

Britain's second special relationship was with the United States. It had been in the making for a number of years, and by the time America formally entered the war in December 1941, it had become a military alliance in all but name. What remained at that point was to construct the necessary machinery.

This was one of the most important tasks addressed at the First Washington Conference—code-named Arcadia—in late December 1941 and early January 1942. At the meeting the representatives of both countries, including President Roosevelt and Prime Minister Churchill, argued their positions, compromised, and then agreed upon the framework for cooperation.[53] In several areas, they were thinking along similar lines. Both were wary of excessive integration. As a consequence, except for a common meeting place in Washington, a combined secretariat, and seven subordinate committees, the Combined Chiefs of Staff, as it came to be called, was to work through its own national staffs and agencies (though the number of British military personnel in Washington mushroomed during the war). Both countries were at the time also cool to having an enlarged body embracing all allies. Hence the Combined Chiefs was to be confined to the two nations.

The British and Americans did not agree, however, on some other matters. Regarding command responsibilities in war theaters, the US preferred that each nation be primarily responsible for certain geographic areas, but Britain wanted the war to "be considered as a whole and not in water-tight compartments." By March, the British had given way. The Americans were to be responsible for the Pacific; the British were to have the dominant say in the "middle area," stretching from Southeast Asia to the Mediterranean; and they were to share control of the rest of Europe and the Atlantic. The British also gave way to the Americans on the composition of theater commands. In this case, the British reluctantly agreed to have integrated staffs with representatives from both countries rather than to allow a theater commander to have his own national staff. In the economic sphere, the United States urged, and Britain finally accepted, the idea of setting up combined boards to oversee their common effort. Thus, during the first six months of 1942, five combined boards—for munitions assignment, shipping, raw materials, production and resources, and food—were established.

How well did these structures work out? The Combined Chiefs developed into a highly successful institution. Though not the ultimate decision maker—this prerogative was reserved for the prime minister and the president—it was in a sense a decision-making body. Following the British precedent, its members were from the army, navy, and air force. It met weekly, the US being represented by its joint chiefs, the British by delegates (the British Joint Staff Mission) "sitting in" for their chiefs of staff. At times, as at allied conferences, the British chiefs themselves took over the discussions with their American counterparts. Their main functions were, not to originate, but to recommend strategies and war requirements to their heads of state, to advise them while the recommendations were being fashioned into a common strategy, and once the decisions were made, to send out orders to the theater commanders for detailed planning. In this way, both national and Anglo-American priorities were interwoven throughout the decision-making process.

Other than a successful relationship with the heads of state, the results the Combined Chiefs achieved were more mixed.[54] Both countries continued to adhere to the "special" relationship established between Churchill and Roosevelt, but as the relationship between the two allies became more unequal, the United States insisted on having more of a say, as at the Cairo Conference on November 24, 1943, when it resurrected the idea of a "United Chiefs of Staff" to include, besides Britain and the US, the Soviet Union and China. The British turned the proposal aside, but the episode does reflect tensions in the alliance. On the other hand, with some exceptions, such as the desire of the US naval chief, Admiral Ernest King, to exclude the British from operations in the Pacific, the division of the war theaters into areas of responsibility generally worked out well. Moreover, by January 1944, every theater had supreme commanders—Americans in the Pacific and for Overlord, Britishers in Southeast Asia and the Mediterranean—and integrated staffs. The other main component, the economic boards, which, except for munitions assignments, were directly under the president and the prime minister rather than the Combined Chiefs, did help bring about better cooperation, although the boards never had much power and declined in importance as American production became predominant. Still, overall the Combined Chiefs benefited both nations.

In sum, then, except at the beginning, it is difficult to fault the organizational structure of the British high command. It did perhaps put excessive power into the hands of Churchill, but given Churchill's devotion to democracy and the parliamentary system, he did not abuse that power. When necessary, the chiefs of staff stood up to him, and they ran the war intelligently, providing for input from the service and civilian ministries while generally dealing with the theater commanders in a thoughtful yet resolute manner. The cabinet secretariat, which held the mechanism together, indeed made a noteworthy contribution, its personnel being small in numbers and unobtrusive, yet exceedingly capable and knowledgeable. In fact, though there was undoubtedly infighting, it is difficult to find a civilian and military agency associated with the war effort that did not fulfill its functions well. And the British, unlike the Germans, appreciated the value of allies. Despite disagreements, the British erected structures which took into account the views of the French and then the Americans, and also the Commonwealth and Empire and associated governments throughout the conflict. The cooperative spirit which emerged was a definite factor in Britain's ability to play a significant part in achieving the Allied victory.

THREE

Running the War

The Personalities

As the organizational aspects determined in part the effectiveness of both nations' high-command systems, so too did the leading personalities involved.[1] Yet the heads of the services, whether designated commanders-in-chief or chiefs of staff, were seldom in the public eye and were certainly never accorded the accolade of war heroes. Fighting commanders such as Rommel, Guderian, von Manstein, Alexander, Montgomery, and Viscount Slim became household words in millions of German and British homes. But with the exception of Göring as a public figure and Dönitz and Andrew Cunningham for their naval exploits, the military chiefs were not well known—or at least appreciated—by their countries' citizens.

The people's perception is understandable, for military forces are concerned with fighting, and the commanders in the field are in the limelight and ultimately responsible for victory or defeat. Still, in the background—and not so much in the background in the twentieth century—general war on a vast number of fronts requires effective overall coordination as well as rendering intelligent military advice to the heads of state. Although one can overstate the great-person theory as a dominant force in shaping events, Brooke, Pound, Cunningham, Portal, and Ismay on the British side, and Halder, Keitel, Jodl, Raeder, Dönitz, and Göring on the German side, deserve to be better known and understood. They were as important in determining the outcome of the war as were the famous British and German warriors we have come to associate with it.

Although one might prefer to look as these individuals on a comparative basis—the head of the German air force and his British counterpart, the commanders of the respective navies, and so on—the wide differences between the two systems make it useful to examine the leaders from each nation individually before arriving at some comparative conclusions. One of the difficulties in separating the commanders-in-chief into their service components is that the British chiefs functioned, to use the overworked term, as a "team." It was through their close working relationship, as well as through Churchill, that the principal decisions of British war policy evolved.[2] Their closeness also helped them stand up to the prime minister when necessary. Churchill might badger, cajole, and bully them, but, as often pointed out by historians, he "did not overrule them." Historians have used the word "overruled" only in the strictest sense—Churchill was extremely forceful—but on major issues he most often deferred to the collective judgment of his chiefs.

Brooke, Portal and Pound (and after Pound's death in October 1943, Cunningham) shared many interests and characteristics.[3] All of them were fighting men by instinct, lovers of the countryside, keen fishermen, quick-witted, and unostentatious by nature. All possessed a sense of humor and were outwardly calm, though often inwardly filled with strong emotions. All of them were intensely loyal to their services, yet willing to compromise for the sake of country. And all worked extremely hard at their jobs—helping to shape strategy and advising the prime minister while staying in constant contact with their commanders in the war theaters. Within this context, some writers, especially those with extensive military experience, have asserted that the chiefs' control over their field leaders was heavy-handed and excessive. On occasion—as in Pound's disastrous scattering of the Arctic convoy PQ 17 in July 1942, or in Brooke's dealings with Mountbatten as Southeast Asian commander in late 1943—it was indeed heavy-handed. But as Ronald Lewin emphasizes, with the widespread use of radio and telephone and telegraph, "a theater commander must automatically expect (and should not think improper) a stream of signals from the center of government." In other words, commanders in the field should not be upset at being pressured from the center, for the main consideration is not simply being subjected to pressure but "the nature of the pressure" being exerted.

Although all of the British chiefs made contributions, the army's first two chiefs of staff, General Sir Edmund Ironside (1880–1959) and General (later Field Marshal) Sir John Dill (1881–1944) were not especially effective, though for different reasons. Ironside, known as "Tiny" because of his 6'4" frame, served as chief of the Imperial General Staff (CIGS) from the war's outbreak until May 27, 1940, when he was replaced by Dill.[4] Although an experienced field commander, Ironside was probably out of his depth as chief of staff. He had never worked as a staff officer at the War Office, and did not like dealing with politicians either, which was another important aspect of his job. As an expert linguist with a vast knowledge of Europe and an enthusiast for mobile warfare, he was perhaps better suited to lead the British Expeditionary Force; but Lord Gort, who had been the CIGS before the war, had been named instead. For several months after stepping down as chief of staff in May, 1940, Ironside held the responsible position of commander-in-chief, Home Forces. However, though liked by Churchill, on July 19 the war cabinet insisted that he give way to the more dynamic and hard-driving Brooke. Upon being told of his release, Ironside wrote in his diary, "I had done my best," and he probably had.

Dill's problem was of a different sort.[5] He, like Ironside, was a sound soldier, and "he was straight, sincere and respected by the Army." Before becoming CIGS, he had served as a corps commander in France and thus had had recent combat experience. But he was never able to deal with Churchill, who, during Dill's eighteen-month tenure, did not always have the kindest things to say about the army. Dill tried to stand up to the prime minister's criticisms usually in written form, but his retorts did not impress Churchill. The constant pressure and hectoring from the latter simply wore Dill out. Desmond Morton, one of Churchill's advisers, related some years after the war: "Winston did not behave well towards Dill. . . . he had little respect for Dill. He had little respect for quiet, intelligent, and well-behaved gentlemen. . . . The Winston-Dill combination would never have worked continuously—far too much difference in temperament and approach to problems."

Given these differences, it is not surprising that Churchill contemplated replacing Dill for several months, and in November 1941 the prime minister finally chose General (later Field Marshal) Sir Alan Brooke as Dill's successor. (Churchill also considered Gort and Vice Chief Archibald Nye for the position before settling on Brooke.) Dill was named governor of Bombay, but instead came to head the Joint Staff Mission after attending the Washington conference (Arcadia) in December. In this post, he performed his greatest service, ably representing Britain's military position in Washington while earning the respect and admiration of the Americans. When Dill died in November 1944 and was buried in Arlington National Cemetery, General George C. Marshall, the US Army chief of staff, said he was lost without Dill's presence. "Your Alan Brooke," Marshall said, "is very good, but no one will ever take the place of Sir John; as far as I am concerned, he is irreplaceable."[6]

Brooke (1883–1963) was different again from Dill and Ironside, though he shared with them a soldiering background.[7] Born of a Northern Irish noble family and brought up in France, he saw extensive combat in World War I. During the interwar period, he served in a number of important leadership positions, including assignments at the Staff College, Camberley; the new Imperial Defense College, which had been founded to promote interservice cooperation at the highest levels; and the newly formed Antiaircraft Command. When the war broke out, he became head of one of the two corps immediately sent to France. The other was given to one of his staff-college mentors, Sir John Dill. Commanding the two divisions under Brooke were the elderly General Dudley Johnson and the hard-driving General Bernard Montgomery. After being responsible for the successful evacuation of most British (and some French) soldiers from Dunkirk, Brooke was selected to command the 140,000 British troops still left in France, but he arrived back on the Continent only during the final days before the French capitulated. After returning to England, as mentioned earlier, he replaced General Ironside as commander-in-chief, Home Forces, and in this capacity worked unceasingly to strengthen Britain's defenses. On November 13, 1941, while visiting the prime minister at Chequers, he was told by Churchill that he was to be the next chief of the Imperial General Staff.

Therefore, in December, at age fifty-eight, Brooke became the new CIGS, a position from which he emerged as an almost legendary figure by war's end. Upon his arrival at the War Office, the atmosphere changed dramatically. Sir John Kennedy has recorded: "It was a delight to work with him. He was quick and decisive; his freshness made a new impact; he infected the War Office and the COS with his own vitality; the change of tempo was immediate and immense."[8] In March he became chair of the Chiefs of Staff Committee, in part because it was the army's turn, but in part because the current chair, First Sea Lord Pound, recognized Brooke's extraordinary dynamism.

Yet Brooke did not dominate the other service heads.[9] He was a patient listener at their meetings, and they made their decisions jointly. This was their strength. They resolved their problems reasonably on the basis of give-and-take. Brooke presided over the proceedings, not as their superior, but as one among equals, and their thinking represented their "collective identity." Because of the never-ending work, Brooke left the running of the army mainly to his gifted deputies, Archibald Nye and General Ronald Weeks.

Brooke is a very difficult person to characterize.[10] He is probably best summed up in a phrase once used to describe him—a man who "thought fast, talked fast, moved fast." At first sight a rather formidable figure, immaculately dressed, with aquiline features, he had an exceedingly quick mind. He seldom needed to hear anything twice before grasping its essence, whether it was a matter of detail or broad strategy. This trait led him to be impatient with individuals slower-witted than he, though he could be gracious to a fault, and those around him, especially his fellow chiefs, considered him a charming companion. His staccato, strong, rather nasal voice added to his reputation as a man in a hurry, as did his efficient, methodical. punctilious way of doing business. He displayed a number of other admirable characteristics as well. He was not given to jealousy or ambition for the sake of ambition, and his few off-duty hours were spent with family or engaging in one of his many hobbies, such as birdwatching, fishing, gardening, or photography. He truly possessed a multisided character.

On the other hand, Brooke was rather aloof and austere, difficult to get to know. His reserved nature seemingly made it difficult for him to understand the more relaxed, less sophisticated American military men with whom he came to associate. Though an excellent field commander, he was not a soldiers' general, not "one of the fellows." Moreover, his diary, parts of which were published a little over a decade after the end of the war, brings out other negative aspects of his personality—his high-strung, volatile temperament, his scornful comments about Churchill, his intolerance of others.[11] The diary had served as his "safety valve" amid the tensions of office. Nevertheless, Sir Arthur Bryant's later inadequate editing of it diminished Brooke's stature for some time until Brooke's papers became available in the late 1970s.

Fortunately, Brooke's positive traits far outweighed his negative ones. Nowhere was this more in evidence than in his dealings with Churchill, whom he handled with tact and resourcefulness. Their relationship did not begin that way. When discussing Brooke for the CIGS appointment, Churchill said to Vice Chief Nye: "When I thump the table and push my face towards him what does he do? Thumps the table harder and glares back at me—I know these Brookes—stiff-necked Ulstermen and there's no one worse to deal with than that!"[12] Within a very short time, however, each had gained the other's respect. Alan Brooke's realism was the perfect complement to Churchill's more imaginative schemes, a check on the latter's impatience and impetuosity. This was probably Brooke's great contribution. He was not an originator. His strength lay in knowing what would and would not work and in his ability to push strategy to completion, not inflexibly, but with a resolve of purpose. Through the combination of practicality and determination, he became not only an outstanding soldier but also "the prime military architect of Britain's successes in the Second World War."[13]

We know a good deal less about Admiral Sir Dudley Pound (1877–1943), the head of the Royal Navy throughout most of the period, than we do about Brooke. Pound left few intimate papers and has not been the subject of a biography. We do know that he had extensive operational and administrative experience, including, in the 1930s, service as second sea lord (personnel) and commander-in-chief of the Mediterranean fleet before becoming first sea lord at age sixty-two in June 1939.[14] We also know that he was a naval person to the core, that he loved the sea, but was probably a better administrator than a commander, and that he effectively kept his staff and the commanders at sea abreast of personnel, operational, and strategic matters.

Pound himself is a study in contrasts.[15] He has been criticized for being slow and going to sleep at meetings, but, as Ismay has pointed out, "on the mention of the word 'destroyer' or of any harbour in any part of the world, he was wide-awake at once and showed that he had been following the discussions more closely with his eyes shut than many of those who had their eyes wide open." The reason for his dozing off was that he suffered excruciating pain from arthritis in his left hip, which affected his sleep and work routine. It also led to a general deterioration in his health, and by the time of his resignation following a stroke in September 1943, he had been ill for some time.

Another contrast is that even though the first sea lord possessed an orderly and logical mind, he was not especially imaginative. He was not resourceful in argument and seldom took a broad view of strategy, but remained naval in outlook. In addition, he did not have intellectual interests and had no hobbies except fishing and hunting. He was hard-working, efficient, outwardly calm, and pleasant in his relations with others. Upon meeting Pound, Sir Claude Auchinleck, the commander-in-chief, Middle East, wrote to his wife, ". . . I like [Pound] very much indeed. He doesn't say much but he is very straight and honest and has a great sense of humor."[16]

Pound and Churchill thought a lot of each other, though sometimes Pound admitted being sorely tried by the prime minister. According to Roskill, Pound's most serious drawback was his tendency to assume too much authority, even for operations at sea. For instance, he—and Churchill—were responsible for allowing the battleship *Prince of Wales* and the cruiser *Repulse* to be attacked and sunk near Singapore after Japan's declaration of war. Then there was Pound's order for the dispersal of Convoy PQ 17, which led to its near destruction. He might also be criticized for not pushing more strongly for the necessary long-range aircraft and other means to turn around the Atlantic battle sooner. Nevertheless, Pound's inclination toward overcentralization was offset to an extent by his fair-mindedness and integrity. He was, after all, commanding what was arguably the finest navy in the world. It is interesting that even during the perilous days of 1940, while the war cabinet and chiefs of staff fretted about the army and the air force, how little concern British leaders expressed about the navy. The presumption seems to have been that somehow, some way, the navy would get the job done. When Pound died on Trafalgar Day, October 21, 1943, Churchill's glowing tribute to "my trusted naval friend" obviously came from the heart.

Pound's successor, Admiral Sir Andrew Bourne Cunningham (1883–1963) was truly a superior combat commander—resolute, courageous, interested in those who served under him.[17] In his two stints as naval commander-in-chief, Mediterranean (interspersed in 1942 with a tour on the Joint Staff Mission in Washington), ABC, as he was called, had been associated with numerous naval victories—as well as with some setbacks. When Pound became incapacitated, Churchill wanted Admiral Sir Bruce Forbes to become first sea lord, but the navy wanted ABC. Admiral Sir Percy Noble, Cunningham's replacement in Washington, reflected the navy's position in a letter he wrote to Cunningham just before the latter's October appointment: ". . . if [Pound] should be unable to go on, I assume that you will in due course, take his place. That is what the whole Navy would like to see, but I know that you personally would view the suggestion with some distaste! All the same, I think for the good of everyone, you ought to do it if it comes your way."[18]

Although they got along well enough, Churchill never really took to Cunningham. Undoubtedly, Cunningham was a formidable person—bluff, extroverted, quick-tempered, with a round face and penetrating blue eyes. While Cunningham was not a gifted strategist, perhaps Churchill feared this determined Scot because of his forceful nature. And Cunningham's replies to Churchill's inquiries were usually shorter and more direct than Pound's had been. ABC was simply too much a fighting sailor, and he admitted that "office work [is] not my strong suit." Days of meetings and indecision clashed with his resolute nature. In August 1944, for example, after a frustrating discussion on the strategy to be followed in Burma, he wrote: "No decisions were reached, in fact a thoroughly wasted day. What a drag on the wheel of war this man [Churchill] is. Everything is centralized in him with consequent indecision and waste of time before anything can be done."[19] Yet Cunningham's primary task was to keep the war machinery running smoothly, and this he did with a cooperative spirit that earned him the respect of his fellow chiefs. In this regard, the navy's confidence in him was indeed justified.

The head of the air force, Air Chief Marshal Sir Charles Portal (1893–1971) was of yet another stripe. He had become chief of the air staff in October 1940, when the able and well-liked Sir Cyril Newall (1886–1963) proved not strong-willed enough to adjudicate the many conflicting air requirements and to deal effectively with the strong personalities that made up Britain's youngest service.[20] Portal represented the RAF's youthful outlook—he was only forty-seven when he took over—but he possessed a sagacity that one often attributes to older persons. Part of the reason why "Peter" Portal seemed so wise and thoughtful was because of his imperturbability. Nothing seemed to bother him, and his aristocratic background—born on a country estate near Hungerford in Berkshire, attended prep school at Winchester, studied at Oxford, where he never finished because of World War I—lent itself to self-control. He was, in addition, very active and competitive and became a first-class pilot during the Great War. During the interwar years, he served in numerous important command and administrative positions, and soon after the war broke out, he became commander-in-chief of Bomber Command until being named air chief in 1940. In this capacity, he reached the pinnacle of military success.

Among the many characterizations of Portal, the one by Sir David Fraser is succinct yet appropriate: "quiet, courteous, master of his subject, intelligent, unruffled and decisive."[21] Though not especially talkative or social, he had a certain modesty, charm, and wit. He knew what he was talking about and could present his arguments persuasively. Like most other proponents of air power, he believed in strategic bombing, but he was just as interested in increasing the total strength of the air force, while at the same time protecting its integrity against the other services. He wholeheartedly believed in working with the army and navy, too, and the spirit of cooperation that he engendered made him an extremely valuable member of the Chiefs of Staff Committee. He was, moreover, exceedingly intelligent. Not only Churchill and the other chiefs, but the Americans as well appreciated his analytic mind and the impartiality with which he appeared to approach and resolve problems. His calm temperament and decisive nature, both integral parts of his personality, add to our positive picture of him.

Yet there was another side to Portal, one well brought out by his biographer, Sir Denis Richards, and by John Terraine.[22] Besides being intelligent, controlled, and quiet, he was also cold and remote in his relations with others.

As Terraine has put it, "down the years he does not warm the heart." He enjoyed the out-of-doors and fishing and doing card tricks, but, except for his closeness with family, he led a relatively solitary existence, working long days and nights at his London office and attending meetings, but seldom visiting command headquarters or air stations. He ate lunch daily at the Travellers Club in Pall Mall, purposely alone, not talking with other members while there or even exchanging greetings with the help. He behaved similarly with his staff and secretaries, whom he treated in a businesslike and correct, but hardly cordial, way.

Portal's main contribution, then, was not in personal relations but in making sure that the air force was functioning well at home and in keeping in constant contact with his commanders overseas. The actual running of the RAF was turned over to his trusted vice chief, Air Chief Marshal Sir Wilfrid Freeman. Portal's other contribution, of course, was his help in fashioning interservice and also combined strategy with the Americans and advising the prime minister, and these duties he performed with great distinction. Churchill thought highly of his air force chief despite—perhaps because of—Portal's ability to examine problems on a rational, objective basis. And he, like the other chiefs, was not afraid to defend his position against Churchill if he thought the issue was vital. Of the many memoranda Churchill sent to Portal, Richards writes that they "suggest a domineering Prime Minister dealing with a Chief of Staff who refuses to be dominated, and who by his skill, good manners, and patience usually ends up the victor in the argument."[23] In this capacity, Portal served the air force and the British nation well.

Although not a decision maker, one other "member" of the chiefs of staff deserves special mention: General Sir Hastings Ismay.[24] Best known as the liaison between Churchill and seemingly everyone else, this tall, well-built, upright army officer, whose broad nose and rather flat face earned him the nickname "Pug," was truly a remarkable individual. Possessed of a quick mind, a cultivated manner, and a strong personality, he was a gentleman in the best sense of the word. He loved good living and was an excellent horseman and games player. He was also a very hard worker with unbelievable stamina who displayed no traces of vanity, jealousy, or undue ambition. He got along well with everyone—the prime minister, the other chiefs, his staff, ministers, civil officials, allies—all those concerned with the British war effort.

As secretary to the war cabinet and the chiefs of staff, his most telling gift was the esteem in which he was held by Churchill. Churchill could talk with Ismay, reason, even rage at him if necessary. Ismay bore these outbursts from his mercurial, exacting boss with equanimity, and his steady, good temper never seemed to fail. When Churchill was upset with what was happening in the Middle East, for example, and wanted to intervene directly, Ismay would talk him out of it or at least attempt to tone down any communication he might send to the field. When the prime minister became exasperated with the American president, Ismay would rewrite the pertinent telegram so that it was less harshly phrased. When Churchill fumed about one of his ministers, Ismay would make sure that the minister was informed firmly, but in a diplomatic way. Ismay, in short, was "a wise interpreter and an immensely tactful conciliator."[25] Churchill realized he needed a person like that, and fortunately for Britain, Ismay was such a person.

Despite their differences, the British chiefs thus complemented one another. Each had characteristics which contributed to a smooth-running war machine from the top: Brooke's dynamism, Portal's calmness, Pound's determination, and Ismay's tact were essential ingredients that made the system work. None was an original thinker, but with the assistance of their staffs and with Churchill's imagination, they were able to forge a joint strategy that saw Britain through its most perilous early years. Then, after the entrance of the United States, they were able to develop a combined strategy with their American partners, which, along with the Soviet contribution, ultimately brought military victory. In both instances, the formulation of joint and combined strategy into a unified whole and the overseeing of its execution, the British chiefs played a stellar role.

On the German side, as noted earlier, there was a lack of cooperation and coordination at the highest level. That the system worked at all was more the result of a cooperative spirit among the various service staffs and at the lower echelons than at the top. Nevertheless, not all of the commanders-in-chief and the chiefs of staff were unintelligent, servile incompetents. Some of them, such as Halder, Zeitzler, and Raeder, were individuals of ability, and others, notably Guderian and Dönitz were simply misplaced, being better suited to operational than staff commands. Even those usually viewed as sycophants—von Brauchitsch, Keitel, Jodl, and Göring—were not completely bereft of talent. Therefore, even though the German service chiefs conjure up a negative image, it is not completely a one-sided picture.

While the dominant service, the army, lost considerable power in relation to Hitler even before the war, not until December 1941, when the Führer took over as commander-in-chief, had its decision-making capabilities become completely eroded. Before then—and during the period of Germany's greatest triumphs—von Brauchitsch and Halder worked in tandem to provide the Wehrmacht with the necessary planning and oversight, restricting themselves to military matters while at the same time trying, though not always successfully, to resist inordinate interference from Hitler and Nazi party officials in the military sphere.[26]

General (later Field Marshal) Walther von Brauchitsch (1881–1948) had become head of the army in the wake of the February 1938 Blomberg-Fritsch scandals, which had helped Hitler cement his control over the army.[27] Like his predecessors, von Brauchitsch had his roots in the general-staff tradition. He had served in World War I as an artillery officer and during the 1920s and 1930s in various command and staff positions, including head of Army Group Command IV at Leipzig, just prior to becoming army commander-in-chief.

From the beginning of his tenure, he had compromised himself with Hitler. At the time he took over, von Brauchitsch was unhappily married, having been separated from his wife for five years. But in return for a divorce so that he could remarry, his wife demanded a sizable financial settlement, which he could not afford. Hitler resolved the problem by reportedly having the party loan von Brauchitsch the necessary money (although after the war he denied ever receiving it). Still, his fate was sealed, particularly since he was a party member and his second wife a devoted National Socialist follower.

Despite his personal problems, von Brauchitsch was an extremely hard worker.[28] Besides receiving numerous reports that dealt with all aspects of the army and keeping informed of war developments, he conferred with Hitler at least every other day and met with his staff and branch chiefs every morning and afternoon, when decisions were made on the spot. In addition, he displayed a correct and gentlemanly, if oversensitive, nature.

It was in his relationship with Hitler that he could not cope. Von Brauchitsch would not speak out against the Führer to his face, and Hitler completely dominated and browbeat him. The commander-in-chief's worsening health—he had suffered a series of heart attacks—as well as the deteriorating situation on the Russian Front finally led to his removal. Even though he recommended Field Marshal Günther von Kluge or General Erich von Manstein to be his successor, by this time Hitler was experiencing difficulties with his recalcitrant generals and decided to take over himself.

General Franz Halder (1884–1972) was willing to stay on as chief of staff. He was of much stronger mettle than the pliable von Brauchitsch. He is also one of the more enigmatic figures of the war. The attempt of Halder's granddaughter, Countess Schall-Riaucour, to depict him as a person truly caught up between his military duty and his moral beliefs is overgenerous, but her view provides a starting point for evaluating his character.[29]

First and foremost, Halder was a military professional. Following in the footsteps of his ancestors, who had served in the Bavarian military for generations, he had been a general staff officer in World War I and, like von Brauchitsch, had held down a number of line and staff appointments during the interwar years. In 1938, he became the chief of operations (*Oberquartiermeister* I) and deputy to his friend, General Ludwig Beck. When Beck resigned as chief of staff in August because of a basic disagreement with Hitler over the timing for attacking Czechoslovakia, Halder, at age fifty-four, took Beck's place. In the ensuing three years he was the driving force in the operational effort, overseeing the planning and execution of the early campaigns. But after 1941, his position deteriorated to the point that by September 1942 it had become intolerable. The final break occurred when Hitler would not allow several German units to withdraw from the Rzhev salient in Russia to more defensible lines, and Halder stepped down.

As brought out by Schall-Riaucour and others, there was another side to this complex individual. He was an exceedingly ethical, devout Christian,

who did not approve of Hitler's lack of morality. Moreover, he was willing
to stand up to the Führer if he considered Hitler wrong, and on occasion
went so far as to ignore orders, as in the summer of 1942 when Hitler
directed a panzer division to be sent from France to the east. Halder's response
was to do nothing. His dislike, perhaps even detestation, of Hitler and his
methods led him to join the military resistance before and during the war.
Although deeply involved at the time of the Czech crisis, and in November
1939, his involvement in resistance efforts then lessened, and he often equivo-
cated instead of taking a resolute stand in backing the various plots. And
though he spent the final months after the July 20 attempt in a concentration
camp, his moral scruples never seemed to overcome his military sense of
duty.

Complicating the picture of Halder are a number of other traits. One
of the first Bavarians to gain prominence on the German general staff, he
has been described as conservative, cautious, and colorless. But those around
him contend he could be lively enough, certainly less stiff-necked than many
of his Prussian counterparts. He was also extremely conscientious, working
long days (horseback riding at 5:30 a.m., eating no lunch, going over reports
and attending briefings late into the night) and taking leave only once at
Christmas time in 1940 during his four years as chief of staff. Furthermore, no one doubted his intelligence. He had an excellent grasp of strategy
and weaponry, and even his avocational interests—mathematics and plant
specimens—show an intellectual bent. In fact, Halder's temperament and
appearance, with his close-cropped hair and pince-nez, resembled those of
a schoolmaster more than a general. Nor did anyone doubt the mutual respect
between him and his staff as they worked together on problems and his
love for the troops in the field. He had his critics—Fedor von Bock and
Göring among the military, and Bernd Gisevius and Ulrich von Hassell among
the conspirators—but he was certainly an honorable man.

Why then, did this upright, reserved, intense, in some ways fearless general
staff officer not break sooner with Hitler? The answer can only be surmised,
for Halder's diary, in contrast to Brooke's, is more a recapitulation of military
considerations than an account of Halder's innermost thoughts. But as Klaus-
Jürgen Müller has indicated, Halder was never able to free himself from
the military structures and ideas that shaped his thinking.[30] He, too, like
Hitler, wanted a stronger Germany; he, too, was anti-Bolshevik, approved
of the "ideological" war against the Soviet Union, and distrusted the masses.
He was also fascinated to an extent by Hitler's Blitzkrieg conceptions and
expansionistic aims, though he hated the man. As a result, despite his efforts
to exonerate himself after the war, and despite his being the "best and bright-
est" of the chiefs of staff, Halder never achieved the true greatness that
might have been his had he been willing to take more decisive steps in
toppling the regime.

Halder's successor, General Kurt Zeitzler (1895–1963), turned out to be a surprise.[31] Hitler had selected the forty-seven-year-old staff officer because he thought Zeitzler, who had been serving as chief of staff to Field Marshal Gerd von Rundstedt's western theater command, would prove more "cooperative" than the critical and pessimistic Halder. Zeitzler was not held in high esteem by many of the field commanders because of his relative inexperience and caustic personality. But even though limited to overseeing developments on the Russian Front, he did not always cave in readily to Hitler's schemes. and he effectively resisted interference in his affairs from other quarters, particularly from Jodl at OKW. And so long as two-thirds to three-fourths of Germany's combat divisions were involved in the east, Zeitzler was bound to have some say in German operations.

The conservative, straightforward, apolitical Zeitzler was not so knowledgeable about strategy as Halder, but he was energetic and hard-working and stuck up for the troops and officer corps. Though demanding and thus difficult to work for, he kept the branches under him working smoothly and maintained contact with the commanders in the field through frequent telephone calls and messages.

Zeitzler's main problem was in dealing with Hitler. At first they seemed to get along well enough, and Zeitzler was able to argue the Führer out of some of his more dubious notions, such as Hitler's insistence on not allowing troops to evacuate parts of the Caucasus region in December 1942 (though Zeitzler never did persuade Hitler to order a timely withdrawal from Stalingrad). During 1943, however, their relations cooled, and Zeitzler repeatedly tried to resign (five times altogether). The last altercation took place in early July 1944 when Zeitzler wanted to remove Army Group Courland near the Baltic before it became completely encircled. Hitler was opposed. In a conversation with Liddell Hart after the war, Zeitzler, who could be as hot tempered as the Führer, recalled their argument in the following terms:

> I told him that I could not be a party to the encirclement of the Army Group Courland. . . . He became very loud and broke off the interview with the words: "I bear the responsibility and not you." I replied just as loudly: "In the same way as you, my Fuehrer, are responsible to the German people, I am responsible to my conscience. And nobody can relieve me of that responsibility, not even you, my Fuehrer." He thereupon became pale with rage. I was prepared for anything. I told him further that it was impossible to win the war by military means. Something had to be done by political means. Hitler then started raving. . . . That was the last time I saw and spoke to Adolf Hitler. From that moment onward I did not do any more duty. I reported sick immediately.[32]

The July 20 attempt on Hitler's life was therefore the occasion, not the cause, for Zeitzler's dismissal. He probably knew about the plot (as did other officers) but was not involved. Nevertheless, this did not prevent the Führer from removing him only hours after the explosion. Hitler even forbade Zeitzler the right to wear his uniform and had Zeitzler's military aide executed for possible involvement.

As the war situation worsened—the summer of 1944 was especially desperate, with Allied land forces advancing rapidly from the east, west, and south and with bombing attacks beginning to have a devastating effect—Hitler decided to appoint General Heinz Guderian (1888–1954), the famous tank commander, his new chief of staff.[33] Originally Hitler had preferred General Walter Buhle, the head of the army liaison staff at OKW, but Buhle had been seriously injured in the July 20 bomb blast. By this time it made little difference. Guderian was still to be responsible for the war in the east, but Hitler was more firmly in control than ever. At the time of the Ardennes offensive, Guderian urged the Führer not to neglect the Russian Front, but to no avail. In late January 1945, he proposed that Hitler seek an armistice in the west, but his appeal was again turned down. Though intelligent enough, Guderian was not particularly effective in his job because he was a much better tactician than strategist.

The final clash came on March 28, when Guderian sought to defend General Theodor Busse of the Ninth Army, whom Hitler was berating at one of his briefings. As the confrontation became more heated, Hitler cleared the room and, in the presence of Keitel and Guderian, informed the latter, who was having heart trouble anyway, that he should immediately go on leave for six weeks until his health improved. In his stead, General Hans Krebs, a friend and drinking companion of General Burgdorf, the Nazi head of army personnel, would serve until Guderian had supposedly recovered. But the war ended before Guderian ever returned. With Krebs as acting chief of staff, Waldemar Erfurth sarcastically summed up the depth to which the position had sunk from Hitler's standpoint with the following comment: "Halder was a know-it-all *[Besserwisser]*, Zeitzler empty-headed and Guderian pig-headed; now in Krebs he [Hitler] had found the perfect chief of the general staff."[34]

As brought out earlier, given the Army High Command's decline in importance, one might expect OKW to assume a more prominent role. But while OKW's power increased, it never became the dominant element in Germany's war machine. In part this was because Hitler never gave the Armed Forces High Command the organizational structure or the freedom and responsibility it needed to function as the overall directing and coordinating body. In part it was because OKW's two leaders, Field Marshal Wilhelm Keitel and General Alfred Jodl, lacked the stature to influence the Führer more than marginally. They simply believed too much in his "genius" to oppose him for any length of time.

Keitel (1882–1946), the weaker of the two, has been pilloried by associates and historians alike for his lack of backbone.[35] It is indeed difficult to paint a very positive picture of this mediocre man, who for seven years did virtually nothing to enhance his potentially powerful position as OKW chief. Keitel was born into a landowning Hanoverian family, was an average student at the Gymnasium, displayed religious convictions, married an ambitious and strong-willed wife, by whom he had six children, and became a general staff officer prior to World War I. After the war, he stayed on in the army and held artillery unit and staff appointments. He worked extremely hard and was a good organizer with outstanding attention to detail, and these attributes brought him to the notice of the army leadership.

In 1934, Keitel became a general during a difficult time and was commanding the 22nd Infantry Division when he was asked to become chief of the Wehrmacht Office, War Minister von Blomberg's unsuccessful project aimed at forming a true joint operations staff. In 1938, after the Blomberg-Fritsch affair, Hitler asked Keitel to head the newly formed Armed Forces High Command. From this point on, he was continually at the Führer's side; however, he never influenced Hitler in any meaningful way, merely echoing his ideas and issuing orders to suit his master's wishes. To Keitel's credit, he was aware of not being up to the job and asked to be replaced on three occasions—fall 1939, December 1941, and September 1942. Hitler always turned him down, and Keitel did not press the matter. Whether he should have been hanged at Nuremberg for his role in the Third Reich may be open to debate, but he certainly did little to resist or even to advise Hitler against pursuing his inhumane and racist notions.

General Jodl (1890–1946) was a more admirable person.[36] He was from a Bavarian military family and, like Keitel, served in numerous artillery and general staff posts in World War I and during the 1920s and early 1930s. In 1935, he became associated with the Wehrmacht Office as chief of the Operational Defense Section *(Abteilung Landesverteidigung)* and, in 1938, was named to command a division in Vienna. Just prior to the war, he was recalled to Berlin to head OKW's operations staff *(Wehrmachtführungsamt)*. His admirers, especially his second wife, Luise, contend that he was not a "yes man" and point to his standing up to Hitler after undertaking an inspection trip to the Caucasus in September 1942. In this instance, Jodl told the Führer upon his return that German troops in the area were already overextended and in particular that a mountain corps was not fit to undertake any further offensive actions. Hitler was so furious with Jodl's defeatist attitude that he "banished" him from eating at his table and refused to shake hands with either Jodl or Keitel for some months. Nevertheless, seldom did Jodl argue with the Führer about his military decisions. Instead, he continued to tailor his briefings to Hitler's liking and to busy himself with responsibilities for the war in the OKW theaters. Jodl seldom visited the areas under OKW, delegating that job to his deputy, General Walter Warlimont, and his staff. Until the final year of the war, Jodl preferred to stay in his office near Hitler and to be briefed by others rather than to involve himself more directly in strategic matters.

Jodl was not devoid of positive traits. Although taciturn, he was respected by his peers as an intelligent, hard-working, decent staff officer who knew his job and the profession in general. What he lacked was the vision to see the broader dimensions of strategy, an area in which he constantly deferred to Hitler. To Jodl's detriment, he never understood the disastrous path on which his leader was moving the country. One might quarrel, as in the case of Keitel, that the guilty verdict meted out to Jodl at Nuremberg was excessive, particularly since Hitler's leadership style was *not* to seek counsel, but there is no doubt that despite doing his duty—a point effectively made by his lawyer at the trial—Jodl, like many others in Nazi Germany, came too much under the Führer's spell to be an effective adviser.

Germany's two naval leaders throughout the war—Grand Admirals Erich Raeder and Karl Dönitz—had some success in their dealings with Hitler. Despite the navy's small size in relation to the other services, both admirals were able to push forward important naval priorities, such as submarine construction, and had some impact on German strategy, particularly with regard to Norway and the Atlantic. Yet these two thoroughly professional naval officers, like their army and air force counterparts, gave in to Hitler's wishes more often than not. Admittedly, their only choices were resignation, compliance, or "playing a game"; nonetheless, their selfish attitudes were disastrous for their country.

The effectiveness of Raeder (1876–1960) as head of the navy can generally be attributed to his long tenure: having become its commander-in-chief in 1928, he thus provided the navy with great stability and unity for an extended period.[37] Born at Wandsbek near Hamburg, he had entered the navy in 1897 and served in World War I with Admiral Franz Hipper and his famous scouting force. After the war, Raeder made the mistake of backing the unsuccessful putsch attempt of Wolfgang Kapp against the Weimar government and was "exiled" for a time to the naval archives to help work on a naval history of the recent conflict. He used the assignment to good advantage. Not only did he write a volume dealing with German cruiser warfare in foreign waters, he also displayed considerable intellectual ability by finishing his doctorate at the University of Berlin. In 1922, he became inspector of naval education. This was followed by two important command assignments before being named naval commander-in-chief at age fifty-two.

Raeder's personal characteristics are a mixture of qualities. He was short, and his body and legs were slightly out of proportion; he was very conscious of both physical "drawbacks." As a person, besides being bright, he was conservative, religious, gentlemanly, and austere. As head of the navy, he ran a tight ship; though respected, he did not like to be criticized or contradicted. As a strategic thinker, he was not a forceful speaker; one might expect Hitler not to be interested in his opinions. The Führer, however, usually listened respectfully to Raeder's advice on naval matters, partly because Hitler admitted being unfamiliar with the intricacies of naval warfare, partly because Raeder shared with the Führer his desire for eventual world mastery. Nor was Raeder hidebound despite being thought of as a person from the "old school" when the war broke out. He favored a balanced fleet and was concerned about having too few surface vessels, but by 1942, he, like Dönitz, was pushing hard for more U-boats.

Nevertheless, in late 1942, with the war going badly, Hitler and Raeder were not getting along. Their disagreements, primarily over types of ships, financial stringencies, and operational concerns, came to a head when German surface vessels, after fierce fighting, failed to stop a British convoy heading for Murmansk on New Year's Eve.[38] After some haggling between the two, Raeder finally resigned. He suggested Admiral Rolf Carls, the commander of the northern group, or Dönitz, whom he disliked, as his replacement. Hitler selected Dönitz. Raeder was given an honorary post and sat out the rest of the war. Because he was then tried and sentenced to life imprisonment at Nuremberg (later reduced to ten years because of his failing health), he was extremely bitter toward the Allies for what he considered unjust punishment. Except in the eyes of "old navy" comrades, his stature further declined after his release, for his largely ghost-written memoirs are a blatant attempt to dissociate the navy from the more horrible aspects of the National Socialist regime.

The same problem also affected the stature of Dönitz (1891–1980).[39] His memoirs, though valuable, must be read with caution, for they are replete with errors and half-truths. In them he underplays his belief in National Socialism, even though, in contrast to Raeder, he was on friendly terms with most of the party hierarchy. Other factors have tarnished Dönitz's reputation as well. He was a brilliant tactical commander, but as head of the navy he had his limitations. He was not a gifted strategist. Despite his insistence that he was given free reign in handling the navy, he was more subservient to the Führer than he was willing to admit.

Still, Peter Kemp and others are correct in asserting that Dönitz's forte was as builder and commander of the U-boat arm, a position he retained even after becoming naval chief at age fifty-one and transferring his headquarters from Paris to Berlin. It was as U-boat chief that he was best able to use his energy, iron will, calm, and resolution. The position also allowed him to be near his sailors, whom he dearly loved and respected. In many ways, he was thought to epitomize the spirit of the "new navy," in contrast to the older, outmoded thinking of Raeder and his staff.

When Dönitz moved to Berlin, however, other qualities were called for. Although able to make a point, he was on the whole a quiet person who seldom challenged the Führer. Around associates and family he was pleasant enough, but he was not a gifted conversationalist. He was diligent, but headstrong, refusing to admit when he was wrong. He increasingly fell under Hitler's spell. Biographer Peter Padfield has noted Dönitz's revealing account of an August 1943 meeting which dealt with Italy after Mussolini's overthrow:

The huge force which the Führer radiates, his unshakeable confidence, his far-sighted judgment of the situation in Italy had made it plain during these days what very poor little sausages we all are in comparison with the Führer, and that our knowledge, our vision of things outside our limited sphere is fragmentary. Anyone who believes he can do better than the Führer is foolish.[40]

Given Dönitz's adulation of Nazi principles, it is little wonder that in May 1945 Hitler selected him as his successor.[41] By that time, Dönitz's inflated ego and self-deception were complete. Even after being sentenced to fifteen years at Nuremberg, he continued in prison to see himself as the head of state who would someday once again be proclaimed by the people to guide the German nation.[42]

Although both Dönitz the ultimate tactician and Raeder the competent strategist were able to gain certain concessions in the naval sphere, their limited outlooks and their delusions about Hitler and his movement in the end led to their undoing. That the navy fared no worse, and in some ways fared better, than the other services is no excuse for their failure to condemn Hitler's immoral actions.

The head of the Luftwaffe, Reichsmarschall Herman Göring (1893–1946), was a well-known public figure outside his role as air force chief.[43] Besides being Hitler's designated successor, he was at one time or another responsible for Prussia, the four-year economic plan, rearmament, and even certain areas of justice. He was also an unofficial foreign policy adviser and a top party leader, the latter position reflecting his longtime comradeship with Hitler during the so-called *Kampfzeit,* or early years of struggle.

He was truly a fascinating if repulsive individual. Born in Bavaria, he became an infantry officer but transferred to the flying service during World War I and became a renowned air "ace" before war's end. After the war, the swashbuckling Göring was restless. After joining the Nazi movement, he played an active part in Hitler's Beer Hall putsch in November 1923. When it failed, he fled to Sweden, but returned and was elected to the Reichstag as a National Socialist representative in 1928. In this position he became a disruptive force in that body's workings. Nevertheless, he gained additional influence inside the party and notoriety outside. By the time Hitler attained power, Göring was one of his most trusted and esteemed lieutenants, and when the Führer openly proclaimed the creation of an air force in March 1935, Göring, already heavily involved in air matters, was at age forty-two the obvious choice to become Luftwaffe commander-in-chief. He held the post until the final days of the war, when Hitler stripped him of his power because he had been seeking a separate peace with the Allies.

Göring was a number of individuals rolled into one. He liked to be called the "Iron Man" (*Der Eiserne*), but he often played the role of a sycophant around Hitler, to whom he was intensely loyal. Matthew Cooper characterizes him further as a study in contradictions: "brutal and kind; brave and cowardly;

refined and coarse; intelligent, vain, humourous and ruthless by turns, an inspiration to some, an object of ridicule and detestation to others." Moreover, after he had firmly established the air force, Göring became lethargic and erratic and often incapable of sustained work. He refused, for instance, to read any policy document longer than four pages. This obese man was also attracted by the gaudy and the luxurious; his dress became more bizarre as time went on, and his country estate, Karinhall, a tribute to ostentatious living. In later years his health showed a marked decline, a result not so much of taking morphine as being overwrought and depressed. Göring's influence, at its height during the 1930s and the early years of the war, had steadily declined. After Stalingrad, he became a political outsider. Hitler still talked with him—he still headed the air force—but his counsel was seldom sought. Near the end, when he was in disgrace, he was replaced by General Robert von Greim, but then reemerged at the Nuremberg trials as the paladin of Nazism: jovial, bluff, cunning, totally corrupt. Göring avoided the gallows by taking cyanide, thus producing a type of mystique surrounding his death, but a mystique which had little, if any, impact on postwar Germany.

Göring's running of the air force reflected his increasingly slothful and unstable nature.[44] Edward Homze has pointed out that "he intervened on large issues but relegated the day-to-day operation of the Luftwaffe to others." This was a source of difficulties because the air force and the air ministry were staffed generally by competent but ambitious, egotistical, highstrung, jealous officers. Field Marshal Erhard Milch (1892–1972) was the key individual until mid-1944, particularly in the area of aircraft production. Although Milch experienced problems—mainly because of air staff and ministry infighting—this former Lufthansa chief executive was able, despite Göring's poor relations with aircraft manufacturers and lack of appreciation of technological innovation, to push production ahead and to reorient it to producing more fighters for air defense as the war progressed. Milch retained his position of power until June 1944, when he gave in to inevitable consolidation, and aircraft production was shifted to Speer's control.

General Hans Jeschonnek (1899–1943), the air chief of staff, was Milch's main rival. A dedicated Nazi, Jeschonnek, the *Wunderkind* of the Luftwaffe, was a true professional, but he was so dedicated to pursuing operational matters that he gave up oversight of other essential areas, such as training and communications, which were delegated to Milch, and supply, which was run by the Luftwaffe quartermaster general. Consequently, coordination among the various air components was lacking. As the air war worsened, Jeschonnek became increasingly isolated, Göring turned more and more to officers other than him for advice, and when Hitler berated Jeschonnek several times after successful Allied air raids on targets in Germany, he had had enough. He committed suicide on August 18, 1943.

A series of successors followed. General Günther Korten (1894–1944) established himself as a strong personality, got along well with Milch and Hitler, and understood air defense (which Jeschonnek did not). Unfortunately, Korten was injured in the July 20 bomb blast and died soon after, and his replacement, General Werner Kreipe (1904–1967), almost immediately got into a heated argument with the Führer and was asked to resign. Though disliked by Göring, General Karl Koller (1898–1951), Korten's head of operations, was next appointed chief of the air staff in November 1944. Koller was not firm enough in his dealings with Hitler, but he did complete the streamlining of air functions begun under Korten. The air staff now coordinated all military aspects of the air war, including aircraft procurement, while the armaments ministry supervised production. In other words, the air general staff was finally operating as an air staff in wartime should.

Nevertheless, while Milch and Jeschonnek and later Korten and Koller were the dominant authorities in the Luftwaffe's daily workings and had some contact with Hitler, the air force's preferred status with the Führer was highly dependent on Göring. When the latter's influence waned, the other air leaders were not allowed to fill the vacuum, in large part because Göring still remained titular head. Hitler's say in directing air policy increased accordingly. The result was that Hitler's interference in air matters, as in other military concerns, continued to rise as German defeats multiplied in number and severity. It was an unfortunate combination of circumstances for the air force and for Germany.

Were Warlimont, Zeitzler, and others therefore correct? Was the British chief-of-staff system truly superior to that of Germany? Based on the foregoing evidence, the answer has to be yes. Organizationally, the German system, with each service directly responsible to Hitler, was unwieldy and cumbersome at best, wasteful and illogical at worst. It put too much power into the hands of the Führer and left his commanders-in-chief and other military advisers with only partial pictures of the war effort. In the early stages of the war, the difficulties were kept within bounds because the army held dominant sway, and the other services cooperated with OKH. But once Barbarossa did not lead to a quick victory, and once altercations between Hitler and army leaders again came to a head, the system's deficiencies became magnified. Each of the services and OKW tended to favor its particular view over the broader view. Plans continued to be written, but not on the basis of give-and-take. Cooperation among the services still existed at staff and combat levels, but it was insufficient at the top. Contact between the high commands and the war theaters was generally maintained, but increasingly subject to Hitler's unwarranted interference. And while some of his advisers continued to disagree with him almost until the end, the disagreements were usually over operational and tactical matters, not basic strategy.

The British, on the other hand, once their problem of excessively slow decision making was overcome, established a sound system. The chiefs of staff spoke as one, and their unity carried weight with Churchill and the war cabinet. They, like their German counterparts, did not have complete pictures, but with the help of staffs and civilian ministries, they developed a comprehensive strategy. They also enjoyed better relations with their allies (except perhaps for Russia) than did the Germans, and this feature of combined warfare further enlarged their outlook. Their planning was thorough, their liaison with field commanders excellent, and their advice to the prime minister sound. To be sure, Churchill was imperious, but he accepted the team idea, which took time but allowed sounder ideas. He also understood that he was subject to the war cabinet and Parliament, not a dictator, but a democrat. What Britain proved was that war by committee (the chiefs-of-staff committee was only one of many that permeated Britain's running the war) did not have to be indecisive.[45] It could be resolute as well.

As for the leaders of Germany's and Britain's high commands, the differences between them were not so marked as was the way their organizations functioned. All were thoroughly professional, dedicated to their individual services, and, with the exception of Göring, extremely hard-working and conscientious. All were roughly the same age, though the naval commanders-in-chief, Raeder and Pound, were a little older than the others. All, except again for Göring, were imbued with a love of country above all else.

The most obvious difference between them is the number of commanders-in-chief and chiefs of staff who served Churchill and Hitler. Once Churchill's military machinery was in place, he made almost no changes. Hitler's changes, particularly after 1941, were constant. Only one change, when Dönitz replaced Raeder, took place at the highest command level (unless one counts von Greim for Göring at the very end), but in the course of time there were ten army, navy, and air force chiefs of staff. The result was a lack of consistency and continuity in German decision making. Moreover, the German high command never seemed to have the breadth of outlook that characterized the British chiefs of staff. No doubt, part of the problem for Germany's military leaders was Hitler's unrealistic aims, but part of it was not only that they seldom challenged him, but also that they actually to an extent shared his outlook. The British chiefs were not any better strategists, but they did stand up to Churchill, and they worked out goals with him that were realistic and attainable. In the forging of strategy, that difference was crucial.

FOUR

Planning the War

The Early Years

Before comparing the strategies of Great Britain and Germany during the war, it is necessary to explicate some basic terms which, though used in previous chapters, now require more precise definition.[1] The most inclusive of these is "grand strategy," by which is meant utilizing a country's total resources—political, economic, social, military, diplomatic, technological, ideological—to forge national objectives. It is also sometimes called "national security policy" or "national strategy," but for our purposes, "grand strategy," because of its broader connotation, seems preferable.

There are two main components of grand strategy—policy and strategy. Policy consists of the domestic and foreign considerations (political, economic, and so on) required to form a national will and which together make up the civilian side of grand strategy. On the other side is military strategy, or the elements necessary to secure a nation's objectives by force or the threat of force. These elements include, among others, force structure, the enemy (real or potential), technology, targetry, leadership, doctrine (the principles by which one fights), and logistics. While our focus is military strategy, it alone is not the only aspect to be considered in war or peacetime. For both policy and strategy interact, and the two are not easy to disentangle. As Lord Strang points out: "Ideally speaking, the rule should be that in preliminary survey policy and strategy should be kept separate; in decision, they should be brought together. But it is not as tidy as that. . . ."[2] In other words, foreign and domestic policy and military strategy become entwined, and one needs to know about the one to comprehend the other. Policy making requires an understanding of strategy, just as military planning requires a knowledge of policy.

Overriding policy and military strategy, however, is grand strategy. Grand strategy is, or should be, the inclusive, determining element in formulating national objectives. Here Clausewitz is still pertinent. Policy may be the dominant force in peacetime, and strategy in wartime, but both concepts are subject to the dictates of grand strategy because both are but parts of the larger whole. This is why heads of state or parliaments have the ultimate say, for they embody a nation's grand strategy.

Military strategy is therefore only a part of grand strategy, but an essential part nonetheless. (Even if absent from a nation's grand strategic calculations, its absence still has to be taken into account.) For both Germany and Great Britain, military strategy reflected a combination of the old and the new, traditions as well as current thinking. Overall for Germany, the new element was Hitler and what has been called his apocalyptic vision, his advocacy of *Lebensraum*, racial purity, and eventual world domination.[3] Hitler's vision was not totally new, however; it was also based on the traditional values and frustrations of Germany's elite, who, along with Hitler, convinced the people that they, too, were not free, but vulnerable and dependent on outside forces. While this elite, including the military, may not have shared with Hitler the extent of his racial dogma or of his goals, it did share with him the desire to break out of the confines of central Europe, even if doing so meant that war became the centerpiece of Hitler's *and* Germany's grand strategy. In this sense, the forces of continuity and discontinuity in German history came together. Hitler's Reich was a combination of past slights and future yearnings.

Britain's goals were more realistic than ideological.[4] In its view, German dominance over the Continent, let alone the world, was unacceptable and must be resisted. To overcome German military might, Britain realized it must mobilize its resources and human power on a vast scale, a commitment both its elite and its citizens, no matter how reluctantly, were willing to undertake. Yet Britain, like Germany, felt vulnerable, though in a different sense. Chamberlain and Churchill and their military leaders considered their resources too meager to meet the enemy head on. They therefore felt obliged to follow the traditional British pattern of gathering allies, wearing down the enemy, and relying on maneuver rather than frontal attack to gain their objectives. Once Germany had been worn down, Britain and its allies would then assume the offensive and emerge victorious. The end goals were limited to defeating the Nazi movement and its Axis allies, reestablishing a balance of power on the Continent, and retaining a worldwide presence with the Commonwealth and Empire at its basic element, though the last goal was controversial and reflected only the aspirations of a portion of British society (including Churchill) instead of a consensus among the nation's leaders. But initially Britain's main concern was its very existence, and within that framework Europe was the crucial battleground, Germany the foremost opponent. From this strategy the British never deviated.

Nevertheless, while Britain and Germany had long-term military goals, the methods by which they sought to attain them were never followed consistently and were subject to numerous deviations as the conditions of the war changed. To understand the twists and turns of their respective strategies, it will be helpful to examine them during three periods: from September 1939 to December 1941, when the Axis dominated the war in Europe and to a degree on its periphery; from 1942 to mid-1943, the transition years, when the war became truly worldwide and the initiative shifted to the Grand Alliance; and from June 1943 to May 1945, when the Allies pushed back the Axis and won the war on all fronts. By juxtaposing their military strategies in this way, the similarities and dissimilarities in their thinking should become apparent.

Even before the war, German planning was subject to an inner contradiction.[5] On the one hand, by 1939, Hitler and the army were thinking in short-term, land-oriented, strategic goals. Initially, additional "living space" was to be gained either at the expense of Poland in the east or from France, Belgium, and the Netherlands in the west. But Hitler also ordered an extensive naval and air buildup that indicated his long-term, worldwide aims, which German naval and air leaders were only too willing to endorse. The problem was that the Führer unleashed the European war long before the air and naval programs were complete. In fact, they had barely begun. Instead of the 25 battleships and pocket battleships envisaged in the naval Z-plan for 1944–46, when the war started the Germans had 5; instead of 4 aircraft carriers, none; instead of 250 submarines, 57. Heavy bombers, which Göring and the air staff preferred, were not built because of raw-material shortages and because the plans for the immediate ground war required fighters, medium bombers, and dive bombers, not four-engined aircraft. The extensive armament buildup was therefore shelved soon after it began, and the exigencies of the continental campaigns took precedence.

Hitler decided in April and May 1939 to attack Poland (Operation White) first.[6] Complementing his military strategy was his diplomatic goal of coming to an accommodation with the Soviet Union so that France and Britain, his main antagonists in the west, would be deprived of their major prospective eastern ally. He hoped that an agreement with the Soviets might even persuade the Western Allies, given their timidity in the Austrian and Czech crises, not to fight at all. Even if Britain and France declared war over Poland, he was determined to fight. When the two western nations stood by their Polish ally, despite Hitler's August 23 bargain with Stalin, World War II began.

The German means for achieving victory was the Blitzkrieg. Although there has been much debate over whether the Blitzkrieg was truly a strategy or a doctrine or simply a concept, there is no doubt as to its effectiveness.[7] It featured tanks and motorized infantry, which, combined with the support of tactical aircraft, would break through enemy lines and advance rapidly beyond the immediate battlefield, causing havoc in the enemy's rear areas. It was further designed to break stalemated lines that had persisted during World War I, to exploit tactical success boldly, and to take advantage of the country's technological advances. In a sense, it was nothing new, merely a technique designed to exploit the existing technology. The necessary coordination between the army and the air force was not particularly effective in Poland, and only by 1941 had the Wehrmacht developed the Blitzkrieg into a well-honed instrument. But it was effective enough even at first to cause the Allies great alarm.

One of the obvious differences between Germany and Britain at the war's inception was that while Germany's strategy was primarily offensive, Britain's was defensive. Defensive thinking had dominated British strategy throughout the late 1930s. By early 1939, it had taken the form of a double strategy: (1) to gather together as many allies as possible to discourage and, if necessary, to resist German aggression; and (2) to defend Britain's vital national and global interests.[8] To accomplish the first goal required diplomacy of the most delicate sort. France was the only active ally who could be relied upon in all instances, though a March 1939 guarantee to Poland was designed to strengthen the latter's resolve and to put pressure on Germany from the east. Among other possible allies, besides the Commonwealth and Empire, Belgium and the Netherlands had reverted to their traditional neutrality; the states of eastern Europe were increasingly subject to German pressures; the Soviet Union was thought to be on the allied side but, after May, was negotiating with the Germans as well as the British; and the United States was unwilling to become directly involved, though it was increasingly sympathetic, as evidenced by its bilateral discussions with Britain in July, in which the secret talks between the two countries intensified and the eventually agreed upon destroyers-for-bases deal was first brought up.[9] Italy and Japan were considered more friendly toward Germany and only remotely as possibilities to become allies. Still, keeping on "tolerable" terms with the Italians and the Japanese was deemed crucial, for they were the only powers, except possibly the Soviet Union, who could threaten Britain's worldwide interests.

Closer to home, Britain's strategy was economic by design and based on the premise that time was on the Allied side and would eventually result in victory.[10] The means they envisaged for carrying out their strategy was to prevent essential supplies from reaching Germany by instituting a blockade and other economic-warfare measures and by destroying the Reich's war-making machine through bombing. The British acknowledged that whereas the first goal, blockade, could be initiated immediately upon the outbreak of hostilities, the second, bombing, was untested and would have to await the buildup of the bomber force. This was beginning, but only slowly, because fighter-aircraft production and radar had to be given a much higher priority in view of the immediate German air threat. British (and French) planning was thus predicated on a long war, which at first would constitute a purely defensive phase. Then after their forces had been strengthened sufficiently, Britain and its allies would eliminate the weaker opponents, such as presumably Italy, on the periphery, and finally would undertake a truly offensive phase in which Germany would be attacked directly.

This was the "considered" strategy followed once the war started on September 1. The Germans broke the Polish army in seven to fourteen days, although it took them nearly a month to take over the western two-thirds of the country. In the meantime, the Soviets began occupying the eastern one-third on September 17. As much as Britain and France would have liked to help Poland, they "were not ready or willing to fight a general war."[11] They declared preparations for a war of at least three years' duration and instituted a blockade, but otherwise confined themselves to probing operations into Germany from the west and, fearing retaliation and the loss of valuable aircraft, undertook virtually no offensive air operations. While historian Williamson Murray is perhaps too severe in condemning the Western Allies for their refusal to link economic pressure on Germany with at least some type of military action, there is no doubt that they showed themselves to be extremely timid. They drove the indirect approach to its illogical extreme, preparing for an attack in the west, while at the same time considering, but not implementing, measures to thwart possible enemy moves into Scandinavia and southeastern Europe. Moreover, British estimates to the contrary, their blockading activities did little to curtail Germany's ability to pursue the war.[12]

After the quick defeat of Poland, which helped Germany solve some of its coal and steel problems, the Germans prepared for new conquests. Their military strategy has been characterized as planning and executing a series of masterful strokes—from Norway and Denmark to France and the Low Countries to the Balkans and North Africa—marred only by a "temporary" setback at the hands of Great Britain in August and September 1940. Even though this version of events is accurate so far as it goes, it fails to bring out the complexity of German decision making between the Polish victory and the June 1941 Russian campaign. Germany's strategy did not move from point to point along a predetermined line, but was undertaken only after a number of alternatives had been weighed and accepted or rejected.

The Norway and Denmark operation (Weser Exercise) reflected the influence of the navy.[13] According to naval thinking, taking Norway would deny that country's coastline to Britain, provide additional anchorages for the naval war, and secure Swedish iron-ore shipments headed for Germany via Narvik.

The campaign also reflected an ad hoc decision. On December 13, 1939, Hitler instructed OKW, not the army or naval high commands, to study the possibility of occupying neutral Norway. His singling out of OKW for the task was not as farfetched as it might seem, for the army was busy planning the projected western offensive, and the naval staff lacked the background to plan a joint land, air, and sea operation of this complexity. In late February 1940, General von Falkenhorst, commander of XXI Corps, and his staff were called in to work out detailed plans in conjunction with OKW. The plans were ready by the first of March, and they now included the occupation of Denmark because Danish airfields were deemed necessary to extend the striking power of the Luftwaffe and thus ensure the undertaking's success. Continuous naval encouragement plus well-founded fears of a possible landing by British troops in Norway made the operation a reality on April 9. The campaign was decided quickly in Germany's favor. Denmark fell without a fight, but in the face of Norwegian and indecisive British and French opposition, it took the Germans two months to gain control of all of Norway, with Narvik not being given up to German forces until June 8.

From a strategic standpoint, the takeover of Norway and Denmark had several important consequences. It cemented Hitler's fascination with Scandinavia, Norway in particular, to such an extent that the area received attention (and troops) out of all proportion to its military worth throughout the war. And, as pointed out earlier, it helped undercut OKH's exclusive right to plan the war. Whether the navy intended this result or not, it certainly fit in with the navy's desire to have a larger say in military strategy and would perhaps help it achieve some of its armament priorities as well.

In contrast to the Norway and Denmark operation, the offensive against France (Operation Yellow) had been planned for some time. Thus, it did not take long for the Führer to resurrect a western operation once Poland's defeat had been assured.[14] On September 27, 1939, during the final days of the Polish campaign, Hitler called his military leaders together and told them that the time was right militarily and politically "to attack France as soon as possible." By October 9, the army had prepared, and OKW had issued, an operational directive which set November 10 as the earliest possible date of execution, though OKH doubted if its forces could be readied that early. From the beginning, the plan called for German units to attack France through neutral Luxemburg, Belgium, and the Netherlands, thus ensuring the protection of the vulnerable Ruhr industrial base at the same time. While the operation was eventually altered from a type of Schlieffen Plan to a strong thrust through the Ardennes Forest aimed at the Channel coast to cut Allied forces in two, Hitler never deviated from the premise that France was to be beaten quickly and decisively.

Nor did Hitler deviate from his ambivalent attitude toward Great Britain. Although he wanted some type of arrangement with the British so as to preclude extended fighting against them (which would also free him to attack the Soviet Union), his directive stipulated occupying as much of the Netherlands, Belgium, and northern France as was necessary "for the successful prosecution of an air and sea war against England." In other words, if the British refused to be accommodating, he would have to defeat them, too.

OKH's premonition that the western operation could not be mounted in November proved correct. A combination of factors, including inclement weather, shortages of soldiers, and other priorities, such as the Norwegian campaign, led to its postponement twenty-nine times. When it was finally launched on May 10, Britain and its French ally could not blame their eventual defeat on surprise, for they had long assumed that Germany would execute one of three possible options during the spring of 1940.[15] The main possibility in their view was a ground and air offensive aimed at France. Britain's problems in working out common strategy with the French military had been substantial, but they finally decided that France, having by far the larger army, would determine the lines for land defense. Britain, having more modern aircraft, would have the dominant say in the use of bomber forces.[16] The plan was greatly affected, of course, by the policies of neutral Belgium and the Netherlands. Though the two countries were pro-Allied in sentiment, their fears of alienating Germany made them reluctant to become involved in mutual discussions. The Allies did, however, receive some detailed information from Belgian officers who secretly visited them dressed in civilian clothes. Nevertheless, French and British plans for moving into Belgium were fraught with difficulties, not least of which was that their proposed defensive line in Belgium, the Dyle River line, would immediately give up one-third of that country to Germany, a fact not lost on the Belgians.[17]

The second option the British feared the Germans might implement was sea and air attacks against the British navy and commerce. The war cabinet thought the navy could handle its commitments, but whether the air force could was another matter.[18] Soon after the war had begun, the British started overestimating the number of German aircraft being produced, an intelligence error which became even more pronounced during 1940. Moreover, Germany's aerial successes in Poland further enhanced the Luftwaffe's reputation and made it imperative to Britain's leaders that they strengthen their defensive air capabilities at breakneck speed—hence the critical need for more fighters and radar stations.

The third, though least likely, alternative for Germany was thought to be a continuation of its waiting strategy, possibly combined with minor operations against the Low Countries, Scandinavia, or the Balkans. France and Britain examined these possible German options with great care. They would immediately assist the Low Countries, though "they had come to the conclusion that there was very little which we could do to prevent Holland being overrun."[19] They believed that they could perhaps effect some delay through air action but that their help would only postpone ultimate German victory.

In Scandinavia, by December 1939, the Allies had decided to intervene (especially to assist the Finns in the Russo-Finnish War), but only if Scandinavian cooperation was first obtained.[20] The Scandinavian countries refused to give up their neutrality, however, and the Allies were further aware that direct aid to Finland might well lead to war with the Soviet Union. In the end, these factors precluded intervention. Finland's defeat in the Winter War by March 13, 1940, took some of the immediacy off a Scandinavian operation, though "a force was still to be held in readiness to deal with a possible German advance into the area."[21] By April 5, the British had prepared forces to land in Norway, but then backed away, contenting themselves with mining Norwegian waters, which was done off Narvik early on April 8. Yet the German assaults, which started on the night of April 8–9, caught British officials in London off guard. The British and French troops eventually sent to near Trondheim and Narvik were ineffective and did little but delay Germany's takeover of central and northern Norway.

As for the Balkans, the Allies realized that their only practical alternative was to try to persuade these nations, particularly Romania, to resist German pressures and to remain neutral.[22] The situation was complicated by possible Italian moves into the region, but the main hope in this case, as among the Balkan countries, was that Italy would continue its policy of neutrality.

During the spring of 1940, the major threat remained to France or to France by way of the Low Countries. This had been the Allied assumption since April 1939, and all efforts were being directed to the short-term goal of building up their defensive strength to resist German aggression.[23] The long-term goal, to be sure, was to pass to the offensive, but the Allies considered themselves far from ready for such an undertaking. In the interim, they were daily increasing their defensive capabilities. By January 1940, they were beginning to feel that France could be adequately defended.

By May their confidence had increased even more. On May 4, their view was set forth in a chief of staff memorandum, entitled a "Review of the Strategical Situation on the Assumption that Germany Has Decided to Seek a Decision in 1940." This document deserves to be quoted at some length because of its insights into British strategy.[24]

2. On the assumption that Germany has decided to seek a decision in 1940, we sum up the following terms:—

    (a) The most likely method by which she might attempt to achieve this object is by a major offensive against Great Britain.

    (b) The main threat to the United Kingdom is an intensive air offensive which, if successful, might culminate in an attempt at actual invasion. Any enemy occupation of the Low Countries would seriously increase this threat. . . .

    (c) We cannot ignore the possibility of the main German attack being directed against France. In this event we estimate that there are at present sufficient land forces to maintain the security of French territory against both Germany and Italy, if adequate air protection and support is provided. In the latter respect, the deficiencies in fighter and bomber aircraft . . . are serious.

In other words, the document, to which the cabinet devoted considerable discussion on May 9, shows how British national security had assumed prime importance. France, it was felt, was generally secure. Even the problem of insufficient air power, Britain's major responsibility, was couched in British terms. The document thus indicates not only a growing confidence but also the primacy of national, not coalition, thinking. The point here is not that Britain did not attempt to do its part once the Battle of France broke out, as some French commentators at the time (and since) have alleged. But the document does suggest that for Britain, even though the defense of France continued to have a high priority, the defense of the homeland, harkening back to the thinking of the 1930s, was considered even more significant.

By May 1, warnings of a German attack in the west had begun to increase.[25] By May 10, it had started, the same day that Churchill replaced Chamberlain following the disastrous course of events in Norway. During the campaign, it soon became evident that Germany still held the initiative. In fact, German forces were more successful than anyone had expected. In five days, their Army Group A broke through the Ardennes. On May 15, the Netherlands capitulated; on May 28, Belgium, and within six weeks, France. Moreover, the other main western antagonist, Great Britain, had now been forced off the Continent. It was a German victory of overwhelming dimensions.

The relative quickness and devastating nature of Germany's military triumph became obvious to Allied leaders early in the campaign. On May 14, French Premier Paul Reynaud wired Churchill that Wehrmacht troops, having crossed the Meuse River in the Ardennes sector, were threatening France itself. The next morning, Reynaud telephoned the British prime minister and declared, almost hysterically, that the Germans had broken through and that the way to Paris was open. Although Churchill did his best to calm Reynaud's fears and to restore the confidence of the French leader, the British already recognized that a complete collapse of their ally was possible.[26] By May 25, after a conference between members of the two governments in which the possibility of French withdrawal from the war was openly discussed, it was obvious on both sides of the Channel that the battle had been lost. In this sense, as suggested by Brian Bond, the heroic Dunkirk evacuation of British and French soldiers between May 28 and June 4 was anticlimactic, as was the equally significant Declaration of Union, which the British proposed to the French on June 16 in a fleeting attempt to keep them in the war. The reaction of the French cabinet to this remarkable gesture for the "closest Anglo-French union" to pursue the war was almost completely negative, in some cases hostile. One French cabinet officer went so far as to comment: "What the proposal amounts to is that we should become a British Dominion."[27] The elements in France seeking an armistice had clearly become dominant, and on June 17 they initiated overtures to the Germans for a possible armistice. On June 22, the armistice was signed, to take effect two days later. The campaign was over, with Germany the clear winner.

In Germany, success brought a sense of travail as well as euphoria. On the positive side, France's defeat brought the previously lukewarm German public around to back the war effort wholeheartedly.[28] Among the general populace, the great victory parade in Berlin in July seemed to symbolize not only the invincibility of the Wehrmacht but also the now accepted achievements of the Third Reich. Workers, whose productivity had declined in part because they feared their social benefits might be eliminated, started working harder for the country. Even the generals, many of whom had sided with

Hitler despite his ideological biases, because he promised action and success, now accepted him as a military genius.

But the victory also had its negative side. Since army leaders considered that Hitler had an unerring grasp of strategy, they tended to concentrate only on the "operational" aspect of strategy and did not take sufficiently into account all of the elements associated with grand strategy. Consequently, there was no overall planning, no true coordination within the military or with the civilian sector at the top. Hitler had little understanding of the economic requirements for the "big" war he was undertaking, though the appointment of Fritz Todt as munitions minister in April 1940 did help to ease some of the difficulties in the armaments industry. The German military deluded itself into believing that the rapid elimination of France meant the era of short wars would continue so long as it could confine its efforts to the Continent. Large stockpiles were not required, only enough for the next victim. The nation and the newly conquered territories could produce sufficient goods for pursuing the war without altogether curtailing consumption at home. It was a false hope. Civilian consumption had already been reduced, and as Richard Overy has argued, Germany's remarkable early military successes were not gained because of the so-called Blitzkrieg economy, but because of "the staff work, leadership, and fighting of the German forces as compared with the weaknesses, poor leadership and wrong intelligence of the Allies."

At the same time during the summer, Germany's foreign policy became more complicated.[29] Germany hoped, even expected, to come to an agreement with Britain, but if the British refused, their ability to thwart Hitler's ambitions would have to be dealt a devastating blow by the Wehrmacht. France had been overwhelmed, but it was essential that its fleet and colonies remain loyal to the newly formed Vichy government. The United States had not become directly involved, but it was alarmed to such an extent that German propaganda had to be slanted more than ever toward keeping the US neutral. Italy had actively joined Germany's side on June 10. While Hitler was generally not displeased with its entrance, it signaled increased German concern about Mussolini's "parallel war" in the Mediterranean.[30]

And then there was the Soviet Union. Though an ally, in June it had completed its takeover of Estonia, Latvia, and Lithuania, while Germany was involved in the west, and parts of Romania also came into the Soviet orbit. The Germans were also well aware that the Russians could switch sides and become Britain's ally. More importantly, the Soviet Union's vast lands and resources, combined with its varied racial makeup, including particularly Jews, made it by far the most attractive military and ideological prospect for Hitler to attain his policy objectives. He had actually never questioned whether the Soviet Union should be attacked and subjugated, only when. Still, Hitler realized that the time might not yet be propitious for such a move, and other Nazi leaders, especially Foreign Minister Ribbentrop, continued to push for a four-power continental bloc of Germany, Italy, Japan, and the Soviet Union (he also tried to bring in France after its collapse), which would be directed against Great Britain with the additional aim of neutralizing the United States. Thus, during July 1940, three different but interrelated alternatives presented themselves to the Germans: peace or war against Britain, involvement in the Mediterranean, and peace or war with Russia.

The second part of Britain's dual strategy now came to the fore—survival. Its outlook was exceedingly bleak. The British government continued unrealistically to think that the economic pressure it was placing on Germany was having an effect. But Italy's entrance into the war on June 10 had transformed the Mediterranean into an active theater of operations and imperiled British interests in that area and beyond. The United States, like many other neutrals, was in shock and promised additional help, but no direct intervention. The Soviets now had what they wanted for the moment in eastern Europe and were not about purposely to alienate their German partner. Far more important immediately, Britain's major ally, France, had been defeated, and the Dutch, Belgians, and Luxemburgers as well. Britain was not exactly alone—the Dominions could provide some immediate assistance. But the governments-in-exile—Norwegian, Dutch, Belgian, French, and others—that were springing up in London could provide little more than a moral boost. It is small wonder that British leaders, while determined to fight on, also talked, at least in private, of a possible negotiated peace.[31]

But the main issue for Britain remained survival. The next three months were deemed critical, and the government called for drastic measures—actions against the French navy, active civil defense at local levels, large-scale evacuations from endangered areas, stringent economic controls—to meet "the imminent threat of attack with which we are now confronted."[32] While Churchill and his military advisers expected possible enemy raids any time after the first of July, they did not anticipate that the Germans could ready a full-scale invasion before mid-month. As General Ironside, who had become commander-in-chief, Home Forces, put it: "I should say that there will be a respite for the Germans to lick their mechanical sores."[33]

The British had long presumed that the fighting at first would be a struggle for air superiority and would include attacks on the aircraft industry as well as on airfields.[34] Hence the main burden would be borne by Fighter Command. Even the navy, no matter how superior, understood the need for fighter protection from enemy aircraft.[35] The navy thought it alone could stave off a seaborne assault for a while but not indefinitely. In the interim, sea mines had to be laid, land fortifications built up, and tank forces deployed to rush to landing beaches quickly, for amphibious operations are most vulnerable during their initial stages. That the British could stand up to the test was not a foregone conclusion.

At first, as mentioned earlier, Hitler thought the British might be willing to come to a compromise settlement.[36] His terms were that if Britain would recognize German preeminence on the Continent and return its African colonies, Germany, for its part, would allow Britain to retain its empire and world-power status. Britain rejected his public and private overtures, and by mid-July he moved to the position, albeit reluctantly, that the British Isles would have to be invaded (Operation Sea Lion). The army undertook the planning, but the navy, which had too few landing craft and had suffered numerous losses of surface ships in the Norwegian campaign, rejected the army's proposed "broad plan" for assaulting the English coast. Instead, they presented a "narrow plan," to be readied by September 15. Hitler went along with the navy's thinking. Whether broad or narrow, the essential prerequisite for the invasion was control of the air. Already, on June 30, the Luftwaffe issued a directive to gain that objective.[37]

The Battle of Britain began on July 10.[38] It reached peak intensity by mid-August. When the Luftwaffe did not achieve decisive results against the RAF (helped by the first effective use of Ultra intelligence), the Germans switched away from concentrating on airfields, antiaircraft batteries, radar stations, and aircraft factories in southeastern England and started attacking London directly on September 7. The battle reached a turning point on September 15, when the Germans suffered horrendous losses. (Although the British estimated 185 German planes shot down, the number was actually only 61.) At the same time, Britain's fear of Germany's planned seaborne invasion began to subside, for without air superiority, a German assault could not proceed. Britain's assumption of German hesitancy was correct, for, lacking air supremacy, Hitler was forced to postpone Sea Lion several times during September. On October 13, he finally called it off, though he stated he hoped it could be resurrected in 1941. Although the Luftwaffe continued to engage in terror bombing for some months, mostly at night, the British (or more accurately the RAF) had achieved a defensive victory. Their initial battle for survival had been won.

Hitler's reluctance to invade England along with a number of discussions he held in the summer of 1940 have led some historians to contend that he never took the operation against Great Britain seriously.[39] But Andreas Hillgruber and Ronald Wheatley have shown conclusively that Hitler did take Sea Lion seriously, at least from the end of July until mid-September, though with decreasing interest after the first of September.[40] Of course, the Soviet Union was never completely absent from Hitler's thinking, as Halder's diary makes clear.[41] But Halder further indicates Hitler's determination to deal with England.[42] The Führer was also impressed by the navy's argument that Britain was the first if not the last to stand in the way of Germany's striving for world power, and even Jodl, one of his closest advisers at the time, considered the British to be the main enemy.[43]

Still, throughout the period Hitler's interest in the Soviet Union never waned.[44] When Britain refused to give in diplomatically and then militarily, he switched his priorities. The Soviets would be defeated first, then Great Britain.[45] Even so, Hitler's resolve to dispose of the USSR immediately was not unalterable in the fall of 1940. Between mid-September and early December, he weighed another possibility—an increased presence in the western Mediterranean and eastern Atlantic.

In Hitler's view, increased German involvement in the Atlantic would accomplish two things: it would weaken Britain by cutting off a number of its important trade routes, and it would set the stage for more far-reaching enterprises.[46] In the aftermath of the French victory, he had stepped up the navy's commercial war against the British, and he further envisaged an "Atlantic empire" which would rival the combined strength of Britain and the United States. To establish such an empire, he needed the help of Vichy France, Portugal, and especially Spain. To the Spanish, he held out as bait the possibility of taking over Gibraltar, and he went so far as to meet and negotiate with Franco for possible bases in Spain, Spanish Morocco, and the Canary Islands. He also considered Portugal's Madeira, Cape Verde, and Azore islands as suitable areas for expansion, the Azores being particularly attractive to him because they could be used in a future confrontation with the United States.

The negotiations never came to fruition. Among the reasons were conflicting claims over territory among the countries involved, a disinclination among them to "assist" Germany anyway, and Mussolini's difficulties in Greece and northern Africa. Moreover, Hitler's concern about the Mediterranean and the Atlantic soon became subsidiary to his one, overriding aim: the defeat of the Soviet Union. Possible warfare in the west was to give way to definite warfare in the east.

On the British side, even while the Battle of Britain was at its crucial stage, Churchill and the chiefs of staff seemed outwardly calm and confident and were, in fact, planning what to do next.[47] Much of the strategy they came up with merely restated earlier thinking: defeat the Third Reich, build up strength while on the defensive, and intensify economic pressure on Germany. There was also a sense of optimism among Britain's leaders, as if the worst were past. They expected 1941 to be a difficult year, a year of attrition, in which they would have to hold on, but they conceived of it as a prelude to passing to the offensive, perhaps as early as the spring of 1942. They rightly judged that Hitler, having failed to beat them, "will probably recoil eastwards," though they did not rule out other possibilities, such as German attacks on British shipping or movements into Egypt, Spain, and northwestern Africa. To redress the balance, US entrance was considered mandatory and to be earnestly sought. In the meantime, however, immediate military measures could be undertaken—raids along the western and northern coasts of Europe, air attacks against German economic targets, operations designed to eliminate Italy from the war. The accomplishment of these short-term—and also longer-term—tasks required not only an emphasis on more light ships, fighter aircraft, radar research, and small arms, but also a return to a balanced building program which stressed capital ships and aircraft carriers, four-engined bombers, and more and better-equipped divisions. The war cabinet even found time to discuss policies for the seemingly distant future, such as the possibility of a postwar international system and a "scheme of social reform for the United Kingdom with particular reference to unemployment, education, and housing."[48]

At this point the intensity of combat between the two belligerents slackened. They continued to engage each other on the high seas and to an extent in the air, but not on land. Although their end goals were still to defeat each other, their means were to be more indirect than direct, and their strategies began to diverge. Britain began dealing with its new foe, Italy. Germany turned against the Soviet Union.

It is difficult to ascertain exactly when Hitler and his advisers decided to launch an eastern offensive.[49] As early as July 21, 1940, and probably earlier, he indicated interest in a possible Russian campaign. On July 31, he asked the army to draw up preliminary plans. Army staff officers had already been working on a plan, which in August became a basis for additional study. In the meantime, Finland and Romania, subjected to further Russian pressure, were now supported by the Germans with weapons and some troops and seen as prospective allies. Planning continued throughout the autumn, during which time the possibility of Ribbentrop's continental bloc, already remote, was eliminated.[50] Soviet Foreign Minister Vyacheslav Molotov visited Berlin in November to try to come to an accommodation with the Germans, but Hitler was not interested and turned aside Molotov's proposal for settling matters in eastern Europe. Similarly, Hitler pushed away the navy's desire to postpone a showdown with Russia until Britain had been disposed of, since by now ideological as well as strategic considerations had become paramount.[51] On December 5, von Brauchitsch and Halder presented to Hitler the army's overall plan.[52] After some discussion, he approved it and turned it over to OKW to prepare a directive. Although he modified an OKW draft so that the occupation of Leningrad was to precede the attack on Moscow, on December 18, Führer Directive No. 21 was issued with the codename changed from Fritz to Barbarossa.[53] Hitler's resolve was now unalterable.

From this point on until Barbarossa's execution on June 22, the changes in the plan were mainly matters of detail. Hitler and OKW intervened on occasion, but planning was almost entirely overseen by the army. Given the problems of length and breadth in attacking the Soviet Union, the role of Germany's allies took on added significance. Romanian, Finnish, Slovak, Hungarian, and Italian divisions were enlisted to take part, though not in the initial onrush.[54] At this point Japan was not to become involved. In fact, it was not even told about Barbarossa. Hitler preferred to have the Japanese tie down British forces and American interests in the Pacific as implied in the Tripartite Pact signed by Japan, Germany, and Italy in September 1940.

Italy presented Hitler with quite a different problem. Mussolini's campaigns had gone badly almost from the start, and by the winter of 1940–41, his forces were in trouble in the Balkans and in northern and eastern Africa. Hitler could do little to help in Ethiopia, but he could intervene in Libya and the Balkans. His reasons were fairly straightforward.[55] He felt obliged to assist Italy. He could not allow extensive British involvement in the Italo-Greek War, for the RAF, which had begun sending units to the area on March 7, could make Greek airfields usable to strike economic targets, such as the Ploesti oil fields, which were essential to the German war effort. And he could not afford instability in the Balkans which could threaten the southern flank during the Russian operation. As a result, he started sending troops to North Africa in February (he had already sent an air corps to Sicily) and took over Yugoslavia, Greece, and Crete in April and May 1941.

No matter how successful, did the Balkan campaigns, as a number of historians have alleged, delay Barbarossa for a crucial five weeks, and therefore help spell defeat for the Wehrmacht? The answer now is no.[56] Van Creveld has shown that of the twenty-nine divisions allocated to the Balkans operation, only three remained in Greece afterward, and the others had already been earmarked for Barbarossa as OKH reserves or could have been readied by mid-May if necessary. Nor were the casualties prohibitive—11,348—except for the airborne losses on Crete.[57] Germany's losses in equipment in the Balkans were negligible, too. The main problem which held up the start of the Russian campaign was a lack of weaponry, ammunition, and other war goods from the Reich. The Germans simply could not get sufficient matériel ready for the units in time. Insufficient equipment rather than combat in the Balkans was decisive in delaying the German offensive until June 22.

But what of Germany's Mediterranean strategy in general? Would a victory over the British in the Mediterranean have made a decisive difference? Was it a viable alternative to attacking the Soviet Union? The answers again are no.[58] According to Gerhard Schreiber, despite the navy's preference for the Mediterranean option, Hitler never seriously considered it an alternative to his ideological and political war against the Soviet Union. While the Mediterranean was significant to the British, it was not of vital significance. Its loss would not have broken Britain's will to continue the war, although the loss would have complicated Britain's need for resources. The point is that Germany, whether involved in Russia or in the Mediterranean, would still have been overextended in terms of matériel and personnel. One might even contend that Germany's force structure was even less suitable for fighting in the Mediterranean, where naval and naval air power were of prime importance, than it was for fighting the Soviets.

When the Wehrmacht unleashed its forces against the Soviet Union on June 22, its success was immediate and far-reaching. On July 3, even the usually pessimistic Halder expected the Red Army to be beaten within fourteen days.[59] On July 8, German formations reached Smolensk, two-thirds of the way from the starting line to Moscow. Three days later, OKW issued a proposal for what was to be done after the Soviets had been defeated.[60] According to the proposal, of a total of approximately 145 divisions, 50 were to be left to occupy European Russia and to push across the Caucasus into Iran and Iraq. Seventeen more were to move across Turkey and North Africa and link up with the forces coming south out of the Soviet Union, while 6 motorized divisions were to be situated in Afghanistan so as to threaten India from the northwest. At the same time, Japan was to move into Southeast Asia and threaten India from the east. The remaining 60 or so divisions were to be used to form a central reserve, prepare for possible operations into Spain and northwestern Africa, and protect German interests in western and northern Europe. No mention of Great Britain was made, but the assumption was that it eventually would be dealt with, too.

Toward the end of July, however, problems began to set in. Soviet resistance stiffened, the Blitzkrieg forces were in need of refurbishing, and Hitler and his military leaders had to decide what to do next.[61] The Führer and several advisers advocated diverting part of the panzer and motorized divisions north and south to help in the investment of Leningrad and in the takeover of the Ukraine. OKH and almost all of the field commanders preferred a concerted drive toward Moscow, pitting strength against strength. An extended argument ensued; in the end, Hitler, as might be expected, had his way. The diversions, which involved 12 ½ mobile divisions, began in mid-August and lasted for approximately one month. The units suffered heavy losses in weapons and personnel, though Guderian's southern thrust did assist in the capture of Kiev.

By August 27, while the diversions were in full swing, Hitler had come around to the Army High Command's position and decided an attack against Moscow should receive top priority. He also acknowledged that "the campaign in the east might not yet lead in the year 1941 to the complete destruction of Soviet Russia's capacity for resistance."[62] Still, he hoped that the Moscow operation would bring the eastern war to a decision before the end of the year. By September 30, despite great logistical difficulties, the forces had been assembled for the assault on Moscow (Operation Typhoon).[63] At first the German offensive resulted in numerous tactical victories, but then the momentum began to slow and came to a halt in the face of tenacious Soviet fighting, the weather, and a lack of supplies and reserves.[64] The Germans made one last, desperate attempt to take Moscow in November and early December, but they fell short of the city, and a major Russian counteroffensive beginning on December 5 sealed the fate of the campaign. Hitler's belief in late August that the war in the east might well extend into 1942 had come to pass.

Hitler further realized that his strategy lay in tatters. The Soviet Union had not been defeated in one bold stroke. Not only was the German military involved in a multifront war, but also a formidable constellation of nations, including the United States, was now arrayed against it.[65] As pointed out earlier, even Hitler at this point had doubts that the war could be won, as he indicated to Jodl in December.[66] Hitler had regained his confidence by February, but no matter how one assesses the war, it is difficult to escape the conclusion that the period between the inception of the Russian campaign and the entrance of the United States was decisive in that the world's two economic giants had now joined the Allied side, and Germany found itself at a grave disadvantage.[67]

From Britain's standpoint, its elation during the fall of 1940 had been short-lived. While the British were not forced to abandon their long-range goals, 1941 was indeed a difficult year for them. It might even be called survival, part two. Early in the year, the military picture was not good but had not reached crisis proportions.[68] Although the Luftwaffe continued its bombing raids against British cities and countryside, the threat of invasion for the moment had passed. The Germans were intensifying their efforts in the Atlantic, while the British and Canadians did the same. There was increasing evidence that Germany would launch an attack against the Soviet Union, which, if it happened, posed as many uncertainties as possibilities. But the theater which caused the British the most immediate concern was the Middle East.

The area itself is so vast and diverse as to defy exact demarcation. For the British it encompassed not only the Levant and Egypt, but also Greece, Crete, and northern and eastern Africa. It was the one region where the British, despite admittedly inadequate resources, hoped to make inroads against the Axis, in this case Italy. Germany's intervention into the Mediterranean put an abrupt end to British designs. The British offensive against Italian forces in East Africa was carried to a successful conclusion, but German troops in Libya, rather than becoming acclimated, undertook an offensive in late March which did not end until Rommel's Africa Corps, with Italian assistance, had captured Cyrenaica (except Tobruk) and reached the Egyptian frontier.

In the meantime, the British had weakened their forces in North Africa by shipping some of them to support the Greeks, but their efforts were inadequate, awkward, and poorly coordinated.[69] The German offensives into Greece and Yugoslavia in April soon put the Balkans and then Crete, in May, under Axis domination. In June, a hurried and ill-conceived British offensive in North Africa (Operation Battleaxe) was a dismal failure. There was better news in Iraq, where Britain overcame a pro-Axis coup by General Rashid Ali by sending soldiers from the British army and the Arab Legion to restore the situation there. In Vichy-controlled Syria, the possibility that Germany might make additional use of the region was eliminated in June and July by a combined British, Australian, and Free French expedition. But these undertakings were accomplished against inferior opponents, not German troops. Churchill, his advisers, and the soldiers in the field were doing their best, but their best did not seem good enough. At one point the prime minister went so far as to sketch "a world in which Hitler dominated all Europe, Asia and Africa and left the U.S. and ourselves no option but an unwilling peace."[70]

As Britain labored in this pessimistic atmosphere, Germany attacked the Soviet Union. Did the June 22 assault save Britain from certain defeat? While the answer can only be surmised, there is no doubt that the German move gave the British some much needed breathing space. Their problems, however, were far from over. Other than immediately accepting the Russians as allies, there was little the British could do to assist them despite Stalin's call for a second front in the west. In fact, the British, like the Germans, became convinced that the Red Army could not last out the summer.[71] That view of the Soviets' tenuous position was reflected on June 25, when the British chiefs placed anti-invasion units in Britain on full alert, an order which was not rescinded until August 2. The British contended they wanted to send all possible aid, but they were in such a sorry state that their assistance was limited to one or two small northern convoys per month. An operation on the Continent was ruled out; military planners stated frankly that "we cannot afford another Dunkirk." They further felt that a continental undertaking would upset Britain's "long term strategical and industrial plan." In other words, even though Russia was in desperate straits, the British were not prepared to alter drastically their "considered" approach to achieve ultimate victory.

Nevertheless, Britain's long-range strategy had already to an extent begun to shift emphasis.[72] The essentials remained the same—to attract allies, especially the United States, since the Soviets were now on the British side; to step up bombing raids by the end of 1941, when Britain's bombing capabilities were expected to reach parity with that of Germany; and to continue to exert economic pressure on Germany to bring about its eventual collapse. In the latter instance British planners admitted that finding vulnerabilities in the German economic infrastructure had proved more difficult than anticipated. Because of untold problems (British as well as German moves), the timetable for assuming the offensive had been pushed back from spring to autumn of 1942. In the interim, large-scale sabotage, subversion, and propaganda were to be undertaken to galvanize opposition on the Continent and weaken Germany's resolve. In a telegram to President Roosevelt, Churchill went further, returning to an old theme that perhaps these measures—air offensive, rigorous blockade, subversion—would "be enough to force Germany to sue for peace." The process could be accelerated by landing forces, relatively small in number, equipped to strike Hitler's Europe. There was "no need for vast armies of infantry as in 1914–1918," for by the time of the invasion Germany's strength would have been "whittled away." What this meant, of course, was that Britain's traditional preference for maneuver over mass continued to be a cardinal feature of its strategy.

The British acknowledged two other theaters of immediate concern.[73] One was the Far East. They realized that in this area their best hope lay in not antagonizing the Japanese, since Britain lacked the resources to redress the balance there. Japanese moves in July into southern Indochina made conditions increasingly ominous, however.

In the Middle East, despite recent setbacks, the British were more optimistic.[74] To be sure, the Mediterranean was closed to British shipping (except for an occasional and usually costly convoy to beleaguered Malta), and precautions had to be taken against internal troubles in Egypt and Palestine. But with Germany occupied in Russia, the Middle East continued to provide the British with the best possibilities for eventual success. The immediate need, however, was to replenish their depleted forces, especially with tanks and airplanes, which could be procured only by way of the Cape of Good Hope and across the Takoradi air route in Central Africa. General Sir Claude Auchinleck had replaced General Sir Archibald Wavell as theater commander, and to Auchinleck's credit, he was not stampeded into precipitous action by the impatient prime minister. The divisions and air groups were brought up to strength and new ones added; by November, they were ready. This offensive (Operation Crusader) was the main action the 1941 Russian respite provided. Churchill and other advisers discussed additional operations, such as one directed against Norway, but nothing came of their schemes.[75] The Russo-German campaign in 1941 was actually more important to the British indirectly, allowing them time to recover, to build up their forces, and to expand war production. In this sense, the Soviets provided more relief to the British than the other way around.

Crusader began on November 18.[76] It was not at first successful, but by December 8, with German and Italian troops short on supplies, Rommel started a skillful but necessary retreat which did not end until January with the British at the El Agheila line, an advance of more than five hundred miles. Though Rommel's army had not been destroyed, substantial British victory (temporary, as it turned out) had been won.

Russia's entrance into the war had therefore prompted Britain to change its strategy only to a limited extent. Tangibly this had meant sending war matériel to the Soviet Union via the northern sea route and taking over the southern part of Iran, with Russia coming in from the north in September to establish a supply corridor. Of much greater significance to Britain, however, was the United States' declaration of war after the bombing of Pearl Harbor.[77] The main reason for Britain's elation was, of course, that America's resources, already a factor, could now finally be put to full use. The years of courting were over; the US was in the war. At the end of 1941, the attainment of this primary objective of British policy overshadowed all other considerations.

Churchill was not slow to seize the initiative. Almost immediately after the United States entered the war, he suggested a full-scale meeting between the two allies.[78] At first Roosevelt and his military advisers wanted to wait until early 1942 because of the emergency caused by the Pearl Harbor disaster and the simultaneous Japanese advance into Southeast Asia and the western

Pacific (in which the sinking of a British battleship and a cruiser weakened still further their meager contingents in Malaya). But Churchill would not be put off. By December 12, he and Roosevelt had agreed to confer in Washington. (At the same time, Foreign Secretary Anthony Eden was sent to Moscow to carry out scheduled talks with the Russians.) Churchill sailed on December 14, arrived on December 22, and set to work, often meeting two and three times a day to hammer out the basis for a common military strategy and to accelerate a victory program in the production of war goods. The intended one week of sessions stretched to more than three, punctuated by Churchill's speeches before the US Congress in Washington, the Canadian Parliament in Ottawa, and a five-day vacation in Florida. By the time the First Washington Conference concluded on January 14, 1942, the two allies had accomplished a great deal.[79]

Strategically, despite Churchill's misgivings before the meeting that the United States might shift its emphasis away from Europe and concentrate on defeating Japan, the Americans quickly reaffirmed the Germany-first strategy agreed upon the previous March. Both allies realized the vital part the United States was expected to play in terms of manpower and matériel, and the talks therefore sought to ensure that supply lines and bases in the Atlantic and the Pacific were protected and in friendly hands. Although plans for a North African amphibious operation were discussed but considered premature, they foreshadowed the successful invasion of November 1942. On a more informal level, Roosevelt and Churchill discussed further steps for cooperation in atomic energy research.

Institutionally, as discussed earlier, there was the establishment of the Combined Chiefs of Staff, by which the British and American chiefs of staff, or their representatives, were to coordinate Allied strategy and see to its execution. While the theater command set up in the Southwest Pacific and Southeast Asia, the ABDA (American-British-Dutch-Australian) command, was soon overtaken by events—the Japanese had already captured Hong Kong and Manila during the conference—it served as the pattern for area commands formed later in the war. In addition, the two allies created five combined economic boards in an effort to ensure that their countries' resources were properly distributed.

Politically, the results were more meager, taking the form only of the "Declaration by United Nations," in which twenty-six nations, after an intense diplomatic effort, agreed to employ their "full resources, military or economic, against those members of the Tripartite Pact and its adherents with which such governments are at war."[80] Besides the United States, Great Britain, the Soviet Union, and China, the signatories included many of the governments-in-exile, the Dominions, and Latin American countries. The declaration actually did little more than "symbolize" the unity and aspirations of the anti-Axis coalition, but it was a start.

The meeting brought about one further achievement: the respective military decision makers who had met only briefly at Argentia Bay in August became better acquainted on an informal as well as a formal basis. Although Churchill and Roosevelt had known each other and corresponded for years, the closer ties fostered among the two countries' military leaders proved to be a positive element for the future. The period of open cooperation, along with continual adjustments, had commenced.

Yet, despite the sense of camaraderie, to what extent had Britain truly altered its long-range strategy? The answer is, somewhat. Britain was now committed to eastern Asia, an area to which Churchill, though not the chiefs of staff, had previously paid insufficient attention.[81] Otherwise, the British had not as yet changed their thinking all that much. Fighting in Asia and the Pacific was bound to have an adverse effect on Britain's ability to supply its major land theater, the Middle East, but the military priorities for Europe remained the same—blockade, bombing, and subversion, followed by an invasion from the west with well-equipped but small forces once Germany had been weakened.[82] The possible date had again been moved back, this time to the summer of 1943, but the significant point for Churchill and his advisers was that the Americans could now be counted upon to play a direct and increasingly important role. What the British failed to realize sufficiently was the degree to which the United States would eventually dictate their still-to-be-formulated "common" offensive strategy.

The year 1941 therefore ended on an optimistic note for the British. But the optimism associated with the coming together of the Grand Alliance was at odds with Britain's situation during the first twenty-eight months of war. Its victories had resembled more holding actions than victories, preventing what might have been even worse calamities. Winning the Battle of Britain had merely averted a probably seaborne invasion; defeating Italian troops in East Africa had eased but not averted potential problems in the Indian Ocean; taking control of Syria and recapturing Iraq had eliminated pro-Axis elements only in those areas. These successes hardly added up to an enviable record.

Nor was the pessimism that prevailed among Germany's military leaders at the end of 1941 a true reflection of their situation during the early years. Most of the victories had been of major proportions—the defeat of Poland in a month; the capture of Norway, providing better access to the Atlantic; the unbelievable fall of France in six weeks, the rapid takeover of Yugoslavia and Greece, cementing Axis dominance over the Balkans; the amazing success of Rommel in North Africa. All of these campaigns confirmed the exceptional abilities of the Wehrmacht and might well have allowed the Germans, had they looked at their difficulties on the eastern front against this background of earlier victories, to accept the setback before Moscow as "temporary."

Other contrasts between the two combatants stand out as well. As noted earlier, one was the difference between an offensive and a defensive war. Almost without exception, Britain was on the defensive against German forces.

Until Crusader, its only offensive undertaking, Battleaxe, in North Africa in June 1941, had failed almost before it started. Even the main arm of the British military, the navy, had performed tasks—blockade and the Battle of the Atlantic—that were defensive in orientation. And the air force's bombing offensive had barely started and had caused virtually no damage to Germany's war-making capacity. The Wehrmacht, on the other hand, given its initial advantage in armaments and more and better trained troops, had almost continuously held the initiative. Their superiority even held in North Africa, where two to three divisions and Italian forces had proved sufficient to put British and Commonwealth soldiers on the run. Germany's ability to defeat its adversaries quickly (except for the Soviet Union) had allowed the Germans breathing spaces between campaigns, thus increasing their effectiveness even further.

On a deeper level, one is struck by the degree to which Britain was "gasping for breath" from the time the war began. Its commitments seemed overwhelming. Defending the United Kingdom and dealing with potential difficulties posed by Ireland were only two of its many worries. Immediate concerns arose in western, northern, and southeastern Europe; less immediate, but nonetheless threatening, situations existed in northern and other parts of Africa, the Middle East, India, Southeast Asia, and the Southwest Pacific. If any one of these areas became a war theater, Britain was obliged to help out. In comparison, Germany's commitments were actually quite limited. It had no empire, though it wanted one, to be concerned about. It was able to conduct a series of land wars confined to Europe and its periphery. It was pursuing a strategy based on calculation rather than on survival.[83]

Nevertheless, every German victory brought in its train more actual or potential enemies. Its assault on Poland led Britain and France to come into the war. The defeat of France brought the Soviet Union and the United States into the strategic picture, especially when Britain was able to hold on in the autumn of 1940. The European allies that Germany gained—Italy and the states of Eastern Europe—would be of some help in the war of annihilation planned against the USSR, but they were not geared to a protracted war based on human power and matériel. The other partner, Japan, might have rendered assistance against the Soviets, but opted to move south and east instead. Britain, however, given its commitments, was trying to attract major and minor allies from 1939 on. Not only did the British enhance their reputation as coalition builders during the conflict, but they also convinced many of the world's nations that, despite their imperial tradition, they were much less of a threat than a resurgent Germany. For many countries, including the United States and the Soviet Union, siding with Britain turned out to be a fortunate choice.

Thus, from the start Britain was conducting its war on a global basis.[84] To do so was filled with risks, but it fit in with Britain's traditional posture in the world, and the British built up their military force structure, with the help of allies, accordingly. Germany, too, wanted eventually to fight a global war, but it decided to establish European hegemony first and geared its force structure to that arena. Even at this level, its resources were insufficient, for Britain convinced most of the rest of the world, though not the USSR and the US before being attacked, that the Germans and their allies must be resisted whatever the cost. In a sense, then, Germany's strategy was riskier than Britain's. It was based on a number of gambles in which more and more nations became increasingly involved against them. As long as Britain remained undefeated, it would contest German supremacy on the Continent. To counter Britain's worldwide strategy, Germany itself had to adopt a broader strategy. It was much like the proverbial race between the tortoise and the hare. The German hare started much faster, but the plodding British tortoise eventually won.

The tortoise-hare analogy can be taken further when one looks at war production. Surely, both nations experienced economic difficulties in preparing for the type of war they wanted. But Britain went into the war more intensely in an economic sense than Germany, devoting 60 percent of its gross national product to the war effort in 1941, a figure Germany reached only in 1943.[85] Overall, between 1939 and 1943, 54 percent of Britain's gross national product went to support the war; in Germany, it was 45 percent. Figures show that Britain's war production also soon surpassed Germany's in many specific areas, as in front-line military aircraft and tanks (including assault guns), for instance (table 4-1).

Granted, the gross figures do not take into account the quality of the weapons or the personnel manning them. Nor do they reflect Germany's substantial lead at the beginning. On September 1, 1939, the Germans had 3,609 combat aircraft; the British, 1,911.[86] The Germans had 3,257 tanks; the British, 1,148. While one could go on and on with qualifying points (for example, Britain's deficiencies were offset to a large degree by France's armaments), the oft-made point, made here again, is that Britain allocated more of its industrial base, though smaller, to war production than did Germany. When the United States and the Soviet Union joined Britain, the potential economic disparity swung overwhelmingly in favor of the Allies. The amazing fact is that economic factors were never fully taken into account in Hitler's and his advisers' calculations.

Given the overwhelming roles played by Hitler and Churchill, to what extent did they dictate strategy during these early years? The answer is that even though both of them received and acted on advice from others, they

TABLE 4-1

Aircraft and Tank Production, 1939–41

| | Aircraft | | | Tanks | | |
	1939	1940	1941	1939	1940	1941
Germany	8,259	10,826	11,776	c. 900	1,643	3,790
Great Britain	7,940	15,049	20,094	969	1,399	4,841

were the driving forces in their countries' war efforts. Churchill contributed a great deal to Britain's long-range strategy, especially in its articulation, but little in the short run, which was largely determined by Axis initiatives, not British desires. Hitler, on the other hand, was the key figure in setting Germany's short-term, calculated goals as well as its long-term aspirations. Unfortunately for him, his military strategy did not add up to a realistic grand strategy.

FIVE

Planning the War

The Middle and Later Phases

Germany's and Britain's strategy between 1942 and 1945 can conveniently be divided into two phases. The first consists of the nineteen months from January 1942 through July 1943, a period of transition, during which the initiative passed slowly, but decisively, to the Allies. The second phase continued through the last twenty-one months between August 1943 and May 1945, when the Allies were everywhere victorious.

In considering Britain's and Germany's strategies in 1942, several points need to be borne in mind. First, despite the relatively recent coming together of the Axis and Allied coalitions against common enemies, by January 1942 Great Britain and Germany had constantly been at war for twenty-eight months. The same could not be said of their partners. Britain's eastern ally, the Soviet Union, had fought Finland during the winter of 1939–40, but it had not become completely involved militarily until mid-1941. The direct role of the United States, of course, had just begun. On the Axis side, Italy had come in in June 1940, but its lack of preparedness and its inability to sustain a long war had become apparent soon after its entrance. Even Japan, though heavily committed against China since 1937, had only recently undertaken aggression against American, British, and Commonwealth forces, thus inaugurating a new phase. In other words, at the beginning of 1942, none of the members of the coalition had been at war as long or at least as intensely as Germany and Great Britain.

Second, while numerous historians rightly see the end of 1941 as the turning point in the war, their view is a retrospective one.[1] In fact, a good case can be made for the traditional notion that late 1942 was the decisive phase. Early in 1942, it was not at all evident that Germany and especially Japan had lost the initiative. Japan was pushing rapidly into Southeast Asia and the Pacific. Germany's navy was achieving spectacular results in the U-boat war off the North American coast as a consequence of the United States' entering unprepared. In January, Rommel was executing a brilliant counter-stroke in Cyrenaica which for the most part offset Britain's advance the month before. By March, the Wehrmacht was finally able to stabilize a line in Russia since the Red Army had for the time being spent itself. Britain's strategic bombing offensive was only having a slight effect on Germany's war economy. If this were not enough, Churchill's health showed signs of deteriorating, and one of his moods of depression had set in.[2] These developments amply demonstrate that even though we now realize that the Allies' vastly superior economic strength would ultimately spell defeat for the Axis, that outcome was not so obvious to contemporary observers. It is within the context of Britain's and Germany's war efforts at an in-between, indecisive stage, that we will examine their strategies for 1942.

Though enemies, Germany and Britain, in regard to strategic planning and action, during the year shared a number of features. Both now accepted that the current struggle would be a long one and were gearing their economies accordingly. Both realized that the war had become one of attrition, not quick annihilation. And while Britain was now directly involved in Asia, both were still concentrating their efforts on Europe and the periphery.

Yet there were differences of emphasis. Germany's possibilities had become more restricted. Realistically, it could not launch a major operation against the British Isles or into neutral Spain without shifting sizable forces west. Nor did it possess the force structure to inaugurate a strategic bombing offensive against Britain. Since its surface fleet had become less and less a factor, except as a "fleet in being," it was forced to focus its naval effort primarily on the U-boat war in the Atlantic. Moreover, the naval war, important as it was, was defensive in orientation. Germany was left with only two possible offensive opportunities—North Africa and the Soviet Union.

This reality did not prevent German military leaders from thinking about complementary campaigns in conjunction with Japan. Their relations with the Japanese were cordial, so cordial, in fact, that on January 18, 1942, representatives of the two nations and Italy initialed a military pact in Berlin.[3] Its provisions divided the world into the Axis powers' spheres of interest. Those areas east of 70° longitude (approximately bisecting the Indian Peninsula) were to be in the Japanese sphere; those west of 70°, in Germany's and Italy's. Germany and Italy were to conduct operations against US and British interests in the Middle East, the Mediterranean and the Atlantic, while Japan attacked Anglo-American forces in the Pacific theater. Operations in the Indian Ocean were to be undertaken jointly. The agreement went so far as to stipulate that if the United States and Britain concentrated their naval effort in the Atlantic, Japan was to send part of its fleet to that area. If, on the other hand, the Western Allies concentrated on the Pacific, Germany and Italy were to move part of their navies there. Despite the vague proposition that Axis forces link up somewhere in the Indian Ocean, the pact itself was the furthest extent of German-Japanese military cooperation.

Soon afterward, the Axis' enthusiasm as well as their ability to effect a linkup began to dissipate. In March, Raeder presented a memo to Hitler recommending a coordinated attack in which Germany would move east by way of Egypt or across the Caucasus, or preferably by both routes, and Japan would advance west, with the goal of meeting in the Indian Ocean. The memo also discussed the possibility of exchanging with Japan Middle Eastern oil for Southeast Asian raw materials. But Hitler only "agreed on principle" to the wide-ranging naval proposal. Nor did the suggestion appeal to OKW and OKH, who, if they favored any operation at all, preferred one closer to home. Japan, for its part, was not all that enthusiastic either. In late March, simultaneously with the Japanese land campaign in Burma, a carrier force under Admiral Chuichi Nagumo inflicted damage on the British fleet and installations in Ceylon and elsewhere in the area. Suffering considerable losses itself, the task force then returned to Pacific waters. This costly undertaking, combined with naval air defeats at Coral Sea and Midway, made Japan extremely reluctant to attempt establishing a major naval presence in the Indian Ocean.

Any German notion to bring about closer coordination with the Japanese in 1942 was hardly more than a pious hope anyway. More promising were the North African and Soviet theaters. In North Africa, where Rommel's and Auchinleck's troops were facing each other astride the Gazala line, the Germans and Italians initially opted for an attack against Malta in June to relieve the supply situation in the central Mediterranean before undertaking an operation at Gazala.[4] But on April 29–30, at a meeting between Hitler and Mussolini, the two leaders, over the objections of the Italian Supreme Command, decided to attack in Libya (Operation Theseus). Once German troops had overrun Cyrenaica, and Tobruk in particular, and had reached the Egyptian border, Rommel's and the Italian divisions were to stand on the defensive. Air units were then to be shifted to help in the assault on Malta (Operation Hercules), presumably to take place by mid-July or early August at the latest. Yet by May 20, less than a week before the Gazala offensive was to begin, the Führer voiced his skepticism about a Malta operation.[5] Instead, Malta was to be retained only as a paper (geistig) operation, and Axis forces were to concentrate on northeastern Africa, with the Suez Canal as the goal.

However, despite all the talk and preparations related to North Africa, Hitler and his army advisers never thought of it as more than a secondary theater.[6] They never supported it with the necessary troops or supplies, in part because of the enormous logistical difficulties within the area, in part because of its vast distance from Germany's economic and military base. Consequently, it was never accorded greater than second or third priority in the German scheme of things. As Hitler remarked to Halder: "This war on the periphery doesn't interest me."

This left the Soviet Union as the main theater. If Hitler could gain victories in North Africa on the cheap, so much the better, but his main interest continued to be directed toward the east. Even during Germany's 1941 Moscow offensive, staff studies were being conducted for a possible advance across the Caucasus into Iran and Iraq and for extensive attacks during 1942 on the southern, central, and northern fronts, the latter to effect the capture of Leningrad.[7] By mid-December 1941, however, with the Red Army's counter-offensive in full swing, the Germans realized such wide-ranging aims would be impossible to carry out during the coming year. This realization, combined with the command shakeup, in which Brauchitsch as well as field commanders Gerd von Rundstedt, Fedor von Bock, Wilhelm von Leeb, Heinz Guderian, and Erich Hoepner were "retired" from their positions, left little opposition to Hitler's desire for a campaign on the southern Russian Front. At first Halder was extremely upset and argued that, except for limited offensives to straighten the lines, German troops should remain on the strategic defensive until the depleted army had been refurbished.[8] Nevertheless, by March 15, he, too, went along with Hitler's plan.

The actual directive for Operation Blue was issued on April 5.[9] As a reflection of the weakened condition of the Wehrmacht and the difficulties involved, the offensive was to be executed, after some preliminary operations, not in one, but in four steps, beginning perhaps in mid-June. The final step was to be the taking of the Caucasus region, which would not only provide a springboard for further German advances into the Middle East, but also cut off the flow of supplies into central and northern Russia from the south and secure the region's oil resources to bolster the German war effort. The directive further revived the possibility of an assault against Leningrad, but only after the southern offensive had been concluded. The German priorities for 1942 were thus set. Hitler's desire for an economic war and for a continuation of the racial war against the USSR was to remain the overriding priority.

Britain's strategic alternatives at first glance seemed almost unlimited. Its interests were worldwide, its production attuned to building a balanced fleet and a strategic air force, its allies possessed of overwhelming economic might. All of these factors should have provided for flexibility in strategic planning. Yet Britain faced difficulties as well. Its Soviet ally had barely averted defeat in 1941, and although the Russians had been able to move many of their factories east before being overrun, their economy was still in disarray. The United States was an economic giant, but its conversion to war production was only in its initial stages. At home, Britain's strategic air arm, Bomber Command, was becoming stronger, but its vulnerability to attack along with its lack of bombing accuracy were causing Churchill and air leaders grave concern. No matter how formidable the navy, its worldwide commitments were outstripping its capabilities. The global nature of the conflict posed more problems than benefits, especially with Japan's moves in Asia helping to drain Britain's already inadequate resources.

Most important, Britain did not hold the initiative. Enemy actions might interrupt or even cancel British offensive plans or operations at any time. This situation did not prevent the British from conducting long-range planning, but it did mean that short-range imperatives might have to take priority.

Britain's strategic possibilities for 1942 and beyond had been set forth in three lengthy, brilliantly written memoranda presented at the Arcadia conference in December.[10] In them, Churchill outlined his offensive thinking. In retaining the Europe-first strategy, he wrote that while he realized developments in Russia were of prime importance, he saw that little beyond sending supplies to the Soviets could be accomplished at this point. (The British had earlier offered to send troops to the Russians, but Stalin had been cool to the suggestion.) Rather, Churchill believed that Russia would be better served by a British and American undertaking in northwestern Africa (Operation Gymnast). This amphibious attack, in conjunction with a British offensive in Libya, would clear North Africa by the end of 1942 and open up the Mediterranean to Allied shipping. Control of that vital sea link would then make it possible for the United States and Britain to turn their full attention to an invasion of the Continent by mid-1943, though the chiefs of staff thought late 1943 or early 1944 more likely.[11] Also by mid-1943, Britain's air forces would be built up to the point that they could assume a significant role in bombing Germany and supporting land operations. Churchill envisaged Anglo-American naval forces regaining the initiative in the Pacific by the middle of 1942, thus setting the stage for further offensive actions in that theater.

Many of Churchill's optimistic views were overtaken by events, but as he pointed out after the war, his ideas eventually came to fruition. Still, it was not easy to arrive at that point strategically. The Soviets not only pressed for military aid but also insisted on a second front to take some of the pressure off them.[12] Despite the Western Allies' knowledge through Ultra that Germany's offensive in southern Russia could not be mounted until May or possibly June, they realized that Soviet participation was crucial. Therefore, in the spring of 1942, they decided to prepare for an emergency landing on the Continent (Operation Sledgehammer).[13] By June, however, even though staff officers continued to hold out the possibility of a continental operation, the British had become convinced that the forces and equipment available for establishing a beachhead in France were insufficient to withstand the German divisions located there, a judgment confirmed by the failure of the Dieppe raid in August. Since Britain and the Commonwealth were to provide the troops for Sledgehammer, its refusal to go ahead was decisive.

At the same time, British leaders understood that their highly publicized, thousand-plane raids against Cologne, Essen, and Bremen could not be sustained because they had made extensive use of training as well as frontline aircraft to launch the attacks. They realized further that Germany's U-boat war against Allied shipping in the Atlantic and elsewhere was becoming more critical than ever before. In fact, First Sea Lord Pound argued that unless that situation were dealt with, an Anglo-American operation to invade the Continent might well have to be delayed.[14]

These concerns brought the Allies back to Gymnast.[15] It had been an on-again, off-again, on-again operation. At Arcadia it looked as if the Allies would move toward the amphibious assault for clearing northwestern Africa, especially since President Roosevelt was favorable to the idea. But his military chiefs were convinced that a continental undertaking in support of the Russians was preferable. After being brought around to their thinking, Roosevelt dispatched General Marshall and Harry Hopkins to London to get assurances. The British seemed agreeable, and the Americans left with the impression that some type of western European operation was in the offing. It turned out that Churchill was not in favor. He continued to hold out for Gymnast. The Americans felt betrayed.

The two parties decided to meet in Washington (Argonaut) in June to resolve their differences. During the discussions, British obduracy began to fade, particularly in light of the fall of Tobruk on June 20, to which Roosevelt responded by making available immediately three hundred Sherman tanks and one hundred self-propelled guns for shipment to Egypt. By the end of the conference, it had been decided to look into both a major continental and a North African operation—and even possibly one directed against Churchill's pet project, northern Norway. Establishing a small beachhead in France in 1942, except in a grave emergency, had been ruled out.

At the beginning of July, however, with the front stabilized in Egypt—albeit sixty miles from Alexandria—Britain again insisted on an extensive operation directed against Africa's northwestern coast. Later in the month, Roosevelt, after sending his military leaders to London to look into the matter, agreed that Gymnast, now renamed Torch, could take place sometime in the fall. The Americans insisted on writing into the agreement "that it be understood that a commitment to this operation [Torch] renders 'Round-up' [the major attack against the Continent] in all probability impracticable of successful execution in 1943, and therefore that we have definitely accepted a defensive, encircling line of action for the Continental European theater, except as to Air operations and blockade. . . ."[16] While Churchill continued to think that a cross-Channel assault might be undertaken in 1943, at least the North African operation was finally scheduled for execution. Though interim in nature, Britain's strategy of using its superior seapower, hence its mobility, to compel the Germans to disperse their land forces was about to commence.[17] Moreover, as President Roosevelt and General Marshall well appreciated, Torch fulfilled their desire to get American soldiers actively into combat in the European arena as soon as possible.

While the British and Americans had been trying to resolve what to do next, the Germans had struck. On May 26, three German and six Italian divisions attacked British, Commonwealth, and Free French units along the Gazala line.[18] For a little over two weeks, the Allies held their own, but by June 10, Rommel's forces had taken a number of strongpoints and forced the British to begin withdrawing toward the Egyptian frontier. On June 20, he turned toward Tobruk, took it in a *coup de main*, then asked Hitler

for permission to proceed into Egypt without stopping at the border as originally planned to shift army and especially air forces to attack Malta. Hitler
consented, and after getting a reluctant Mussolini to agree, Rommel advanced
into Egypt. By June 30, he was at El Alamein—but his soldiers were at
the end of their tether.[19] On June 25, he was down to eighty tanks in commission; by July 1, fifty-five; on July 3, twenty-six. Only approximately four
thousand German and six thousand Italian troops remained available for combat. With no supplies or reinforcements in sight, Rommel stopped active
fighting. He expected to resume the attack, but as late as July 21, he estimated
that it would still be another four to five weeks before he could return to
the offensive.[20]

Much more important from the German standpoint was the Russian campaign. After blunting a Soviet operation around Kharkov in May and undertaking a series of small, preliminary attacks, on June 28 the Wehrmacht's offensive
on the southern front began.[21] Germany's 67⅔ divisions, supported by 12½
Rumanian, 7 Hungarian, 3 Italian, and 1 Slovakian, were at first overwhelmingly successful. The first two steps of Operation Blue, now renamed Brunswick, which entailed closing to the Don River, were accomplished by July
8–9. Two weeks later, as a result of additional, substantial gains, Hitler abandoned the originally planned four-step approach and decided to carry out
steps three and four simultaneously. Instead of advancing quickly toward Stalingrad as stipulated in step three, one of the two army groups, Field Marshal
Maximilian von Weichs's Army Group B, was to proceed toward Stalingrad,
while Field Marshal Wilhelm List's Army Group A, with most of the armor,
was to race toward the Caucasian oil fields, some as far as seven hundred
miles away. OKH issued the plan as Directive No. 45, with the additional
provision that most of Manstein's Eleventh Army, which had just taken Sevastopol, was to be detached north to help in a future attack against Leningrad.[22]
In other words, three operations were to be implemented: one to secure
important areas in the Caucasus (codenamed Edelweiss), one to capture
Stalingrad (Heron), and one to take Leningrad and link up with the Finns
(Northern Lights).

This dispersal of forces in the east (additional German units, including
several Panzer divisions, had also been sent west) along with stout Soviet
resistance proved fatal to German designs.[23] Units of Army Group A were
unable to reach all of their Caucasian objectives, and fighting bogged down
with Red Army troops still in control of the mountain passes. By September,
German problems in taking Stalingrad, as well as having an extended flank
north and northwest of the city, had also become apparent. At the same
time, Hitler provoked another leadership crisis. On September 9, he relieved
List of his command and Hitler himself took over as head of Army Group
A. On September 24, he replaced the worn-out and defeatist Halder with
General Kurt Zeitzler as army chief of staff. Halder's departing words to
Zeitzler were "God be with you." On September 30, Zeitzler expressed doubts

about getting sufficient forces readied for the Leningrad attack, and on October 14, Hitler ordered that all offensive operations in the east, except for the Stalingrad battle and some local operations, were to cease and that German soldiers were to stand on the defensive. In effect, as Hillgruber has emphasized, Hitler by this point had given up his worldwide thinking and had moved to a "holding" strategy.[24] Moreover, Hitler's October order stated that any offensive in 1943 would once again take place in the east. What he conceived of as his historic mission to defeat Russia and to eliminate the Jews and other "undesirable" elements would continue.

For Britain, the summer crisis, which included fears that the German thrusts might threaten Britain's oil interests in southern Iran, had passed.[25] It could now look forward to executing Torch, though the original target date of October 15 was pushed back to November 8. In Egypt, after having stopped Rommel's attack at Alam Halfa at the beginning of September, British and Commonwealth forces started preparing their own operation, scheduled to begin in late October. Also by this time, British intelligence was convinced that, despite the heavy fighting, "Germany is unlikely by military action this year to put Russia out of the war." It was therefore conceivable that Britain's weary months of disappointment and frustration, which had included a journey by Churchill to Moscow to inform Stalin personally that there would be no second front in 1942, were about to come to an end.

The beginning of the end occurred on October 23, when British, Commonwealth, and Free French divisions unleashed their attack at El Alamein. At first, they made little headway, but by November 4, they had forced Rommel's outmanned and underequipped troops into retreat. On November 8, American and British forces landed in Morocco and Algeria and started moving eastward. On November 19, the Soviets struck north and south of Stalingrad and soon trapped Germany's Sixth Army and other Axis units inside and west of the city. While the speed of the Allies' advances in each instance varied, the initiative had obviously shifted. A sense of optimism began to prevail among their leaders. As Charles K. Webster and Noble Frankland have written: "As the Grand Alliance began to emerge from the straits to which it had been reduced by German and Japanese advances, more and more attention came to be focused upon the means of achieving victory rather than upon those of averting defeat."[26]

Nevertheless, the Allies still had numerous problems to work out. The most important was how to bring the greatest possible power to bear on Germany. By the late fall of 1942, the British, Americans, and Soviets were all convinced that the strategy for victory in Europe would be a conventional one in which the enemy would have to be confronted and defeated in a series of land campaigns. The navies and air forces would be of help, but winning the Atlantic battle, though crucial, would merely be a prerequisite to clear the way for a western invasion. The strategic air forces would "be developed, not as an instrument of outright victory, but as the means of softening Germany at the centre so that the armies could prevail from the edges."[27] As early as September 20, air Commander-in-Chief Portal had acknowledged: "It will likely be agreed by all of us [the chiefs of staff] that we must ultimately occupy Germany with land forces. The only difference of opinion seems likely to be on how to do so with the least delay and without prohibitive cost in life."[28]

Such differences of opinion were to be examined by the Big Three at Casablanca. Stalin, however, demurred because of pressing developments on his western front. His refusal was probably tied to his displeasure at having no second front, which led him to agree to exploratory talks with the Germans for a possible peace settlement.[29] Roosevelt and Churchill decided to meet in any event, for the military issues they needed to resolve were both immediate and far-reaching. The conference (Symbol) took place January 14–24. The results were, in effect, a "military" victory for the British. Agreements reached at Casablanca in a sense represented compromises between short-range opportunities and the eventual goal of a cross-Channel invasion, but on no vital point did Churchill and his military advisers give way.[30]

The military decisions for European matters all bore a British imprint.[31] The defeat of the U-boat menace in the Atlantic was deemed essential to pursuing the war and was accorded top priority. Every effort was to be made to supply the Soviets with war matériel, but no immediate invasion from the west was envisaged. Instead, the US and Britain agreed to continue their buildup in Great Britain for an operation into France by late summer or autumn of 1943, but only if conditions—for instance, a German collapse (Operation Rankin)—warranted such a move. Meanwhile, North Africa was to be cleared. That effort would be followed by an invasion of Sicily (Operation Husky), which would possibly help entice Turkey into the war on the Allied side. The British had examined the possibility of a Sicilian operation and others in the Mediterranean as early as 1940 and again in 1941. America's agreement amounted to a major concession on its part, for US leaders still preferred a cross-Channel attack, even a small one.[32] Although nothing beyond the invasion of Sicily was stipulated, both allies were well aware that the Mediterranean option had, for the time being, carried the day.

Another significant decision at Casablanca was to increase the role of air power. In the strategic air war, America's desire to employ daylight bombing was agreed to; Britain was to step up its night attacks. Air leaders made the further point, on the basis of their experiences in North Africa, that large tactical air forces would also constitute an important ingredient in assisting in subsequent land operations.[33] The buildup of tactical air forces, combined with the use of additional aircraft in the naval war, meant that the Allies had opted for a general air strategy based not only on long-range bombing, but also on extensive support of land and sea forces. This broad application of air power the Germans could not match.

The other Casablanca military decisions dealt with the Southeast Asian

and Pacific theaters. Included, among other provisions, was a possible operation to recapture part of northern Burma in 1943 as a prerequisite to opening
a land route to China, but nothing definite was approved. In political matters,
besides unsuccessfully attempting to undercut General de Gaulle as leader
of the Free French, Roosevelt announced the unconditional-surrender formula.
The president wanted to assure Stalin that the Western Allies would never
seek a compromise peace, only the total elimination of the Axis as warring
nations. Even though Churchill had not given his approval when Roosevelt
made his statement to the press, there is no doubt that the prime minister
agreed with the policy and that it had been a part of Britain's grand strategy
for some time.[34] Overall, then, it was obvious at the conclusion of the
Casablanca conference that the British and the Americans had approved a
broad-based military strategy with the widespread use of sea, land, and air
components.

Germany's options for 1943 continued to be much more limited. As the
year began, conditions in North Africa and the Soviet Union remained critical,
and the situation did not improve until the Russo-German front finally stabilized in March, more than a month after the fall of Stalingrad. In a further
blow, Axis troops were defeated in North Africa in May.[35] During this time,
Hitler's holding strategy took further shape.[36] Preparations were to be undertaken to meet possible Allied operations into Spain, Sardinia, Sicily, Italy,
and the Balkans as well as to increase defensive readiness in western Europe.
The Luftwaffe also started thinking more in terms of a defensive war; the
number of fighters produced rose from an average of 435 per month during
the last half of 1942 to 753 in the first half of 1943.[37] In the submarine
war, despite Grand Admiral Raeder's removal in favor of Dönitz, the navy
expected even greater success in 1943 than it had had in 1942, since more
than twenty new submarines per month were being built.[38] In March, it
looked as if Dönitz's expectations were being realized, since he estimated
that 875,000 tons of Allied shipping had been sunk. (He considered 700,000
tons per month would be sufficient to turn the tonnage war in Germany's
favor.) Only two months later, the Atlantic battle shifted dramatically in favor
of the Allies. German naval leaders were not sure of all the reasons, but
they were fully aware that their losses in the Atlantic had more than doubled,
from twelve in April to thirty-one during the first twenty-two days of May.[39]
In the face of these prohibitive losses, Dönitz called off his wolfpacks on
May 24. Although he did not lose Hitler's confidence and hoped to revive
the U-boat campaign at some future date, the Battle of the Atlantic had
entered a new, less decisive, phase.

In the meantime, Hitler and his advisers had once again turned toward
the east. They had already decided to make their main effort against the
Soviet Union in 1943, especially since 163 of the German combat divisions
were stationed there.[40] The only question was the form the German operation
would take. In this instance, Hitler deviated from his holding strategy, and

in March he decided to eliminate the Red Army salient west of Kursk.[41] Designated Operation Citadel, it was a tactical undertaking, but it could in Hitler's thinking serve as the first of a number of offensives designed to consolidate Germany's position in the east. The operation was important to the Führer, if for no other reason than to demonstrate to the world and to the populace at home that German troops still held the initiative.

Citadel experienced difficulties from the start. It could not be readied by mid-April as hoped, and at a conference with his staff and commanders on May 3, Hitler decided that the offensive should be put off again until the number of German tanks, including new Panther tanks, could be increased substantially. By the time Citadel commenced on July 5, the Soviets, aided by excellent intelligence, were ready. After heavy fighting, they not only blunted the two-pronged German attack, but then started an offensive of their own. Rather than easing Germany's problems on the Russian Front, Kursk only made them worse.

Given the myriad of difficulties Germany now was facing on all fronts, how could Hitler ever expect to win? The answer seems to be that he and his closest associates decided that by withdrawing only as a last resort and by destroying as many of the enemy as possible in the process, the result might lead to a dissolution of the unstable opposing alliance that would allow Germany to turn the war again in its favor.[42] In this regard, the Führer rejected Mussolini's plea in April 1943 to come to an understanding with Russia so as to concentrate on the west, but he began to believe that if Germany could exploit fundamental antagonisms between Britain and the United States, even their partnership might not last. While this thinking strikes one today as exceedingly unrealistic, it does help substantiate the notion that Hitler early on thought the unnatural Grand Alliance would come apart. So long as the Third Reich's propaganda machine succeeded in convincing its people and its troops that the war must continue or grave retributions from the enemy would surely follow, Germany would carry on.

Allied staff officers shared this latter sentiment. They did take into account that Germany might collapse, but they truly believed that the Wehrmacht would continue fighting and made their plans accordingly. Their problem was that, despite mounting victories, the cooperative mood at Casablanca soon dissipated.[43] The Americans felt they had been taken in by Britain's Mediterranean strategy and even suspected that the British wanted to avoid a cross-Channel attack altogether. Britain, for its part, believed that the US was trying to shift its primary focus from Europe to the Pacific. The western partners had already agreed that a further meeting to "adjust" the common strategy they had worked out at Casablanca might be necessary. The result was a third Washington conference (Trident), held May 12–25.[44]

During the meetings it became evident that American strategic thinking had become more sophisticated and that the nature of the western alliance was changing, with the US assuming a more prominent role. It was also apparent that the Americans were not going to yield to the British on almost every point as they had at Casablanca. Nevertheless, except for the agreement that the atomic bomb be developed as a joint enterprise, few new decisions were made. The Allies continued to emphasize that control of the Atlantic was crucial, that the strategic air offensive should be pursued, and that Russia should be assisted. But they differed on how best to render assistance. In the end, the Americans leaned toward Britain's plan to assault the Italian peninsula once Sicily, now scheduled for invasion on July 10, had been taken. They also wanted to keep other options open in the Mediterranean, including a possible assault against Sardinia. Further, they insisted that preparations be intensified for a full-scale invasion of the Continent launched from the UK with a target date of May 1, 1944.

Thus acknowledging that "the Mediterranean momentum" could not be halted altogether, US leaders also realized that the Pacific and Asian theaters gave them a significant lever for keeping in check what they considered unrealistic British "aspirations" in the Mediterranean. American concern about the Asian war took concrete form in their pressing for more aid to China by way of Burma, and their ally went along with the idea. But when Britain subsequently brought up that its forces, particularly naval, might start to play a role in the Pacific, the US resisted British involvement.[45]

While Trident did not erase all of the suspicions between the two countries' leaders—in part these misgivings led to an August conference at Quebec—the broad lines of assaulting Hitler's Europe had been drawn. The main effort was to be a spring 1944 attack from the west with Soviet help (as yet uncoordinated) from the east. The British and Americans hoped that their landings in Sicily would quickly lead to success, and they eventually agreed to an invasion of the Italian mainland, which would not only knock Italy out of the war, but also, especially from Britain's standpoint, present additional opportunities in the area. The Americans thought this might mean a British adventure in the Balkans, but British historians generally accept Ronald Lewin's assertion that "at no time . . . did Churchill advocate a military penetration of the Balkans *on a major scale.*"[46] Another issue, that of insufficient personnel and equipment, particularly landing craft, continued to raise its head; however, despite the frustrations, by mid-1943, the Western Allies were convinced that the war was won if they did not make a strategic misstep.[47] This the British and American chiefs were determined to avoid. They still argued over strategic aims and never developed a full-scale politico-military strategy, but at least they were resolving their differences as true and equal partners.

Mid-1943 also provides a convenient place to break the narrative to comment briefly on the significance of intelligence, war production, and military manpower in the war efforts of the two belligerents. Obviously these elements were of utmost importance to both sides, but their ability to utilize them effectively differed substantially.

Of the three areas, intelligence is the most difficult to assess. Even though a great deal of documentation has become available, portions still remain classified, and the declassified portions seldom tell us the extent to which intelligence information influenced decisions at the front. In operational matters, historians usually have either to *assume* that there is a link between the deciphered messages and the decisions made or to depend on recollections of the individuals involved to get an answer, for the relevant materials in the theaters were closely held and destroyed after being used.

Nonetheless, at least three generalizations can be ventured.[48] First, cryptographic intelligence was the most reliable source of information on the enemy, more accurate than reports from spies or POWs or other sources. Yet the cryptographic information was most valuable when backed up by other intelligence, especially from photo reconnaissance and ground patrols at the tactical level. Second, British intelligence, particularly cryptographic, was superior to that of Germany. David Kahn has given a number of possible reasons, including Allied knowledge of the Enigma machine, the most important cryptographic source; better and different types of Allied machines; fragmentation of Germany's organization as compared with the more unified Anglo-American effort; more talented people (Germany's expulsions and extermination of Jews was a factor here); greater German reluctance to face reality; and better Allied luck.[49] The third generalization is that no matter how good the intelligence was during the war, it was less important than the abilities of the troops and the quality and quantity of their equipment. What timely intelligence did was to give the possessor an advantage, but it did not assure victory. This had to be earned on the battlefield.[50]

Germany's cryptographic record is mixed. Its intelligence experts, who were scattered among twelve separate agencies, were generally unable to crack the Allied army and air force codes (except those of the Soviets), but their *B-Dienst* (Observation Service) did gain numerous successes in the naval sphere.[51] It was able, for instance, to decrypt the British naval administrative code during the assault on Norway. The knowledge thus gained helped the German navy to avoid the British fleet at critical junctures. Even more noteworthy is *B-Dienst's* record in the Battle of the Atlantic, during which its personnel read portions of one or more naval codes from September 1939 to August 1940, and then after a break because Britain changed its codes, again from September 1941 to June 1943 (except for problems in late 1942 and early 1943). The decrypts allowed the Germans to forecast the areas through which the Allies would route their convoys, sometimes as early as ten to twenty hours in advance, and to act accordingly. But at the end of 1942 the British assumed their "convoy" cipher system was insecure and undertook measures to introduce a new one. By June 1943, the new deciphering system was in place, and it virtually cut off *B-Dienst's* ability to read the British codes (except for the merchant naval code, which it took the British until December to make secure).

German cryptographers also had some, albeit limited, success in influencing the land campaigns. They were somewhat effective in the east, where General Reinhard Gehlen's Foreign Armies East used a variety of methods as well as cryptographic intelligence to assemble important information, which at times Hitler and his advisers disregarded because it did not accord with what they wanted to hear. In the west, Germany's achievements were even more limited. The Germans did on occasion in 1944 get warnings of Allied bombing raids in France which allowed their troops to take cover and to shift equipment to other places. They also broke the encoded messages of the US attaché in Cairo, Colonel Bonner Fellers, whose reports assisted Rommel in his January 1942 counterattack in Cyrenaica. Still, as Kahn points out, German communications experts failed to decrypt strategic communications. Thus, their intelligence did not have as much impact on grand and military strategy as it might have had.

Britain's successes, helped along by the Poles, French, and Americans, were at times dramatic and they were achieved among all of the services.[52] The most significant source was codenamed Ultra, the process whereby cryptographers located in Bletchley Park, forty-five miles northwest of London, were able to decipher and distribute to selected users a number of messages sent by the German air force (from May 22, 1940, to the end of the war), by the navy (May 1941–February 1942, and from December 1942 to the end); and by the army (first intercepted during the last half of 1940, but only decrypted with regularity after mid-1942 and still subject to a three-to-seven-day delay). The German equipment which sent the encryptions were the air force and naval Enigma machines and the army *Geheimschreiber* machine (called Fish by the British).

Britain's breaking of various German service codes had an impact on both its strategy and its operations. In terms of strategy, decryptions from Enigma and Fish allowed the Allies to build up and update a generally accurate order of battle on the German armed forces and its European associates in all theaters. Knowing what Germany was doing also enabled Britain to give the Soviet Union warnings of impending German actions, which at least in the case of Barbarossa went unheeded. On the other hand, Ultra decrypts made it possible for the Western Allies to gain insights into Soviet operations in the east, thus partially overcoming Soviet reticence to inform the British and the Americans of their intentions.[53] The Allies were further able to follow changes in German thinking about Italy, the Balkans, and western and northern Europe as these areas moved from potential to active war theaters.

In terms of operations, the list of known Ultra-related achievements is even more impressive. Ultra helped immeasurably in North Africa, especially between May 1942 and May 1943. During this time, Hinsley concludes: "The British forces . . . were supplied with more information about more aspects of the enemy's operations than any forces enjoyed during any important campaign of the Second World War."[54] Specifically, the ability to decipher German messages made a significant contribution to Britain's realizing Rommel's operational and supply difficulties at the end of June 1942 and to Montgomery's stopping Rommel's subsequent Alam Halfa offensive at the beginning of September. In the Atlantic, Ultra played an equally important role. When the Allies were unable to decipher the German navy's new Triton code between February and December 1942, they suffered considerable shipping losses. The same occurred when the Germans instituted a new rotor sequence for their machines during the first twenty days of March 1943. As a result, U-boats sunk 40 of the 202 Allied ships that made up the eastbound convoys. However, the Allies soon overcame the difficulty and turned the Atlantic battle in their favor during the next two months. Although longer-range bombers, new radar, and more naval escorts obviously played a part in the turnaround, historian Jürgen Rohwer, the foremost expert on submarine warfare during the war, contends that "if I had to place the many factors which decided the outcome of the Battle of the Atlantic in the spring of 1943 in an order of precedence, I would place 'Special Intelligence' or 'Ultra' at the top."[55]

By 1944, most Allied commanders were relying on Ultra for a good deal of their information on the enemy. Ultra obviously assisted in both the deceptions and the execution of the Normandy campaign before, during, and after the June assault.[56] It helped to halt Germany's Mortain counteroffensive on August 7. It allowed the US Seventh Army commander, General Alexander Patch, Jr., to move his troops boldly north after the French Riviera landing on August 15, and also permitted him to check a German attack in Alsace at the end of December. Ultra did not lead the Allies to foresee the Ardennes offensive earlier in the month, but it was still considered such an important source that "whenever a message came in labeled with five Zs [the most urgent category], the head of the Special Liaison Unit [which received the information] had to take it personally to the commander, no matter what time of day or night."[57] This does not mean that Ultra was always foolproof. As General Elwood Quesada, the US commander of IX Tactical Air Command, indicated in a 1975 interview: "On some occasions, *Ultra* information would be erroneous. We went on many wild goose chases as a result of *Ultra*. . . . *Ultra* was a very fine tool that also had its drawbacks."[58] Still, the results it achieved were indeed of major proportions and did affect the course of the war.

The Western Allies, of course, used other intelligence sources besides Ultra. The Americans' ability to decrypt Japanese naval and diplomatic codes was second in importance only to the British achievement.[59] Not only did Magic, as the American process was codenamed, give the Allies vital information about the Pacific theater (especially significant in the Midway victory of early June 1942), the diplomatic messages sent to Japan by Baron Hiroshi Oshima, the ambassador to Germany, contained significant data about the war in Europe. For example, from Oshima the Allies in August 1943 learned that the Luftwaffe had definitely decided to step up aircraft production and to give priority to building fighters rather than bombers. In October they received an indication that Hitler was thinking about concentrating on British and American instead of Soviet forces. There are other examples of Magic's value as well. Nevertheless, while extolling the importance of intelligence, it is necessary to emphasize again the crucial point made by General Leo Hepp, the wartime chief of staff in the German army signals branch. At a conference in 1978, he reminded the participants: "Allied material superiority was the crucial factor, not Ultra."[60]

No one at the 1978 conference, which centered on the influence of Ultra, disputed Hepp's statement. In other words, historians and other authorities still believe economic considerations were the overriding factor in determining the war's outcome.[61] This topic has been examined elsewhere in great detail, but seldom on a comparative basis. For our purposes, it is sufficient to discuss German and British war production in two major categories—tanks and aircraft—for these weapon systems give us a good idea of the magnitude of Allied economic superiority.

The figures for tank production (table 5-1) show clearly that no matter how good the Germans' tanks and tank crews were, they could not match the British, let alone the Americans and Soviets, on anything like an equal basis.[62] With Britain having available four times as many new tanks as the Germans in 1942 and 1943, and twice as many during the first six months of 1944, there was no way the Germans could compete with the Allies, despite having accorded tanks top priority in their armaments program during the first four months of 1943.[63]

In aircraft production, the totals also clearly demonstrate Allied superiority (table 5-2).[64] The main point in this instance is that by the time the Germans reached parity with the British in 1944, the United States' contribution had become overwhelming, even though part of the US total was being sent to the Pacific and Asia. And these figures do not take into account growing Soviet air might.

When one breaks down the totals into types of aircraft being constructed, despite differences in classification, the figures indicate the changing nature of the air war (table 5-3).[65] While Germany shifted almost exclusively to producing fighters, many for defensive purposes, the British and the Americans

Table 5-1
Tank Production, 1942–44

	1942	*1943*	*1944 (1st 6 mos.)*
Germany	4,137	5,996	4,402
Great Britain	8,611	7,467	2,474
From Overseas	9,253	15,933	6,670
Total British	17,864	23,400	9,144

Table 5-2
Aircraft Production, 1942–44

	1942	1943	1944
Germany	15,556	25,527	39,807
Great Britain	23,672	26,263	26,461
From Overseas	5,898	6,710	11,414
Total British	29,570	32,973	37,875
United States	47,836	85,898	96,318

built up a balanced force of both fighters and bombers. What the figures here do not show is that many of the British bombers were long-range, four-motored Lancasters suitable for strategic bombing. Nor do they show that, despite increased German aircraft production, German losses during some months of 1943 more than offset the increases, so that "the number of aircraft in frontline units began to decline noticeably."[66] As with tank production, the Germans clearly could not compete with the Allies in the air.

In comparing the sizes of the British and the German armed forces, one finds that the two were on a more equal footing.[67] In 1939, the population of Greater Germany was approximately 79.5 million; that of the United Kingdom, 47.7 million. The figures for the active strength of their armed forces throughout the war show that both nations rapidly increased the size of their military establishments through mid-1941, and that the numbers generally leveled off between 1942 and 1944 (table 5-4). They also reveal that Britain was vastly inferior in total forces. The Commonwealth and Empire made up part of the disparity, but their numbers alone were insufficient. Britain obviously required outside assistance, which was provided by the United States. American human power, though partly allocated to the Pacific, was crucial, and US forces grew from 1.7 million in mid-1941 to 9.2 million in mid-1943 to 11.5 million in mid-1944. Both during and after the war, the British well understood the telling importance, though somewhat wistfully, of having allies. They further recognized that their "considered" strategy had paid off in another way: while the Germans suffered approximately 8,333,000 military casualties, Britain's total losses were 755,439.[68]

During the last twenty-one months of the European war, between August 1943 and May 1945, Britain and Germany found their roles reversed from what they had been at the beginning. If Germany had at first held the initiative, it was now clearly in the hands of Britain and its allies. In place of German victories was a series of stunning British successes. Although Britain had initially fought for survival, it was now Germany's turn. The Wehrmacht was, in effect, reacting, improvising, and finding itself limited to short-term

TABLE 5-3
Aircraft Production (By Type)

	Germany				Great Britain		
	1942	1943	1944		1942	1943	1944
				Fighters (incl.			
Fighters	7,128	15,151	30,511	Lt. Bombers)	10,663	11,103	10,730
Bombers	4,428	5,019	2,596	Bombers	5,439	7,352	7,903
Transports	588	1,176	504	Transports	—	209	889
Trainers	1,150	2,280	3,215	Trainers &			
Seaplanes	228	264	156	Others	5,942	4,825	2,877
Others	2,034	1,637	2,825	Naval	1,082	1,720	2,939
				Recce	546	1,054 ⟨	1,123
Totals	15,556	25,527	39,807	*Totals*	23,672	26,263	24,461

objectives, while Britain had the benefit of preparing much broader, more deliberate, and better calculated moves.

By August 1943, in the wake of defeats at Kursk and in Sicily, Germany's already diminished strategic options had narrowed even further. In fact, the Germans had little alternative but to intensify the holding strategy they had been forced to adopt since October 1942 in the hope of making the war so costly that the Allied coalition would fall apart.

In the meantime, while the Red Army was advancing in the southern and central sectors, the Western Allies were meeting at Quebec (Quadrant) to coordinate their strategic thinking. As in the past, military considerations dominated the meeting.[69] Except for the establishment of the Southeast Asia Command, the military decisions, reached only after numerous and frank discussions, reaffirmed the strategic directions of the previous May: a cross-Channel attack in 1944 targeted for May; the invasion of Italy with the object— easier now that Mussolini had been overthrown—of eliminating Italy from the war; a continuing emphasis on keeping sea communications open and on bombing Germany; a number of 1944 battles projected for the Pacific to take advantage of Japan's dwindling resources; and limited offensives in northern Burma. There were also compromises. Although the Allies agreed that the invasion of northern France was to have highest priority, the Americans insisted on examining the possibility of a landing in southern France to assist Overlord. The British, for their part, wanted more flexibility for other possible operations in the Mediterranean, including plans for seizing Sardinia and Corsica, vigorous pressure in Italy to draw off German forces from Russia and elsewhere, the establishment of air bases in Italy to strike at central and east European targets, and measures to step up material assistance to Balkan resistance groups. In both matters—a landing in southern France and additional Mediterranean undertakings—each ally reluctantly went along at

Table 5-4
Armed Forces (In Millions)

	June 1939	June 1940	June 1941	June 1942	June 1943	June 1944
Germany	1.366	5.600	7.200	8.635	9.555	9.100
Gr. Britain	.480	2.273	3.383	4.091	4.761	4.967
GB + Empire	.600	—	3.800	4.500	5.100	5.200

least with making plans for what the other proposed. By the end of Quebec, even the usually pessimistic General Brooke, though not completely satisfied, felt that he had at least made some headway in proving to the Americans the close relation that existed between cross-Channel and Italian operations. And US leaders, although still suspicious of Britain's Mediterranean designs, were pleased to have its leadership reiterate that the main Anglo-American effort in 1944 was to come from the west, not the south. Compromises and overall cooperation, not confrontation, had prevailed. (Another example of their cooperation was the British decision to send their strategic planning papers to US planners in Washington twice a week.)[70]

Events soon after Quebec bore out Allied optimism. On September 8, the beleaguered Italian government exited from the war. A little earlier, British landings on the peninsula near Reggio and at Taranto had succeeded. By early October, despite determined German opposition to an amphibious assault at Salerno, British and American forces had cleared southern Italy and taken Naples and the Foggia airfields in the process. In addition, Sardinia and Corsica fell to the Allies, led by Free French troops, thereby further opening up the western Mediterranean to Allied shipping. In the east, the Soviets punched holes in the German lines, which allowed them to advance beyond the Dneiper in the south and to capture Smolensk in the center by the end of September.

In October, however, Germany's holding strategy again began to have an effect. To be sure, the Russians continued to win tactical victories, especially on the southern front, but German opposition was stiffening. The same was true in Italy, where Hitler had decided not to withdraw and where German forces were holding their own behind a series of defensive lines north of Naples. With Italy now out of the war (at least temporarily), the Germans completed taking over the previously Italian-occupied areas in southern France and Yugoslavia and strengthened their defensive presence throughout the Balkans.[71] They also took over Rhodes from the Italians and retook other islands in the Dodecanese chain which the British had occupied after the Italian surrender. In the air war, the Luftwaffe marshaled its fighter and antiaircraft resources to deal the Americans a devastating setback in their attack on Schweinfurt.[72] As a result, the US decided to limit its daylight bombing raids to close-in targets. Bomber Command's attacks over Germany at night were also subject to substantial losses. (Only by early 1944 did the Americans overcome the problem by starting to use P-51 Mustangs as long-range escorts.)

Hitler also began to see possibilities for his Fortress Europe concept in the west. On November 3, on the basis of a detailed appraisal from Field Marshal von Rundstedt, his commander-in-chief west, the Führer issued a directive which spelled out a change of emphasis.[73] Rather than to concentrate on the Soviet Union, he had decided to concentrate on defeating an Anglo-American invasion from the west. In Hitler's view, this was where the next decisive battle would be fought, perhaps as early as the following spring. His goal was to repulse the enemy at the water's edge. Should that prove impossible, the enemy "must be hit by a counterattack delivered with all our might." All measures were to be directed to this task: fortifications were to be strengthened; strongpoints made invulnerable; air, sea, and land units, especially armored divisions, built up and increased in number so that the "Anglo-Saxons" would be dealt a devastating blow. Hitler ended the directive with the injunction: "I expect that all staffs will make a supreme effort toward utilizing the time which remains in preparing for the expected decisive battle in the West."

Thus Germany's agenda for 1944 had been determined: defeat the antici-pated attack in the west and at the same time undertake holding actions in the east and south, giving ground only when absolutely necessary. Moreover, Hitler not only insisted that Göring have a bomber force readied to strike London after the first of the year but also announced that the revenge weapons, the V-1 and V-2, were nearing operational readiness.[74] Although the February "Baby Blitz" turned out to be a miserable failure and the V-weapons encoun-tered production and design problems which held up their introduction until June and September 1944, the strategic designs set forth by German planners in late 1943 indicate that Hitler still thought he had a chance to turn the war in his favor.

The British, on the other hand, were resolved to retain their hard-earned initiative. They also recognized that the war had reached a critical stage in which additional coordination, including more with the Soviets, was essen-tial. This time Stalin agreed to a conference—the place yet to be determined—in late November. Prior to the meeting, the American, British, and Soviet foreign ministers and other officials got together in Moscow toward the end of October to discuss various issues and to make preparations for the larger conclave. At Moscow, it was evident that significant political as well as military items would be placed on the forthcoming agenda. The British, for example, had already begun post-hostilities planning.[75]

It also soon became evident that, despite the "friendly atmosphere" at Moscow and the subsequent agreement to meet at Tehran, all was not well, at least among the military leaders of the Big Three. The British were particu-larly perturbed with the Soviets. Field Marshal Brooke indicated after the war that part of the problem was that Britain was always giving and never getting anything in return.[76] A November 24 note from the chief British liaison officer in Moscow makes clear one of the reasons for Brooke's discontent:

> We have done our best to play the game with the Soviets by providing generous opportunities for Soviet officers and Engineers to study our forces and in the provisions of intelligence on the enemy and very ample information about our equipment. On this score we have nothing with which to reproach ourselves. The picture from the Soviet side is entirely different and it can be observed that they have done little to reciprocate our efforts to cooperate with us. . . .[77]

Brooke also had doubts about the Americans. On November 11, he wrote in his diary: "I feel that we shall have a pretty serious set-to which may strain our relations with the Americans, but I am tired of seeing our strategy warped by their short-sightedness [with regard to the Mediterranean]," a sentiment he recorded again on November 20.[78] General Frederick Morgan, the head planner for Overlord, noticed while in Washington that the US joint chiefs felt the same way. Upon leaving for Cairo and Tehran, he indicated "they had left muttering imprecations about the adjectival British and their perfidy, particularly in relation to their Mediterranean ambitions."[79]

The desire among the British and Americans "to put the other straight" was not helped at Cairo (Sextant), where the two allies met between November 22 and 26 before going on to Tehran.[80] The British chiefs were upset because so much time was devoted to discussing the Asian situation, especially China, since Jiang Jie-shi (Chiang Kai-shek) had been invited there to meet with Churchill and Roosevelt. They were further displeased with American organizational schemes to establish a single supreme commander for the Mediterranean and western Europe combined and to form a united chiefs of staff committee of the United States, Britain, the Soviet Union, and China.[81] The British were able to sidetrack both US proposals as unworkable, though they did agree to supreme allied commanders, but one for the Mediterranean (SACMED) and one for the west (SCAEF). The chiefs also disagreed on the agenda of common issues they wanted to discuss with the Soviets.[82] Finally having resolved their differences, they proposed that the following military issues be brought up, but not in any particular order: coordination of Anglo-American and Soviet offensives in Europe, Italian operations, measures to entice Turkey into the war, supplies to Russia, strategic bombing, and the possible use of Soviet air bases against Japan. They decided not to broach three other matters—shuttle bomber bases in the western USSR, air transport routes between the west and the Soviet Union, the exchange of weather information—and relegated these items to discussions among their respective military representatives in Moscow.

After the hurried and less-than-satisfactory talks at Cairo, the British and Americans proceeded to Tehran (Eureka), where they met their Russian counterparts for four days of intensive talks interspersed with less formal conversations and sumptuous meals and banquets. The Big Three were finally together. As might be expected from three such powerful, confident, yet different leaders, their discussions were wide-ranging. Nonetheless, military issues dominated three of the four plenary sessions.[83] By the time the conference was over, the leaders had decided regarding Europe that the Yugoslav partisans be supported with additional supplies, that attempts be made to get Turkey into the war, and that operations in Italy be continued with the aim of reaching the Pisa-Florence-Rimini line. But they spent most of their time discussing the supreme operation for 1944—Overlord.

The cross-Channel attack was to be launched in May (the British chiefs expected it would be the end of the month), and the Soviets agreed to help by unleashing their own offensive at approximately the same time. Overlord was to be assisted also by another operation, the invasion of southern France (Anvil), on as large a scale as landing craft would allow. While the Western Allies had talked about Anvil at Quebec and had had planners look into such a possibility (the planners had been skeptical whether it would "assist" Overlord), nothing definite had been decided.[84] On this issue, Stalin had taken the lead. At the November 28 session, during which Churchill had brought up landings at the head of the Adriatic or in southern France as possible options, Stalin had commented: "The best course would be to make 'Overlord' the basic operation for 1944, and once Rome had been captured, to send all troops available in Italy to Southern France. These forces would then join hands with 'Overlord' forces when the invasion was launched. France was the weakest spot on the German front."[85] President Roosevelt agreed with Stalin's suggestion, though it was decided (for the time being) to launch Anvil simultaneously with the cross-Channel attack. Therefore, Stalin's remark and his insistence on a second front, as historians have pointed out numerous times, played a role in determining western strategy.[86] While historians continue to argue over Stalin's motives, there is no doubt that Roosevelt, in his desire to get along with the Soviet dictator because of his anticipated official role after the war, at times supported Stalin's views in preference to those of Churchill. As General Kennedy, Britain's top planner, noted after Tehran: "The Russians and the Americans have had their way. Time will show whether this is justified."[87] He added ". . . the conclusions [at Tehran] have hardened our strategical policy and have committed us, more deeply than before, to courses of action which, it is true to say, we should not have adopted had the conduct of the war been entirely in our own hands. It is not at all impossible that these courses will prove to be right. . . . We will certainly put our whole effort into making a success of them."

With regard to Asia and the Pacific, the three powers were generally in accord. The Western Allies were especially cheered by Stalin's "concession," brought up at Moscow the previous October, to enter the war against Japan once Germany had been defeated. But the British and Americans disagreed over one of the proposed operations. Both had agreed, after the first meeting in Cairo, that the main effort against Japan would come from the Pacific and that Southeast Asia would have to play a subsidiary role.[88] The Americans, however, still wanted a seaborne assault against the Andaman Islands (Buccaneer) in conjunction with operations in northern Burma designed to get assistance to Jiang by land as well as by the now functioning air route. Churchill was opposed to Buccaneer. Upon the return of the delegations to Cairo, the Americans finally gave in. Actually, Buccaneer's postponement did not come about because of Churchill's persuasive powers, but because the Anglo-Americans lacked sufficient landing craft to carry out Overlord, Anvil, and Buccaneer all in the spring of 1944. The old problem of not having enough landing craft had once again raised its head, and it had become obvious that nothing, including Buccaneer, was to be done to jeopardize Overlord or Anvil.

Not until the final days at Tehran were political questions formally examined. Although Churchill has contended that the political discussions were "more remote and speculative," he, along with Roosevelt and Stalin, certainly appreciated their vital significance.[89] On the other hand, they probably did not realize the extent to which their talks would help shape the postwar world. As with the military concerns, Stalin got most of what he wanted.[90] The session concentrated on central and eastern Europe, though Iran's "continuing" independence was also agreed upon. In regard to central Europe, the leaders concurred that Germany should be dismembered, while disagreeing on the specifics to bring this about. The European Advisory Commission, set up at Moscow, was to continue developing policies for the area. The situation in eastern Europe was more complicated. It was decided (1) that Finland retain its independence, (2) that Königsberg and the northern portion of East Prussia become Soviet territory, and (3) that the Curzon Line serve as Poland's eastern border. Otherwise, except for Stalin's demand that a "friendly government" be established in Poland, specifics were avoided.

Churchill, Roosevelt, and their chiefs of staff returned to Cairo, where their talks between December 3 and 7 dealt with implementing the military decisions reached at Tehran.[91] Besides canceling Buccaneer, they reiterated that "nothing must be undertaken in any other part of the world which hazards the success" of Overlord and named General Dwight Eisenhower to command the cross-Channel attack. They also discussed a possible amphibious landing to capture Rhodes, but after talking with Turkey's evasive president, Ismet Inönü, who declined to enter the war, an Aegean operation was not in the offing. Upon renewing their commitment to keep the Atlantic clear of U-boats and to support the strategic bombing offensive, the Western Allies declared the Cairo-Tehran-Cairo meetings over.

The importance of those meetings cannot be overstated.[92] They determined the final strategy for the war in Europe and pointed the direction for ending the conflict in Asia and the Pacific. The main Anglo-American effort in Europe was to come from the west, with Soviet forces advancing and occupying areas from the east. Further, the acceptance of the Pacific strategy meant that the United States would dominate operations in that theater and that Britain and the Soviets would assume a secondary role, except perhaps in southeastern and northeastern portions of Asia.

Tehran had other repercussions as well. It had drawn the Soviets closer to the Western Allies. As a result, British and American fears of a possible German-Soviet deal subsided. Because of the concessions gained, the USSR was now inextricably bound to the west. Yet despite their emphasis on cooperation, the Russians were still wary of their "friends" and refused to share military plans and detailed information with them. They would remain partners at arm's length.

The atmosphere at Tehran also provided evidence that Roosevelt was beginning to believe that the Soviet Union and the United States would be the dominant powers after the war and that Britain would have a lesser part to play.[93] Churchill, in his heart of hearts, possibly realized this too, but he was determined to do all that he could to ensure that Britain would have a say in shaping postwar developments.

While the Allied decisions at Tehran and Cairo prescribed their strategic priorities for 1944 and into 1945, Germany's guarded optimism, apparent in November 1943, eroded during the next seventeen months until at the end Hitler's Reich lay prostrate. Apprehension commenced soon after the Führer's November directive in which he indicated that the major effort to turn back the Allies was now to be prepared in the west. At a December meeting with his military staff, while still exuding confidence, he pointed to one of Germany's most urgent problems: the Allies could attack almost anywhere at any time.[94] "I have the feeling," he said, "that they want to operate on very broad fronts." Besides France's Channel coast, where he expected an invasion was certain, he named other possibilities, including southern France, the Bay of Biscay area, and Norway. These possibilities related only to the west, not to the other threatened areas in southern or eastern Europe or to the air war, all of which were important to consider.

Therefore, Germany did not have the "luxury" of preparing only for the anticipated landing in the west, but had to consider numerous contingencies.[95] If the Allies undertook an amphibious operation in the Balkans, additional troops and equipment were to be rushed there from other theaters (Operation Gertrude). The same would apply to an assault launched against Italy's northwestern Ligurian (Marder 1) or northeastern Adriatic (Marder 2) coasts. Provisions, though limited, were also made for an attack against Denmark (Hanna) and Norway (Falke). In February, the German commanders in the west and OKW became apprehensive about possible Allied operations in southern France and Portugal and moved several divisions south of the Loire just in case. German fears about their southwestern flank lessened when they learned that the Allies had shipped a number of experienced combat divisions from Italy to the United Kingdom. But the idea that British and American forces would initiate diversionary attacks before or during the cross-Channel operation had become deeply embedded in the minds of Hitler and his military advisers.

In the meantime, Hitler had directed Field Marshal Rommel to oversee the intensified defensive buildup along the Channel. He and the theater commander, von Rundstedt, did what they could to have more permanent fortifications erected, foreshore obstacles and mines installed, coastal divisions upgraded, and armored divisions shifted west.[96] There is no doubt as to the importance Hitler attached to repelling the invasion. In a March 20 speech to his western commanders, he declared: "The destruction of the enemy's landing attempt means more than a purely local decision on the Western front. It is the sole decisive factor in the whole conduct of the war and hence its final result." As a consequence of the stepped-up measures begun in November 1943, the Germans had by May 1944 assembled fifty-eight divisions, ten of them armored, behind a relatively formidable system of coastal defenses.

Still, the Atlantic Wall defenses were never so formidable as the Wehrmacht wanted or hoped because Allied actions even during the relatively "quiet" spring of 1944 did not allow the Germans to concentrate solely on the west. The Allied amphibious landings at Anzio and repeated, though unsuccessful, attempts to break through the German defenses south of Rome kept up the pressure in Italy. British and American strategic bombing attacks took a heavy toll, though the British suffered a setback in their night-bombing raids, which culminated at Nuremburg at the end of March. In the east, Hitler ordered Wehrmacht units to occupy an increasingly recalcitrant Hungary, and the Red Army undertook a series of offensives, relieving Leningrad in January, capturing Vinnitsa and other Ukrainian cities in March, and forcing the Germans to give up Odessa in April. Then, except for in the Crimea, where the German Seventeenth Army was able to evacuate some but not all of its forces by sea, there was a lull on the Russian Front while the Soviets prepared their next offensive thrusts.

The Western Allies were involved in their own preparations. Despite subsequent comments that the "ease" of the Overlord landing showed that the US and Britain should have undertaken the operation earlier, intelligence experts at the time did not share this retrospective view. A December 20 Combined Intelligence appreciation indicated that "in spite of the loss of her Italian ally, her failure in Russia, and her difficulties in the Balkans, and in spite of the intensification of the Allied bombing offensive, Germany's strategic situation had not deteriorated 'anything like as rapidly as probable in early autumn.'"[97] The appreciation went on: although Germany's productive output was declining, "the central control of her economic machine remained unbroken, her work-force remained well disciplined and her population was adequately fed." In other words, Germany was not on the verge of collapse, and the Allies could expect rugged fighting in the months ahead.

British and American expectations centered on Overlord. With Eisenhower's selection as Supreme Commander Allied Expeditionary Forces (SCAEF), they redoubled their efforts. The Normandy coast between Le Havre and Cherbourg had been agreed to as the landing area the previous August, but the original plan for a three-division seaborne assault was recognized to be inadequate, and the number was raised to five, plus airborne and commando units, to ensure initial success.[98] Moreover, because the Allies rightly believed that the Germans would rush additional forces to the invasion sector, they undertook numerous deceptions, including several carried out by the Soviets, to keep the Wehrmacht off stride.[99] Perhaps the most ingenious and successful ruse was Britain's ability through double agents to mislead the Germans into thinking that the Western Allies had thirty-five to forty more combat divisions in the United Kingdom than the thirty-nine they actually had at their disposal.[100] This deception, along with others, such as a bogus army in Scotland, led the Germans to expect a second major attack long after Overlord had been launched, an attack which, of course, never came.

Another Allied concern in preparing for Overlord was how best to utilize their sea and air forces. It was not an issue of inadequate numbers, but rather of having certain types of naval craft and airplanes at the right time. The air problem turned out to be especially difficult to resolve.[101] With the strategic-bombing offensive having come into its own, and with its belated emphasis on defeating the Luftwaffe and its related infrastructure beginning to pay dividends, bomber force commanders did not want to divert their Fortresses, Liberators, and Lancasters to support Overlord until the last moment. Only after numerous meetings and arguments did they reluctantly go along with the use of their bombers during the "softening up" phase, and then only after the highly respected Air Chief Marshal Sir Arthur Tedder, Eisenhower's deputy, was given the additional duty of overseeing the Overlord bombing effort, directed primarily at the transportation system in France. While attacks on aircraft factories, oil plants and other targets farther inland continued, though at a reduced rate, the Allies now had sufficient heavy bombers as well as other aircraft (nearly 13,000 total) to take full advantage of their air superiority at the time of the invasion.

The often described naval problem revolved around inadequate landing craft.[102] Only in April, when LSTs, LCIs, LCTs, and other craft were sent to England from the Mediterranean, did the Allies feel confident that they had enough of this precious commodity (eventually numbering 4,126) to assure Overlord's success.

Actually, the landing craft had become available because the British and Americans had on March 21 postponed the projected operation in southern France.[103] Its postponement had been the result not only of a lack of landing craft, but also of difficulties in Italy, where the Germans continued to resist tenaciously. At least until Rome was taken, the Allies decided, the troops and pilots scheduled to take part in Anvil would have to remain in Italy. The sacrifice of Anvil to the exigencies in Italy and the necessities for Overlord did not mean that its postponement was permanent, and the issue continued to strain Anglo-American military relations until it was finally decided in early July to go ahead with Anvil on August 15.

Insufficient landing craft also played a role in the scaled-down operations on the other side of the globe in Burma. As discussed earlier, it had led to the cancellation of an amphibious attack on the Andaman Islands, and Japanese offensive and defensive moves against the British, Indian, Chinese, and American troops in northern and central Burma were still keeping the Allies at bay. Part of the problem in the theater also stemmed from the British and American agreement at Cairo that the Pacific strategy was to receive first priority and Burma was to be of only secondary importance, a policy the British chiefs reaffirmed on several occasions during the spring.[104] Despite their agreement, however, Churchill had his doubts about the Pacific priority. On February 25, he again brought up one of his pet projects, a landing in Sumatra (Culverin).[105] When the chiefs of staff voiced their opposition, the prime minister backed down. But he continued to search for a strategy in which British troops, operating from India, might be deployed without being subordinated to the Americans, as would be the case in the Pacific. In the end, Churchill had to confine his ambitions in Southeast Asia to "liberating" Burma. The instance shows once again that his thinking was often national, not coalition-oriented.

Meanwhile, Allied strategy in Europe began to unfold. Field Marshal Alexander's offensive in Italy started on May 11 (Diadem).[106] It was designed not only to take Rome and advance northward but, more immediately, to link the divisions in the Anzio bridgehead with the main forces to the south and to tie down as many German soldiers as possible. On both counts, Diadem succeeded. Rome was taken on June 4.

In the east, the Soviets started their attack on June 22 (Operation Bagration). Their 166 rifle divisions, 2,715 tanks, and 5,327 aircraft opened gaping holes in the German lines.[107] The collapse of Germany's Army Group Center was followed in some places by a 450-mile Soviet advance, which only came to a halt before Warsaw. The failure of the Red Army to support a Polish uprising in that beleaguered city gave rise to much resentment in the west, though Churchill and other British leaders already realized there was little they could do directly to influence events in eastern Europe.[108]

In the time between the southern and the eastern offensives, Overlord was launched. On June 6, along sixty miles of Normandy beaches, Allied troops came ashore and soon secured a beachhead. For the next month and a half, despite Allied control of the air, the Germans held their own. They were able generally to contain the beachhead, especially in the Caen area, and on June 12 they began striking London with one of their vaunted miracle weapons, the V-1 flying bomb. Although the V-1 caused great alarm and some damage, British officials knew that countermeasures could be directed against it (mainly from fighters and antiaircraft guns) and that its effects could therefore be limited.[109] In fact, even the V-2 rocket, impossible to defend against when first launched in September, was too late to have more than a minimal impact on the Allied war effort.

During the summer, Germany's own efforts deteriorated at home and at the fronts. Allied bombing of the Reich was beginning to cause widespread dislocations. In the west, on July 15, Rommel warned that the situation was reaching "crisis proportions."[110] Two days later, the renowned field commander was seriously injured when his staff car was strafed by Allied aircraft. He was eventually sent home to recuperate. On July 20, some Wehrmacht "traitors" attempted to kill Hitler. While he was only slightly injured, several of his advisers, including the Luftwaffe chief of staff, were killed by the bomb blast. A purge of those involved and implicated followed. On July 23, Allied troops in Italy reached the Arno River, 175 miles above Rome, thereby punctuating the extent of their gains in that theater. Two days later, strong American forces on the western end of the Normandy beachhead started moving south and then turned east. The ensuing dash across France would not end until mid-September near the German border.

American insistence that Anvil go ahead in southern France had forced the British reluctantly to give way. While the Germans knew the date and the approximate location of the amphibious assault, they could do nothing to stop it.[111] On August 15, the operation, renamed Dragoon for security reasons, was launched against the French Riviera coast around St. Tropez and was immediately successful. Even Churchill, who had done his best to have it canceled, preferring an attack at the head of the Adriatic instead, was on hand and seemed to enjoy a magnificently "good show."

Elsewhere, the Russian juggernaut continued its drive west and south. On August 23, Romania surrendered. Two days later, the same day Paris was liberated, the Romanians declared war on Germany. During September, an insurrection took place in Slovakia, and Finland and Bulgaria ended their participation on the Axis side. As a result, large portions of eastern Europe were coming increasingly under Soviet domination. Only in the north in Norway, where approximately 290,000 German soldiers were stationed, did conditions remain relatively quiet.[112]

In this atmosphere of Allied victories and German defeats, Churchill and Roosevelt and their advisers gathered for a second meeting at Quebec (Octagon).[113] The conference, which took place between September 12 and 19, addressed primarily the relation between the European and the Pacific and Asian theaters. At this point the war's outcome was certain; the main problem was one of timing. Could the war against Germany be brought to a successful conclusion in 1944 so that additional forces could be transferred for use against the Japanese? Many of the participants at the meeting thought so. Churchill, however, did not share their optimism. From his viewpoint, there was still a lot of fighting to be done, especially since almost all of the large harbors along the French and Belgian coasts remained in German hands, and this situation could cause a grave logistics bottleneck. Thus the decisions made at Quebec were for the most part tentative. The Western Allies did agree that at the war's conclusion the British would occupy northwestern Germany, the Americans the southwestern portion, and the Soviets, subject to their approval, the area to the east of the British zone. They also emphasized that the strategic air forces were to continue "the progressive destruction and dislocation of the German military, industrial and economic systems." But while they desired an increase in British naval, air, and land units in Southeast Asia and the Pacific (except for the US chief of naval operations, Admiral King), the shift depended on the outcome of the battles in western Europe—and in Italy.[114]

Churchill's fears turned out to be warranted. By mid-September, the rapid American and French advance through southern France came to a halt in the Vosges Mountain approaches of eastern France. In Italy, the Germans, having decided to make a stand north of Rimini on the Adriatic coast and in front of Bologna in the center, held on tenaciously into the winter. So long as the Allies could not (or would not) spare additional troops for the Italian front, they lacked sufficient strength to push to the Po River and beyond. On the northern part of the western front, British and American divisions reached the German frontier near Aachen, but an attempt to secure a bridgehead over the lower Rhine at Arnhem in the Netherlands failed. Then there was the problem of the ports. Le Havre fell on September 12, Brest on September 18, and Calais on September 30, but given the destruction and bombing, they were in no shape to be put to immediate use. Even more crucial, because of its large berthing facilities, was Antwerp, which had been captured on September 3. However, the Allies' failure to take its approaches until two months later brought on the logistics crisis that Churchill had feared. In part, the crisis had been the result of faulty Allied planning.[115] The planners had anticipated that only by D-Day plus 360 would their forces reach the German border, for they expected the Germans to fight a stubborn, river-by-river defensive war across France. Instead, the Allies were approaching Germany in the Aachen region by D + 95. Part of the reason also was that Hitler had decided to hold on to the major harbors at all costs. As he remarked to General Jodl on July 31:[116]

> We must be clear with each other, Jodl. Which places [in the West] do we want to hold under all circumstances because they provide additional supply possibilities for the enemy? We cannot throw away the harbors that can keep the enemy from having unlimited manpower and material at his disposal. Thus, if the enemy is no longer able to get a number of the productive ports, then that is about the only brake we can put on his already almost unlimited possibilities for movement . . . we must therefore decide that a certain number of troops are simply going to have to be sacrificed to save others.

In this sense, the Atlantic Wall strategy did eventually prove of worth to the Germans.

After ruminating for over a month about a possible operation in the west, in September Hitler opted for an offensive in the Ardennes area, with the ultimate goal of recapturing Antwerp and dividing Allied forces in the area.[117] While no one among the Army High Command, including General Guderian, the chief of staff, favored such a vast operation, the Führer remained adamant that twenty-five divisions, ten of them panzer, be readied for a western offensive (Operation Watch on the Rhine). When OKH and the western commanders proved unable to persuade him to cancel it, they proposed a "modified" solution, a less ambitious plan to remove an Allied salient west of Aachen. Hitler was not convinced and insisted that the Ardennes attack be executed. Preparations for the operation therefore continued throughout the autumn.

On the Allied side, optimism continued despite the military slowdown. In October, while Churchill was involved in power brokering with Stalin in Moscow over the fate of eastern Europe, British and American military leaders retained the hope that, despite the logistical problems, the European war could be won by the end of the year.[118] On October 23, the US joint chiefs and the British staff mission in Washington, reflecting Marshall's views, thought that Eisenhower should "conduct operations with the objective of completing the defeat of Germany by 1 January."[119] On October 19, the British added a note of caution: "Although we are in complete agreement with the US Chiefs of Staff as to the desirability of making an all-out effort to defeat Germany this year, . . . the present operations which are designed to open the port of Antwerp are essential to the completion of the administrative build-up, without which the offensive cannot be sustained."[120]

Eisenhower agreed, for it fit in with his thinking, first discussed in August, of attacking Germany from the west on a broad front. This was not what Field Marshal Brooke and the other British chiefs had in mind. They preferred a single thrust led by Field Marshal Montgomery's forces into northern Germany. The dispute, after several relatively minor attacks in November and with Eisenhower equivocating at times, came to a head on December 12.[121] At a meeting among the military leaders in London, which Churchill also attended, Eisenhower set forth his strategy. There was to be an initial phase, beginning almost immediately, with the objective of closing to the Rhine. This was to be followed by a second phase, starting in late May when the possibility of flooding was past, of two thrusts, one north of the Ruhr along a Münster-Hanover axis, the other south along the Frankfurt-Cassel axis. Although Brooke disagreed vehemently and pressed for a concentrated effort in the north, Eisenhower's strategy was adopted.

Four days later, the Germans, having waited for their forces to get ready and for cloudy weather to negate Allied air supremacy, struck in the weakly held Ardennes area. Though surprised, the Americans survived the initial shock, stopped the German attack short of the Meuse River, and then, depending mostly on their own resources, eliminated the German bulge by January 1945.[122] While the attack had upset Allied plans, Germany's "last, desperate gamble" had ended in failure and it had used up its last operational reserves in the process.

Nineteen forty-five turned out to be a year of never-ending Allied victories. On the Russian Front, the Soviets began an offensive on January 12 which swept through Poland to the Oder by early February. There the Germans held. The Red Army had to content itself with finally taking besieged Budapest to the south and pinning down German forces which eventually had to be evacuated by sea along the Baltic coast to the north. In the west, the Allies, having recovered from the Ardennes battle and complementary German attacks in Alsace and in northern Italy, proceeded to launch their own offensives in February to close to the Rhine (Operations Veritable and Grenade). Although Allied navies continued to guard against the U-boat threat and although the air forces sustained some losses on their strategic bombing runs, the sea and air wars had for all intents and purposes been won.[123]

Meanwhile, Stalin, Churchill, and Roosevelt met together for the second and last time at Yalta (Argonaut).[124] Stalin had not particularly wanted to have a conference at all, and only after months of wrangling did he agree to one, though on Soviet soil. The issues addressed between February 4 and 11 were both military and political, but the ones remembered today are primarily the latter. They included, among others, plans for dealing after the war with Germany, Poland, Iran, and Japan, and measures for establishing a United Nations. Nevertheless, military strategy also received considerable attention. The discussions dealt with numerous topics, from situation reports on the various fronts to proposals on ways to prevent the Germans from shifting troops from one front to another, to talks between the Americans and the Soviets about Russia's entry into the Asian war.[125] Despite subsequent charges of a Yalta "sell-out" in which American naivete has been contrasted with British realism and Soviet cunning, the participants at the time seemed to be fairly well pleased with the results and with their "growing cooperation and understanding."[126]

Although the friendly atmosphere at Yalta soon gave way to mutual suspicions, Allied victories did not abate. In the Pacific, the Americans were rapidly advancing toward Japan. In Burma, on March 20, Field Marshal Viscount Slim's Fourteenth Army overcame frustrations to take Mandalay and raced to Rangoon, capturing it on May 2 just as the monsoons set in.[127] In Italy, on April 9, US and, later, British divisions began their last offensive and soon liberated the rest of that country. At the same time, the Allies were pushing into Germany from both the east and the west. On March 7, American 9th Armored Division troops discovered that a bridge over the Rhine at Remagen had not been destroyed, took it, and secured and enlarged a bridgehead on the eastern bank. Later in the month, American and British forces made additional crossings at Oppenheim south of Mainz and near Xanten north of the Ruhr. With these moves, the advance into the heart of Germany proceeded at a rapid pace from the east and the west.

At the end of March, General Eisenhower queried the Soviets as to when and where they expected to launch their frontal attack so that the Allies could coordinate their plans.[128] Eisenhower indicated that he hoped to effect a junction with the Red Army in central Germany somewhere along the Erfurt-Leipzig-Dresden axis and in southern Germany and Austria in the Regensburg-Linz area. Stalin replied the next day, agreeing that the Western Allies and Soviets should meet as Eisenhower proposed. He added that the main Soviet offensive would probably not start until mid-May with a secondary operation toward Berlin, which he asserted had lost its former "strategic significance." The British chiefs were terribly upset with Eisenhower's inquiry, for they were convinced of the desirability, both psychological and political, "of Anglo-American forces capturing Berlin as soon as possible."[129] But the US joint chiefs backed Eisenhower. The American plan assured that Soviet Marshal Georgi Zhukov's and Marshal Ivan Konev's groups of armies, who hurried up their offensive to begin on April 16, would win the race to Berlin. For a variety of reasons, including the relatively short distance of the Red Army from Berlin, the Soviets might have won the race anyway, but it became a disputed issue in the Cold War that followed.

From the standpoint of the Soviets and their allies, Hitler's actions during these last hectic days reached the height of unreality.[130] Ensconced in his underground quarters below the Reich chancellery gardens, the Führer and his advisers continued to direct depleted units and to shift nonexistent divisions from place to place to stem the tide. On April 30, the charade came to an end when Hitler committed suicide. His designated successor, Grand Admiral Dönitz, understood the reality of the situation and came to terms, his emissaries surrendering to the Western Allies on May 7 and to the Soviets on May 9. The European war was over.

What do the events during the middle and later stages tell us about the nature of German and British strategy? For one thing, it is striking how the direction if not the specifics of both countries' strategies was set forth during the early rather than later phases of the conflict. Before the end of 1941, the Germans had attacked east, west, and east, thereby creating new, powerful enemies in the process; had combined with Italy and Japan, assuring a world-wide war; and had failed to develop a force structure, especially the sea and air components, commensurate with its commitments. Britain, on the other hand, had withstood the initial onslaught, giving hope to those countries overrun; had gained the support of strong, eventually overwhelming allies; and had thought in terms of a balanced force, including long-range bombers and aircraft carriers, to overcome its Axis adversaries. In a sense, then, the path the war took had been set before the middle and later phases ever began.

In addition, despite allegations to the contrary, it is evident that military leaders on both sides, with the crucial exception of Hitler, understood the functioning of grand strategy. General Jodl, in his cell at Nuremberg, ticked off many of the elements—foreign and domestic policy, economic mobilization, propaganda, leadership of the people—and Halder and Zeitzler comprehended grand strategy as well.[131] So did Churchill, Brooke, Portal, and Ismay. Whether all of them always acted on their understanding is another matter.

Another, oft-made observation, which, nonetheless, bears repeating, is that both Britain and Germany emphasized military, not political, goals between 1942 and 1944 and in some cases into 1945. Germany's thinking throughout the period is not difficult to fathom. During most of it, Germany was fighting a defensive and terroristic war, in which the main consideration, again except in Hitler's view, was survival.[132] There was little looking ahead, few thoughts about long-range policies, even less about the future shape of the world. While a reactive war does not rule out political objectives, it does limit the range of possibilities.

Given the composition of the Grand Alliance, Britain's strategy was also primarily military rather than political, economic, or diplomatic in character.[133] Political and economic matters were discussed, and at times acted upon, but the main thrust of the coalition was military. Whether at Washington, Casablanca, Quebec, or Tehran, military strategy was in the forefront. Even at Yalta, part of the agenda was devoted to attempting to coordinate activities in the various war theaters. Perhaps the military emphasis was inevitable because of the broad and complicated nature of the conflict, in which the Allies as late as April 1945 were fighting not only in Germany, Austria, and Italy, but also in Burma and the Pacific. Nonetheless, political considerations were often shoved aside.

The makeup of the alliance affected Britain in another way. Its leaders realized it would be increasingly inferior in military might to the Soviets and the Americans and that it would have to gear its thinking accordingly.[134] As a consequence, there was little the British could do to alter military or political developments in eastern Europe. It ended up having an important say in Greece and wanted to influence events in Yugoslavia and Poland, but the Soviets determined the military strategy in the east, which, in turn, determined the political outcome.

A more complex relationship existed between the British and the Americans. At first, British thinking prevailed with land operations centered in the Mediterranean. But after 1943, even though the Mediterranean remained an active combat theater, the main Anglo-American emphasis shifted to the west and continued there until the end. In Asia and the Pacific, the Americans predominated almost from the start. Even in Burma, where the US wanted to set up closer links to the Chinese Nationalists, Britain did not have the major say. Still, the Western Allies agreed on the significance of the Battle of the Atlantic and the strategic bombing offensive and cooperated in these vital undertakings.

Finally, from an operational standpoint, the willingness of the Anglo-Americans to develop balanced forces gave them alternatives the Germans could not exercise. In the Atlantic, additional naval escort groups, escort carriers, long-range aircraft, the new ten-centimeter radar and direction-finding equipment, and Ultra intelligence allowed British, Canadian, and American personnel to turn the battle in their favor. In the air war, strategic bombing may not have been decisive in the theater, but it did destroy military targets, dislocate German industry, and, more specifically, delay the introduction of jet aircraft and new types of submarines into service.[135] In other words, the Allies utilized the potential of naval and air power much more fully than did the Germans. Overall, then, Allied preponderance in all areas—sea, air, and eventually on land—lead to the conclusion that it is perhaps surprising that the Germans held on as long as they did.

Fighting the War, 1939–1940

When one turns to the carrying out of British and German strategy, several difficulties immediately become apparent. First is the impossibility of analyzing all of the many operations in which the two nations were involved. The emphasis here, therefore, will be on only eleven campaigns, which, nevertheless, represent a cross-section of the land, sea, and air commitments of both sides. Second is the problem of discussing even these selected operations at a tactical level, for to do so would be prodigious and merely repeat much of the fine work done by official historians and other writers. The following chapters, then, will focus primarily on the planning phases and only secondarily on the tactical details of the operations, with some observations ventured as to the latter's overall significance.

In 1939 and 1940, four operations predominated. None of the four—the Polish campaign, the battles of France and Britain, or the British blockade—was traditional in the nineteenth-century or World War I–sense of the term. Although motorized and air formations had been used with some effect during 1918, their use during World War II in the Polish and French campaigns was far more extensive and significant. The Battle of Britain was almost exclusively fought in the air, although naval elements did play a role, and there was also the possibility of a German amphibious operation should the Luftwaffe gain local air superiority. Even the blockade, while based on World War I precedents, featured new elements which led the British to describe what they were doing as "economic warfare." In other words, despite the contention that the Second World War was merely a continuation of the First, it was from the beginning a much different type of war.

Hitler and his military commanders instituted this different type of warfare against Poland.[1] At first, after the bloodless subjugation of Czechoslovakia in March 1939, the Führer was not sure whether to strike east or west. During April and May, he decided that since the Poles could not be relied upon to remain neutral if Germany attacked France and the Low Countries, they would have to become the first "military" victim. On April 3, 1939, he had General Keitel of OKW issue orders to start plans for a possible offensive, codenamed Operation White, any time after September 1.[2] On April 11, OKW clarified Hitler's position in another directive, which stated:

"The present attitude of Poland requires, over and above the plan 'Frontier Security East' [the defensive plan in force], the initiation of military preparations, to remove if necessary any opposition from this direction forever."[3] The directive added that "the political leaders" hoped to isolate Poland diplomatically so that it would be a localized war, and that within these parameters "the task of the Wehrmacht is to destroy the Polish Armed Forces."

On April 27, the Army High Command (OKH) presented the Führer its initial plan.[4] Because of a possible attack from the west, staff planners called for a quick victory against the Poles. The main German force was to advance out of Silesia toward Warsaw, while other divisions swung behind the capital from the north and south in a large pincer movement to cut off any possible Polish retreat to the east. The land armies were to be divided into two groups. Army Group North was allotted two armies, the Third and Fourth, with Air Fleet 1 in support. Its task was to push from Pomerania across the corridor to link up with forces in East Prussia, and then to assist them in a two-pronged drive south, one toward and the other around Warsaw. Army Group South was to have three armies, the Eighth, Tenth, and Fourteenth, and Air Fleet 4 for support. Its mission was to engage the bulk of the Polish army west of the Vistula River, defeat it, and then take Warsaw. At the same time, additional divisions were to thrust around Warsaw from the south and connect with the northern pincer. Hitler approved the plan and had it given over to the army groups for detailed preparations.

On May 23, at a secret meeting with his military leaders, the Führer proclaimed his resolve to crush Poland.[5] Germany's goal, he admitted, was not, as he had stated for diplomatic reasons, control of Danzig, but rather "a matter of expanding our living space in the East and making food supplies secure. . . ." He preferred, he said, to deal with Poland first before turning west, where England was the main enemy, but he felt that the western adversaries would have to be defeated sooner or later in any event. He therefore asked that preparations be made for a long war. He also indicated that it might be possible to persuade the Soviet Union to remain disinterested while Poland was being overrun.

From this point on, until the September 1 invasion, Hitler followed two paths—the diplomatic attempt to isolate the Poles from their western allies by coming to an agreement with the Soviet Union; and the military preparation for a local, six-to-eight week war against Poland. In the diplomatic sphere, he was only partially successful. On August 23, after feverish negotiations, he was able to have von Ribbentrop conclude a nonaggression treaty with the Russians, which included a secret protocol that divided eastern Europe into spheres of influence.[6] According to the agreement, the Germans were to have the western half of Poland and Lithuania, and the Soviets were to control Finland, Estonia, Latvia, eastern Poland, and Bessarabia. Still, the announcement of the pact did not separate the British and the French from their Polish ally, as Hitler had hoped, and he decided to take several more days—the invasion had been set for August 26—to try to drive the Poles and their western partners apart.

At the same time, military planning had been moving ahead and generally followed the guidelines set forth in the OKH plan. By July, a detailed plan was ready. On August 22, the day before the von Ribbentrop–Molotov signing, Hitler assembled his military commanders at the Berghof for a final meeting.[7] He told them that "a conflict with Poland had to come sooner or later. I had already made this decision in the spring, but I thought that I would first turn against the West in a few years, and only after that against the East. But the sequence of these things cannot be fixed." Halder cryptically summarized part of the Führer's speech as follows: "Polish-German relations unbearable. . . . Time for solution now ripe; therefore strike. Political risk involved cannot be avoided. There are no great decisions without risks."

When negotiations with the West broke down, Hitler decided to take the risk—even of a two-front war.[8] On the night of August 31, he had SS troops stage an incident at a border radio station near Gleiwitz in which Germans were supposedly killed by Polish troops (the dead Germans were actually murdered concentration-camp prisoners). At 4:45 a.m., Wehrmacht forces began streaming into Poland.

Figures indicating the forces involved on the two sides at the beginning (table 6-1) belie some significant differences.[9] Germany's eastern totals do not include thirty-one divisions, many of them admittedly second-rate, numbering about 950,000 troops stationed in the west. Nor do they show that the German total included fifteen panzer and motorized divisions as compared with Poland's one panzer and eleven cavalry brigades. The obvious disparity in tanks and aircraft becomes even more pronounced when one takes into account that many of Poland's tanks and aircraft were outdated.

Besides its numerical and material advantages, Germany had a truly impressive list of commanders, many of whom achieved future greatness: Fedor von Bock was head of Army Group North with Hans von Salmuth as his chief of staff; von Rundstedt, commander of Army Group South, with von Manstein his chief of staff; Günther von Kluge, Johannes Blaskowitz, Wilhelm List, Hoth, Hoepner, and Guderian among the army and corps commanders; Albert Kesselring and Alexander Lohr, heads of the air fleets. Some of Poland's commanders and troops displayed great valor, but the aforementioned factors,

TABLE 6-1

Opposing Forces for the Polish Campaign, September 1939

	Troop Strength	Divisions	Tanks	Combat Aircraft	Ships
Germany					
Eastern Front	1.5 million	53 1/3	3,257	2,721	40
Poland	1.3 million	43	750	900	50

when combined with German superior offensive doctrine and training, put the Poles at a serious disadvantage.

Germany's military superiority soon became clear. In the north, von Kluge's Fourth Army advanced rapidly across the corridor and reached East Prussia by September 3.[10] On September 4, Fourth Army began moving the rest of its armored and motorized forces to East Prussia. The next day, Hitler himself was driven across the corridor and took time to talk with some of the troops and their commanders. When he talked with Guderian, the latter recommended that more Panzer IIIs and IVs be produced. That same day, OKH ordered Third Army, strengthened by units from Fourth Army, to undertake a two-pronged offensive on both sides of the Vistula toward Warsaw. The eastern prong, as envisaged in the original plan, was to move around the capital and head toward Brest-Litovsk.

In the south, three armies, spearheaded by General Walter von Reichenau's Tenth Army, engaged portions of the spread-out Polish Army.[11] While there was some hard fighting, German armor, supported by infantry and by Air Fleet 4, broke through the Polish defenses and approached Warsaw by Septem-

Map 6-1: Polish Campaign, 1939

ber 8. The Poles counterattacked and had to be beaten back in a series of battles west of the Vistula between September 7 and 11. At the same time, German formations started circling behind Warsaw from the south. On September 17, the northern and southern pincers closed fifty miles south of Brest-Litovsk. Polish units held out in Warsaw until September 28 (the government had already evacuated), but by then the campaign had long been decided. The Germans had won a decisive, localized victory.

In the west, Poland's French and British allies had mobilized on the first of September and declared war on Germany on the third, but had undertaken no wide-scale offensive.[12] The British dispatched four divisions and four fighter squadrons of sixty-four planes to France, but only nine French divisions advanced a maximum distance of five miles along the German border. On September 27, with the Polish campaign having been decided, the French began withdrawing their forces back into the Maginot Line. In the air, the Allies were equally timid, generally confining their efforts to reconnaissance, attacks on enemy shipping, and propaganda-leaflet drops behind enemy lines.[13]

Far to the east, the Soviets decided to speed up their timetable for entering and came in on September 17.[14] When staff officers at Hitler's headquarters learned of Russia's entrance, one of them quipped, "Against whom?" Opposed by such token resistance, the Red Army proceeded to occupy the eastern one-third of Poland. Toward the end of the month, the two eastern "allies" overcame their distrust of each other and agreed to alter their previously agreed upon spheres of interest in eastern Europe. The Soviet Union was now to get Lithuania, and the Germans, more of central Poland. Both Hitler and Stalin seemed satisfied with the alteration.

The Wehrmacht could look back on the campaign with a good deal of satisfaction.[15] German casualties had been high—44,000—but Polish losses were 253,000, not including those missing. In addition, the Germans lost 300 tanks and 560 aircraft. On the more positive side, at the highest command level, Hitler had generally allowed the Army High Command to conduct the operation as it had seen fit. OKH had directed that any reports for the Führer be cleared first through the army commander-in-chief, von Brauchitsch, and Hitler had stipulated that any sizable transfer of troops from the east to the west was his, not the army's, decision. Nevertheless, except for his insistence on hurrying up the transfer of motorized forces to East Prussia and his demand that Eighth Army alter its attack plans, he had seldom intervened. At the tactical level, the army was not especially pleased with reports of a lack of coordination among the armored, infantry, and air elements and undertook measures to correct the deficiencies, but military leaders could not help but be pleased with the overall effectiveness of Germany's Blitzkrieg tactics and with the excellent combat flexibility exhibited by the various staffs. As Hans Umbreit concluded: "The superiority and mobility of the German military had surprised both friend and foe."

Besides wanting to help Poland, but feeling unable to do so with any degree of effectiveness, the British during the fall of 1939 undertook two main military strategies.[16] Among a number of military options examined, the one adopted was to build up their forces at home and their defensive strength in France. The other strategy was to invoke a blockade.[17] Blockade was, of course, nothing new to the British, who had used it extensively throughout their history and most recently during World War I. The principle of taking advantage of their naval power had remained the same. By World War II, new elements had entered the picture, however. In fact, as early as 1936, British officials rejected the term "blockade" as too restrictive for modern, total war, and began to use "economic warfare" instead.

After the war broke out, Britain organized quickly for the economic battle. Because the French were already involved in the planning, the measures undertaken had their concurrence and participation. On September 3, the same day Britain entered the war, the Ministry of Economic Warfare (MEW) was established with Sir Frederick Leith-Ross as director general. MEW was divided into four departments—plans, foreign relations, prize contraband control, and intelligence.[18] Although the plans department was incorporated into the other branches in December, the remaining departments engaged in three types of activities: legislative, which dealt with parliamentary acts and legal measures for controlling trade with the enemy; diplomatic, which related to discussions with neutral nations to limit their trade with Germany; and military, which included contraband control, blockade, seizure of enemy exports, and even air attacks against economic targets, although the latter did not come into play until May 1940.[19] While all three were interrelated and involved representatives from other ministries, the military activities, led by the navy, were deemed crucial. To be sure, the navy had additional tasks, such as securing sea communications and protecting military and civilian shipping, but its ability to control all seaborne trade intended for the enemy— whether direct or indirect—was also considered of vital importance.[20]

The system at first was to work as follows: Ships suspected of carrying contraband goods to neutral countries were to be intercepted and diverted to bases for examination.[21] As in World War I, there were to be two types of contraband—absolute and conditional. Goods were considered absolute contraband if they fell into one of four categories: (1) arms and ammunition; (2) fuel and means of transportation; (3) means of communications; and (4) coin, bullion, and currency. Conditional contraband was defined as food and clothing. During the first month, ships bound for neutral countries were invited to call voluntarily at the contraband control bases, but naval patrols were to bring in any ship trying to avoid voluntary compliance. The British control bases were at Kirkwall in the Orkneys for ships sailing in the North Sea and farther north and west; at Ramsgate and Weymouth for ships coming through the English Channel; at Gibraltar for eastbound traffic in the Mediterranean, and at Port Said and Haifa for ships using the Suez Canal or in the eastern Mediterranean. France also set up control bases at Le Havre and Dunkirk along the Channel; at Marseilles and Oran for western Mediterranean traffic; and at Dakar and Casablanca for ships coming from South America. Once a ship reached the control port, its cargo was examined. Then the Contraband Committee decided if none, some, or all of the consignment should be seized. Seized cargo was placed in custody of the Prize Court, which determined what should be done with the goods. At times the owner was compensated, at times not. By the end of September, control had been tightened when additional auxiliary ships assumed patrol duties, although some ships bound for neutral harbors inevitably slipped by the British and French patrols.[22]

During the fall, a number of refinements were made in the basic system.[23] One was the "hold back" guarantee, which allowed certain seized ships to proceed to a neutral port if the captain guaranteed not to deliver any cargo still being considered as possible contraband and to return it to the Allied control base should the Contraband Committee determine that the item be seized. Another was to have the ship manifest sent in advance to the contraband port, so that when the ship arrived at the control base, the inspectors merely had to check to see whether the manifest was correct. A third, begun on December 1, was the use of navicerts (called Mewcerts in the Mediterranean), documents obtained from British foreign missions in the country of origin. Shippers applied for navicerts by listing cargo that might be construed to be contraband and, if they were wise, all other goods as well. The list was usually "referred" to the economic warfare ministry, which decided whether or not listed articles were contraband. At times, officials deferred a decision until the items themselves were checked in transit, but not as their usual practice. Once issued, the navicert indicated that the ship did not have contraband and should be allowed to pass. All of the measures just described were designed to reduce delays of goods bound for neutral nations near Germany.

The Allies also introduced additional features to cut off, or at least to cut back, unwarranted trade with the enemy. Among them were blacklisting, enemy export control, and war trade agreements with neutral nations. The Black List Committee, which included French representatives, was established on September 4.[24] The committee was to list firms outside Germany suspected of trading with the enemy or definitely under German control. There were two lists. The main list was the Statutory List, originally with 278 names but rapidly expanded, which was made known to the general public. Any company engaging in trade with these firms (or persons) was subject to prosecution. The other list, actually called the Black List, was confidential and at this time included the names of only twelve firms thought to be trading with Germany. MEW was to pressure friendly companies not to deal with the "suspect" firms.

The control of enemy exports came about in reprisal for German measures against British and neutral ships.[25] The precipitating event occurred on November 18, when a Dutch liner hit a German mine and sank with the loss of

140 lives. On November 23, British officials, again with French representation, decided to institute the Enemy Exports Committee, which was to oversee the detention of merchant ships sailing from German or neutral ports (mainly from the Netherlands and Belgium) and carrying enemy goods. Goods determined to be German were to be seized. It was hoped that such seizures would also have an adverse effect on Germany's already tenuous foreign-exchange problem. The system started on December 4, but during the first month measures were applied leniently so as not to upset the neutrals. During January stricter enforcement was imposed, although the harshness of the procedure was mitigated to an extent by the use of certificates of origin. These documents, issued to neutral exporters, stated that, after investigation, British officials were satisfied that the shipper's goods were not of enemy origin and could proceed without being inspected.

The British also attempted to sign war trade agreements with European neutrals.[26] The agreements were designed to prohibit the export to Germany of goods which had reached the neutrals through Allied controls and further to "limit the sale to Germany of other goods to 'normal' pre-war figures." Britain, in return was to facilitate the passage of goods covered by the agreements through its control points and not to demand individual guarantees against reexport. Agreements with some countries, because of their location as well as German or internal pressures, were never signed, as with the Baltic states, the Soviet Union, and Italy. The British were able after laborious negotiations to get agreements with Sweden and Belgium in December 1939, with Greece in January 1940, and with Norway, Denmark, and the Netherlands in March. However, any effect the agreements might have had was soon obviated by Germany's spring victories in northern and western Europe.

Another important function undertaken by MEW was intelligence.[27] In this case, the ministry, with the assistance of other agencies and the military branches, basically dealt with two areas. One was blockade intelligence to help in the day-to-day contraband activities. After several months, officials were receiving the information they considered necessary. The second, economic warfare intelligence, was the more difficult area. Not only did information on the enemy's war-making capacity and potential prove hard to obtain, especially after the outbreak of the war, but practical problems with the other intelligence-producing agencies and insufficient personnel hampered MEW as well. Although the problems were eventually overcome, the consequence was that, during the remainder of 1939 and into 1940, Britain's appreciation of the German war economy was often both incomplete and inaccurate.[28] For example, the navy in September 1939 estimated the Germans would have built a total of 129 U-boats by March 1940; on that date they actually had completed 67. Air Force intelligence thought that Germany constructed 13,330 aircraft in 1940; in effect it produced 10,826. The War Office believed that German factories turned out more than 2,000 tanks between September 1939 and June 1940; the true number was 755. The extent to which MEW was involved in working out these figures is difficult to determine, but the results, even though they came closer to reality in 1940, were obviously far from satisfactory.

An area of concern in which MEW was more intimately involved was the German procurement of oil and iron ore. The British rightly considered these two products essential to Germany's war effort, and they also readily appreciated German vulnerabilities here. Regarding iron ore, Narvik, the ice-free Norwegian port through which Swedish mine operators shipped most of their ore to Germany during the winter months, was deemed most vulnerable.[29] Officials at the ministry examined the issue from all angles. They ascertained that Germany needed about nine million tons of Swedish iron ore annually "if she is to avoid a major industrial breakdown" and examined a number of alternatives to halt the shipments—a naval force placed off Norway, minefields, military occupation of Narvik and the railway leading to it, sabotage—although it would be difficult to get lasting results in the last instance since the rail lines were electrified.[30] All of these options presented problems, not the least of which would be the violation of Norwegian or Swedish neutrality. Furthermore, even if ore shipments to Germany via Narvik were stopped, would the stoppage be decisive? It was on this issue that the idea of military intervention floundered.

Despite the desire to intervene, especially after the November Soviet invasion of Finland—since British and French occupation of northern Norway and northern Sweden would ease getting supplies to the Finns—the Allies realized that cutting off ore shipments from Narvik alone would be insufficient. During the summer, ore traffic from Lulea on the Gulf of Bothnia and other Swedish ports would continue and could be expanded, so that unless one were able to stop the export of all Swedish iron ore to Germany, the Germans could still get enough ore for their military needs.[31] The Allies therefore pinned their slim hopes on open Swedish and Norwegian cooperation. It was not forthcoming. Ironically, the amount of Swedish iron ore reaching Germany in January and February 1940 did decline sharply from the year before. During these two months in 1939, 937,427 tons had reached Germany; in 1940, only 359,000 tons. The reasons were that Swedish workers who controlled the railway and docks at Narvik were not cooperating with the Germans; the ships transporting the ore to Germany had to stay within Norwegian territorial waters, and such navigation required Norwegian pilots; and much of the ore normally shipped to German Baltic ports was held up by exceptionally cold weather. Oxelosund in southern Sweden, for instance, was frozen in "for the first time in living memory." In the end, the Allies did little.[32] The conclusion of the Russo-Finnish Winter War on March 13 took some of the urgency off getting supplies (or troops) to Finland. The British did sow some mines in Norwegian waters off Narvik in early April, but the Norwegian protest to British authorities was still uresolved when the Germans struck north on the night of April 8–9.

In regard to oil, the vulnerable area was neutral Romania. The British at first did not know exactly how much oil Germany needed, but they knew that Romania supplied them with approximately 80 percent of their imported needs.[33] Embarking on a policy of preemptive buying, the Allies were able to purchase 351,000 tons of Romanian oil during the fall of 1939. In December, however, they learned that while the Romanian government agreed to allow the Allies purchases of up to 2,000,000 tons per year, Germany would be allowed up to 1,300,000 tons (the true figure turned out to be 1,560,000 tons as the British learned in April 1940). Another Allied measure was the purchase of tugs and barges using the Danube and of railway oil-tank cars so as to preclude their use for shipments to Germany. Such means—the purchase of oil and transport—did have some effect. The British also threatened to cut off exports to Romania.

Nevertheless, 324,300 tons of Romanian oil reached Germany between September and December 1939. During the first four months of 1940, the British and French continued to try to limit the flow; however, they were aware that, besides Romanian oil, the Germans were receiving some oil from the USSR and from the evasion of contraband control (mainly through Italy). They estimated further that Germany itself would produce 2,400,000 tons of synthetic oil during 1940 (the actual total was 3,348,000 tons). The Allies therefore found themselves in a losing proposition, and German victories in the west plus Russian moves in the east spelled the end of Romania's attempt to carry out an evenhanded oil policy.

Overall, how did the various economic measures work out for the British?[34] In early 1940, they acknowledged that their efforts so far had not been decisive in regard to oil and iron ore and that intelligence estimates lacked precision. Nevertheless, they did feel that the contraband-control system had become relatively effective. Despite protests from neutral countries, or perhaps because of them, delays at the control ports had been reduced substantially. For example, the average stay at Ramsgate was reduced from 11.9 days in September to 6.1 in December, and at Weymouth, from 11 to 7.6 days. At Kirkwall, in part because of the trade agreement with Sweden, by the end of December the average stay had been decreased to 3.6 days. Moreover, control bases had been added at Falmouth and Invergordon; and at Italy's request, at Aden; and for the "tricky" central Mediterranean traffic, at Malta, to expedite the inspection of goods in that area. Surely, the distinction between absolute and conditional contraband, as in World War I, was seldom heeded ("since a totalitarian country like Germany had all goods at least subject to governmental agencies") but the Contraband Control Committee met daily (sometimes twice a day) and dealt with 1,816 cases by the end of the year, thus indicating the extent of their activities. In addition, some of the attempts to improve the contraband system had worked; others had not. On the positive side, navicerts proved their worth. Initially they applied to goods shipped from the United States, Argentina, Brazil, and Uruguay. During December, the first month of operation, 7,447 applications were processed and only 1,889 rejected, though others were left undecided. Throughout the following months, the number more than doubled, as did the rejections. The extension of navicerts to other Latin American nations never took place, however, because of the changed situation brought on by the spring fighting. On the negative side, the "hold back" guarantees were less successful because many of the shippers refused to return goods declared contraband after the British had allowed them to be sent on.

As a result of the blockade, the amount of tonnage seized between September and December 1939 totaled approximately 527,471 tons, with September 16–22 having the highest weekly total of 109,747 tons. After this date, cargoes were no longer openly manifested to Germany; thus for the rest of the year the total averaged about 20,000 tons seized per month. The figure for the first three months of 1940 was about 10,000 tons per month. Highest in the category of tonnage seized were ores, metals, and related manufactures (196,188 tons) and oil products (135,053 tons), followed by oilseeds, nonmetallic minerals and products, and foodstuffs, including some tea bound for Hamburg.[35]

Among the British, such figures contributed to a sense of guarded optimism, which was still evident in a thorough ministry report that assessed the blockade during the first four months from a somewhat different perspective.[36] It concluded that even though it was "difficult to gauge" the blockade's effects after so short a period,

> it would be a great mistake to measure the efficiency of the control by the tonnage of goods seized. . . . The most important effect of seizure was . . . psychological. Trade of a suspect character was held up for a long, sometimes indefinitely long period, and was made correspondingly hazardous and costly. The fear of seizure induced firms to give destination undertakings, apply for navicerts, and make great efforts to clear themselves of suspicion.

These factors, plus the virtual elimination of German merchant shipping on the high seas, led the British to believe that despite numerous problems, including the increased supply of raw materials from Russia, their economic warfare was having an adverse effect on Germany. This idea persisted into 1940. After the fall of France and the entrance of Italy, when the main method of contraband control was changed from interception at sea to control at the point of origin through compulsory navicerts, the British still refused to abandon the use of blockade as an integral part of their strategy.[37] Even at the end of 1940 and into 1941, when it became all too clear to the British that the economic measures they had instituted so far were having only a limited effect, they continued to hold on to economic warfare as part of their strategy for winning the war. Only during 1942 did they begin to emphasize other methods, especially strategic bombing, as the primary means of attempting to limit the enemy's resources. But in this respect, as with the

earlier measures, the Allies were much less successful than they had anticipated.

The second part of Britain's strategy in 1939 was to build up its military
strength for a number of possible contingencies. The most likely possibility
was a German decision to attack France. The British and the French had
had a falling out after World War I, and only the renewal of Germany's
aggressive posture in the 1930s had brought them back together. In March
1939, secret staff conversations between the two nations intensified. When
both entered the war on the side of Poland, their collaboration became wide-
ranging and close despite "the awkward fact that the two countries did not
greatly care for each other."[38]

With Britain's and France's declaration of war on September 3, preparations
for an eventual western campaign started in earnest.[39] The two countries
did little to assist Poland, for they preferred to remain on the defensive
"until our strength has been developed."[40] Even bombing operations were
generally ruled out, since they "would lead us to no permanent military
result, but would cause unnecessary loss of aircraft."[41] Yet the British were
convinced it would be a long war and accordingly planned for one of at
least three years' duration. Their goal was to build up a total of fifty-five
divisions, twenty of which were to be formed within the first year.[42] Though
seldom discussed, the assumption was that the French, augmented by British
land and, especially, air forces, were to assume the offensive, perhaps in
1942 after Germany had been weakened by blockade.

British personnel began moving to France sixteen days after war was declared. Using the already worked out W-4 plan, four divisions with 150,000
soldiers were transported to northern France and in place along the Franco-
Belgian frontier by October 12.[43] By about the same time, twelve RAF squadrons—four fighter, six army cooperation, and two bomber—had been deployed
to French airfields.[44] More were to arrive when ready.

Anglo-French plans not only dealt with Germany, but also depended on
their relations with neutral Italy, Belgium, and the Netherlands. While Italy
had opted not to enter the war, it was obviously "allied" with Germany.
This meant that Britain and France would have to maintain a military presence
in the Mediterranean and along the Franco-Italian border "until we are certain
that Italy will not turn hostile."[45]

Belgium and the Netherlands presented different problems. Both nations
were more friendly toward the Allies than toward Germany, but both were
determined to remain neutral and not antagonize their eastern neighbor.
As a result, cooperation with Britain and France was virtually nil. Some information was exchanged, but not much. This left the Allies in a quandary
as to what to do. They expected that if the Germans attacked in the west,
they would come through Belgium and possibly the Netherlands. Allied threats
to limit their support of the Dutch and the Belgians to air attacks and to
retain their forces behind the Franco-Belgian boundary and "leave them to

their fate" were of no avail in dealing with two neutrals.[46] Britain and France decided they would have to defend them in any event.

After examining several options, General Maurice Gamelin, the French supreme commander, came up with Plan D, or the "Dyle Plan,"[47] which Allies' leaders accepted on November 17. According to the plan, the French Seventh Army was to advance on the left into the southern Netherlands near Breda and link up with Dutch forces. Belgian divisions, after meeting the enemy along the Albert Canal–River Meuse line, were to fall back on Antwerp and defend that area. To their right, the British Expeditionary Force under Lord Gort was to deploy along the Dyle River between Louvain and Wavre. Two additional French armies—the First and the Ninth—were to cover the sector between Wavre and the French border. The objective was to establish a continuous defensive line approximately from Breda through Antwerp, Wavre, and Namur to Givet in France. Despite reservations expressed by some of the French and British army commanders and the lack of cooperation from the Belgians and the Dutch, the Dyle River plan was executed when the Germans finally attacked on May 10.

Throughout the period of the Phony War, uncertainties and frustrations with the neighboring neutrals were only one of many Allied difficulties. Of more import was to gauge what the Germans would do. After the rapid defeat of Poland, both the British and French high commands expected a German invasion during the autumn.[48] Initially, Gamelin in particular believed that the main assault would come through Belgium, though he did not rule out other possibilities, even perhaps an attack against the Maginot Line. Although no attack came, the Allies were correct to the extent that the Germans were planning a western offensive, and rumors of an invasion continued to keep them on edge during the winter and spring months.

While the major war decisions were reserved for the British and French parliaments through their war cabinets and while the actual running of the war was turned over to their respective chiefs of staff, coordination and discussion of strategy between the two countries at the highest level was vested in the Supreme War Council. Formed at the outbreak of the war, it consisted of the heads of both governments, who met along with one other civilian minister from each country and their staffs to thrash out common problems and to adopt policies for pursuing the war. Chamberlain and Daladier, and after March 20, 1940, Paul Reynaud, met nine times between September 12 and the start of the battle for France. The meetings were held on both sides of the Channel, usually in Paris and London.[49] They were often preceded by conferences between the countries' chiefs of staff, who were able to discuss their common effort and to recommend changes in strategy before meeting with their civilian superiors.

The issues taken up by Chamberlain and his French counterparts were knotty and far-reaching. The buildup in France and the difficulties associated with Belgium and the Netherlands occupied a good deal of their time, but they also examined possible measures for relieving Finland, meeting German aggression into the Balkans, and handling numerous contingencies in the Middle East and North Africa. By the beginning of 1940, as they became more confident that the "situation" in the west could be dealt with, they were increasingly turning their attention to other matters. By March, their confidence had grown to the point that they felt any German offensive in the west could be defeated.[50] Plans for moving into Belgium had been worked out in detail and were to be acted on with or without a Belgian "invitation." While the Allies assumed that they could render little assistance to defend the Netherlands, they would help that country as best they could with naval and air power. As for France, British joint planners admitted that "the Germans hold a position of strategic advantage" on the western front, but "taking into account the French frontier fortifications, the Allies forces now in the field should be capable of stopping a German offensive against France." Despite acknowledged deficiencies in equipment and aircraft, this optimistic attitude prevailed until the invasion.

Meanwhile, the buildup continued. Additional British divisions had been formed and brought over to France.[51] Eight had arrived by January, and two more by April, bringing the total to ten, the number the British said they could contribute at this point. More vital was the RAF contingent, which was to supplement France's admittedly dated and inadequately equipped air force. The RAF's 27 squadrons sent to the Continent were divided into two main groups.[52] One was the Air Component of 13 squadrons with 64 Hurricane fighters and 162 Lysander and Blenheim reconnaissance aircraft. The other was the Advanced Air Striking Force of 14 squadrons with 160 outdated Fairey Battles, 32 Blenheims, and 32 Hurricanes. The British total came to 450 aircraft, though other squadrons were scheduled to be sent over when hostilities began, and some of the RAF units stationed in England were expected to provide additional help.

The much larger British air contingent which remained in the United Kingdom—1,400 first-line aircraft as of April 1—was a source of constant irritation to the French.[53] In their view, why not bring more of them to France? The British countered that air facilities in France did not allow for servicing and defending many more squadrons than were there and that the dispatch of large numbers of additional fighters to France would denude Britain of its own air defense. This had been the British position from the start; it hardened during the first eight months of the war. On September 16, Britain had acknowledged that France was in dire need of aircraft and antiaircraft assistance "to stem a German land advance."[54] The appreciation went on:

> There would be an immediate request for us to send fighters to France and there is no doubt in extreme circumstances we might have to do so. It would, however, be a matter of utmost difficulty for administrative reasons, and apart

from the fact that we should have to weaken the air defense of this country in order to assist France, our fighters would only be able to operate with a reduced degree of efficiency if they were transferred to France.

On January 23, 1940, British planners presented their military leaders with a position paper which set forth the contingencies they felt Britain faced.[55] The first was that "adequate provision must be made for the defence of . . . Great Britain and British sea communications against air attack." Listed second was "holding the Western Front." After Germany's April attack on Denmark and Norway, British joint planners argued that the operation might be "an easy way of alleviating, for the time being, their [German] economic difficulties."[56] If that were the case, the planners contended, Germany might concentrate on Britain rather than on France, or they might "attack both the Allies simultaneously, and their air force is sufficiently large to enable them to launch a formidable air offensive on this country while maintaining adequate air superiority on the Western Front." By May, as discussed earlier, British leaders came around to the position that "although we cannot ignore the possibility of the main German attack being directed against France," the most likely course of action would be an unrestricted air offensive against the United Kingdom, followed by an invasion.[57] This British concern for its own security, while understandable, no doubt helped nourish France's already skeptical view of British resolve.

While the Allies prepared for a western attack, they assumed that "the Germans were also likely to be making good use of the present period of military inactivity."[58] Their assumption was, of course, correct. Hitler had brought up the idea of a western offensive at the end of September, 1939, and on October 8, he ordered the army to prepare a possible operation.[59] According to Keitel, Hitler wanted to attack as early as October 25, but realistically he envisaged mid-November as the earliest time for launching the assault.[60] By October 19, OKH had completed a definite plan.[61] It resembled the Schlieffen Plan of World War I, with the main thrust coming through central Belgium, but it predicated the destruction of the Allies in the Low Countries and northern France rather than primarily on French soil. To Hitler, time was of the essence, mainly because of economic problems at home; thus an operations order was sent out on November 5 for the attack to commence a week later. The army, however, was opposed, because it had insufficient supplies and munitions, as were the air leaders, who feared bad weather. Hitler was therefore forced to delay.

From this point until the May attack, Operation Yellow, as it was called, was postponed twenty-nine times, mostly during the winter months.[62] When a German plane on January 10 was forced to land in Belgium, a major who was captured had the Yellow plan on him and had failed to destroy it. Belgian officials bent their official neutrality to the extent of showing it to the French. The Germans appreciated that the plan might be compromised, and Hitler, who had some reservations about the proposed operation anyway, wanted it changed. General von Manstein, the chief of staff of Army Group A, having opposed the original plan for some months, had drawn up one of his own. It called for the major thrust to be made farther south in the Ardennes sector near the Belgian-Luxembourg border instead of through central Belgium. Halder of OKH was skeptical of Manstein's scheme, for the Ardennes forest was a formidable barrier, but Hitler was interested despite his hatred of the haughty Manstein, who, he explained, "was not my type."[63] Manstein met with the Führer on January 17, and the latter accepted Manstein's plan. Halder now generally came around to Manstein's thinking, and by January 24, OKH had prepared a new version of Yellow.

It was a bold plan.[64] Instead of allotting the main weight of the attack to Army Group B in the north, the plan now called for shifting it to Army Group A in the center. Army Group A was to receive most of the panzer and motorized divisions, which, once infantry divisions had led the initial attack, were to exploit the infantry push by driving through the Ardennes, crossing the Meuse River between Dinant and Sedan, and then advancing rapidly across northern France in the direction of the Lower Somme River and the coast. This move was designed to cut the Allies in two, with the result that the Belgian, Dutch, British, and some French armies would be caught in the north while the bulk of the French and a few British forces were left in the south. In the meantime, Army Group B to the north was to occupy the Netherlands quickly with one of its armies and prevent the Dutch from linking up with the Allies. The other army was to move into Belgium. Army Group C to the south was to launch a cover operation against the Maginot Line and defend that sector in case of a French attack. In addition, the army groups were to be supported by two air fleets. While Halder and Manstein continued to haggle over the use of the armored forces—Halder wanted some pauses in the operation once an area had been taken over to consolidate their gains; Manstein advocated the utmost speed all the way to the Channel—the plan was set.[65]

On March 15, Hitler told his western commanders that he would determine the actual invasion date, since it would depend on political considerations, though he also wanted good weather for the Luftwaffe. The political issue he had in mind was a March 18 meeting with Mussoloni, during which, without giving any specifics as to the timing, Hitler "invited" the Italian dictator to join against the western powers.[66] Mainly for the prestige, Mussolini wanted to become involved, but he knew his forces were not yet ready, and he thus gave no definite commitment. Another issue, though not political, was the Scandinavian campaign, which began on the night of April 8–9. Though only one of the divisions earmarked for the French offensive—the 3rd Mountain Division—was used against Norway and Denmark, the first stages of the operation did make extensive demands on the Germans, especially the navy, so that it obviously had an impact on selecting the starting date for the western offensive. Accordingly, for the operation now called *Siche-lschnitt*, or "cutting motion made by a sickle," the attack day was set for May 10.

The forces assembled by both sides for the battle were more equal numerically than has been sometimes alleged (table 6–2).[67] The facts behind the figures show, however, that Germany's army forces were superior. Its troops were all German, and many of them were more experienced, were better trained, and possessed higher morale than their Allied counterparts, who were grouped into 104 French, 10 British, 22 Belgian, and 8 Dutch divisions.[68] In the critical area of tanks, the Allies not only had more, but they were as good as those of the Wehrmacht.[69] The Germans had increased their total of Panzer IIIs and IVs from 314 on September 1, 1939, to 725 on May 10, 1940, but they still had 2,389 of the lighter Panzer Is and IIs.[70] A number of the Allied tanks, most of which were French, were also too light, but they had more than 1,000 Char B, Char D, and SOMUA tanks, which were comparable to the German Panzer IIIs and IVs. The Germans had a decided advantage in aircraft. On invasion day, they had 1,736 fighters, 2,224 bombers, and 700 reconnaissance aircraft; the Allies had 1,590 fighters, 710 bombers, and 719 reconnaissance planes, and 850 of these front-line aircraft were located in Great Britain. The British sent sixteen additional squadrons to France during the fighting (some of them only for a day), but their main fighter, the Hurricane, was no match for the German Messerschmitt Bf 109. The Luftwaffe overcame British and French opposition and gained air superiority as early as May 12. Their superiority should not mask the fact, however, that both sides suffered substantial losses in pilots and aircraft during the battle. This weakening of German air strength was a factor in their defeat in the subsequent Battle of Britain, for their aircraft production and pilot-training capacity was insufficient to make up the deficiencies in such a short time for the specifically British combat that followed.[71]

Nevertheless, German superiority in the air and on land does not alone explain the magnitude of their victory. At least three additional reasons need to be pointed out. One was that French civilian leadership was in disarray. Although Reynaud had taken over in March and Daladier stayed on as Minister of Defense, large numbers of critics on both the left and the right still hounded the government. While such a situation is normal in a democracy, it is not the condition in which a nation wants to fight a war. Second, General Alphonse Georges, the head of Allied forces in the north, was excellent, but Gamelin,

TABLE 6-2
Opposing Forces for Battle of France, May 1940

	Allies	Germans
Divisions	144	141
Tanks	3,383	2,445 (on hand)
Aircraft	3,079	5,446

the supreme commander, and even Lord Gort were not of the quality of Halder, von Bock, von Rundstedt, von Kleist, and von Leeb, or of their subordinate commanders. Third, and most important, a series of critical errors at the beginning crippled the Allied effort. French intelligence failed to recognize the extent to which German forces were concentrated in front of the Ardennes sector.[72] They estimated that the Germans had thirty-seven divisions under Army Group B in the north, whereas they had only twenty-one. In the south, German divisions under Army Group C were estimated at forty-one; they had only twenty. In the decisive Army Group A area, the French Second Bureau thought the Germans had only twenty-six divisions, while the true figure was forty-five. The French also failed to detect that the Germans had forty-five divisions in reserve instead of about thirty as estimated. Moreover, their failure to pinpoint the large armored forces of eight divisions opposite the Ardennes was compounded by the failure of French leaders to identify the crucial German thrust when it started on May 13. Even when recognized, the German drive between Sedan and Dinant was not met in strength but piecemeal.[73] The quality of the forces developed by the Germans and Allied errors were therefore more significant in explaining Germany's convincing triumph than the quantity of its troops and equipment.

The campaign itself can be divided into two main phases. During the first, the revised Yellow plan was carried through. In the main thrust, German divisions cut a swath through Luxembourg and southern Belgium and then into France, reaching the sea in eleven days. There followed a mopping up stage in which the Allied forces that remained in northern France and Belgium were rounded up or forced to evacuate to England. During the second phase, Operation Red, which started on June 5, the Wehrmacht swept across the rest of northern and central France with such speed that, by June 17, what remained of the British forces were either captured or being pushed off the Continent, and the French were seeking an armistice. On June 22, it was signed. In just six weeks, the Germans had won a victory of truly remarkable proportions.

When one looks at the tactical turning points, it is obvious that the decisive phase took place quite early in the campaign. At 5:35 a.m. on May 10, von Rundstedt's Army Group A crossed the Belgian and Luxembourg frontier.[74] By the end of the day, the Fourth, Twelfth, and Sixteenth armies and Panzer Group von Kleist had reached a line approximately eighteen to thirty miles west of the starting line from Malmedy in Belgium south through Bastogne to Arlon. The next day, in sunny weather, armored units crossed the Ourthe River and, on May 12, reached the Meuse River. Barely pausing at this formidable barrier, German armor on May 13, with the help of engineers and with outstanding close air support from Air Fleet 3, established bridgeheads over the Meuse at Dinant and Sedan. On May 14, the bridgeheads were enlarged and additional crossings made. The advance to the Somme River and the Channel coast now commenced. Despite constant concern about their southern

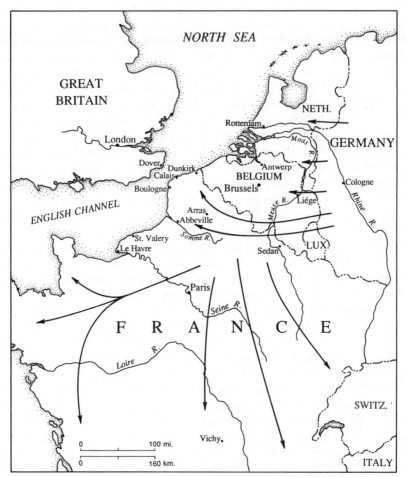

Map 6-2: Battle of France

and northern flanks, German armored and motorized columns were given "full reign" and captured the area around Arras (though not the city) on May 18, reached Abbeville on May 20, and the coast on May 21. The initial goal of dividing the Allies in two had been accomplished.

Meanwhile, to the north, Army Group B's Eighteenth Army, with airborne and air support, advanced into the Netherlands, prevented a strong linkup between French and Dutch forces, and overwhelmed the Dutch in five days.[75] On May 15, the Dutch capitulated. In Belgium, specially trained German units took the Eben Emael fortress on the first day, and the Sixth Army drove west against only slight opposition. By May 14, they were engaged against Belgian, British, and French troops along the Dyle River line.

While the Allied forces had advanced (pulled back in the case of some

Belgian units) to their positions with a minimum of difficulties and were holding their own against the enemy, their main problems were the German movements to the north and south.[76] The defeat of the Dutch freed the German Eighteenth Army to attack French, Belgian, and remnants of Dutch formations north and east of Antwerp. By May 18, the Germans were advancing rapidly and, with the Allies in retreat, took Brussels uncontested on May 21. In the French First, Sixth, and Ninth Army areas to the south opposite German Army Group A, the situation was even more serious. By May 14, the German drive across the Meuse had French military and civilian leaders in a near panic. At 7 p.m., as mentioned briefly above, Premier Reynaud wired Churchill and exclaimed: "Germany intends to deliver a mortal blow toward Paris. The German Army has broken through our fortified line south of Sedan. . . ."[77] The next morning at 8:30, Reynaud telephoned Churchill and in great agitation said: "We have been defeated. We are beaten; we have lost the battle. . . . The front is broken near Sedan; they are pouring through in great numbers with tanks and armoured cars."[78] Churchill tried to calm Reynaud and assured him of British support. He then offered to come over for talks, and did so the next day. Nevertheless, it was obvious that even at this early stage—six days after the fighting had begun—the situation for the Allies was in grave doubt.

In the north, the British Expeditionary Force (BEF) of nine divisions had no alternative but to fall back.[79] This was accomplished in three stages, starting on the night of May 16 and completed on May 19, by which time most of the British soldiers were in place along the Scheldt River. That same day, Lord Gort's chief of staff telephoned London to indicate that, given the widening gap to their right, it might be necessary to withdraw the BEF toward Dunkirk on the coast and "to fight it out there."[80] Field Marshal Ironside, the army chief of staff, and Churchill realized that this meant probable evacuation. They instructed Gort instead to move his forces toward Amiens to link up with the French to the south.[81] Although Gort ruled out such an extensive operation, which would have required breaking through the German lines, he had already decided to undertake a counterattack west of Arras to prevent that important transportation center from being surrounded. On May 21, a small British force advanced up to ten miles against German units and relieved the city.

This move frightened the Germans, for they were well aware of their exposed corridor across northern France.[82] They therefore held up an Army High Command order to have panzer units advance toward the ports of Boulogne and Calais until their forces were strengthened with infantry troops around Arras. This being done by May 22, the German tanks headed off toward Boulogne and Calais. By this time, the Germans realized that less than 50 percent of their armor was in commission and "barely capable of defensive action."[83] Accordingly, on May 23, amid fears of an Allied attack against the corridor from the north and south, von Rundstedt, with Hitler's concurrence, ordered the panzers to stop.[84] The halt order, as it turned out, was a logical decision, since the Allies, now under General Maxime Weygand, were planning just such an operation. But it never came off, and not until May 25 were the panzers ordered to push toward Boulogne and Calais, and more importantly, to Dunkirk, where the Allies had set up a defensive perimeter to cover the evacuation of their soldiers. On May 26, the panzers were moving forward again.

The British had hurriedly been making their plans for an eventual evacuation. On May 27, Operation Dynamo was put into effect.[85] During the next nine days, under almost unbelievable conditions, and despite Belgium's surrender on May 28, the British were able to remove 338,226 British and French soldiers from the beachhead.[86] At first, there was a good deal of confusion, since French commanders on the scene received almost no guidance from their superiors. Moreover, the British were directed to have their troops taken off in British ships, and the French were to remove their troops in the even fewer French ships.[87] On the night of May 30–31, however, the British commanders received word that equal numbers of French and British soldiers were to be loaded onto the British ships, so that by June 4, 224,885 British and 112,547 French, plus some Belgian, troops had been removed.

Was the "miracle of Dunkirk" truly a miracle? As brought out by Liddell Hart and many others, no doubt the German decision to halt their panzers before advancing toward Dunkirk was crucial.[88] Nonetheless, for our purposes here, the question is, not so much whether there was a miracle, but what happened to cause the delay?[89] Four explanations, some already alluded to, stand out. First of all, the British counterattack at Arras did concern the Germans. They feared that the Arras attack might be the preliminary to a much more extensive undertaking to cut the corridor in two, which had to be prevented at all cost.[90] Hence, there was a need to refurbish their depleted armored forces for the expected major Allied counterattack. A second reason, related to the first, is that the Germans wanted to conserve their tanks for the subsequent push south, a task that was expected to be arduous and ultimately more significant than taking Dunkirk. The enemy in the north had already demonstrated that it could fight with "extraordinary tenacity," and on May 26, Army Group A went so far as to order that Dunkirk be assaulted by artillery fire rather than by tanks. Moreover, at a meeting on May 27 between Halder and all of the theater commanders and members of their staffs, the army chief of staff emphasized preparations for the southern offensive and said little about the Dunkirk operation.[91] A preparatory order for the southern assault was given the next day. In other words, as important as Dunkirk was, its primary importance in the eyes of the Germans was to bring the operation to a speedy conclusion so that they could concentrate on an attack to the south. A third, though subsidiary, explanation for the Dunkirk delay was the concern of Hitler and others about marshy Flanders, where so much blood had been spilled during World War I and where German armor could get bogged down. Fourth, and finally, there was Göring's assurance that the Luftwaffe alone could handle the job. On May 26, he blustered to Hitler: "Only [British] fishing boats are coming over; I hope the Tommies are good swimmers."[92] Here, the Luftwaffe was unsuccessful because it never established complete air supremacy over the beaches and did not have a sufficient night-flying capability to prevent the Allied forces from escaping. Although the British lost extensive material, including 7,000 tons of ammunition, 90,000 rifles, 1,000 heavy guns, 2,000 vehicles, 8,000 Bren guns, and 400 antitank guns, at least most of their best soldiers had been saved to fight another day.[93]

For the French, the evacuation meant the immediate transshipment back to France, not only of their own troops, but also those of the British. By this time, France was in desperate straits, and a "peace with Germany" faction of civilian leaders had formed in Paris. Given the political turmoil and declining support, Reynaud asked and expected the British to provide additional assistance. On June 2, he requested the urgent dispatch of three more British divisions and fighter aircraft (later specified as 320) to France.[94] Only with these forces, and more to come, he stated, could the tide of battle be turned in favor of the Allies.

While the British wanted to help for both "strategic and political reasons," they had decided as early as mid-May that they would have to resist exorbitant French demands since they had to retain some forces, especially fighter aircraft, for their own defense.[95] Churchill therefore agreed to send over two divisions, the first to be ready in seven days, to add to the two British divisions already there, and to bring up to strength the nine British air squadrons also still in France.[96] At this point, he said, he could do little more, except to use the bombers and fighters based in the United Kingdom for their common effort, since the troops evacuated from Dunkirk had to be entirely reequipped and "British fighter aviation had been worn to a shred" during the recent fighting. It now became apparent to the French as well as to the British that there was a limit beyond which Britain would not go. France would have to depend mainly on its own resources for the upcoming battle.

France was not up to the task. It had been shocked by the Wehrmacht during Operation Yellow, and German dominance continued during Operation Red. On June 5, the Fourth, Sixth, and Ninth armies under Army Group B, with air support, moved out of their Somme River and Oise-Aisne Canal positions. At first, the French provided stout resistance, but the Germans, spearheaded by their armor, eventually broke through the Allied defenses, crossed a number of river barriers, and captured Rouen on June 9.[97] That same day, to the east, Army Group A's three armies—the Second, Twelfth, and Sixteenth—started their own attack.[98] Their divisions soon crossed the Aisne River and began moving to the southeast. On June 10, the Italians finally entered the war. While French forces held their own along the Alpine front, the French government hardly noticed; it had begun leaving Paris, heading first for Tours and then later for Bordeaux. Paris was declared an open city, and the German 87th Division had the honor of occupying it on June 14. At this stage, the French were in such confusion that even German Army Group C, opposite the Maginot Line, started a limited offensive of its own. By June 17, the French had had enough and sued for an armistice.

For the British, June was indeed a trying month. General Dill had by now replaced Field Marshal Ironside as chief of the Imperial General Staff, and on June 2, Dill named General Alan Brooke, most recently a corps commander in Belgium, to head the new BEF effort in the south of France. By the time Brooke arrived there on June 12, he could do little but oversee the evacuation of British forces—some of whom had only just arrived—from the Continent. A disaster of major proportions had already occurred at St. Valéry, where the navy, because of fog at night and German air superiority during the day, could not remove approximately 10,000 troops of the 51st Highland Division. The troops were captured. From other French ports, however, the navy was able to evacuate 191,870 troops, of whom 144,171 were British and the remainder French, Polish, Czech, and Belgian.[99] It was also able to save some 2,292 vehicles, 315 guns, and 5,197 tons of equipment.

Ultimately as important as the military events that were unfolding were Britain's political relations with the French. By the time of Germany's renewed June offensive, relations between the two nations had become quite strained. The British genuinely wanted to assist their ally, but not to the extent of putting their own country in jeopardy. The French thought the British were holding back deliberately and could do much more to help out. Churchill and Reynaud supported each other as best they could, but Reynaud's critics inside France were rapidly gaining strength. On June 15, he indicated his willingness again to have the government continue the fight, even from North Africa if necessary, but his resolve did nothing to quell the opposition.[100] On the same day, when General Weygand reported that "coordinated resistance is no longer possible," it was obvious that Reynaud's days as premier were numbered unless something unforeseen happened.

It almost did. British officials, with the help of French emissaries in London, were preparing a document of monumental historical importance.[101] A draft of the document, known as the Declaration of Union, was presented to the British war cabinet and discussed on the afternoon of June 16. It was amended, and then telephoned to Reynaud to put before his ministers, with whom he was meeting that evening to decide whether the government should go on. Edward Spears, the British liaison officer with Reynaud, said he was told by others who attended the meeting that "it acted like a tonic on M. Reynaud, who said that for a document like that he would fight to the last."

In it, the British proposed that both governments declare an "indissoluble union" of the two countries in which they would share, among other things, "joint organs of defence, foreign, financial and economic policies"; common citizenship; a single war cabinet which would direct the armed forces and "govern from wherever it best can"; and an "association" of the two parliaments. In a final flourish, the declaration concluded: "The Union will concentrate its whole energy against the power of the enemy no matter where the battle may be. And thus we shall conquer." It was truly a remarkable gesture.

Since Reynaud had been so favorably impressed by the declaration, Churchill proposed to meet with the French premier the next day off the coast of Brittany in the hope of dissuading the French from seeking an armistice. However, at 10:10 p.m., after Churchill had left for a train that was to take him to the coast for embarkation, he received word from his ambassador in Paris that a ministerial crisis was taking place and that the meeting for the next day was off. Shortly thereafter, word was received that Reynaud had resigned. Spears reported that the French leader had read the declaration twice to his cabinet, but without fire or conviction, and that "it had fallen flat." His supporters explained that, when he found little enthusiasm for the British proposal, he had become discouraged himself. The pro-surrender faction thus won out.

The next morning, the new French government, under Marshal Pétain, asked the Germans for an armistice. Sir Stafford Cripps, then ambassador to the Soviet Union, was probably close to the mark in explaining the declaration's failure when he wrote to Lord Halifax on August 8, 1940: "The last-minute attempt by His Majesty's Government to hold the two countries together by substituting for the Alliance a more permanent form of union was too sudden and unexplored, and raised in such circumstances too many points which were capable of causing alarm and prejudice in the minds of many Frenchmen of all classes for it to meet with success."[102]

With the armistice signed on June 22, to take effect on June 24, the British had to decide quickly how to deal with their former French ally. They had already concluded that their basic objective at this point was survival and that they would do whatever was necessary to realize that objective. They had tried to work with the French and to support them—Churchill and other ministers had met with them at Supreme War Council meetings nine times during the fighting, most often attempting to raise their flagging morale—but now was a time for action. The prime minister received advice from numerous quarters. A letter from G. B. Shaw, of all people, echoed the sentiment of most Britons about what the country should do:[103]

Dear Prime Minister,
    Why not declare war on the French and capture her fleet (which would gladly strike its colors to us) before A.H. [Adolf Hitler] recovers his breath?
    Surely that is the logic of the situation?
                                                            Tactically,
                                                            G. Bernard Shaw

Measures similar to those suggested by Shaw had already been contemplated and were set in motion. French soldiers and sailors in the British Isles (around 21,000) were allowed to return home if they wished, but this policy was not to apply to France's most precious remaining asset, its naval ships.[104] As early as June 7, First Sea Lord Pound and government officials had decided that it might be necessary under certain circumstances "to sink the French Fleet" and that the Royal Navy would not hesitate to do so.

On July 3, the British struck. French ships harbored in Metropolitan France were beyond reach, but those in the United Kingdom were taken over. Those at Mediterranean ports in northern Africa were immobilized or sunk; only three of the French ships moored at Alexandria and Mers el-Kebir managed to get away. The British thereby demonstrated their resolve to retain dominance of the seas, even at the expense of their former French partner. The new Vichy government understandably responded by breaking relations with Britain. The last thread of the alliance had been quickly cut.

Still, British determination to carry on could not mask the fact that during May and June 1940 the Wehrmacht had won an overwhelming victory. The reasons were in part a result of bold German planning, well-trained troops, and superior military leadership at all levels; and in part because the Allies, the French in particular, were poorly organized, emphasized outdated defensive thinking, and failed to appreciate the revolutionary nature of German tactics.[105] Two British measures that might have made a difference—strategic bombing and timely intelligence—were either too little, as in the case of bombing, where they did not strike targets east of the Rhine until May 15, and then only sporadically and with little effect; or too late, as in the case of strategic intelligence, where, even though the British began decrypting German air force Ultra signals after May 20, they were not yet able to put them to effective use in the field. That step would have to wait until later.[106]

In terms of losses during the Battle of France, however, a rather startling fact emerges. Troop casualties—156,492 for the Germans as compared with 2,291,240 for the Allies (including 1,900,000 French prisoners of war and missing)—were what one might expect.[107] So were the tank losses, 753 for the Germans, approximately 3,300 for the Allies. But in aircraft, the Germans had 1,428 destroyed; the French and British, 1,701. Of the latter figure, 944 were British. In other words, the Luftwaffe lost more aircraft (and pilots) in the Battle of France than did the RAF. Despite the magnitude of Germany's triumph, its air force had been substantially weakened just prior to its greatest challenge, the Battle of Britain.[108]

During the French campaign, Hitler reached the pinnacle of his military success. Though not to the extent later on, he was heavily involved in the operation from his two headquarters—flying to the front, making suggestions, at times even changing orders.[109] While his interferences did cause tensions with the military staffs, especially OKH, on the whole, as at Dunkirk, he went along with what the army proposed. The result was a "shared" victory in which Hitler was now accepted as a military genius; and his advisers, seen as the ultimate practitioners in carrying out his wishes. Hitler's stature with the military—and the people—was the highest it had ever been.

Churchill, on the other hand, had just been appointed prime minister at the beginning of the battle. Nevertheless, he had acquitted himself well. He had instituted some organizational changes, thus bringing the war under more central direction. He had uplifted British morale and had demonstrated throughout a genuine concern for the French ally. Despite the stinging defeat, he faced the future with outward calm and resolve. Whether his resolve, and that of the British military and citizenry, could be translated into victory against the seemingly invincible German juggernaut, however, was far from certain.

In regard to the preparatory phase for the Battle of Britain, one perception seems to dominate all others: whereas the British prepared well for the battle, the Germans did not.[110] A good deal of the blame for Germany's confused planning has to be placed on Hitler, although jealousies among the services also played a part. Contrary to those for the Battle of France, where the Führer and his military advisers demonstrated a sure hand during the planning and execution phases, preparations for the battle with Britain suffered as the top leaders vacillated on priorities. On May 21, in the flush of success as German forces reached the Channel, Hitler directed the services to look into the possibility of invading Britain. The services had already examined the possibility in preliminary studies in 1939 and had concluded that a direct attack could be undertaken only if local air superiority had been achieved beforehand. A naval study issued on May 27, 1940, confirmed the difficulty of invading England. As the Battle of France drew to a close, Hitler started pursuing two possible courses of action. One was to gain a compromise peace with the British whereby Britain would not be invaded and would retain its empire. In return, it would be allowed to participate with Germany in dividing the French colonial areas and would see that Germany's "lost empire" was restored.[111] Confident that Britain would accept his diplomatic solution, Hitler pursued it, with modifications, into July. During the same time, he made it clear to the services that the possibility of an invasion could not be ruled out.[112] On June 23, interservice planning began. After General Jodl of OKW had presented a memorandum indicating that a campaign against the British Isles and its empire was a definite possibility, the Führer on July 2 ordered that the services start their own planning, with the stipulation that they take into account the necessity of air superiority before a landing could take place.[113]

Two weeks later, the Führer issued Directive No. 16, "Preparations for a Landing Operation against England."[114] In it he called for an invasion, if necessary, along a broad front from Ramsgate to west of the Isle of Wight once the prerequisites of sea and air superiority had been attained. Preparations for the operation (Sealion) were to be ready by the middle of August. In fact, by this time, July 16, a plan drawn up by the army had been nearly completed.[115] Though subsequently altered in detail, it was presented on July 17. The assault was to be undertaken by portions of thirteen infantry divisions, plus two airborne divisions, which were to land between Ramsgate and Lyme Regis, a coastal distance of some 265 miles. Ninety thousand seaborne troops were to land initially, with up to 260,000 coming ashore by the end of the third day. A second wave of six panzer and three motorized divisions was to follow. Nine more infantry divisions were to form a third wave. The goal was to have thirty-one divisions disembarked within a month, by which time the army envisaged that German forces would have broken out of their beachhead and, with Luftwaffe support, taken over most of the country.

Almost immediately the navy protested. Grand Admiral Raeder pointed out that it would be impossible for the navy to transport such a huge force across the Channel and to land it on so many widely dispersed beaches, and that enemy ships, defenses, and mines would also cause grave difficulties. An unspoken point, but one German leaders well understood, was that naval losses in Norway had depleted the fleet to the point that only one cruiser (the *Hipper*), three light cruisers, eight destroyers, twenty-six submarines, and forty to fifty torpedo and patrol boats would be available for Sealion.[116] They further realized that it would take considerable time to assemble the invasion fleet, which was to consist primarily of large river barges towed across the Channel.

Meanwhile, on July 19, Hitler delivered a speech before the Reichstag in which he roundly condemned the "war policy" of Churchill and his followers, but he still left open the possibility of negotiations. The British rebuffed the offer. Two days later, Hitler further discussed his thoughts about the landing with von Brauchitsch, Raeder, and air force Chief of Staff Jeschonnek. He expressed his concern about mounting the invasion and said it might be necessary to consider other plans, namely, an attack against the Soviet Union. On July 31, he instructed that plans for such an eventuality be carried forward.

Throughout the period, the navy continued to object to the army plan. On July 31, Hitler met with von Brauchitsch, Raeder, Keitel, Jodl, and others at the Berghof to elicit their views.[117] Raeder stated that the navy could not be ready until September 15, for it would take that long before barges and transport ships were ready and minesweeping and minelaying tasks were accomplished. He reiterated that the invasion was being planned on too wide a front, especially since the Lyme Bay region to the west was heavily defended. He also stressed that even though he had opted for September for the invasion, it was still an inopportune time because of the weather; May and June were much better. The Führer and his army advisers did not favor waiting until spring, but they were otherwise impressed with Raeder's arguments. As a result, Hitler agreed that plans were to go ahead for the landing on a broad front, though it might be scaled down in the future. In the interim, he had decided to emphasize control of the air. If the results were not satisfactory, preparations for the invasion were to be halted; if the Luftwaffe attained air superiority, the attack should proceed. He set September 15 as the date by which Sealion was to be ready. On the day after the meeting, OKW distributed to the three services Führer Directive No. 17, "For the Conduct of Air and Sea Warfare against England," to serve as a guideline for the preliminary phase.

Throughout August, the army-navy disagreement over Sealion continued, though both services acknowledged that the navy would probably get its way. By September, a revised plan had been worked out.[118] It featured a much smaller landing area, fewer divisions taking part, and a slower rate of reinforcement than did the original plan. Instead of landing from Lyme Bay to Ramsgate, German forces, with air support, were to assault beaches along a seventy-mile front between Folkestone and Brighton. Rather than thirteen first-wave seaborne divisions and a total of thirty-nine (including two airborne) to be landed within a month, nine were to undertake the initial attack and twenty-three to come ashore within six weeks. The plan provided that two Sixth Army divisions be held in readiness for the Lyme Bay region, but gave no projection as to when they might be used.

By this time, the navy and the army were both having doubts about Sealion unless air superiority was achieved. Hitler eventually came around to the same conclusion. On September 13, he tentatively decided to terminate the operation but, with the air battle raging, put off a definite decision until the next day. He then delayed Sealion again until September 17, but on that date he postponed it. Not until October 12 did he call it off definitely until the spring of 1941. Although the Wehrmacht continued to assemble barges and undertook exercises along the French coast for purposes of deception, Sealion was never resurrected.

Britain's plans for defending the home islands had been in the gestation stage for a number of years. By the time the war broke out in 1939, the British had already developed techniques, such as radar, and soon set about training air observers and antiaircraft gun crews to establish the rudiments of an air defense system. They also assumed that the Germans might unleash a "total air war" against Britain or attack British seaborne trade to weaken the country before mounting a direct assault.[119] Realizing that the navy and air force were the first line of defense, they decided to strengthen them further, concentrating especially on the production of up-to-date fighters.[120] But they knew they must also strengthen their land forces and streamline their home defense system for the upcoming battle.[121]

During June, with the Battle of France in its final throes, Britain used every resource available to build up its defensive capabilities. Instructions were sent out for laying mines, erecting and using field fortifications, and deploying the land, sea, and air units properly.[122] Provisions were made to utilize the Flying Training Command, Naval Auxiliary Patrols, and Local Defence Volunteers (LDVs) in case of an invasion.[123] These forces were not expected to repel a landing on their own, but it was hoped that they would augment the regular units, whose numbers were increasing, particularly with the addition of troops from the continent and from the Commonwealth and Empire.

There were numerous problems. Many of the soldiers were not properly equipped, and the shotguns and hunting rifles used by many of the LDVs were hardly a match for the automatic weapons and grenades of the German army.[124] Nor were the tank traps and four-inch artillery pieces expected to provide much of a defense against the panzers.[125] When he took over as commander of Home Forces on July 19, General Brooke commented: "I knew well . . . the unpreparedness of our defences, the appalling lack of equipment, and the deficiency of training and battle-worthiness in the majority of our formations."[126]

Amidst this mixture of British resolve, activity, and uncertainty, the air battle began. Although the most intense phase took place between mid-August and mid-September, a preliminary, or contact, phase had started on July 10. During this extended, early stage the Germans were still in the process of building up airfields and facilities in the west and replenishing their supply of aircraft and crews. They thus concentrated their effort primarily on probing British coastal defenses and attacking harbors and convoys. The missions undertaken at this time by both sides were arduous, and there was some combat—the British lost 150 fighters; the Germans, 286 aircraft—but not to the extent of the fighting later on.[127]

German air forces leaders obviously had additional goals in mind besides operations over the Channel.[128] Their basic plan was to strike British airfields, aircraft factories, and supporting facilities in southeastern England, with the object of wearing down the RAF so as to attain eventual air superiority. Officially, the air campaign was seen as the preliminary phase prior to invasion; unofficially, Göring and his associates "hoped that air action alone would force Britain to sue for peace."[129]

As mentioned above, on August 1, Hitler instructed the Luftwaffe to prepare for all-out combat against the RAF. Having indicated to Göring that he would for the most part leave the execution of the air war to the Reichsmarschall, he spent this period at the Berghof or in Berlin.[130] The air staffs had already been working on detailed plans, which were to be ready by August 5.[131] Three air fleets were to take part. Field Marshal Kesselring's Air Fleet 2 and Field Marshal Hugo Sperrle's Air Fleet 3 were to bomb and strafe targets in the southeast up to London, and General Hans-Jürgen Stumpff's smaller Air Fleet 5, based in Norway, was to strike targets farther north. There were several postponements due to weather, but attack day (Eagle Day), was finally set for August 13.

Both countries went into the battle with impressive air armadas. Although sources vary as to the total figures, the Germans on August 10 had available in the west approximately 2,621 front-line aircraft, of which 2,355 were serviceable; the British had only 1,720, with 1,154 serviceable.[132] The disparity in number of fighters was not so great as that in overall strength. The Germans had a total of 1,152 with 963 serviceable; the British, 1032, with 687 serviceable. Breaking down the figures still further, the Luftwaffe had 702 of its most effective fighter, the Messerschmitt Bf 109, in service; the British, 598 Hurricanes and Spitfires.

Besides aircraft, an essential component for Britain was its air defense system. It included, among other elements, 52 operational radar stations, 1,300 heavy and 700 light antiaircraft guns, and at least 3,500 searchlights. Moreover, for the first time, the British were able to put Ultra intelligence to use. At this stage, its value was not so much in aiding the conduct of operations as it was in indicating Germany's possible intentions and its order of battle.[133] On July 6, for example, an Ultra decrypt revealed that instead of 2,500 German bombers capable of dropping 4,800 tons of bombs, as the British had thought, the Luftwaffe had only 1,250 bombers that could drop 1,800 tons. Between August 10 and 24, a variety of intelligence sources, including Ultra, indicated that an invasion was not to be expected within the next two weeks. On September 7, the large number of barges collected at French and Belgian ports was a tip off that an amphibious attack might take place at any moment. Such information was indeed of inestimable value during Britain's attempt to stave off the Luftwaffe.

The most intense period of the battle began on August 13 and consisted of four main phases.[134] From the thirteenth to the twenty-third, the Luftwaffe focused on British airfields, facilities and radar stations in southeast England. Between August 24 and September 6, the Germans extended their attacks to RAF and other military installations around London, and toward the end of their most successful, second period, started bombing British aircraft factories and other plants associated with the air industry. In an effort to get the RAF to engage more directly, on September 7, the Germans began day and night bombing missions on targets throughout the London area, and this third phase continued through September 19. Having suffered severe casualties, they then switched mainly to night bombings and indiscriminate attacks on London and other cities. The Germans undertook this fourth phase, known as the Blitz, in the faint hope of forcing a quick decision so that the invasion could proceed. Though unsuccessful, the Blitz continued into the spring of 1941. While causing damage, it failed to dislocate British industry and was less intense than the phases that preceded it.

Three days during the battle, which was punctuated by periods of bad weather as well as changes in tactics, were most important. One was August 15, when the Luftwaffe sent up 1,786 fighter and bomber sorties, including planes from Air Fleet 5 in Norway, to bomb Britain's airfields.[135] The British responded with 974 fighter sorties of their own. While the British lost 34 fighters, the Luftwaffe lost 75 (the British estimated 182). Germany's Air Fleet 5 was found to be so ineffective at such a long range that it was withdrawn from the battle; most of its combat planes were transferred to France toward the end of August. In addition, the twin-seated Messerschmitt Bf 110 was found to be too slow and required escort to be of further use.

Another important day was August 18. Although the Germans flew only 750 sorties, at this point they realized that the vaunted Ju-87 Stuka dive bomber, in the face of mounting losses, was too vulnerable to fighters and antiaircraft fire. It was removed from further combat.

September 15, Battle of Britain Day, is also considered a key turning point. On this day, the Luftwaffe flew about 1,320 sorties, and Fighter Command undertook 733. The most important figure, however, is the 185 German aircraft supposedly shot down. Although after the war the actual number was found to be only 61, news of immense German losses at the time greatly heartened British leaders and the public, especially since they lost only 26 aircraft and 13 pilots during the day's fighting. The outcome had the opposite effect on Hitler and his advisers, who had anticipated a substantial victory by September 15, and it undoubtedly played a role in his calling off Sealion on September 17. Although both sides did not realize it at the time—even Ultra gave the British no precise answer as to when the invasion was postponed—the Battle of Britain had passed its most critical stage.[136]

The main reason usually given for Britain's defensive victory and Germany's initial defeat was Göring's decision on September 3 to shift the focus of attack from British airfields and other facilities supporting the air effort in the southeast to London itself. This decision gave the hard-pressed RAF a reprieve, during which it recovered to continue the battle.

While this reason is no doubt valid, at least five other reasons are in the background. One is the matter of numbers. The Luftwaffe was never able to overcome the RAF fighters to such an extent that it gained a decisive numerical advantage. Fighter Command suffered considerable casualties in both aircraft and pilots, but it always had enough fighters in commission during August and September—the lowest was 631 on August 18, the highest 740 on August 25—to provide a stout defense.[137]

Second, the Germans seriously underestimated British aircraft production and repair capabilities.[138] Whereas German intelligence estimated that the British built 2,790 fighters during 1940, they actually produced 4,283. During August and September, the Germans thought that the British were building 280 per month; the actual figures were 476 for August and 467 for September. These numbers were more than enough to make up for the 359 and 363 fighters lost during these two months. Moreover, the Germans did not emphasize attacks on British repair facilities, which by mid-July were putting planes back into service at a rate of 160 per week. Britain's replacement capabilities in both new and repaired planes therefore substantially exceeded its losses throughout the battle despite a temporarily negative gain-loss ratio in late August and early September.

Third, Germany did not possess suitable aircraft for the air campaign they undertook.[139] They did not have strategic bombers, and their medium bombers did not have sufficient accuracy, range, or bomb load to attack all of Britain's fighter facilities or to destroy its aircraft industry. Among the fighters, the Bf 109 was equal to the Spitfire and superior to the Hurricane, but it did not have the range to escort bombers all the way to their targets. Consequently, British pilots often waited until the 109s had to return to their bases and then engaged the vulnerable bombers with considerable effect.

Fourth, their defense system gave the British a decided advantage.[140] After radar or air observers picked up incoming German aircraft, information was sent to group headquarters (10, 11, or 12 Group) and then on to sector stations, which controlled a number of airfields in their areas. Operators at these stations informed the squadrons at airfields of the enemy raid and the number of aircraft in general needed to intercept the Luftwaffe attackers. The operators then communicated with the pilots in the air by radio, thus assuring a coordinated effort throughout the period from detection to interception. This system allowed the British to avoid using their fighters unnecessarily, to hold some of them back if required, and to allocate them to a number of different tasks. For instance, while half of 11 Group's squadrons might engage the enemy's fighters, the other half could be employed against its bombers. Or, if the enemy attacked in waves, as it usually did, some of 11 Group's fighters might meet the first wave, and others would be used for successive waves, while the squadrons of 10 and 12 Group would protect targets around London or along the southern coast. An additional help for the RAF was that Fighter Command was able to rotate depleted squadrons from the southeastern part of the country with full squadrons farther north. During the September 7–19 period, however, when the Luftwaffe was concentrating on London, Fighter Command was not able to rotate its squadrons and could only replace pilots who were lost. On the whole, however, the RAF's was a flexible system that made optimal use of its defensive posture.

Fifth, and finally, is the question of leadership. Göring was more heavily involved in the battle than in any other operation throughout the war, and there seems little doubt that he thought the Luftwaffe could defeat the RAF with or without an invasion to follow. Although he should have turned the running of the campaign over to subordinate commanders, there is no reason to believe that they would have conducted the operation differently. They collectively thought that the RAF fighters had to be brought to battle, and attacking London directly achieved that result. In the end, the Luftwaffe suffered too many losses in aircraft and pilots to have a decisive effect. A further leadership factor was that since Hitler had confidence in Göring, he was the logical choice to direct the air offensive.

Churchill also retained confidence in his enigmatic commander, Air Chief Marshal Sir Hugh Dowding.[141] Dowding, as head of Fighter Command, had been the key individual in persuading Churchill not to give France what he considered excessive air support at the expense of Britain's own defense. During the battle over Britain, Dowding made sure that sufficient fighters and, more critically, pilots, were available so as not to lose control of the air. The actual running of the air campaign was in the hands of the group commanders, most notably Air Vice Marshal Keith Park of 11 Group. Park's tactic of using squadrons to intercept the enemy far forward was thought to be erroneous by 12 Group Commander, Air Vice Marshal Sir Trafford Leigh-Mallory, who advocated instead the use of a "big wing" of fighters to deal a knockout blow to the attacker. Even though Park's method was successful, a British board of inquiry after the battle decided that Leigh-Mallory's technique would have been better, and the Australian Park was shunted off to head Fighter Training command. Dowding himself was retired from service and given other tasks, including a goodwill tour to the United States. Britain's aerial victory was at the time obviously not perceived in official quarters as the triumph it would later be judged.

Overall, the results of the Battle of Britain show that the Luftwaffe lost 1,733 aircraft between July 10 and October 31, and the RAF, 914.[142] Just as important, between August 8 and September 30, the Germans suffered 501 Bf 109 pilot casualties, but the RAF had only 342 Hurricane and Spitfire pilot casualties. While Britain's Bomber and Coastal commands played only a limited role, they did help by patrolling the coasts and attacking German airfields and troop and shipping concentrations across the Channel.[143] Bomber Command also flew a retaliatory raid of eighty bombers against Berlin on August 25. Though of tangential importance, the raid brought the war more directly to the German homeland and presaged developments to come. Whereas after the battle the British were convinced that air power must serve a variety of roles, the German air force reverted to a tactical-support orientation.

And so the Germans, having been dealt a setback, now turned to an eastern strategy and away from one that emphasized air and ultimately naval power as well as warfare on land. During 1939 and 1940, it had won impressive victories against Poland, Norway and Denmark, and especially France and the Low Countries and considered its failure to subdue Britain as temporary. Germany's forces still held the initiative. During the fall of 1940, Hitler and his advisers looked at a number of options, though by the end of the year they had definitely decided that the Soviet Union was priority number one.

As for the British, their problems were far from over. In fact, one might contend that they had just begun. Despite France's defeat, Britain had survived the initial onslaught, but it did not possess the military strength to face the Wehrmacht directly on land. With Italy having come into the war on Germany's side, increased commitments in the Mediterranean and Africa meant that the British blockade and holding strategy would be strained even further. The United States was increasing its assistance, and even the Soviet Union might some day be of help, but their entrance into the war on the British side was as yet only a hoped-for wish. In the interim, the British were consigned to attacking the enemy on the periphery and building up their forces at home and in the Commonwealth and Empire for the battles to come.

SEVEN

The Russian Front, 1941–1943

One of the most striking aspects of Germany's campaigns in the east is the extent of its commitment to that theater once operations had begun.[1] Between 1941 and 1944, approximately three of Germany's four million combat troops were deployed in the east. The army and air force, despite horrendous losses, had available about 2,700 first-line aircraft and 3,000–3,500 tanks and assault guns at the time of their three major offensives against the Russians. Even after the Normandy landings, the proportion of German forces on the eastern front remained higher than in the west until late 1944, when the distribution became more even. In terms of casualties, John Erickson estimates that of 13,600,000 total German casualties, 10,000,000 were suffered in the east. Furthermore, not only was the Wehrmacht obsessed with achieving a military victory over the Russians, Germany's civilian leaders, along with many of its military personnel, were equally determined to take over the area and its resources and to subjugate or exterminate its inhabitants for the "good" of the Reich. In other words, from the beginning, warfare in the east was conceived as an ideological as well as a traditional military conflict.

The three campaigns that dominated Germany's offensive effort were Operation Barbarossa/Typhoon between June 22 and December 1941; Operation Blue/Brunswick from June 28, 1942, to February 1943; and Operation Citadel between July 5 and 19, 1943. The geographic extent and the duration of each are indicative of Germany's declining fortunes. Barbarossa was launched during an optimistic period along a 1,250-mile front (1,600 if one includes the Finnish sector). Despite tactical reverses, German forces were generally successful until stopped before Moscow. Operation Blue, later renamed Brunswick, opened along a 450-mile front in southern Russia. It, too, was marked by initial German successes, but, as in the case of Barbarossa, Hitler had overreached himself. The campaign came to a halt in the Caucasus and at Stalingrad. Citadel was undertaken along a 150-mile front to eliminate a Soviet salient west of the city of Kursk. Although huge amounts of men and matériel on both sides were poured into the battle. Hitler soon recognized the futility of the offensive and, prodded also by the Allied landing in Sicily on July 10, called off Citadel after nine days, although portions of the offensive continued for another week. While these elementary facts surrounding Barbarossa/Typhoon, Blue/Brunswick, and Citadel give only a incomplete picture of Germany's demise, they do make clear that its defeat was intimately tied in with horrendous losses suffered on the eastern front.

Preliminary planning for Barbarossa had started long before its execution.[2] On July 21, 1940, when Hitler indicated to the service chiefs (with Jeschonnek representing Göring) that studies be undertaken for a possible campaign against the Soviet Union, Brauchitsch produced an outline plan for possible execution in the fall. On July 31 at a meeting at the Berghof, the Führer informed his generals that he was contemplating a spring operation and ordered OKH to undertake the necessary planning. By August 5, General Erich Marcks of the OKH staff had produced a plan which called for German troops to conduct a campaign along a broad front in four stages, with the main push toward Moscow. The final goal, a line from Archangel in the north to Rostov in the south, was expected to take nine to seventeen weeks to accomplish. The navy was to control the Baltic sea lanes, and the air force was to support the army. Since both the navy and air force were heavily involved against Great Britain, they were to be brought into the overall planning only at a later date. From this point on, OKH's operation staff began the strategic planning process, although a parallel OKW study prepared by Lieutenant Colonel Bernhard von Lossberg advocated primarily a northern push rather than one against Moscow. By the end of October, with the invasion of Britain no longer in sight, the army's operations staff under General Friedrich Paulus had drafted a plan which emphasized surprise and concentration to overcome Soviet numerical superiority. It further stressed the critical importance of rapid movement so as to engage the enemy as far forward as possible. Like Marcks's study, Paulus's plan also called for the main effort to be north of the Pripet Marshes toward Leningrad and Moscow, but in this case the plan specified that the operation was to be launched anytime after May.

Additional planning and war games took place during November and early December. Although Raeder and others during these months warned Hitler of the dangers of a possible two-front war, by this time, he had definitely decided to attack the Soviet Union.[3] On December 5, Halder presented the army plan to the Führer. Resembling the previous army studies and drafts, this version proposed three primary thrusts. One was an advance out of East Prussia toward Leningrad; the second, from Poland toward Minsk and then Smolensk; and the third, from the south toward Kiev. An eventual offensive toward Moscow was also featured. A total of 105 infantry and 32 armored and motorized infantry divisions was estimated as necessary for conducting the entire operation. While Hitler agreed to the army proposal, he indicated his preference for concentrating on economic goals, and the decision as to whether to move directly toward Moscow was left open. The plan was then turned over to OKW to draft the implementing directive.

On December 18, Führer Directive No. 21 was issued.[4] There was one important alteration to the OKH plan. Reflecting von Lossberg's view, instead of having German forces advance immediately toward the capital, they were now to capture Leningrad and Kronstadt first. Then they were to attack and occupy Moscow. Only if Soviet resistance was crumbling were both operations to be undertaken simultaneously. Why Halder did not argue with the Führer over this basic change is unclear. Perhaps he did not wish to risk Hitler's ire at this point. Perhaps he thought that the thrust toward Moscow would become obvious once the offensive was in progress. In any event, this difference between the Führer and OKH was papered over for the time being. During the campaign, however, it reappeared, and then with a vengeance.

Otherwise, except for the elimination of one of the pincer movements from Lemberg (Lvov) in the south, Directive No. 21 generally conformed to the OKH plan. The bulk of the Red Army was to be destroyed by "deep penetrating armored spearheads" from the north, center, and south. This first, decisive stage was to take eight to ten weeks. The remaining Russian soldiers were then to be pursued relentlessly, and, during the second stage, besides taking Moscow, German formations were to seize the economically important Donets River basin in the south. The final objective was a line stretching from the Volga River to Archangel (later changed by propaganda officials to Astrakhan and Archangel, or the AA line). The area to the east, especially the Ural industrial complex, was to be neutralized by the German air force. Finnish and Romanian units—plus other Allies later—were to assist in the north and the south. Preparations for the operation were to be concluded by May 15. Unless unforeseen circumstances intervened, Operation Barbarossa was soon to become a reality.

During the winter and spring, Italian setbacks in Africa and the Balkans and a Japanese neutrality pact with Russia were still insufficient to sway Hitler from his now determined course of action: a life and death struggle against the Soviet Union. As a result, the changes in Barbarossa were primarily matters of detail, not of substance. On January 31, deployment instructions were issued.[5] They paralleled the December directive but specified more clearly the roles of the Luftwaffe—destruction of the Soviet air force as well as support of the ground forces. On March 17, the December directive was altered to reflect changes in the northern and southern portions of the operation.[6] Twelfth Army, rather than to undertake a sweeping movement out of Romania, was now merely to tie down the enemy in that area. In the northern and middle Finnish sectors, OKW instead of OKH was to issue the necessary orders. In addition, Hitler made it clear to the military that the campaign was more than simply a military struggle; it was also an ideological one in which he envisioned the liquidation of the "Jewish-Bolshevik intelligentsia." Most of the generals, including Halder, seemed to accept Hitler's premises.

The German diversions into Yugoslavia and Greece during April and in Crete in May, which involved twenty-nine Wehrmacht divisions, were not the decisive factor in putting off Barbarossa. German planners had originally set May 15 as the earliest possible, not the final, execution date for Barbarossa, and late spring rains meant that that date would have to be set back. More important, as brought out earlier, the main reasons for the delay were the difficulty of getting ready and the lack of equipment from the Reich rather than operations in the Balkans. On April 30, Hitler met with his advisers and declared June 22 as the attack day (B-Tag). As throughout the planning process, the military leadership did not protest, for they shared with Hitler the conviction that the Wehrmacht would defeat the Soviets soundly in a swift battle of annihilation. Their usual pessimism had given way to unbridled optimism.

Throughout the period, Britain's involvement in the potential Russo-German conflict was minimal. The Germans accepted that the Soviets would ally with the British once warfare in Russia had broken out, but by that time it would be too late for Stalin and his comrades to stave off ultimate defeat. During the spring, Churchill, through Ultra intercepts, was able to inform Stalin of a possible German attack; the Soviet dictator, however, seemingly swept aside these warnings, along with information from his own intelligence services.[7] As it turned out, Stalin did not exclude the possibility of an invasion but expected Germany to make peace overtures toward the British, or perhaps even conclude a pact with them, before turning toward Russia. He was therefore surprised and unprepared for the onslaught when it came.[8]

While both sides realized the Soviets could ultimately muster more forces than the Germans, at the beginning the opposing forces were relatively equal (table 7-1).[9] The 148 German combat divisions (plus 4 in Finland) consisted of 19 panzer (plus 3 brigades), 14 motorized, 111 infantry, 1 cavalry, and 2 mountain divisions. Added to this number were 14 Romanian and 21 Finnish divisions ready to enter the battle, and other allies were to furnish troops soon after the fighting commenced. The German forces' 3,350 tanks included 281 Panzer Is, 743 IIs, 808 35-ton Czech and 38-ton models, 979 IIIs, and 444 IVs.[10] In addition, the Wehrmacht had 7,184 artillery pieces (4,760 light guns, 104 88s, 2,252 heavy guns, and 68 special high-angle and flat trajectory guns), 600,000 motor vehicles, and 625,000 horses.[11] Of the 2,713 German aircraft, 2,080 were in service on June 22—approximately 1,200 were bombers, 750 fighters, and 130 reconnaissance aircraft.[12] A number of Germany's allies—Italy, Finland, Romania, Hungary, Croatia, and Slovakia—contributed another 900 aircraft to the Axis cause. Nevertheless, the aircraft total was little more

TABLE 7-1
Opposing Forces at the Onset of Barbarossa, June 1941

	Germany	USSR
Divisions	148	170 and 2 brigades
Personnel	3.6 million	2.9 million
Tanks	3,350	1,800 heavy and medium
Aircraft	2,713	1,540 (plus many older)

than two-thirds of the 5,446 (some of them admittedly second-rate) the Luftwaffe had available at the onset of the Battle of France. In other words, the Germans started the much more demanding Barbarossa campaign with less air strength than they had had the year before. Losses over France and Britain and a relatively static production rate obviously had hampered air preparations in 1941.[13]

Looking at the German order of battle from another angle shows that 28 of the divisions were under Field Marshal von Leeb's Army Group North.[14] Six of these were armored and motorized divisions of General Hoepner's Panzer Group 4. In Field Marshal von Bock's Army Group Center were 50 divisions, with an equivalent of 10 armored and 6 motorized divisions as part of Guderian's Panzer Group 2 and Hoth's Panzer Group 3. Von Rundstedt's Army Group South of 40 German divisions included 6 armored and 3 motorized divisions under von Kleist's Panzer Group 1. Thirty divisions were in reserve. The infantry commanders of the various armies included a number of famous generals—George von Küchler, Ernst Busch, Adolf Strauss, Günther von Kluge, Maximilian von Weichs, and Walter von Reichenau. Providing air support to Army Group North was General Alfred Keller's Air Fleet 1 with 592 aircraft (including transports).[15] Supporting the crucial Army Group Center was Field Marshal Kesselring's Air Fleet 2 with 1,367 aircraft, and assisting Army Group South was General Lohr's Air Fleet 4 with 887 aircraft. The small Air Fleet 5 was to handle special assignments in the north. As for the navy, its forces were concentrating on the trade war in the west, and its activities in the Baltic were therefore limited primarily to defense and supply duties. Nevertheless, the German army and air force, in both quantity and quality, presented the Russians with a truly formidable opponent.

Barbarossa basically went through three phases.[16] During the first phase, the month between June 22 and July 22, the Wehrmacht made large gains, although advances in the south were not so great as those on the central and northern fronts. The second phase, between July 22 and September 29, featured a German pause to rest and refurbish, diversions of mobile forces north and south, and preparations for the assault against Moscow. The last phase, Operation Typhoon, started on September 30 and lasted until the Soviet counteroffensive on December 5, during which time the Germans were engaged in a bitter struggle against the Red Army while attempting to bring the operation to a successful conclusion.

The June 22 attack indeed surprised the Russians, and initial reports gave every indication of an early victory for the Germans. On the morning of the invasion, Army Group Center reported that its Fourth Army was making good progress against slight resistance and that its Ninth Army was encountering only weak opposition and light artillery fire.[17] The next day, it was noted in OKH's war diary that "in all places along the eastern front, they were exploiting their successful surprise attack of the first day," that "the Luftwaffe

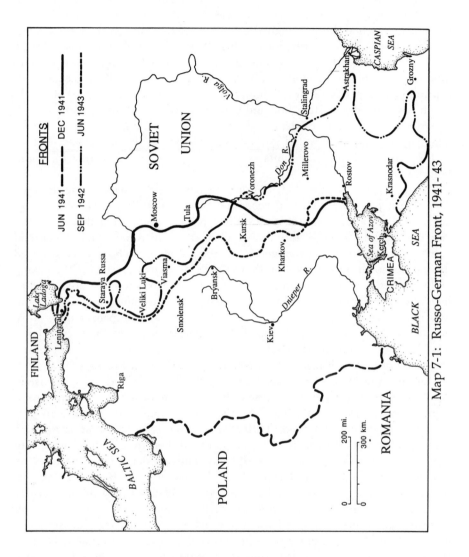

Map 7-1: Russo-German Front, 1941- 43

had achieved air mastery," and that "enemy border defenses had been breached in many places."[18] In the north, on July 1, Riga was taken, and to the east, on July 5, the city of Ostrov. The latter victory opened the way toward Leningrad. At the same time, Finnish troops advanced toward Leningrad from the north. In the south, Lvov was captured on June 30, and mobile formations reached Zitomir, eighty miles west of Kiev on July 9. In the center, German forces swung north on the Pripet Marshes and approached Minsk on June 24. The city fell on June 28. During the first seventeen days of fighting, 324,000 Red soldiers, 3,300 tanks, and 1,800 artillery pieces were captured on the central front alone. On July 8, the battle for Smolensk, 400 miles from the starting line and 230 miles west of Moscow, commenced. Despite fierce Soviet resistance, it and the surrounding area were finally taken by July 22. The initial goals of Barbarossa had been reached, but all of the army and air force units were in desperate need of refurbishment before moving on.

While the forces paused, Hitler and his advisers decided what to do next. The Führer had always favored economic goals in the north and south, especially in the Ukraine. Keitel, Jodl, and von Kluge supported that view, but von Brauchitsch, Halder, and almost all of the field commanders advocated a drive toward Moscow. Although Halder did not object to temporary armored diversions north and south, for their timely use could result in the taking of numerous prisoners, he much preferred the Moscow alternative. Hitler had already sent out a directive proposing the diversion on July 19, but four days later he rescinded it and acknowledged that the panzer units were not yet ready to undertake the northern and southern operations. Nevertheless, Hitler still wanted Hoth's Panzer Group 3 to advance to the Leningrad area and Guderian's Panzer Group 2 to move south to east of Kiev.[19]

During August, the generals continued to press for a Moscow offensive. On August 4, Hitler met with a number of his commanders at Army Group Center headquarters at Borissov. Neither he nor they were willing to give way, and during the discussion Hitler went so far as to accord Moscow third priority after the investment of Leningrad in the north and an advance into the Donets area in the south. He did not render a decision at the meeting but retired to his headquarters to think the matter over. By August 12, his position was clear. Although issued in terms of flanking movements, Hitler ordered that armored and motorized divisions move north to protect the eastern flank while Leningrad was encircled and that the exposed southern flank of Army Group Center be relieved by the southern diversion. Despite the army's persistence in disputing Hitler's decision—the effort included a meeting at Hitler's headquarters on August 24 in which a supposedly enraged Guderian as well as other army leaders backed down before the Führer—one panzer and two motorized divisions from Hoth's panzer group had already been ordered north on August 15.[20] The second phase of Barbarossa had, in effect, begun.

In the northern diversion, Hoth eventually sent six of his fourteen divisions to help Army Group North.[21] Five were mobile—the 18th Motorized, 20th Motorized, 12th Panzer, 19th Panzer, and 20th Panzer—and one infantry—the 110th. While three of the divisions assisted in turning back a Soviet attack south of Lake Ilmen, the other three, constituting General Rudolf Schmidt's XXXIX Corps, were dispatched in the direction of Leningrad. Here some of the heaviest fighting of the campaign took place.

In the meantime, on August 27, Hitler decided on a Moscow operation after all. An overjoyed Halder now wanted to break off active fighting in the north as soon as possible—he set a deadline of September 15—so that the divisions could prepare for the Moscow offensive scheduled for the end of September. But the fierce combat in the Leningrad region did not abate. Though virtually encircled, Soviet troops with civilian help were holding out courageously in the city. The German attempt to link up with the Finns east of Leningrad was not accomplished either, in part because the Finns would not advance farther than the territory they had lost in the Winter War of 1939–40. Field Marshal von Leeb of Army Group North received permission to retain the mobile formations for several extra days, but on September 17, some of them began pulling out and moving south. However, Schmidt's corps was still too heavily engaged to be relieved. By September 24, the 12th Panzer division was down to 4,487 men and had 54 tanks in commission, about one-third of its allotted complement.[22] The 28th Motorized had only 5,940 troops; 18th Motorized had 8,512. These weakened divisions never did move south. Eventually they disappeared from the order of battle altogether, and their remaining soldiers were integrated into other units. The other two mobile divisions—the 19th and 20th Panzers—were in better shape, but the 19th was facing such stiff opposition that it could not withdraw until October 1. Only the 20th Panzer was able to return in time to participate in the initial drive toward Moscow. Therefore, of the five mobile divisions involved in the northern diversion, only one returned on time for Typhoon.

In the south, the goal of Guderian's Panzer Group 3's diversion was to push south and meet up with armored formations from Army Group South east of Kiev.[23] Six divisions—the 3rd, 4th, 17th, and 18th Panzer and the 10th and 28th Motorized—started the operation. Though in a weakened condition because of the extended fighting just prior to the August 25 starting date, they advanced fifty miles the first day, entering the Ukraine by evening. Nevertheless, General Baron Geyr von Schweppenburg's XXIV Armored Corps already showed signs of strain because of insufficient gasoline and supplies. By August 29 with only one of Geyr's three divisions capable of offensive operations, the southerly thrust had come to a halt. Relief soon arrived in the form of one and a half armored divisions, the SS Reich Division and Gross Deutschland Regiment, and on September 1, with two days' supply of gasoline now available, the advance resumed.

Assisted by seven infantry divisions from General Baron von Weichs's

Second Army protecting the western flank and by three and a half of Panzer Group 2's mobile formations on the eastern flank, the remaining armored forces made substantial progress. On September 10, Guderian began anticipating a junction of his panzer divisions with Army Group South. On the night of September 14, the encircling movement was achieved, and the trap closed east of Kiev. During the ensuing week, nearly 400,000 prisoners were taken in the pocket that had been formed. Kiev itself fell on September 19. Three days later, Guderian's and von Weichs's depleted divisions were directed to return north and to prepare for the Moscow operation. The good news for the Germans was that all of the seven and a half mobile divisions involved in the Ukranian diversion were available for Typhoon. The bad news was that both the northern and the southern diversions had obviously enacted a heavy toll in fatigue, casualties, and destroyed and damaged equipment.

Only a herculean logistics effort made the Moscow offensive, the third and final phase of Barbarossa, possible. By September 29, the mobile formations had a three-to-five days' supply of gasoline and adequate ammunition and provisions for the initial push.[24] By utilizing divisions from Army Groups North and South, the Germans were able to assemble a force of 70 attack divisions, including 14 panzer and 8 motorized divisions, although their tank strength was only 60 percent of establishment. They were supported by Air Fleet 2 with 1,387 aircraft. Facing them, the Soviets had 92 smaller divisions and 13 tank brigades, but only 770 tanks and 364 planes were available.[25]

Typhoon was designed to converge on Moscow from three directions. The southern thrust began on September 30, those from the north and center two days later. In all instances, the Wehrmacht once again made sizable gains. Army Group Center reported that "the enemy at least at the time of the attack was surprised. Its defensive measures have been less than expected."[26] Hitler seemed confirmed in his view that Soviet forces were at the end of their tether. By October 4, Orel in the south, Vyasma in the middle, and Kalinin in the north had been taken. Only on October 7 did Army Group Center show signs of slowing because of a lack of gasoline. On that same day, the first snow fell. By October 12, infantry divisions had begun replacing the wornout panzer formations, a process which continued throughout the month.[27] The supply effort simply could not be sustained, however. In November and early December, the Wehrmacht unleashed several desperate attempts to take Moscow, but the last one fell twenty-one miles short of the capital. A Soviet counterattack, bolstered by forces returning from the east, started on December 5 and succeeded in driving back the hard-pressed German soldiers. By this time, the infantry units were down to 50 percent of their combat strength.[28] The number of tanks in commission for Panzer Army 2 was 168, or 17 percent of its normal number, and only 960 of the 1,960 front-line aircraft available in the east, or 50.1 percent, were ready for operations. In effect, Hitler's belief that the Red Army was in worse shape than the Wehrmacht had proved to be incorrect.[29]

On December 8, Hitler called for German forces, except those in the Crimea, to go over to the defensive.[30] About this time, the army underwent a leadership crisis, in which a number of field commanders and also army head von Brauchitsch were dismissed from their positions. The Führer, as discussed earlier, took over as army commander-in-chief. One of his first orders was to exhort the troops not to retreat under any circumstances.[31] While the commanders at the time widely denounced the order as ridiculous and impractical, most historians now accept the fact that by not engaging in a general retreat and by withdrawing only as a last resort, German forces averted what might have been an even worse disaster.

During the entire time, between June 22 and the end of December, the British contribution to the Russian cause was meager at best.[32] Other than immediately allying with the Soviets, sending a small expedition to Spitz-bergen Island, convoying an occasional northern shipment with war equipment, warning them of the impending Moscow counterattack, and jointly taking over a corridor in Iran for the future transport of supplies, the British were able to do little. On September 13, Stalin requested his western ally to send twenty-five to thirty divisions to southern Russia to help out. Even if the Iranian route could have handled such a large contingent of troops, the British at best thought they could spare two divisions. They felt to offer the Russians such a paltry contribution would be little more than an insult. Churchill and his unofficial American ally did attempt, however, to establish cordial relations with the Soviets, and even though Stalin's responses to their notes were often filled with suspicion and ingratitude, the foundation for a more meaningful relationship began to evolve.

In the end, against the expectations of the British and the Americans as well as the Germans, the Soviets held out. The obvious question is, how was this possible? In this instance, as is often the case, the reasons were a combination of German errors and Soviet fortitude. Despite the campaign's overriding importance, the Germans were simply not prepared for the personnel and equipment losses they suffered. Their casualties in the six months after June 22 totaled 918,000, or approximately 28.7 percent of all their soldiers in the east.[33] Their loss of 3,254 panzers and assault guns and 6,000 aircraft meant that the Luftwaffe exhausted more than its entire eastern inventory during the last half of 1941. In other words, German resources as well as their productive capacity were insufficient to overcome the attrition and the maintenance and repair difficulties brought on by Barbarossa. Only a larger economic infrastructure would have allowed them to fight the protracted war in which they now found themselves.

The Soviets, too, suffered horrible losses. By the end of 1941, OKH estimated that Germany had taken 3.5 million prisoners, and that the Soviets had lost 20,000 tanks and 2,300 aircraft. While these figures are undoubtedly high, at least for tanks, they do show the extent of Russia's problem. Yet the Red Army's replacement capabilities were greater than those of the Germans.[34] Whereas the 30 divisions in OKH's reserve were soon expended and allied reinforcements proved disappointing, in part because of a lack of equipment, Soviet combat soldiers on December 1 totaled more than 4 million, a larger number than they had started with on June 22. Moreover, once having overcome the initial defeats, Soviet troops acquitted themselves well and often fought tenaciously against the German invader. In addition, although the Soviet air force was virtually destroyed at first, it was beginning to recover by year's end, and Russian tank forces had proved much more formidable than the Germans had expected. With the failure of Barbarossa, Germany knew it was in for a long war, an alternative that Hitler had hoped at all cost to avoid. As brought out in the German "official" history, his political and ideological conceptions had been too unrealistic to secure the victory he and his commanders sought.

When, then, was the decisive moment in the Barbarossa campaign? Rather than one specific turning point, probably an accumulation of errors—unrealistic goals, underestimation of the enemy, insufficient resources—led to its failure. Once Germany became enmeshed on its eastern front, it could not, or would not, extricate itself until the campaign was drawn to its bloody conclusion. When the end came in 1945, it was far worse than the Germans could ever have imagined.

As early as November 11, 1941, Hitler realized that Moscow could probably not be taken. He proposed for 1942 a series of eastern offensives, the most important of which was to secure the Caucasian oil fields.[35] OKH had already been thinking along the same lines and had started planning another eastern campaign.[36] By December, with losses on the southern front and with the Soviet counteroffensive west of Moscow, Hitler decided that wide-ranging offensives all along the front were no longer feasible and that an attack in the south was the best option available.

December was a decisive month in other ways. The large number of army commanders dismissed or retired included, not only von Brauchitsch, but also the heads of all three eastern army groups—von Rundstedt, von Bock, and von Leeb (the latter on January 15). Hitler's "take over" as army commander-in-chief, with all of the prerogatives associated with that position, meant, among other things, that the military latitude given to field commanders in the east would seldom be tolerated in the future.[37] In addition, it now became the normal procedure for OKH and its chief of staff to have the dominant say in the east and for OKW to oversee the other theaters. The December crisis also had broader, grand strategic implications.[38] Hitler's desire for a "world Blitzkrieg" had been thwarted, but the war of extermination against the dreaded Soviet enemy still begged solution. To defeat the Soviet Union—and Britain and now the United States as well—would require large increases in war production. Hence, in Hitler's eyes, a southern offensive to capture the rich oil and coal regions of the USSR was more imperative than ever. Halder, though skeptical for a while of any eastern undertaking, also eventually accepted the importance of gaining control of additional Soviet resources.[39] As a result, during January, large increases were called for in the armament and tank-production programs.[40]

By February, even though Russian counterattacks continued, Hitler had regained his confidence, and throughout the spring he became obsessed with preparing for a new summer offensive against the Soviets.[41] Since his military critics were gone and Halder had come around to his thinking, no one stood in his way. On February 12, OKH issued a directive for regrouping and refurbishing its forces in the east prior to their use during the summer.[42] The directive also placed special emphasis on an operation in the south.

During March, the Red Army offensives finally came to a halt and the front stabilized. On March 28, OKH showed its basic agreement with Hitler by presenting him with a plan which closely paralleled his wishes.[43] It proposed, after preliminary operations, several southern thrusts, of which the final goal, to be reached by September, was the Caucasus. In the meantime, operations on the central and northern fronts were to await the outcome of the southern offensive. Hitler naturally approved the army plan, and he turned it over to OKW to write an implementing directive. He then made substantial revisions to the earlier draft before it was issued. Operation Blue was truly to be Hitler's campaign.

On Easter Sunday, April 5, Führer Directive No. 41 was transmitted to the subordinate commands.[44] The operation was to be mounted along the 450-mile southern front. Preliminary attacks, including ones to complete the take over of the Kerch and Crimean peninsulas to the south, were to be completed first, however. Since German forces could not be readied all at once, the main operation was to be "carried out . . . in a series of successive attacks, which were, however, connected or supplementary to each other." Divisions in the northern attack, which was to begin any time after June 15, were to break through the front south of Orel, drive forward, and occupy Voronezh, a distance of some 125 miles.[45] This initial phase was to be completed by July 15. The Voronezh formations were then to head south along the Don River to support a second attack, which was to have been launched from around Kharkov. These two thrusts were to form a pincer that would destroy large numbers of Russian soldiers west of the Don. Once this objective had been accomplished, by about August 15, a third phase was to be instituted. The Don force was to move southeast and meet a third mobile group already advancing out of the Taganrog-Artemovsk area west of Rostov. The combined armies were then to proceed to Stalingrad, approximately 300 miles from the starting line. During the final phase, German units were to advance from several directions another 300 miles into the Caucasus. The directive made clear that an extended flank to the north would pose a definite problem and that German, along with Hungarian, Italian, and Romanian, troops would have to be deployed there to shield the main offensive. The air force's tasks were to gain air superiority and to support the advancing armies. The navy was to help, if possible, by assembling a fleet in the Black Sea to assist in supplying the southern armies.

During May, the Germans prepared for a limited offensive south of Kharkov, but before it could be launched, the Russians, on May 12, undertook their own assault to gain the city.[46] The Germans soon blunted the attack, taking an estimated 200,000 Soviet prisoners in the process. Meanwhile, between May 8 and 18, the German Eleventh Army took over the Kerch Peninsula. On June 7, it attacked the besieged Sevastopol in the Crimea and finally captured it nearly a month later. Any threat to Operation Blue from the south was thus erased.

On May 27, Blue was still scheduled to start on June 15, but on June 1, OKH decided to postpone Blue as well as two preliminary operations east of Isjum and at Volchansk.[47] The Volchansk attack was finally carried through between June 10 and 15, and the Isjum assault, between June 22 and 25. As a result, Blue was reset for June 28.

At the time of the attack, the Germans had assembled 67⅔ of its own divisions, including 9 panzer and 5 motorized formations.[48] Its Romanian, Hungarian, and Italian allies initially contributed 22½ divisions plus 1 Slovakian security division. The southern forces were divided into two army groups, South and A. Field Marshal von Bock's Army Group South was to direct the northern portion and control three armies—the Second, the Fourth Panzer, and the Sixth. Von List's Army Group A, which was to handle the southern sector, also had three armies under it—the First Panzer, the Seventeenth, and the Eleventh, although the last, heavily involved in the Crimea, was not available for the initial stages of Blue. On the central and northern fronts, the Wehrmacht had 98⅔ additional German and foreign SS divisions as well as one Hungarian and one Spanish division. Of a total field-army strength of 3,950,000 soldiers in all theaters, 2,847,000 were deployed in the east.[49] In addition, the Germans had 3,300 tanks and approximately 2,750 aircraft, of which 1,500 were allocated to the southern offensive.[50] Opposing them, the Soviet forces numbered 5,100,000 troops along the entire front, with 3,900 tanks and 2,200 combat aircraft, although a considerable proportion of their forces were located in the center rather than in the south when the German offensive opened.

The German initial attack was immediately successful. Mobile forces made considerable advances, and on June 30th, the codename for the operation was changed from Blue to Brunswick.[51] On that same day, the second thrust east of Kharkov began. On July 2, the two pincers met. There followed a series of discussions among Hitler, Halder, and von Bock, the commander of Army Group South, soon to be renamed Army Group B. At first, Hitler gave Bock permission to take Voronezh to the east across the Don, but after Bock's forces seemingly had difficulties capturing it, Hitler forbade using the armored divisions for such a minor objective as Voronezh. He relented on July 6, however, after portions of Hoth's Fourth Panzer Army had already occupied the city. During this time, most of the Russian soldiers were able to retreat east of the Don, with only 70,000 troops caught in Germany's first envelopment.

Hoth's army then headed southeast to meet the First Panzer Army, which, having hurried up its timetable, began a third thrust on the southern portion of the front on July 9. Although both armies made substantial gains, Hitler was still disappointed with the "slow" progress of Army Group B's mobile divisions after leaving Voronezh. On July 13, he had von Bock replaced by General von Weichs. Though Bock protested that any problems the motorized divisions had had was a result of insufficient fuel, the change of command was not rescinded, and von Bock was never recalled to active duty. At the same time, Hitler decided to transfer Hoth's panzer army from Army Group B in the north to Army Group A in the south so that it could assist in the encirclement of Russian forces in the great bend of the Don. On July 17, the Führer instructed the panzer armies to change course and help in taking Rostov. Even though the tactic worked and the city fell on July 23, the anticipated large number of Soviet prisoners again did not materialize, and German armor had been used for a task better left to infantry divisions.

Nevertheless, also on July 23, an elated Hitler decided it was no longer necessary to have German forces first move toward Stalingrad and then, with other divisions, pull out of the Rostov area to concentrate on reaching the Caucasus. Instead, his Directive No. 45 stipulated that both operations were to be undertaken at the same time.[52] Army Group A, with the bulk of the armor, including most of the Fourth and First Panzer armies, was to destroy the Red Army formations that had escaped southeast of Rostov, clear the area along the Black Sea, and then head toward the Maikop, Grozny, and Baku oil fields. Maikop was less than two hundred miles away, but Grozny was nearly four hundred miles to the southeast, and Baku, seven hundred miles. In addition, he split von Manstein's Eleventh Army. Only two of the seven divisions were to assist in the Caucasus push; the other five were to move north and to help prepare for the capture of Leningrad. Thus began a series of orders and counterorders that did little but dissipate Eleventh Army's contribution and disperse Wehrmacht forces in general. Army Group B, for its part, was to move forward to Stalingrad, crush the Soviet armies expected to be concentrated there, occupy the city, and then have mobile divisions proceed along the Volga to Astrakhan so as to block that waterway. After both operations got underway, Hitler again changed his mind on the disposition of forces. On July 31, he had most of Fourth Panzer Army redeploy so that it could push toward Stalingrad from the south.

During August and September, the offensives continued but, as Earl Ziemke has stated, "without attaining any of the major objectives." Seventeenth Army did not clear the Black Sea coast. Maikop was taken on August 9, but its oil-field equipment had already been destroyed. Grozny was not reached because the mobile formations lacked fuel. The Fourth Panzer and General

Friedrich Paulus's Sixth Army closed in on Stalingrad, but the city remained in Soviet hands. Despite 2,490,000 German troops deployed in 163½ divisions plus 648,000 other Axis soldiers in 51⅓ divisions, the Red Army was holding its own.[53]

Another German leadership crisis ensued during September. As pointed out earlier, Jodl was sent to examine the situation on the Caucasus front, where he concluded that List's army group was overextended and that a mountain corps should be held back rather than advancing farther. When Jodl gave his report to the Führer, the latter was so enraged that he thought about dismissing both Jodl and Keitel. Eventually he decided merely not to eat with them. Nevertheless, relations between Hitler and his OKW associates were cool for some months. List was dismissed, and Hitler himself assumed command of Army Group A, a position he relinquished only on November 23 to von Kleist as the Stalingrad crisis deepened. Perhaps more significantly, on September 24, Halder was retired and replaced by a relative unknown, General Kurt Zeitzler, whose most recent assignment had been as chief of staff to von Rundstedt in the west. Upon reporting to Hitler's new headquarters near Vinnitsa in the Ukraine, Zeitzler relates, he found "a most peculiar atmosphere and situation as a result of the stalled [eastern] offensive. This atmosphere was indescribable and for a general staff officer who had served at the front incredible. Mistrust and exasperation everywhere. No one seemed to trust anyone else, and Hitler mistrusted everyone."[54] To Zeitzler's credit, he set about to restore Hitler's trust in OKH, to render him timely advice based on accurate information, and to support the field commanders while allowing them as much operational latitude as possible. He never succeeded in reaching any of these goals, though he did exclude Jodl from briefing the Führer on developments on the Russian Front, thereby cutting off OKW from exercising any substantial influence in that theater. Yet by now, Hitler was heavily involved in all the major and some minor decisions related to Brunswick.

During October, it became clear that the main German effort would continue against Stalingrad.[55] On October 14, Hitler directed that all offensive operations, except those still in progress—meaning Stalingrad and some local battles—were to cease and German armies were to go over to the defensive.[56] The situation at Stalingrad remained inconclusive. By this time the Germans had bridgeheads up to the Volga, thereby denying its use to the Soviets to transport supplies north, and half of the city was under German control. However, German infantry strength was low, its ammunition and fuel at times were running out, and its extended flank to the north was of increasing concern. Moreover, the Soviets were building up their forces in the area, and though Hitler was well aware of the threat, he did not expect a Soviet offensive until December.

But on November 19, the Red Army and Air Force struck. Despite the heavy summer and fall losses, the Soviet field army had increased to 6,124,000 troops, with 77,734 guns and mortars, 6,956 tanks, and 3,254 aircraft.[57] Over one million troops were located in the Stalingrad sector alone. The Germans still had 258 divisions and 16 brigades in the east, of which 66 divisions and 13 brigades belonged to their satellites, but virtually all of the formations were underequipped and under strength. The Russians had an equivalent of 416 divisions. They first attacked the Romanian Third Army north of the city and broke through its lines by early afternoon. The next day, Soviet divisions broached the Fourth Panzer and Romanian Fourth Army lines south of Stalingrad. By the 23rd, they had surrounded and cut off German forces in a cauldron thirty-five by twenty miles west of, and including, the city. About 240,000 German, Romanian, and Croatian soldiers were trapped in the pocket.

The Germans appreciated the problem at hand, but none of the proposed alternatives were carried through with sufficient resolve or timeliness. The vain though talented von Manstein was named commander of the new Army Group Don, to be made up of the embattled Sixth, Fourth Panzer, and Third and Fourth Romanian armies. Sixth Army's Paulus was to direct operations inside the pocket. One of the selected alternatives was to take Göring up on his boast that the trapped Axis units could be supplied by air. About 600 tons of supplies per day were required; the best the overextended Luftwaffe ever averaged was approximately 120 tons per day. On December 12, German panzer forces, after numerous delays, started executing another alternative by opening a drive to reach Paulus's beleaguered formations. At one point, von Manstein's armor got to within thirty miles of the pocket. At this juncture, Paulus might have had his forces attempt to break out, but he had been directed by Hitler to stay put until the time was right. It never became right, and Manstein broke off the attempt on December 23. With cold weather, heavy combat, and a lack of essential supplies exacting a terrible toll, the Sixth Army could not be saved. On January 22, Paulus asked his superiors for permission to open surrender negotiations. Though refused permission and ordered to continue resisting, by January 31, German units had no alternative but to begin laying down their arms, a process which ended on February 2. The cost for the Germans was approximately 238,000 soldiers lost. It was a staggering defeat.

After Stalingrad, Stalin decided on a series of offensives all along the front. Germany's Army Group A had already in January extricated itself from the Caucasus region, part of its troops by way of Rostov and part across the Kerch Peninsula to the Crimea, and the Red Army proceeded to overextend itself by undertaking too many operations all along the front. The operations ended in March with the noose around Leningrad loosened to some extent, but with no meaningful Soviet gains. In fact, Kharkov in the Ukraine, which had been taken by Russian forces in February, was retaken by the Germans by mid-March, and Army Group South advanced all the way to the Donets River before stopping. The front now stabilized, and the combatants began preparing for another round.

Throughout 1942, British assistance to the Soviets continued to be minimal.[58] British leaders wanted to help their eastern ally in some tangible way, but with the strain on resources created by Japanese advances in Southeast Asia and the Pacific and by German and Italian forces in North Africa, there was little the British felt they could do. They did ship some goods to Russia via the northern route, but the convoys had to be stopped periodically because of heavy losses, and the Persian transportation corridor was still not well developed. The Soviets had the obvious solution—open up a second front in the west. Despite American as well as Soviet pressure, however, Churchill and the British chiefs were reluctant to undertake such an operation. In Soviet eyes, the Anglo-American invasion of northwestern Africa was hardly an adequate substitute. For a short time, Stalin seemed interested in Churchill's proposal to send a combined British and American air force to the Caucasus region, but the dictator's interest in the project flagged when his own situation brightened on his southern front. Another British–US proposal, regarding the exchange of technical information was likewise turned aside. The Soviets continued to be suspicious of their western partners throughout the war.

For the Germans, 1942 had indeed been a calamitous year. Hitler and the other German leaders, if not the public, understood the magnitude of the catastrophe. What had started so promisingly in late June had ended in disaster the following February. They now realized that they had had insufficient forces and equipment to carry out the operations they had attempted in 1942 and that they increasingly had had to turn to their allies for help in their struggle against the Soviet Union.[59] They also rationalized that their Axis partners—in North Africa and in Russia—had let them down and were responsible for many of their difficulties. Now more fully in control than ever before, Hitler believed the situation could be turned again in Germany's favor: despite Stalingrad, the Wehrmacht was still a substantial force which could hold its own against any enemy; and if the German military fought hard enough and long enough, the unnatural coalition arrayed against them might well fall apart. What Hitler and his cohorts failed to appreciate sufficiently was that with all of the human and material resources the Allies now had at their disposal, the Germans had no chance of winning at all.[60]

Fighting during the spring of 1943 did not completely abate. The Germans pulled out of several exposed salients—one at Demjansk south of Lake Ilmen in February and in the Rzhev-Vyasma area in March—and some local actions took place all along the front as well.[61] The main concern for both sides, however, was what to do next. For the Germans, several considerations had to be taken into account. Their forces had suffered horribly during the past six months, and many of the OKW and OKH generals thought that the best solution might be for the Wehrmacht in the east to remain on the defensive throughout 1943. Lending support to this view was the added possibility that the Allies would launch an invasion of southern or western Europe. The only way the Germans could defend those areas was by withdrawing units from the Soviet theater. Nevertheless, although Hitler was relatively subdued during the spring and did not rail at his commanders for the recent defeats, he could not bring himself to accept a defensive orientation. From his standpoint, to stay on the defensive for a prolonged period was unthinkable, especially since it would probably mean giving up certain areas, including prime industrial and agricultural land in southern Russia.

On March 13, therefore, Hitler had OKH issue Operation Order No. 5.[62] Titled "Directive for the Conduct of the War during the Ensuing Months," it emphasized Germany's preempting anticipated Soviet offensives by undertaking an offensive of its own. Hitler and his advisors concluded that the best place to conduct an operation was a 125-by-75-mile salient west of Kursk, which could be attacked by von Kluge's Army Group Center from the north and by von Manstein's Army Group South from the south. By straightening out this deep bulge along with other places along the front, the Germans would not only consolidate their defenses, but also keep the Russians off balance for some months.[63] The order stipulated no specific date for the operation, but because of the necessity of attacking after the muddy period but before the Soviets could get their forces ready, the army groups were to report their intentions to OKH by March 25. The order further indicated that, following the Kursk operation and anytime after the first of July, an operation against Leningrad might well be mounted.

Later in March, as a result of Hoth's Fourth Panzer Army's clearing an area west of the Donets River in the south, an opportunity seemed to present itself for taking over a bulge southeast of Kharkov and west of Kupyansk. The favorable situation led Hitler to order plans be drawn up for two operations, Hawk and Panther. The plans were to be worked out immediately so that German forces could proceed once the swollen Donets had receded. The three armies given responsibility for conducting Hawk and Panther—the First and Fourth Panzer armies and Armeeabteilung Kempf—were lukewarm about the offensives, for their divisions were badly in need of rest and refurbishment. Reflecting their concern, an order from Hitler on April 2 stipulated that Hawk, the projected thrust across the river, was to begin by April 17. If that proved impossible, then Panther, the assault designed to close to the Krasnaya River, was to be implemented instead anytime after May 1. If neither were possible, German formations were to turn their attention to the Kursk operation, now codenamed Citadel. The three offensives were closely related, for if Hawk and Panther succeeded, Soviet forces south of the Kursk salient would no longer pose a flanking threat while Citadel was being carried out.

Hawk and Panther were never executed, however. The main reason was that during the first two weeks of April, Hitler definitely decided on the

Kursk operation.[64] On April 15, OKW circulated the pertinent Operation Order No. 6, the introductory section of which made clear Hitler's resolve: "the best formations, the best weapons, the best leaders, large amounts of ammunition are to be assembled at the [Kursk] strongpoint. Every officer, every enlisted man must be imbued with the decisive significance of this attack. The victory at Kursk must shine like a beacon for the world."[65] The assaults were to be carried through in a traditional manner, with mobile forces moving out of Belgorod in the south and from south of Orel in the north and the pincers coming together at Kursk. The air force was to begin moving all available aircraft near the salient to help out. The order further emphasized the importance of speed and deception. The earliest date the operation could be implemented was May 3, and preparations for Panther, among other measures, were to serve as a cover for the actual operation. The order was now turned over to the army groups for detailed planning.

At the time the order was issued, Hitler realized the risks involved. The Red Army was strong both north and south of the bulge, and the movement of additional Soviet forces toward Kursk had already been detected. These factors, combined with protests from the German army commanders, especially from General Walter Model of Ninth Army, that they could not get their troops ready by May 3, led to Citadel's being postponed a number of times. It turned out that on May 3 Hitler called for a meeting of his commanders and other leaders the next day at Munich to set a new date.[66] In attendance were Manstein and Kluge among the field commanders, and Keitel, Jodl, Zeitzler, Luftwaffe Chief of Staff Jeschonnek, and Guderian, recalled as inspector for armored forces, among his advisors. A lengthy discussion ensued. Manstein, who favored an early operation, warned that it had to take place soon to be a success. Kluge was definitely in favor as was Zeitzler and Jeschonnek, although they, too, wanted the operation executed as quickly as possible. Guderian, who hated von Kluge (the feeling was mutual), was opposed, since he expected that the resulting heavy tank losses could not be replaced readily. According to Seaton, Model was not at the meeting, but a letter he had written and made available at the conference clearly indicated his opposition on the grounds of the Soviet buildup in the area. With all of the conflicting opinions, Hitler did not render an immediate decision. He said he wanted to talk with Speer first. After meeting with his armaments minister, the Führer decided to put off Citadel until June 12, when more Panther tanks and assault guns were expected to be available.

Hitler was still uneasy, however, and suggested to Zeitzler later in May that the attack come directly from the west, not from the north and south as had been worked out.[67] It took all of Zeitzler's persuasive powers, plus detailed tables showing the supply and personnel changes that would be required for such an operation, to get Hitler to retain the original plan. At a conference at OKH headquarters on June 10, the military leaders again brought up to Hitler, as they had in April, the possibility of waiting for the Russians to strike first rather than assuming the offensive themselves. Saying that the forces were not ready, in part because the Panther tanks were still not available, Hitler again set back the start of Citadel but gave no specific date for its execution. Meanwhile, both sides continued to build up their forces. On June 18, OKW recommended that Citadel be abandoned and proposed the formation of two strategic reserves to counter possible Allied moves from the south and west as well as to be available for the eastern theater. Hitler responded that, while he appreciated OKW's proposal, he had decided that Citadel go ahead. On June 21, he set July 3 as the day for the attack. Four days later, he pushed back the starting date another two days to July 5. Though seemingly delayed interminably, Citadel was finally to be executed.

After all the procrastinating, why had Hitler opted for the offensive at all?[68] No doubt, his desire to regain the initiative in the east played a role. Just as significant, he felt it would strengthen the morale of the people at home, renew the confidence of the troops at the front, reinvigorate the friendly powers, and restrain neutral countries from joining the enemy. In his mind, these factors made Citadel well worth the risk.

The disparity between the two opponents becomes apparent when one looks at the total numbers.[69] Whereas the Germans had approximately 3,064,000 troops in the east, the Soviets, according to German estimates, had 5,755,000, and although the Italian units had departed, the German total included about 225,000 Romanian, Hungarian, and Spanish soldiers. As for tanks and antitank guns, the Russians had approximately 7,855 and 21,050, the Germans 2,088 and 8,063. For the Kursk battle, the Red Army had initially assembled 1,300,000 personnel and 3,600 tanks; the Wehrmacht, 900,000 men and 1,950 tanks.

Still, one should not underestimate the German force in the sector, for it was formidable. Model's Ninth Army, which was to lead the northern spearhead, had 6 panzer, 1 motorized infantry, and 8 infantry divisions. Backing them up were 730 aircraft of Air Fleet 6. To hold the western portion of the salient, the Second Army had deployed 7½ infantry divisions. Hoth's Fourth Panzer Army of 6 panzer, 5 motorized infantry, and 7 infantry divisions were to be used for the southern thrust, with the 9 divisions of Armeeabteilung Kempf serving as flanking support. Providing air support were 1,100 aircraft attached to Air Fleet 4. In all, the Germans had readied 42 divisions and 1,830 aircraft for the offensive. Moreover, the 1,950 tanks included at least 90 of the powerful 60-ton Tiger tanks with an 88-mm gun and 200 45-ton Panthers with a 75-mm gun. Nevertheless, Germany faced the problem that the Russians, through their own sources as well as through the British, knew where the offensive was coming and consequently had erected a series of defensive barriers designed to blunt the German thrusts. Within two to three miles of the front lines, Soviet soldiers and civilian workers had dug three to five trench lines with numerous weapon emplacements. They had constructed similar emplacements between six and eighteen miles to the rear. A third set of trenches lay at least twenty-five miles back. In between, every village and hill had been amply fortified, and interspersed among the defenses were some 400,000 mines. Such defenses proved impossible for the Germans to overcome.

Between 3:30 and 5:00 a.m. on July 5, the German assaults began.[70] In the south, divisions of the Fourth Panzer Army, spearheaded by Tiger and Panther tanks, attacked along a thirty-five-mile front and advanced up to six miles in some places.[71] On July 6 and 7, despite heavy rains, the German thrusts continued to make progress, but the Soviet defenses were proving formidable, and Red Army reserves were being quickly brought forward. Even more significant were the huge numbers of tanks being massed and moved into battle by both sides. These armored armadas reached upwards of 100 to 200 tanks on occasion, so that eventually 4,000 Russian panzers and nearly 3,000 German panzers and assault guns were involved. Although total losses can only be surmised, the "Gross Deutschland" division went from 300 tanks at the start to only 80 on July 7, and it is certain that Soviet tank strength was reduced to less than half of what it had been at the beginning, with overall Wehrmacht losses being considerably higher.

On July 8, plagued by a lack of air superiority, German momentum, particularly in the north, began to slow. The army group commanders, von Kluge and von Manstein, had used up all of their reserves and had to start calling on divisions from other nearby armies to keep the offensives going. By July 12, Model's northern thrust had stalled completely north of Oklhovatka, and Soviet counteroffensives now began to have an effect. The farthest German penetration had been about eight miles.[72] Also on July 12, in the south, the situation for Hoth's panzer army looked more promising, but a Wehrmacht attempt to take Prokhorovka failed. The casualties on both sides were so heavy that Soviet historians have termed the day's fighting the "slaughter at Prokhorovka."[73] By this time the Germans were losing the initiative, but von Manstein did not call off the southern operation until July 19. The Germans in this sector had penetrated about twenty-two miles at most before the momentum shifted.

In the meantime, three events occurred that had a direct impact on Citadel.[74] Two were strong Soviet offensives north and south of the salient. The one in the north, directed against the German Second Panzer Army, opened on July 12. The Russian move forced von Kluge to divert four divisions and artillery and rocket projectors intended for the Kursk battle to stem the tide east of Orel. Hard combat in this area, known to the Red Army as the Bryansk sector, continued into August. The Germans held on tenaciously, but finally, on August 5, they had to give up Orel and withdraw west. The Soviet southern push, in what was called the Mius sector, commenced on July 17. Though the Soviet move had been anticipated by the Wehrmacht, the new German Sixth Army was forced to give ground, and Red Army troops were able to cross the Mius River. In this instance, the Germans feared that their southern flank at the Kursk salient was threatened and sent armor south to assist in containing the Soviet Mius offensive. Yet in the end, the Red Army could not be stopped. On August 5, Belgorod was taken, and later that month, Kharkov. The Russians now held the initiative on both the southern and the central fronts.

The third event was Hitler's announcement on July 13 that Citadel was not to continue. At the time, von Manstein and von Kluge were meeting with the Führer at his headquarters, and Manstein protested against having to break off the battle, which he mistakenly thought could possibly still succeed. Hitler responded that, even though Citadel was to stop, he would allow Manstein additional time to deal the Russians a limited defeat and thus cut down the possibility of their undertaking an immediate counteroffensive. Hitler made it clear that he was greatly concerned not only about the Soviet threat north and south of Kursk, but also about the Anglo-American landing on Sicily, which had begun four days earlier. In his opinion, since Italian opposition had shown itself weak and Wehrmacht divisions were too few in number, the only way the situation could be restored was to shift German troops there from the east. On July 17, he started to have forces withdrawn from the salient by ordering the II SS Panzer Corps, with three motorized divisions and one infantry regiment, from the area. Initially, it was to assist against the Red Army push to the Mius sector, but once that Soviet drive had been halted, the entire corps was to be sent to Italy. However, that in the end only one division—the SS Adolf Hitler—and II SS Corps personnel were eventually transferred to Italy underlines once again the difficulties the Germans were having in meeting their many commitments.

Citadel therefore ended in almost total failure. Whether it lasted eight days, when Hitler called for it to cease, or fourteen, when Manstein acknowledged that his southern push could not meet its objectives, the result was the same. The Germans had waited too long, had "telegraphed" their plans, and had suffered crippling casualties. The Soviets estimated 70,000 Germans killed, and 2,952 tanks and 1,392 aircraft destroyed.[75]

While these figures are undoubtedly too high, they make us realize that the German losses had been devastating. This time, moreover, the Soviet counteroffensives did not come to a halt until they had achieved large-scale advances. In fact, by the end of 1943, Kiev in the south and Smolensk in the center were firmly in Russian hands, and the siege around Leningrad in the north was about to be lifted. After Kursk, if not before, the Soviets had definitely assumed the upper hand. It would continue that way until the end.

A comparison of Barbarossa, Blue/Brunswick, and Citadel makes clear the futility of Germany's campaigns in the east. While it might be argued that the Germans should never have attacked the Soviet Union in the first place, the fact remains that once they became enmeshed, they could not or would not extricate themselves from the struggle. Leaving aside their bestial treatment of the population, in which the military was also deeply involved, the Germans simply did not have the resources to prevail against the Soviets in an extended land war.[76] The Wehrmacht had been able to ready relatively comparable numbers in the east in 1941 and in 1943—about 3,000,000 combat troops, 2,700 aircraft, and 3,000 tanks—but the extent of their operations continually decreased, so that by the time of Kursk, their offensive was more of a spoiling action than a true strategic undertaking.

Their strategic vision diminished as well. In 1941, the German goal was to establish control over most of European Russia by the end of the year. By 1942, their objective was to take over all the industrial and oil-producing regions in the south. The implication was that the accomplishment of these tasks would eventually lead to Russia's demise, but no date was set as to when this might ever occur. In 1943, it is difficult to discern any overall strategy except that Germany hoped to hold on, to keep the Red Army and air force off balance with small attacks, and perhaps to build up its own strength to the point that the Wehrmacht could do something meaningful in the east in the future. This type of thinking was not conducive to bringing the war, any war, to a successful conclusion.

The British assistance to the Soviets, and that of the Americans and the Canadians, remained in the area of supplies. At first, Stalin and the other Kremlin leaders might have been willing to accept divisions and air wings, but the Western Allies were in no position to provide them. By the time the British and the Americans could provide more than token forces, the Soviets did not want them. Supplies, especially in the form of trucks and jeeps, industrial equipment, and raw materials, were readily accepted, but the more than 10,000 tanks sent between June 1941 and April 1944 were less sought after because the Soviets preferred to use their own.[77] Since they had the superior medium T-34 tank, one can hardly fault their preference. When the British pressed for closer relations and coordination, except on matters associated with the establishment of a second front and postwar boundaries, the Soviets were seldom interested. At times the British were less than forthright in their overtures to the Russians—as when they proposed exchanging technical information but intended to make sure that nothing truly significant was exchanged—but Soviet conduct toward its allies was also self-serving and less than candid. As a result, the Grand Alliance went through its ups and downs; throughout, Stalin never trusted the British sufficiently to deal with them as true partners. Given the longstanding apprehension and animosity the Soviets felt toward the west during the interwar years, their wary attitude might be condemned but is nonetheless understandable.

EIGHT

North Africa and Sicily, 1941–1943

A telling point, discussed earlier, about German strategy is the disparity between its effort in the east and that in the other theaters. Between 1941 and 1943 while the Germans had at least 3,000,000 combat troops, 3,000 tanks, and 2,700 aircraft deployed along the Soviet front, on the other land front, North Africa, the numbers until toward the end in 1943 never exceeded 55,000 soldiers, 332 tanks, and 500 aircraft. Even taking into account Germany's Italian partner, the totals still never approached those in Russia. Throughout the period, the Wehrmacht actually had more troops in noncombat theaters, such as western Europe and Norway, than in Africa.[1]

Given this disparity, one might contend that it is unnecessary to devote an entire chapter to the African campaign and the carry-on operation in Sicily. But if the region was only of secondary importance to Germany, it was, of course, extremely important to Great Britain. For the British, it was early on the major land theater in their confrontation with Germany; they knew that its loss would present them perhaps with insuperable difficulties in their ability to defeat the enemy through the indirect approach. They considered it, in effect, second in significance only to protecting the sea lanes and defending the United Kingdom itself.

One must then ask, if the Mediterranean was so important to Britain, why not devote more than a chapter to it? Why not examine the 1943–45 campaigns on the Italian mainland as well? The answers to these questions return us to our original premise: the goal is not to look at all of the major operations on both sides, but to discuss only selected campaigns that reflect their respective strategies. Italy was a significant theater; however, its importance pales when compared with the Allied campaigns in the west and those of Germany in the east and west. Therefore, the Italian theater will not be discussed separately, but only as it relates to those operations during the later stages of the conflict which are under discussion here.

The Mediterranean is, of course, a vast and awkward theater in which to fight. Although most of the combat between 1941 and 1943 centered in northeastern Africa, it might have at any time expanded in focus, as it did into Greece, Syria, and Iraq in 1941, into northwestern Africa in late 1942, and then into Sicily, the Italian mainland, and the eastern Mediterranean during the last half of 1943. The area was also plagued by poor communications and the need to bring almost everything long distances from the outside.[2] Besides that, the indigenous populations were not always enthusiastic about the Allied (or Axis) cause they were expected to support. The region, in short, presented both sides with considerable problems.

From the time the British entered the war, they well understood the area's strategic importance and the necessity of eventually moving substantial forces there.[3] When Italy came in on June 10, 1940, the British had to begin turning the necessity into reality. With the Mediterranean Sea, except for an occasional convoy, closed off to Allied shipping, the task became increasingly arduous and time-consuming. Supplies now had to be routed around the Cape of Good Hope, and although some aircraft could be sent by way of Malta, many of them had to come across the Takoradi air route, which was opened up in Central Africa by early 1941.[4] The buildup proceeded, but at a very slow pace. Nevertheless, British and Commonwealth forces were sufficient to rout Italian troops in Libya and eastern Africa during the winter of 1940–41, and these operations, combined with Italian setbacks in Greece, induced Germany to become involved in the area.

From the onset of their involvement—first in the form of air units, then land formations—the Germans breathed new life into the languishing Italian effort. In late March 1941, Rommel and his soon-to-be-acclaimed Afrika Korps quickly launched an offensive that took advantage of Britain's diversion of forces to Greece. The result was that Rommel drove the overextended and depleted British divisions back to the Egyptian frontier, although the British did retain Tobruk. When the British attempted in mid-June to relieve the Tobruk garrison and to retake eastern Cyrenaica in the hastily conceived Battleaxe offensive, they failed miserably, although Allied forces did undertake the operations to reassert control over Syria and Iraq. By this time, Churchill had already decided that a change was in order, and he replaced his Mediterranean commander, Field Marshal Sir Archibald Wavell with General Sir Claude Auchinleck. Wavell was shuttled off to Auchinleck's old position as commander-in-chief India.

In this atmosphere of frustration and declining fortunes, exacerbated by the loss of Greece and Crete, the British decided to try again in Libya. The operation was to be called Crusader, and at this point it was designed merely to relieve the situation by retaking Cyrenaica and also to regain dominance of communications in the eastern Mediterranean.[5] But while troops and equipment were becoming available in increasing numbers in the United Kingdom and from the United States, the chiefs of staff were reluctant to send large numbers of men and amounts of material to Egypt in case Germany defeated the Soviets quickly—a distinct possibility in Britain's view—and then turned toward a relatively undefended British Isles.[6] Therefore, army Chief of Staff Dill recommended caution. The buildup in the Middle East was to move ahead, but a possible German attack against the United Kingdom also constantly had to be kept in mind.

This constraint did not seem to deter Churchill.[7] He was trying to be patient, but he kept querying Auchinleck as to whether anything could be done to speed up a renewed Libyan offensive. He was not above applying tangible pressure either. On July 17, he asked the chiefs of staff whether Auchinleck intended to undertake an offensive before winter.[8] If not, the next convoy should be confined to 25,000 men; if Auchinleck was contemplating an offensive earlier, more ships could be made available for transporting additional troops, along with 150 more tanks. While Churchill's motives were not lost on Auchinleck, he refused to be stampeded into action. In his opinion, "to launch an offensive with the inadequate means at present at our disposal is not . . . a justifiable operation of war, and is almost certain to result in a further lengthy postponement of date on which we can assume [an] offensive [can have a] reasonable chance of success."[9] Given the differences that were arising between Churchill and his Mediterranean commander, the chiefs of staff welcomed the prime minister's suggestion to have Auchinleck come to London for consultation.

The meeting at the end of July seemed to clear the air.[10] Auchinleck was determined not to begin a major operation until sufficient tanks and trained personnel to man them were in place, and he did not think they would be ready until early November. Churchill reluctantly gave way, but only for the moment. After having traveled to meet with the Americans at Argentia Bay, at which time he discussed, among other things, the importance of the Middle East in Britain's overall strategy, he once again started to badger Auchinleck. Once again Auchinleck stood firm. On August 22, he telegraphed the prime minister: "I have to chose [sic] between a problematical limited success in October or a probably complete success early in November. . . . I have no hesitation in advocating patience and the big objective."[11] Auchinleck, backed by Dill, was to have his way.

On September 2, Auchinleck issued a directive to General Sir Alan Cunningham, commander of the soon-to-be-created Eighth Army and brother of the naval admiral, to prepare an offensive against Axis forces in Cyrenaica.[12] Cunningham was to study two possibilities: a large-scale turning movement to the south through Jalo to cut the enemy's supply lines, perhaps as far west as Benghazi; and a thrust along the coast toward Tobruk with feints to the west and south. After examining the alternatives throughout the month, Cunningham and his staff presented their outline plan to Auchinleck on September 28. Cunningham preferred the direct thrust, for in his view an offensive to the south would lose both time and the element of surprise. But rather than having the main British force advance along the coast, he opted for XXX Corps, with almost all of the armor, to launch a strong attack northwest in the center, with XIII Corps undertaking a holding action at the Egyptian frontier along with a subsidiary attack near the coast on the right. Later, XIII Corps was to swing west, but only after XXX Corps had engaged and defeated Rommel's armor near Gabr Saleh. This move was the key to the entire plan. The relief of Tobruk was considered important, and the garrison there was to make a sortie south when needed, but the plan depended on Rommel's fighting XXX Corps tanks in the vicinity of Gabr Saleh. Cunningham was confident that Rommel would take the bait and seek to do battle there.

To assist the British main force, special long-range groups were to take over Jarabub and Jalo in the desert and secure a landing ground in the area for air attacks.[13] In addition, RAF fighters and bombers were to gain air superiority over the battle zone and also to fly air cover for the navy, which was to support the operation with naval gunfire and raids along the coast and to fulfill supply functions. While rejecting any major landing attempt, the navy agreed to undertake several diversions, including dummy convoys from Gibraltar and Malta to draw off enemy aircraft.[14]

Once Auchinleck accepted the plan on October 3, there were few changes. The XXX Corps commander, General Willoughby Norrie, voiced strenuous objections, advocating an immediate assault directed at Sidi Rezegh, just south of Tobruk, instead of the engagement at Gabr Saleh. Despite doubts, Cunningham stayed with his original plan. After extended staff discussions in Cairo and in London, however, it was decided that if Cyrenaica fell rapidly, preparations should be made for a possible advance on Tripoli to liberate that important port city. The British hoped that such a move would even hasten Italy's collapse.[15] Another change that took place was that Auchinleck had to postpone Crusader twice, the first time from November 1 to November 15 and then to November 18 because of the late arrival of an armored brigade and the need for additional training.

Churchill's reactions to the delays were predictable. He was trying to get along with Auchinleck, but he began to wonder whether Crusader would ever be launched. His fertile mind started to conjure up all kinds of other projects. His impetuousness caused his military advisors considerable frustrations, especially General Kennedy, the head of the joint planning staff. At this time, according to Kennedy, "whenever an idea, however wild, was thrown up, [Churchill] ordered detailed examination or plans, or both, to be made at high speed. Our stables were so full of these unlikely starters that we were hard put to give the favourites the attention they deserved. To cope wth the situation adequately, it would almost have been worthwhile to have two staffs: one to deal with the Prime Minister, the other with the war. . . ."[16]

Meanwhile, additional troops and supplies continued to be moved in, training proceeded apace, and preliminary actions were carried out. One particularly difficult operation was the replacement of Australian soldiers at Tobruk, demanded by their government, with British and Polish troops.[17] The relief by sea took place in three stages between August 19 and October 25; by the time it was over, 18,263 had been evacuated, and 19,552 brought in. The cost of these dangerous night operations was only three ships lost and one damaged, although throughout the eight-month siege of Tobruk, the British lost thirty-four merchant vessels and warships, with another thirty-three damaged. Besides the buildup, preliminary activities took the form of extensive naval and air bombardments, which were especially devastating on Axis shipping and ports. In October, 63 percent of the enemy ships dispatched from Italy to Libya were sunk in transit, and the percentage for November was 77 percent sunk or damaged.[18] Only 8,400 tons of merchant ship goods reached Libya during November, and air and naval forces stationed in Malta as well as in Egypt could take credit for a job well done.

Nevertheless, relations among the three services regarding the use of air power remained delicate and had to be worked out with care.[19] The air force wanted to support the navy, but in its own way. The navy desired additional air cover for its ships and resented the RAF's seemingly cavalier attitude toward the special training needed for flying over the sea. In the end, Air Marshal Tedder gave in and assigned a small air group—201 Group of 68 aircraft—to assist the navy and sent an air force officer to Alexandria to serve as a liaison with the fleet. With the army, the issue was over who should exercise ultimate control over the aircraft. The RAF wanted to cooperate with the land units, but insisted it needed to retain control of its aircraft so as not to dissipate its effort. The army desired that control be parceled out among its corps commanders. In this instance, Auchinleck, who had been upset with the lack of air support previously, now "seemed to appreciate the importance of air matters," and allowed the air force ultimate control so that its aircraft might be used, not only to assist the army, but also, if warranted, for bomber attacks and other missions. Although subject to initial problems, this concept of centralized control of air assets, championed by the tactical air commander Air Vice Marshal "Mary" Coningham, was to become a principal tenet of RAF thinking and was later adopted by the US Army Air Forces as well.

By November 18, the Crusader formations had been assembled. It was truly a mixture of types of units and nationalities. The main striking force, XXX Corps, consisted of the 7th Armored and 1st South African divisions and the 4th Armored and 200th Guard brigades. The XIII Corps was made up of the New Zealand and 4th Indian divisions and the 1st Tank Brigade. At Tobruk were the 70th Division and 32nd Tank Brigade, and the 2nd South African Division was in reserve. In addition to other attached units, such as antitank regiments and antiaircraft batteries, were two long-range desert groups. The total was equivalent to nine divisions, or about 118,000 troops in all.[20] Sprinkled among the British, Indian, South African, and New Zealand formations were small contingents of Australian, Free French, Polish, Belgian, and Greek soldiers.

The all-important tanks numbered 738, backed by considerable reserves, but the number is misleading. The 199 infantry tanks, 339 Cruisers, 173 American Stuarts, and 25 other light tanks could be stopped by German antitank guns and were inferior to the Panzer IIIs and IVs. The British tanks—Matildas, Valentines, and Cruisers—were armed with nothing more than

2-pounder guns, which had an insufficient armor-piercing capability. The Stuart light tanks were faster and more reliable and had a slightly more powerful 37-mm gun, but their vulnerability and short radius of action without refueling were definite liabilities which soon became apparent in the subsequent fighting. Moreover, a number of the British tanks, though part of the order of battle, were inoperable.

The British buildup in the area had been especially impressive in regard to aircraft and ships. By the time of the offensive, they had approximately 775 aircraft, including those at Malta, of which 670 were serviceable. Among the total were 256 Hurricane fighters and 84 Blenheim light and 100 Wellington medium bombers.[21] The navy had 4 battleships, 1 aircraft carrier, 10 cruisers, 29 destroyers, and 30 submarines, including Force H at Gibraltar and the smaller Force K at Malta.[22]

The Axis forces presented the British with a formidable challenge, for they, too, were being readied for an offensive to begin on November 20. Although the British did not know the exact date, they did know through Ultra that the enemy was planning an operation against Tobruk in the near future.[23] The Axis formations consisted of ten divisions, three of which were German—the 21st and 15 Panzer divisions and the 90th Light Division. The combined German and Italian strength equaled that of Eighth Army—119,000—of which 65,000 were German.[24] Their tank strength was less, however, with 386 and no reserves, though the British advantage was offset to a degree because the Germans possessed not only excellent antitank weapons, but also 139 Mark III tanks and 35 Mark IVs. Tedder in the Middle East and Churchill at home disagreed over whether the British had more aircraft than the Germans, but the British finally concluded that they had an edge because, of the 798 estimated Axis total, 435 were thought to be Italian.[25] In actuality, the Germans and Italians had only 611, of which 181 were in Greece and Crete, and only 35 of them were the celebrated Messerschmitt Bf-109Fs. The British, however, did not realize the disparity.[26] Overall, then, when Crusader started, the British had at least a slight advantage in total strength. Whether their strategy, initiative, and tactical abilities would prove superior was another question.

Prior to the November 18 starting date, the British carried out two commando raids.[27] One was an attempt on the night of November 17 to capture what was thought to be Rommel's headquarters near Beda Littoria. Not only did the attack fail and result in heavy casualties, but Rommel was not there, being in Athens until the evening of November 18. The final irony is that Beda Littoria was no longer his headquarters anyway. The other raid was a parachute drop aimed to destroy aircraft and other equipment at airfields near Gazala. In this case the raiders were dropped in the wrong place, never reached the airfields, and, as in the headquarters debacle, suffered heavy losses.

Crusader itself was fought in two main phases.[28] During the first phase, which started in foul, rainy weather and lasted between November 18 and December 7, the combatants battled on relatively even terms, with one side seemingly gaining the upper hand for a while, and then the other. At first, on November 18, the British XXX Corps advanced against token opposition to Gabr Saleh, but contrary to General Cunningham's expectations, Axis forces refused to do battle. The next day, the British dispersed their armor, and by November 20, heavy fighting broke out. Despite their air superiority, which continued throughout the campaign, the British on the ground had difficulties holding their own.

British and Polish units moved out from Tobruk to help, but they had little effect. On November 23, both sides suffered severe casualties near Sidi Rezeqh. The Germans later called the day the "battle of the Sunday dead" because of their staggering personnel and panzer losses (75 out of 162). Rommel then disengaged most of his motorized formations and undertook a flanking movement to his right toward the Egyptian frontier in the hope of cutting off British supplies and perhaps forcing them to withdraw. Although the counterattack surprised the British, it eventually came to a halt, in part because of British resistance, including assistance from long-range penetration groups, in part because Rommel's force ran out of gasoline. By this point, General Cunningham had lost his grip and was thinking defensively. Auchinleck, who now had Churchill's full confidence and encouragement, had no such illusions, and on November 26 he replaced Cunningham with General Neil Ritchie, Auchinleck's deputy chief of staff. Auchinleck remained the driving force behind the British effort. He exhorted his troops in a widely disseminated message: "You have got your teeth into [the enemy]. Hang on and bite deeper and deeper and hang on till he is finished. . . . There is only one order 'Attack and Pursue.'"[29]

Rommel's "dash to the frontier wire" had allowed the British to recoup in the Sidi Rezegh area, and on November 27, they linked up with Tobruk garrison. On November 30, Auchinleck relayed a birthday message to Churchill from his XIII Corps commander: "Corridor to Tobruk clear and secure. Tobruk is as relieved as I am."[30] Despite continued strong fighting during the next week, in which the Germans retook Sidi Rezegh and for several days broke the linkup with Tobruk, the battle had become one of attrition. Under these circumstances, Auchinleck and Ritchie, with their ability to replenish their forces, were bound to gain the upper hand. On November 30, the Germans had been reduced to 57 tanks; by December 7, to 30. The British had approximately 160. With no reinforcements in sight, Rommel began withdrawing his forces to the Gazala area to the west.

During the second phase, between December 7 and January 12, the British followed the Germans all the way across Cyrenaica to the El Agheila line. The offensive was more cautious than it might have been because Auchinleck

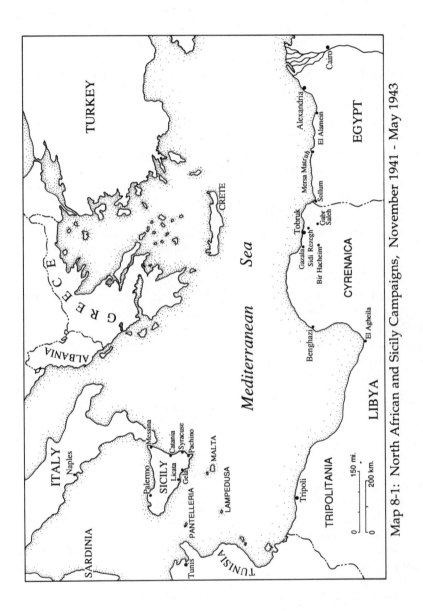

Map 8-1: North African and Sicily Campaigns, November 1941 - May 1943

thought the Axis would make a stand at Gazala. When the German forces began retreating from their Gazala positions on the night of December 16, the British, with excellent air support, started in pursuit. Early on December 24, Auchinleck learned through Ultra that the Germans were abandoning the port of Benghazi.[31] That evening, the elated Middle Eastern commander wired Churchill: "Royal Dragoons occupied Benghazi this morning. The Army of the Nile send you hearty greetings for Christmas."[32] By January 12, Rommel had withdrawn to El Agheila on the western edge of Cyrenaica.

Although Crusader was now over, the story does not quite yet come to an end. By this time, the British had their own problems.[33] They were stretched to the limit, with some equipment shipped by sea to Tobruk, but not enough. In any event, as Tobruk was about three hundred miles from El Agheila, it was necessary to send large truck convoys across the desert, and still the amount of supplies, especially gasoline, reaching the front was insufficient to support a large force. This limitation had dictated that the pursuing army be a relatively small one. Rommel was able to take advantage of Britain's difficulties. He replenished his forces by means of improved sea transport and caught the British off guard. On January 21, he began pushing them back across Cyrenaica. On February 5, Axis units reached the Gazala line, only forty miles west of Tobruk. Here the front stabilized, and the combatants started preparing for the next round.

However, the British had won a substantial if incomplete victory. They had suffered fewer casualties—17,700 to the enemy's 37,400, of whom approximately 29,000 had been surrounded, captured, and listed as missing.[34] While the losses in aircraft and tanks were much less favorable—440 British as compared with 463 Axis aircraft, and an estimated 600 British (including numerous breakdowns) as opposed to 340 enemy tanks—Britain and its allies had relieved Tobruk and had seized the initiative in driving the Axis out of Cyrenaica.[35] Yet the British had not been able to eliminate Rommel's forces completely, the naval situation in the central Mediterranean had deteriorated with the loss of surface vessels and the arrival of additional Luftwaffe units in Sicily, and the army had again been found wanting in terms of organization, equipment, and tactics.[36] They had not been able to keep their forces supplied as they moved across the desert and thus were extremely vulnerable by the time they reached El Agheila. Rommel and his troops exploited that vulnerability to the fullest. Moreover, though one might argue with Sir Michael Carver's contention that the German Mark IIIs and IVs were not really superior to the British tanks, there can be no doubt of the Wehrmacht's vast superiority in antitank and heavy artillery guns. Nor is there any doubt about Germany's superior tactics and Britain's failure to concentrate their armor and to coordinate their motorized infantry, artillery, and tanks effectively.

British strategy also proved defective. Rommel did not take up the battle immediately at Gabr Saleh as anticipated, and the opposing armies continued to engage indecisively for more than two weeks before the Germans had to begin withdrawing because of lack of reinforcements. In the end, the British had won because of material superiority, not because of better tactics or strategy.[37]

Several questions surrounding Crusader remain to be answered. For one thing, what was the role of Ultra? According to the British official history, the British received good information from cryptographic and other sources throughout the operation.[38] Ultra was particularly helpful in determining enemy supply and order of battle, but of less assistance in gauging Rommel's operational intentions. For example, the British received no information of his intended November 24 counterattack until after it had been executed. Ultra did allow planners at the end of the month to appreciate the Axis' increasingly tenuous supply situation and to plan accordingly. On the other hand, even though the British learned of the enemy withdrawal from Gazala during the night it took place, they could not prevent it. No information was received to anticipate Rommel's counterstroke of January 21. In other words, though helpful, Ultra was not of decisive importance.

The second question is, how did Crusader fit in with Britain's overall strategic picture at the time? In the long run, the situation brightened substantially, for not only had Britain assumed the initiative, but the Soviet Union had undertaken its counteroffensive to relieve Moscow and the United States had formally entered the war. In the short run, however, Britain's position remained precarious. One of its most significant difficulties was that open involvement in eastern Asia and the Pacific had now added a new dimension. With regard to the Middle East and North Africa, warfare in the Far East meant that any possibility of advancing into Tripolitania would have to be postponed.[39] It meant further that some of the resources intended for the Middle East as well as forces already in the theater would have to be diverted east, as started happening when seven fighter and four light bomber squadrons were removed early in 1942 and sent to India.[40] Even while Crusader was in its final stages, the long shadow that the Far East would cast on Middle Eastern operations was already apparent. A January 3 War Ministry telegram to Auchinleck stated: "'Crusader' should be exploited to the greatest extent possible subject to the condition that it must not (repeat not) prevent the dispatch of essential reinforcements to the Far East."[41] Britain's material advantages, evident during the offensive, were now in jeopardy because of the new front in Asia. American resources were expected eventually to redress the situation, but in a sense prospects in the Middle East in January were less favorable than they had been two months earlier at Crusader's onset. This fact became painfully clear to the British when Rommel executed his successful January counterattack and retook western Cyrenaica.

The next round took place along the Gazala line in May 1942. During the spring, both sides had replenished and reinforced their depleted forces. For the Axis, the increase in weaponry and equipment had already become evident the previous December, for the supplies which reached Rommel's forces had allowed them to undertake the January counterstroke. Between February and May, incoming matériel averaged about 60,000 tons per month, an amount Rommel at the time said was inadequate but which he later admitted had been sufficient.[42] The increases in tanks and aircraft are especially noteworthy. Whereas the Axis had only 182 serviceable tanks on February 3, by April 14 they had 377, and by May 6, 438.[43] The number of aircraft in commission rose from 397 on April 4 to approximately 635 on May 20.[44] The Axis supply situation improved further when Benghazi, which was closer to the front than Tripoli and which had a capacity of 2,700 tons per day, began receiving supplies, and when the Axis were able to make use of air transports to supplement naval shipments. During April alone, the Germans and the Italians moved 10,827 personnel by air to North Africa.[45] As for the British, though their pace was slowed by commitments to the Far East and by fears for their northern flank in Iraq and Iran, by the time Germany attacked on May 26, they had a force of 843 tanks, with another 145 in reserve, and 320 aircraft at hand plus about 680 more in the theater.[46]

Meanwhile, planning proceeded. Though Auchinleck had beaten the Axis to the punch in November, this time Rommel preempted the British and struck first. The initial step in that direction occurred in February 1942, when Hitler authorized German and Italian planners to begin preparing for an attack against Malta.[47] In mid-March, Rommel flew to Hitler's eastern headquarters, where they agreed that Malta was to be subjected to a combined German and Italian invasion in early June, a decision with which Mussolini concurred on March 18.[48] Only after Malta had been captured was a North African offensive to be undertaken, presumably in the summer. But at this point, Rommel and the German theater commander, Field Marshal Kesselring, started to have doubts about attacking Malta first, especially since the British were building up their strength in Cyrenaica and could be expected to launch their own offensive anytime after the end of May.[49] They therefore advocated striking the British before they could complete their refurbishment and before the assault on Malta. When Kesselring on April 28 reported a conversation he had had with the Führer in which the latter had said that the Malta operation (Hercules) should probably still take place first, unless the enemy attacked in North Africa beforehand, the stage was set for another conference between Hitler and his Africa Corps commander.

The meetings took place at Klessheim Castle and the Berghof on April 29–30.[50] Besides Rommel and Hitler, Mussolini and both leaders' entourages were in attendance. While part of the discussion was devoted to conditions and a renewed offensive in Russia, the main topic was how to deal with the Mediterranean theater. By the time the meetings were over, Rommel had convinced the Führer and "perhaps" Mussolini that it would be better to attack first at Gazala about the end of May, capture Tobruk, which he hoped could be accomplished in six days, and then advance to the Egyptian frontier before turning against Malta. Once eastern Cyrenaica had been taken,

Rommel was to stand on the defensive. As a corollary, he was to shift air forces west to assist in the execution of Hercules. During the conference, the relative position of the supposed partners was obvious: Germany would continue to dictate strategy in the Mediterranean, and Italy would have to go along whether it wanted to or not. As the Italian foreign minister, Count Ciano, related in his diary:

> Hitler talks, talks, talks. Mussolini suffers—he who is in the habit of talking himself, and who, instead, practically has to keep quiet. On the second day, after lunch, when everything had been said, Hitler talked uninterruptedly for an hour and forty minutes. . . . Mussolini automatically looked at his wrist watch, I had my mind on my own business. . . . Those, however, who dreaded the ordeal less [?more] than we did were the Germans. Poor people. They have to take it every day, and I am certain there isn't a gesture, a word, or a pause which they don't know by heart. General Jodl, after an epic struggle, went to sleep on the divan. Keitel was reeling, but he succeeded in keeping his head up.[51]

Following the meeting, Rommel and his staff proceeded to draw up detailed plans.[52] Although the Germans codenamed the operation Theseus and the Italians called it Venezia, even at the time, the offensive was usually referred to simply as the Gazala campaign. It was to consist of two parts. One was a diversion by Axis forces to keep the British occupied in the north along the coast. The other was the main thrust, in which panzer and motorized formations were to wheel south of Bir Hacheim, the southern anchor of the Gazala line. Once the flanking movement had been accomplished, Axis armor was to push quickly behind the British and Commonwealth units along the front and attack them from both the west and the east. The capture of Tobruk was to follow, with the initial portion of the operation expected to take four days. Next would come the advance to the Egyptian frontier. In addition to the land forces, air groups from Italy and Crete, as well as those in Africa, and small naval craft, including submarines, were to lend support. A special battle group, Kampfgruppe Hecker, was to land by sea behind the lines, undertake reconnaissance, and block the coastal road, Via Balbia, thus hampering enemy troops when they withdrew to the east.[53] Though no starting date was stipulated—the actual attack day was to be given out the night before—Axis forces were to be ready anytime after May 20. The entire campaign was to be completed within a month so that units could be redeployed for the Malta assault.

During the two weeks prior to Rommel's May 26 offensive, two significant developments took place. The first occurred at a situation conference on May 21 during which Hitler gave his opinion that Italy did not have "the necessary attacking spirit" to execute the complicated Malta operation and suggested it be given up and "prepared only in spirit."[54] This meant, of course, that Hitler was skeptical of the Malta operation even before Gazala was launched, and he hinted he might even change his prior April agreement with Mussolini should Rommel succeed in taking Tobruk. Second was Britain's decision to stand on the defensive.[55] This had been the result of Ultra decrypts which indicated that the Afrika Korps commander was planning an imminent attack and of Auchinleck and Ritchie's realization that they were in no position to undertake an offensive of their own at least until mid-June. Their foreknowledge of Axis designs was not so helpful to the British as one might expect, for they still did not know the day of attack or Rommel's actual battle plan, and thus positioned themselves in linear fixed defenses with armor too far to the rear. But the information they had did allow them to prepare for what Rommel might do.

By the evening of May 25, the Axis forces were ready. Their rested and refitted army was made up of nine divisions plus the Hecker commando group.[56] The divisions included three panzer—the German 15th and 21st and the Italian Ariete; two motorized—the German 90th Light and the Italian Trieste; and four Italian infantry formations. Another Italian armored division was to be sent in during the battle. Tanks on hand numbered 560, of which 228 were Italian and 332 German. The German tanks included 50 Panzer IIs, 242 IIIs, and 40 IVs, with 77 more reserve. The Axis also had 485 artillery, 576 antitank, and 64 heavy antitank guns. The number of serviceable aircraft, excluding transports, was 635.[57]

The British forces were smaller, with six divisions, four independent brigades, and 320 aircraft immediately available.[58] But they had 843 tanks at the front and considerable reserves—145 tanks, four divisions, several independent brigades, and about 680 aircraft—which could be called upon as reinforcements. Reserves of this magnitude were simply not available to the Axis.

With regard to intelligence, both sides had access to large numbers of enemy cryptographic messages, the Germans by way of the American military attaché in Cairo, the British through Ultra.[59] Although the Axis and the British did not decrypt the information quickly enough to use it tactically, for the battle was fought at too fast a pace, they did benefit strategically. The British, for example, often knew of the Axis' intentions and strengths, and after the fall of Tobruk on June 21, Auchinleck was well aware of Rommel's combat and logistical problems. In fact, this information made an important contribution to the Eighth Army's willingness to hold fast to Alamein in July. Fortunately for the Allies, during the same month the Americans changed ciphers, and Rommel was therefore deprived of this valuable source of information about British plans and deployments. Nevertheless, as Hinsley has pointed out, Rommel's victories during the Gazala campaign were less attributable to intelligence "than to his superiority in direction of battle and in the quality and handling of his tanks."

Like Crusader and the other North Africa operations, the Gazala campaign was fought in phases, in this case, four.[60] During the first phase, between May 26 and June 15, the opposing forces engaged in fierce combat, with first one side, then the other, seemingly gaining an advantage. Eventually Rommel's divisions gained the upper hand. During the second phase, between June 16 and 21, the victorious Axis forces added to their laurels by taking the once considered impregnable fortress at Tobruk. During the third phase, between June 22 and 30, they advanced past the Libyan frontier 220 miles into Egypt, where they ran into prepared British defenses at El Alamein. Here, during the final phase, between July 1 and 20, the Germans and Italians were finally stopped.

The first three weeks of the campaign were crucial. Once the Axis forces overcame Britain's Gazala position, their momentum carried them all the way to El Alamein before they could be halted. At first, on May 26, their plan seemed to be working. At 2 p.m., Italian infantry formations began engaging the enemy along the Gazala line.[61] That evening, German and Italian armored and motorized divisions started moving south of Bir Hacheim to get around and behind the British. On May 27, the panzers and other armored vehicles swung north, destroyed substantial British armor, and moved as far as El Adem south of Tobruk. They also encountered American-made Grant tanks, which they found to be "very formidable," for the first time. Moreover, as British resistance began to stiffen, the German and Italian supply situation behind the British lines was becoming precarious. The next day, Rommel was able to get some supply trucks through a gap in the lines, but, now facing even more formidable opposition, he gave up the immediate goal of taking Tobruk. What followed was a series of blows and counterblows, in which the Axis, led by the Afrika Korps, turned back the British armor in a series of encounters highlighted by the "cauldron" battles of June 5–6; invested and finally captured Bir Hacheim, where Free French forces had been holding out, on June 10; and overwhelmed the British tanks at Knightsbridge on June 11 and 12. By June 15, the British and other allied units were in retreat toward the Egyptian border. Rommel accurately summarized the period in his diary: "It began very badly for us, but in the fluctuating fighting which followed we succeeded—partly by attacks with limited objectives, partly in defence—in smashing the British forces one by one, despite the courage with which they fought."[62] On June 15, he wrote to his wife, Lu: "The battle has been won and the enemy is breaking up."

The next Axis objective, and the one Rommel most coveted, was Tobruk. It was not, however, the defensive bastion it had been in 1941, and in fact the British at this point never intended that the forces there withstand a second siege.[63] But the speed with which the Germans and Italians took it surprised everyone, including Churchill, who was crestfallen when he heard the news while meeting with the Americans in Washington. Rommel's task was eased because the British had had to withdraw their fighter aircraft from the area to bases farther east, thereby depriving the Tobruk garrison of their support. By June 19, Rommel had his forces in place. The next day, they stormed Tobruk's outer perimeter and soon overran portions of it. By the morning of June 21, the fortress was in Axis hands. The cost for the British was heavy—32,000 soldiers taken prisoner, 100 tanks lost, and numerous guns and other weapons destroyed. The Axis triumph was particularly sweet for Rommel, who was promoted to field marshal. He now called on all units to reassemble and "prepare for further advances."[64]

Between June 22 and 30, the Axis did just that. First, however, Rommel had to receive permission to set aside the original plan of going on the defensive preliminary to the attack on Malta.[65] He therefore cabled the German liaison officer in Rome, General Enno von Rintelen, to get Mussolini's approval for the change in plan. The Duce still preferred to invade Malta first. Hitler than contacted Mussolini and persuaded him to give way, and the Malta operation was put off until August. The change was made also over the opposition of the German navy, whose ability to get supplies to North Africa had become increasingly difficult because of the British air and naval units stationed on the island. Nevertheless, the supply problem did not seem to deter Rommel. His forces managed to capture Mersa Matruh, taking more prisoners in the process, and to pursue the fleeing enemy farther into Egypt. In the interim, on June 25, Auchinleck took over from Ritchie and prepared to do battle at the El Alamein line.

On July 1, Rommel's units, though exhausted and depleted, attacked. The British were also exhausted, but they held on, in part because of Auchinleck's knowledge that the Axis was in even worse shape than they were. In fact, on July 1, Rommel was down to 55 tanks and just over 2,000 infantry at the front.[66] By July 2, the number of tanks in commission had decreased to 35; on July 3, to 26. On July 4, Rommel went on the defensive. While he made several subsequent attempts to break through, British counterstrokes and air superiority, coupled with inadequate Axis reinforcements, brought the offensive to an end. On July 21, Rommel acknowledged temporary defeat and estimated that it would take almost four to five weeks to rehabilitate his formations before they could advance again—that is, if they suffered no further losses and if much needed personnel and supplies arrived on time.[67] The British, in effect, has survived the first battle of Alamein.

Yet, overall, between May 26 and July 21, Axis forces had once again proved far superior.[68] Despite heavy losses, in both men and equipment, on the two sides, the Germans and Italians had advanced 290 miles, their farthest easterly penetration during all of the North African campaigns, almost to Alexandria itself. In the field, Rommel had outgeneraled his British counterparts, and his imaginative use of armor had left the opposition almost in a daze. Surely, the Axis had experienced difficulties, such as grave logistics problems, increasingly aggravated the farther their forces moved east from their supply ports, and a lack of air support. But the German air force and army still had to be pleased, for they always considered North Africa of secondary importance to Germany, and yet, Rommel had kept the British, in what was Britain's primary land theater, completely unhinged throughout the summer of 1942. It is little wonder that John Terraine has called Gazala "the nadir of British military fortunes during the war."

This type of thinking was not lost on Churchill. Despite the July victory at El Alamein, Auchinleck no longer had the prime minister's confidence. For a while, the British chiefs of staff, led by Brooke, stood by their Middle Eastern commander, but by early August, they, too, realized Auchinleck had to go.[69] On August 6, while on the way to tell Stalin that the second front would be in northwestern Africa, not in France as the Soviet leader wanted, Churchill informed Auchinleck of the change in command. The downhearted commander, who had done everything he could to keep the confidence of the prime minister and to inform him of developments in the theater, would not accept another post for some months but finally agreed in mid-1943 to return to his old position as commander-in-chief, India. On August 15, his successor, Field Marshal Alexander, was already in place in North Africa, and Lieutenant General Bernard Montgomery had become head of Eighth Army. Originally, General W. H. E. "Strafer" Gott, an experienced corps commander, was to assume the Eighth Army post, but on August 7, he was killed in an airplane crash, and Montgomery was called in as his replacement. At about the same time, a number of the corps commanders and top staff officers in what was called the Cairo purge were replaced as well. Alexander and Montgomery had few command and staff holdovers with which to begin again.

The irony is that the Alexander-Montgomery team, in which the vain and publicity conscious Montgomery soon became the dominant force, did not really have to begin again. Auchinleck and his chief of staff, General Eric Dorman-Smith, had already formulated defensive and offensive plans which Montgomery could use. And Montgomery did use them, though he never attributed their origin to anyone but himself. In any event, both Auchinleck and the new Eighth Army commander agreed that it would be at least mid-September before replacements and equipment could be readied to assume the offensive.

In the meantime, Rommel made another attempt to get around the El Alamein line, this time by going south of it.[70] The British knew it was coming, and once Rommel moved his armor and motorized infantry east of the line, on August 31, he ran into stout British defenses at Alam Halfa ridge. In a series of battles during the next several days, he was turned back. Outgunned, outmanned, and perilously low on fuel, a fact known to the British through Ultra, Rommel called off the offensive on September 3 and removed his forces to the west. Montgomery had won his first desert battle.

By now, Montgomery had started preparing for their own offensive, Operation Lightfoot.[71] Montgomery's initial appreciation appeared on August 19, only a week after he had taken over.[72] In it, he called for one corps of infantry to break through the northern sector of the forty-mile front and to establish a bridgehead through the minefields. This move, in his view, would force Rommel's tanks to do battle. They were to be met and defeated by a British armored corps that had advanced through the gap provided by the infantry, while the latter assumed a defensive posture. A third corps was to keep Axis units busy on the southern portion of the front. Sea, air, and special forces were to be used for various tasks, including the disruption of German and Italian communications in the rear. No specific starting date was mentioned, but the object was "to destroy the enemy's forces in the area they now occupy" and not to allow them "to withdraw any elements back to Cyrenaica." Churchill stopped by on his way back from Moscow and indicated he was pleased with what was happening, wiring back to the War Cabinet on August 21: "I am satisfied that we have lively, confident, resolute men in command working together as an admirable team under a leader of the highest military quality. Everything has been done and is being done that is possible, and it is now my duty to return home as I have no part to play in the battle which must now be left to those in whom we place our trust. . . ."[73]

During September, the date for Lightfoot was set for October 24, although Churchill wanted it earlier. In a tactic reminiscent of Auchinleck a year earlier, Alexander, after several exchanges of telegrams, wired the prime minister on September 21: "If I were obliged to carry out this operation before my target date [October 24], I should not only be not satisfied with the chance of success, but I should be definitely apprehensive as to the result."[74] Churchill wired back: "We are in your hands and of course a victorious battle makes amends for much delay. Whatever happens we shall back you up and see you through."

Also in September, Montgomery began to become apprehensive about the original plan. Eighth Army's training was not so far advanced as he would have liked and the enemy defenses were much stronger than anticipated.[75] On September 6, he therefore decided to have the infantry, while still within the enemy's defense lines, widen the breach north and south by "crumbling" the Axis' forward troops. Then, when Rommel's armor started to engage the British infantry, they were to be pounced upon by British tanks, with artillery support, and destroyed closer to the front than previously envisaged.

Throughout the summer and early fall, the British were aided by a large influx of new troops, tanks, and aircraft coming by way of the Cape of Good Hope and the Takoradi air route. The buildup intensified in July with the arrival of the 8th Armored and 44th Infantry divisions. Additional personnel and equipment reached the area in August and September. For a while it was feared that some of the forces might have to be diverted to Iran and Iraq, but once the German threat of coming through the Caucasus had subsided, they were put to use at El Alamein. Their formations were further augmented by supplies from the United States, including 300 Sherman medium tanks and 100 self-propelled 105-mm guns, although the immediate American contribution was less than the British had hoped for.[76] Moreover, the number of air squadrons in the Middle East rose from 46 in May to an equivalent of 104 in October, and Air Marshal Tedder wired his superior, Air Chief Marshal Portal, in London, that cooperation with the "new army regime" was much improved.[77] The RAF demonstrated its strength in the preliminary air attacks prior to Lightfoot; between September 8 and October 23, they flew 10,815 sorties, and the Americans contributed 704, with combined losses of only 79 aircraft.[78]

By October 23, the forces had been assembled. The comparative strengths of the two sides give some idea of Britain's advantages in men and matériel (table 8-1).[79] Britain and its allies had the equivalent of 12 divisions, of which 4⅔ were armored. Most of the tank forces had been grouped under X Corps, which was to exploit the gap opened by XXX Corps' infantry and to engage the enemy's armor. The other corps, XIII, was to undertake a strong diversion along the southern portion of the line. Opposing the Allies were 4 German divisions with 54,000 soldiers and 8 Italian divisions with 50,000. Thus while the number of Axis divisions equaled that of the British, and four of the German and Italian divisions were armored, the troop total was much lower.

With regard to tanks, guns, and aircraft, the British included 170 Grant and 252 Sherman tanks in their inventory, the latter being equipped with 75-mm guns that could counter the German 88-mm guns. The best tanks the Germans had were 169 Panzer IIIs and 38 IVs. Among the field and antitank guns, the British now had 848 6-pounders for antitank tasks; thus their approximately 850 25-pounders could be switched to their proper role as artillery guns. The Germans had 86 of their renowned 88s. Of aircraft, the British not only had more based near the front, but also could augment their numbers much more readily than could the Axis. The British advantage in air reserves could be replicated in other areas of weaponry as well.

Another advantage Britain had was its high morale. Part of it no doubt stemmed from its manpower, matériel, and air superiority, but some must also be attributed to Montgomery's dynamic leadership. No matter what one thinks of him as a person, he was a highly competent professional who was

TABLE 8-1
Opposing Forces at El Alamein, October 1942

Allies		Axis
195,000	Troops	104,000
1,039	Tanks	527
435	Armored Cars	192
908	Field and Medium Guns	518
1,451	Antitank Guns	850
530	Serviceable Aircraft	350

able to infuse into his soldiers a sense of resolve and confidence that seemed to have been lacking in North Africa for many months.

Still, Montgomery did not expect to have an easy time of it, for the Axis had set up a defensive cordon at Alamein two to four miles in depth that featured extensive minefields with the Afrika Korps placed close behind it. In fact, just prior to the attack, he told his senior officer to be prepared for a "dogfight" of at least a week before a breakthrough could be achieved.[80] In other words, Montgomery fully anticipated that positional, rather than mobile, warfare would dominate the initial stages of the battle.

Montgomery's surmise proved correct, and the first thirteen days of combat between October 23 and November 4 brought the British some anxious moments.[81] At 10 p.m. on October 23, after a twenty-minute, 500-gun artillery barrage, XXX Corps infantry began penetrating the Axis defenses. By 5:30 the next morning, they had advanced far enough through the enemy minefields that X Corps armor could start moving through the cleared areas. They could not break through, however, and Rommel, who had been in Semmering near Vienna recovering from a liver ailment and high blood pressure, returned on the evening of October 26 to take over direction of the Axis troops. He promptly counterattacked on October 27 and 28, but his forces were repulsed. Meanwhile, the British regrouped. On October 30, Montgomery issued another plan, Operation Supercharge, designed to attack a little south of the original offensive surge in the hope of achieving a breakthrough.[82] On the night of November 1–2, after a day's delay to get ready, the infantry divisions, led by the 2nd New Zealand, assaulted the Axis positions. Again it was difficult fighting, but by November 3, the British armor had gained the upper hand, and Rommel had started to pull back. At first, Hitler refused to give permission, but finally, on the next evening, he and Mussolini agreed to a withdrawal.[83] The second battle at Alamein thus ended as the first—with a British triumph—but this time British troops were in a position to exploit it.

Now began the second phase, between November 5 and 23, during which the Axis retreated to the El Agheila position, some 620 miles from the starting line. While the Allies landed in Morocco and Algeria and began to become a factor far to the west, Tobruk fell to the British on November 13, and Benghazi, on November 20. By November 23, forward elements had reached the Axis defenses at Agheila. Here, the Allies stopped. The exploitation of Alamein was over, and new operations now had to be designed to drive the enemy out of Africa. Montgomery has been criticized for being over cautious during the pursuit phase, and perhaps he was, especially in light of Rommel's depleted forces.[84] But in his own defense, Montgomery summed up his thinking in a letter to Alexander on November 19 as follows:

> I have got to be careful at this stage not to do anything still and have a setback. We have been up to Benghazi several times before and have then had

a disaster which negatived [*sic*] all the success gained. I do *not* intend that that should happen this time; if I accepted the advice of all the people who give it to me we should not be where we are now; and if I accepted a good deal of the advice I am now receiving we might well have a disaster.[85]

The victory at Alamein might therefore be seen as less than complete, but it was, nonetheless, construed by Churchill and the people at home as a resounding one. In retrospect, besides the resolve of Britain's troops, three reasons stand out to explain Rommel's defeat. First, Alamein was above all a battle of attrition, and in that type of combat, Britain was bound to have the advantage. Not only did it start the fighting with twice as many soldiers and tanks, but its reserves were far more plentiful and available. The Axis' stretched and vulnerable supply lines could simply not keep pace. Although the British had nearly half of their tanks immobilized during the first thirteen days, they still had 537 in commission and another 67 in reserve on November 6.[86] At this point, the Axis had only about 60, 36 of them German. Even at the end of the pursuit, the British had 525 tanks serviceable; the German Afrika Korps, 35.[87] In terms of personnel, the British by November 4 had suffered 13,560 casualties; the Axis, 26,000 dead and missing. These losses Britain could replace; the Axis could not replace theirs without a dramatic change in strategy. The change came about with the Allied invasion of north-western Africa and Rommel's loss of Cyrenaica. These Allied operations prompted Hitler to send large numbers of troops to Tunisia, and while their presence did halt the Allied momentum in North Africa for awhile, it could not alter the ultimate outcome.

Second, although Montgomery's tactics at Alamein and immediately after-ward might be questioned, he did make good use of air superiority. Not only did the fighters and fighter bombers virtually rule the skies, but also on occasion the RAF made use of bombers, as when they broke up an enemy counterattack on October 28 and bombed Tobruk harbor on November 3.[88] During the height of the battle, 1,000-plus Allied sorties per day were not uncommon, while the best the Luftwaffe could muster was between 100 and 250.[89] Overall, between October 23 and November 4, the Allies flew 11,631 sorties, an average of 833 per day.[90] The Western Desert Air Force kept up the pressure across Cyrenaica by relocating to forward airfields as the offensive progressed.[91] The result was that between November 5 and 25, the Allied air effort amounted to 4,278 sorties, or about 200 per day. Tedder put his finger on another aspect of the air contribution when he informed Portal that "cooperation between fighters and bombers and between British and Americans in Desert [Air Force] is first class, and the operational organisation is working like clockwork, with excellent mutual confidence." Although this level of cooperation was not always to be exhibited between the British army and air components, everyone recognized the RAF's stellar role at Alamein and how prominent a feature it had become in desert warfare.

Third, and finally, the victory owed a good deal to British intelligence.[92] In addition to Ultra, which allowed them to appreciate the enemy's supply and manpower problems, the British also effectively utilized air reconnaissance, army tactical intelligence, and long-range penetration groups to assess Rommel's difficulties. One group, in what was called Operation Road Watch, was placed along the Via Balbia behind the lines to count Axis vehicles as they withdrew, thereby verifying or modifying the information gleaned from Ultra. Such measures may not have spelled the difference between victory and defeat, but they obviously rendered valuable assistance to the Allied cause.

How then does Alamein and the subsequent expulsion of the Axis from North Africa fit into Britain's long-term strategy? Is Churchill's boast that "after Alamein we never had a defeat" correct? The answer to the first question helps explain why Alamein is considered a turning point. In a sense it vindicated Britain's strategy of striking the enemy at vulnerable points and keeping the effort spread out, but it accomplished more than that. It was a "British" victory of substantial proportions that assisted in calming Churchill's critics at home. It and Operation Torch helped open the Mediterranean, thus relieving Malta and reforging the normal sea links with the Middle East, South Asia, and beyond. And both Lightfoot and the Northwest African landings meant that the Anglo-American locus of power would remain in that theater for some time to come, and that Britain's immediate goal of eliminating Italy from the war was now in the forefront despite American reservations. As to whether Alamein was the first in a series of never-ending military successes, one has to be wary that Churchill's gift for memorable phrases does not lead one to lose sight of its accuracy. The Allies from the fall of 1942 on won numerous, stunning victories; at the same time, they suffered setbacks along the way, as in Italy, in the air war, and in the Ardennes. These and other setbacks reflected Germany's ability to hold on despite its many difficulties. As the Germans demonstrated during Second Alamein, they would not succumb easily. Most of the Allied victories would be hard earned.

The British and the Americans found this out during the Tunisian fighting, which dragged on for five months before the reinforced German and Italian forces were defeated. The Allies gained some compensation, however, in the form of 250,000 prisoners, when all of Tunisia finally fell by May 10, 1943.

Yet, more important for the Allies from a strategic standpoint was to decide what to do next. As examined earlier, this question threatened to bring the United States and Great Britain on a collision course.[93] A strategic stalemate was averted at the Casablanca conference, where the issue was to be decided, because the Americans did not have a consensus among themselves and at this point were willing to compromise and because the British did not push their ally too far in a Mediterranean direction. The US had only reluctantly agreed to Torch, and they further realized that operations in North Africa had made it difficult, if not impossible, to launch a major landing against western Europe in 1943. While the Americans preferred a 1943 cross-Channel attack, they were not adamant. The British were, and they defended their Mediterranean preference with skill. They had debated the issue at length throughout November and December 1942, and it was mainly on the insistence of General Brooke that the Mediterranean option, Sicily in particular, was adopted.[94] Therefore, when the British arrived at Casablanca for the January meeting, they had already agreed among themselves on the course they wished to follow and had prepared a full-blown outline for a Sicilian operation. By January 18, the Americans, led by General Marshall, had given way, and the British chiefs were careful not to push for Mediterranean operations beyond Sicily, although they, and even their American counterparts, realized that the invasion of Sicily probably meant that Italy, rather than northern France, would be next.[95]

What has not been adequately appreciated was the length of time Britain had been involved in planning operations against Sicily as a step toward eliminating Italy from the war. As early as December 1940, only five months after Italy had entered the war, British staff officers drew up a plan, codenamed Influx, to occupy the island "in order to deny it to the Germans."[96] The plan was based on the premise that Italian morale would have deteriorated to a point that an occupation would be possible. The British move was designed to beat Germany to the punch. The operation was not as illogical as it might seem, for Italy, at the time being beaten back by a smaller British contingent in Egypt and also by Allied troops in Greece, was thus in trouble militarily. But the moment soon passed when Germany entered the theater, first with air units in Sicily, and then with land and air forces in North Africa.[97]

Still, Sicily was not forgotten. In October 1941, the British planned another attack against the island, Operation Whipcord, designed to relieve the siege of Malta, open the Mediterranean to British shipping, and cut off Axis supplies to Libya.[98] The operation was to take place in November or December and would take advantage of the conditions created in North Africa by Crusader. Cover operations into Norway were to be used as a deception. The hastily prepared Whipcord was short-lived, however, because of insufficient shipping. It was abandoned by the end of October.[99]

The idea of an operation into Sicily was revived again toward the end of September 1942.[100] This time the British examined the operation thoroughly within the context of whether it should be launched at all, or whether the capture of Sardinia, Corsica, Crete, or some other option should be pursued instead. The planning depended on the success of Torch and Lightfoot in North Africa, and once they succeeded, it was more urgent than ever to prepare for the next move. While the British joint planners preferred Sardinia, they did not rule out Sicily as a possibility, and at this juncture, Brooke came to the fore.[101] He proceeded to reject the advice of his joint planners and fended off any other opposition, including that of Eisenhower, the Torch commander, who at this point also favored Sardinia.[102] By January 10, just prior to Casablanca, an outline had been prepared, and Churchill and all of the British Chiefs accepted Sicily, now called Operation Husky, as the preferred choice.[103] Brooke had carried the day.

When comparing the three outlined plans for capturing Sicily—Influx, Whipcord, and Husky—one finds interesting the extent to which the operation changed. Forces for Influx, the December 1940 plan, were to take over the island against expected light Italian opposition. The equivalent of two divisions, one from Britain and one from Egypt, plus an armored brigade, eight combat air squadrons, and a relatively small naval escort were all that were considered necessary for the undertaking. Ten months later, the new plan, Whipcord, still featured land units coming primarily from the United Kingdom and the Mediterranean theater, but with Germany's presence in the area, the force was to consist of three infantry divisions, approximately two armored brigades, and twenty-seven air squadrons as well as a substantial naval task force. By the time Husky was being worked on in late 1942, the number of units to be involved had risen to nine infantry divisions (four of them American), two armored brigades, five parachute brigades, and ninety-five air squadrons, along with a much larger naval contingent. In addition, instead of having the land forces concentrated at a single point from which to fan out across the island, as in the case of Influx, where the landing was to be carried out at Catania on the east coast, Whipcord called for British formations to land in two areas—Catania in the east and Palermo in the west—and then proceed to take over the island. When the outline for Husky was issued in early January 1943, the planned dispersion had become even more pronounced, with seven different beaches and ports around the island eventually scheduled for landings. In all three instances, planners estimated that it would take the navy twenty-five to twenty-eight days to get all of the necessary troops and supplies, including reinforcements, to the combat zone. Nonetheless, what the comparison makes clear is that, over the course of two years, plans for Sicily had been altered from a preemptive attack to an assault of major proportions.

Was Husky then as it evolved a continuation of Britain's "soft underbelly" theory by which it would attack the enemy at its weaker parts?[104] The answer, according to Sir Michael Howard, is that it was not so much a case of Britain's dedication to a peripheral strategy as it was, at this point, the fullest extention of the victory being won in North Africa. In the view of the British leaders, the Mediterranean emphasis would further relieve shipping difficulties, eventually provide additional air bases for bombing European targets, hasten Italy's military collapse, and cause further strains on the German war machine, even to the point of forcing the Germans to divert part of their resources from the Russian Front and thus assisting Britain's eastern ally. Britain's focus on the Mediterranean was not designed to forestall the Russians in Europe; rather its main goal was to engage the enemy continuously in battle in what the British considered the most effective way possible, and not to have their troops stand idle while a cross-Channel assault was being readied. In this sense, Britain's Mediterranean strategy had become more opportunistic than peripheral, and Husky was an integral part of that strategy.

After Casablanca, the Husky plan, which differed little from Britain's preconference outline, was turned over to Eisenhower's staff for additional planning.[105] Though under Eisenhower, the British Mediterranean commanders—Alexander, Cunningham, and Tedder—still had considerable input. In this way, much to Eisenhower's initial displeasure—for it upset his established procedures—Husky became truly a combined enterprise. Eisenhower's integrated headquarters in Algiers made the plans, which then had to be coordinated with the British land, sea, and air commanders. The result was a lot of wrangling among the various senior officers and their staffs, but in the end, an effective overall plan was produced.

The process was not without its difficulties, however. While the arduous fighting in Tunisia did not upset the planning, it did dictate Husky's timing and deflected the attention of Eisenhower, Alexander, and others from concentrating solely on Sicily. Moreover, Eisenhower seemed somewhat overwhelmed by all of the intricacies involved and the various constituencies he had to satisfy. Not only did the combined chiefs and Churchill and Roosevelt have a keen interest in the plan but the British commanders, now bursting with confidence, also wanted a definite say in the preparations. While staying with the idea that the landings, focused in the southeast and northwest, were to be widely dispersed, on March 22, the American supreme commander suggested that one of the secondary attacks at the southwestern port of Sciacca, designed to capture an airfield and thus provide air support for the western assaults, be eliminated because of shipping and manpower problems.[106] On March 25, the British chiefs voiced their opposition to dropping the Sciacca attack. Eisenhower withdrew his proposal. He did manage, however, to get extra forces from England for the southeastern landing, which had been advocated by Alexander, and eventually additional assault craft as well.

Perhaps reflecting recent setbacks in Tunisia, Eisenhower was also concerned about German troops in Sicily and went so far as to send the British chiefs a memo stating that two Wehrmacht divisions on the island might be sufficient reason to force a postponement of the operation, now set for July 10. Churchill's reply, by way of the chiefs of staff, was a stinging retort to Eisenhower's pessimism.[107]

If the presence of two German divisions is held to be decisive against any operation of an amphibious character open to the million men now in North Africa, it is difficult to see how the war can be carried on. Months of preparations, seapower and air power in abundance, and yet two German divisions are sufficient to knock it all on the head. . . . I trust the Chiefs of Staff will not accept these pusillanimous and defeatist doctrines, from whomever they come. . . . I regard the matter as serious in the last degree. We have told the Russians that they cannot have their supplies by the Northern convoy for the sake of 'Husky', and now 'Husky' is to be abandoned if there are two German divisions (strength unspecific) in the neighbourhood. What Stalin would think of this, when he has 185 German divisions on his front I cannot imagine.

There were no more warnings of possible disaster from Eisenhower and his headquarters.

Another problem, discussed previously, came to a head during April. In a confrontation that shows him at his best and worst, Montgomery, who was to direct the British land forces, insisted that the southeastern landings were not sufficiently strong and called for US divisions to come ashore just to the left of the British and to form a flanking force as the campaign unfolded. A change of this nature would eliminate the Palermo and other western landings, and not only the Americans, but also Admiral Cunningham and Air Marshal Tedder were opposed to Montgomery's proposal.[108] The leaders involved met at Algiers on May 2 to reconcile their differences. Alexander now backed Montgomery, and Eisenhower and his chief of staff, Bedell Smith, also gave in to the obstinate Eighth Army commander. On May 3, Eisenhower telegraphed the combined chiefs that all of the theater commanders now agreed that the assault would be concentrated in the southeast. Montgomery, in his now-becoming-familiar self-congratulatory tone, wrote to Alexander on May 5 to explain his position as follows:[109]

As far as the world is concerned, and particularly the enemy, Eighth Army is still controlling the battle in this corner of the battle area.

And this is true; because I myself am here and I direct operations, making the plans and controlling the policy.

And this must go on; the enemy must not have any reason to think that I have pulled out.

By May 10, as the Tunisian fighting wound down, a new outline plan had been prepared. Three days later, Churchill and Roosevelt and the combined chiefs approved it while meeting in Washington.[110] Before the conference adjourned, Eisenhower confirmed that July 10 was still the projected assault day.

The revised plan, issued at the end of May, provided for seven British, Canadian, and US divisions to land along the southeastern coastline of the 10,000-square-mile island in a predawn attack.[111] Preliminary naval gunfire and air bombardments were to neutralize Axis shipping and to gain air superiority. Just prior to the seaborne attacks, airborne brigades were to land beyond the coast to assist in the taking of airfields and the ports of Siracusa on the eastern shore and Licata (later abandoned) on the western end of the beachhead. Once the Americans had moved from the west and the British from the east to join near Ragusa, and after Augusta and Catania harbors and the Gerbini group of airfields had been captured, the Allies were to take over the rest of the island, with the Americans protecting the British flank as the latter overcame the expected heart of the enemy defense around Messina.

The outline above does not do justice to the complexity of Husky.[112] The operation was to be mounted and assembled from four widely scattered areas— the United States, Britain, Algeria and Tunisia, and Egypt. It required a gigantic Allied naval armada, divided into two task forces, to lift the forces to the area, and a huge air force to soften up the enemy defenses, cover the invasion beaches, and carry out the first large-scale Allied airborne attack. This large expenditure of men and matériel, especially landing craft, ruled out any possibility of even a small cross-Channel landing in 1943.

In the preliminary operations, the British and increasingly the Americans carried out a series of activities. One of the most important was the capture of the islands of Pantelleria and nearby Lampedusa for use as air bases from which to attack Sicily.[113] On June 11, after days of heavy air and naval bombardment, the British 1st Infantry division landed on Pantelleria. The small German contingent had already left, and although there was some enemy air resistance, the Italians surrendered without a fight. The same occurred on Lampedusa on June 12 and 13. An American fighter group was in place on Pantelleria by June 26.

In addition, in the softening up process, Allied air forces flew a total of 12,962 Husky-related sorties between June 13 and July 3.[114] In the week prior to the assault, 8,799 sorties were flown, and an increasing number of them were bomber attacks against targets in Italy to slow the flow of reinforcements south. Air Marshal Tedder asserts that by invasion day, July 10, the Germans did not have a single airfield in Sicily fully operational.

By this time, the Allies had readied what was considered then and now a truly formidable combined force.[115] It consisted of portions of nine divisions initially; with reinforcements, it was to reach 14⅔ divisions (8⅓ British). Ten and one-third were to be infantry, the equivalent of 2⅓ armored, and 2 airborne. The naval task forces totaled 2,590 ships and landing craft, of which 1,614 were British, 945 American, and 31 Belgian, Polish, Norwegian, Greek, and Dutch. The fleet among this number consisted of six battleships, two aircraft carriers, 18 cruisers of various types, 119 destroyers, and 23 submarines. The Allied forces (minus transports) were made up of 3,462 aircraft, of which 2,510 were serviceable, and many of them were fighters based on Malta, Pantelleria, and other smaller islands. Although Eisenhower and Alexander, Cunningham, and Tedder were in overall command, leading the tactical forces were Generals Patton and Edwin House and Admiral H. Kent Hewitt for the Americans; and Montgomery, Air Vice Marshal Harry Broadhurst, and Admiral Sir Bertram Ramsay for the British. All of them, except for House, had had extensive experience in combat operations.

The Axis' situation in the Mediterranean had deteriorated substantially during 1943. They had tried to build up their forces on Sicily, for despite successful Allied deception measures during the spring and early summer, by July they expected the island to be invaded, though they did not know exactly where.[116] Consequently, they spread out their equivalent of eight divisions in the western and eastern parts of the island. The best two were the German Hermann Göring division, with 99 serviceable tanks (13 Tigers), and the 15th Panzer Grenadier division, with 60 tanks. The navy consisted almost solely of portions of the Italian fleet, and included five capital ships and two cruisers. Their air forces were composed of 1,750 aircraft in all of Italy, Sicily, and Sardinia. It is estimated that about 775 German aircraft were within range of Sicily; on the island itself, 289 (143 serviceable) were German, and 145 (63 serviceable) were Italian. The Allies had already attained air superiority at the time of the landings, so that the Axis forces confined themselves mainly to raids against the invasion fleet.[117] The supreme Axis commander for the area was Field Marshal Kesselring, with General Alfredo Guzzoni heading the Italian forces.

The Allied invasion began with airborne formations landing after midnight behind the coast.[118] Although helpful in easing the task of the seaborne forces, it eventually became apparent that the airborne operations had not been as successful as first thought.[119] In all, the British and Americans had undertaken four drops, two on the night of the invasion and two additional ones on July 11 and 13. The drops involved 8,416 troops. Most of the British operations were conducted with gliders; on July 10, only 12 of the 137 gliders landed in the correct zone, and 50 of them came down in the sea. In the American zone, paratroops in the first drop were scattered over an area fifty to sixty miles long, and on the July 11 drop, the transporting aircraft were fired upon by friendly ships and land-based antiaircraft, with the result that the aircraft suffered severe losses and damage. Nevertheless, Allied leaders continued to believe in the potential of airborne operations, and utilized them extensively in future campaigns.

The amphibious landings went much more smoothly, in part because of air superiority, in part because of a lack of enemy resistance on the beaches. Beginning at 2:45 a.m. and continuing until about 6 a.m., the first wave struck at seven different beaches along 100 miles of Sicilian shoreline. Four and one-third divisions of the British Eighth Army—the 5th, 50th, 51st, 1st Canadian, and 321st Infantry Brigade—landed in the southeastern corner between south of Siracusa and west of Pachino. Three American Seventh Army divisions—the 1st, 3rd, and 45th—assaulted beaches farther west between south of Scoglitti and west of Licata. The attack forces soon established themselves and started moving inland. By the end of the day, considerable gains had been made, and Pachino airfield on the extreme southeastern tip was in British hands. The onslaught continued the next day. It was found that more personnel and equipment could be offloaded over the beaches than anticipated, and these beach unloadings, plus those at several ports, enabled an estimated 163,100 soldiers, 14,200 vehicles, and 596 tanks to be brought ashore by midnight of July 11.

On July 12, US and Canadian units joined their beachheads at Ragusa. Although Axis resistance, especially below Catania, was stiffening, on July 14 plans began to be formulated for reducing the rest of the island. Two days later, Alexander issued his plan. It called for the British XIII Corps to move north along the eastern coast and around Mt. Etna toward Messina, while XXX Corps drove north to split the island from north to south before it, too, pushed east toward Messina. The US Seventh Army was to protect the flank. Once XXX Corps had reached the northern coast, the Americans were to advance toward Palermo and liberate that area. General Patton, who had already positioned part of his force for a westerly move, was greatly upset, and his protest to Eisenhower resulted in a change of plans. While part of General Omar Bradley's II Corps thrust north, the other part was to capture Palermo and the rest of the western half of the island. After this had been accomplished, the Americans were to shift their forces east toward Messina. On the evening of July 22, Palermo was taken, thus vindicating Patton's plan.

In the meantime, Allied aircraft were producing devastating results, particularly against interdiction targets. The early capture of numerous airfields in Sicily eased the flying burden, and thirty fighter squadrons were operating from them by July 23. On invasion day, the Allies flew 2,543 sorties, and between July 10 and 22, British, American, and some French pilots flew 18,389 more, or an average of 1,657 every twenty-four hours. Between July 22 and August 17, when the campaign ended, they flew another 36,884 sorties, with an increasing proportion bomber and fighter bomber rather than fighter missions. By the time it was over, the Allies had flown 57,816 sorties for an average of 1,482 per day.

During the midst of the July fighting, two events of overriding strategic significance took place. One was the overthrow and arrest of Mussolini by the Fascist Grand Council on July 25. This move understandably alarmed the Germans, who intensified their plans to take over the peninsula and those areas in southern France and the Balkans occupied by the Italians. Italy was still nominally an ally, however, and any open break would compound Germany's military problems, already reaching crisis proportions in Russia. Hitler therefore decided to wait before moving. The new Italian government under Field Marshal Pietro Badoglio also found itself in a dilemma. Italian leaders wanted to exit the war, yet not alienate their German partner unalterably for fear of reprisals. In mid-August, after preliminary contacts, the government began secret negotiations with the Allies, but not until September 3 (announced on September 8) did they reach an agreement. Soon after the announcement, the Germans swiftly occupied the country and the other Italian-occupied areas. The second event, precipitated by Mussolini's fall, occurred on July 26, when the combined chiefs ordered Eisenhower to assault the Italian mainland as soon as was practicable. To carry through on this decision, as discussed in May at the Washington conference and subsequently at Eisenhower's headquarters but not formally agreed upon, meant not only an attempt to eliminate Italy, but also an ongoing commitment in the Mediterranean, until, and as it turned out, Germany was defeated on all fronts.

By August 1, the Allies were in position for the final drive to liberate Messina. The Germans and Italians held a line from south of Catania on the east coast through Triona to San Stefano in the north. With the Americans pushing from the west and the British from the south, the outnumbered Axis forces could do little but hold on as long as possible so that they could get as many of their troops and equipment across the Straits of Messina as possible. The British took Catania after fierce fighting on August 5, and on August 11, the Axis pull out started in earnest. Allied aircraft tried to prevent the evacuation, but German and Italian flak was so heavy that the British and American pilots could not prevent it. By the time Patton's Seventh Army, followed closely by the British, entered Messina on August 17, 60,000 German and 75,000 Italian soldiers had gotten away.[120]

The campaign was over. Sicily had been taken in thirty-nine days. Although sources differ as to the exact figures, it is estimated that the Axis had 167,000 casualties, many of them Italians who surrendered *en masse*.[121] Allied casualties numbered 31,158. Even more one-sided were the losses in aircraft. About 740 Axis planes were destroyed in combat, and another 1,100 (600 German), on the ground.[122] Allied aircraft losses were less than 400.

Tactically, Husky was a very important amphibious operation for the Allies.[123] According to Martin Blumenson, it was a vast improvement on the rudimentary techniques employed for Torch; it introduced new communications and command procedures; it made use of new equipment, such as landing ships and a two-and-a-half-ton amphibious truck called the DUKW; and it featured new methods for beach organization and supply. And though it did not make effective use of aircraft for close air support of ground troops, it did impress on the Americans as well as on the British, who were already convinced by their experiences in North Africa, the overriding importance of tactical air forces.

As for intelligence, the Allies received no indication how Germany and Italy reacted to the Sicilian invasion, but they did receive a good deal of tactical information.[124] On July 14, for instance, the Allies learned that the enemy had decided to abandon the western half of the island, and on the same day it became apparent that it was reinforcing the eastern half. It also became clear from Ultra and other sources that the Luftwaffe was withdrawing its fighters to the mainland, an operation carried through between July 16 and 22. But the Allies were not sure about Axis plans to evacuate the island until August 10, even though Kesselring had stated his plans for a general evacuation much earlier. Overall, then, Ultra continued to be helpful, but the "bits and pieces" picked up were not put together in time to influence the outcome of specific operations.

In regard to strategy, one might ask whether the Husky invasion plan, which emphasized concentration on force, was the best choice. Its success in thirty-nine days would seem to justify its use, although Eisenhower on August 5 indicated that perhaps victory could have been achieved sooner had he pushed harder during the early stages of the campaign.[125] Possibly we should view the operation from a different perspective. In looking back on Husky, Admiral Cunningham indicated that although the plan as carried out was a good one, he was "perfectly confident that any of the alternative plans would [also] have succeeded."[126] In other words, Cunningham was contending that, given Allied naval and air superiority, dispersal instead of concentration might have been just as effective.

Although the British did not pause after Sicily to reflect on what had been accomplished during the earlier North African campaign, it was obvious that they had learned a great deal. Despite the Crusader victory in late 1941 and early 1942, they had been frustrated by the subsequent Axis counterattack and even more humiliated by Rommel's May 1942 Gazala offensive. British leaders knew that, besides more equipment and personnel, they also required more resolute commanders at all levels, further training of their troops, and better coordination among the ground, sea, and air components. The improvements that came about for the British were not so dramatic as they were incremental. It is difficult to put an exact date to the turnabout, but by Second Alamein, it was well underway. Although the Axis, especially the German, forces still fought tenaciously, the Allies had by now started to improve on some of Germany's techniques, such as the use of tactical air power and long-range reconnaissance groups, and had added elements of their own, including effective landing craft and other devices for amphibious warfare. In this way, the North African and Sicilian experiences aided the Allies in preparing and refining subsequent joint and combined operations as well as in giving them added confidence for the battles ahead. Overall, the British realized that the turnabout also owed much to the increase in men and matériel. They had made some progress without the United States at their side, but with the infusion of American arms and later their manpower, sufficient resources were finally at hand to make a visible difference. In fact, by the end of the Sicilian campaign, each of the Allied partners had roughly the same number of combat troops—168,000—involved in the fighting.[127] This process the British well understood and appreciated. For them, the corner had not only been reached, but also turned, and they faced the future with greater optimism than ever before.

NINE

The Battle of the Atlantic

When considering naval and air aspects of World War II, two points almost immediately come to mind. One is the dominant roles that tradition and geography assumed in the forging of Britain's and Germany's naval and air strategies. The other is that naval and air power were both separate and highly integrated features of these two countries' war efforts. They were separate in the sense that, in certain instances, most notably the Battle of the Atlantic and the strategic bombing offensive, either the naval or the air element predominated. If other military services were involved, as in the case of long-range search aircraft, they were subordinate to the main service component. But they were more often integrated with the other services, in that both combatants constantly utilized two or three elements when conducting combined arms or amphibious operations. In these cases, the land, sea, and air components fused with one another, though in varying proportions.

Seapower, of course, had been the cornerstone of British strategy for centuries. Without it, in Britain's view, not only would vital sea communications be imperiled, but also eventually the British Isles themselves.[1] This thinking had led the British over the years to build up and retain a strong, balanced fleet designed to protect the trade routes and to ply the world's oceans. It also led them, for technological and strategic reasons, to develop air power. While they well understood the offensive potential of this new type of warfare, they further appreciated how vulnerable warships had become in its wake, as evidenced during the early encounters in the North Sea and the Norwegian campaigns. This factor, along with the Battle of Britain and an increasing number of land operations, caused the British to move toward a balanced air as well as a naval arm.

For the Germans, the situation was not quite so straightforward. They, too, appreciated the potential of sea and air power.[2] They, too, wanted to develop balanced air and naval forces that included offensive long- and short-range and defensive components. That they started the European war almost before their "balanced" building program had commenced, however, forced the Germans to fight according to short-term requirements and to continue their age-old reliance on land warfare. The concepts of a balanced fleet and air force were put off and finally abandoned. This turn of events did not mean that Hitler and the other military leaders were ignorant of the naval and air components, for they often took them into account in their planning. It meant merely that they were so dependent on the exigencies of the moment that immediate needs had to take priority. Aircraft were built increasingly to support land operations and eventually to defend the homeland and occupied territories from air attacks. The navy became more dependent on the submarine as it evolved into the main weapon in the commerce war being fought in the Atlantic. The interesting point is that even though these air and naval wars were separate and undertaken directly by the Germans to protect their production and to subject the Allies to prohibitive shipping losses, they were linked indirectly to bringing about victory in the land campaigns. In this context, land operations always took priority for the Germans, and air and sea considerations were subordinate to them.

Nevertheless, various aspects of the air and naval wars do deserve our attention. In the naval sphere, the Battle of the Atlantic is the obvious choice, for both sides devoted substantial resources and energy to it. While it is impossible here to examine this long and extended campaign in all of its ramifications, it is possible to deal briefly with the early phases and its aftermath and to concentrate on its high point between December 1942 and May 1943 and still gain an appreciation of its importance. It is also possible, in this way, to get an understanding of how the Battle of the Atlantic fit into Germany's and Britain's overall strategies.

What has been called "the most prolonged and complex battle in the history of naval warfare" went though a number of phases.[3] As analyzed by Jürgen Rohwer, during the first phase, between September 1939 and March 1940, the Germans undertook raids by surface vessels and with their small submarine fleet. In retrospect, the damage they inflicted then was relatively minor. During the second and third phases, between July 1940 and December 1941, the German effort expanded dramatically because they were able to make use of Norwegian and French Bay of Biscay harbors and anchorages. Though the sinking of the battleship *Bismarck* in May signaled a virtual end to the use of capital ships as raiders, the U-boat gained in significance, and by the end of 1941, 249 were in commission. Nevertheless, the number of Allied sinkings decreased during the autumn months as German U-boats were drawn to North African and Norwegian waters and as Ultra and more convoy escorts became available to the British. During the fourth phase, between December 1941 and July 1942, German submarines resumed extensive operations, and they were particularly effective against US shipping in the western Atlantic. During the fifth phase, between August 1942 and May 1943, the intensity of the battle increased even more, with the German submarine force putting its maximum effort into the mid-Atlantic air gap and the Allies doing everything they could to counter it. By May 1943, the Allies had achieved success, though the possibility of Germany's resurrecting the battle remained until the end.

Through all the various phases, the German goal continued to be the same: to eliminate Allied ships coming across the Atlantic and thereby seriously undermine the Allies' ability to carry out operations in Europe and the periphery. German naval leaders never went so far as to claim that they could halt the flow of goods and personnel entirely, but they did think their U-boats could have a devastating effect on Anglo-American plans. To do so, the *Kriegsmarine* believed, required two related conditions. First, the number of U-boats had to increase faster than they were lost. The production rate was set at twenty per month, which approximated the German output of new U-boats in mid-1942.[4] Second, the German navy had to sink at least 700,000 tons of Allied and neutral merchant shipping per month.[5] This figure—from Donitz's perspective—would be sufficient to overcome the capabilities of US and British shipyards to replenish their merchant fleet.

The pertinent figures for 1942 show the extent to which the German navy achieved its goal (tables 9-1 and 9-2).[6] The Germans accomplished the 700,000-ton objective in four of twelve months and approached the figure in five others. Of the 7.79 million tons sunk, 6.27 million tons were sunk by submarines, or 80.5 percent of the year's total. With regard to the number of submarines, German shipyards put 238 into service and lost only 88 in combat, for a gain of 150. By the end of the year, 393 U-boats were in commission, and naval leaders expected this figure to rise even further in the months ahead.

No wonder the British were worried. They thought that the U-boat could be defeated by a combination of naval support groups; long-range, shore-based aircraft; radar; shipborne high-frequency, direction-finding (HF/DF) equipment; and continuous radio intelligence. But they still feared that the balance might not shift in their favor in time. In terms of ships and aircraft, they realized they needed more fast escort vessels, including escort carriers, and

TABLE 9-1
Allied Merchant Ship Losses, 1942

	Tonnage (Ships)
January	419,907 (106)
February	679,632 (154)
March	834,164 (273)
April	674,457 (132)
May	705,050 (151)
June	834,196 (173)
July	618,113 (128)
August	661,133 (123)
September	567,327 (114)
October	637,833 (101)
November	807,754 (134)
December	348,902 (73)
Date Unknown	2,229 (2)
Total	7,790,697 (1,664)

TABLE 9-2
German Submarines, 1942

	Gains (Losses)
January–March	49 (12)
April–June	59 (10)
July–September	61 (32)
October–December	69 (34)

more four-engined bombers equipped to range far out to sea. More new 10-centimeter radar on the aircraft were needed, for the enemy could detect Britain's 1½-meter radar, thereby avoiding surprise attacks. More ships had to be outfitted with HF/DF. These elements were crucial to the Allies, for only with added surface mobility could they effectively hunt down the U-boats when the latter moved into position to fire their torpedoes. Through Ultra, the British had been able to decrypt German naval radio traffic with regularity between July 1941 and February 1942, but when the *Kriegsmarine* installed new Enigma machines on its U-boats, the British were unable to decipher its messages again until December. This regained capability was obviously a breakthrough of major proportions.

Churchill and the chiefs of staff were well aware how tenuous the situation was. In October 1942, he wired Roosevelt, "First of all, I put the U-boat menace. This I am sure is our worst danger."[7] Pound, in a note to the prime minister on November 23, went further, writing that the situation in the North Atlantic "is such that we cannot allow it to continue as at present. The Minister of War Transport has represented that if our convoys continue to be knocked about in the Atlantic . . . there are signs that the merchant seamen may refuse to sail."[8] Members of Parliament even began debating the possibility of appointing a supreme commander for the Atlantic battle, a suggestion with which British naval leaders for the moment did not concur.[9] Yet the feeling that something must be done—and soon—permeated into the next year. At the Casablanca conference in January, the "defeat of the U-boat" was accorded top priority.[10] In other words, the Battle of the Atlantic had become the overriding concern of both American and British military leaders. The question was whether this concern could be translated into action in time to stave off defeat.

As the battle reached its crucial phase, the elements for conducting it, including the leaders, the types of forces and equipment, and the tactics involved were for the most part in place. The German naval leadership was highly centralized in the person of Dönitz, and became even more so in late January after he became head of the navy as well as retaining his position as commander-in-chief, U-Boats. Although Dönitz did not completely deemphasize the need for heavy surface ships, as some military leaders had predicted, his involvement in the U-boat war continued unabated.[11] Not only did he integrate his U-boat staff with the Naval High Command in Berlin, he also replaced or transferred a number of commanders whose ideas did not coincide with his own. In this way, he put his own people into key positions, such as the more pliable Admiral Wilhelm Meisel as Naval High Command chief of staff, though he did leave Rear Admiral Eberhardt Godt to conduct the day-to-day submarine activities in the west. The navy might have benefited from a better relationship with the Luftwaffe, but it was never close. Although the Germans did at times make use of aircraft for anticonvoy work, it was a minor factor in the U-boat war.

The Allied command structure was more decentralized.[12] The Admiralty through First Sea Lord Pound exercised overall operational control in the eastern half of the Atlantic, and the US Navy, the western half. During April 1943, the Canadian Northwestern Atlantic Command took over operational responsibility for northern convoys west of 47°, and the British command, Western Approaches, under Admiral Max Horton for those east of that line. The American Tenth Fleet assumed control over the central and southern Atlantic routes. Britain's Coastal Command, though operationally under the Royal Navy since December 1940, remained administratively under the RAF, and many of its squadrons, flying from bases in Iceland and the United Kingdom, were heavily involved in the naval war.[13] Coastal Command was headed by Air Chief Marshal Sir Philip Joubert de la Ferté until February, and then, by Air Marshal Sir John Slessor. Directing the exceedingly important Submarine Tracking Room was Captain Rodger Winn, and the Plotting Room, Commander Richard Hall. US Captain Kenneth Knowles undertook similar duties on the other side of the Atlantic.

By December 1942, the Germans had about 400 U-boats in service, but after taking into account those being worked up, involved in training, and stationed in other waters, on March 1, only 182 were in the Atlantic.[14] Of the 182, 70 were in operational areas, 44 on the way out or back, and 68 in French or German North Sea harbors, thus approximating the usual one-third on station, one-third coming or going, and one-third in port. The most common type of submarine was Type VIIC, followed by Type IXC (table 9-3).[15]

While the submarines' endurance was extended by using refuelers, called "milk cows," the U-boats did have several drawbacks. Their inability to sustain

TABLE 9-3
German Submarine Characteristics

	VIIC	*IXC*
Tons	500	740
Range in Miles	8,850	13,450
Maximum Surface Speed	17	18.2
Maximum Submerged Speed	7.6	7.3
Torpedoes	14	22

maximum surface and underwater speeds for long periods made it impossible for them to follow effectively fast ships, such as troop ships. Furthermore, their dependence on batteries for underwater propulsion increased their vulnerability by forcing them to surface at night to recharge their batteries.

To combat the U-boat, the Allies emphasized escort groups and shore-based aircraft along with effective radar and Ultra intelligence. The escorts groups, which were to protect the forty-to-sixty-ship convoys, eventually reached twelve in number, to include seven British, four Canadian, and one US group.[16] Each group contained six to nine ships, including destroyers, frigates, and corvettes, and in late March, the British and Americans also reintroduced escort carriers with up to twenty aircraft each. The shore-based aircraft posed a difficult, though not insuperable, problem for the Allies. So long as they had to depend on long- and medium-range aircraft with ranges from 600 to 1,800 miles, there were gaps in the air coverage over the Atlantic, especially in "the Gap," which stretched from south of Greenland to the Azores. Here U-boats could lie in wait beyond the effective operational range of the B-17 Fortresses, B-24 Liberators, Halifaxes, Whitleys, and Wellingtons. The solution, of course, was to extend the range of the patrol aircraft to more than 2,000 miles, and specially modified, very long range Liberators were found to be particularly suitable. Their availability would make it impossible for the U-boat packs to assemble and deploy, since the latter's ability to concentrate on convoys and position for attack depended on surface maneuverability. Although the Liberators had started coming into the inventory in mid-1942, they still numbered only 18 in February 1943. But more were on the way, and Liberators, flying from Newfoundland and Labrador, were eventually expected to have a significant effect. As a further advance, the Allies started fitting ships with new direction-finding equipment and aircraft with short 10-centimeter radar that the U-boats could not yet detect. Radar and increasing airpower made the U-boats especially vulnerable, and it was not certain whether their commanders, despite a growing submarine fleet, could cope with all of these increasingly formidable Allied countermeasures.

Also by this time, the tactics employed on both sides had for the most part become standardized.[17] The Germans normally used wolfpacks. They followed the basic principles of centralized control, concentration, and, if possible, mass attack. U-Boat Command controlled all phases except the attack itself. The Germans collected their six-to-twenty-boat packs at sea on both sides of the Atlantic with at least one on the eastern and one on the western ends of the convoy lanes. Each wolfpack was given a name—*Draufgänger* (Daredevil), *Falke* (Falcon), *Habicht* (Hawk), and so on—although the length of time they remained in existence, like the number of submarines in each group, varied considerably. The groups would await the convoys, and if contact were made, they would shadow and attack the enemy for as long as possible across the Atlantic. After refueling as necessary, often northeast of Bermuda, the wolfpacks would be in position to move in the opposite direction. After breaking off on the eastern side, those U-boats with sufficient fuel would join a new group, and the others, which either had too little fuel or were damaged or had expended their torpedoes, returned to base. The commanders usually fired their torpedoes on the surface at night because their U-boats were less likely to be detected. The limited range and accuracy of the torpedoes dictated that the submarines had to get close to the potential target. When a convoy was located during the day, it was usually shadowed and then attacked at night. The best chance for the wolfpacks to succeed was on the first night, since after that time the enemy's defenses often became progressively stronger.

The Allied convoys were designated by letters, HX for fast eastbound North Atlantic crossings, SC for slow ones. When going west, the letters were ON for fast, ONS for slow. The more southerly convoys, plying between New York or Norfolk and Gibraltar or Casablanca, between the West Indies and Britain, or along the western and eastern Atlantic coasts, also had their own letter designations. A convoy normally set out in the early afternoon so as to establish its route order before dark. The fast convoys had a minimum speed of 10 knots; the slower ones, 7½ knots. They were arranged, depending on the number of ships, in 7 to 14 columns with 3 to 5 ships per column. Ideally, the space between the columns was 1,000 meters, and between the ships in line, 500 meters. All were given a tactical number used for keeping in radio contact with one another. The convoy commodore was in charge of the convoy. The senior officer of the escort (SOE) was in charge of the entire operation, but he commanded through the commodore. In practice, they worked as a team, but the SOE was really in command. The primary antisubmarine weapon used by the escort vessels was the depth charge, although it could also be dropped effectively from aircraft at very low altitudes (best at fifty feet above the surface).[18]

Besides working directly with convoys, Coastal Command, and to a limited extent Bomber Command, undertook two other antisubmarine missions.[19] One was to patrol the Bay of Biscay and to attack surface U-boats as they proceeded to and from ports. Although these actions did bring results during the last half of 1943 and did slow down the submarines in reaching their rendezvous points, since they had to submerge constantly, the Bay of Biscay patrols were not a telling factor during the battle's crucial phases and were called off after March. The other mission was to have Bomber Command destroy the U-boat bases themselves, but though some damage was done to surrounding facilities, the attacks had little effect on the submarines and their heavily protected pens.

The Atlantic battle had reached its crucial stage by December 1942. Both sides realized it was moving toward a climax. The Allies knew they had to clear the sea lanes if they wanted to get sufficient men and matériel across the Atlantic. Otherwise, their ability to launch a cross-Channel attack would be sharply curtailed and perhaps even impossible to carry out. The German

U-boat commanders were just as determined to prevent large numbers of ships from coming across. For our purposes, it is unnecessary to follow all of the many actions, but it will be helpful to summarize the battle between December 1942 and May 1943 and to highlight some of the combat and other activities in which both sides were involved.[20]

In December, the German success rate declined sharply from that of the previous month, in large part because of unbelievably horrible weather. Nevertheless, the Germans managed to deal Allied convoy ONS 154 a devastating blow by sinking fourteen of its ships. Bad weather also plagued the Germans in January, although they did sink a number of stragglers. Toward the end of the month, Dönitz again exhorted his wolfpacks to converge aggressively on any sighted convoy. U-Boat Command radioed its commanders: "Your aim is to get at the convoy again and again as quickly as possible."

During early February, the Germans' new zeal paid off.[21] Group *Pfeil* (Arrow) with eleven boats, made contact with Allied eastbound convoy SC 118 on February 4 and sank seven ships within three hours two nights later. The damage was done by Baron von Forstner's U-402 and Captain Franke's U-262, both of which had gotten inside the convoy. By the time it was all over on February 8, ten merchant ships had been sunk. First Sea Lord Pound tried to put the best possible face on the attack. In a memorandum to Churchill, he wrote: "Having regard to the large number of U-boats operating around the convoy, possibly 20, it is considered that the losses were not heavy."[22] But he knew better. Although the loss of ten ships was high, though not inordinately so, the significant point was that the sixty-three-ship convoy had been heavily escorted by ten vessels and aircraft from Iceland and had still suffered a substantial loss. Pound pointed out that when a very long range Liberator had been in the vicinity, as on the day of February 6, the wolfpack had had to submerge. After the Liberator had had to break off its patrol, the devastating attack had taken place. He indicated further that once the convoy came within range of UK-based Fortresses, only one more ship had been lost. Hence there was an urgent need for more very long range aircraft. Throughout the rest of February, the Germans could point to some additional successes, especially against westbound convoys, but not enough to have a major impact.

Throughout the winter and spring, as already mentioned, the information gleaned from Ultra was a considerable factor in the Atlantic battle. Most of the decryptions dealt with routine matters—repairs being done on the U-boats while at sea, rendezvous points, arrival and departure orders for the wolfpacks, German radio transmitter frequencies, weather reports. Messages of this nature were exceedingly helpful in building up information on all aspects of the U-boat effort, but were seldom of tactical value. Given that the U-boats were in a sense homes-away-from-home for the sailors, the messages at times had a morale-boosting aspect.[23] On December 14, for example, U-boat headquarters informed U-125 that a "daughter was born to

Seaman 1st Class Radtke. Mother and daughter well." On December 31, headquarters performed the proxy marriage of Radioman 3rd Class Schoppmann-Ketting on U-515 to his bride on shore. That same day, Dönitz radioed his submariners: "U-boat men: The new year will see us, as all three previous years, uninterrupted in battle. Wherever we may be, whether in contact with the enemy, from the North Cape to the Cape of Good Hope, from the coast of America to the Mediterranean, or in the preparation and construction of new U-boats and equipment, we have only one goal: to strike the opponent. . . . Everything for our German home. Long live the Führer."

Of greater operational significance were messages dealing with U-boat location, operations, and condition.[24] On December 9, for instance, U-441 was reported returning to Brest with only a limited diving capacity, and its location was given. On December 10, submarine commander Manseck reported to headquarters that he had torpedoed two freighters and then gave his location as 55°10′N and 21°05′W. The British found out with little delay that on December 14, Group *Ungestürm* (Storm) of nine boats had set up a patrol line west of Ireland and was moving slowly in a westerly direction. Two days later, U-boat Command radioed the *Raufbold* (Brawler) wolfpack the following instructions: "Stick it out with convoy. Their escort is powerless in this weather. Since conditions are extremely favorable for attack and since we know from experience that torpedoes will run in foulest weather, attack according to opportunities." Such information was bound to be of considerable assistance to the Allies.

The prime example of Ultra's value occurred during the first twenty-two days of March. On March 1, the Germans introduced a new rotor on their Atlantic U-boat cipher machines. This put the Allies "in the dark" for three weeks. When combined with Germany's success against the Allied convoy cipher, the result was that the battle turned dramatically in favor of U-Boat Command. Its wolfpacks seemingly had little difficulty locating the approximately fifty-ship eastbound convoys. The consequence was that four of them in succession were heavily attacked.[25] On March 6, U-boat 405 sighted convoy SC 121. Despite air patrols and a sea escort of one destroyer, one frigate, and three corvettes, two wolfpacks converged on the convoy, and by the time the U-boats had broken off on March 10, thirteen ships had been torpedoed and sunk. On the same day, German submarine group *Neuland* (New Land) made contact with the faster HX 228 convoy and torpedoed four freighters on March 10 and 11. The Allied sea escort of six to nine ships had difficulties with the weather, and the attacks had taken place in the Gap beyond the range of shore-based aircraft.

Even more devastating attacks were registered by wolfpacks *Raubgraf* (Robber Baron) and *Stürmer* (Attacker) against HX 229 and SC 122. *Raubgraf* consisted of nine U-boats and *Stürmer* nineteen of a total of thirty-eight in North Atlantic waters. HX 229 and SC 122 together comprised about one hundred ships. SC 122 was escorted by seven ships, and an eighth for a time. HX229 was inadequately escorted by two destroyers and two corvettes, as well as by one destroyer and air escorts for several days. On March 15, the attack groups cited the two convoys. By March 16, the slower SC convoy had caught up with HX 229, and the fighting began. Between March 16 and March 18, the wolfpacks sank twenty convoy ships in the Gap. Although the submarine commanders sank only one additional ship after March 18, the operation continued for two more days. At 5 p.m. on March 19, U-boat Command urged its submariners that "in spite of aircraft, try absolutely to get ahead in order to be near the convoy when darkness falls. Take advantage of last chance tonight, since operation will be discontinued tomorrow at dawn."[26] On March 20, it was over. While the Allies had lost twenty-one ships, the U-boats had suffered no losses, though they had had one sunk by enemy aircraft after the attacks had been broken off.[27] On March 21, Dönitz congratulated the crews of the *Raubgraf* and *Stürmer* groups with the following message: "Appreciation and recognition for the greatest success yet achieved against a convoy. After the extraordinarily successful surprise blow of the first night, tough and energetic pursuit, despite strong air and surface defense, brought splendid successes to the submarines in their attacks both by day and night."[28]

For the Allies, the results during the March 1–20 period had indeed been devastating. Although 155 of the convoy ships had arrived safely, 32 had been sunk, and 9 of those that reached port had been damaged by torpedoes.[29] The casualty figures for Allied shipping worldwide for the twenty days were also high. Among the North Atlantic merchant ships, 67, including stragglers, had been sunk, and altogether, 85 had been lost, for a total of more than half a million tons of shipping.[30] German losses had been 6 U-boats. The Allies realized that part of the problem stemmed from Germany's introduction of a new rotor on its Enigma machines.[31] They also realized that the enemy had known the convoy routes and surmised that the Germans had deployed "contact" U-boats along the routes.[32] What the Allies failed to appreciate was that the German intelligence B-Dienst was reading about 80 percent of the British messages during this time. This problem was not rectified until June 10, by which date the Allies were able to get their codes changed.

During the last eleven days of March, conditions changed again, in large part because the Allies had rebroken the German cipher. German U-boats briefly made contact with the next two eastbound convoys—HX 230 and SC 123—but only one convoy straggler was sunk. U-boat group *Seeteufel* (Sea Devil) also sighted westbound Convoy ON 173, but achieved no successes. For March 20–31, the total for all North Atlantic operations was only ten ships, far below the sixty-seven sunk during the first twenty days. Ironically, on March 31, Hitler agreed to have the number of submarines produced per month doubled from twenty to forty.

During April, the course of the battle did not change appreciably. The U-boats continued to locate some of the convoys, including westbound ones, and exact some losses, but not so many as to be prohibitive to the Allies. On the other hand, submarine losses were not prohibitive either. Wolfpack *Löwenherz* (Lionheart) of fifteen boats intercepted and sunk five ships from Convoy HX 231 southeast of Greenland. The *Lerche* (Lark) group of ten submarines torpedoed and sunk three more from HX 232, and the *Meise* (Titmouse) group sank one from HX 233. The results did not approach the magnitude of March, and Dönitz toward the end of April decided to change tactics.[33] Allied radar was warning the convoys of possible German surface attacks at night, and the air and sea escorts were forcing the U-boats to remain submerged so long that they could not keep up with the convoys during the day. Dönitz therefore ordered that the U-boats surface during daylight hours to recharge their batteries and to fight off any surprise attack, especially from aircraft, with their 37-mm deck gun. This change proved disastrous, for the U-boat gun was no match for undetected low-flying aircraft.

During May, the Allies gained the upper hand. Although at least three wolfpacks were operating, they either had difficulty finding the expected convoys or were subjected to strong enemy defensive measures if contact was made. On May 4–6, the Germans sank twelve ships from westbound ONS-5, but at a cost of seven U-boats. On May 8 U-Boat Command indicated that the recent eastbound convoys had obviously known the location of the U-boat patrol line and had sailed south of convoys.[34] The only explanation, they surmised, was a security leak, and a thorough investigation was launched. As for a break in their Enigma codes, they thought it "improbable." Meanwhile, submarine losses mounted. On May 21, a message from headquarters to its U-boat commanders made explicit the severity of the situation:

> With the last two North Atlantic convoys we have gotten nowhere. . . . Now if there is anyone who thinks that combatting convoys is therefore no longer possible, he is a weakling and no true U-boat captain. The battle in the Atlantic is getting harder, but it is the determining element in waging the war. Keep yourselves aware of your high responsibility and do not fail to understand that you must answer for your actions. Do your best with this convoy [HX 239]. We must smash it to bits. If circumstances permit, do not submerge from aircraft. Shoot and ward them off. Make surface escapes from destroyers whenever possible. Be tough, get ahead and attack. I believe in you.[35]

Despite the exhortation, eight U-boats were lost in the attempt to overcome the Allied forces protecting HX 239. With an estimated thirty to forty U-boats sunk during the first three weeks of May, Dönitz on May 23 alerted the wolfpacks that they would have to shift their U-boats south, and he confirmed this move the next day.[36] Although he expected to resume the battle once appropriate countermeasures had been developed, he had acknowledged, in effect, "temporary" defeat.

The Allies were not able to confirm the victory definitely until early June, when its true significance became apparent as a result of decrypted signals.

But they were already aware in late May that the battle was turning decisively in their favor.[37] At the Trident conference in Washington, Churchill on May 24 "indicated that there might be as many as 30 [U-boat] sinkings in May. If this continued, a striking change would come over the scene." On May 26th, the vice chief of the naval staff, Sir Henry Moore, reported to the Anti U-Boat Committee "that the number of U-boats operating in the Atlantic at the present time was estimated to be considerably less than last week" and "there seemed little doubt that May would prove to be the best month since the beginning of the war." On May 30, Pound wrote to Cunningham: "The U-boat war is going well at the moment and I think some of the Huns are getting cold feet." Thus, when the victory came, it was appreciated but not unexpected.

The figures for Allied merchant ships and tonnage lost and German submarines lost from January to May 1943 tell the story (tables 9-4 and 9-5).[38] March was the critical month for the Allies, and May for the Germans. Except for May, the number of U-boats placed in service exceeded losses. These figures make it evident that Dönitz was correct in thinking that the battle was not irretrievably lost but might be renewed if effective countermeasures, such as "snorkels," which would allow U-boats to remain submerged while recharging their batteries, could be brought into operational use.

As mentioned previously, the Allied victory can be attributed to a number of factors—naval support groups, including escort carriers; shore-based air patrols; shortwave radar; direction-finding equipment; and Ultra intelligence. To these five factors should be added a sixth: the various Allied conferences and committees which not only looked into the U-boat problem, but also took steps to see that it was overcome.

All of the Allied military leaders recognized the significance of the naval support groups. At the beginning of 1943, however, they had insufficient destroyers, frigates, and corvettes to meet all of their convoy commitments.[39] Assuming adequate air cover, Allied planners estimated that a minimum of

.TABLE 9-4

Total Allied Merchant Ship Losses and North Atlantic Losses, January–May 1943

	Tonnage (Ships)	North Atlantic Losses Tonnage (Ships)
January	261,359 (50)	176,691 (27)
February	403,062 (73)	288,625 (46)
March	693,389 (120)	476,349 (82)
April	344,680 (64)	235,478 (39)
May	299,428 (58)	163,507 (34)
Totals	2,001,918 (365)	1,336,650 (228)

TABLE 9-5
**German Submarine Losses and North Atlantic Losses,
January–May 1943**

	Gains (Losses)	North Atlantic Losses
January	21 (6)	2
February	21 (19)	14
March	27 (15)	12
April	18 (15)	12
May	28 (41)	36
Totals	115 (96)	76

seven operational escort ships per convoy was necessary to combat the wolf-packs. Although the number of escorts required would be fewer on routes where there were fewer U-boats around, the planners still felt that 309 destroyers and 653 ocean-going escorts (over 200 feet in length) would be necessary to fulfill their minimal requirements. Yet on January 1, only 258 destroyers and 500 other escorts were available—a deficiency of 204 ships. Taking into account attrition through sinkings and extended repair work, the Allies further estimated that it would be July or August before sufficient additional vessels could be constructed to reach the 758-ship minimum. It would be a long spring and summer in 1943.

The difficulty was alleviated to an extent by moving escorts from the less to the more threatened waters and by reintroducing of escort carriers in late March—they numbered three in the North Atlantic by May. Moreover, troop ships, including the *Queen Mary* and the *Queen Elizabeth*, were too fast for submarines to shadow and attack, hence were able to sail alone or in convoys that did not exceed four ships. Yet, although the number of destroyers and other escorts in service was rising every month, another report in March showed that without air support, twelve operational support ships per convoy were now thought necessary if the convoys were not to be overwhelmed by the ever larger wolfpacks.[40]

The escort problem could be solved in the near term only by emphasizing another factor, long-range patrol aircraft with a range of over 2,000 miles. As in the case of support groups, leaders recognized that sufficient air patrols were an effective antidote to the U-boat.[41] The difficulty again was having enough in the "North Atlantic danger zone" to have an effect. All types of aircraft were considered important—short-range Hudsons and Swordfish torpedo aircraft, medium-range Wellingtons, long-range Catalina flying boats and Halifaxes, Fortresses, and Liberators—and some of these could be moved from less endangered areas and away from Bay of Biscay operations. Nevertheless, the key aircraft was deemed to be the specially modified, very long range Liberator. At Casablanca, the leaders had been told that 80 would probably be sufficient, 60 on the British side of the Atlantic and 20 on the

American and Canadian side. By the end of March the total was revised to 260 to reflect more realistic estimates and the use of Liberators at night as well as during the day.[42] Also at the end of March, the Americans, who had allocated large numbers of Liberators for reconnaissance duties, especially in the Pacific, agreed that their use in the North Atlantic should have top priority.

The figures are indicative of the change that took place. As of March 1, the British had only 25 very long range Liberators flying from Iceland and Northern Ireland; the Americans and Canadians had none in their area. On April 16, at a combined chiefs meeting, Air Marshal Foster pointed out to the American representatives that as of that date "there was [still] not a single VLR aircraft operating west of Iceland."[43] General Arnold, head of the USAAF, replied that Liberators were on the way. By May 5, the British had 62, the Americans and Canadians 17, although not all of them, of course, were operational on any given day.[44] This number fell short of the March estimate of 118 very long range bombers projected to be in service by May, but when one adds 17 Gibraltar-based Liberators to the 79 operating in the North Atlantic, the total of 96 aircraft is relatively close to the projected figure. By the end of May, the number having taken another jump to 178, there were enough VLR aircraft (including some Halifaxes) deployed in Central and North Atlantic waters to have a substantial impact. The Allies had quickly closed the gap.[45]

The figures for Coastal Command sightings and attacks during May reveal another interesting aspect of the story (table 9-6).[46] The number of sightings in May reached a crescendo of 81 during the third week and then diminished sharply to 27, reflecting Dönitz's closing down of the North Atlantic battle.

Two other, technological factors helped the pilots and ship commanders. The one for aircraft was the 10-centimeter radar whose beams the Germans could not detect. Installation of the new radar, which replaced the longer, but compromised, 1½ meter radar, had begun in January 1943, and by March it had been placed on many of the aircraft.[47] Because the radar made it possible to locate submarines on the surface at night and in foggy weather, this advantage made patrol aircraft truly a formidable opponent. Escort ships, on the other hand, made effective use of automatic direction-finding equipment, which allowed them to intercept radio messages between U-boats that were near by. Once a submarine was located, the escort could move toward it, force it to dive on short notice, and then attack with depth charges.

Just as significant was the role of Ultra.[48] Since the Germans, through B-Dienst, also had broken the Allied codes, it is difficult to ascertain why the British and Americans were more successful. Part of the reason is probably the diligence with which the Allied analysts performed their task. According to Admiral Cunningham, "every submarine leaving an enemy harbour was tracked and plotted, and at any moment Capt. C. R. B. Winn could give the numbers, likely position and movement of all the U-boats at sea. His

TABLE 9-6
Coastal Command Actions, April–May 1943

	Sightings	*Attacks*
April 26–May 2	33	25
May 3–9	39	33
May 10–16	42	30
May 17–23	81	43
May 24–30	27	17

prescience was amazing." The Allies were able to put together into a meaningful pattern all the scraps of information they received—U-boat headings, enemy operational plans, passage reports, position reports while on station, information while returning, fuel on hand, details on new equipment, even general situation reports. The results were not applied to offensive actions until June 1943, but were used solely for evading the enemy. Rohwer indicates that between mid-July 1942 and the end of May 1943, the Anglo-Americans managed to reroute 105 out of 174 North Atlantic convoys, or about 60 percent, around the German wolfpacks without being spotted. Of the 69 that the U-boats located, 23 escaped without loss, 40 sustained minor losses, and only 16 lost more than four ships. Ultra obviously proved its worth.

The final factor was Allied committees and conferences. Most important of these was Britain's Anti-U-Boat Warfare Committee.[49] It met weekly from November 4, 1942, through mid-1943, and its significance was underlined by Churchill's chairing the initial meeting and by his continuing interest in its discussions. Though preceded by other naval warfare committees, one as early as March 1941, and supplemented by the Inter-Allied Anti-Submarine Survey Board, the Anti-U-Boat Committee served as the catalyst in overcoming Germany's effort in the Atlantic. When the services differed over allocations of aircraft, it determined that some twenty new Halifaxes projected for Bomber Command were to be given to Coastal Command instead. When questions arose as to whether antisubmarine patrols in the Bay of Biscay were to receive priority, it decided that the Atlantic patrolling was to be given precedence. When Allied leaders at Casablanca called for the deployment of more naval escorts and shore-based aircraft in the North Atlantic, the committee requested material assistance from the Americans and made sure that anti-U-boat forces were increased. In fact, it had provided the American and British participants at the meeting with the necessary data on which to base their decisions. The committee's constant concern was rewarded, it will be recalled, when at the conclusion of Casablanca, measures for combatting the U-boat were accorded "first charge on the resources of the United Nations."[50] Admirals Sir Percy Noble and Sir Max Horton, commanders-in-chief, Western Approaches, had been saying the thing for the past year, but the committee gave their warnings new urgency.

In addition, the Anti-U-Boat Committee studied new techniques and weapons for the submarine war. On February 5, for example, it devoted most of its time to discussing the operational research of Professor Pat Blackett. Based on a wide range of statistics, his report, one of several, emphasized the value of adequate air cover; the relative unimportance of the size of convoys, at least those having between twenty and sixty ships; and the significance of convoy speed. He noted, for instance, that slow eastbound convoys had suffered 1.75 times more losses than the fast convoys, and that increasing the speed from seven to nine knots had reduced losses by 43 percent. Information such as this obviously assisted the committee a great deal in making its recommendations.

Conferences among the Allies also helped in the combined effort. Besides Casablanca and the May Trident meeting in Washington, during which the U-boat problem was investigated extensively, the Canadians talked the Americans into calling the Atlantic Convoy Conference during early March.[51] Although the British thought little could be gained from such a meeting, US, British, and Canadian naval and air representatives were able to go over a number of common issues and to recommend several actions. It was at this meeting that the Allies agreed to have the Canadians and British "take complete charge of the northern trans-Atlantic convoys, except for the short leg between Halifax and Boston or New York," and to have the Americans take over the responsibility for those using central and southern Atlantic routes. The American reason for the change was US Admiral King's desire to concentrate his country's ships on the more southerly routes that were serving American forces in the Mediterranean and his preference for US escorts to be under US command, although he did allow an escort carrier group to be employed farther north under the Royal Navy. Another important point discussed at the conference was that the U-boat menace, as Admiral Sir Percy Noble put it, was "becoming every day more and more an air problem." Accordingly, every effort was to be expended to bring additional very long range aircraft into the Atlantic theater as soon as possible, especially for bases in Newfoundland and Labrador. The Atlantic Convoy Conference proceedings did, then, bring about some positive changes in Allied procedures and, perhaps more important, demonstrated the Allies' resolve to turn the battle in their favor.

All of these factors were instrumental in winning the Battle of the Atlantic. Ultra intelligence played a significant part in rerouting the convoys. Ten-centimeter radar and direction-finding equipment enabled locating the submarines. Once the U-boats were found, naval and carrier escorts and shore-based aircraft pressed home their attacks. While shore-based aircraft were involved in 52 percent of the submarine losses, surface escorts had a hand in 39 percent of them (table 9-7).[52] Overall, both naval and air leaders must have been pleased with the contributions their servicemen had made during the battle.

In the aftermath of the May turnaround, two points—one for each side—

TABLE 9-7
Submarine Kills, April–May 1943

Surface Escorts	16
Carrier Aircraft	2
Carrier Aircraft and Surface Escorts	2
Shore-Based Aircraft and SurfaceEscorts	4
Shore-Based Aircraft	25
Other Causes	7
Total	56

soon became clear. One, the Allies would not relax their war against the U-boat, and, in fact, they intensified it. Two, the German navy truly considered the diversion of its submarines to other waters to be temporary and expected to renew the North Atlantic offensive at a future date.[53] In its view, once improvements could be developed, such as the snorkel, they might well be able to resume attacks against the northern convoys. Moreover, U-boat production, despite Allied bombings, continued at a rate of twenty to thirty per month. With the introduction of new types of submarines having underwater speeds of up to seventeen knots, the battle, the Germans felt, could be turned once again in their favor.

But the Germans could not overcome the growing Allied anti-U-boat forces.[54] In June, the Allies began emphasizing again Bay of Biscay operations, and with the addition of ten-centimeter radar and Liberators on loan from Newfoundland, they sank twenty-five submarines in the area over the summer. At the same time, bombers stepped up attacks on German submarine plants and assembly yards. While not cutting off U-boat production, the raids decreased the rate of production and delayed the introduction of the faster submarine Types XXI and XXIII until early 1945. In addition, not only did the *Kriegsmarine* lose 141 U-boats during the last six months of 1943, it also lost ten refueling vessels, so that only two were left at the end of the year. In September 1943, the Germans, armed with new search receivers and acoustic torpedoes, attempted to resume the North Atlantic battle, but during the two months in which wolfpacks operated, only nine Allied merchant ships were lost at a cost of twenty-five U-boats. Despite continuing Allied vigilance and the understandable fear that the Germans might revive the submarine war at any moment, the U-boat campaign had, in effect, been won in mid-1943.

When one places the Battle of the Atlantic into a broader framework, at least five conclusions can be drawn. The first, often repeated in this chapter, is that the defeat of the U-boat was attributable, not to a single factor, but to a combination of factors, including naval support groups, air patrols, radar, and radio intelligence. This trend, evident in May 1943, continued throughout the rest of the year. Of the 141 U-boats sunk between June 1 and December

31, the Germans lost 30 to surface vessels, 5 of which were shared kills; 22 to escort carriers with 1 shared; and 71 to shore-based aircraft with 4 shared. Over 50 percent of the kills are thus attributable to Liberators, Wellingtons, and other RAF aircraft, but their success would not have been achieved without naval escorts, the fleet air arm, and technological advances.

Second, the Battle of the Atlantic by 1943, at least for the British, provides "an example of inter-Service cooperation at its best."[55] Although Coastal Command remained an integral part of the RAF, "operational direction" was in the hands of the Royal Navy. It was a centralized system which puzzled many, but because of the give-and-take that existed between the Admiralty and the Coastal Command headquarters, the results were exemplary. In August 1943, Captain Vest of the US navy described this air force–navy relationship in the following terms: "For two years I have been trying to find an official definition of [Britain's] 'operational direction' without any success. In fact, it is quite unusual to find two people who agree as to just what it means. However, in this particular case it seems to work fairly well, with few exceptions." The Germans certainly would have benefited had their navy and Luftwaffe developed such a relationship.

Third, the Allied triumph in the Atlantic ensured a western invasion of the Continent in 1944. This victory, coupled with the almost simultaneous opening of the entire Mediterranean to shipping, eased Britain's logistics difficulties worldwide. With regard to preparations for Overlord, the increase in cargo and troops arriving in the United Kingdom was dramatic.[56] In May 1943, the amount of matériel brought across was 251,832 tons. In June, it more than doubled to 542,001 tons and reached a 1943 peak of 1,018,343 tons in October, declining only slightly to 910,482 tons in December. The number of troops also rose, from 19,220 in May to 49,972 in June. By October, the total was 105,557; by December, 133,716. There is something to be said for Roskill's contention that the Atlantic battle might have been won six months earlier had the Admiralty pushed more strongly for additional aircraft, but Roskill's assertion is a retrospective one. [57] In mid-1943, leaders on both sides of the Atlantic seemed relieved that the tide of battle had turned so quickly.

Fourth, Dönitz's assumption that the tonnage war could be won by sinking 700,000 tons of Allied shipping per month was far wide of the mark. Already by the third quarter of 1942, the British, American, and other Allies were putting into service more merchant vessel tonnage than was being sunk, and the figure of 468,000 deadweight tons gained between July and September continued to rise in succeeding quarters (table 9-8).[58] As Rohwer has put it, "the Allied shipbuilding yards . . . won the tonnage war."[59]

Since construction gains exceeded losses beginning in mid-1942, might one contend that the Atlantic battle was not really in jeopardy in March 1943, or at least that the threat is overstated?[60] The answer has to be yes. There was some apprehension among Admiralty officials in late March, but

TABLE 9-8

Allied Gains in Merchant Shipping
(In Thousands of Deadweight Tons)

October–December 1942	+ 942
January–March 1943	+ 1,937
April–June 1943	+ 4,037
July–September 1943	+ 3,691
October–December 1943	+ 3,885

this view was not shared by those closer to the battle. Beesly states that the idea of defeat "was never held even privately by [those in] the Tracking Room," and staff officers at Western Approaches Command headquarters, who directed the convoys, recorded that while the situation at the time was difficult, they expected it to improve, as it in fact did in April. By early 1943, British military leaders felt that though they did not know the timing, victory in the Atlantic was inevitable. To them, it was not a matter of if, but when. In this instance, their optimism was not misplaced.

Fifth, and finally, the Battle of the Atlantic exonerated those in Britain who believed in a multidimensional navy. Although Pound early in the war displayed a decided preference for naval surface forces, he eventually came to realize the importance of shore-based aircraft in fighting on the high seas. The Germans, on the other hand, opted almost exclusively for the submarine. When this course failed to be decisive in mid-1943, they decided to try to improve the U-boat so that the battle could be resumed. By this time, the possibility of relying more on a surface fleet or on aircraft was no longer a viable alternative. The result was that they were simply not equipped to wage a world war against a foe with many more tools at its disposal.

TEN

Strategic Bombing vs. Air Defense

When comparing the Allies' strategic bombing offensive with Germany's defensive effort against it, one is struck by the relative importance the two sides attributed to those aspects of their air strategies. For the British, and later in combination with the Americans, there was never any question as to the significance of strategic bombing. It was part of their overall strategy from the beginning. While their military leaders, especially those from the army and navy, at times questioned the proportion of effort being devoted to it, none of them seriously called for its cessation. The Germans, on the other hand, were not overconcerned with Britain's strategic bombing during the war's early years. They undertook countermeasures, of course, but so long as the enemy bombing raids on their war production did not result in excessive damage, they could use their fighter aircraft more for operations on the land fronts than primarily for air defense. Britain's thousand-plane raids in May and June 1942 did cause genuine alarm; however, since hundreds of training aircraft took part, they could not be sustained. Only in 1943, first with the raids against the Ruhr and then with the devastating attacks on Hamburg, did Germany begin to shift substantial resources to meet the Allied aerial threat. Even at this point, Hitler and Göring were reluctant to allocate their aircraft solely to air defense duties. Only the pressure of seemingly continuous Allied bombings forced the Luftwaffe to become essentially a defensive force. By the time it did so, in late 1943, Allied air power had become so formidable that it could not be overcome. Despite some subsequent reverses, for all intents and purposes, by May 1944 the Allies had won the air battle.

During 1940 and 1941, Britain's bombing offensive and Germany's countermeasures were in their infancy.[1] Yet several features of their respective air policies became evident during this early period. One was Britain's emphasis on "area bombing" at night.[2] Although Bomber Command did not adopt a formal policy on area bombing until February 1942, it was already in practice during 1941, in part because the RAF high command was wedded to a prewar deterrent conception of bombing enemy cities, in part because bombing attacks against specific long-range targets, such as synthetic oil plants, had proved disappointing. In addition, almost from the beginning, most of Bomber Command's raids had been undertaken at night to limit losses.[3] In this way, the

British hoped to have an effect on German morale and cause at least some damage to the urban centers.

The German response to Britain's attacks was, of course, to develop an air defense system.[4] It started in July 1940 when General Josef Kammhuber was appointed to establish a night fighter division. Even though Hitler halted Kammhuber's use of the night fighters and bombers for intruder attacks against air bases in Britain, Kammhuber was able to erect a combination of searchlight belts and defensive boxes, called *Himmelbett*, or four-poster beds, in the west. The boxes, ground control intercept stations set about twenty miles apart so as to give overlapping coverage, at first did not work very well, for the acoustical devices on which the ground controllers and pilots depended were seldom able to locate the approaching bombers. With the introduction of *Freya* and *Würzburg* radar, however, the Bf 110 night fighters, supplemented by searchlights and antiaircraft batteries, became a formidable system. Each ground control intercept station had *Freya* radar, which was used for early warning, and two short-range *Würzburg* sets, one to track the incoming bomber and one to track the German fighter so that the pilot could be directed to the enemy. Even though each station could engage only one aircraft at a time, the belt was constantly being "thickened" so that by the end of 1941, it was inflicting considerable losses on the British bombers. It did not develop into what it might have become because the Germans were constantly diverting fighters for use in the land theaters, but the number of aircraft assigned to night air defense duties rose from 116 in September 1940 to 250 a year later, and the number of heavy flak, four-gun batteries increased from 791 to 967.

In a sense, Germany's early system worked adequately. Not only did Britain's bomber loss rate rise from about 1.7 percent in the spring of 1941 to 2.5 percent in the early summer, to 3.9 percent per aircraft sortied in the late summer and fall, but damage from the attacks was less than might have been expected.[5] The relative ineffectiveness of the raids was known to the British as well. An August 1941 report prepared by civil servant D. M. Butt, and based on June and July photographs and aircrew reports, indicated that very few bombers were hitting the assigned targets.

The accuracy problem was only one of several plaguing Bomber Command's effort.[6] Another was that while the number of operational squadrons increased from 39 in March to 54 in November and the average number of sorties per 24-hour day nearly doubled from 57.7 to 107.6, the sortie total during the fall months was about the same as it had been during the summer and was even slightly lower than the number of aircraft dispatched a year earlier in September 1940.[7] Moreover, the number of tons of bombs dropped in September 1941 was only a little higher than that of the year before (2,781 tons to 2,307). Part of the problem was that production could not meet British expectations. The British had hoped to expand substantially the number of heavy bombers coming on line, but they were to be disappointed.[8] In April

1941, for instance, they had expected 59 bombers to be produced. The actual figure had been 27. They anticipated 90 in July, but a July report indicated the total was expected to be only 67, and shortfalls were also predicted for October and for January 1942.

Despite Churchill's championing of strategic bombing, all of these problems led him to question Bomber Command's most precious assumption: that the strategic bomber was a "war-winning weapon." Air leaders continued to adhere to the belief that the bomber had unique capabilities, and Portal went so far as to call for a 4,000-bomber force to strike the enemy's cities, but Churchill noted on September 27, 1941: "It is very disputable whether bombing by itself will be a decisive factor in the present war. On the contrary, all that we have learnt since the war began shows that its effects, both physical and moral, are greatly exaggerated."[9] On October 7, he amplified his thoughts: "Everything is being done to create the Bombing force desired on the largest possible scale, and there is no intention of changing this policy. I deprecate, however, placing unbounded confidence in this means of attack. . . . One has to do the best one can, but he is an unwise man who thinks there is any *certain* method of winning the war, or indeed any other war between equals in strength."[10] In other words, he would continue to back the strategic bombing campaign, but he considered it only one of the methods for achieving victory.

British air policies in 1942 reflected Churchill's realism. Military leaders hoped that strategic bombing would have an impact, but they were aware that there was a limit to what could be accomplished. It was, in fact, a year of ups and downs in which the stage was set for more far-reaching successes. It was not a year of sustained, decisive operations. Those would have to await 1943 and early 1944.

At first during 1942, Churchill seemed optimistic about the possibilities of aerial bombing. Upon his return from the Arcadia meeting in Washington, he wrote: "In order to wear down the enemy, and hamper his counter-preparations, the bombing offense of Germany from England and of Italy from Malta and, if possible, from Tripoli and Tunis, must reach the highest scale of intensity."[11] In his view, this would be possible because the number of British first-line aircraft had now surpassed that of Germany and because both the Americans and the Russians would add their considerable resources to the air war. He went so far as to note that "there is no reason why a decisive victory of the air should not be established even before the Summer of 1943, and meanwhile heavy and continuous punishment inflicted upon Germany."

Still, in the near term, there remained the twin problems of insufficient aircraft coupled with aircraft losses and the air crews' inability to hit the assigned targets. Several February bombing directives, which set forth the basis for the year's fighting, reflected an admixture of hope and caution.[12] They were hopeful that Bomber Command could make a greater effort against targets inside Germany by use of a new navigational aid, codenamed Gee, which was to come into service in March. It was believed that the increased tempo of attacks "would hearten and support the Russians" and "would further depress German morale." But there was also a cautious tone to the directives. Gee, which permitted navigators to get a radar fix on transmissions, could be employed only for targets within a 350-mile radius of stations in England. Thus, it could best be used against industrial areas in the Ruhr and the Rhineland, with the northwestern coastal cities as alternatives, although raids farther inside Germany might be undertaken "when really favourable conditions" existed. In addition, Gee was expected to be a temporary solution, "because it will probably only be a short time before the enemy institutes effective counter-measures," a forecast which came true in August when the Luftwaffe succeeded in jamming Gee transmissions.

Then there was the question of German morale. Here it was not so much a matter of assessing the effects of the bombing on the population as it was an admission that area bombing was the only type of mission with which the British might cause some damage. Their emphasis on area bombing did not mean that senior RAF officers had given up entirely upon precision bombing, but it did mean that their belief in its efficacy was a fleeting one.

This type of thinking persisted into the spring.[13] Raids against the Reich might eventually force the Germans to transfer some of their fighters and antiaircraft guns to the west, and the attacks were thought to be having some effect against urban targets, such as at Lübeck and Rostock in northern Germany and at the large Renault factory outside Paris. However, an appraisal of recent bombings by Justice John E. Singleton, issued on May 20, indicated that "whatever target is chosen there are always difficulties in finding it, and many of the bombs carried are wasted or are ineffective." Singleton called for a sustained air effort, but his report was filled with caveats. He did state, for instance, that "the bomber strength of the Royal Air Force is increasing rapidly, and I have no doubt that, if the best use is made of it, the effect on Germany's war production and effort will be very heavy over a period of twelve to eighteen months, and such as to have a real effect on the war position." But in his summation, he wrote:

> I do not think that great results can be hoped for within six months from "air attacks on Germany at the greatest possible strength." I cannot help feeling that the six-month period ought to be looked upon as leading up to, and forming part of, a longer and more sustained effort, than as expected to produce results within that limited period of time. Much depends on what happens in Russia. The effect of a reverse for Germany, or of lack of success, would be greatly increased by an intensified bombing programme in the autumn and winter, and if this was coupled with knowledge in Germany that the bombing would be on an increasing scale until the end, and with the realisation of the fact that the German Air Force could not again achieve equality, I think it might well prove the turning point—provided always that greater accuracy can be achieved.

The report therefore contained something for critics and proponents alike. Air leaders were pleased that Singleton acknowledged the importance of the air offensive. They also admitted that he was correct in his assessment that greater bombing accuracy was required, and Portal feared that "any failure on our part to effect a radical improvement may well endanger the whole of our bomber policy."[14] First Sea Lord Pound picked up on the call for greater accuracy as well as the point that no great results could be expected within the next six months to advocate, as he had before, that bombers could be put to better use in the near term by attacking U-boat construction facilities or by helping protect the sea lanes. Field Marshal Brooke, with army forces stretched in North Africa, wanted more bomber support for the army.[15] Despite the success of the Cologne thousand-plane raid, Air Marshal Harris, head of Bomber Command since February, did not help the strategic bombing cause by writing directly to Churchill in June and recommending that all Coastal Command, Middle Eastern, and Army Cooperation Command "bomber-type aircraft" be returned to Bomber Command immediately and that the "highest possible priority" be given to producing heavy bombers.[16] Although Churchill was impressed by the raids, he knew that Harris's thinking was unrealistic. Thus area bombing would continue on as great a scale as possible, but not to the exclusion of other tasks.

Meanwhile, Germany's defensive strategy for attacking the British bomber formations continued along the so-called Kammhuber Line, with radar providing early warning and directing fighter squadrons, particularly night fighter squadrons, to their prey. These measures, along with searchlights and antiaircraft guns, forced the British to go around the defensive boxes until they realized they could overwhelm the individual control stations, which could only deal with one enemy bomber at a time, by using compact bomber streams.[17] Even after the thousand-plane raids, the Germans did not emphasize fighters for defensive purposes, but continued to prefer them at the land fronts instead. While the number of antiaircraft batteries did rise, the number of fighters produced and deployed for defensive purposes remained relatively steady throughout 1942, and so long as bomb damage was not excessive and enemy sortie totals did not average many more than 100 per day, the Luftwaffe was content not to alter appreciably its existing system.[18] Its reluctance to invest more effort into air defense was also shared by Hitler, Göring, and Jeschonnek, and although the Führer was increasingly disillusioned with Göring and started to intervene more and more in air matters, their agreement on this matter meant that air defense of the Reich was not given top priority.[19]

Nevertheless, important strides were made in the air battle on both sides during 1942, notably in terms of navigational aids, aircraft, and techniques. This was especially true with the British. Besides Gee, which allowed radar pulses from Britain to be displayed on a cathode ray tube inside the aircraft, enabling the navigator to plot the plane's position, the RAF came up with two other devices, Oboe and H2S.[20] Although the devices were not introduced until December 1942 and January 1943, research on the two new radars had been going on for some time, and Oboe and especially H2S eventually exerted considerable influence on the evolution of strategic air power. Oboe was a bearing and distance device which permitted an aircraft to fly along a radio beam until a predetermined point was reached for bombing. The beam was the result of directional signals sent out from Britain, and they picked up the echo reflected by the aircraft. A controller in England directed the course of the aircraft through a pulse which was audible to the pilot and sounded similar to the musical instrument of the same name. If the plane deviated from the correct course, there was an easily recognizable variation in the pulse. When the aircraft approached the target, it gave off another signal—a series of dashes followed by a series of dots. When the dots ceased, the bombadier released the bombs. Though highly accurate, it could be used only by a small number of aircraft at any one time. Its range was limited because its transmission was straight-line and the curvature of the earth meant the angle, hence the plane's altitude, had to be increased for the bombers to receive it. Thus, Oboe was used more for marking targets than for the bomb runs themselves.

H2S (the American equivalent was H2X) was less accurate, but it showed great promise because the equipment could be carried exclusively in the aircraft. It consisted of a transmitter which scanned the surface below to pick up radio echoes and displayed the result on a cathode ray tube indicator. Since different kinds of ground gave different responses, as did land and water, it allowed the navigator to make out shapes, such as coastlines, rivers, and builtup areas, and the shapes could then be used as points of reference to establish the plane's position and that of the intended target. While H2S was difficult to interpret and its emissions could be picked up by the enemy, it was later to evolve into the standard blind-bombing device. First, however, it had to be refined.

Another advance for the British was the introduction of the four-engine Lancaster bomber.[21] When compared with early British models, the Lancaster was truly a magnificent aircraft. It could be flown at a maximum speed of 266 mph at a ceiling of 20,000 feet and could carry a normal bomb load of 16,000 pounds. Its 1,660-mile range was unequaled among the British bombers. Its only flaw was that its eight .303 machine guns were inadequate against enemy fighters. The Lancaster had arrived just in time, for its predecessor, the twin-engined Manchester, had proved a disappointment; the aging Hampdens needed to be replaced; and the slower Whitleys could now be shifted to Coastal Command. By the end of the year, the Lancaster, as well as four-engined Stirlings and Halifaxes, constituted the bulk of the long-range bomber force.

With regard to techniques, in addition to using the bomber stream to overwhelm single German boxes, the British came up with a Pathfinder force to mark targets and thus improve bombing accuracy. It was first used in

August 1942, and the methods employed, including flares, did increase the concentration of bombs near a target.[22] But the number of Lancasters, Stirlings, and Halifaxes (and later Mosquitoes) that were used as Pathfinders was limited, and the technique, because of wind and other factors, was still of greater assistance for area, rather than precision, bombing. Another technique that showed great potential in the air war was Ultra, but in 1942 it was used mainly for order of battle information and contributed little to operations, in part because the Luftwaffe made little use of wireless traffic in the west.[23] By 1943, however, Ultra information did help in developing the means to counter German radar and to frame more effective bombing policies.

The German innovations were not so extensive, but *Lichtenstein* radar, introduced on board some of the aircraft, improved the Luftwaffe's night-fighting capabilities. With it, fighters could locate individual bombers at close range after having been vectored by ground radar operators to the vicinity of the enemy plane. Also by late 1942, the defensive aircraft the Germans would use for the remainder of the war were now appearing in substantial numbers.[24] The twin-engined Messerschmitt Bf 110G, with a maximum speed of 342 mph and two 30-mm cannon, two 20-mm cannon, and two 7.9-mm machine guns as armament, became the main night fighter. It was comple-mented by Junker JU-88C aircraft with a maximum speed of 307 mph and three 20-mm cannons and four machine guns. Two single-engined fighters—the Bf 109G and the Focke Wulf 190A—became the primary day fighters, though they were also used later at night. The 109 had a maximum speed of 386 mph, but was too lightly armed, having one 30-mm cannon or one 20-mm cannon plus two 13-mm machine guns. The highly maneuverable FW 190, though produced in fewer numbers than the 109, had a maximum speed of 389 mph and four 20-mm cannon and two 7.9 machine guns. These fighters, along with the JU 88 and antiaircraft artillery, became the backbone of the German defensive effort.

Only two of the major British bombing operations during 1942 can be highlighted. One is the famous May 30–31 thousand-plane raid on Cologne. The other is much less well known, but more typical, an October 5–6 assault against Aachen.

The Cologne attack was one of three thousand-plane raids, the other two being against Essen on June 1 and Bremen on June 25, but it was the most spectacular, both in publicity and in results.[25] Although a number of other successful operations, including ones against Lübeck and Rostock, had already been launched during the spring, none was on the scale that Air Marshal Harris desired. He therefore came up with the idea of a thousand-plane attack designed to saturate an entire city with bombs and mentioned the possibility to Portal on May 18. Portal then spoke to Churchill, and both thought it an excellent idea. On May 20, Harris set forth his reasoning in a memo to Air Vice Marshal W. A. Coryton of 5 Group.[26] In it, Harris "proposed to put over the maximum possible force of bombers on a single and extremely important town in Germany with a view to wiping it out in one night or at the most in two." To accomplish the task, he said he needed practically every aircraft capable of carrying a useful bomb load, and he hoped to get hold of training aircraft as well as others, possibly from Coastal Command, in addition to the 700 Bomber Command could make available. He also stipulated that as many incendiary bombs as possible be used in proportion to high-explosive bombs. He set the date for May 28 "or the first suitable night thereafter." The primary target was to be Hamburg, but Cologne, designated as the alternate, was eventually selected.[27] On May 30, the weather was deemed suitable for Operation Millenium to proceed.

Bomber Command was able to assemble 1,047 aircraft for the raid. The forces consisted of 602 Wellingtons, 131 Halifaxes, 88 Stirlings, 79 Hampdens, 73 Lancasters, 46 Manchesters, and 28 Whitleys. Approximately 620 of them were from Bomber Command, 423 from training units, and only 4 from other sources (and none from Coastal Command).[28]

As for the attack itself, it took place during a moon period; thus no flares were used. Eight hundred eighty-three planes reached the target, and they attacked in three waves. The force was led by Gee-equipped aircraft which dropped mainly incendiary bombs. They were followed by bomb groups with a mixture of incendiary and high-explosive bombs. Within ninety minutes, the raid was over.

Later reconnaissance photos showed extensive damage from the 1,455 tons of bombs dropped. Local records confirm the devastation. They indicate that 3,300 buildings were destroyed and 9,510 damaged, as well as 13,010 homes destroyed and 28,630 damaged, and that nearly all of the destruction was caused by incendiaries rather than by high-explosive bombs. Civilian and military casualties were recorded as 475 killed and 5,027 injured. Nonetheless, the victory was tarnished somewhat when British intelligence learned in July that, within two weeks of the raid, the city was again functioning almost normally.

The British lost 43 aircraft, about half from flak and half from night fighters. Another 7 bombers crashed on landing. Of the 116 damaged, 12 had to be written off, thus making a total loss of 62 and a loss rate of 5.9 percent. Also, 291 crewmen were lost in the operation.

The most cogent assessment of the raid remains that of Webster and Frankland:[29]

> This was an impressive demonstration of what Bomber Command might achieve if it was expanded. It was no more than that for, with a front-line operational strength which was, in 1942, seldom much in excess of and often much less than 400 aircraft, Bomber Command could not sustain such efforts without disrupting its whole training organisation, and, therefore, its future. . . . Public opinion was naturally uplifted by the Cologne success at a time of sore trial on other fronts. It expected, indeed, too much from Bomber Command and did not realise how exceptional the circumstances were.

But Harris had his bombers undertake two additional raids before standing down the large force.[30] On the night of June 1–2, 956 bombers (the early totals indicated 1,004) attacked Essen. Little damage was done to the city and none to the Krupp works, at a cost of 36 aircraft, most of which were claimed by antiaircraft fire. The same applied to Bremen, where, on June 25–26, 904 bombers (the original figure was 1,074) were dispatched. While some damage was done to the city and the Focke Wulf aircraft factory, none was exacted on the dock area, which was the primary objective. The Bremen raid included Coastal Command and Army Cooperation Command, along with Bomber Command aircraft. Forty-nine planes were lost, again mostly from flak. Although neither attack was as spectacular as that against Cologne, both showed that a concentrated force could achieve mass destruction even against well-defended targets.

After the thousand-bomber raids, attacks against German cities continued, though at a reduced rate. Also during the summer, the US Eighth Air Force began bombing targets in France in preparation for its expanded role as more of its bombers became operational. Typifying British activity was a raid undertaken against Aachen on October 5–6.[31] In this attack, 257 aircraft—101 Wellingtons, 74 Lancasters, 59 Halifaxes, and 23 Stirlings—were involved. The force made little use of Pathfinder aircraft, which had come into use in August, because of poor weather conditions. The results of the attack were disappointing in that some damage was caused—22 buildings were hit—in or near Aachen, but most of the bombs fell at Lütterade, a Dutch town 17 miles to the west, where 800 houses were damaged. Ten aircraft were lost in the raid and 6 more crashed in England, for a loss rate of 6.2 percent, demonstrating that German countermeasures were still effective at this point.

Nineteen forty-two was therefore primarily a year of preparation for the Allies.[32] There was little quantitative improvement, for whereas 506 Bomber Command aircraft per day were available in November 1941, only 515 were available on a daily average in January 1943. However, there had been a qualitative improvement as Lancasters and Mosquitoes came into the inventory, and new radar navigation and bombing aids as well. Yet "the damage inflicted on Germany up to the end of 1942, while no means negligible, had [had] but little effect on her war production or the morale of her population."

Figures for 1942 confirm the theme of Allied preparation. A monthly breakdown of Middlebrook and Everitt's figures for total sorties, based on the number of aircraft dispatched, bomber losses, and loss rates, yields no clear pattern (table 10-1).[33] During the better weather of summer months, the British effort reached its highest point. British losses also increased, but the loss rate remained fairly constant throughout the year. What the figures do not show is that besides the 1,418 bombers shot down or written off, Bomber Command also had 2,724 damaged, which meant a considerable number were unavailable for some days or months while being repaired. Nor do they show the increase in the number of four-engined Lancaster sorties dispatched, from 149 in May to 864 in September, and the replacement of Manchesters, Hampdens, and Whitleys.[34] The result was that while the number of front-line bombers with crews remained steady at about 400 per day into the fall of 1942, and even decreased to less than 350 per day in September, aggregate bomb tonnage rose considerably from 3,125 tons in May to 6,688 in June, and remained at 5,509 in September despite the discontinuation of the thousand-plane raids. In retrospect, 1942 represents only the beginning, for by June 4–5, which represents the midpoint in the war between Britain and Germany, Bomber Command had flown only 18 percent of its total sorties, suffered 23 percent of its airplane losses, and dropped 6 percent of the bomb tonnage it would expend throughout the conflict.[35]

Still, British leaders had little cause to be satisfied, for the number of bombers available to Bomber Command was far below expectations.[36] The shortfall was in part a consequence of having to divert bombers to land theaters, including the Middle East, India, and Southeast Asia, and to Coastal Command. Chief of the Air Staff Portal complained that such diversions had deprived Bomber Command of 28 squadrons that it might have put to use in 1942. In part it was also the result of overestimating the number of aircraft the United States could make available to Britain during the year.[37] British production had risen from 20,094 in 1941 to 23,672 in 1942, including an increase in heavy and medium bombers from 3,275 to 5,439, but it was now stretched almost to the limit and not expected to climb much higher. During the same time, arrivals from the United States had risen only modestly, from 4,473 aircraft in 1941 to 5,898 in 1942, and 3,504 of them had been shipped to British overseas commands and to Commonwealth countries rather

TABLE 10-1
Bomber Command, 1942

	Sorties	*Losses*	*Percentages*
January	2,230	58	2.5
February	1,138	75	6.6
March	2,259	79	3.5
April	4,038	134	3.3
May	2,727	109	4.0
June	4,938	212	4.3
July	4,117	180	4.3
August	2,605	134	5.1
September	3,581	172	4.8
October	2,567	107	4.1
November	2,217	66	2.9
December	1,799	92	5.1
Totals	34,216	1,418	4.1

than to the United Kingdom itself. The US Eighth Air Force had started its activities, but its 1,426 total sorties dispatched in 1942 were minor in comparison with Bomber Command's 34,216.[38] More substantial improvements would have to wait until later.

From the German standpoint, the figures confirm increasing concern, but not undue alarm.[39] The number of heavy antiaircraft batteries rose from 967 in 1941 to 1,148 in 1942, the number of single engine fighters in the west increased from 292 to 457, and night fighter totals rose from 500 in September to 654 in December. Aircraft being produced for defensive purposes increased from 379 per month in June to 536 in December, while those completed for offensive uses increased at a similar rate, from 485 in June to 594 in December. Despite a reticence at the highest levels to develop a large defensive force, a system was evolving, though not at the expense of offensive tasks. This picture would change, however, in 1943.

The change came about for three very practical reasons. First, British bomber might increased to the point, as Frankland has put it, that "the power of area bombing became formidable."[40] Second, the US moved from a subordinate role to one approaching equality and willing cooperation in the strategic air war. Third, Germany's ability to combat the aerial onslaught could not keep pace.

The Allies' intensified offensive accorded well with Churchill's and Portal's thinking.[41] Both had come to accept that strategic bombing alone could not bring about victory, but they felt it would make a vital contribution to smoothing the way for a land invasion of the Continent. For this reason the bombing of Germany should not be interrupted, but should be given the highest priority, except perhaps for temporary diversions to support other operations. It was to be nourished and have a life of its own, a life which was to parallel and complement the preparations for the cross-Channel attack.

Their thinking was given definite shape at Casablanca in January 1943. The Allies determined that first importance was to be allotted to bombing German submarine bases and construction yards; second, Germany's aircraft industry; third, transportation targets; fourth, synthetic oil plants; and fifth, other war industries.[42] Although Harris did not like to have his bombers used to strike sixteen-foot reinforced concrete submarine pens, his air crews did so, though with little effect. The attacks on submarine construction yards were not particularly effective either, and they were scaled down as US forces took over more of that role. But the Americans, because of their emphasis on daylight bombing, became convinced that the second priority, knocking out the aircraft industry—expanded to include all elements of Germany's fighter component—was crucial to their success. By June 3 they had issued a directive calling for the destruction of Germany's fighter strength as the immediate objective. The operation was codenamed Pointblank. Harris went along with the directive, though he himself expanded it to include virtually all of Germany's economic infrastructure, thus negating some of the impact

Pointblank might have had, had it been concentrated more on the aircraft industry. This move allowed Bomber Command to continue attacking a broad range of targets. Harris's "reinterpretation" was actually a mistake, for the Luftwaffe fighter force would soon become as serious a threat for the British as it was for the Americans. But at least the Allies were grappling for how best to utilize their increasingly powerful bomber fleets.

Germany's air defense system, based as it was on ground-control interception, early warning radar, large central plotting rooms, searchlights, antiaircraft guns, and night fighters, continued to be improved, but only after July 1943 did the Luftwaffe move toward giving it top billing.[43] British attacks had had some effect during the spring, especially those in the Ruhr area; however, the Hamburg raids, starting on July 25, were the turning point. At a meeting in August, German air leaders were united in their view that air defense must now receive the highest priority. Specific measures were undertaken to strengthen their defensive posture, including increased fighter production, withdrawal of fighter units from Russia and the Mediterranean to the Reich, and the diversion of twin-engined fighters from night to daylight tasks, while adding to their firepower with a rocket adapted from the army's 21-cm mortar.

Only Hitler seemed reluctant to go along. In July he had allowed for some increase in the number of fighters deployed in the west, but his immediate reaction to the Hamburg raids was to insist that a bomber force be readied to retaliate against London. Throughout that last week in July he was more concerned—perhaps understandably—with Mussolini's fall from power than with Hamburg. According to his air production chief, Erhard Milch, not until the October Schweinfurt attack did Hitler concede that defense of the Reich was to have precedence over all other air needs. Nevertheless, the Führer never gave up on his idea of retaliating against Britain, a threat that took definite form in an ineffective bomber raid against London in February 1944 and in his pressing ahead to make the V-1 flying bombs and the V-2 rockets operational.

Meanwhile, despite Hitler's reluctance, the Germans during 1943 added more aircraft and antiaircraft guns and developed new aids and tactics to improve their defensive capabilities.[44] The aircraft included more of the usual Bf 110s, Bf 109s, FW 190s, and some JU 88s, although the night-fighting Heinkel 219, with a maximum speed of 385 mph, also began to appear in small numbers during the autumn. More flak, which fired up to 15,000 feet, with the fighters operating above that height, meant more 88-, 105-, and 128-mm guns. Among the new aids were a better onboard radar, the *Lichtenstein* SN2, which could lock on a target at a relatively long range and could not be jammed by Window, the aluminum strips introduced by the Allies during the Hamburg raids. In addition, upward firing cannon, called jazz music *(schräge Musik)*, were emplaced to hit the undefended belly and vulnerable fuel tanks from below. The new tactics included Wild Boar and Tame Boar. Wild Boar was used at night by single-engine-fighter pilots, who first received information about incoming bombers but then, rather than being vectored to the target, free-lanced and took advantage of searchlights to silhouette enemy aircraft. The technique resulted in heavy German losses, however, in part because there was no blind-flying equipment on board the fighters. More effective was the Tame Boar tactic, by which Luftwaffe ground controllers picked up British signals and then used constant radio contact to direct the twin-engine-fighter crews into the bomber stream. The effectiveness of these numerous measures became all too apparent to the British and Americans during the aerial combat of late 1943 and early 1944.

Like those of the Germans, Allied improvements in aids and aircraft during 1943 were both quantitative and qualitative.[45] Changes included production of more Lancasters; the phasing out of Wellingtons, except for mine-laying operations; the use of the versatile Mosquito twin-engined bomber; and, most important, the addition of large numbers of American bombers and fighter escorts, especially the P-51 Mustang late in the year. In terms of aids, besides more widespread utilization of Oboe and H2S, the Allies overcame their hesitation to use aluminum strips to confuse German radars for fear of like reprisals and introduced the Window with devastating effect during the July Hamburg raids. Only in the winter of 1943–44 did the Luftwaffe find an effective countermeasure, the *Lichtenstein* SN2 radar, and even then, the Allied advantage was never completely erased.

What the Anglo-American advantages added up to was greater accuracy and more aircraft attacking the assigned targets. Over the year, these were evident in three major British offensives, one against the Ruhr area between March and July, the second against Hamburg in late July and early August, and the third, the Battle of Berlin between November 1943 and the end of March 1944.

The first Battle of the Ruhr consisted of 43 major raids, but only two-thirds of them were directed at nine Ruhr cities and the rest against other "deep" European targets from Milan to Stettin.[46] One of the benefits the British derived from striking Germany's industrial heartland was that Oboe radar and Pathfinder aircraft could be used for marking the targets. The disadvantage was that German defenses in and around the Ruhr were the most extensive in the Reich. Of the 24,355 sorties Bomber Command flew between March 5 and July 24, it lost 1,038 aircraft for a loss rate of 4.3 percent, which is 86 percent of the 5 percent figure considered prohibitive.

Typical of the Ruhr operations was an attack on Dortmund on the night of May 23–24. In this raid, the first major undertaking in nine days, 826 aircraft were dispatched—343 Lancasters, 199 Halifaxes, 151 Wellingtons, 120 Stirlings, and 13 Mosquitoes. Pathfinders were able to take advantage of the excellent weather to mark the targets clearly. The results, despite the loss of 38 aircraft, almost half of which were the undependable Halifaxes, were gratifying for the British, as there were nearly 2,000 buildings destroyed and 1,900 enemy ground casualties.

Even more indicative of growing Allied air might were the famous Hamburg raids.[47] They involved six attacks in all, four by Bomber Command and two by the US Eighth Air Force. The British attacks totaled 3,091 sorties, and those of the Americans, 626, the latter being daylight attacks on July 25 and 26. The first British raid on the night of July 24–25 featured the use of Window and H2S radar for marking purposes. Of the 791 aircraft dispatched, 347 were Lancasters, 246 Halifaxes, 125 Stirlings, and 73 Wellingtons. Seven hundred twenty-eight planes dropped 2,284 tons of bombs in 50 minutes at a cost of 12 aircraft, or only 1.5 percent, lost. Enemy ground deaths were approximately 1,500.

It was during the second British attack on July 27–28 that the term Hamburg "fire" raids became a reality. The massive devastation was actually due not so much to incendiary bombs as to a combination of other factors. For one thing, it was hot—80-plus degrees—with a low, 30 percent humidity, and the city was dry. For another, the Germans had few fire trucks available, since they were putting out fires in the western part of the city. And finally, the bombs were concentrated in the industrial parts of Hamburg, where too little oxygen caused the firestorms from which about 40,000 died and 16,000 multistoried apartment buildings were destroyed. After the raid was over, most of the citizens left the city for temporary safety. Seven hundred twenty-nine aircraft of 787 dispatched—353 Lancasters, 244 Halifaxes, 116 Stirlings, and 74 Wellingtons—dropping 2,326 tons of bombs, had caused the horrible destruction. Seventeen aircraft were lost for a rate of 2.2 percent.

On the night of July 29, Bomber Command returned to Hamburg with 777 aircraft—340 Lancasters, 244 Halifaxes, 119 Stirlings, 70 Wellingtons, and 4 Mosquitoes for diversionary purposes. Although the 2,318 tons of bombs dropped by 707 aircraft caused no firestorm, the exhausted Hamburg fire department could do little to check the fires that broke out throughout the city. The British lost 28 aircraft for a rising loss rate of 3.6 percent.

The least successful of Bomber Command's Hamburg raids was the last one, on August 2–3. It took place during a large thunderstorm over Germany, so that no Pathfinder marking was possible. The 740 aircraft dispatched—329 Lancasters, 235 Halifaxes, 105 Stirlings, 60 Wellingtons, and 5 Mosquitoes—inflicted only scattered damage on Hamburg, and some of the bombers attacked alternate targets in northern Germany. Attrition was 30 aircraft for a loss rate of 4.1 percent.

In the near term, the Hamburg raids were a resounding success for the Allies. They had dropped nearly 11,000 tons of bombs, caused nearly 50,000 deaths and 40,000 injured, and wreaked untold havoc everywhere in the city. Bomber Command had lost only 87 aircraft and the Americans 43, for a combined loss rate of 3.0 percent. In an optimistic—perhaps over- optimistic—mood, Allied air leaders began readying their crews for further, even more ambitious undertakings.

For the Germans, the attacks had been devastating, but, as it turned out, the effect on morale was temporary. At the highest levels, as discussed earlier, the Germans had become convinced that something had to be done to stop the Allied bombers. They therefore responded with a series of measures—more fighter aircraft and antiaircraft guns coupled with better aids and tactics—to stiffen their defenses. At this point, a true air war was in the making.

Between August and November, Bomber Command strength remained static, although there were some improvements, as in the equipping of some of the Halifaxes with Hercules engines.[48] Even more significant was the rise in the number of American bombers, some of which flew from bases as far away as North Africa to strike targets in Austria and at Ploesti, and there was also a gradual extension of fighter escorts. On the German side, the number of fighters and antiaircraft in the west as well as inside Germany also continued to rise, thereby setting the stage for the crucial battle for air superiority.

At first, the battle did not work out well for the Allies. Besides the Eighth Air Force defeat at Schweinfurt in October was Britain's exceedingly costly all-out assault on Berlin.[49] It started on the night of November 18–19 and carried on for nearly four and a half months. Not only Berlin was attacked; the total of 32 raids were aimed at other German cities as well, culminating in the disastrous raid on Nuremberg at the end of March 1944, in which 11.94 percent of the RAF bombers failed to return. At this point, the Normandy campaign began to assume top priority, and the strategic bombing offensive, with the Americans playing an increasing role, continued, but at a reduced rate.

Representative of Bomber Command's difficulties was the third raid on Berlin, which took place on December 2–3. Although 458 aircraft—425 Lancasters, 18 Mosquitoes, and 15 Halifaxes (the Stirlings and Halifax IIs and Vs could not get high enough)—were dispatched, 40 were lost for a loss rate of 8.7 percent. The problems were many—the difficulty Pathfinders had in identifying the targets, the scattering of the bomber stream by high winds, many enemy fighters lying in wait. Most of the bombs were dropped south of the city, with damage confined to about 140 buildings, and with 36 persons killed and 105 missing. Murray is particularly critical of the Berlin battle strategy. He writes: "Harris embarked on a strategy that was direct and obvious, that maximized the exposure of his bombers to fighter attacks, that minimized the potential of evasion, and that took place during the year's worst weather."

Nevertheless, events in 1943 demonstrated numerous gains for the Allies in their bomber offensive. Nowhere is this trend more apparent than in the numbers involved. To be sure, with regard to Bomber Command sorties and losses, the increase is not altogether evident (table 10-2).[50] The figures reveal that the sortie total, as in 1942, reached its peak during the summer. But the interesting point is that whereas Bomber Command dispatched 34,216

TABLE 10-2
Bomber Command, 1943

	Sorties	Losses	Percentages
January	2,718	106	3.9
February	5,192	112	2.16
March	5,498	175	3.2
April	5,687	270	4.7
May	5,508	259	4.7
June	5,690	276	4.85
July	6,051	193	3.2
August	7,822	294	3.9
September	5,844	197	3.4
October	4,665	160	3.4
November	5,225	159	3.05
December	4,322	203	4.7
Totals	64,222	2,404	3.8

sorties in 1942, the number reached 64,222 in 1943, an increase of 87.7 percent. As might be expected, the number of aircraft lost also went up, from 1,418 in 1942 to 2,404, but still at an acceptable rate of 3.8 percent as compared with 4.1 percent in 1942. Just as significant was the increase in aggregate bomb tonnage, which rose from 5,509 tons in September 1942 to 14,855 tons a year later.[51]

However, the most important new element, as emphasized earlier, was the American contribution. The figures, as set forth in Craven and Cate, show that in December, Eighth Air Force had surpassed Bomber Command in the number of sorties (table 10-3).[52] This number would increase even more rapidly when Fifteenth Air Force came on line at Italian bases. Indeed, the British effort continued to grow, too—from 5,844 Bomber Command sorties in September 1943 to 14,543 in September 1944—but even this phenomenal rise was overshadowed by the number of bombers and crews that became available for the United States during 1944.[53] No wonder Churchill had been so steadfast and determined to gain American support.

The American contribution to Britain in aircraft also continued to grow, but at a rate slower than hoped for.[54] In 1943, the US sent 2,418 aircraft directly to the United Kingdom and 4,292 to British overseas commands and to their Commonwealth partners. This 6,710 total is up only slightly from the 5,898 in 1942. When the number of aircraft from the United States is combined with Britain's total production of 26,263, including 7,352 bombers, however, the increase was of a magnitude that Germany simply could not match.

Germany's failure does not mean it did not try to redress the situation. While one might question whether the Hamburg raids alone turned the Luft-

TABLE 10-3
8th Air Force Heavy Bomber Missions, 1943

	Sorties	Losses	Percentages
January	354	18	5.1
February	526	22	4.2
March	956	19	2.0
April	450	28	4.9
May	1,649	67	4.1
June	2,107	93	4.4
July	2,829	109	3.9
August	2,265	107	4.7
September	2,829	83	2.9
October	2,053	173	8.4
November	3,849	93	2.4
December	5,179	172	3.3
Totals	25,046	974	3.9

waffe in a defensive direction, there is no doubt that, by the end of the year, it had become a defensive force.[55] With regard to aircraft production, the Germans produced a total of 25,527 in 1943 as compared with 15,556 in 1942, and most of the increase was in the area of fighters—from 7,128 to 15,151. Of this number, more and more were being used for defensive purposes, and there were 1,650 in the west at the end of 1943 as compared with 1,045 a year earlier. It might be argued that more should have been done earlier to convert the fighters over to defensive tasks, for they never surpassed those produced for offensive purposes. Still, the defensive orientation was finally taking precedence. Not only did the number of aircraft utilized for defense increase, but the number of heavy antiaircraft batteries also rose, from 1,148 in 1942 to 2,132 in 1943. Armaments Minister Speer estimated that by this time one-third of the optical industry was producing gunsights for flak and about one-half of the electronics industry was engaged in building radar and communications components for air defense.

Yet, several additional statistics need to be brought into the German picture. First of all, the Germans suffered horrible fighter aircraft and pilot casualties during 1943.[56] For instance, Air Fleet 3, which was responsible for western Europe and part of the Reich, lost 87 fighters in January but its losses per month climbed to 334 in July and remained near or above 250 for the rest of the year. Murray asserts that, in all theaters, the Luftwaffe lost an average of about 25 percent of its fighters per month, including an unbelievable 41.9 percent in October, and that their losses were never less than 19 percent throughout the year. The Luftwaffe fighter groups also lost 2,967 pilots, a number becoming increasingly difficult to replace. The other important statistic is of Allied bombing's impact on German fighter production.

Whereas the Germans were able to produce 1,134 in June and 1,263 in July, production dropped to 985 in November and to 687 in December. Although the monthly figures rose again in 1944, it is difficult to avoid the conclusion that the Lancasters, Stirlings, Halifaxes, Fortresses, and Liberators did have an adverse effect on Germany's fighter aircraft industry.

Nineteen forty-three, then, was for the Allies a year of substantial accomplishments, but they did not achieve outright air superiority. This would have to await the first half of 1944. Unlike the turning point in the Battle of the Atlantic, a specific date when the Allies truly gained the upper hand is difficult to determine for the offensive-defensive air confrontation unfolded like a seamless web. Several events stand out, however. One was the United States' "Big Week" air offensive.[57] Between February 20 and 25, the Americans unleashed a series of attacks against the German aircraft industry that showed they had truly recovered from the Schweinfurt disaster the previous autumn. The raids caused some damage to the targets on the ground, but, more important, the bombers now flew with large numbers of escorts that decimated the Luftwaffe fighter force. US P-38Js, P-47Ds, and especially P-51Bs engaged and, in effect, defeated the German fighters during the spring of 1944. It did not happen all at once, for the attrition of American bombers remained high. But their losses could be borne. For the Luftwaffe, however, single-engined fighter losses reached 33.8 percent of its total force in February, a phenomenal 56.4 percent in March, 43.0 percent in April and 50.4 percent in May. Despite increased production and the formation of an Air Fleet Reich for better coordination to defend the homeland, such attrition was prohibitive. By the end of May, the Allies had achieved daylight air superiority.

It is even more difficult to specify the date when air superiority at night came about.[58] Ironically, the defeat at Nuremberg in March 1944, where the RAF lost 95 of its 795 aircraft dispatched, may well have had a beneficial effect in forcing air leaders to change their thinking. But it was another external event, an ordered concentration on pre-invasion bombing for the Normandy campaign, that helped Bomber Command regroup from its losses. Upon Harris's insistence, raids against German cities were to continue, but Overlord targets assumed more and more of a priority. By the time Bomber Command returned to concentrating on industrial and oil targets—and also began using an extensive daylight bombing force—air superiority had become an accomplished fact. The Command's loss-rate percentages tell the story. Between November 18, 1943, and the Nuremberg raid on March 31, 1944, it lost 3.8 percent of its total sorties. Between the end of March and June 5, the figure plummeted to 2.2 percent, and between June 6 and August 16, it decreased even further to 1.6 percent and remained at about 1.0 percent for the rest of the war. And this decline in the loss rate came about at the same time that the number of Bomber Command sorties per day soared, from 219.8 in late 1943 to 650.6 in the summer of 1944. The air war had finally been won.

How then does the Allies' strategic bombing offensive and Germany's air defense of the Reich fit into the broader strategic picture? There is no doubt that it represents a classic confrontation of weapon vs. counterweapon, and in this case, offense won out. It is also evident that both sides devoted considerable resources to the air war. The Germans, for instance, produced 11,776 front-line aircraft in 1941 as compared with 39,807 in 1944, and 23,805 of the latter were day and night fighters.[59] The weight of the aircraft produced, although not so dramatic, also rose from 88 million pounds in 1941 to 163 million pounds in 1944. In terms of antiaircraft guns, the numbers were 14,575 completed in 1941 and 58,745 in 1944. Yet in the end, the German effort was woefully insufficient. Germany simply did not have the resources to rival Allied production. The British front-line aircraft total for 1941 was 20,094, with 4,473 more coming from the United States.[60] By 1944, the British figure had risen only to 26,461, but 11,414 more arrived from the US, and the crucial factor by this point was that the Americans were producing aircraft in huge numbers—96,318 in 1944 alone. In total weight, the increase was even greater. In 1941, the weight of the aircraft produced by the US and Britain was 168.5 million pounds (81.5 US). In 1944, it was 835.6 million pounds (650.6 US). So long as neither side developed a technological breakthrough of overwhelming proportions, and neither side did, Germany was bound to lose the air battle.

Both sides made mistakes. The Germans should have devoted more resources to air defense earlier, particularly to building fighter aircraft, but the Luftwaffe had been constructed as an offensive tactical force, not a defensive one.[61] By the time air leaders acknowledged its fundamental significance in mid-1943, it was too late. The British mistake was their belief in the strategic bomber as a war-winning weapon.[62] Given the theories of Douhet, Trenchard, Mitchell, and others during the interwar years, the bomber was expected to cause untold devastation on the enemy's heartland, and it was also expected to be able to defend itself. Both of these myths died slowly. British experts at first overestimated the material damage done to the German economy, and only a succession of reports, some as early as 1941, finally convinced RAF leaders that better aids and more aircraft were necessary to have an impact. Both Allies, though at different times, finally realized that their long-range bombers were exceedingly vulnerable and required effective fighter escorts. When the right escorts were found, they played a vital role in turning the air war in the Allies' favor.

Strategic bombing, therefore, was not so decisive as its proponents thought it would be. Nevertheless, it did have important consequences.[63] Even though German arms production increased, the bombing limited the rate of increase. It also caused shortages in electrical power and in certain raw materials. It further forced vast resources to be devoted to antiaircraft and repair work, disrupted the smooth flow of war supplies, and caused the dispersal of numerous industries. Without the bombing offensive, none of these benefits would have been accomplished on a major scale.

Still, strategic bombing was only one factor, and often a subordinate one, in the overall war strategy.[64] When Britain was fighting for its survival, fighter, not bomber, production was emphasized. When the Battle of the Atlantic became crucial to Allied policy, Coastal Command assumed a dominant role, and Bomber Command was forced to undertake raids against submarine bases and construction yards. When Overlord took precedence, the bomber forces were diverted to support that operation. In fact, from 1942 on, strategic bombing was looked upon as a means to help clear the way for an invasion of the Continent, not as a decisive factor in itself. In this light, perhaps Lord Zuckerman is right in contending that the British and Americans did not really have an air strategy, but that their focus was dictated by the circumstances at the time.[65] On occasion, the bombing offense assumed the highest priority; on occasion, it did not. And this was probably as it should be, for air power proved its worth primarily because it was an extremely flexible instrument of war that could be used to fulfill a number of missions, some of them separate, but some of them in concert with other services. It is in this light that the contributions of the air forces should be acknowledged and appreciated.

ELEVEN

Burma and Western Europe, 1944–1945

Although the Allied victories during the final stages of the war have been described elsewhere as "stunning," the word is in a sense misleading. For although Allied operations resulted in victories, they were far from overwhelming until toward the very end. Only in the spring of 1945 did Allied conquests on land reach truly monumental proportions, as in the races for Rangoon, Berlin, and the Po Valley. Until that time, Allied wins were for the most part hard-fought rather than stunning.

Four examples of these hard-fought victories, eased by naval and air supremacy, were the Imphal-Kohima battles during the spring of 1944, the Overlord campaign at mid-year, the Ardennes setback in December, and the Veritable-Grenade operations in early 1945. All four were important to the Allies, though for different reasons. The turning back of the Japanese at Imphal and Kohima in far eastern India actually set the stage for the conquest of Burma. The Normandy landing established the Soviets' long-desired second front, although, as pointed out repeatedly, the Germans had already been engaged in a multifront war for some years. Hitler's gamble to strike a devastating blow against the Anglo-Americans in the Ardennes caught them by surprise, but in the end it weakened the Wehrmacht still further and hastened its demise. And in the Veritable-Grenade offensives, the Western Allies were able to close to the Rhine and thus clear the way for their final push into the heart of Germany to join with their Soviet ally.

The Burma theater presented an exceedingly complex situation.[1] Called the CBI, or the China-Burma-India theater, by the Americans, not only was it caught between developments in India and in China as well as those in Southeast Asia, it was also caught between Allied desires to defeat Germany and Japan as quickly as possible. As a consequence, Burma was accorded a low priority, for it was always considered tangential to a rapid victory over the Axis.

Another Allied problem with regard to Burma was that the Americans and the British had different goals for the area.[2] Although not always consistent, the US wanted to concentrate on operations in northern Burma and to use it as a supply conduit for Jiang Jie-shi's forces in China. It had also sought to establish air bases in south-central and, if possible, even in southern China from which to bomb Japan. Even though the process proved very difficult—in part for logistical reasons and in part because of Japanese summer offensives in 1944—the Americans remained adamant about supporting the Chinese Nationalists, as they did long into the postwar era. The goals for Britain's leaders were more ambivalent. In the back of their minds was always the issue of maintaining the empire, though this objective was seldom stated in forthright terms. From a military standpoint, it meant trying to reestablish a presence throughout Southeast Asia, especially in the former colonies now under Japanese domination. In the end, to accomplish this goal, they had to take Burma in a series of arduous land campaigns from north to south, although they had hoped to avoid this difficulty by undertaking amphibious assaults along the Bay of Bengal and had made plans accordingly.

A third problem for the British was that while they provided most of the personnel and part of the equipment, the Americans dictated the strategy for the theater. After mid-1943, though there was some give-and-take between the two allies, if the United States insisted on a certain course of action, that was the strategy adopted. And because the US looked upon Burma as secondary to their preferred strategy of advancing through the Pacific, Britain eventually had to go along with that, too. The US thinking was not wrong, as the British chiefs of staff fully recognized, but it did cause constant frustration in what came to be called the "forgotten theater" by planners in London and participants alike.

All of these factors—Burma's low priority, Anglo-American differences, the US dominance of strategy—caused an additional problem, that of exercising command. At first, the commander-in-chief, India, assumed control over the area, but in August 1943, the Allies decided to create a theater command.[3] The selection fell on Vice-Admiral Lord Louis Mountbatten, a popular choice with the Americans, who had agreed to have a Britisher, but who had vetoed the leading candidate, Air Chief Marshal Sir Sholto Douglas, because of his derogatory remarks about the US air force. Despite his young age, Mountbatten was especially suited to the job, since he had served as head of Combined Operations and since Allied leaders at this point were seriously considering a series of amphibious operations. Nevertheless, some of the "old heads" among the British military establishment had reservations about Mountbatten. Brooke was concerned about his young age and appointed an experienced chief of staff, General Sir Henry Pownall, "to pull him through." The naval commander in the region, Admiral Sir James Somerville, resented Mountbatten, though he was a navy man, and the same applied to the lethargic army commander, General Sir George Giffard, and the air force commander, Air Chief Marshal Sir Richard Peirse, who was involved in an unsavory love affair with the wife of the commander-in-chief, India. Perhaps as a reflection of the theater's low priority, Mountbatten was unable to relieve these less-than-cooperative commanders until eleven to fifteen months after his appointment. In the interim, he built up a relatively large, interservice, interallied staff that eventually functioned fairly well. Yet there was also the question of

Mountbatten's relations with the top American leader in the theater. General Joseph Stilwell was a good fighter but thoroughly disliked by almost all the British officers because of his brash and abrasive manner. Although nominally under Mountbatten, the outspoken Stilwell had a tendency to go his own way and used his many positions, including one as Jiang's chief of staff, to voice his criticism to the US joint chiefs. The result was difficulties and misunderstandings all the way around until Stilwell's recall to the United States in October 1944 eased some of the tensions. In other words, there was at times as much friendly friction as enemy fog among the Allies in Southeast Asia.

During early 1943, the Allies outlined plans for Burma that included overland preliminary operations to establish bridgeheads over the Chindwin River in northwestern Burma and to set up airfields near Akyab on the western coast before the monsoons set in May.[4] These actions were to be followed by operations for the reconquest of all of Burma, which, with the help of Chinese forces, were scheduled to start by the winter of 1943–44 at the earliest.

By April and May 1943, the British had come to view the plans as over-ambitious. British revisions turned out by their joint planners now narrowed the near-term objectives to "improving the air transport route into China . . . and increasing supplies to China."[5] This new plan was to be achieved after the monsoon period in part by advances from Imphal across the Chindwin and by the capture of Akyab, thus acknowledging that the earlier scheme to take these areas before the monsoon had never been carried through. The new plan also called for the use of Chinese forces from Ledo in extreme northeastern India and out of Yunnan province in China to assist by advancing into northern Burma. And finally, if the Akyab operation, this time seaborne, succeeded, it was to be followed by another amphibious assault on Ramree Island farther south.

By the time of the May Trident conference in Washington, the British had become even more cautious. At the meeting, Field Marshal Wavell, commander-in-chief, India, ended his pessimistic formal presentation by saying: "An unsuccessful operation into Burma would be almost worse than no operation at all."[6] By the end of the conference, however, after long discussions, the Allies had decided that they must do something. They therefore returned at least partially to their earlier thinking and directed that air and sea forces be increased so that the amount of goods flown into China would reach ten thousand tons per month; that operations be undertaken in northern Burma to contain Japanese formations, to cover the China air route, and to allow continued construction of a road from Ledo to link up with the Burma Road; and that amphibious assaults be directed against Akyab and Ramree Island. They also stipulated that preparations continue for a large amphibious operation to the south, implying that a major land offensive in southern Burma could be avoided.

By August, Allied policy regarding Burma had become an admixture of hope and fear. At the Quadrant meeting in Quebec, where the Southeast Asia Command was created, Burma was highlighted when the swashbuckling Lieutenant Colonel Orde Wingate, who had gained fame in leading long-range penetration groups in Burma, and previously in North Africa, made a presentation. But reality was also setting in. For one thing, Allied leaders realized that amphibious requirements in Europe and the Pacific put seaborne operations projected for the Bay of Bengal in jeopardy.[7] Moreover, preparations for offensives out of India had been slowed by disastrous floods in Bengal, and British planners further estimated that an all-weather road across northern Burma, along with a four-inch oil pipeline, could not be finished until 1946, that is, if northern Burma were rapidly cleared of the enemy. By the time the conference was over, the Allies had limited their near-term goals to offensive operations in northern Burma "with the object of establishing land communications with China and improving and securing the air route," thus not only reflecting the American view, but also reaffirming part of the thinking adopted by the Allies in Washington the previous May. The operations were not expected to begin, however, until mid-February, halfway through the dry season, because of training and supply difficulties. Otherwise, the Allies agreed to look into an amphibious attack against Sumatra (Churchill's preference), with a target date for the spring of 1944, and offensives south from northern Burma (Roosevelt's preference), with a target date of November. Nothing definite was set.

British planners then dutifully looked into trying to fulfill the Quebec directive. By October, on the basis of plans already worked out by the commander-in-chief, India's staff before he had relinquished his command in Southeast Asia, the planners proposed a number of offensives converging from different areas, with the help of long-range penetration groups, to liberate northern Burma.[8] Several of the thrusts, as before, were to be undertaken by Chinese formations. To ensure Jiang's support, the British further proposed an amphibious operation against the Andaman Islands in the Bay of Bengal, although they knew that Japanese forces now received most of their supplies by land rather than by sea as Jiang presumed. The British further realized that the diversion of vital air transports from airlifting goods to China to taking part in the North Burma operations might induce Jiang not to participate.[9] They decided, nonetheless, that the northern Burma offensives must go ahead. (As it turned out, British fears of losing air transports were unwarranted, for additional American aircraft made it possible to raise the amount of supplies transported to China "over the hump" from 6,719 tons in September to 13,450 in December.)[10] At a meeting between Jiang and Mountbatten in mid-October, the Chinese Nationalist leader went along with Britain's plan.[11] Thus, by November, the agenda for 1943–44 was taking shape with a seaborne assault against the Andaman Islands, codenamed Buccaneer; a subsidiary operation into the Arakan; and three offensives into northern Burma from the west and north, assisted by long-range penetration groups operating in the rear.

The plans went awry during the next several months. At the first Cairo meeting in late November, which Jiang attended, the British and Americans seemed to favor the Andaman Island landing. By the time of the second meeting after Tehran, which Jiang did not attend, the Western Allies had decided to abandon Buccaneer because of commitments to Overlord and the invasion of southern France (Operation Anvil).[12] Buccaneer's cancellation caused further reverberations, for Jiang now refused to commit Chinese forces fully to the northern Burma offensive. This factor, and the continuing problem of insufficient resources, led to a scaling-down of the northern Burma operations and the delay of part of them until at least mid-March. Added to this, when Buccaneer was called off, Mountbatten had tried to salvage what he could by advocating a smaller amphibious attack for the Arakan, with the eventual objective of taking Akyab (Operation Pigstick). On January 6, it, too, was canceled because it required "more naval forces than envisaged."[13] An additional point, becoming apparent to both Brooke and Mountbatten, was that operations in northern Burma would inevitably lead to more and more undertakings "on an ever-increasing scale until the whole of Burma is in our hands."[14] According to the thinking at the time, these offensives would require extensive naval as well as land and air forces.

By the beginning of February 1944, operations planned for early in the year no longer included clearing northern Burma, but were to consist of a number of limited offensives to "set the stage" for the eventual taking over of the area.[15] One, the Arakan offensive, Operation Cudgel, had already started, with XV Corps divisions, supported by RAF aircraft, undertaking preliminary operations along the Mayu Mountain range. A more extensive attack was to begin on February 6, with the eventual goal of capturing the entire Arakan sector and developing airfields there. The second, Operation Gripfast, was to be an offensive out of Imphal in which IV Corps was to advance southeast to Kalemyo on the Chindwin River. The third was to be a Chinese attack from Ledo, commanded by General Stilwell, with the object of reaching Myitkyina to ensure that at least part of the road designed to link up with the Burma Road could be constructed. The other part could not be completed unless the Chinese agreed to move their forces west from Yunnan, an unlikely prospect given Jiang's opposition at this point. All of these operations were to be assisted by the long-range penetration groups, including one operated by the Americans.

At this juncture, another element entered the picture: the Japanese forestalled the Allies by launching offensives of their own. The first phase began on February 4 with an attack against the Arakan region, followed by an all-out assault against Imphal launched between March 8 and 15. In all fairness to the British, they were not surprised. They had received information as

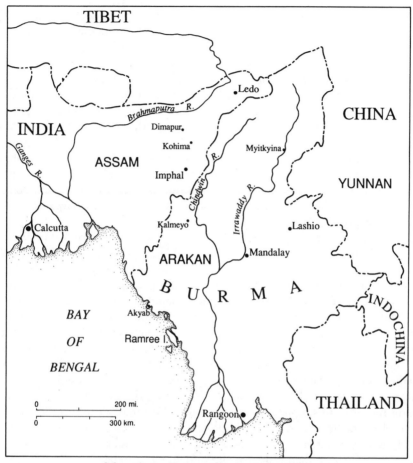

Map 11-1: Burma Campaigns, 1944

early as mid-November that the Japanese were building up their forces in Burma and by December 1 began anticipating a Japanese spring offensive.[16] In fact, Viscount Slim and his subordinate commanders were confident that they could withstand a Japanese attack and greatly weaken enemy forces in the process. Despite savage fighting, in the end British confidence was not misplaced.

It is well to remember that the combat took place along the seven hundred-mile India-Burma frontier and in northern Burma amidst a mass of jungles, rivers, and mountains with a most inhospitable climate to match. The number of Allied ground forces continued to rise throughout the period.[17] In November 1943, they had the equivalent of six British and Commonwealth and two Chinese divisions. By March 1, the figure had reached a combined total of approximately eleven and one half divisions, and by April 19, at the height of the fighting, fifteen and one-third divisions. The formations were allotted as follows: XV Corps on the Arakan front consisted of four and one-third divisions; IV Corps around Imphal, four and two-thirds divisions; XXXIII Corps at Kohima, the equivalent of two divisions; the Chinese-American Ledo force, three and one-third divisions; and the long-range penetration groups, also called Chindits, equal to an oversized division. Each independent column within the long-range groups, if fully manned, was made up of 404 soldiers and eleven Burmese specialists. Although the total number of Allied combat troops in the region varied, in late April, the figure was 319,200. Facing them were 216,000 Japanese.

A much larger discrepancy existed in the respective air forces.[18] In November 1943, the Allies had 723 aircraft (excluding transports), of which 204 were flown by Americans. By the end of the year, they had a combined total of nearly 1,000, and by the summer of 1944, the number had jumped to 1,500. Two British air groups, which included some Indian, Canadian, and Dutch squadrons, covered the Arakan and Imphal regions, and the American forces supported Allied units in northern Burma. On February 20, the number of crucial transports in the theater was 374, and this number increased by another 79 in April, when more C-47 Dakotas arrived on loan from the Mediterranean.[19] The original 374 C-46s and C-47s were deployed in the following manner: 151 were designated for flying the Hump; 69 for transport inside India; 11 to support directly the small US force; 55 to drop in supplies to the long-range penetration groups and the Ledo force; and 88 to support the British and Indian formations. Again, though numbers varied at different times, the Japanese had only 161 aircraft. Further indicating the differential between the two sides, Kirby relates that, whereas the Allies between March 10 and July 30 flew 29,600 fighter sorties (18,860 British and 10,800 US), the Japanese flew 1,750.

The total strength of Allied forces serving under Southeast Asia Command in April 1944 was 1,189,133.[20] Of these, 952,923 were British and Commonwealth troops; 175,468 American; 57,942 Chinese; 2,000 French; and 800 Dutch. Looked at from another angle, 1,008,715 were soldiers, 109,518 airmen, and 70,900 sailors. What these figures indicate is that, despite being labeled the "forgotten theater," the area was the object of a considerable Allied investment.

Although the Imphal-Kohima battles dominated the fighting in the Burma theater during the spring and into the monsoon period of 1944, they were only part of the larger mosaic, in which five interrelated, yet at times separate, operations took place.[21] Three of them, the Arakan, Imphal, and Kohima fighting, were initiated by the Japanese. The two others, the Ledo and Chindit combat and the Yunnan operations, were instituted by the Allies.

The Japanese strategy was to commence its campaign in the Arakan, draw off British forces there, and then strike at Imphal. The goals of the so-called March on Delhi were actually much less ambitious than the name implied. What the Japanese wanted to do was to preempt the British; gain control of the crucial supply lines, especially those which might be extended into China; and perhaps capitalize on national unrest in India by promoting the Indian National Army and its leader, Subhas Chandra Bose, who sided with the Axis and did not believe in Gandhi's nonviolent approach.

The Arakan fighting started on February 4, and Japanese forces soon surrounded the 7th Indian Division in what was known as the Box. However, rather than withdrawing, General Frank Messervy's division held its ground and was supplied by air until its relief on February 24. British XV Corps divisions checked the other Japanese offensive thrusts and, in some cases, drove the enemy back. By mid-March, the British were advancing, though slowly, and took over a number of favorable positions before the onset of the monsoon in May. Though both prelude and sideshow to the main battle, the Arakan fighting was important to the British, for it lifted their morale and showed that Indian and British soldiers could defeat a determined, strong Japanese force.

In early March, approximately 250 miles to the north, the Japanese Fifteenth Army unleashed its forces to capture Imphal and to sever Britain's main road link in northeastern India. Imphal itself is 70 miles inside India. After a preliminary operation on March 8, the Japanese concentrated two divisions to take this capital city of Manipur state and the plain that surrounds it. Divisions of General Sir Geoffrey Scoones's IV Corps stood in the way, and, reminiscent of the tactics employed in the Arakan, they stood their ground. Often supplied from the air, they successfully fended off the Japanese. The latter did not give up easily, however, and they continued to try to take Imphal on into May. During the bitter combat, IV Corps received timely reinforcements, some flown in from the Arakan, and valuable air support from 221 Air Group. By late May, the British were even attacking Japanese lines of communications, and they fought into the monsoon period to open the road again from Imphal north to Kohima on June 22. The initiative had now definitely shifted to the British side.

During the Imphal fighting, the Japanese also attempted to take Kohima, a supply base astride the Imphal-Dimapur road. On April 5, the Japanese closed in on Kohima and put it under siege. Even though the British had to give up the town, Colonel Hugh Richards's 2,500-man garrison, of whom 1,000 were noncombatants, continued to hold out on a nearby ridge; on April 20, it was relieved by a column advancing from Dimapur. Elements of XXXIII Corps then proceeded to secure the region, and the Japanese had to retreat. Having suffered a combined total of 60,843 casualties in the Kohima and Imphal battles, the Japanese were never able to recover from these devastating losses.[22]

In the meantime, Stilwell's Chinese divisions had advanced south from Ledo, and by April 14, lead elements were 42 miles north of Myitkyina. The Chindits, though originally slated to devote part of their effort to cutting Japanese supply lines to the Imphal region, concentrated almost solely on assisting the Ledo force. Although the long-range groups achieved some spectacular successes, the difficulties in keeping them supplied, their heavy losses, and their insufficient armament to meet fully equipped ground troops, have led some military experts to question whether the effort was worth it.[23] Nevertheless, despite Wingate's death in a plane crash on March 24, the special forces caught the imagination of the public back home. To this day, their operations are depicted in heroic terms. There is no doubt that one of the groups, US Colonel Frank Merrill's Marauders, spearheaded Stilwell's drive and allowed the capture of Myitkyina airfield sooner than expected on May 17, although it took the Allies another 79 days to take Myitkyina itself on August 3. Providing a contrast to the success of the Ledo force, the Chinese formations which Jiang finally released moved out of Yunnan on May 10 but experienced slow going. By July, they had made only slight progress against outnumbered but nonetheless superior Japanese soldiers.

Overall, the British suffered only 27,776 casualties, as against 65,978 for the Japanese, in these Burmese operations. The Allies had won a number of victories and had wrested the initiative from their opponent.[24] As Lord Mountbatten summed it up: "In this fighting we had not only prevented the enemy from invading India and cutting our vital lines of communication, but also had broken and defeated his main force at Burma, thus paving the way for our complete reconquest of the country."

The Allied efforts in Burma came to a climax with the taking of Rangoon in May 1945. Yet it was not an easy goal for the Allies to reach. The Pacific option continued to cast a long shadow on the Burma theater, as did operations in Europe. The attempt to nourish China never did work out particularly well. Bombing raids against Japan from airfields in Chengtu proved disappointing, and the effort was switched so that the raids could be conducted solely from the Marianas.[25] The airfields in southern China—to be used primarily for bombing Taiwan—were never developed because of Japanese offensives there. And though the Burma Road was reopened in January 1945, it never carried much cargo. In fact, the airlift over the Hump remained the main means for getting supplies to China until war's end.[26]

Yet, throughout the last half of 1944 and into 1945, the British insisted that Burma could not be "forgotten." Brooke on several occasions said that "contact with the enemy must be maintained" and that they "must undertake some form of operation."[27] He preferred an amphibious assault against Rangoon over the planned land campaign, for a Rangoon landing might well have the added advantage of avoiding the house-to-house combat that had slowed the capture of Myitkyina. But he and the other chiefs of staff did not dictate a strategy for the area and let events take their course. Indeed, events took their course with a series of offensives in which Slim's Fourteenth Army fought through the 1944 monsoon, liberated Mandalay in March 1945, and then, after some preliminary moves, covered the final three hundred miles to Rangoon within a month, arriving there on May 1 just after the rains had started. They found the capital empty. The Japanese had already left.

Some would argue that the campaign was a hollow victory, particularly in light of what happened in Burma and in China after the war. Possibly it was, but this view does not take into account the reality of the situation at the time. Large numbers of troops had become involved in the theater, and they could not be shifted readily elsewhere because of insufficient transport. India, though a considerable distance from much of the fighting, certainly provided a better supply base than was available in the Pacific, where the US was wary of a major British presence in any event. British military leaders further understood that their relative power position in the world was changing, but they also assumed that, given the American attitudes and the Chinese Nationalist weakness, they might well be called upon to serve as a stabilizing influence in Southeast Asia during the postwar period. What occurred was that Allied long-term strategy was overtaken by events. The clearing of northern Burma, though late, necessitated further operations. But by then the Pacific theater had become the preferred area for defeating Japan, and China lost its operational significance. Consequently, taking Burma as a prelude to further Southeast Asian operations became an obvious choice. It happened much more quickly than expected, however, not only because of Japanese decline but also because the British Indian Army had become a first-rate force. The beginning of that process had come about primarily during the Imphal and Kohima fighting in the spring of 1944.

Although the Allied effort devoted to Burma reached considerable proportions, it still is almost insignificant in comparison with Operation Overlord, the largest and most complex Anglo-American operation of the war.[28] Because the many dimensions of this vast and complicated campaign are difficult to capture, it is probably best examined chronologically. Within that context, 1942 may be seen as the year of preliminaries, 1943 as the year of preparation, and 1944 as the year of execution.

The Normandy campaign had its genesis even before 1942. Soon after the Battle of France, British planners began considering moves for a return to the Continent. With the entrance of the United States and the formation of the Grand Alliance at the end of 1941, the possibility of an invasion became a definite probability. The main questions from this point on were ones of timing and extent. At first, Churchill told his American ally that small mobile forces would probably be all that were required, for he and his advisers envisaged a continental operation only after Germany had been substantially weakened by blockade, bombardment, and sabotage. But Britain's unrealistic early strategy and the pressure of events dictated otherwise. The Soviet Union kept insisting on a second front to siphon off some of Germany's strength to the west, and the British and Americans responded by preparing a limited operation on France's western coast, called Sledgehammer, for execution in the fall of 1942. However, despite America's willingness to launch Sledgehammer, the British felt that the gesture, though noble, was doomed to failure and insisted it not be implemented. They preferred and eventually got the northwestern African invasion instead. Although Stalin was far from mollified and remained suspicious of his allies' intentions, the Western Allies were probably correct in not carrying out Sledgehammer, as the disastrous raid at Dieppe in August amply demonstrated.

At the same time, British and American planners continued preparations for a major landing on the Continent. The buildup for the invasion from Britain was codenamed Bolero, and the actual invasion, targeted initially for 1943, was called Roundup. Although the combined chiefs were to exercise overall control, their small planning staff was inadequate to look into all the details for such a massive undertaking. This task was turned over in 1942 to the specially appointed joint Commanders Council under General Sir Bernard Paget in Britain and to the Operations Division of the War Department in the United States. The British in particular compiled extensive information on practically all of the beaches from the Netherlands to the Bay of Biscay and weighed the various factors that would make for a successful invasion.[29] These included, among others, the nature of the beaches, winds, and tides; the area's suitability for airfields; the distance from the United Kingdom (affecting both sea voyage and air cover); the nature of the hinterland for subsequent operations; and enemy defenses. During its early deliberations the Commanders Council concluded that the Caen sector of Normandy was the most favorable landing site because of its well-situated beaches, nearby ports, and relative lack of German fortifications.

Still no decision was made, and the question of timing also remained open. By September 1942, if not earlier, the Western Allies had decided that a full-scale invasion of the continent would be necessary.[30] Most of the military and civilian leaders (though not Churchill) agreed, however, that Torch in North Africa had probably set back the possibility of a major attack in the west until 1944, though it did not rule out securing a "permanent foothold" in 1943 "as a preliminary to more extensive operations later." They also realized that a number of problems remained to be solved, such as insecure supply lines across the Atlantic, inadequate landing craft, and insufficient troops and fighter aircraft in Britain. In fact, American forces in the UK numbered 180,000 at the end of September; because of Torch, US strength dipped to 107,801 at the end of February 1943.[31]

This did not prevent plans from being drawn up. At the Casablanca conference, besides opting for an invasion of Sicily, which virtually ensured 1944 as the invasion date, the Allies designated that a chief of staff to the Supreme Allied Command (COSSAC) take over the planning for the cross-Channel attack. General Sir Frederick Morgan was soon selected. Though not confirmed in the position until April, he was already in the process of selecting a combined, interservice staff to work out plans. Their task was eased considerably since they already had previous staff studies, materials compiled for Sledgehammer and Roundup, and experiences of early seaborne raids and operations to draw upon.[32] The planners received further details about the projected invasion in late May. As specified at the Trident conference, they were to expect an assault force of 9 divisions (two airborne), with 20 more divisions ready for movement to the battle area, naval forces of about 3,300 assault ships and landing craft, and air forces with about 11,400 aircraft. The target date, set for May 1, 1944, represented a compromise between the Americans, who wanted April 1, and the British, who preferred May 1 or June 1.[33] The plan was to be presented to the combined chiefs by August 1, and it was to include a deception as well as an operational component.

Morgan's planners had already determined that the Pas de Calais or the Normandy area near Caen were the best possible places for the attack. While the Americans worked on an outline plan for the projected Normandy assault, the British worked on one against the Pas de Calais.[34] They then held an exercise in June and decided on Normandy as the most logical choice.

By July 27, the provisional plan was ready.[35] Its conclusion was that "our initial landing on the Continent should be effected in the Caen area, with a view to the eventual seizure of a lodgment area comprising the Cherbourg-Brittany group of ports (from Cherbourg to Nantes)." Within the bridgehead, airfields near Caen and Cherbourg port were to be developed. The assault was to be mounted along a three-divisional front east of but not including the Cotentin Peninsula with the object of seizing the general line from Grandcamp east to Bayeux and Caen. The followup and buildup phase was to feature capturing Cherbourg and enlarging the bridgehead into Brittany. Within fourteen days, it was believed that 18 divisions and about 14 airfields would be available in France. Morgan warned, however, that Overlord, as it was now called, might not succeed unless three conditions were met: (1) that German fighter forces in northwestern France be substantially reduced; (2) that the Germans have no more than 12 quality divisions in the region and their buildup be limited to 15 divisions in the two months following the invasion; and (3) that the operation be a tactical surprise, hence the need for deception measures.

Although Churchill and others immediately pointed out that the initial seaborne assault was too weak and should be expanded to include the eastern shore of the Contentin Peninsula, Morgan's outline was approved at the Quebec conference in August. The possibility of a limited operation for 1943 was also discussed, but it was not given serious consideration and was confined to deception measures because of developments in Italy and on the Soviet front. Yet the leaders at Quebec engaged in protracted arguments, not so much over the Overlord plan, but over the extent to which operations in Italy should be emphasized at the expense of Overlord.[36] The Americans feared that their western partner might concentrate on the Mediterranean to such a degree that the Normandy landing might not be undertaken at all. Their concern seemed verified when Brooke expressed reluctance to shift seven divisions (three British and four American) from the Mediterranean to Britain. On the other hand, the British wanted Overlord, but their resolve was not so unswerving as that of the United States, for they also desired to take advantage of the situation in the Mediterranean now that Sicily was virtually in Allied hands and Mussolini had been overthrown. In the end, the British agreed to have the seven divisions eventually transported to the United Kingdom. Nevertheless, the Americans were still apprehensive of British designs and insisted that the possibility of a landing in southern France, brought up by Morgan in May, be examined, too, as further support for the cross-Channel attack. Therefore, although both sides left the meeting relatively satisfied, there was still the nagging feeling between the two that neither one could quite trust the other. More important, however, the decisions adopted at Quebec ultimately led them into a western orientation and relegated Italy to a secondary theater.

This conclusion was not so apparent at first. During the succeeding months, the COSSAC staff worked on details and their plan was briefed to the Soviets, first at the Moscow foreign ministers' conference in October and then at the Tehran Big Three meeting in late November. Stalin was pleased with the operation, for which the total number of divisions had now been raised to thirty-five instead of twenty-nine. One alteration made at the meeting was that the target date was shifted back to "sometime" in May, which the British and Americans knew meant the end of May.[37] Stalin also used the occasion, as discussed earlier, to push for the southern France operation to complement Overlord. The western partners concurred, although the British insisted that Italy was to be kept "aflame" until the Allies had reached the Pisa-Rimini line, unless operations there should put Overlord in jeopardy of being launched.[38]

Thus the European agenda for 1944 was thought to be set. The Anglo-Americans were to attack from the west and undertake a simultaneous landing in southern France, while the Soviets unleashed an offensive from the east. In the meantime, the campaign in Italy was to be supported to the greatest extent possible.

While a number of difficulties, such as getting enough landing craft, remained to be solved, another, major problem that had not been dealt with was the selection of a supreme commander. Churchill and Roosevelt had told Stalin at Tehran that the issue would be settled shortly, and the choice was made at Cairo following the Tehran conclave. General Morgan had been concerned about the matter for some time and had kept pointing out the necessity of having someone in charge.[39] That both Brooke and Marshall were considered for the job gives an idea of the overriding priority Overlord had assumed. Both would have accepted it with alacrity, but the prime minister and the president turned instead to General Dwight Eisenhower because of his extensive experience as a commander in the Mediterranean. Eisenhower's naval and air chiefs had already been named, Air Chief Marshal Sir Trafford Leigh-Mallory and Admiral Sir Bertram Ramsay, the latter being selected when Churchill overruled the navy's choice, Admiral Sir Charles Little.[40] The rest of Eisenhower's top staff and commanders were drawn from the Mediterranean and included General Bedell Smith as his chief of staff, Air Chief Marshal Tedder as deputy commander, and General Montgomery over Alexander as ground commander.[41]

Almost immediately after Eisenhower's arrival in January 1944, alterations in the basic plan were suggested. Montgomery, reflecting Churchill's view, contended that the number of assault divisions should be raised from three to five, that the rate of reinforcements and supplies be accelerated, and that the extent of the invasion frontage be expanded from twenty-five to over fifty miles and include the eastern shore of the Cotentin.[42] Eisenhower agreed, and the changes were made by February 1.

From then until the middle of April, the revised plan was amended in detail but not in substance. The final plan called for portions of five divisions to attack the Normandy coast at dawn, preceded by three airborne divisions that were to link up with the seaborne forces, thereby expediting their movement into the interior.[43] On the right, the ground forces were to be under the US First Army, with the 4th and 1st infantry divisions leading the assault. On the left was to be the British Second Army with the 50th, 3rd, and 3rd Canadian infantry divisions. The airborne formations were the US 82nd and 101st and British 6th divisions. Once the Allies had secured a lodgment, they were to expand the bridgehead, take Cherbourg, and secure the Brittany ports before beginning their drive across France, estimated at D-day + 60. Tide and moon considerations had dictated June 5, 6, or 7 as the invasion date.

The navies were to clear the sea approaches, provide task forces to transport the troops across the Channel, give fire support before and during the landings, and protect the invasion armada from enemy ships. The air forces were considered especially important during the preliminary phase, with attacks designed to gain air superiority and to reduce enemy supplies and personnel from reaching the front. At the time of the landing, the air forces were to provide transports and gliders for the airborne troops and to lend support to the soldiers as they came ashore and moved into the interior. Both strategic and tactical air forces were to take part.

On May 15, Eisenhower and his staff gave a final briefing before civilian and military leaders at St. Paul's School. While some of the commanders emphasized the difficulties involved, it was obvious that Overlord was ready for implementation. D-Day had been set for June 5.

To arrive at that point, a number of aspects had had to be addressed and resolved. Most of them have been mentioned above: port capacity, landing craft, diversionary operations, intelligence, the French Resistance, and air power. Because of their role in Overlord's success, they deserve further comment.

The question of sufficient port capacity to supply the invasion force had come up early and often during the planning discussions. By 1943, planners had recognized that the harbors near the preferred site, the Normandy beaches, could not be captured immediately and that additional resources would have to be unloaded over the beaches. This led the Allies to consider erecting two artificial ports, codenamed Mulberries, behind the invasion sector.[44] They were to be built in England and towed across the Channel for installation. They consisted of two essential elements—breakwaters of sunken ships and hollow, floating, concrete caissons, called Phoenixes, which could be sunk after being brought over, and a series of floating piers connected to the beach by a treadway that would allow the larger ships to unload. They were to be in place soon after the beaches were cleared of the enemy. Scholars recently have come to question whether they were worth the effort, especially since the one in the American zone was destroyed during a June 19 storm, and the one in the British zone damaged, and since it was found that supplies were unloaded more effectively over the beaches than through the Mulberries. Nevertheless, there is no doubt that they provided great "psychological" value.

There is also little doubt that the landing-craft crisis was solved by the cancellation of Anvil on March 21.[45] While its cancellation was not permanent— it was resurrected and launched on August 15—it did ensure Overlord of sufficient assault craft, an issue which had become particularly acute when the invasion was expanded to a five-division front. From the beginning, the problem had been one of landing craft's competing with other naval building priorities and the related problem of constructing enough of the right types of craft to fulfill the many needs and locations where they were being used. A succession of transfers from the Mediterranean, plus a small extra increment from the United States, however, assured the Allies that there would be sufficient landing craft tanks (LCTs), landing craft infantry (LCIs), larger landing ship tanks (LSTs), and other types to support the assault.

Another problem was to set up effective diversionary measures. They were especially important to the Allies since they hoped to achieve tactical surprise and since deceptions can be particularly effective in misleading the enemy. The directive issued at Quebec made this point clear when it had stipulated that COSSAC develop a deception plan to complement the operational plan for Overlord.[46] The ruses took almost every conceivable form, from camouflage to misleading radio traffic to placing commanders in wrong locations, such as Montgomery in Algiers and General Patton in Scotland. The most elaborate deceptions were fake operations supposedly aimed at other landing areas. Plan Zeppelin, for example, was designed to deceive the Germans into thinking an invasion would be directed against the Balkans.

Plan Ferdinand and others were to simulate operations in the western Mediterranean, Fortitude North was to confuse the Germans into believing that a landing would take place in Norway or Denmark. The most successful, however, was Fortitude South, an assault supposedly aimed at the Pas de Calais. In this case, as discussed earlier, the British were able, through false reports and double agents residing in England, to give the Germans a false order of battle. The ruse had already begun in late 1942. By December 1943, German intelligence reported that the Allies had in the United Kingdom approximately 64 infantry, armored, and airborne divisions ready for combat, whereas they actually had only 25.[47] On February 1, the total had risen to 67; on April 1, 77; and on June 1, 88. The real number was 39, including two Polish and French divisions. The amazing aspect of the deception is that it continued to operate after the invasion, for the Germans thought that a second invasion directed against the Pas de Calais was in the offing, and they kept some of Fifteenth Army deployed there until the end of July. Germany's coastal divisions could obviously have been put to better use elsewhere.

On a more tactical level, the Allies undertook three bogus operations the night before the landings that also proved effective.[48] One was the dropping of dummy parachutists across a wide area of Normandy, and one of the drops drew a regiment stationed near Bayeux away from the invasion zone. The others were simulated naval attacks directed toward beaches near Cherbourg and in the Pas de Calais. In these instances, "coastal force craft, fitted with special equipment and supported by aircraft, approached close to their prospective beaches simulating the threats of landings. This was carried out largely by radio countermeasures, the use of smoke, and sonic warfare in which gramophone records, sound effects, and shouting voices were designed to represent noisy ships coming to anchor." These operations led German fighter and E-boat patrols to search the threatened areas most of the night.

Tied in with the deception measures was the gathering of timely intelligence.[49] By the time of Overlord, Ultra cryptographers were reading much of the army and air force and all of the naval traffic in the west. This, when combined with other Ultra and Magic information and verified by reconnaissance flights and Resistance sources, gave an excellent picture of what the Germans were doing. It was particularly valuable to aircrews in their preinvasion attacks and allowed them to neutralize many of the coastal batteries and radar sites, and to damage or destroy numerous airfields, bridges, roads, and rail lines in the interior. The assistance rendered by intelligence before the landings was to continue unabated on D-Day and beyond.

The role played by the French Resistance is more difficult to assess, for it was more important in the political rejuvenation of the country than it was as a military force.[50] In addition, its military activities were more significant after, rather than before, the invasion. Nevertheless, Resistance members helped to pin down rail movements and location of troops and clarify the enemy's military organization and command structure. At times, they even captured documents that were sent on to London. In accomplishing these tasks, and others, Resistance members rendered real intelligence assistance to the Allies. Their help took on added dimensions, such as sabotaging trains and harassing enemy soldiers, once the Allies had established themselves on French soil. Yet, despite their undoubted heroism, their military exploits have perhaps become greater in retrospect than they were at the time.

An Allied effort which is beyond dispute, however, is the important part played by air power. In this instance, the issue was the extent of the support for Overlord. The tactical air forces would assuredly be heavily involved throughout the preparatory and execution phases, but General Carl Spaatz, the commander of US Strategic Air Forces in Europe, comprising both Eighth Air Force in Britain and Fifteenth Air Force in Italy, and Air Chief Marshal Harris were opposed to diverting their bomber forces from attacks against strategic targets in Germany to raids against Overlord targets in France, although Harris was not as adamant on this point as Spaatz.[51] Eisenhower understandably wanted all aircraft, including strategic bombers, under his control to ensure a unified and maximum effort in support of Overlord. The main preinvasion goals, according to Tedder, Eisenhower's deputy, should be to devastate the enemy transportation system in the west, especially rail centers, and to eliminate the German air force, as these steps were essential to the operation's success. Spaatz agreed that gaining air superiority was crucial, but he preferred attacking oil instead of transportation targets, which he insisted would "be a misdirection of effort," since "the transportation 'cushion' is so large, and essential traffic so small." Portal and Eisenhower presumably settled the controversy on March 27.[52] They would assume responsibility for a comprehensive air plan, and Tedder as their representative would oversee the air portion for Overlord. It was understood that Overlord would not absorb the entire strategic air effort, but that portion not put directly under Overlord, that is, the strategic bombing offensive, was to be directed jointly by Portal and Eisenhower. Control was to pass to Eisenhower on April 14.

It was an ingenious solution, but opponents of the so-called Transportation Plan, and there were others besides Spaatz and Harris, now brought up a previously discussed problem and tied it to the bombing raids against transportation targets, which had already begun. According to Lord Cherwell, Churchill's scientific adviser, large-scale bombings would inflict excessive casualties on the French population. On this matter, he had the sympathy and support of Churchill. The issue was debated throughout April and into May at a series of late night Defence Committee meetings and at War Cabinet meetings as well.[53] Most of the meetings conformed to a pattern. Those who opposed the bombing would express their concern about the French civilians. Those in favor would indicate that the casualties of the previous week were less than anticipated. The participants would then agree to continue the bombings for another week, though some railway-center targets were deleted when casualties were expected to be too high. Finally at a cabinet meeting on May 2, an exasperated Eisenhower remarked: "It appears to me that if we are not prepared to bomb France we should never have entered on Overlord." This chilling comment and Roosevelt's disinclination to intervene in what he perceived as the theater commander's prerogatives, put an end to the dispute. Churchill went along.

The extended arguments were beside the point anyway, for by mid-April, Allied airmen were involved in a highly effective dual campaign against oil targets inside Germany and transportation and aircraft-related targets in France.[54] By May 15, of the 94 targets selected for bombing, 40 had been destroyed or rendered inoperative, and 30 more seriously damaged. Moreover, civilian casualties had been relatively low, 6,062 killed as of May 21 according to a German report.

As D-Day approached, the Allied air offensive, especially against targets west of Paris, intensified. For example, on June 2, Allied aircraft flew 4,397 sorties and concentrated on hitting coastal batteries, radar installations, rail centers, factories, bridges, and roadways. On June 3, the number was 3,722; on June 4, 3,367, though few at night because of the weather; and on June 5, 5,338.[55] Overall, between April 1 and June 6, the Allies flew 195,200 sorties, 71,800 of them by the RAF, and 123,400 by the USAAF.[56] Total bomb tonnage was 195,400 tons, considerably higher than the 132,500 tons estimated on March 3. To be sure, the cost had been high—1,953 aircraft lost. But the effort had caused substantial damage to enemy transportation, industrial, and military targets that could affect Overlord, and, more important, had virtually cleared Normandy's skies of the Luftwaffe before the invasion ever began.

Throughout the period of Allied planning and preparations, the Germans had not been inactive.[57] In fact, the measures they undertook, though defensive, often paralleled those of their adversaries. At first, after the conquest of France and the Low Countries, the Wehrmacht's emphasis was on invading and defeating Britain, and it took only minimal defensive precautions. With the loss to the RAF and the turn toward the Soviet Union, Germany relegated the west to a minor theater, at least in terms of land operations. When Barbarossa did not work out, however, western Europe again became an area of concern, not from an offensive, but from a defensive, standpoint. As early as December 1941, this concern took concrete form in an OKW directive, which stated that "the coastal regions of the Arctic Ocean, North Sea, and Atlantic Ocean controlled by us are ultimately to be built into a 'new Westwall' so that we can repel with certainty any landing attempts, even of the strongest forces, with the smallest possible number of permanent assigned field troops."[58] From this directive and the more broadly based Führer Directive No. 40 of March 1942 evolved the system of fortifications known as the Atlantic Wall.

As reports persisted into 1942 that Britain might attempt to secure a land front on the Continent (a not unfounded suspicion), the wall began to take shape. It was based on the premise that so long as the bulk of German ground and air forces were engaged elsewhere, fortifications and firepower would have to make up for manpower. Divisions were to be stationed in the west, but often for formation and refurbishment, not for permanent defensive duties. In this way, the west became a training ground and source of troops for the east. Nevertheless, at the same time, a defensive orientation was evolving. German planners were convinced that any major enemy attack would have to secure a port, and thus the main Channel and Bay of Biscay harbors were to be fortified for all-around defense so that they could withstand assaults from either the sea or the landward sides.[59] In addition, they decided that anywhere along the 2,100-mile coastline from the Spanish border to the Netherlands might be invaded; it was most endangered from the tip of Brittany to the Dutch port of Ijmuiden, since that sector was within range of Allied fighter aircraft. The Germans therefore decided to concentrate their effort on the ports and along the Channel coast, and then to fill in the areas in between as best they could. In a measure to show Hitler's resolve, he named the capable Field Marshal Gerd von Rundstedt to replace the ailing Field Marshal Erwin von Witzleben as commander-in-chief, West. Von Rundstedt's job was to oversee the defensive buildup. By the end of 1942, foreign and German workers, supervised by Organisation Todt, had constructed 3,105 permanent defenses of reinforced concrete (mostly near the harbors), and had emplaced about 790 coastal artillery guns. Forty-three divisions (in part consisting of units being prepared for the east) were now in the area.[60]

During 1943, improvements continued, with 8,478 total permanent structures built and 2,692 artillery pieces above 75 mm in place by year's end.[61] Although the number of divisions decreased to 41, the figure had been considerably lower earlier in the year, and more were on the way. The reason for the optimism was that the Führer, so long deflected from focusing on the west because of his overriding concern for the eastern and to an extent, the Italian fronts, had decided that western Europe must no longer be neglected. As discussed previously, Hitler on November 3 issued Führer Directive No. 51, based on a staff study compiled by von Rundstedt.[62] In the directive, Hitler said he realized that the "Anglo-Saxons" were preparing their long-expected invasion and that it could begin anytime after February. Time was therefore of the essence. The directive called for a vast effort to upgrade the defensive posture in the west, which was to include, not only more and improved fortifications, artillery, and infantry divisions, but also first-rate mobile divisions. In a move reminiscent of von Rundstedt's appointment, he directed Field Marshal Rommel to inspect the defenses in the theater and then make recommendations for their improvement.

Rommel began his task in December, and soon was chosen to head Army Group B, the tactical command in control of the most threatened Channel sector. In this position, though still under von Rundstedt, Rommel became the driving force in the defensive buildup. It took various forms. The major ports were declared fortresses and made capable of withstanding even long sieges. True to their earlier pronouncements, the Germans began to fill in the coastal stretches between the harbors with beach obstacles of various types, land mines, and tank traps as well as additional permanent fortifications and gun emplacements. Behind the beaches, numerous lowlying areas were flooded, and long spears, called Rommel Asparagus, were placed in fields to serve as antiairborne devices. By the end of May, the number of permanent defenses reached 13,078, though this number included 942 in the south of France; 3,301 artillery pieces; 6,508,380 land mines (Rommel wanted 50 million); and about 500,000 foreshore obstacles.[63] Fortunately for the Allies, who landed on a rising tide, only three of six rows of obstacles planned for the Normandy beaches had been laid by June 6.

In terms of personnel, the increase was more steady than spectacular. From December 1943, when forty-one divisions were combat ready and seven more being formed, the total reached fifty-eight just prior to the invasion.[64] Some of them were "static" divisions, immobile and capable only of defensive operations, but at least some of them were now fully manned, with three instead of two regiments as had been the case in December. Moreover, there were ten panzer and panzer grenadier divisions in the theater; by June, they had 1,347 tanks among them.[65] Still, during the spring, their placement had been the subject of a command controversy, in which Rommel had insisted the divisions be placed close to the coast. Runstedt had preferred them farther to the rear. The disagreement was more bitter and prolonged between Rommel and General Baron Leo Geyr von Schweppenburg, the armored group commander, than it was between the two field marshals, however.[66] The upshot of the controversy was a compromise in which Hitler gave Rommel and the soon-to-be-organized Army Group G, under General Johannes Blaskowitz, tactical control over three each of the mobile formations, while he placed the other four under his personal command as part of an OKW-Reserve. This decision helped lead to a weak armored response on D-Day, when their timely intervention was sorely needed. Nonetheless, despite the panzer problem—and there were others, such as interservice frictions among the army, navy, and air forces in the west—by the time of the landing the Germans could still commit a fairly respectable force behind a fairly formidable defensive barrier.[67] It was not a barrier to be taken lightly.

Yet there was still another problem for the Germans. They did not know when and where the invasion would take place. They had long assumed that it would be somewhere along the Channel, but early in 1944 they began to fear that the Allies might assault southern France, Portugal, or the Bay of Biscay, and they made plans for other contingencies as well.[68] When they learned that the Allies had shipped a number of combat divisions from Italy to Britain, they returned to their original conviction that it would be a cross-

Channel operation, but they lacked evidence of the time and place. Air reconnaissance over England was meager at best, and their turned double agents were obviously of no help either. At the end of April, Hitler ordered reinforcements into Normandy, where the landing actually occurred. He had taken into account the location of American troops in Britain, a report on an amphibious exercise in Devon, where the flat terrain resembled that in Normandy, and his belief that the Allies would land near Cherbourg, but his order was based on surmise and not on any definite knowledge. During May, both von Rundstedt and Rommel were aware that Allied aircraft were involved in an effective interdiction campaign against the entire transportation network in the west, against the Seine River bridges in particular, but they and their staffs could not figure out whether these attacks meant that the Allies would strike north or south of the Seine.[69] Nor do the Ultra intercepts between May 30 and June 6 indicate that the Germans found out. Even on the eve of the assault, when German forces in the Pas de Calais region intercepted messages of Allied intentions, this information reached Seventh Army headquarters in Normandy only a few hours before the seaborne landings began. In short, the Allies had achieved one of Morgan's preconditions—a tactical surprise.

Besides a lack of foreknowledge, part of the reason for the initial success of Overlord was the weather. Originally scheduled for June 5, the assault was postponed because of inclement weather, and the Germans even relaxed their defensive readiness because of it. In fact, most of the commanders were on their way to Rennes for a war-game exercise to be held on June 6. Rommel had taken advantage of the lull to return home for a few days to help his wife celebrate her birthday and to talk with the Führer about conditions in the theater. Eisenhower, however, on the basis of an improving weather forecast, decided at 9:45 p.m. on June 4 to go ahead with the attack after a twenty-four-hour delay. Overlord was accordingly set for June 6.

The figures for the opposing forces at the beginning of the campaign are revealing (table 11-1).[70] Of the 58 German divisions, 46 were deployed along the coast: 3 in the Netherlands; 18 in the most threatened Fifteenth Army sector; 14 in the Seventh Army area, where the invasion actually took place; 4 along the Bay of Biscay; and 7 along the French Mediterranean coast. Two reserve divisions were in the interior. Among the 10 panzer and panzer grenadier divisions, 3 were located north of the Seine, 4 between the Seine and the Loire rivers, and the other 3 in the south of France. Although the number of tanks per division varied widely (the 17th Panzer Grenadier had none at all), the total figure of 1,347 consisted of about equal numbers of Mark IIIs, Mark IVs, and Mark V Panthers, along with some captured French and Russian models. A battalion of Tiger tanks had also arrived on June 1, but it was not involved in the initial fighting.[71]

The thirty-nine Allied divisions were made up of twenty American, fourteen British, three Canadian, one French, and one Polish. Eleven were ar-

TABLE 11-1

Opposing Forces on the Eve of Overlord, June 1944

Germany		Allies
58	Combat Divisions	39
1,873,000	Total Number of Troops	2,876,439
561	Ships and Landing Craft	6,939
919	Aircraft	12,837

mored and four airborne. The discrepancy between the two sides in the total number of land, sea, and air personnel—about 2.9 to 1.9 million—is partially explained by the fact that the entire Allied logistical effort was located in the United Kingdom, while that of Germany was divided between the Reich and the west. But part of the reason is also because of the vast differences in the air and sea components.

The German naval total of 561 ships and craft under Navy Group West is even less impressive when one realizes that most of them were minesweepers and patrol vessels. The group had no capital ships, and its 5 destroyers and 49 submarines (35 in commission) were stationed along France's Atlantic coast rather than on the Channel. The Allies, on the other hand, had 1,213 warships among its 6,939 ships and craft. The combat vessels included 7 battleships, 23 cruisers, 105 destroyers, and 63 frigates and destroyer escorts. By nationality, 79 percent of the total were British, 16.5 percent American, and 4.5 percent others.

The difference was even more marked in air power. Germany's Air Fleet 3 had 919 aircraft in the theater, 510 of which were operational prior to the invasion. The Luftwaffe total of about 275 sorties on the day and evening of June 6 would indicate that the actual number in commission was probably fewer.[72] The Allies had no such problem. They had 5,409 fighters; 3,467 heavy bombers; 1,645 medium, light, and torpedo bombers; and 2,316 transports and troop carrier aircraft for a total of 12,837, thus outstripping the estimate in August 1943 that there would be 10,883.[73] Total sorties for June 6 and the night of June 6–7 were 12,617.[74] When Allied sorties on the eve of D-Day are added in, the number rises to 14,507.

The advantages were not all on the Allied side, however. The Germans did have a system of coastal defenses, not so strong or deep as they would have liked, but formidable nonetheless. They also had highly mobile panzer formations in the rear, and Hitler's contention that the German soldier was still a superb fighter was to be borne out once again in the days ahead.[75]

The Overlord campaign consisted of three phases—the invasion, the expansion and buildup of the lodgment, and the breakout.[76] Each of the phases gives us insights into both Allied and German strengths and weaknesses.

The invasion began with airborne drops commencing just after midnight. They were more scattered than had been hoped, but by morning most of the units had gathered themselves and were moving toward their bridge

Map 11-2: Western Front, 1944-45

or causeway-holding objectives. Naval and air bombardments before dawn
had reached their peak about 6:00 a.m. A paltry three German torpedo boats
were all that challenged the invasion armada. At 6:30, the forces began streaming ashore along a sixty-mile front, Americans on the right, British and Canadians a little later on the left. Only at Omaha Beach, where the US First
Division was landing, were great difficulties encountered. German artillery
fire was heavy, the foreshore obstacles had not been cleared sufficiently, and
Allied assault teams and shore parties remained pinned on the beaches for
approximately four hours. Only at 11 o'clock did German fire abate, thus

allowing the US forces to move across the beach and establish themselves. By the end of the day, lead units had moved inland about one mile. Throughout the day, they and the other formations were supported by six squadrons of Spitfires flying low cover and three squadrons of P-47s flying high cover along the beaches. The seaborne troops linked up with the airborne units, and by day's end, except at Omaha, the land forces had advanced up to six miles. This was short of Caen, an important D-Day objective that served as a transportation hub, but it was still enough to ensure the security of the lodgment. Even more impressive that first day was that 155,615 Allied soldiers (including 23,400 airborne) had landed on the Continent. Allied casualties were approximately 10,540.

While the weak German response can be attributed partly to the weather, it was also caused by the failure of the panzer divisions to move quickly. The Germans knew of the airborne landings soon after they began. At 2:30 a.m., one of the three panzer formations in the region was directed to prepare to move forward. By 3:25, the huge seaborne invasion fleet had been located, and by 4:00 a.m., all three of the armored divisions had been put on alert. At 4:25, they were ordered to move toward the expected landing zone. OB West asked OKW headquarters on several occasions to release the Panzer Lehr division near Chartres and the 12th SS Panzer near Evreux to theater control. But Jodl would not release them without Hitler's approval, and he would not disturb the Führer, who was sleeping. At 7 o'clock, OKW ordered the Panzer Lehr and 12th SS Panzer divisions to stop. By the time Hitler's permission was secured, it was 2:30 in the afternoon, and Allied air power was so overwhelming that the two divisions could not move until after dark. They did not arrive at the front until June 8 and 9. The only major German counterattack was mounted by elements of the 21st Panzer Division, but it made little headway against the British forces. By evening, the Germans were well aware that the Normandy assault was the beginning of the much-vaunted invasion, but they continued to believe that it would be followed by another cross-Channel attack during the coming weeks.

During the second phase, between June 7 and July 25, the Allies expanded their beachhead and built up their forces, though against strong opposition. The expansion was achieved by attaining a number of tactical objectives. British and American units joined their sectors near Port-en-Bessin on June 9. Although the Germans knew of Allied intentions, US divisions fought through difficult-to-traverse hedgerow country and sealed off the Cotentin Peninsula on June 17. They then closed in and took Cherbourg on the tip by June 27. Cherbourg's capture proved to be a disappointment, however, since German demolitions prevented it from being put to effective use until September. The British Second Army had even more difficulties. They tried repeatedly to take Caen, but were unable to capture it until July 8, and they never got into a war of movement until the American breakout toward the end of July relieved the pressure on the British portion of the front.

The problems experienced by Second Army has led historians to note serious deficiencies in their effort and to accuse Montgomery of altering the facts to indicate that Britain's primary role *from the beginning* was to hold down German armor so that the US could break out at the western end of the lodgment.[77] There is a good deal of truth in their contention, for some of the British divisions at this point were fought out, and the strategy of holding and wearing down the Germans was instituted in July rather than in June.

In the meantime, the second part of the Allied plan, to build up their forces, went ahead. By the end of June, the Allies had 26 divisions and a total of 861,838 personnel deployed in France. This number was only about 80 percent of the planned buildup because the gales, which had put one of the Mulberries out of commission, had slowed the process. By July 25, the Allied total on the Continent had jumped to 36 divisions and 1,452,000 troops (812,000 US and 640,000 British), and this number was approximately a month ahead of what had been projected. Ninety percent of the forces and supplies had been unloaded over the beaches.

Two other factors help explain the Allies' success. One was Ultra. It and the other intelligence sources were truly a boon. On occasion, Allied cryptologists were able to decode German messages within an hour and a half after they were sent by the Germans.[78] Within a week of the landings, Montgomery, Bradley, and the other commanders had precise information on the location of enemy land, sea, and air formations throughout the region. According to Ralph Bennett, Ultra also allowed the Allies to influence the tactical course of battle on at least five occasions during June and July.[79] It led to an air strike on June 10 that paralyzed General Geyr von Schweppenburg's Panzer Group West for a number of days. It permitted American units on June 13 to snuff out a 17th Panzer attack aimed at Carentan; it helped in Cherbourg's capture on June 27; and it assisted British forces on July 9 to halt a 19th SS Panzer division thrust. Ultra further made known to Bradley, as Twelfth Army Group commander, the low state of German morale before the July 25 breakout, and there were probably other instances of Ultra's assistance as well. Thus, during Overlord, Ultra had an effect on both the strategic and the tactical level. Its influence was to continue until the end.

The other factor was the oft-repeated role of the air forces. Despite the fact that coordination between Montgomery and Air Marshal Coningham, the head of Second Tactical Air Force, was poor, the Allies were able to construct 13 fighter airstrips by June 27, and this number increased considerably during the ensuing weeks.[80] Overall, up to June 30, these airfields and others in Britain allowed British and American pilots to fly 163,403 sorties while losing only 1,508 aircraft. By contrast, Germany's Air Fleet 3 flew 13,829 sorties at a cost of 808 aircraft. The devastating effect of Allied power led General Geyr at one point to declare that the enemy did not possess "air superiority (*Luftüberlegenheit*)," but rather "air mastery (*Luftherrschaft*)," in his sector.[81] Another aspect of the air war, already mentioned, was that the extensive use of fighters, fighter bombers, and bombers for Overlord did not prevent Allied strategic aircraft from attacking targets farther inland, so that during July, Germany's oil production was only 42 percent of what it had been the previous April.[82]

Once the Germans had recovered from the initial shock, they did everything they could to contain the Allied beachhead. The navy had virtually ceased to be a factor as a result of Allied bomber attacks at Le Havre and Boulogne on June 14–15, and the Luftwaffe had to limit its operations primarily to reconnaissance flights and hit-and-run actions at dusk. But the ground forces were reinforced to 16½ divisions by the end of June, and 8 of them were panzer divisions. The Führer had met with Rommel and von Rundstedt on two occasions and had tried to overcome their mounting pessimism. At the June 17 meeting near Soissons, he was so elated that the V-1s had been unleashed against England that he contended no retreats in the west were necessary. At the June 29 meeting at Berchtesgaden, he continued to advocate no withdrawals, and the exchange became so heated that both field marshals expected to be relieved of their posts, but only von Rundstedt was recalled and replaced by Field Marshal Günther von Kluge. Rommel's and Rundstedt's main concerns were the Allied buildup and mounting German casualties. Both of these concerns were magnified in July, when Allied forces in the area reached nearly 1.5 million men, and German casualties, including those taken prisoner, rose to over 100,000 soldiers by July 17. Allied casualties were about the same—110,380—but the disparity in forces and firepower was too great for the Germans to overcome.

On July 25, the Americans started advancing south from St. Lô. Six days later, the Germans finally concluded that there would be no second invasion and ordered Fifteenth Army divisions to leave their coastal positions in the Pas de Calais. On August 3, instead of having Patton's newly activated Third Army turn west and clear Brittany as originally intended, Bradley found the Wehrmacht in disarray in the east and ordered the bulk of Patton's forces to turn in that direction. With that move, the Americans began to push across France at a rate thought to be impossible. British and other American armies also commenced their own drives to the east, and there followed a series of offensives—the invasion of the French Riviera, the disappointment of failing to trap large numbers of German troops in the Falaise pocket, the taking of Paris—which ended only near the German frontier on September 15.

One result, described earlier, of the Allies' rapid advance was that it had been much more decisive than planners had anticipated. Rather than reaching the German border by D + 360, during which the Germans were expected to give up territory only after hard fighting, the Allies had reached it by D + 95. The dash across France had another result: a logistics crisis for the British and Americans. Instead of abandoning the Channel and Bay of Biscay ports, the Germans had left soldiers behind to fight to the last.[83]

These isolated troops fought with such ferocity that the Allies had difficulty liberating the areas. Most of them finally fell to the Allies during the autumn, but by that time it was impossible to mount any more major offensives until 1945. In that sense, the Atlantic Wall continued to be a factor long after it had been overrun.

In retrospect, Overlord points to a number of other conclusions.[84] Two of them relate to the often discussed importance of economic factors in twentieth-century warfare and the implication of the Allies' western strategy on the future shape of Europe. Also interesting is how early in the war Allied *and* German decisions were made regarding western Europe. After basing its initial strategy on the hope that the area would be overrun by a smaller number of troops, by the fall of 1942 Britain had come to realize that a major invasion would be required, and the Americans accepted this position from the time they entered the war. The Germans had settled into a defensive stance at about the same time, especially after the 1942 Russian campaign failed to bring about the desired results.

Another observation is that conditions before Overlord well illustrate the problem of military commitments. Such commitments helped determine the timing and form that the western invasion took. From an Allied standpoint, their adoption of strategies to clear the Mediterranean and the Atlantic was logical, but it meant that these areas had to be made safe for shipping before Overlord could proceed. Their emphasis on naval and aerial might also meant that they would make use of these components to the maximum extent possible. For the Germans, their fixation on the Soviet front virtually assured that defensive measures would predominate in the other theaters. And given all of their commitments and land-based thinking, it could be assumed that they would stress fortifications and firepower in the west, particularly once the war became one of attrition. The earlier development of longer-range rockets and jet fighters might have altered Germany's thinking, but they arrived too late to have much of an impact.

A further observation related to Overlord is the issue of concentration of force. Despite being limited to operations in Europe and on the periphery, Germany after 1941 became so spread out that it could not concentrate on one theater without jeopardizing others. Their attempt to build up the Atlantic Wall was therefore constrained by what was happening elsewhere. Only in late 1943, when western Europe became seriously threatened, did it receive a high priority. Even then, it could not be defended everywhere, so that the Germans continued to concentrate their effort on the ports and along the Channel coast. The differing views of the British and Americans on this matter caused considerable friction between them. Though the distinction can be overdrawn, Britain generally favored a peripheral strategy that took advantage of the enemy's weak points before delivering a fatal blow, while the US preferred to mass its forces and meet the enemy head-on. In this sense, Overlord represents a compromise between their opposite viewpoints.

They selected the Normandy beaches, not the Pas de Calais, the most heavily defended sector. Yet they concentrated on a single operation rather than undertaking a series of assaults along the coast. Admittedly, the French Riviera campaign might be construed as a follow-up attack, but its late implementation more immediately affected operations in Italy than it did Overlord during its initial stages. The irony is that it was the Americans who insisted on the southern France invasion, and the British who wanted to concentrate Allied forces in Italy and Normandy. This reversal of roles was to continue in the subsequent campaigns across western Europe and into Germany.

The decisions surrounding Normandy also reflect the relationship between national and coalition interests. For their military planning in the west, the Germans seldom had to take into account the views of its Axis partners; the Western Allies were seemingly involved in one compromise after another. From the decision not to establish a bridgehead in France in 1942 to the agreement to launch a major attack, their protracted discussions were filled with mutual suspicions. Even the decision to undertake Overlord had to be reaffirmed a number of times because the two allies seemingly did not trust one another. In the end, their differences were reconciled and a common strategy agreed upon. Although they continued to disagree on elements of strategy into 1945, the true spirit of compromise evident in Overlord, where both partners truly had to subordinate aspects of their national policies to achieve a common goal, perhaps helps explain their long-lasting friendship in the postwar world, a friendship few other countries have equaled.

A final question trails off into the realm of speculation: Could Overlord have been planned differently and still have succeeded? Here, as not in the case of the Sicilian operation, the answer seems to be no, for conditions were quite different. Germany's military presence in France was much more prominent than in Sicily, and portions of the Atlantic Wall, as in the Pas de Calais, would have presented the Allies with extreme difficulties. Furthermore, despite all their resources, the Allies did not have sufficient personnel and some specific types of equipment on hand to carry out several large amphibious attacks. They were better off concentrating on one. We are left with the conclusion that Overlord was the correct strategy, and it was not the relatively easy undertaking we have since presumed it to be.

During the summer of 1944, the situation for Germany was becoming truly desperate. Not only was there the breakout at St. Lô, there was also a Russian offensive that was leading to large-scale advances on the central front and an Allied advance that was making substantial headway north of Rome. In the midst of these staggering defeats, the July 20 attempt on Hitler's life occurred. Though unsuccessful, it caused the Führer some injury, and it obviously had wide-ranging repercussions within the Wehrmacht, including the removal or elimination of many officers suspected or involved in the plot. While recovering at his eastern headquarters, Hitler at a conference on July 31 said that he considered the west to be a crucial front and that sometime in the future he himself would have to take over responsibility for that theater. From this statement eventually evolved Germany's Ardennes offensive, or Operation Watch on the Rhine.[85]

Although conditions continued to deteriorate during August, Hitler announced at a staff meeting on August 19 that twenty-five divisions were to be readied in the west for a November offensive "when the enemy cannot fly."[86] Early in September, the Führer accorded the western front the highest priority for new artillery and assault guns and reaffirmed it for tanks. He also recalled von Rundstedt as commander-in-chief, West in the wake of von Kluge's suicide. On September 16, he told his staff that he had selected the Ardennes as the place for the attack, with Antwerp as the ultimate objective. Nine days later, he asked Jodl and his staff to prepare alternative plans for a western operation and to have a deception component for the plans. Jodl presented five possible options to Hitler on October 9. Although none of them coincided exactly with his wishes, they formed the basis for the finished product. On October 21, Hitler approved Watch on the Rhine and the next day revealed the plan to von Rundstedt's chief of staff and to Field Marshal Walter Model, commander of Army Group B.

Three armies under Army Group B were to take part. General Erich Brandenberger's Seventh Army was to protect the southern flank, but the key to the offensive was the two panzer armies. SS General Sepp Dietrich's Sixth Panzer Army was to be on the right. It was to capture the Meuse River bridges on both sides of Lüttich, advance to the Albert Canal, and then move northwest along it all the way to Antwerp. General Hasso von Manteuffel's Fifth Panzer Army was to form the second prong on the left. It was to cross the Meuse north and south of Dinant and push in a northerly direction toward Antwerp, making sure in its westerly swing to cover the Sixth Panzer Army's thrust from the east. The immediate and essential goal for the armored forces was to get across the Meuse quickly, perhaps by D+2, but the long-range objective was to destroy "enemy strength north of the line Antwerp-Brussels-Luxembourg, which would bring about a decisive change on the western front." This change would separate American and British forces and "perhaps even alter the entire course of the war."[87] The operation was to be ready by November 20, with the attack to start anytime after November 25.

The generals thought the plan too ambitious. While not disagreeing that some type of operation was necessary, Rundstedt, Model, and Manteuffel recommended, at a meeting with Jodl on November 3, a "small solution [kleine Lösung]." Part of the operation would still come out of the Ardennes, but part of it would take place farther north near Aachen. The resulting pincer movement would clear the Aachen salient of American troops and extend German control past Liège and the Meuse. Yet the final goal was still a long way from Antwerp. The next day they learned that Hitler had rejected the proposal, for it did not accord with his bigger solution, though he did go along with Manteuffel's suggestion to postpone the starting date into December. On November 26, the attack day was set for December 10.

The final plan had appeared on November 10. It followed OKW's original version to a large degree, but this time Fifteenth Army was brought in to guard the northern flank and rear of Sixth Panzer Army as it drove toward Antwerp, and Army Group H in the Netherlands was to come in during the final stages to help destroy the Allied forces. The air portion was to be handled by the recently created Luftwaffe Command West.

On December 2, Hitler again met with his western commanders (except von Rundstedt, who sent his chief of staff, Westphal) at the Reich chancellery, but he would agree only to slight modifications in the projected operation. On December 11, the day he began a series of final briefings with staff officers and commanders at his western headquarters near Bad Nauheim, the offensive was postponed to December 15, and then on the following day pushed back to December 16.[88] At the meetings, Hitler indicated that he had already decided during the fall that Germany must continue to defend itself, especially since separate negotiations with its enemies had been ruled out because of their repeated demands for an "unconditional surrender." In his view, the west presented better opportunities at this time than did the east. The distances to cover were shorter, fuel could be transported more cheaply, and strategic objectives reached more easily. Also, he did not regard the Americans and the British as such formidable opponents as the Red Army or the Soviet political leaders. He had therefore decided to deal the Western Allies "a powerful blow" before their forces reached the Rhine because Germany needed a respite in its continuing defensive struggle. Whether the reasons he gave for his decision should be taken at face value might well be questioned, but there is no doubt that he considered the Ardennes risk to be worth it. Only time would tell whether this gamble would succeed as so many had in the past.

One factor in Germany's favor was that its offensive took the Allies by surprise. Historians have been puzzled by the lack of foreknowledge to this day, particularly because of all the information the Allies were receiving.[89] In fact, several intelligence officers did pick up on the Ardennes as the place for an attack, but their opinions were dismissed. Part of the reason for the Allies' being surprised is that they thought the Germans were incapable of mounting a strong offensive at this point; enemy movements of troops or supplies were taken as measures to stiffen its defensive posture rather than as preparations for an offensive of its own. Part of the reason also stems from effective Wehrmacht deceptions and secrecy. Most of the movements were carried out at night. Only those who needed to know were told about the attack in advance. German signals made it known they were preparing a counterattack west of Cologne instead of in the Ardennes. All of the major formations were given bogus names. The Armed Forces Command Netherlands was called Fifteenth Army. Fifteenth Army, which was to cover the northern flank, was renamed Group von Manteuffel. General von Manteuffel himself was commander of Fifth Panzer Army, and that armored force was called Military Attack Command on Special Assignment. Sixth Panzer Army became Rest and Refitting Staff 16. Even the codename for the operation, Watch on the Rhine, had a misleading defensive connotation. These measures obviously had an effect, for even after the attack began, the Americans at first still thought it was a spoiling action rather than a major offensive.

The numbers of forces for both sides at the start are rather deceptive, for the Allies brought in substantial reinforcements during the battle. Nevertheless, the Germans had assembled a respectable force.[90] Army Group B's ration strength was 501,755 soldiers. They were divided into four armies and had 41⅔ divisions. Few of the Fifteenth Army's 11 divisions became involved, but all of the other armies' divisions did. They included Seventh Army with 4 infantry divisions, Fifth Panzer Army with 9 (4 armored), and Sixth Panzer Army also with 9 (4 SS armored). In reserve were 8⅔ divisions, of which 2⅔ were armored. The panzer and panzer grenadier formations had 753 tanks for the opening phase—328 Panzer IVs, 410 Panther Vs, and 15 Tiger VIs. The Germans had, in addition, 833 assault guns, especially effective as an antitank weapon and for infantry support, and 3,409 artillery pieces. Although Göring had promised 1,500 planes, only about 1,000 were available for the battle.

By contrast, the Ardennes sector was lightly held by the Americans. Only five divisions, one of them armored, were in the area when Germany launched its attack.[91] They did have 242 medium tanks, 182 tank destroyers, and 504 artillery guns, but these numbers were unimpressive alongside Germany's much larger totals. The offsetting elements were the numerous Allied ground reinforcements within reach and the huge air armada that could be switched to targets in the region if necessary. These elements proved to be the decisive factors.

On December 16, after an hour-long artillery barrage and even the use of V-weapons aimed at Liège and Antwerp, the Germans unleashed their ground forces at about 6:30 a.m. along a sixty-mile front.[92] By 9:25, lead elements, helped by hazy weather, had advanced two to three miles against slight opposition, but by afternoon, their progress had slowed considerably. By nightfall, it had become apparent that, except for the Fifth Panzer Army in the center, there had actually been little progress at all and that the important transportation hub at St. Vith, an opening-day objective, had not fallen. On December 17, the skies brightened for the first of several days, and Luftwaffe fighters could be used effectively. But so could Allied aircraft, and St. Vith continued to remain in Allied hands.

By the time Fifth Panzer Army took St. Vith on December 21, valuable time had been lost. In fact, von Manteuffel in retrospect has contended the German offensive had failed as early as December 18, when the panzer armies did not reach the Meuse. This does not mean that they did not try. Sixth Panzer Army on the right was by now acting more as a covering force for Fifth Panzer Army rather than the other way around, and Fifth Panzer, spearheaded by Battle Group Peiper, succeeded in going around or crossing a number of Ardennes barriers. However, they could not dislodge the American 101st Airborne division from another important transportation center, Bastogne. The road network that centered in Bastogne was the key to any large-scale German advance, but they could not get the American soldiers, though surrounded, to capitulate. Several factors were involved. Eisenhower's command had finally reacted strongly to the threat, and US Third Army divisions, instead of preparing their own offensive, raced north to relieve the Bastogne defenders; British units were beginning to play a role; and, more important immediately, better weather allowed Allied pilots to bring in much-needed supplies and to clear the skies of German aircraft. The Allies' 3,000 sorties per day was an exceedingly significant factor in curtailing the German ground forces during this crucial phase. On December 26, Patton's divisions lifted the siege at Bastogne.

In the meantime, German plans had gone awry across the entire front. A German infiltration force dressed in American uniforms under Lieutenant Colonel Otto Skorzeny and paratroopers under Colonel Friedrich von der Heydte had not reached their objectives. On the right, Sixth Panzer Army had virtually come to a standstill along Eisenborn Ridge, and on the left, Seventh Army had made some gains but had never reached the Ourthe River, let alone the Meuse near Givet, the original goal. On December 24, Fifth Panzer Army had come to within five miles of Dinant on the Meuse, but the Second Panzer Division could not advance farther because of strong Allied attacks and a lack of fuel. It proved to be the Wehrmacht's farthest penetration.

The Germans continued to try to take Bastogne even after its relief and also readied Sixth Panzer Army divisions for a renewed attack toward Liège. But except for an effective Luftwaffe raid against Allied airfields on January 1, little of consequence took place from a German standpoint on the Ardennes front. They undertook a devastating secondary attack to the south in Alsace and then another in northern Italy, but the main offensive had, in effect, already come to an inglorious end.

On December 30, Patton started a southern counterattack, and Montgomery, once he had gotten his forces rearranged, began one from the north five days later. The northern drive was led by the American First Army with some assistance from Britain's XXX Corps, and on January 8, Hitler reluctantly agreed that his forces could undertake a tactical withdrawal from the tip of the bulge. By mid-month the Allies had retaken about one-half of the lost area, and by January 28, they were back approximately to the starting line. On February 1, Eisenhower called on his armies to prepare for closing the Rhine north of Düsseldorf as soon as possible. Combat in the west was ready to enter a new phase.

German casualties had been heavy—80,000 to 90,000, with about 13,000 dead.[93] Total Allied casualties were about the same, 80,987 Americans and 1,408 British. In all, approximately three British divisions (55,000 soldiers) were involved, but as the casualty figures show, they were lightly used. On the other hand, eventually thirty-one American divisions (600,000 troops) took part. The number of German divisions that saw action was twenty-nine (about 500,000 men).

On the tactical level, the Ardennes battle again underlined the importance of Allied air superiority. It has been impossible to determine the number of German sorties, but an estimate of 1,000 planes lost during the campaign is not unreasonable. For the Allies, the figures help substantiate that it was primarily an American show. Of 63,741 total sorties dispatched between December 16 and January 16, 51,594 were flown by US flyers and 12,147 by those of the RAF. The Anglo-Americans lost 647 aircraft.

After the operation began, Ultra also made a difference.[94] On December 20, for instance, the Allies located Battle Group Peiper, and they also knew it was short of fuel and ammunition. On December 26, they realized through enemy messages that the tide of the battle was turning, and on December 28 and 30, they knew of Germany's difficulties in getting its drive toward Liège organized. There were, of course, numerous other disclosures. Most of the signals were being deciphered with little delay. The Germans were not so fortunate, for the small amount of intelligence they gained proved of little benefit.

Strategically, Hitler's Ardennes operation—for it was truly his in conception and outlook—was a disaster for the Germans.[95] It was unrealistic to expect their armies to reach Antwerp or, for that matter, the Meuse, and the latter failure casts doubt on even the small solution advocated by the generals. The offensive used up valuable panzer and air formations as well as reserves needed for defense of the Reich. As pointed out by Army Chief of Staff Guderian, and others, it also weakened the German military in the east and helped contribute to Russia's highly successful January 1945 offensive against an increasingly demoralized foe.

On the other hand, the Ardennes campaign did shake Allied, in particular American, confidence. The Americans hurriedly sent over the rest of the US strategic reserve from the States to strengthen the western theater. In doing so, they left the cupboard bare for future major operations in the Pacific.[96] The campaign also led British planners to revise their estimates for the end of the war in Europe. In late October 1944, they had thought it would be over sometime between January 31 and May 15, 1945. By December 8, they had changed it slightly to sometime between January 1 and June 30. But by January 22, during the final stages of the Battle of the

Bulge, they had decided that unless the Soviet offensive succeeded beyond expectations so that the war might be concluded in April, the end date would probably be between June 30 and November 1. Fortunately for the Allies, their ability to pick up the pace from both the east and the west made these dates far wide of the mark, but they do demonstrate that the German offensive had a substantial impact on Allied deployments and thinking.

Eisenhower's February 1 order that Allied armies close to the Rhine north of Düsseldorf was not unexpected. Indeed, Allied planning for such an operation had been in train for some months. It was conceived of as the first of three steps that would carry Allied troops to the heart of Hitler's Reich: an advance to the Rhine, its crossing, and then pursuit of the enemy and occupation of his homeland. By late 1944, the main Allied problem was not if they would reach that great river barrier, but when and where. The when depended on many factors—offensive, defensive, and logistical—and thus could not be predicted with any sense of assurance, but the where could be examined with more precision. On this question, British-American military relations again became severely strained.

The controversy revolved around Eisenhower's—and the US joint chiefs'—contention that Germany should be attacked along a broad front and Montgomery's—and the British chiefs'—assertion that Allied forces should be concentrated for a strong push across northern Germany. At the Quebec Octagon meeting in August 1944, the British had reluctantly given in to Eisenhower's wishes so long as the planned southern thrust was a subsidiary undertaking.[97] But they continued to fear that Eisenhower would give more preference to US offensives in the south. Their surmise was correct, for the Americans held such a preponderance of power in the west that they insisted on having their own area of operations and on not being subjected to British control. They would cooperate, but they would not accept a secondary role. Although the British continued to press for a single, northern thrust, they were never able to get the Americans to go along. At Malta, before the conference at Yalta, Allied leaders reaffirmed the broad-front strategy.[98]

Despite their reluctance, the British agreed that Eisenhower's February order should be implemented. The operations could be mounted with little delay because they had already been planned the previous December.[99] At that time, Allied planners had proposed three different offensives. The first, called Operation Veritable, was to have First Canadian Army drive southeast from Nijmegen and clear the area between the Meuse and the Rhine. The second, undertaken by Twelfth US Army Group, was to be a major drive northeast across the Roer River to opposite Düsseldorf on the Rhine. Both offensives were to begin any time after January 1. They were to be preceded by a third operation, in which the British Second Army was to eliminate an enemy salient known as the Roer River salient between Geilenkirchen and Roermund. The target date for the third operation was December 12, though both planners and commanders knew that they could never get it launched by then. After these three operations, and others to the south, had been completed, they hoped to attack across the Rhine in mid-March.

These plans were upset by Germany's Ardennes offensive. Still, by mid-January the Bulge was being cleared, and a British attack north of the Ardennes sector, which was actually the carrying out of the earlier plan to eliminate the Roer salient, put the Allies in a position to undertake their offensives to reach the Rhine between Nijmegen and Düsseldorf. These January actions set the stage for Operations Veritable and Grenade.[100]

As set forth in a modified February 4 directive issued by Twenty-First Army Group, Veritable was still to feature the First Canadian's pushing southeast out of Nijmegen in a series of steps until it reached a line from west of Geldern to Xanten on the Rhine. The offensive was to start along a relatively narrow six-mile front, but it was eventually to expand to twenty miles by the time Veritable reached its final objectives about forty miles distant. It was to take place in terrain that was exceedingly difficult to traverse, with areas along the rivers flooded and an undulating forested region in between that included the dense, state-owned Reichswald in the north and several smaller woods to the south. The Germans had set up three defensive belts in the region: one west of the Reichswald; one, an extension of the West Wall, through the forest to west of the towns of Goch and Geldern; and a third from Rees on the Rhine to west of several forests and then on to Geldern. The Germans were also helped by the uncertain weather that was typical this time of year.

The second main operation, Grenade, was also like its predecessor in that it focused on crossing the Roer River around Jülich and then heading northeast to link up with the Canadian-British force, but this time it specified that General William Simpson's Ninth US Army would be under Montgomery's command. The river crossing was to be executed along a seventeen-mile front, followed by an advance to the Rhine, a distance of forty to fifty miles, as rapidly as possible. The area to be covered was not so rugged as that faced by the First Canadian Army, since most of it was a flat plain leading toward Cologne. But the Germans had also erected defensive barriers across the area—on the east bank of the Roer, and two others two and six miles behind the river. The Allied plan was to have the Canadian-British force start first, tie down the Germans, and thus allow the Americans to the south to break through and catch the enemy in a vise west of the Rhine. Accordingly, attack day for the Canadian First Army was set for February 8, and for the American Ninth Army, February 10. The British Second Army was to hold the zone between the two attacking armies, and the American First Army was to cover Simpson's right flank as his Ninth Army advanced north and northeast. Air support was to be provided by Air Marshal Coningham's Second Tactical Air Force and General Richard Nugent's American XXIX Tactical Air Corps, though fighter bombers and medium and heavy bombers from other units were also to be called upon as needed.

One of the Allies' primary concerns was that the Germans possibly expected "a major offensive designed to reach the Rhine in the north." This fear was verified by Ultra intercepts in early February and substantiated further when it was learned that German reinforcements were arriving in the region between Cologne and the Dutch border.[101] The Allies therefore decided to try to disguise the exact location of the attacks, not to hide the fact that they would take place. In this respect, they were successful, for the Germans thought that the initial Allied offensive would come somewhere between Venlo on the Meuse and Roermond farther south rather than from near Nijmegen. Even after Veritable was launched, the Germans labored under this mistaken idea until the strength of the First Canadian Army's thrust convinced them otherwise.

The forces and command structure at the beginning were as follows: Both Veritable and Grenade were under Montgomery's overall control, but tactical command for Veritable was exercised by the head of the First Canadian Army, General Henry Crerar.[102] Crerar's two corps had seven infantry and three and one-third armored divisions, plus assorted artillery and antiaircraft units, but an interesting feature of Crerar's forces was its truly integrated nature— eight British and two and one-third Canadian divisions. General Sir Miles Dempsey's supporting Second British Army had two infantry, one airborne, and one armored division. General Simpson's Ninth US Army for Grenade had three corps, with ten divisions positioned along the Roer River and one more in reserve, making a total of eleven. Four additional divisions from First US Army were to cover the flank. The total number of ground troops for both operations was approximately 640,000, with 380,000 of them American and 260,000 British and Canadian. The Americans also had more tanks, 1,394 to about 500 for the British, but the disparity can be explained in part by the fact that Ninth Army would be operating in an area well suited for tanks. The Allies further had nearly 3,000 artillery pieces and were able to utilize a number of special weapons, such as tanks equipped with flame throwers or long arms that could detonate mines.

The number of aircraft that took part has been impossible to determine, especially since the medium bombers of Ninth Bombardment Command, the heavy bombers of Bomber Command and Eighth Air Force, and the fighters of IX Tactical Air Command were involved only sporadically. The operations were supported primarily by 1,300 aircraft of the Second Tactical Air Force and about 450 of the XXIX Tactical Air Command. The German opposition on both fronts was ten and two-thirds Fifteenth Army infantry divisions, backed up by five reserve divisions, four of which were armored. Still, they were severely under strength, since there were only 276 tanks and assault guns in all of Army Group B, the command responsible for the area, and the number of aircraft was minuscule.

Nevertheless, the outmanned and outgunned Germans acquitted themselves well, particularly in the Veritable fighting. It began at 10:30 a.m. on February 8 after a prolonged Allied artillery bombardment and bomber attacks the night before.[103] Parts of five divisions moved out of their attack positions south of Nijmegen and made good progress, moving southeast and securing a foothold in the difficult-to-penetrate Reichswald by nightfall. The Allied advance had been up to four miles in some sectors, and the ground troops had been supported by 1,211 Second Tactical Air Force fighter and fighter-bomber sorties. On the next day, German resistance stiffened, especially when portions of the 116th Panzer and 15th Panzer Grenadier divisions entered the battle. Although the British were approaching the important town of Cleves by evening, they were also being held up by extensive flooding, which often required the use of duplexdrive amphibious trucks (DUKWs) to get supplies to the forward troops. At the same time, another factor entered the picture. The Americans, who were to start Grenade the next day to ease the pressure on the British and Canadian forces, found that the Germans at the last minute had opened the discharge valves on one of the main Roer River dams. The resulting flooding of the countryside meant that Grenade had to be postponed for some days. Growing German resistance could now be concentrated against the Veritable force.

The British and Canadians managed to enter Cleves on February 11. Few houses were left standing by the time it was completely taken the next day. The British XXX and Canadian II corps continued to push southeast, but only slowly. During this time, the skies cleared for several days, and on February 15, Allied air forces flew 9,066 sorties, the largest total since the Normandy fighting. Many of the attacks were directly or indirectly related to Veritable. Also, while Ultra and other intelligence information did not change the course of the battle, it did help by giving the location and movement of the enemy formations.[104] Yet the Germans did not crack, although the heavily defended town of Goch fell on February 19. Corps Commander Horrocks aptly described this stage of the fighting as "a slogging match as we inched our way forward through mud and rain."

However, on February 23, the logjam began to break when the Americans were finally able to start Grenade. The Roer was still over its banks, but with the use of assault boats and footbridges, elements of four divisions began at 3:30 a.m. to cross the river. They soon established themselves on the other side. By the end of the day, some of the assault teams had advanced four to five miles and had taken the towns of Jülich and Baal. They had been ably supported by 613 sorties of XXIX Tactical Air Command. The next day, they started to expand the bridgehead north and northeast. On February 26, the British and Canadians mounted an offensive of their own (Operation Blockbuster) to overcome the Germans' third defensive belt and to pin down the German forces, while the Ninth Army pushed ahead from the south. By February 28, Simpson's divisions had achieved a breakthrough, and the next day, they entered the major industrial city of München-Gladbach and Neuss, opposite Düsseldorf. Also on that day, March 1, US and British soldiers made contact for the first time. Despite continued heavy fighting, especially in the First Canadian Army sector, victory was in sight.

During the operation's final stage, the Allies naturally wanted to capture one of the Rhine bridges—there were eight in the area—before they could be blown. General Simpson thought that one of them between Düsseldorf and Urdingen could be secured. In several instances, however, Montgomery would not allow even a try, and his unwillingness not to make an attempt became a further point of dispute between Montgomery and the American commanders. Nevertheless, Geldern, one of the final objectives, fell on March 4, and Xanten, the last strongpoint, on March 9. By the night of March 10, Allied forces were holding the west bank of the Rhine from Nijmegen to Düsseldorf. The next step, the crossing of the river, could now proceed.

This step was not as difficult as it might have been, for not only had the Allies closed to the Rhine in the Nijmegen-Düsseldorf sector, but by this time US divisions had also cleared the west bank all the way south to Koblenz. More important, as is well known, on March 7, a bridge at Remagen south of Bonn was unexpectedly captured intact by American troops before it was destroyed, and a substantial bridgehead was established on the eastern side of the river before it collapsed. This unforeseen good fortune certainly eased the problem for Patton's Third Army, which crossed near Oppenheim on the night of March 22–23, and Montgomery's 21st Army Group, which crossed at a number of places between Osoy and Rees the next night. The latter operation, Plunder, was an extension of the Veritable-Grenade offensives. With the support of airborne forces and more than seven thousand air sorties, it was eminently successful. By March 28, Montgomery had declared that the "Battle of the Rhine" had been won, and the battle for Germany, including the taking of the Ruhr, was ready to enter its final phase.[105] Despite all of the postwar controversy regarding the carrying out of that final phase, the war in Europe ended with Germany's surrender on May 8, much to the jubilation of the British and the relief of the German population.

Still, the fighting during Veritable and Grenade had been difficult.[106] The equivalent of 25 Allied divisions had been involved, 13 British and Canadian and 12 American, and they had suffered a combined total of 22,900 casualties. German casualties had been much higher. From their 9 divisions that had taken part, the Germans had lost an estimated 89,000 troops. Even more alarming was that 51,000, or 57 percent, of the total had been taken prisoner, which showed a serious deterioration in morale even though the soldiers had been fighting on German soil.

The Allies could also be heartened by several other factors. Air power had continued to play a prominent role during Veritable-Grenade. Despite unfavorable weather, between February 1 and March 11, Second TAF flew 21,976 sorties, XXIX TAC nearly 7,000, and, though total numbers are not available, other air formations helped out as well.[107] Moreover, although it cannot be proved, Germany's horrendous losses before the Rhine may well have lowered their resistance during the final stages when everything fell apart. If that is indeed the case, then the hard-earned Veritable-Grenade victory undoubtedly assisted in bringing about that result.

On a broader level, Veritable-Grenade also shares at least three elements in common with the Imphal-Kohima battles, the Normandy landings, and the Ardennes fighting. First, all four illustrate forcefully—even more so than other operations discussed here—the importance of Allied material superiority. In Burma, which was so difficult to support logistically, the Allies were still able to supply some of their forces with air drops at critical times and eventually to overcome Japan's initial advantages with more troops and equipment. In Normandy, Allied naval and air superiority was an obvious advantage of considerable magnitude, and aerial dominance was also of crucial significance in the Ardennes and Rhineland combat. Furthermore, by this time, the Allies (and the Germans) were experimenting with all types of new equipment, including flame-throwing Crocodile tanks and troop-carrying turretless Kangaroos and amphibious Buffaloes, and similar experiments were being tried in other theaters, such as Italy, as well. Still, Allied superiority was not so much a matter of new or better weapons—for the German and Japanese equipment was often as good, and in some cases better—as it was simply that the Allies had so many more of them—and personnel—that the Axis could not expect to compete in a war of attrition.

Second, it is truly amazing, though understandable, how international the opposing armies had become during the latter stages. The Allied forces in Burma were predominantly British and Indian soldiers, but Chinese, American, Burmese, and other European and Commonwealth personnel were also represented, and the Japanese also used Burmese and Indian troops. Although not emphasized, the Germans at Normandy as well as the Allies had a definite international flavor, for they were using military and labor battalions from around the world. This trend was not so evident on the German side in the west later on, but the Allies had not only become more international, but also increasingly integrated, as was particularly apparent by the time of Veritable-Grenade. British troops continued the trend begun earlier of serving under Canadian army commanders, and not always the other way around. The Americans retained tactical control of their forces, except for two divisions that were shifted to the British Second Army during the early fighting, but Britain's Twenty-First Army Group exercised overall command. And British and American air leaders at times got along better among themselves than they did with their own countrymen. Certainly, there was a limit to their cooperation—Bradley, for instance, did not want Simpson's Army serving under Montgomery—and national pride and objectives remained in the forefront of the coalition. At the tactical level, however, the Allies on numerous occasions fought together as true partners.

And third, as discussed at the beginning of the chapter, during Veritable-Grenade and the other operations, the Axis still managed to give a good account of themselves. The Japanese fought tenaciously in northeastern India and northern Burma, and the Germans did likewise in western and eastern Europe and also in Italy. There were lapses—as in the Soviet 1944 summer offensive and the Anglo-American drive across France—and there were pullbacks—as in southeastern Europe and southern France. But on the whole, as exemplified at Myitkyina, in front of Caen, and at Xanten, the Axis continued to be a determined, stubborn foe until almost the very end. While their strategic goals and especially their hubris should be condemned, their ability to fight well and often courageously cannot help but be admired.

Conclusion

Ultimately, when future historians write about the twentieth century, they may well focus their attention on the moribund nature of the nation-state and how the demise of that outdated institution was speeded along by events during the century's fourth decade. They may also note that the people at the time, no matter how misguided, became caught up in the decade's most important act, the last major national war, the so-called Second World War, to such an extent that the world has never been the same. The two nations examined here, Great Britain and Germany, certainly fit into the mold of the extreme nationalism epitomized by the conflict. Their leaders filled their populations with patriotic fervor and clothed their ideas in national rhetoric to a degree seldom paralleled in human history. And the military personnel who served their nations—both top and bottom—served them willingly and at times heroically. There were, to be sure, dissidents at home and deserters at the fronts, but, on the whole, the morale of the populace and soldiers remained surprisingly high despite the carnage wrought by the two sides. It was truly an amazing time.

We have looked at the leaders of these two nations and at how they and the high-command systems they fashioned developed strategies and then tried to ensure that the strategies were carried out. It was an ongoing process. Nonetheless, it is difficult to escape the conclusion that, despite German superiority in the operational and tactical spheres, the British had superior leadership, high-command structures, and strategy.

The leaders of both countries were remarkable individuals, although one in a negative rather than positive sense. Unlike Ozymandias, neither of them will be forgotten, for both left an indelible imprint on the war and on the time in which they lived. Hitler's beliefs lay in National Socialism and the destiny of Germany, and these beliefs were related to his themes of additional living space, hatred of Jews, and eventual world domination. Even though his third theme was not evident to the German populace, it was apparent to his military advisers, and most of them also accepted his ideas about race and space at least to some extent. Except for the war's early stages, when Chamberlain was in control, Britain's prime ministership was in the hands of Churchill, whose main beliefs were grounded in democracy as exemplified by the British parliamentary system, balance-of-power considerations, and defense of the empire. In all three aspects, he had the support of his military advisers. His theme of defeating the Axis, with Germany as the number-one enemy, was realistic and accepted by them as well. These goals contrast markedly with the grandiose schemes of Hitler.

Yet the Führer dominated Germany's short-term and long-term goals to a much greater degree than Churchill did Britain's. In fact, Churchill's primary contribution was to infuse the country's long-term aspirations with his spirit rather than to dictate the details of that spirit.[1] Hitler, on the other hand, was not satisfied with directing the Reich's war effort and overseeing its strategy. As Charles Burdick has written, the Führer was a gambler, a person seeking a rapid decision. "He had to win quickly before an effective opposing system came into play, but his lack of experience, understanding, or education" as contrasted with Churchill's background precluded success. Given his proclivities, Hitler became increasingly involved in details of strategy rather than allow a collective endeavor.

Another significant contrast between the two leaders was their view of allies. Churchill realized Britain could not prosecute the war without them. He willingly went to considerable lengths to gain the support of the Soviet Union and the United States along with that of his Commonwealth friends. While relations between Britain and its allies did not always work smoothly, they were certainly superior to those between Germany and its partners, whom Hitler treated at best as conveniences and often with outright contempt. Only with Mussolini, though not with Italy, did he develop a satisfactory relationship, and he still never dealt with the Italian dictator on anything like an equal basis.

A further crucial difference between Hitler and Churchill was in their treatment of military advisers. Both understood the need for advisers, but between Hitler and his service chiefs arose a type of competition in which he was constantly trying to prove himself, often at their expense. Hitler disliked being contradicted and generally gathered around him lackeys who did not speak out against his more unrealistic notions. If they did show signs of opposition, and some of the bolder staff officers and field commanders on occasion did, they might well find themselves relieved of their posts. The result was a good deal of turnover among the commanders-in-chief and chiefs of staff and discontinuity at the highest levels. The service staffs therefore concentrated on operational matters at the expense of strategic considerations, which they left primarily to Hitler. The Führer exacerbated the problem by setting up an unwieldy decision-making system which left each of the military chiefs (and the heads of armaments and the SS) to deal with him individually, not on a unified basis. Consequently, there was no true general staff speaking as one, but only a number of individual representatives whom Hitler dominated or cajoled as he saw fit.

In Britain, however, once the military and civilian leaders overcame their slowness in decision making, the system instituted by Churchill worked well. At first, Churchill had difficulty finding military advisers he could get along with, but after he found them, there were few changes at the top. The chiefs of staff argued among themselves, but once they reached a decision, they stood by it and resolutely defended it even when the prime minister voiced his opposition. He might fume at them, but he seemed to appreciate their willingness to stand up to him, and there developed a true sense of collegiality between him and the service heads. In this respect, they served their nation more effectively than did their German counterparts.

The strategy which evolved for the two countries also presents some interesting comparisons. When one assesses economic, political, and military aspects of their respective strategies, one is struck in the last instance with the relative simplicity of Germany's military strategy in contrast with that of Great Britain. A good deal of the reason no doubt was Britain's difficulty in forging a common strategy with equal or superior economic partners, a situation Germany did not face; but part of it can also be attributed to Germany's aggressive moves and Britain's having to react not only to them but also to those of Italy and Japan through 1942. Only when the initiative passed to the Grand Alliance could Britain pursue the war on a more calculated basis, yet again within the framework of the Big Three and their often differing goals.

Germany's relatively simple strategy was opportunistic and not based on any overall plan, although the Führer's ideas about space, race, and, to a degree, world dominion obviously conditioned the planning process. In 1939, Poland was to be the victim. When it became thus, with the blessing and some actions from the Soviet Union, France and the Low Countries were next. The conquest of Norway and Denmark intervened, but only to a limited extent, and the Battle of France in May and June 1940 turned out to be Germany's greatest triumph. But Britain did not capitulate, and when diplomatic efforts failed, Hitler decided on an invasion to bring them to heel. When Luftwaffe failed, however, in its attempt to gain air superiority, the Führer decided to pursue other alternatives. One possibility was an increased presence in the eastern Atlantic, but another one, an invasion of the Soviet Union, was more intriguing and fit in well with his economic and racial thinking. During 1941, and for at least three years thereafter, defeat of the Soviet menace became Germany's foremost goal. Interestingly, Germany even at this point could not concentrate solely on Russia because of Italy's problems in the Balkans and in northern and eastern Africa. While Germany's involvement in those areas did not particularly set back its 1941 campaign against the Red Army and air force, it did bring about an ongoing commitment in southeastern Europe and the Mediterranean which Germany could ill afford. Despite numerous tactical victories against the Soviets, a strategic victory of annihilation was not achieved. As a result, Hitler determined that the main effort for Germany would continue in the east in 1942, with a secondary commitment in North Africa. During the summer, the Wehrmacht again dealt the enemy substantial defeats on both fronts. Then difficulties set in.

During the fall of 1942, Germany had to move toward a holding strategy. This aspect of its strategy has not been examined in detail in the context of the early years, but even though it was generally reactive and brings into sharp relief Germany's problem of overcommitment, the adherence to it in the later years shows also that the Germans would not succumb easily. In 1943, they did deviate from their holding pattern to attack the Soviets in the Kursk salient. Otherwise, they suffered defeat after defeat—in the Atlantic, in Tunisia and Sicily, in western Russia, and increasingly in the air. Still, the Germans had some "cushion" in Europe, and this allowed them to hold out. But the situation did not brighten in 1944. They were beaten in the south, west, and east and had to pull out of substantial portions of Europe. They also lost the air battle, but at the end of the year, they managed to make one last, desperate attempt in the Ardennes forest to redress the balance in the west. When this offensive, too, failed, they could do little but await their fate since Hitler refused to sue for peace. At war's end, Germany's relatively simple, but unrealistic, strategy lay in tatters, and the country, prostrate.

Britain's strategy was more complex in large part because of its worldwide geographic reach. When the war broke out in 1939, its long-term strategy centered on blockading the enemy and defending Britain and western Europe, although the eventual bombing of Germany and defense of the Commonwealth and Empire were also elements of its thinking. All aspects of that strategy were dealt a severe blow with the defeat of France. Nevertheless, economic warfare and strategic bombing remained important components of their war planning, and to them were added subversion and the future invasion of the Continent. Once the RAF prevailed in the Battle of Britain, the country's goals for Europe, as defined by Churchill and the chiefs of staff, remained the same; but outside Europe, the battles being fought in the Mediterranean and the Atlantic also assumed a high priority. These objectives continued into 1941, but other elements entered the picture when Japan became an enemy and the Soviet Union and the United States active allies.

At this juncture, December 1941, we find a lag effect in Britain's strategy. Churchill continued to talk in terms of blockade, bombing, subversion, and an eventual assault against western Europe with relatively small numbers of troops. With Britain and the Commonwealth fighting in Asia and the Pacific as well as in Africa and the Atlantic, however, this strategy was bound to change. During 1942, in concert with the United States, Britain's strategy was brought more into accord with reality. Bombing and sea communications remained important considerations, but blockade and subversion were finally seen as ineffective or insufficient and were dropped as major strategic objectives. Japanese advances pushed British forces into India, and the United States, with its emphasis on the Pacific, started to dominate that region. Although not acknowledged at the time, this meant that Britain would be relegated to a subsidiary role in the area.

Yet, in the European theater, the British wanted to strike at Germany in some effective way. By the fall of 1942, they realized that the defeat of the Wehrmacht would require an invasion from the west, but for the moment, this was not thought plausible even on a limited scale. They therefore opted for two widely separated attacks to drive the Axis out of Africa, and despite initial American reluctance, operations mounted in Egypt and Northwest Africa in October and November gained complete success by mid-1943. In the meantime, the Red Army halted the Germans at Stalingrad, and that theater also entered a new phase.

By the time of the Casablanca conference in January 1943, a comprehensive Allied military strategy was in the making.[2] Besides the addition of the unconditional-surrender formula at a press conference, the main elements as set forth at the end of the meeting were as follows:

(1) Intensify the Anti-U-Boat war.
(2) Expand the Anglo-American bomber offensive.
(3) Keep the pressure on in the Mediterranean by attacking Sicily after clearing North Africa. No further operations were designated, but additional measures should be designed to knock Italy out of the war as soon as possible.
(4) Continue to supply goods to Russia.
(5) Undertake additional offensives in the Pacific.
(6) Begin operations to reopen the Burma Road to China.
(7) Increase American air presence in the China-Burma-India theater.
(8) Concentrate forces to the greatest extent possible in the United Kingdom for a return to the Continent.

The Americans, of course, were concerned about Britain's true commitment to number eight, but those elements, with several additions and subtractions, provided the framework for the military decisions that were reached at the subsequent wartime conferences. They became, in effect, the bases of Anglo-American strategy for the remainder of the war.

In 1943, the Battle of the Atlantic was virtually won, the bomber offensives intensified, and Sicily overrun. Pressure was kept on in the Mediterranean with the September invasion of the Italian peninsula, and the flow of supplies to Russia increased substantially. In the Asian theater, America's Pacific strategy became the prime factor, although operations in Burma and concern about China continued until the end of the war and, in the latter case, beyond. Also, throughout 1943, the Allies reaffirmed their resolve to go ahead with the western landing, and the Normandy assault was launched in June 1944. Even though developments in the Balkans came up in military discussions, the single main addition to the US-British list at Casablanca (besides atomic weapons) was the invasion of southern France. This possibility, in support of Overlord, was brought up repeatedly in 1943, and finally agreed to at

Tehran. But it was postponed in March 1944, in deference to Overlord, only to be resurrected again and carried out in August. By this time, Germany was being subjected to horrendous defeats on land and in the air, and though its "annual collapse" was put off until 1945, when it came, Germany was devastated. If winning is the key ingredient of any military strategy, then the Allies' strategy was by all accounts remarkably successful.

A further question one might ask is, when did the United States come to dominate its British partner in terms of strategy? While some historians, including this one, believe that date is mid-1943, others put it as early as Operation Torch or as late as Tehran. But perhaps the attempt to find an exact date is misplaced. For it was definitely a combined strategy in which Britain determined the agenda, though not necessarily the timing, for Europe, and the US, for the most part, went along. In the Pacific, the Americans set the course, and the British, again with some misgivings, agreed to lend their support. Despite heated arguments and festering disputes between them, theirs was in this sense a true partnership.

Even though this study has not emphasized the economic and political aspects of the war, they obviously played significant roles in the working out of Britain's and Germany's military strategies. In the economic realm, Britain was not only on the winning side because of Soviet and American help, but also because it was more realistic in its appraisal of the conflict at the beginning. From the first, Britain planned on a long war and geared its production accordingly. Despite a lower manufacturing capacity than Germany's and despite the Reich's head start in armaments, Britain passed Germany in annual aircraft production in 1940 and in tank production in 1941. When the Germans moved to a full war economy in early 1942, it was too late, for although they could now surpass the British in war equipment as well as in manpower, they were eventually dwarfed by the combined economic might of Britain, the Soviet Union, and the United States. In the end, then, Britain's economic thinking was the more realistic of the two.

In politics in the broad sense, neither side was especially successful, for neither developed a comprehensive grand strategy. In the case of Germany, its strategy had no finite, end goals. The Germans started the war, but had no idea of when it should stop, and they ruled the areas they conquered according to short-term exploitative practices rather than on a long-term basis. Britain's situation was different, but it, too, stressed military at the expense of political objectives, in part because of the fragile nature of the Grand Alliance, in part because of the exigencies of the war itself. Britain and its allies did initiate steps to bring about a lasting peace, but the pull of nationalism was too strong to assure that result. While many elements of the subsequent Cold War were beyond Britain's power to influence, a more realistic appraisal of its problems at home and in the Commonwealth and Empire still might have eased its burdens after the conflict.

On the operational level, among the many conclusions that can be drawn from the eleven campaigns we have examined on each side, three might be highlighted. First is that intelligence was a factor in many of the battles, and in this regard, British intelligence was superior, although the Germans did achieve successes, as on the Soviet front in 1943 and in the Atlantic campaign. Second, what was a minor theater to one side was not necessarily minor to the other. The foremost example is the differential between Germany's major effort in Russia and its peripheral one in North Africa, whereas the British, despite logistical difficulties, considered North Africa their primary land theater between 1941 and mid-1943 and devoted considerable resources to it. On the other hand, given Britain's wide-ranging commitments, it never concentrated its combat strength to the extent that Germany did against the Soviet Union.

Third, Allied operations were more varied and involved more interservice cooperation than did those of Germany. Certainly, many of the British and German operations we have discussed made extensive use of land and air components, and the Anglo-American strategic bombing against Germany's defensive air campaign was undertaken primarily by one service on each side. In the Battle of the Atlantic, however, the Allies called on both naval and air elements, while the Germans depended almost solely on its naval arm; and in the amphibious assaults, from Torch through Overlord and Dragoon, all three Allied services were heavily engaged. The disparity in numbers is not so apparent in the largest land operations—France, Barbarossa, and Normandy—where the number of troops at the battles' outsets varied between 1.8 and 3.6 million on each side. The real difference is in the amphibious undertakings, where, in addition to the land forces, the Allies marshaled 2,590 ships and craft and 3,462 aircraft for Sicily, and an astounding 6,939 ships and craft and 12,837 aircraft for Overlord. These numbers again give credence to the role that Allied economic superiority played in achieving victory.

Several other overall observations about Germany's and Britain's conduct of the war might be ventured in closing. First of all, after fifty years, perhaps our view of World War II has become too retrospective. Did the participants, for instance, in contrast to historians, actually see the turning point in Europe as late 1941, or is it more proper to see it as a year later when Germany truly lost the initiative? Was the Allies' overwhelming economic might a foregone conclusion when the Soviet Union and the United States entered the war, or did their potential power have to become a reality first, as it did on an upward curve in 1942 and 1943? In tactical operations, do we make too much of Britain's hanging by a thread during the crucial phases of the battles of Britain and the Atlantic, especially since those at the top who were directing the battles were confident that their forces could hold out and eventually triumph? Is our judgment of Germany's failure at Normandy conditioned by our knowledge of the subsequent race across France? In this light, possibly we have focused excessively on looking back at the war instead of trying to look at it through the lenses of those who experienced it first-hand.

The war also makes evident that democracies can fight wars effectively. To be sure, they do not normally fight well unless provoked, but once provoked, they can do amazingly well. There is no doubt that modern warfare requires centralized decision making; nevertheless, in this instance Britain proved that war by committee could and did work. This conclusion is somewhat reassuring in an era that produced Mussolini, Stalin, and Hitler as well as Churchill, Roosevelt, and Gandhi.

Appendix

CODE NAMES

Anvil	Anglo-American plan for landing in southern France; launched as Operation Dragoon, August 1944.
Arcadia	Anglo-American conference in Washington, December 1941– January 1942
Argonaut	Anglo-American conference in Washington, June 1942; also Allied conference at Yalta, February, 1945.
Bagration	Soviet offensive against German forces on central front, June 1944.
Barbarossa	German offensive against the Soviet Union, 1941.
Battleaxe	British attack in North Africa, June 1941.
Blockbuster	British-Canadian attack in Hochwald, February–March 1945.
Blue	German offensive against the Soviet Union, June 1942; renamed Operation Brunswick, June 30.
Bolero	US buildup in the United Kingdom for Operation Overlord, 1942–43.
Brimstone	British plan for invasion of Sardinia.
Brunswick	German offensive against Soviet Union, 1942; superseded Operation Blue.
Buccaneer	British plan for invasion of Andaman Islands, 1943.
Citadel	German operation against Kursk salient, July 1943.
Crusader	British offensive in North Africa, November 1941–January 1942.
Cudgel	British operation along the Arakan coast, Burma, 1943–44.
Culverin	Projected Anglo-American operation against Sumatra, 1943–44.
Diadem	Anglo-American offensive to capture Rome, May 1944.
Dragoon	Anglo-American invasion of southern France, August 1944; superseded Operation Anvil.
Dynamo	British evacuation operation from Dunkirk, May–June 1940.
Edelweiss	German offensive to capture Caucasus region, 1942.
Eureka	Allied conference at Tehran, November–December 1943.
Falke	German contingency plan to reinforce Norway, 1944.

Ferdinand	Anglo-American deception plan aimed at western Mediterranean, 1944.
Fortitude-North	Anglo-American deception plan for Norway and Denmark, 1944.
Fortitude-South	Anglo-American deception plan for Pas de Calais, 1944.
Freya	German radar device for air defense, introduced 1940.
Fritz	Original German codename for attack on Soviet Union, 1940.
Gee	British aerial radar aid, introduced 1942.
Gertrude	German contingency plan to reinforce the Balkans, 1944.
Grenade	US Ninth Army offensive to clear area west of the Rhine, February–March 1945.
Gripfast	British plan to advance in Indaw-Kathay area, Burma, 1944; preempted by Japanese attack.
Gymnast	Original codename for Anglo-American assault of northwestern Africa, 1942; renamed Operation Torch.
Hanna	German contingency plan to reinforce Denmark, 1944.
Hawk	German plan for offensive in Soviet Union, 1943.
Hercules	German plan to capture Malta, 1942.
Heron	German attack against Stalingrad, 1942.
Himmelbett	German air defense system in west, introduced 1940.
Husky	Anglo-American invasion of Sicily, July–August 1943.
Influx	British plan to occupy Sicily, 1940–41.
Lichtenstein	German aircraft radar, introduced 1942.
Lightfoot	British offensive against Axis forces at El Alamein, October–November 1942.
Magic	American decryptions of Japanese radio messages.
Marder 1	German contingency plan to reinforce Italy's Ligurian coast, 1944.
Marder 2	German contingency plan to reinforce Italy's Adriatic coast, 1944.
Millennium	British bomber raid against Cologne, May 1942.
Mulberries	Anglo-American artificial harbors erected on Normandy coast, June 1944.
Northern Lights	German plan for offensive in northern Russia, 1942.
Oboe	British blind-bombing radar device, introduced 1942.
Octagon	Anglo-American conference at Quebec, September 1944.

Overlord	Allied invasion of Normandy, June–July 1944.
Panther	German plan for offensive in Soviet Union, 1943.
Pathfinder	British aircraft used for making targets, introduced 1942.
Phoenixes	Portion of artificial harbors erected by Allies on Normandy coast, June 1944.
Pigstick	Proposed British landings along Arakan coast, 1944.
Plunder	Anglo-American operation to cross the Rhine north of Düsseldorf, March 1945.
Pointblank	Anglo-American strategic bombing offensive, 1943–44.
Quadrant	Anglo-American conference at Quebec, August 1943.
Rankin	Anglo-American plan for return to the Continent should Germany collapse, 1943.
Red	German operation against Anglo-French forces, June 1940; continuation of Operation Yellow.
Rommel Asparagus	German antilanding stakes emplaced in Normandy, 1944.
Roundup	Anglo-American plan to invade western Europe, 1943.
Schräge Musik	German fighter aircraft cannon, introduced 1943.
Sea Lion	German plan to invade Great Britain, 1940.
Sextant	Allied conferences at Cairo, November–December 1943.
Sichelschnitt	German attack against France and the Low Countries, May–June 1940.
Sledgehammer	Anglo-American plan for limited invasion of France, 1942.
Supercharge	Second stage of British offensive at El Alamein, October–November 1942.
Symbol	Anglo-American conference at Casablanca, January 1943.
Tame Boar	German fighter aircraft tactic, introduced 1943.
Theseus	Axis attack at Gazala, May–June 1942.
Torch	Anglo-American landing in Northwest Africa, November 1942.
Trident	Anglo-American conference at Washington, May 1943.
Typhoon	German offensive aimed at Moscow, 1941.
Ultra	British decryptions of German radio messages.
V-1	German pilotless bombs, introduced June 1944.
V-2	German long-range rockets, introduced September 1944.
Venezia	Italian codename for Axis Gazala offensive, May–June 1942.

Veritable	British-Canadian offensive to close to the Rhine, February–March 1945.
Watch on the Rhine	German attack in the Ardennes, December 1944.
Weser Exercise	German invasion of Norway and Denmark, April–May 1940.
Whipcord	British plan to invade Sicily, 1941.
White	German invasion of Poland, September 1939.
Wild Boar	German fighter aircraft tactic, introduced 1943.
Window	Tinfoil strips introduced by British to confuse German radar, 1943.
Würzburg	German radar device for air defense, introduced 1940.
Yellow	German offensive against France and the Low Countries, May–June 1940.
Zeppelin	Anglo-American deception plan aimed at the Balkans, 1944.

Notes

PREFACE

1. Notable exceptions include Alan S. Milward, *War, Economy, and Society: 1939–1945* (Berkeley: University of California Press, 1977); and Andreas Hillgruber, *Der Zweite Weltkrieg, 1939–45: Kriegsziele und Strategie der grossen Mächte* (Stuttgart: Kohlhammer, 1983).

2. Richard J. Overy, *The Air War, 1939–1945* (London: Europa, 1980), 127, 209–210.

3. Russell F. Weigley, *Eisenhower's Lieutenants: The Campaigns of France and Germany, 1944–1945* (Bloomington: Indiana University Press, 1981), 727–730.

ONE. DIRECTING THE WAR

1. Robert Sherwood, *Roosevelt and Hopkins: An Intimate History* (New York: Grosset & Dunlap, 1950), 243.

2. Percy Ernst Schramm, *Hitler: The Man and the Military Leader*, trans. Donald S. Detwiler (Chicago: Quadrangle Books, 1971), 110.

3. Brief comparisons are undertaken in David Kahn, *Hitler's Spies: German Military Intelligence in World War II* (New York: Macmillan, 1978), 542–543; and Ronald Lewin, *Churchill as Warlord* (New York: Stein & Day, 1973), 20–21.

4. See Gerhard Schreiber, *Hitler Interpretationen, 1923–1983: Ergebnisse, Methoden und Probleme der Forschung* (Darmstadt: Wissenschaftliche Buchgesellschaft, 1984). Among the many biographies of Hitler, the best is Joachim Fest, *Hitler*, trans. Richard and Clara Winston (New York: Vintage, 1975). Also useful are Alan Bullock, *Hitler: A Study in Tyranny*, rev. ed. (New York: Harper, 1964); and for his early years, Bradley F. Smith, *Adolf Hitler, His Family, Childhood and Youth* (Stanford, CA: Stanford University Press, 1968), and Helm Stierlin, *Adolf Hitler: Familien perspektiven* (Frankfurt a.M., Suhrkampf, 1975). For insights into his military role, see Gert Buchheit, *Hitler der Feldherr: Die Zerstörung einer Legende* (Rastatt: Grote, 1958); Schramm, *Hitler: The Man;* Albert Speer, *Inside the Third Reich*, trans. Richard and Clara Winston (New York: Macmillan, 1970); William Carr, *Hitler: A Study in Personality and Politics* (London: Edward Arnold, 1978); John Keegan, *The Mask of Command* (New York: Penguin, 1987); and the popular Sebastian Haffner, *The Meaning of Hitler*, trans. Ewald Osers (London: Weidenfeld & Nicolson, 1979). Psychological studies include Robert G. L. Waite, *The Psychopathic God: Adolf Hitler* (New York: Signet, 1977); and Wolfgang de Boor, *Hitler: Mensch, Übermensch, Untermensch: Eine kriminal psychologische Studie* (Frankfurt a.M.: R. G. Fischer, 1985).

5. Schramm, *Hitler: The Man*, 134–135; and Haffner, *Meaning of Hitler*, 6–7.

6. Speer, *Inside the Third Reich*, 306–307.

7. Eberhard Jäckel, *Hitler in History* (Hanover, NH: University Press of New England, 1985), 90–91.

8. Ibid., 38.

9. Gerhard L. Weinberg, "Reflections on Running a War: Hitler, Churchill, Stalin, Roosevelt, Tojo," Phi Alpha Theta Lecture, State University of New York at Albany, 1986, 4; and Hermann Graml, "Wer bestimmte die Aussenpolitik des Dritten Reiches?" in Manfred Funke et al., *Democratie und Diktatar . . . Festschrift für Karl Dietrich Braeher* (Düsseldorf: Droste, 1987), 236.

10. Martin L. Van Creveld, "War Lord Hitler: Some Points Reconsidered," *Euro-*

pean Studies Review, 4 (Jan 1974): 72; Gerhard Engel, *Heeresadjutant bei Hitler, 1938–1943* (Stuttgart: Deutsche Verlags-Anstalt, 1974), 74–75; and Keegan, *Mask of Command*, 267–268.

11. Heinz Assmann, "Some Personal Recollections of Adolf Hitler," trans. Roland Krause, *U.S. Naval Institute Proceedings*, 79 (Dec 1953): 1291–1293.

12. Engel, *Heeresadjutant*, 80.

13. Horst Boog, *Die deutsche Luftwaffenführung, 1935–1945: Führungsprobleme-Spitzengliederung-Generalstabsausbildung* (Stuttgart: Deutsche Verlags-Anstalt, 1982), 519–520.

14. Among others, see Assmann, "Some Personal Recollections," 1290, Van Creveld, "War Lord Hitler," 74; Edward N. Peterson, *The Limits of Hitler's Power* (Princeton: Princeton University Press, 1969), 431–432; Felix Gilbert, ed., *Hitler Directs His War: The Secret Records of His Daily Military Conferences* (New York: Oxford University Press, 1950), 25–26; Werner Maser, *Hitler: Legend, Myth and Reality*, trans. Peter and Betty Ross (London: Allen Lane, 1973), 280; and Henry Ashby Turner, ed., *Hitler—Memoirs of a Confidant*, trans. Ruth Hein (New Haven: Yale University Press, 1985), 87.

15. Waite, *The Psychopathic God*, 481.

16. Van Creveld, "War Lord Hitler," 79.

17. Milan Hauner, *Hitler: A Chronology of His Life and Times* (London: Macmillan, 1983); Keegan, *Mask of Command*, 274–275; and Max Domarus, hrsg., *Hitler: Reden und Proklamationen, 1932–1945* (Würzburg: Verlags Schmidt Druckerei, 1963), II, 2276.

18. Henry Picker, hrsg., *Hitlers Tischgespräche im Führerhauptquartier, 1941–42* (Stuttgart: Seewald, 1963), 37–54; Percy Ernst Schramm et al., hrsg., *Kriegstagebuch des Oberkommandos der Wehrmacht, 1940–1945* (Frankfurt a.M.: Bernard & Graefe, 1961), I, 140E; Hugh R. Trevor-Roper, ed., *Hitler's Secret Conversations, 1941–1944*, trans. Norman Camison and R. H. Stevens (New York: Farrar, Straus, & Young, 1953), xi–xiii; W. H. Tantum IV and E. J. Hoffschmidts, eds., *The Rise and Fall of the German Air Force (1933 to 1945)* (Old Greenwich, CT: WE Inc., 1969), 414–415; Speer *Inside the Third Reich*, 318–319; Eugene Davidson, *The Trial of the Germans* (New York: Collier, 1966), 362; Fest, *Hitler*, 668–671; and Nicholus von Below, *Als Hitlers Adjutant, 1937–1945* (Mainz: Von Hase & Koehler, 1980), 208.

19. See the interesting memoirs of one of his secretaries, Christa Schroeder, *Er war mein Chief . . .* , hrsg. von Anton Joachins-Thaler (München: Langen Müller, 1985).

20. Werner Jochmann, hrsg., *Adolf Hitler: Monolog im Führerhauptquartier, 1941–1944: Die Aufzeichnungen Heinrich Heims* (Hamburg: Albrecht Kraus, 1980), 84; and Fest, *Hitler*, 671. See also Speer, *Inside the Third Reich*, 323.

21. The best one-volume biography is Henry Pelling, *Winston Churchill* (New York: Dutton, 1974). Martin Gilbert's exhaustive eight-volume biography, *Winston Churchill* (Boston: Houghton Mifflin, 1966–88), a continuation of Randolph Churchill's work, is the definitive account; volumes 6 and 7 are especially pertinent. The best book on Churchill as war leader is Lewin, *Churchill as Warlord*. An excellent short sketch is contained in Kahn, *Hitler's Spies*, 542–543. An insightful psychological study is Anthony Storr's in Alan J. P. Taylor et al., *Churchill Revised: A Critical Assessment* (New York: Dial, 1969), 229–274. An analysis of the strengths and shortcomings of Churchill's magisterial *The Second World War* (6 vols. [Boston: Houghton Mifflin, 1948–53]), is Raymond Callahan, *Churchill: Retreat from Empire* (Wilmington, DE: Scholarly Resources, 1984).

22. Gilbert, VI, *Finest Hour*, 165–166; and ibid., VII, *Road to Victory*, 341–342; Sir John R. Colville, *The Fringes of Power: Downing Street Diaries, 1939–1955* (London: Hodder & Stoughton, 1985), 124–129; Sir Arthur Bryant, *The Turn of the Tide* (Garden

City, NY: Doubleday, 1957), 12 (based on the Alan Brooke diaries); Sir John W. Wheeler-Bennett, ed., *Action This Day: Working with Churchill* (New York: Macmillan, 1968), (Colville) 48–51, 53, and (Jacob) 174; Lewin, *Churchill as Warlord*, 5–6; J. R. M. Butler, *Grand Strategy*, Vol. 2, *September 1939–June 1941 (History of the Second World War, United Kingdom Military Series)*, 249–250; Sir Stephen Roskill, *Churchill and the Admirals* (London: Collins, 1977), 274–275; Elisabeth Barker, *Churchill and Eden at War* (London: Macmillan, 1978), 307; R. W. Thompson, *Churchill and Morton* (London: Hodder & Stoughton, 1976), 48, 73; and Admiral Sir Andrew B. Cunningham Correspondence (Viscount Cunningham of Hyndhope), ADD MS 52561, 20 September 1940, British Museum Library.

23. Colville, *Fringes of Power*, 143.

24. Robert Rhodes James, ed., *Winston S. Churchill: His Complete Speeches, 1897–1963* (New York: R. R. Bowker, 1974), VI, 6331.

25. Taylor et al., *Churchill Revised*, (Storr) 231, 171–273.

26. Cunningham Correspondence, MS ADD 52577, July 6, 1944, BML; and Colville, *Fringes of Power*, 280.

27. Among others, see Wheeler-Bennett, ed., *Action This Day*, (Colville) 71; Colville, *Fringes of Power*, 29; Bryant, *Turn of the Tide*, 13; and Barker, *Churchill and Eden*, 307.

28. Thompson, *Churchill and Morton*, 198–199; Warren F. Kimball, ed., *Churchill and Roosevelt: The Complete Correspondence* (Princeton: Princeton University Press, 1984), II, 442; and Taylor, *Churchill Revised*, (Storr) 230–238.

29. Wheeler-Bennett, ed., *Action This Day*, (Colville) 67, and (Normanbrook) 26.

30. Bryant, *Turn of the Tide*, 12; Lewin, *Churchill as Warlord*, 6–9; and Thompson, *Churchill and Morton*, 71, 163.

31. Lord Hastings Ismay, *The Memoirs of Lord Ismay* (London: Heinemann, 1960), 185.

32. Colville, *Fringes of Power*, 124–127; Wheeler-Bennett, ed., *Action This Day*, (Normanbrook) 25, and (Colville), 57.

33. Thompson, *Churchill and Morton*, 198–199.

34. Kenneth Harris, *Attlee* (New York: Norton, 1983), 206; Colville, *Fringes of Power*, 122; Wheeler-Bennett, ed., *Action This Day*, (Colville) 48–53; Kenneth Rose, *The Later Cecils* (New York: Harper & Row, 1975), 168; and Thompson, *Churchill and Morton*, 86.

35. Colville, *Fringes of Power*, 128; Barker, *Churchill and Eden*, 26; and Ernest L. Woodward, "Some Reflections on British Policy, 1939–45," *International Affairs*, 31 (1955): 280.

36. Thompson, *Churchill and Morton*, 48; and Roskill, *Churchill and the Admirals*, 276.

37. Ronald Lewin, *Ultra Goes to War* (London: Hutchinson, 1978), 184; Wheeler-Bennett, ed., *Action This Day*, (Colville) 61; and Butler, *Grand Strategy*, II, 249–250.

38. Wheeler-Bennett, ed., *Action This Day*, (Colville) 62; Roskill, *Churchill and the Admirals;* and Sir David Fraser, *Alanbrooke* (New York: Athenaeum, 1982), 210–211.

39. Colville, *Fringes of Power;* and Winston S. Churchill, *The Second World War* (Boston: Houghton Mifflin, 1948–1954).

40. WM 111(41), 11.11.1941, CAB 65/20, Public Record Office; Gilbert, VI, *Finest Hour;* John N. Kennedy, *Business of War* (London: Hutchinson, 1957), 60–62; Barker, *Churchill and Eden*, 16; Wheeler-Bennett, ed., *Action This Day;* and Gerald Pawle, *The War and Colonel Warden . . .* (New York: Knopf, 1963).

41. James Leasor, *War at the Top: Based on the Experiences of General Sir Leslie Hollis* (London: M. Joseph, 1959), 71.

42. Gilbert, ed., *Hitler Directs His War*, 29; Horst Boog et al., *Das Deutsche*

Reich und der Zweite Weltkrieg, bd. 4, Der Angriff auf die Sowjetunion (Stuttgart: Deutsche Verlage-Anstalt, 1982), 1079; and Hauner, *Hitler,* vii.

43. Essays in H. W. Koch, ed., *Aspects of the Third Reich* (London: Macmillan, 1985) summarize the various arguments.

44. There is also the dispute among historians as to whether Hitler had a "program," or series of steps *(Stufenplan),* that would lead to German overseas expansion. See Hillgruber, *Der Zweite Weltkrieg.* For a rejoinder, based on economic considerations, see Hartmut Schustereit, *Vabanque: Hitlers Angriff auf die Sowjetunion 1941 als Versuch, durch den Sieg im Osten den Westen zu bezwingen* (Herford und Bonn: Mittler, 1988).

45. Koch, ed., *Aspects of the Third Reich,* 185, and (Carr) 487–488; Klaus Hildebrand, hrsg., *Deutsche Frage und europäisches Gleichgewicht: Festschrift für Andreas Hillgruber zum 60, Geburtstag* (Köln: Bohlau, 1985), (Watt) 150–164; Timothy W. Mason, *Arbeiterklässe und Volksgemeinschaft: Dokumente und Materalen zur deutschen Arbeiterpolitik von 1936 bis 1939* (Opladen: Westdeutscher Verlag, 1975); and Walther Hofer, "Fifty Years On: Historians and the Third Reich," *Journal of Contemporary History,* 21 (Apr 1986): 225–251. A balanced analysis is in Ian Kershaw, *The Nazi Dictatorship: Problems and Perspectives of Interpretation* (Baltimore: Edward Arnold, 1985).

46. Jäckel, *Hitler in History,* 38.

47. Pelling, *Winston Churchill;* Thompson, *Churchill and Morton,* 118; and Maurice Matloff and Edwin M. Snell, *Strategic Planning for Coalition Warfare, 1941–1942* (Washington: USGPO, 1953), 29–30.

48. Wilhelm Deist et al., *Das Deutsche Reich und der Zweite Weltkreig,* bd. 1, *Ursachen und Voraussetzungen der deutschen Kriegspolitik* (Stuttgart: Deutsche Verlags-Anstalt, 1979), 31, 708; and Van Creveld, "War Lord Hitler," 65.

49. Roskill, *Churchill and the Admirals,* 278; Wheeler-Bennett, ed., *Action This Day,* (Normanbrooke) 24; and Colville, *Fringes of Power,* 127.

50. Haffner, *Meaning of Hitler,* 25–31; and Colville, *Fringes of Power,* 128.

51. Peterson, *Limits of Hitler's Power,* xiv–xv, 430–431; Leonard Krieger, "Nazism: Highway or Byway," *Central European History,* 11 (Mar 1978): 3–22; Colville, *Fringes of Power,* 307–402; and Gilbert, VI, *Finest Hour,* 595.

52. Among others, see Berenice A. Carroll, *Design for Total War: Arms and Economics in the Third Reich* (The Hague: Mouton, 1968); Willi A. Boelcke, hrsg., *Deutschlands Rüstung im Zweiten Weltkreig: Hitlers Konferenzen mit Albert Speer, 1942–1945* (Frankfurt a.M.: Akademische Verlagsgesellschaft, 1960); Karl Hardach, *The Political Economy of Germany in the Twentieth Century* (Berkeley: University of California Press, 1980); and William K. Hancock and Margaret Gowing, *British War Economy* (London: HMSO, 1949).

53. Kimball, ed., *Churchill and Roosevelt,* II, 479; Karl Dietrich Bracher, *The German Dictatorship: The Origins, Structures, and Effects of National Socialism,* trans. Jean Steinberg (New York: Praeger, 1970), 404; and Carr, *Hitler,* 84–85.

54. Among others, see Van Creveld, "War Lord Hitler," 67–71, 77; Walter Warlimont, *Inside Hitler's Headquarters* (New York: Praeger, 1964), 183, 277–278; Sir Basil H. Liddell Hart, *The German Generals Talk* (New York: W. Morrow, 1948), 297–298; Engel, *Heeresadjutant,* 75; Keegan, *Mask of Command,* 243; Ismay, *Memoirs of Lord Ismay,* 163; Sir Arthur Bryant, *Triumph in the West* (Garden City, NY: Doubleday, 1959) 77 (based on Alanbrooke diaries); Wheeler-Bennett, ed., *Action This Day,* (Jacob) 198–199; William D. Morgan Papers, WDM 1/3, Imperial War Museum; Admiralty, 19th January 1940, ADM 205/7, PRO; and Gilbert, VI, *Finest Hour,* 166.

55. Thompson, *Churchill and Morton,* 71–72; Wheeler-Bennett, ed., *Action This Day,* (Jacob) 200–202; Churchill, *Closing the Ring,* 65–66; R. J. Overy, "Hitler and Air Strategy," *Journal of Contemporary History* 15 (Jul 1980): 418; Edward L. Homze,

Arming the Luftwaffe (Lincoln: University of Nebraska Press, 1976), 51; Carr, *Hitler,* 78–79; and Albert Speer, *Infiltration,* trans. Joachim Neugroschel (New York: Macmillan, 1981), 83.

56. Keegan, *Mask of Command,* 300; Speer, *Inside the Third Reich,* 394; Overy, "Hitler and Air Strategy," 405; Cunningham Correspondence, MS ADD 52561, 1 December 1940, BML; Wheeler-Bennett, ed., *Action This Day,* (Normanbrooke) 27–28; Lewin, *Churchill as Warlord,* 266; Leasor, *War at the Top,* 168–169; and Fraser, *Alanbrooke,* 396–397.

57. Ronald Lewin, *Hitler's Mistakes* (New York: Morrow, 1984); and Roskill, *Churchill and the Admirals.*

58. Kahn, *Hitler's Spies,* 536–538; Lewin, *Churchill as Warlord,* 75; and Van Creveld, "War Lord Hitler," 57–58.

59. See, for example, Frederick W. Deakin, *The Brutal Friendship: Mussolini, Hitler and the Fall of Italian Fascism* (New York: Harper, 1963); Jürgen Förster, *Stalingrad: Risse im Bundnis 1942/43* (Freiburg i.Br.: Rombach, 1975); Burkhart Mueller-Hillebrand, *Germany and Its Allies in World War II* (Frederick, MD: UPA, 1980); Lewin, *Churchill as Warlord;* and Kimball, ed., *Churchill and Roosevelt,* I, 3–4.

60. A solid synthesis of international developments in the late 1930s and Chamberlain's role in them is Christopher Thorne, *The Approach of War, 1938–1939* (New York: St. Martin's, 1968). A negative appraisal of Chamberlain, based on extensive documentation, is Williamson Murray, *The Change in the European Balance of Power, 1938–1939: The Path to Ruin* (Princeton: Princeton University Press, 1984).

61. Sir Keith Feiling, *The Life of Neville Chamberlain* (London: Macmillan, 1946); Gerhard L. Weinberg, *The Foreign Policy of Hitler's Germany: Starting World War II, 1937–1939* (Chicago: University of Chicago Press, 1980); and David Dilks, *Neville Chamberlain,* vol. 1, *Pioneering and Reform, 1869–1929* (Cambridge: Cambridge University Press, 1984). A shorter, balanced view of Chamberlain's character is in Robert Rhodes James, *Anthony Eden* (London: Weidenfeld & Nicolson, 1986), 172–173.

62. Colville, *Fringes of Power,* 35–36.

63. Dilks, *Neville Chamberlain,* 329, 386.

64. Feiling, *Life of Neville Chamberlain,* 402; and James, *Anthony Eden,* 163.

65. As cited in Feiling, *Life of Neville Chamberlain,* 415.

66. As cited in ibid., 417.

67. Michael Glover, *The Fight for the Channel Ports: Calais to Brest, 1940* (Boulder, CO: Westview Press, 1985), 14.

68. Ivan Maisky, *Memoirs of a Soviet Ambassador: The War, 1939–1943,* trans. Andrew Rothstein (New York: Scribner's, 1967), 100.

69. Bryant, *Turn of the Tide,* and *Triumph in the West;* and Brian Bond, ed., *Chief of Staff: The Diaries of Lieutenant General Sir Henry Pownall* (London: Leo Cooper, 1975), II, 171.

70. Cunningham Correspondance, Add MS 52577, 8 August 1944, BML.

71. Haffner, *Meaning of Hitler,* 50–51; and Koch, ed., *Aspects of the Third Reich,* 190–191.

72. See, among others, KTB/OKW, II, 1503; Schramm, *Hitler: The Man,* 183; Klaus Reinhardt, *Die Wende vor Moskau: Das Scheitern der Strategie Hitlers im Winter 1941/42* (Stuttgart: Deutsche Verlags-Anstalt, 1972); and Klaus Reinhardt, "Das Schietern des deutschen Blitzkriegs Konzeptes vor Moskau," in Jürgen Rohwer and Eberhard Jäckel, hrsg., *Kriegswende: Dezember 1941* (Koblenz: Bernard & Graefe, 1984), 199–209.

73. Maser, *Hitler,* 271–277; and Fest, *Hitler,* 726–727.

74. Haffner, *Meaning of Hitler,* 151.

75. Domarus, hrsg., *Hitler: Reden,* II, 1579, 1606.

76. Ibid., 1697–1704.

77. Ibid., 1772, 1827; Helmut Heiber, *Hitlers Lagebesprechungen: Die Protkoll-fragmente seiner militärischen Konferenzen, 1942–1945* (Stuttgart: Deutsche Verlags-Anstalt, 1962), 368; and François Genoud, ed., *The Testament of Adolf Hitler: The Hitler-Bormann Documents, February–April 1945*, trans. R. H. Stevens (London: Cassell, 1961), 32–34.

78. Wheeler-Bennett, ed., *Action This Day*, (Colville) 85; and James, ed., *Winston S. Churchill*, VI, 6330–6331, 6681, and VIII, 6697.

79. Ibid., VI, 6631.

80. John Hiden and John Farquharson, *Explaining Hitler's Germany: Historians and the Third Reich* (London: Batsford, 1983), 14.

81. DO (42)6, 22.1.42, CAB 69/4, PRO.

82. As cited in Harris, *Attlee*, 569.

TWO. RUNNING THE WAR: THE ORGANIZATION

1. Lewin, *Churchill as Warlord*, 183.

2. Bryant, *Triumph in the West*, 35.

3. Warlimont, *Inside Hitler's Headquarters*, 541; and Kurt Zeitzler, "Stellung-nahme zu der Ausarbeitung 'Die oberste Führung des deutschen Heeres (O.K.H.)' im Rahman der Wehrmachtführung," *Foreign Military Studies*, MS# P-041ii, 14, NA.

4. August Winter et al., "Das Oberkommando der Wehrmacht," FMS, MS# T-101, Anlagenband II.-Nr. 2, s. 4–6, NA.

5. KTB/OKW, I, 198E.

6. Zietzler zu Heinrici, 23.2.54, Nachlass 63/15, Bundesarchiv-Militärarchiv; and Warlimont, *Inside Hitler's Headquarters*, 264.

7. Franz Halder and Burkhart Muller-Hillebrand, "Die oberste Führung des deutschen Heeres(OKH) im Rahman der Wehrmachtführung," FMS, MS# P-041a, 7, NA. This Foreign Military Study is part of OKH Project #7 conducted after the war. The group of 33 essays by German military leaders and staff officers is the most extensive study of Army High Command. It is available in English translation from the National Archives on microfilm under T517/1-4 and also from University Publications of America, *The German High Command, 1938–1945*. A synopsis is also available from the National Archives under FMS, T111, "The German High Command—OKH—Within the Framework of the Armed Forces," No. 173, Roll 4. Other helpful books on the army are Albert Seaton, *The German Army, 1943–45* (New York: St. Martin's Press, 1982); and Matthew Cooper, *The German Army, 1933–1945: Its Political and Military Failure* (London: MacDonald & Jane's, 1978).

8. Van Creveld, *Fighting Power*, 43.

9. Alfred Zerbel, "Aufbau und Arbeitsweise der obersten Feldkommandostelle des Heeres," FMS, MS# P-041b, 4–17, NA.

10. Ernst Klink, *Das Gesetz des Handelns: Die Operation "Zitadelle" 1943* (Stutt-gart: Deutsche Verlags-Anstalt, 1966), 40; Zerbel, "Aufbau und Arbeitsweise," 4–17; and [OKH], Operationsabteilung Nr. 112872/43 g.Kdos., "Stellung des Chef des Generalstabes des Heeres der Spitzengliederung der Wehrmacht und Gliederung des Generalstabes des Heeres," National Archives Microcopy Nr. T78, roll 534, frames 821–822.

11. The branches affected were intelligence, central, Luftwaffe General, and dep-uty for operations.

12. Zeitzler, "Stellungnahame," 68–69.

13. Ibid., 17. An excellent account of Schmundt's activities is Dermot Brad-ley and Richard Schulze-Kossens, hrsg., *Tätigkeitsbericht des Chefs des Heeres-personalamtes General der Infanterie Rudolf Schmundt fortgeführt von General*

der Infanterie Wilhelm Burgdorf, 1.10.1942–29.10.1944 (Osnabrück: Biblio-Verlag, 1984).

14. Heinz Guderian, "Spitzenvertretung des Panzertruppe in der Obersten Führung des Heeres 1938–1945," FMS, MS# P-041p, 22–24, NA.

15. OKW, [Spitzengliederung 1944], T-78/520/497, NA.

16. Zeitzler zu Heinrici, N63/15, BA-MA; Heidemarie Grafin Schall-Riaucour, *Aufstand und Gehorsam; Offiziertum und Generalstab im Umbruch: Leben und Wirken von Generaloberst Franz Halder, Generalstabschef, 1938–1942* (Wiesbaden: Limes Verlag, 1972), 104; Fritz Freiherr von Siegler, hrsg., *Die höheren Dienststellen der deutschen Wehrmacht, 1933–1945* (München: Institut für Zeitgeschichte, 1953); and Warlimont, *Inside Hitler's Headquarters*.

17. Heinz von Gyldenfeldt, "Die Feldkommandobehorde," FMS, MS# P-041c, 47, NA.

18. As quoted in Pierre Galante, *Operation Valkyrie: The German Generals' Plot against Hitler,* trans. Mark Howson and Gary Ryan (New York: Harper, 1981), 199.

19. Winter et al., "Das Oberkommando der Wehrmacht," (Warlimont) FMS T101, 80, NA.

20. KTB/OKW, I, 184E.

21. Warlimont, *Inside Hitler's Headquarters,* 52, 196–198. The previously cited FMS, T101, is the most thorough study of Armed Forces High Command. Its overall title is "The German Armed Forces High Command: A Critical Study of Developments, Organization, Missions and Functioning from 1938 to 1945," and it is available on microfilm from the National Archives, No. 173, roll 3, and also from Charles B. Burdick and Donald Detwiler, eds., *World War II German Military Studies,* vols. 4–5 (New York: Garland, 1979).

22. OKH, [Spitzengliederung 1942, Herbst], T-78/521/503, NA; OKW, "Kriegsspitzenliederung des Oberkommandos der Wehrmacht, Heft 1," 1.3.1939, T-77/777/5502815-5502842, NA; Zerbel, "Aufbau und Arbeitsweise," 11–14; Burkhart Müller-Hillebrand, "Die organisatorischen Aufgaben der obersten Heeresführung vom 1938 bis 1945 und ihre Lösung," FMS, MS# P-041f, 43–44, NA; Zeitzler, "Stellungnahme," 98–103; KTB/OKW, I, 170E; and Ernst Klink, "The Organization of the German Military High Command in World War II," *International Review of Military History,* 47 (1980): 179.

23. Warlimont, *Inside Hitler's Headquarters,* 8–9; Klink, "The Organization of the German Military High Command," 136; Gyldenfeldt, "Feldkommandobehorde," 26–27; Wilhelm Keitel, "Einzelheiten zur Führung des Heeres durch Hitler als Ob. des Heeres seit 19.12.4941 bis Winter 1942–43," N54/7, BA-MA; and Zeitzler, "Stellungnahme," 81–82.

24. Zeitzler to Heinrici, N/63/15, BA-MA.

25. Heinz Guderian, *Panzer Leader,* trans. Constantine Fitzgibbon (New York: Dutton, 1952), 326–327.

26. The best study is Michael Salewski, *Die deutsche Seekriegsleitung, 1935–1945,* 3 vols. (Frankfurt a.M.: Bernard & Graefe, 1975). Dated but still useful is Anthony Martienssen, *Hitler and His Admirals* (New York: E. P. Dutton, 1949). A popular account is Cajus Bekker [pseud.], *Hitler's Naval War,* trans. Frank Ziegler (Garden City, N.Y.: Doubleday, 1974).

27. Boog, *Die deutsche Luftwaffenführung,* 344; KTB/OKW, I, 171E; Roland E. Krause, "The German Navy under Joint Command in World War II," *US Naval Institute Proceedings,* 73 (Sep 1947): 1033–1034; and Keith W. Bird, *German Naval History: A Guide to the Literature* (New York: Garland, 1985), 708.

28. Overy, *Air War,* 130.

29. Boog, *Die deutsche Luftwaffenführung,* is outstanding. Boog has summarized

his findings in "Higher Command Leadership in the German Luftwaffe, 1935–1945," *Proceedings of the Eighth Military History Symposium, US Air Force Academy* (Oct 1978): 128–158; and in "The Organization of the German Air Force High Command, 1935–1945," *International Review of Military History* 47 (1980): 95–106. Other accounts include Overy, *Air War;* idem, *Goering: The 'Iron Man'* (London: Routledge & Kegan Paul, 1984); Matthew Cooper, *The German Air Force, 1933–1945: An Anatomy of Failure* (London: Jane's, 1981); and Williamson Murray, *Luftwaffe* (Annapolis: Nautical & Aviation Co., 1985). Less satisfactory is Cajus Bekker [pseud.], *The Luftwaffe War Diaries,* trans. Frank Ziegler (Garden City, N.Y.: Doubleday, 1968).

30. Halder and Müller-Hillebrand, "Die oberste Führung," 12–13; Speer, *Inside the Third Reich;* and Willi A. Boelcke, hrsg., *Deutschlands Rüstung im Zweiten Weltkrieg: Hitlers Konferenzen mit Albert Speer, 1942–1945* (Frankfurt a.M.: Akademische Verlagsgesellschaft, 1960). See also Franz W. Seidler, *Fritz Todt: Baumeister des Dritten Reiches* (München: Herbig, 1986); and Gregor Janssen, "Todt et Speer," *Revue d'histoire de la deuxième guerre mondiale,* 21 (Oct 1971): 37–53.

31. Boelcke, hrsg., *Deutschlands Rüstung,* 6; and Karl-Heinz Ludwig, *Technik und Ingenieure im Dritten Reich* (Düsseldorf: Droste, 1974), 402–403.

32. Speer, *Inside the Third Reich,* 312. A more negative view of Speer is Matthias Schmidt, *Albert Speer: The End of a Myth,* trans. Joachim Neugroschel (New York: St. Martin's, 1984).

33. Hans Buchheim, "Command and Compliance," in Helmut Krausnick et al., *Anatomy of the SS State,* trans. Richard Barry, Marian Jackson, and Dorothy Long (New York: Walker, 1968), 270–274; George H. Stein, *The Waffen-SS: Hitler's Elite Guard at War, 1939–1945* (Ithaca, NY: Cornell University Press, 1966); and Bernd Wegner, "My Honor Is Loyalty: The SS as a Military Factor in Hitler's Germany," in Deist, ed., *The German Military,* 220–239.

34. Bernd Wegner, *Hitlers politische Soldaten: Die Waffen-SS, 1933–1945* (Paderborn: Ferdinand Schöningh, 1982), 329.

35. The other offices included the Army Administrative Office, the Prisoner of War Service, and the Army Personnel Reinforcement Service (Krausnick et al., *Anatomy of the SS State,* [Buchheim] 273–274).

36. KTB/OKW, I, 154E; Klaus-Jürgen Müller, "The Army in the Third Reich: An Historical Interpretation," *Journal of Strategic Studies,* 2 (Sep 1979): 123–152; Matthew Cooper, *The German Army;* and Van Creveld, *Fighting Power,* 146.

37. KTB/OKW, I, 170E; Halder and Müller-Hillebrand, "Die oberste Führung," 3; and Van Creveld, *Fighting Power,* 36, 137.

38. WM 8(39) 51, 8.9.1939, CAB 65/1, British Public Record Office; Lewin, *Churchill as Warlord,* 32–34; MC(40)69, "Revised Composition," 5 April 1940, CAB 83/5, PRO; J. R. M. Butler, *Grand Strategy,* vol. 2, *September 1939–June 1941* (London: HMSO, 1957), 507; and John Colville, *Man of Valour: Field Marshal Lord Gort* (London: Collins, 1972), 173. An excellent book on the army is David Fraser, *And We Shall Shock Them: The British Army in the Second World War* (North Pomfret, VT: Hodder & Stoughton, 1985).

39. Hastings Ismay, *The Memoirs of Lord Ismay* (London: Heinemann, 1960), 109.

40. Roderick Macleod and Denis Kelly, eds., *Time Unguarded: The Ironside Diaries, 1937–1940* (London: Constable, 1962), 144–145.

41. Among the many studies, see Ismay, *Memoirs,* 160–162; Butler, *Grand Strategy,* II; and *Central Organization for Defence* (London: HMSO, 1946).

42. As quoted in Gilbert, VI, *Finest Hour,* 324.

43. Lewin, *Churchill as Warlord,* 32–34; Wheeler-Bennett, ed., *Action This Day,* (Jacob) 163; Fraser, *Alanbrooke,* 210–211; and Ismay, *Memoirs,* 109.

44. Winston S. Churchill, *Their Finest Hour* (Boston: Houghton Mifflin, 1949),

16–17; Gilbert, VI, *Finest Hour*, 324; John Ehrman, *Grand Strategy*, vol. 5, *August 1943–September 1944* (London: HMSO, 1956), 17–18; idem, *Grand Strategy*, vol. 6, *October 1944–August 1945* (London: HMSO, 1956), 316–320; and S. S. Wilson, *The Cabinet Office to 1945* (Public Record Office Handbooks: No. 17) (London: HMSO, 1975), Annex 7b. For Churchill's view of the importance of a war cabinet, see his *The Gathering Storm* (Boston: Houghton Mifflin, 1948), 402.

45. The seventeen subcommittees were Bolero accommodation (for the buildup of US forces in Britain), bacteriological warfare, chemical warfare, defense of aerodromes, active air defense, invasion (of Britain), Victor (Home Forces invasion exercise), defense of bases (ports), defense arrangements for the Indian Ocean, floating airfields, airfields (for Overlord), movement and transportation (for the invasion of Northwest Africa), research and development priorities, night air defense, post-hostilities planning, smoke (warfare), and technical warfare. See Wilson, *Cabinet Office;* and Sir Ronald Weeks, *Organisation and Equipment for War* (New York: Cambridge University Press, 1950), 5–18.

46. Gilbert, VI, *Finest Hour*, 322; J. M. A. Gwyer and J. R. M. Butler, *Grand Strategy*, vol. 3, *June 1941–August 1942* (London: HMSO, 1964), 427–428; Wilson, *Cabinet Office*, Annex 7b; Fraser, *Alanbrooke*, 207–209; and John M. Lee, *The Churchill Coalition, 1940–1945* (Hamden, CT: Archon, 1980), 22. For an overview of Churchill's "early" years, see Alex Danchev, "The Central Direction of the War, 1940–41," in John Sweetman, ed., *Sword and Mace: 20th Century History of Civil and Military Relations in Britain* (London: Brassey's, 1986), 57–78.

47. Gwyer and Butler, *Grand Strategy*, III, 427–428; and Bryant, *Triumph in the West*, 358–359.

48. Bryant's introduction in Fraser, *Alanbrooke*, 21.

49. Wheeler-Bennett, ed., *Action This Day* (Jacob), 195–196; Arthur Marder, *Winston Is Back: Churchill at the Admiralty* (London: Longman, 1972), 5; and Morgan Papers, "Lord Alanbrooke," WDM 1/3, IWM.

50. Kennedy, *Business of War*, 146.

51. Denis Richards, *Portal of Hungerford: The Life of Marshal of the Royal Air Force Viscount Portal of Hungerford* (New York: Holmes & Meier, 1977), 200–203; and Fraser, *Alanbrooke*, 107, 530.

52. MR(39) 1, "Anglo-French Liaison," 19 September 1939, CAB 85/2, PRO; Butler, *Grand Strategy*, II, 9–10; JP(40) 14th Meeting, 6 March 1940, CAB 84/2, PRO; Colville, *Man of Valour*, 133; and Eleanor M. Gates, *End of the Affair: The Collapse of the Anglo-French Alliance, 1939–1940* (Berkeley: University of California Press, 1981), 59–60.

53. Gwyer and Butler, *Grand Strategy*, III, 383–387; Warren F. Kimball, ed., *Churchill and Roosevelt: The Complete Correspondence* (Princeton: Princeton University Press, 1984), I, 292; Francis L. Loewenheim et al., eds., *Roosevelt and Churchill: Their Secret Wartime Correspondence* (New York: Saturday Review Press, 1975), 189; Maurice Matloff, *Strategic Planning for Coalition Warfare, 1943–1944* (Washington: USGPO, 1959), 6; Richard M. Leighton and Robert W. Coakley, *Global Logistics and Strategy, 1940–1943* (Washington, USGPO, 1955), 213, 255–257; COS(41), 429th Meeting, 20.12.41, CAB 79/16, PRO; WP(41) 303, 19 December 1941, CAB 66/20, PRO; and Lyle F. Ellis, *Victory in the West*, vol. 1, *The Battle of Normandy* (London: HMSO, 1962), 4.

54. COS(43) 791(o) (Part I) 31 December 1943, CAB 99/25, PRO; Christopher Thorne, *Allies of a Kind*, 721; Ehrman, *Grand Strategy*, V, 205; and Leighton and Coakley, *Global Logistics*, 255–257. For a more positive appraisal, see Alex Danchev, *Very Special Relationship: Field Marshal Sir John Dill and the Anglo-American Alliance, 1941–1944* (London: Brassey's, 1986).

THREE. RUNNING THE WAR: THE PERSONALITIES

1. Halder and Müller-Hillebrand, "Die oberste Führung," 13.
2. Gilbert, VI, *Finest Hour,* 325.
3. Fraser, *Alanbrooke,* 206; and Ronald Lewin, *The Chief: Field Marshal Lord Wavell, Commander-in-Chief and Viceroy, 1939–1947* (New York: Farrar, Strauss, Giroux, 1980), 43–44.
4. Brian Bond, *British Military Policy between the Two World Wars* (New York: Oxford University Press, 1980), 333–334; Colville, *Man of Valour,* 143; and Macleod and Kelly, eds., *The Ironside Diary,* 387. The date in the Ironside diary is July 19, 1940.
5. Kennedy, *Business of War,* 161; Colville, *Man of Valour,* 144–145; Thompson, *Churchill and Morton,* 58; and Gilbert, VI, *Finest Hour,* 1234. More sympathetic to Dill is Alex Danchev, "'Dilly-Dally,' or Having the Last Word: Field Marshal Sir John Dill and Prime Minister Winston Churchill," *Journal of Contemporary History,* 22 (Jan 1987): 21–44.
6. As quoted in Kennedy, *Business of War,* 284. Dill's "Washington" career is dealt with in Danchev, *Very Special Relationship.*
7. Bryant, *Turn of the Tide,* 6–7, 26; and Fraser, *Alanbrooke.* The Alanbrooke papers are located at the Liddell Hart Centre.
8. Kennedy, *Business of War,* 181.
9. Fraser, *Alanbrooke,* 204–206.
10. The outstanding biography is Fraser, *Alanbrooke.* Other insights can be gained from Richards, *Portal,* 202–207; Michael Carver, ed., *The War Lords: Military Commanders in the Twentieth Century* (London: Weidenfeld & Nicolson, 1976), (Cook) 519–520; Bryant, *Turn of the Tide,* 6, 26; Lord Cunningham of Hyndhope, *A Sailor's Odyssey* (London: Hutchinson, 1951), 661; and Morgan Papers, "Lord Alanbrooke," WDM 1/3, IWM.
11. Basil H. Liddell Hart, "Western War Strategy: A Critical Analysis of the Alanbrooke Diaries," *Journal of the Royal United Services Institution,* 105 (Feb 1960): 53.
12. As quoted in Fraser, *Alanbrooke,* 202.
13. Ibid., 538.
14. The best treatment is in Stephen Roskill, *Churchill and the Admirals* (London: Collins, 1977). See also Stephen Roskill, *The War at Sea, 1939–1945,* vol. 2, *The Period of Balance* (London: HMSO, 1960), 15–17; and Cunningham Correspondence, Pound to Cunningham, 24 July 1939, Add MS 52560, BML. The few papers associated with Pound are deposited at Churchill College, Cambridge.
15. Roskill, *Churchill and the Admirals;* Kennedy, *Business of War,* 161, 309; Cunningham, *A Sailor's Odyssey,* 583–584; Bryant, *Turn of the Tide,* 246–247; Ismay, *Memoirs,* 316–317; Richards, *Portal,* 199; Cunningham Correspondence, 24 July 1939, Add MS 52560, BML; and Colville, *Fringes of Power,* 176.
16. As quoted in John Connell [pseud.], *Auchinleck* (London: Cassell, 1959), 267.
17. Roskill, *Churchill and the Admirals;* Richards, *Portal,* 211–212; Carver, ed., *War Lords,* (Kemp) 464; Cunningham, *A Sailor's Odyssey,* 474; Fraser, *Alanbrooke,* 30; and H. Kent Hewitt, Oral History, Naval History Division Reel 24/17–19. Cunningham's correspondence at the British Museum Library is also valuable.
18. Cunningham Correspondence, Noble to Cunningham, 1 October 1943, ADD MS 52571, BML.
19. Cunningham Correspondence, 8 August 1944, ADD MS 52777, BML.
20. Richards, *Portal,* 167–169; and John Terraine, *A Time for Courage: The Royal*

Air Force in World War II (New York: Macmillan, 1985), 251–252. The Portal Papers, which concentrate on the war years, are at Christ Church, Oxford.

21. Fraser, *Alanbrooke*, 30. See also Richards, *Portal;* Allen Andrews, *The Air Marshals: The Air War in Western Europe* (New York: Morrow, 1970); Anthony Verrier, *The Bomber Offensive* (New York: Macmillan, 1969), 96; Roskill, *Churchill and the Admirals*, 136; Leasor, *War at the Top*, 12; Terraine, *A Time for Courage*, 253–256; and Cunningham, *A Sailor's Odyssey*, 657.

22. Richards, *Portal;* and Terraine, *A Time for Courage*, 684.

23. Richards, *Portal*, 187.

24. Wheeler-Bennett, ed., *Action This Day*, (Jacob) 196–197, and (Martin) 157; Kennedy, *Business of War*, 239; and Gilbert, VI, *Finest Hour*, 1053.

25. Leasor, *War at the Top*, 11.

26. Müller, "Army in the Third Reich," 138.

27. Records of the Department of State Special Interrogation Mission to Germany, 1945–46, Record Group 59, National Archives Microcopy M-679, roll 1, frame 207; Seaton, *German Army*, 83, 104; and Klaus-Jürgen Müller, *Das Heer und Hitler: Armee und nationalsozialistisches Regime, 1933–1940* (Stuttgart: Deutsche Verlags-Anstalt, 1969), 268.

28. von Gyldenfeldt, "Feldkommandobehorde," 41–43; Schall-Riaucour, *Aufstand und Gehorsam*, 122–124; Seaton, *German Army*, 162–163; and Engel, *Heeresadjutant*, 116–117.

29. Schall-Riaucour, *Aufstand und Gehorsam*. See also Halder KTB, I, xvii–xviii; Cooper, *German Army*, 99–100; Galante, *Operation Valkyrie;* Harold Deutsch, *Hitler and His Generals* (Minneapolis: University of Minnesota Press, 1974), 32; and Koch, ed., *Aspects of the Third Reich*, (Koch) 288–289. Halder's papers are located at the Bundesarchiv-Militärarchiv but are subject to restrictions.

30. Müller, "Army in the Third Reich," 142.

31. Zeitzler, "Stellungnahme," 68–69; Cooper, *German Army*, 445–446; Carr, *Hitler*, 84; and Seaton, *German Army*, 193–194, 231. Zeitzler's papers at the Bundesarchiv-Militärarchiv are also valuable.

32. As quoted in Cooper, *German Army*, 355–356.

33. "The German Army High Command," (Guderian) FMS, MS# T-111, 109; Guderian, *Panzer Leader*, 332, 356–357; Cooper, *German Army*, 534; Carver, ed., *War Lords*, (Strawson) 310; and Seaton, *German Army*, 235. A popular account is Kenneth Macksey, *Guderian—Panzer General* (London: Macdonald & Jane's, 1975).

34. Waldemar Erfurth, *Die Geschichte des deutschen Generalstabes von 1918–1945* (Göttingen: Musterschmidt, 1957), 321.

35. Warlimont, *Inside Hitler's Headquarters;* Guderian, *Panzer Leader*, 464; John W. Wheeler-Bennett, *The Nemesis of Power* (New York: Macmillan, 1961), 429; Eugene Davidson, *The Trial of the Germans* (New York: Collier, 1966), 330–341; and Helmut J. Schmeller, *Hitler and Keitel: An Investigation of the Influence of Party Ideology on the Command of the Armed Forces in Germany between 1938–1945* (Fort Hays, KS: Fort Hays State College Press, 1970). For a more sympathetic picture, see his memoirs, Walter Görlitz, hrsg., *Generalfeldmarschall Keitel: Verbrecher oder Offizier? Erinnerungen, Briefe, Dokumente des Chefs OKW* (Göttingen: Musterschmidt, 1961). His papers are available at the Bundesarchiv-Militärarchiv.

36. State Department Interrogation, RG 59, M-679/1, NA; Davidson, *Trial of the Germans*, 342–343; Guderian, *Panzer Leader*, 464–465; and Warlimont, *Inside Hitler's Headquarters*, 45–47. Jodl's papers at the Bundesarchiv-Militärarchiv include some important speeches as well as correspondence and a war diary.

37. Salewski, *Die deutsche Seekriegsleitung*, I and II; Erich Raeder, *My Life*, trans. Henry W. Drexel (Annapolis: US Naval Institute, 1960); Jost Dülffer, "Determinants of German Naval Policy, 1920–1939," in Deist, ed, *The German Military*, 155;

and Davidson, *Trial of the Germans,* 368–371. Raeder's papers are available at the Bundesarchiv-Militärarchiv.

38. Michael Salewski, "Von Raeder zu Dönitz: Der Wechsel im Oberbefehl der Kriegsmarine 1943," *Militärgeschichtliche Mitteilungen* 7 (1973).

39. Salewski, *Die deutsche Seekriegsleitung,* II; Peter Padfield, *Dönitz: The Last Führer: Portrait of a Nazi War Leader* (London: Victor Gollancz, 1984); Carver, ed., *War Lords,* (Kemp) 474–483; and Karl Dönitz, *Memoirs: Ten Years and Twenty Days,* trans. R. H. Stevens (Cleveland: World, 1959). Dönitz's papers are available at the Bundesarchiv-Militärarchiv.

40. As quoted in Padfield, *Dönitz,* 316.

41. Salewski, *Die deutsche Seekriegsleitung,* II, 594.

42. Albert Speer, *Spandau: The Secret Diaries* (London: Collins, 1976).

43. The best study is Overy, *Goering.* Other helpful characterizations are in Alfred Price, *Luftwaffe Handbook, 1939–1945* (New York: Scribner's, 1977), 91; Homze, *Arming the Luftwaffe,* 238–239; Cooper, *German Air Force,* 9–10; Speer, *Inside the Third Reich,* 276; and Asher Lee, *Goering—Air Leader* (London: Duckworth, 1972). A broader treatment is Roger Manvell and Heinrich Fraenkel, *Herman Goering* (London: Heinemann, 1962).

44. Homze, *Arming the Luftwaffe,* 236–240; Boog, *Die deutsche Luftwaffenführung;* Boog, "Higher Command Leadership," 137–139; Cooper, *German Air Force;* Murray, *Luftwaffe,* 198; and Karl Koller, *Die letzte Monat: Die Tagebuchaufzeichnungen des ehemaligen Chefs des Generalstabes der deutschen Luftwaffe von 14 April bis 27 Mai 1945* (Mannheim: Norbert Wohlgemuth, 1949), 106–107. See also David Irving, *The Rise and Fall of the Luftwaffe: The Life of Field Marshal Erhard Milch* (Boston: Little, Brown, 1974), which is one of his best, though still flawed, works. For a rejoinder, see Theo Osterkamp, *Tragodie der Luftwaffe? Kritische Begnungs mit dem gleichmassigen Werk von Irving/Milch* (Neckargemünd: Vowinckel, 1971).

45. Fraser, *Alanbrooke,* 209–210.

FOUR. PLANNING THE WAR: THE EARLY YEARS

1. Bernard Brodie, *War and Politics* (New York: Macmillan, 1973), 1–2; D. Clayton James, "American and Japanese Strategies in the Pacific War," in Paret, ed., *Makers of Modern Strategy,* 703; John M. Collins, *Grand Strategy: Principles and Practices* (Annapolis: U.S. Naval Institute, 1973), 14; and William Strang, "War and Foreign Policy: 1939–45," in David Dilks, ed., *Retreat from Power: Studies in Britain's Foreign Policy of the Twentieth Century,* vol. 2, *After 1939* (London: Macmillan, 1981).

2. Ibid., 97.

3. Paret, ed., *Makers of Modern Strategy,* (Geyer) 573–574, 596. See also Deist, et al., *Das Deutsche Reich,* 1, 711–716.

4. Michael Howard, *The Mediterranean Strategy in the Second World War* (New York: Praeger, 1968), 22–23; J. M. A. Gwyer and J. R. M. Butler, *Grand Strategy,* vol. 3, *June 1941–August 1942* (London: HMSO, 1964), 350–351; and Brian Bond, "Dunkirk: Myths and Lessons," *RUSI Journal,* 127 (Sep 1982), 7.

5. Jost Dülffer, *Weimar, Hitler and die Marine: Reichspolitik und Flottenbau, 1920–1939* (Düsseldorf: Droste, 1972), 557–562; Bird, *German Naval History,* 556–557, 615; Overy, "Hitler's War," 273; and Overy, *Air War,* 20–23. See also Deist et al., *Das Deutsche Reich,* 1.

6. Maier et al., *Das Deutsche Reich,* 2, 79; and Gerhard L. Weinberg, *The Foreign Policy of Hitler's Germany: Starting World War II, 1937–1939* (Chicago: University of Chicago Press, 1980), 560–580.

7. Larry H. Addington, *The Blitzkrieg Era and the German Staff, 1865–1941* (New Brunswick: Rutgers, 1971); Trevor N. Dupuy, *A Genius for War: The German Army and General Staff* (London: Macdonald & Jane's, 1977), 257; Paret, ed., *Makers of Modern Strategy*, (Geyer) 584; and Matthew Cooper, *The German Army*, vii.

8. Hillgruber, *Zweite Weltkrieg*, 15.

9. Sir R. Lindsay (Washington) [to Foreign Office], Telegram, 1 July 1939, ADM 205/1, PRO.

10. Butler, *Grand Strategy*, II, 71, 551; and Hillgruber, *Zweite Weltkrieg*, 21.

11. Paret, ed., *Makers of Modern Strategy*, (Geyer) 575–576; WP(39)19, "Air Policy," 11.9.39, CAB 66/1, PRO; and Murray, *Change*, 340–352.

12. Hinsley et al., *British Intelligence*, I, 227–231.

13. Salewski, *Die deutsche Seekriegsleitung*, I, 175–212; Warlimont, *Inside Hitler's Headquarters*, 66–89; Paret, ed., *Makers of Modern Strategy*, (Geyer) 587; Bird, *German Naval History*, 683; and Carl-Axel Gemzell, *Raeder, Hitler und Skandinavien: Der Kampf für einen Maritimen Operationsplan* (Lund: C. W. K. Gleerups, 1965).

14. "Berichte des ehemaligen Stellvertretenden Chefs des Wehrmachtfuhrüngsstabes General der Artillerie Warlimont," OQu Nr. 172/39 g.K.Chefs., "Weisung Nr. 6 für die Kriegsführung," 9.10.1939, T-77/1423/942–943, NA; [OKW], "Notizen zum Kreigstagebuch," 7.4.1941, T-77/869/5616131–5616134, NA; von Below, *Als Hitlers Adjutant*, 217; Hillgruber, *Zweite Weltkrieg*, 38; and Bernard R. Kroener, "Squaring the Circle: Blitzkrieg Strategy and Manpower Shortage, 1939–1942," in Deist, ed., *German Military*, 288–290.

15. COS(40), 217, "Possible German Actions in the Spring of 1940," 24.1.40, CAB 80/7, PRO.

16. Butler, *Grand Strategy*, II, 157; and Brian Bond, *France and Belgium, 1939–1940* (London: Davis-Poynter, 1975), 90.

17. WM 87(40), 10.4.40, CAB 65/6, PRO.

18. WM 7(39), 7.9.39, CAB 65/1, PRO; and Hinsley et al., *British Intelligence*, I, 227–228.

19. WM 76(40), 27.3.40, CAB 65/6, PRO.

20. WP(39) 179, 31.12.39, CAB 66/4, PRO.

21. David Dilks, "Great Britain and Scandinavia in the 'Phoney War,'" *Scandinavian Journal of History*, 2 (1977), 50. See also Richard Petrow, *The Bitter Years: The Invasion and Occupation of Denmark and Norway, April 1940–May 1945* (New York: Morrow, 1974); and, from a Norwegian perspective, Johannes Andenaes, Olav Riste, and Maque Skodvin, *Norway and the Second World War* (Oslo: Tanum, 1966).

22. Butler, *Grand Strategy*, II, 69.

23. JP(40)61, "Review of the Present Strategical Situation," 19 March 1940, CAB 84/11, PRO.

24. WP(40)145, "Review of the Strategical Situation on the Assumption that Germany Has Decided to Seek a Decision in 1940," 4.5.40, CAB 66/7, PRO. See also Butler, *Grand Strategy*, II, 172–173.

25. WM 109(40), 1.5.40, CAB 65/7, PRO; and WM 114(40), telegram, 7.5.40, CAB 65/7, PRO.

26. Gates, *End of the Affair*, 377; and Bond, *France and Belgium*, 133.

27. Sir Edward L. Spears, *Assignment to Catastrophe*, vol. 2, *The Fall of France, June 1940* (London: Heinemann, 1955), 298.

28. Deist, ed., *German Military*, (Kroener) 291; Paret, ed., *Makers of Modern Strategy*, (Geyer) 584; Murray, *Strategy for Defeat*, 69; and Overy, "Hitler's War," 283, 290.

29. Wolfgang Michalka, *Ribbentrop und die deutsche Weltpolitik, 1933–1940: Aussenpolitische Konzeptionen und Entscheidungsprozesse im Dritten Reich* (München: W. Fink, 1980), 256–260, 305; Hillgruber, *Zweite Weltkrieg*, 38; Maier et al., *Das*

Deutsche Reich, 2, 419; and Gerhard Schreiber, "The Mediterannean in Hitler's Strategy in 1940," in Deist, ed., *German Military*, 242–254.

30. MacGregor Knox, *Mussolini Unleashed, 1939–1941* (New York: Cambridge University Press, 1982), 117–119.

31. David Reynolds, "Churchill and the British 'Decision' to Fight on in 1940," in Richard Langhorne, ed., *Diplomacy and Intelligence during the Second World War: Essays in Honour of F. H. Hinsley* (Cambridge: Cambridge University Press 1985), 154.

32. JP(40)248, "Urgent Measures to Meet Attack," 15 June 1940, CAB 84/15, PRO.

33. Ironside Diaries, 346–347. The entry is May 30, 1940.

34. JP(39)16, "The Possible Future Course of the War: Appreciation," 16 September 1939, CAB 84/7, PRO.

35. Pound to Cunningham, 20 May 1940, Cunningham Correspondence, ADD MS. 52560, BML; COS(40)397, "British Strategy in the Near Future," 26.5.40, CAB 80/11, PRO; and WP(40)178, "Invasion of the United Kingdom," 29.5.40, CAB 66/8, PRO.

36. Hillgruber, *Hitlers Strategie*, 144–156; and Ronald Wheatley, *Operation Sea Lion: German Plans for the Invasion of England, 1939–1942* (Oxford: Clarendon, 1958).

37. Der Oberbefehlshaber der Luftwaffe, Führungsstab Ia Nr. 5835/40 g.k.(op.), "Allgemeine Weisung für der Kampf der Luftwaffe gegen England," 30.6.40, RL 2 II/27, BA-MA.

38. Derek Wood and Derek Dempster, *The Narrow Margin* (London: Hutchinson, 1961); COS(40) 300th Meeting, 7.9.40, CAB 79/6, PRO; Lewin, *Churchill as Warlord*, 52; and Terraine, *A Time for Courage*, 255.

39. See, for instance, Barry Leach, *German Strategy against Russia, 1939–1941* (New York: Oxford University Press, 1973), 9.

40. Hillgruber, *Hitlers Strategie*, 171, and Wheatley, *Operation Sealion*, 133–134. See also Hillgruber, "England's Place in Hitler's Plan for World Domination," *Journal of Contemporary History*, 9 (Jan 1974): 5–22.

41. Halder, *Kriegstagebuch*, I, 373–375, and II, 51. The entries are for 26.6.40, 30.6.40, and 1.8.40.

42. Ibid., II, 30, 45, 51. The entries are for 22.7.40, 30.7.40, and 1.8.40.

43. Gerhard Schreiber, "Zur Kontinuität des Gross- und Weltmachtstrebens der deutschen Marineführung," *Militärgeschichtliche Mitteilungen*, 26 (1979): 130–131; Hillgruber, "England's Place," 16–18; and Hillgruber, *Hitlers Strategie*, 157.

44. Boog et al., *Das Deutsche Reich*, 4, 15–16.

45. Warlimont, *Inside Hitler's Headquarters*, 134.

46. Hillgruber, *Hitlers Strategie*, 273–277, 323–331; and Deist, ed., *German Military* (Schreiber). See also Charles Burdick, *Germany's Military Strategy and Spain in World War II* (Syracuse: Syracuse University Press, 1968).

47. WP(40) 362, "Future Strategy," 4.9.40, CAB 66/11, PRO; WP(40) 229, "The Strategical Outlook," 28.6.40, CAB 66/9, PRO; Colville, *Fringes of Power*, 233; Gilbert, VI, *Finest Hour*, 845–847; and Gwyer and Butler, *Grand Strategy*, III, 32.

48. WP(40) 322, "Post War Policy," 19.8.40, CAB 66/11, PRO. See also Correlli Barnett, *The Audit of War: The Illusion and Reality of Britain as a Great Nation* (London: Macmillan, 1986).

49. Genoud, ed., *Testament of Adolf Hitler*, 66, 90; Gerd R. Ueberschar und Wolfram Wette, hrsg., *"Unternehmen Barbarossa": Der deutsche Überfall auf die Sowjetunion 1941: Berichte, Analysen, Dokumente* (Paderborn: Ferdinand Schöningh, 1984), 99; and Deist, ed., *German Military*, (Schrieber) 249–251.

50. Michalka, *Ribbentrop und die deutsche Weltpolitik*, 269.

51. *Fuehrer Conferences*, II, 1940, 41.

52. KTB/OKW, I, 203–209.

53. Ibid., 233. The actual directive is in Hubatsch, *Hitlers Weisungen*, 84–88; and the English translation in Trevor-Roper, ed., *Hitler's War Directives*, 93–98.

54. John Erickson, *The Road to Stalingrad: Stalin's War with Germany* (New York: Harper & Row, 1975), 83–84.

55. George E. Blau, *The German Campaigns in the Balkans (Spring 1941)* (Washington: US Department of the Army, 1953), 48; and Deist, ed., *German Military*, (Schreiber) 271.

56. Martin van Creveld, "The German Attack on the USSR: The Destruction of a Legend," *European Studies Review*, 2 (Jan 1972): 69–86. For a more detailed treatment, see idem, *Hitler's Strategy, 1940–1941: The Balkan Clue* (London: Cambridge University Press, 1973).

57. *Die Berichte des Oberkommandos der Wehrmacht, 1939–1945*, (München: Verlag für Wehrwissenschaften, 1983), bd. 2, 155–156.

58. Deist, ed., *German Military* (Schreiber); and Bird, *German Naval History*, 585.

59. Halder, *Kriegstagebuch*, III, 38. The date is 3.7.1941.

60. Abteilung Landesverteidigung Nr. 441187/41 g.K. Chefs. (I op), "Krafteverteilung des Heeres nach Abschluss der Ostoperationen," 11.7.1941, T-78/346/6304079–6304080, NA; and Hillgruber, *Zweite Weltkrieg*, 48–49.

61. Alan F. Wilt, "Hitler's Late Summer Pause in 1941," *Military Affairs*, 45 (Dec 1981): 187–191.

62. DGFP, D, XIII, 423. The date is 27.8.1941.

63. Oberkommando des Heeres, GenStdH/Org. Abt. (I) Nr. 702/41 g.Kdos. Chefs., "Panzer-Nachschub Ost vor Beginn der Operation der H.Gr. Mitte," 15.9.41, T-78/430/64022198–6402205, NA.

64. Reinhardt, *Die Wende vor Moskau*, 180–181.

65. Boog et al., *Das Deutsche Reich*, 4, 1086.

66. Schramm, *Hitler: The Man*, 161. See also Reinhardt, *Die Wende vor Moskau*, 262; and Carr, *Hitler: A Study*, 98.

67. Hillgruber, *Zweite Weltkrieg*, 68.

68. Butler, *Grand Strategy*, II, 380; Gwyer and Butler, *Grand Strategy*, III, 22; and JP(40)815(s), "Review of Strategic Situation," 30 December 1940, CAB 84/25, PRO.

69. Robin Higham, *Diary of a Disaster: British Aid to Greece, 1940–1941* (Lexington: University of Kentucky Press, 1986); and Geoffrey Warner, *Iraq and Syria, 1941* (London: Davis-Poynter, 1974).

70. Colville, *Fringes of Power*, 382. The date was May 2, 1941.

71. Hinsley et al., *British Intelligence*, II, 482; and JP(41)691, "Assistance to Russia," 23 August 1941, CAB 84/34, PRO.

72. JP(41)444, "Future Strategy," 13 June 1941, CAB 84/31, PRO; and JP(41)549, "Future Considerations and Requirements," 17 July 1941, CAB 84/32, PRO.

73. Butler, *Grand Strategy*, II, 506–507.

74. Ibid., 529.

75. DO(41), 64th Meeting, 15.10.41, CAB 69/2, PRO.

76. Gwyer and Butler, *Grand Strategy*, III, 237–244.

77. Ibid., 343, 403.

78. WM(41), 126th Meeting, 10 December 1941, CAB 65/20, PRO; and Churchill, *Grand Alliance*, 658–698.

79. Gwyer and Butler, *Grand Strategy*, III, 357–359; and Dilks, ed., *Retreat from Power* (Strang), 77–78.

80. Washington—Arcadia, December 1941–January 1942, CAB 99/17–18, PRO;

and James MacGregor Burns, *Roosevelt: The Soldier of Freedom* (New York: Harcourt, Brace, Jovanovich, 1970), 176–178.

81. Roskill, *Churchill and the Admirals*, 208.

82. Richard M. Leighton and Robert W. Coakley, *Global Logistics and Strategy, 1940–1943* (Washington: USGPO, 1955), 951.

83. Deist, ed., *German Military*, (Koerner) 298.

84. Overy, *Air War*, 46, 204; and Paret, ed., *Makers of Modern Strategy*, (Geyer) 574–575.

85. Earl Ziemke, "Military Effectiveness in the Second World War," in Allan R. Millett and Williamson Murray, eds., *Military Effectiveness*, 3 vols. (Winchester, MA: Allen & Unwin, 1988), III, 284–285; M. M. Postan, *British War Production* (London: HMSO, 1952), 186; Boog, *Die deutschen Luftwaffenführung*, 90; and United States Strategic Bombing Survey, *The Effects of Strategic Bombing on the German War Economy* (Washington: Overall Economic Effects Division, 1945), 163.

86. Maier et al., *Das Deutsche Reich*, 2, 268; and Overy, *Air War*, 23.

FIVE. PLANNING THE WAR: THE MIDDLE AND LATER PHASES

1. See, among others, Manfred Messerschmidt, "La stratégie allemande, 1939–1945: conception, objectif, commandement, réussite," *Revue d'histoire de la deuxième guerre mondiale*, 25 (Oct 1975) 1, 22.

2. Robert Rhodes James, *Anthony Eden* (London: Weidenfeld & Nicolson, 1986), 262.

3. Hillgruber, *Zweite Weltkrieg*, 89; Johanna Menzel Meskill, *Hitler and Japan: The Hollow Alliance* (New York: Atherton Press, 1966); and Gerhard Weinberg, *World in the Balance: Behind the Scenes of World War II* (Hanover, NH: University Press of New England, 1981), 43–44.

4. Andreas Hillgruber, "Zwei neue Aufzeichnungen über Führer-Besprechungen aus dem Jahre 1942," *Militärgeschichtliche Mitteilungen*, 1 (1972): 119–120; Oberkommando per Panzerarmee Afrika, Abt. Ia Nr. 31/42 g.Kdos.Chefs., 30.4.42, T313/426/8719631, NA; and Barnett, *The Desert Generals*, rev. ed. (Bloomington: Indiana University Press, 1982), 139.

5. KTB/OKW, II, 102–104, 370–373.

6. Carver, ed., *War Lords*, (Douglas-Home) 280–281; Andreas Hillgruber, "La politique et la stratégie de Hitler dans le bassin Méditerranéen," in Comité d'histoire de la deuxième guerre mondiale, *La Guerre en méditerranée, 1939–1945* (Paris: Éditions du Centre Nationale de la Recherche Scientifique, 1972), 157; and Kahn, *Hitler's Spies*, 393.

7. OKH/Op. Abt. IIb Nr. 1550/41 g.K., "Studie Kaukasus," n.d., T78/336/6292480, NA; Organisations-Abteilung (I) Nr. 3493/41 g.Kdos., "Vortragsnotiz," T78/346/6304307–309, NA; and Klaus Reinhardt, *Die Wende vor Moskau*, 292.

8. Halder, *Kriegstagebuch*, III, 332, 401.

9. Hubatsch, hrsg., *Hitlers Weisungen*, 183–191; and Kurt Zeitzler, "Die Operationen der l. Panzerarmee vom 22.6.1941 bis Frühjahr 1943," N63/54, BA-MA.

10. Churchill, *Grand Alliance*, 543–557.

11. Gilbert, VII, *Road to Victory*, 20.

12. Gwyer and Butler, *Grand Strategy*, III, 337; Hinsley et al., *British Intelligence*, III, 91–95; JP(42)243, "Offensive Operations," 7 March 1942, CAB 84/43, PRO; and DO(42)27, "Enemy Intentions," 20.3.42, CAB 69/4, PRO.

13. Michael Howard, *The Mediterranean Strategy in the Second World War* (New York: Praeger, 1968), 28–30; and CCS 78/1, "Landing Craft," June 24, 1942, CAB 88/6, PRO.

14. COS(42)71(o), "Future Strategy," 21.3.42, CAB 80/61, PRO.
15. Paret, ed., *Makers of Modern Strategy*, (Matloff) 684–685; Kimball, ed., *Churchill and Roosevelt*, I, 398–399; Ismay, *Memoirs*, 249–250; and Bryant, ed., *Turn of the Tide*, 277, 347.
16. CCS 94, "Operations in 1942/43," July 24, 1942, CAB 88/6, PRO.
17. Gwyer and Butler, *Grand Strategy*, III, 563; and Maurice Matloff, *Strategic Planning for Coalition Warfare, 1943–1944* (Washington: USGPO, 1959), 13.
18. Ian S. O. Playfair, *The Mediterranean and the Middle East*, vol. 3, *The British Fortunes Reach Their Lowest Ebb*, (London: HMSO, 1960), 219–252; and KTB/OKW, II, 107, 440.
19. Der Dtsch.Gen.b. H.Qu.d.ital.Wehrmacht Nr. 5107/42 G.K., 25.6.42, T78/431/6402457–6402458, NA; and Walter Baum and Eberhard Weichold, *Der Krieg der "Achsenmächte" in Mittelmeerraum: Die Strategie der Diktatoren* (Göttingen: Musterschmidt, 1973), 237–238.
20. Panzerarmee Afrika Ia Nr. 80/42 g.Kdos.Chefs., "Beurteilung der Lage und des zustandes der Panzerarmee Afrika am 21.7.42," 22.7.42, T78/431/6401500, NA.
21. Institut für Marxismus-Leninismus, *Geschichte des Grossen Vaterländischen Kriegs der Sowjetunion* (Berlin: Deutscher Militärverlag, 1964), III, 491; KTB/OKW, II, 52–61; GenStdH/OpAbt (III)Pruf. Nr. 57687, "Zahlenmässige Übersicht über die Verteilung der AOK, Gen.Kdos., Divn., u. Heerestruppen," 15.6.42, T78/431/6402424, NA; and Erickson, *Road to Stalingrad*, 362.
22. Hubatsch, *Hitlers Weisungen*, 196–200; and Oberkommando des Heeres, GenStdH/Op. Abt. (Ia) Nr. 420551/42 g.Kdos.Chefs., "Decknamen," 25.7.42, T78/431/6402505, NA.
23. OKW/WFSt Nr. 551213/42 G.Kdos.Ch., 9.7.42, T78/431/6402478-6402480, NA; Zeitzler, "2 Jahre Chef des Generalstabes des Heeres in zweiten Weltkrieg," N63/18, BA-MA; OKH-GenStdH-Op.Abt. I Nr. 420767/42 g.Kdos.Chefs., 30.9.42, T78/431/6402713, NA; and Der Führer, GenStdH-Op Abt (I) Nr. 420817/42 g.Kdos.Chefs., "Operationsbefehl Nr. 1," 14.10.42, T78/431/6402726, NA.
24. Hillgruber, *Zweite Weltkrieg*, 97.
25. WP(42)372, "Future Operations," 23.8.1942, CAB 66/28, PRO: COS(42)357, "Review of the Situation in the Middle East," 2.8.42 CAB 66/27, PRO: CCS 103, "Operation Torch," August 25, 1942, CAB 88/7, PRO; JIC(42)358 (Final), "Basic Strategic Policy," 18 September 1942, CAB 84/49; and Kennedy, *Business of War*, 194. See also Keith Sainsbury, *The North African Landings, 1942: A Strategic Survey* (London: Davis-Poynter, 1976).
26. Charles Webster and Noble Frankland, *The Strategic Air Offensive against Germany, 1939–1945*, vol. 1, *Preparation* (London: HMSO, 1961), 311.
27. Ibid.
28. COS(42)288(o), "Future Strategy," 30.9.42, CAB 80/64, PRO.
29. Keith Eubank, *Summit at Tehran* (New York: William Morrow, 1985), 60–61.
30. Paret, ed., *Makers of Modern Strategy* (Matloff), 688; and COS(42)452(o), "Future Strategy," 13.12.42, CAB 80/66, PRO.
31. CCS 135/2, "American-British Strategy in 1943," January 3, 1943, CAB 88/8 PRO; and JP(43)140 (Final), "European Strategy—1943–44," 7.4.43, CAB 79/60, PRO. The decisions are summarized in Herbert Feis, *Churchill, Roosevelt, Stalin: The War They Waged and the Peace They Sought* (Princeton: Princeton University Press, 1957), 105–107.
32. Kennedy, *Business of War*, 174, 177; and Kimball, ed., *Churchill and Roosevelt*, II, 48.
33. Overy, *Air War*, 74, 83.
34. COS(43)33(o), "Symbol," 28.1.43, CAB 80/67, PRO: and Kitchen, *British Policy towards the Soviet Union*, 122.
35. Erickson, *Road to Berlin*, 63; Ian S. O. Playfair and C. J. C. Molony, *The*

Mediterranean and the Middle East, vol. 4, *The Destruction of the Axis Forces in Africa* (London: HMSO, 1966), 429–462.

36. GenStdH/Org.Abt.(I) Nr. 1002/43 g.K.Chefs., "Personal—u. Materialplanung des Heeres 1943," 6.2.43, T78/431/6402951, NA; OKW/WFSt, Op. Nr. 66303/43 g.K.Chefs., "Gisela," 9.2.43, T78/431/6402964, NA; OKW/WFSt. Op. Nr. 661055/43 g.Kdos.Chefsache, 12.5.43, T78/431/6403140, NA.

37. Murray, *Luftwaffe*, 104.

38. Speer, *Inside the Third Reich*, 356; and KTB/OKW, III, 143.

39. Jürgen Rohwer, "The U-Boat War against the Allied Supply Lines," in Hans-Adolf Jacobsen and Jürgen Rohwer, eds., *Decisive Battles of World War II*, trans. Edward Fitzgerald (New York: Putnam's, 1965), 306.

40. GenStdH/Op Abt (III) Pruf. Nr. 93237, "Zahlenmässige Übersicht über die Verteilung der Divisionen," 4.11.42, T78/431/6202780, NA; and Zeitzler, "Abwehrschlachten," N63/60, BA-MA.

41. OKW/GenStdH/Op Abt Nr. 430163/43 g.Kdos.Chefs., "Operationsbefehl Nr. 5," 13.3.43, KTB/OKW, III, 1420–1421; Der Führer, OKW, GenStdH, Op. ABt. (I) Nr. 43024643, g.Kdos.Chefs., "Operationsbefehl Nr. 6 (Zitadelle), 15. April 1943, KTB/OKW, III, 1425–1427; and Ziemke, *Stalingrad to Berlin*, 124–129.

42. Paret, ed., *Makers of Modern Strategy* (Geyer), 574–575; Ivone Kirkpatrick, *Mussolini: Study of a Demogogue* (New York: Harper & Row, 1954), 507; and Andreas Hillgruber, "England's Place in Hitler's Plans for World Domination," *Journal of Contemporary History*, 9 (Jan 1974), 18–21.

43. Kimball, ed., *Churchill and Roosevelt*, II, 121.

44. COS(43)281(o), "Trident," 3 June 1943, CAB 80/70, NA: Kimball, *Churchill and Roosevelt*, II, 217; Lee, *Churchill Coalition*, 65; Bryant, ed., *Turn of the Tide*, 504; Ehrman, *Grand Strategy*, V, 7; and Paret, ed., *Makers of Modern Strategy* (Matloff), 688–689.

45. Kimball, *Churchill and Roosevelt*, II, 332.

46. Lewin, *Churchill as Warlord*, 195. Italics in the original. See also Elisabeth Barker, "Problems of the Alliance: Misconceptions and Misunderstandings," in William Deakin et al., eds., *British Political and Military Strategy in Central, Eastern, and Southern Europe in 1941* (New York: St. Martin's, 1988), 40–53.

47. Kennedy, *Business of War*, 288; and Paret, ed., *Makers of Modern Strategy* (Matloff), 696.

48. This section is based on the pathbreaking works of F. H. Hinsley et al., *British Intelligence;* and of David Kahn, *Hitler's Spies*, and idem, *Kahn on Codes: Secrets of the New Cryptology* (New York: Macmillan, 1983).

49. Kahn, *Kahn on Codes*, 113–118.

50. This is the main thesis of Ronald Lewin, *Ultra Goes to War* (London: Hutchinson, 1978).

51. Hinsley et al., *British Intelligence*, II, 176–177, 553-554, 634-641; Kahn, *Hitler's Spies*, 217–222; Kahn, *Kahn on Codes*, 104–106; and Keegan, *Mask of Command*, 273.

52. Hinsely et al., *British Intelligence*.

53. Ibid., III, 19–20.

54. Ibid., II, 380.

55. Jürgen Rohwer, "Ultra and the Battle of the Atlantic: The German View," in Robert W. Love, Jr., ed., *Changing Interpretations and New Sources in Naval History: Papers from the Third United States Naval Academy History Symposium* (New York: Garland, 1980), 442. See also the British participant, Patrick Beesly, *Very Special Intelligence: The Story of the Admiralty's Operational Intelligence Center, 1939–1945* (London: Hamish Hamilton, 1977); and idem, "Special Intelligence and the Battle of the Atlantic: The British View," in Love, ed., *Changing Interpretations*, 414–415.

56. See Ralph Bennett, *Ultra in the West: The Normandy Campaign, 1944–45* (London: Hutchinson, 1979); and Kahn, *Kahn on Codes,* 110–112.

57. Charles B. MacDonald, *A Time for Trumpets: The Untold Story of the Battle of the Bulge* (New York: Morrow, 1985), 61.

58. General Elwood P. Quesada Interview, 12–13 May 1975, 3, USAF Historical Research Center.

59. Kahn, *Kahn on Codes,* 93–94, 107–109; and Hinsley et al., *British Intelligence,* III, 294. See also Carl Boyd, "The 'Magic' Betrayal of Hitler," in Michael B. Barrett, ed., *Proceedings of the Citadel Symposium on Hitler and the National Socialist Era* (Charleston, SC: Citadel Press, 1982), 83–89.

60. Kahn, *Kahn on Codes,* 74.

61. Besides the pertinent official histories, see, among others, Alan Milward, *War, Economy and Society, 1939–1945* (Berkeley: University of California Press, 1977); Alan P. Dobson, *US Wartime Aid to Britain, 1940–1946* (New York: St. Martin's, 1986); and Richard Overy, "Hitler's War and the German Economy: A Reinterpretation," *Economic History Review,* 33 (May 1982): 272–291.

62. United States Strategic Bombing Survey, *The Effects of Strategic Bombing on the German War Economy* (Washington: Overall Economic Effects Division), 163; and Great Britain, Central Statistical Office, *Statistical Digest of the War* (London: HMSO, 1975), 148.

63. Hauner, *Hitler,* 181–183.

64. USSBS, *Effects of Strategic Bombing,* 149; and Great Britain, *Statistical Digest,* 152, 156–157; and Overy, *Air War,* 74.

65. USSBS, *Effects of Strategic Bombing,* 149; and Great Britain, *Statistical Digest,* 152.

66. Murray, *Luftwaffe,* 135–136, 180.

67. USSBS, *Effects of Strategic Bombing,* 207, 215–216; Great Britain, *Statistical Digest,* 8–9; and William K. Hancock and Margaret Gowing, *British War Economy* (London: HMSO, 1949), 366. The British Empire totals for 1940 were not available.

68. Great Britain, *Statistical Digest,* 13; Ueberschar and Wette hrsg., *Unternehmen Barbarossa,* 402; and Martin K. Sorge, *The Other Price of Hitler's War: German Military and Civilian Losses Resulting from World War II* (Westport, CT: Greenwood, 1986), 63.

69. COS(43)480(o), "Quadrant," 23 August 1943, CAB 80 /73, PRO; Hinsley et al., *British Intelligence,* III, 11; Bryant, ed., *Turn of the Tide,* 579–587; and Matloff, *Strategic Planning for Coalition Warfare, 1943–1944,* 242–243.

70. JP(43)306, "Combined Planning," 31 August 1943, CAB 84/56, PRO.

71. AOK 19, "Kriegstagebuch," 29.8.43, T312/977/9167902; Obkdo. von Sodenstern, 394/43 g.Kdos., 20.8.43, T312/977/9168361, NA; and Hinsley et al., *British Intelligence,* III, 12–13.

72. Noble Frankland, *The Bombing Offensive against Germany: Outline and Perspectives* (London: Faber & Faber, 1965), 83.

73. Der Oberbefehlshaber West, Ia Nr. 352/43 g.Kdos.Ch., "Beurteilung der Lage Ob. West am 25.10.43," 28.10.43, T311/27/7032424–7032475, NA; and Hubatsch, *Hitlers Weisungen,* 233–237.

74. Murray, *Luftwaffe,* 237–238.

75. Churchill, *Closing the Ring,* 237–254.

76. Bryant, ed., *Triumph in the West,* 121.

77. COS(43)729(o), "British Military Relations with the USSR," 24 November 1943, CAB 80/76, PRO.

78. Bryant, ed., *Triumph in the West,* 60, 65.

79. Sir Frederick E. Morgan, *Overture to Overlord* (New York: Doubleday, 1950), 227.

80. The minutes of the Cairo meeting are located in CAB 99/25, PRO.

81. Richards, *Portal,* 269–270.

82. CCS 407 (Revised), CCS 407/1, "Collaboration with the USSR," 25–26 November 1943, CAB 88/20, PRO.

83. COS(43)791(o) (Part II), CCS, 132nd Meeting, 25 February 1944, CAB 80/77, PRO; Ehrman, *Grand Strategy,* V, 175–182; and Churchill, *Closing the Ring,* 345–346.

84. AFHQ, A93528, "Operations to Assist Overlord," 27 October 1943, RG 218, CCS 381, France (7-28-43), sec. 1, box 561, NA.

85. COS(43)791(o) (Part II), "Eureka, 1st Meeting," 25 February 1944, CAB 80/77, PRO.

86. Paret, ed., *Makers of Modern Strategy,* (Matloff) 689; Kitchen, *British Policy towards the Soviet Union,* 174; and Eubank, *Summit at Teheran,* 421–422.

87. Kennedy, *Business of War,* 314.

88. CPS, 92d Meeting, "Sextant," 29 November 1943, CAB 88/51, PRO.

89. Churchill, *Closing the Ring,* 346.

90. Eubank, *Summit at Teheran,* 420–424.

91. CCS 423/2, 5 December 1943, CAB 80/77, PRO; and Hinsley, *British Intelligence,* 3, 16–17.

92. Eubank, *Summit at Teheran,* 431, 487–489. Also informative is Keith Sainsbury, *The Turning Point* (New York: Oxford University Press, 1986), 293–309.

93. Barker, *Churchill and Eden,* 204.

94. Heiber, hrsg. *Hitlers Lagebesprechungen,* 440–443.

95. Adjutant des Chefs des Generalstabes des Heeres Nr. 576/43 g.Kdos. Chefs, 23. Dezember 1943, T78/310/6262659, NA; Ob West, Ia Nr. 1409 geh.Kdos., "Lagebeurteilung durch Ob. West," 14.2.44, T311/22/7026193, NA/ OKW/WFSt/Op. Nr. 560/44 g.Kdos.Chefs., "Verstarkung des Küstenverteidigung und Reserve im Bereich des AOK, 7, AOK 1, und AOK 19," 18.2.44, T78/317/6271383–6271384, NA; and Armeeoberkommando 1, Ia Nr. 14/44 g.Kdos.Chefs., "2. Fall aa," 3. Februar 1944, T312/28/7535029, NA. See also Alan Wilt, *The Atlantic Wall: Hitler's Defenses in the West* (Ames: Iowa State University Press, 1975), 130–132.

96. Wilt, *Atlantic Wall,* 116–129; and Liddell Hart, ed., *Rommel Papers,* 466.

97. Cited in Hinsley et al., *British Intelligence* III, 43.

98. Detailed accounts of Overlord are in Lyle F. Ellis, *Victory in the West,* vol. 1, *The Battle of Normandy* (London: HMSO, 1962); and Gordon Harrison, *Cross-Channel Attack* (Washington: USGPO, 1951).

99. Gilbert, VII, *Road to Victory,* 700.

100. Generalstab des Heeres, Fremde Heere West, "Kraftverteilung Gross brittanien und Nordirland," 31 Dez 1943–31 Mai 1944, T78/646/896–911. See also Alan Wilt, "The Summer of 1944: A Comparison of Overlord and Anvil/Dragoon," *Journal of Strategic Studies,* 4 (Jun 1981): 187–195.

101. CCS 166/11, "Revised Directive for Combined Bomber Offensive," 13 February 1944, CAB 88/9, PRO. See also, among others, Tedder, *With Prejudice,* 519–521; and Hastings, *Overlord,* 39–45.

102. See, for example, Roskill, *War at Sea,* III, 2.

103. COS(44)278(o), "Operation 'Anvil,'" 21 March 1944, CAB 80/81, PRO.

104. JP(44)47(Final), "South-East Asia Command—Future Operations," 19 February 1944, CAB 79/70, PRO; and JP(44)136(Final), SEAC—SEACOS 158, 159, and 160," 19 May 1944, CAB 84/63, PRO.

105. Gilbert, VII, *Road to Victory,* 693–695, 712.

106. See, among others, Dominick Graham and Shelford Bidwell, *Tug of War: The Battle for Italy, 1943–1945* (New York: St. Martin's, 1986).

107. Erickson, *Road to Berlin,* 214. Andreas Hillgruber puts the eastern collapse

in a wider perspective in *Zweierlei Untergang: Die Zerschlagung des Deutschen Reiches und das Ende des europäischen Judentums* (Berlin: Siedler, 1986), 26–32. Hillgruber's book sparked a controversy among historians because he seemed more concerned about the fate of Germans and their culture at the end of the war than the destruction of European Jewry. See Konrad Jarausch, "Removing the Nazi Stain? The Quarrel of the German Historians," *German Studies Review*, 11 (May 1988): 285–286.

108. Colville, *Fringes of Power*, 480; and COS(44)113, "Policy towards Western Europe," 23.6.44, CAB 80/44, PRO.

109. Hinsley et al., *British Intelligence*, III, 48–49.

110. KTB/OKW, IV, 1572.

111. Armeegruppe G, 12 Aug 1944, T311/140/7185931, NA; Armeegruppe G, "Lagebeurteilung," 7 August 1944, T311/140/7185871, NA; and XL 6079, 132045Z/44, DEFE 3/118, PRO.

112. Earl Ziemke, *The German Northern Theater of Operations, 1940–1945* (Washington: Headquarters, Department of the Army, 1959), 310.

113. Ehrman, *Grand Strategy*, V, 401–402, 505–524.

114. COS(44)875(o), "Octagon," 9 October 1944, CAB 80/88, PRO; and COS(44)293(o), 31 August 1944, CAB 79/80, PRO.

115. PS-SHAEF(44)13(Final), "Post-Neptune Planning Forecast No. 1," 27 May 1944, RG-331, SHAEF SGA 381, NA.

116. Heiber, hrsg., *Hitlers Lagebesprechungen*, 593–594.

117. Hermann Jung, *Die Ardennen-Offensive, 1944-45; Ein Beispiel für die Kriegsführung Hitlers* (Göttingen: Musterschmidt, 1971), 102–104, 218–219.

118. The percentages of the famous Moscow trade-off were that the Soviets would have a 90 percent say in Romania, the British 10 percent. In Greece, the British would have the 90 percent say, Russia 10 percent. As for Hungary and Bulgaria, they finally agreed to 80 percent Russian, 20 percent British. In Yugoslavia, it was to be 50-50. (Gilbert, VII, *Road to Victory*, 993, 1001.)

119. Telegram from JSM, Washington, to Chiefs of Staff, 23 October 1944, AIR 8/1348, PRO.

120. JP(44)275(Final), "Operations in Europe," 29 October 1944, CAB 79/82, PRO.

121. COS(44)399th Meeting(o), 12 December 1944, CAB 79/84, PRO.

122. For an evaluation of Britain's contribution, see MacDonald, *Time for Trumpets*, 611–614.

123. ANCFX, XF No. 18/o/1005, "War Diary for 16–31 Dec 44," 5 February 1945, ADM 199/1400, PRO; and Murray, *Luftwaffe*, 276.

124. Russell Buhite, *Decisions at Yalta: An Appraisal of Summit Diplomacy* (Washington, DC: Scholarly Resources, 1986), 1–11.

125. Details of the military discussions are contained in Argonaut Conference, CAB 80/92, PRO.

126. Gilbert, VII, *Road to Victory*, 1212.

127. Callahan, *Burma, 1942–1945*, 143–160.

128. Ziemke, *Stalingrad to Berlin*, 467.

129. CCS 805/4, "Plan of Campaign in Western Europe," 4 April 1945, CAB 88/36, PRO: and CCS 805/5, "Plan of Campaign in Western Europe," 6 April 1945, CAB 88/36, PRO.

130. See, among others, Hugh R. Trevor-Roper, *The Last Days of Hitler* (London: Macmillan, 1950); and Lev Bezymenski, *The Death of Adolf Hitler: Unknown Documents from Soviet Archives* (New York: Harcourt, Brace, 1968.).

131. Schramm, *Hitler*, 110.

132. Paret, ed., *Makers of Modern Strategy*, (Geyer) 593.

133. Among the many historians who have written on this point, see Lisle Rose, *After Yalta* (New York: Scribner's, 1973), 72–73.

134. Kitchen, *British Policy towards the Soviet Union*, 268; Dilks, ed., *Retreat from Power*, (Strang) 81; and Paret, ed., *Makers of Modern Strategy* (Matloff) 691–692.

135. Hinsley et al., *British Intelligence*, III, pt. 1, 50–51.

SIX. FIGHTING THE WAR, 1939–1940

1. The most authoritative account of the Polish campaign is Klaus Maier et al., *Das Deutsche Reich und der Zweite Weltkrieg*, bd. 2, *Die Errichtung der Hegemonie auf dem europäischen Kontinent* (Stuttgart: Deutsche Verlags-Anstalt, 1979), 79–135. Also helpful are the works of Nikolaus von Vormann, *Der Feldzug 1939 in Polen: Die Operationen des Heeres* (Weissenburg: Prinz-Eugen Verlag, 1958); Jacques Mordal [pseud.], *La guerre commence en Pologne* (Paris: Presses de la Cité, 1968); Telford Taylor, *Sword and Swastika: Generals and Nazis in the Third Reich* (Chicago: Quadrangle, 1952), 256–350; and two articles by Hans Roos, "Die militärpolitische Lage und Planung Polens gegenüber Deutschland vor 1939," *Wehrwissenschaftliche Rundschau*, 7 (1957): 181–202, and "Der Feldzug im Polen vom September 1939," *Wehrwissenschaftliche Rundschau*, 9 (Sep 1959): 491–512. The planning phase is well covered in Robert M. Kennedy, *The German Campaign in Poland, 1939* (Washington: USGPO, 1956). For the diplomatic activities, especially those of Britain and France, see Nicholas Bethell, *The War Hitler Won: The Fall of Poland, September 1939* (New York: Holt, Rinehart & Winston, 1972); and the more popularized Anthony Reed and David Fisher, *The Deadly Embrace: Hitler, Stalin and the Nazi-Soviet Pact, 1939–1941* (London: Michael Joseph, 1988). One of the most important battles is described in Rolf Elble, *Die Schlacht an der Bruza im September 1939 aus deutscher und polnischer Sicht* (Freiburg: Rombach, 1975); and the Polish side in Josef Garlinski, *Poland in the Second World War* (London: Macmillan, 1985), and in Michael A. Peszke, "Poland's Preparations for World War II," *Military Affairs*, 43 (Feb 1979): 18–24.

2. Gerhard Weinberg, *The Foreign Policy of Hitler's Germany: Starting World War II, 1937–1939* (Chicago: University of Chicago Press, 1980), 560.

3. Germany, Auswärtigen Amt, *Documents on German Foreign Policy, 1918–1945*, ser. D, vol. 6 (Washington: USGPO, 1956), 224–227. For a brief description of the earlier defensive plan, see Alfred Jodl, "Strafverfahren des Generalobersten a.D. Alfred Jodl," 9.9.45, N69/14, BA-MA.

4. Maier et al., *Das Deutsche Reich*, II, 93–97.

5. DGFP, D, VI, 575–580; and Weinberg, *Starting World War II*, 580.

6. DGFP, D, VII, 246.

7. DGFP, D, VII, 200–201; and Halder, *Kriegstagebuch*, I, 23–26. The translation is from DGFP, D, VII, 558. See also Winfried Baumgart, "Zum Ansprache Hitlers von den Führern der Wehrmacht am 22. August 1939," *Vierteljahrshefte für Zeitgeschichte* 16 (Jan 1968): 120–149; and Hermann Boehm, "Zur Ansprache Hitlers vor den Führern der Wehrmacht am 22. August 1939," *Vierteljahrshefte für Zeitgeschichte* 19 (Jul 1971): 294–304. Boehm, as fleet commander-in-chief, German navy, attended the conference.

8. Halder, *Kriegstagebuch*, I, 40–41; and Albert Seaton, *The German Army, 1933–1945* (New York: St. Martin's, 1982), 117.

9. Maier et al., *Das Deutsche Reich*, II, 2; Roos, "Feldzug im Polen," 500–502; and Helmuth Greiner, *Die Oberste Wehrmachtführung, 1939–1943* (Wiesbaden: Limes, 1951), 51–52.

10. For the northern push, see Heeresgruppe Nord, "Kriegstagebuch," 1–12 September 1939, RH 19II/2, BA-MA; Roos, "Feldzug im Polen," 508–509; and Guderian, *Panzer Leader*, 54–55.

11. For the southern operations, see Heeresgruppe Sud, 'Kriegstagebuch, 12.8.39–3.10.39," T311/236/11–184, NA; and Roos, "Feldzug im Polen," 503–511.

12. Bethell, *War Hitler Won*, 419; Alistair Horne, *To Lose a Battle: France, 1940* (Boston: Little, Brown, 1969), 83; DGFP, D, VII, 478; COS(39) 1st Meeting, 2 September 1939, CAB 79/1 PRO; and COS(39)51, "Despatch of Additional Fighter Squadrons and AA Batteries to France," 26.9.39, CAB 80/3, PRO.

13. WP(39)13, "Weekly Résumé," 8.9.39, CAB 66/1, PRO; and WP(39)28, "Air Operations and Intelligence," 14.9.39, CAB 66/1 PRO.

14. Gerhard L. Weinberg, *Germany and the Soviet Union, 1939–1941* (Leiden: Brill, 1954), 53–54; and von Vormann, *Feldzug 1939*, 153–172.

15. Maier et al., *Das Deutsche Reich*, II, 133–134; DGFP, D, VII, 548; Halder, *Kriegstagebuch*, I, 50; Williamson Murray, "The German Response to Victory in Poland: A Case Study in Professionalism," *Armed Forces and Society* (Wtr 1981): 285–298; and Görlitz, hrsg., *Generalfeldmarschall Keitel*, 216–217.

16. WP(39)13, "Weekly Résumé," 8.9.39, CAB 66/1.

17. By far the most comprehensive treatment is William N. Medlicott, *The Economic Blockade*, 2 vols. (London: HMSO, 1952–59).

18. Ibid., I, 64–65.

19. "Handbook of Economic Warfare," July 24, 1939, FO 837/3, PRO.

20. WP(39)13, "Weekly Résumé," 8.9.39, CAB 66/1.

21. Medlicott, *Economic Blockade*, I, 52, 70–75, 83; and MEW, n.d., "Contraband Control and Enemy Export Control in 1939," FO 837/170, PRO.

22. WP(39)101, "Weekly Résumé," 28.10.39, CAB 66/3, PRO.

23. MEW, "Contraband Control," FO 837/170; and Medlicott, *Economic Blockade*, I, 87–102.

24. MEW, "1st Meeting of the Black List Committee," 4 September 1939, FO 837/65, PRO; Ministry of Economic Warfare, "War Trade Lists No. 1," October 1939, FO 837/48, PRO; and MEW, November 1939, FO 837/66, PRO.

25. Medlicott, *Economic Blockade*, I, 113–114; Ministry of Economic Warfare, November–December 1939, FO 837/115, PRO; and MEW, "Contraband Control," FO 837/170, PRO.

26. Medlicott, *Economic Blockade*, I, 54–58. For another side of Britain's campaign to control neutrals, see Robert Cole, "The Other 'Phoney War': British Propaganda in Neutral Europe, September–December 1939," *Journal of Contemporary History*, 22 (Jul 1987): 455–479.

27. Medlicott, *Economic Blockade*, I, 65–69.

28. Hinsley et al., *British Intelligence*, I, 226–231.

29. WP(39)57, "Norway and Sweden," 29.9.39, CAB 66/2, PRO.

30. JP(39)102, "Stoppage of Iron Ore from Narvik," n.d., CAB 84/9, PRO; COS(39)168, "Stoppage of Export of Swedish Iron Ore to Germany," 20.12.39, CAB 80/6, PRO; and Butler, *Grand Strategy*, II, 101.

31. Medlicott, *Economic Blockade*, I, 145–146; COS(39)181, "Military Implications," 31.12.39, CAB 80/6, PRO; and WP(39)180, "Stoppage of Iron Ore to Germany," CAB 66/4, PRO.

32. Medlicott, *Economic Blockade*, I, 191–192.

33. Medlicott, *Economic Blockade*, I, 250–259; WP(39)134, "German Oil Supplies," 20.11.39, CAB 66/3, PRO; WP(40)26, "German Oil Supplies," 19.1.40, CAB 66/5, PRO; Hinsley et al., *British Intelligence*, I, 241–242.

34. JP(40)88(S), "Major Strategy of the War," 8.4.140, CAB 84/11, PRO; MEW, "Contraband Control," FO 837/170, PRO; MEW, 31st Dec 1939, FO, 837/134, PRO; and Medlicott, *Economic Blockade*, I, 84–100.

35. MEW, "Minutes of 60th Meeting of Contraband Committee," 3rd Nov 1939, FO 837/133, PRO.

36. MEW, "Contraband Control," FO 837/170.

37. Hinsley et al., *British Intelligence*, I, 240–248; and Gwyer and Butler, *Grand Strategy*, III, 510.

38. Michael Glover, *The Fight for the Channel Ports: Calais to Brest, 1940* (Boulder: Westview Press, 1985), 13.

39. Among the excellent books on the Allied side of the Battle of France, see Horne, *To Lose a Battle*; Lyle F. Ellis, *The War in France and Flanders, 1939–1940* (London: HMSO, 1953); Guy Chapman, *Why France Fell* (London: Cassell, 1968); Adolphe Goutard, *The Battle of France, 1940,* trans. A. R. P. Burgess (New York: L. Washburn, 1959); the compact Henri Michel, *La défaite de la France (Septembre 1939–Juin 1940)* (Paris: Presses Universitaire de France, 1980); and the synthesis in Maier et al., *Das Deutsche Reich,* II, 235–327. A popular account is Richard Collier, *1940: The Avalance* (New York: Dial, 1979). The British side is also well covered in P. H. M. Bell, *A Certain Eventuality: Britain and the Fall of France* (Lexington, MA: Saxon House, 1974); the Belgian in Brian Bond, *France and Belgium, 1939–1940* (London: Davis-Poynter, 1975); and Franco-British diplomacy in Eleanor M. Gates, *End of the Affair: The Collapse of the Anglo-French Alliance, 1939–1940* (Berkeley: University of California Press, 1981). Specific topics are dealt with in Jeffrey A. Gunsburg, *Divided and Conquered: The French High Command and the Defeat of the West, 1940* (Westport, CT: Greenwood, 1979), and idem, "Coupable ou non? Le rôle du Général Gamelin dans la défaite de 1940," *Revue historique des armées,* 4 (1979): 145–163; Glover, *Fight for the Channel Ports*; Basil Karslake, *1940: The Last Act: The Story of the British Forces in France after Dunkirk* (Hamden, CT: Archon. 1979); Ride Belot, *La Marine française pendant la campagne 1939–1940* (Paris: Plon, 1954); David Dilks, "The Twilight War and the Fall of France: Chamberlain and Churchill in 1940," *Transactions of the Royal Historical Society,* 28 (1978): 61–86; Faris R. Kirkland, "The French Air Force in 1940: Was It Defeated by the Luftwaffe or by Politics?" *Air University Review,* 36 (Sep–Oct 1985): 101–118; James Marshall-Cornwall, "A Proposed Refuge in Brittany—June 1940," *RUSI Journal,* 121 (Jun 1976): 78–82; Leon Noel, "Le project d'Union Franco-Britannique de juin 1940," *Revue d'histoire de la deuxième guerre mondiale,* 6 (Jan 1956): 22–37; and Emile Wanty, "La défense des Ardennes en 1940," *Revue d'histoire de la deuxième guerre mondiale,* 11 (Apr 1961): 1–16. The entire June 1953 issue of *Revue d'histoire de la deuxième guerre mondiale* is devoted to "La campagne de France."

40. COS (39)34(JP), "The Possible Future Course of the War," 16 September 39, CAB 84/7, PRO.

41. WM2(39), 4.9.39, CAB 65/1 PRO.

42. Macleod and Kelly, eds., *Ironside Diaries,* 106.

43. COS(39)38th Meeting, 5.10.39, CAB 79/1, PRO.

44. [RAF], "Strength and Disposition of the RAF Component," 15 January 1940, AIR 35/278, PRO.

45. COS(39)34(JP), "Possible Future Course," CAB 84/7.

46. JP(39)27, "Staff Conversations with Belgium," 15 September 1939, CAB 84/7, PRO. See also D. O. Kieft, *Belgium's Return to Neutrality* (Oxford: Clarendon Press, 1972); and the documents in *Les relations militaires Franco-Belges, Mars 1936–10 Mai 1940* (Paris: Centre de la Recherche Scientifique, 1968).

47. COS(39)117(JP), "German Invasion of Holland," 10 November 1939, CAB 84/9, PRO; GHQ(O), "GHQ Operation Instruction No. 36," 17 April 40, WO 197/58, PRO: and Bond, *France and Belgium,* 51–56.

48. COS(39)54, "Possibility of German Attack in the West," 28.9.39, CAB 80/3, PRO; and WP(39)65, "General Gamelin's Observations," 2.10.39, CAB 66/2, PRO.

49. The minutes of the meetings are contained in CAB 99/3, PRO.

50. JP(40)65, "Certain Aspects of the Present Situation," 23 March 1940, CAB 84/11, PRO; and SWC(39/40), 6th Meeting, March 28, 1940, CAB 99/3, PRO.

51. WP(40)27, "Strength and Organization of the British Expeditionary Force in France," 20.1.40, CAB 66/5, PRO; and JP(40)88(S)PD, "Major Strategy of the War," 8.4.40, CAB 84/11, PRO.

52. [DMO], March 1940, WO 106/1597, PRO; and Terraine, *A Time for Courage,* 122.

53. JP(40)88(S)PD, "Major Strategy of the War," CAB 84/11.

54. COS(39)(34)JP), "Possible Future Course," CAB 84/7.

55. COS(40)216(S), "The Major Strategy of the War," 23/1/40, CAB 80/104, PRO.

56. JP(40)88(S), "Major Strategy of the War," 8.4.40, CAB 84/11, PRO.

57. WP(40)145, "Review of the Strategical Situation," CAB 66/7, PRO.

58. COS(40)270, "Certain Aspects of the Present Situation," 26.3.40, CAB 80/19, PRO.

59. Besides in Maier et al., *Das Deutsche Reich,* II, the German side of the Battle of France is well covered in Hans-Adolf Jacobsen, *Fall Gelb: Der Kampf um den deutschen Operationsplan zur Westoffensive 1940* (Wiesbaden: Steiner, 1957); and in two books of documents, idem, *Dokumente zur Vorgeschichte des Westfeldzuges, 1939–1940* (Göttingen: Musterschmidt, 1956); and *Dokumente zum Westfeldzug, 1940* (Göttingen: Musterschmidt, 1960). A popular version is Telford Taylor, *The March of Conquest: The German Victories in Western Europe, 1940* (New York: Simon & Schuster, 1958). On plans, see John Mearsheimer, *Conventional Deterrence* (Ithaca, NY: Cornell University Press, 1983), 67–133. Specific aspects of the campaign are explored in James E. Mrazek, *The Fall of Eben Emael: Prelude to Dunkerque* (Washington: Luce, 1970); Volkmar Regling, *Amiens 1940: Der Deutsche Durchbruch südlich vom Amiens 5. bis 8. Juni 1940* (Freiburg: Rombach: 1968); Robert Jackson, *Air War over France, May–June 1940* (London: Ian Allen, 1974); Herman Teske, *Bewegungskrieg: Führungsprobleme einen Infanterie-Division im Westfeldzug, 1940* (Heidelberg: K. Vowinckel, 1955); Lee Kennett, "German Air Superiority in the Westfeldzug, 1940," in F. X. J. Homer and Larry D. Wilcox, eds., *Germany and Europe in the Era of Two World Wars* (Charlottesville: University Press of Virginia, 1986): 141–156; C. J. DeJong, "La préparation de l'attaque allemandes sur la Hollnade en 1940," *Revue d'histoire de la deuxième guerre mondiale,* 5 (Oct 1955): 1–16; Hans-Adolf Jacobsen, "L'erreur du commandant allemand devant Dunkerque," *Revue Historique de l'Armée* (1958): 63–74; and Jacobsen, "Der deutsche Luftangriff auf Rotterdam, 14 Mai 1940; Versuch einer Klärung," *Wehrwissenschaftliche Rundschau* 7 (Mai 1958): 257–285).

60. Keitel, "Lebenserinnerungen," N54/5, BA-MA.

61. Maier et al., *Das Deutsche Reich,* II, 19, 245–247.

62. Ibid.

63. Engel, *Heeresadjutant bei Hitler,* 74–75.

64. Heeresgruppe A, G.Kdos., "Kriegstagebuch West, II, Teil," 22.2.40, RH 191/37, BA-MA; and Der Oberbefehlshaber des Heeres, GenStdH Op. Abt. (Ia) Nr. 130/40 g.Kdos., "Neufassung der Aufmarschanweisung 'Gelb,'" 24. February 1940, RH 191/38, BA-MA.

65. Der Chef des Generalstabes der Heeresgruppe A Ia Nr. 508/40, g.Kdos., 5.III.40, RH 191/38, BA-MA; and Heeresgruppe A, G.Kdos., "Kriegstagebuch West, II. Teil," 6.3.40, RH 191/37, BA-MA.

66. Maier, et al., *Das Deutsche Reiche,* II, 309.

67. Ibid., 282.

68. The point of Germany's having better doctrine, organization, and training is made persuasively by Williamson Murray, who shows that German commanders

instituted extensive corrective measures to overcome what they considered "deficiencies in Poland" (*The Change in the European Balance of Power, 1938–1939: The Path to Ruin* [Princeton: Princeton University Press, 1984], 338).

69. Russell H. S. Stolfi, "Equipment for Victory in France in 1940," *History* 52 (Feb 1970): 1–20.

70. Maier et al., *Das Deutsche Reich*, II, 268.

71. Murray, *Luftwaffe*, 40–43; and Overy, *Goering*, 171.

72. Hinsley et al., *British Intelligence*, I, 130–134.

73. Stolfi, "Equipment for Victory," 19–20.

74. Army Group A's decisive role is covered in Heeresgruppe A, G.Kdos., "Kriegstagebuch West, II. Teil," 10–21 Mai 1940, RH 191/37, BA-MA.

75. For Army Group B actions, see Obkdo. Heeresgruppe B, Ia, G.Kdos., "Kriegstagebuch Nr. 4," 10–21 Mai 1940, AL 1433, Imperial War Museum.

76. M.O. 4, "War Office Summary of Operations," 14–15 May 1940, WO 106/1673, PRO.

77. WM 122(40), 14.5.40, CAB 65/7, PRO.

78. Churchill, *Their Finest Hour*, 37. The 8:30 hour is the time given in COS(40) 133rd Meeting, 15.5.40, CAB 79/4, PRO. In Churchill's recollections, the time given is 7:30.

79. BEF activities are followed in M.O. 4, "War Office Summary of Operations," 16–21 May, 1940, WO 106/1673, PRO; and BEF [Messages], 16–19/5/40, WO 106/1682, PRO.

80. WM(40), 130th Conclusions, Confidential Annex, 19.5.40, CAB 65/13, PRO.

81. DO(40), 4th Meeting, 19.5.40, CAB 69/1.

82. Heeresgruppe A, g.Kdos., "Kriegstagebuch West, II. Teil," 21–31 Mai 1940, RH 191/37, BA-MA.

83. Gruppe von Kleist, 23.5.40, RH 191/38, BA-MA.

84. Heeresgruppe A, Chef d.Gen.Stabes, "Lagenbetrachtung 23/24.5," 24.5.40, RH 191/38, BA-MA; and Heeresgruppe A, Ia, 24.5.40, RH 191/38, BA-MA.

85. BEF, "Emergency Operations," 27.5.40, WO 106/1682, PRO. Excellent accounts of the Dunkirk operation are those of Hans-Adolf Jacobsen, *Dünkirchen: Ein beitrag zur Geschichte des Westfeldzuges, 1940* (Neckargemünd: Vowinckel, 1958); and David Divine, *The Nine Days of Dunkirk* (New York: Norton, 1959). Jacobsen has summarized his findings in Jacobsen and Rohwer, eds., *Decisive Battles*, 29–68. Valuable additional material is contained in Bond, *France and Belgium;* and idem, "Dunkirk: Myths and Lessons," *RUSI Journal* 127 (Sep 1982): 3–8. Other studies on aspects of Dunkirk are Gregory Blaxland, *Destination Dunkirk: The Story of Gort's Army* (London: William Kimber, 1973); Norman Franks, *The Air Battle of Dunkirk* (London: William Kimber, 1973); and Patrick Turnbull, *Dunkirk: Anatomy of a Disaster* (New York: Holmes & Meier, 1978).

86. Churchill, *Their Finest Hour*, 100.

87. War Office, "War Office Note on Dunkirk Evacuation," 3 May 1941, WO 106/1618, PRO.

88. Basil H. Liddell Hart, *The German Generals Talk* (New York: Morrow, 1948), 81–84.

89. This question is explored in depth in Bond, *France and Belgium*.

90. Heeresgruppe A, g.Kdos., "Kriegstagebuch West, II. Teil," 26. Mai 1940, RH 191/37, BA-MA.

91. Heeresgruppe A, g.Kdos., "Kriegstagebuch West, II. Teil," 27. Mai 1940, RH 191/37, BA-MA.

92. Engel, *Heeresadjutant bei Hitler*, 81.

93. Gilbert, VI, *Finest Hour*, 478.

94. WM(40), 152nd Conclusions, Confidential Annex, 2 June 1940, AIR 8/287, PRO.
95. COS(40)418(JP), "British Policy in Relation to the Situation on the Western Front," 1.6.40, CAB 80/12, PRO.
96. WM(40), 154th Conclusions, Confidential Annex, 4.6.40, CAB 65/13, PRO; and Edward L. Spears, *Assignment to Catastrophe*, vol. 2, *The Fall of France, June 1940* (London: Heinemann, 1955), 68.
97. Heersgruppe B, g.Kdos., "Kriegstagebuch Nr. 5," 5–20 Juni 1940, RH 191/106, BA-MA.
98. Heeresgruppe B, g.Kdos., "Kriegstagebuch West," 8–19 Juni 1940, RH 191/48, BA-MA.
99. Glover, *Fight for the Channel Ports*, 182–186; Terraine, *A Time for Courage*, 159; and Q(M)2a, "Personnel Returned from BEF," 15/8/40, WO 106/1752, PRO. See also Roderick Grant *51st Highland Division at War* (London: Ian Allen, 1977).
100. CUS(40), 182nd Meeting, 15.6.40, CAB 77/5, PRO.
101. WM 169(40), "The Declaration of Union," 16.6.40, CAB 65/7, PRO. The sequence of events is masterfully set forth in Llewellyn Woodward, *British Foreign Policy in the Second World War*, 5 vols. (London: HMSO, 1970–1976), I, 276–282. See also Spears, *Assignment to Catastrophe*, II, 315.
102. WP(40)310, "Sir S. Cripp's View on the Post-War Position of the British Empire," 8.8.40, CAB 66/10, PRO.
103. Quoted in Colville, *Fringes of Power*, 171.
104. WM(4) 179th Conclusions, 24.6.40, CAB 65/8, PRO; Gilbert, VI, *Finest Hour*, 633–638; and First Sea Lord's Records, 7 June 1940, ADM 205/4, PRO.
105. Maier et al., *Das Deutsche Reich*, II, 27–28; Samuel J. Lewis, *Forgotten Legions: Germany's Army Infantry Policy, 1918–1941* (New York: Praeger, 1985), 106; and Overy, *Goering*, 103.
106. Hinsley et al., *British Intelligence*, I, 143–144.
107. Maier et al., *Das Deutsche Reich*, II, 282, 294, 307; Horne, *To Lose a Battle*, 584–585; Murray, *Luftwaffe*, 44; and Terraine, *A Time for Courage*, 162–164.
108. Murray, *Luftwaffe*, 42–43; and Homer and Wilcox, eds., *Germany and Europe*, (Kennett) 153.
109. Keitel, "Lebenserinnerungen," N54/64; and Horne, *To Lose a Battle*, 535–536.
110. Maier et al., *Das Deutsche Reich*, II, 382. Among the many fine studies of the aerial campaign, see Derek Wood and Derek Dempster, *The Narrow Margin* (London: Hutchinson, 1961); Basil Collier, *The Defence of the United Kingdom* (London: HMSO, 1957); Francis K. Mason, *Battle over Britain: A History of the German Air Assaults on Great Britain 1917–18 and July–December 1940* . . . (London: McWhirter, 1969); Udo Volkmann, *Die Britische Luftverteidigung und die Abwehr der deutschen Luftangriffe während der 'Luftschlacht um England' bis zum Juni 1941* (Osnabrück: Biblio, 1982); and the more popular works of Len Deighton, *Fighter: The True Story of the Battle of Britain* (New York: Knopf, 1979), and Armand Van Ishoven, *Luftwaffe in the Battle of Britain* (New York: Scribner's, 1980). German plans for invading Britain are well covered in Ronald Wheatley, *Operation Sea Lion: German Plans for the Invasion of England* (Oxford: Clarendon, 1958); and Karl Klee, *Das Unternehmen 'Seelöwe': Die geplante deutsche Landung in England, 1940* (Göttingen: Musterschmidt, 1958). Klee has also edited *Dokumente zum Unternehmen, 'Seelöwe': Die geplante deutsche landung in England, 1940* (Göttingen: Musterschmidt, 1958), and his conclusions are summarized in Jacobsen and Rohwer, eds., *Decisive Battles*, 73–94. Specific aspects are dealt with in Hillgruber, "England's Place"; Friedrich-Karl von Plehwe, "Operation Sealion, 1940," *RUSI Journal*, 118 (Mar 1973): 47–58; David

Reynolds, "Churchill and the British 'Decision' to Fight on in 1940," in Richard Langhorne, ed., *Diplomacy and Intelligence during the Second World War: Essays in Honour of F. H. Hinsley* (Cambridge: Cambridge University Press, 1985), 147–167; Walter Ansel, *Hitler Confronts England* (Durham, NC: Duke University Press, 1960); Tommy J. Smith, *Ultra in the Battle of Britain: The Real Key to Success* (Alexandria, VA: Defense Technical Information, 1980); and Peter Wykeham, *Fighter Command: A Study of Air Defence* (London: Putnam, 1960).

111. Hillgruber, *Hitlers Strategie*, 60, 144.

112. Heeresgruppe B, g.Kdos., "Kriegstagebuch Nr. 5," 23.6.40, RH 19II/106, BA-MA.

113. Klee, *Dokumente zum Unternehmen 'Seelöwe,'* 298–302.

114. Hubatsch, hrsg., *Hitlers Weisungen*, 61–65.

115. Wheatley, *Operation Sea Lion*, 40–41, 152–155.

116. Hillgruber, *Hitlers Strategie*, 168; and Butler, *Grand Strategy*, II, 285–286.

117. Halder, Kriegstagebuch, II, 46–50.

118. Wheatley, *Operation Sea Lion*, 95–96, 155–159.

119. MR(J)(40)10, "Possible German Action in the Spring of 1940: Appreciation," January 22, 1940, WO 193/785, PRO.

120. COS(40)394, "British Strategy in a Certain Eventuality," 26.5.40, CAB 80/11, PRO.

121. COS(40)395, "The Control of Home Defence Operations," 26.5.40, CAB 80/11, PRO.

122. Head of Military Branch, "GHQ Operation Instruction No. 1," 5 June 1940, ADM 205/7, PRO; and Admirality, 11 June 1940, ADM 205/7, PRO.

123. Wood and Dempster, *Narrow Margin*, 203–204; and WM 170(40), 17.6.40, CAB 65/7, PRO.

124. Collier, *Defence of the United Kingdom*, 123.

125. Head of Military Branch, "GHQ Operation Instruction No. 3," 15 June 1940, ADM 205/7, PRO.

126. Bryant, ed., *Turn of the Tide*, 155.

127. Collier, *Defence of the United Kingdom*, 450.

128. [ObdL], "Besprechung Reichsmarschall," 21.7.40, RL 2II/30, BA-MA.

129. Jacobsen and Rohwer, eds., *Decisive Battles*, (Klee) 73–74.

130. Hillgruber, *Hitlers Strategie*, 675.

131. [ObdL] 31.7.40, RL 2II/30, BA-MA.

132. Collier, *Defence of the United Kingdom*, 452; and WO 4, "Summarised Order of Battle," 9.8.40, PREM 3/29, PRO.

133. Hinsley et al., *British Intelligence*, I, 180; and Gilbert, VI, *Finest Hour*, 655, 726, 773.

134. As summarized in Terraine, *A Time for Courage*, 182.

135. The figures that follow are taken from Collier, *Defence of the United Kingdom;* Wood and Dempster, *Narrow Margin;* and Air Ministry War Room, Daily Summaries, 13 August–29 September 1940, AIR 22/12-13, PRO.

136. Gilbert, VI, *Finest Hour*, 780.

137. Air Ministry War Room, "Strength of Aircraft, Searchlights, Balloons and AA Guns," n.d., AIR 22/33, PRO.

138. Maier et al., *Das Deutsche Reich*, II, 402–406; and Wood and Dempster, *Narrow Margin*, 199–201.

139. Murray, *Luftwaffe*, 1; and Overy, *Goering*, 172.

140. Carver, ed., *War Lords*, (Lyall) 207–210; and Report from Hdqrs., No. 11 Gp to Hdqrs. Ftr. Cmd., "German Air Strikes on England—8th Aug–10th Sept," 12 September 1940, AIR 16/690, PRO.

141. Gilbert, VI, *Finest Hour*, 658; and Wood and Dempster, *Narrow Margin*, 411–413.

142. Overy, *Air War*, 34; and Murray, *Luftwaffe*, 55–56.

143. Richards, *Portal*, 159.

SEVEN. THE RUSSIAN FRONT, 1941–1943

1. The best general study of the Russo-German front is John Erickson, *The Road to Stalingrad: Stalin's War with Germany* (New York: Harper & Row, 1975); and idem, *The Road to Berlin: Continuing the History of Stalin's War with Germany* (Boulder, CO: Westview Press, 1983). Especially noteworthy is Erickson's coverage of Soviet operations. Despite being laced with Soviet Marxist rhetoric, the Soviet official history (Institut für Marxismus-Leninismus, *Geschichte des Grossen Vaterländischen Krieges der Soweitunion*, trans. 6 banden [Berlin: Deutscher Militärverlag, 1964]), is also valuable. Other works of note are Albert Seaton, *The Russo-German War, 1941–1945* (New York: Praeger, 1971); the journalist Alexander Werth, *Russia at War, 1941–1945* (New York: Dutton, 1964); and Alan Clark, *Barbarossa: The Russian-German Conflict, 1941–45* (New York: W. Morrow, 1965), although Clark's discussion of diplomatic and political developments is flawed. A survey which casts doubt on German intelligence successes in the east is David Thomas, "Foreign Armies East and German Military Intelligence in Russia, 1941–1945," *Journal of Contemporary History*, 22 (Apr 1987): 261–301.

2. The definitive account is Horst Boog et al., *Das Deutsche Reich und der Zweite Weltkrieg*, bd. 4, Die Angriff auf die Sowjetunion (Stuttgart: Deutsche Verlags-Anstalt, 1982). Also outstanding on the later stages of the campaign is Klaus Reinhardt, *Die Wende vor Moskau: Das Scheitern der Strategie Hitlers im Winter 1941/42* (Stuttgart: Deutsche Verlags-Anstalt, 1972). Reinhardt's views are summarized in "Das Scheitern des deutschen Blitzkriegskonzeptes vor Moskau," in Jürgen Rohwer und Eberhard Jäckel, hrsg., *Kriegswende, Dezember 1941* (Koblenz: Bernard & Graefe, 1984), 199–209. Another excellent book of essays is Überschär and Wette, hrsg., *Unternehmen Barbarossa*. Memoirs by some of the leaders are contained in Heinz Guderian, *Panzer Leader*, trans. Constantine Fitzgibbon (New York: Dutton, 1952); Erich von Manstein, *Lost Victories*, trans. Anthony G. Lowell (London: Methuen, 1958); and Hermann Hoth, *Panzer-Operationen-Die Panzergruppe 3 und der operative Gedanke der deutschen Führung, Sommer 1941* (Neckargemünd: Vowinckel, 1956). A biography is Walter Charles de Beaulieu, *Generaloberst Erich Hoepner—Militärisches Porträt Panzerführers* (Neckargemünd: Vowinckel, 1969). Aspects of the campaign are dealt with in Andreas Hillgruber's brilliant *Hitlers Strategie;* idem, "Das Russland-Bild der führenden deutschen Militärs von Beginn der Angriffs auf die Sowjetunion," in Alexander Fischer, Günther Moltmann, und Klaus Schwabe, hrsg., *Russland, Deutschland, Amerika, Festschrift zum 80: Geburtstag Fritz Epsten* (Wiesbaden: Steiner, 1978), 296-310; George E. Blau, *The German Campaign in Russia: Planning and Operations, 1940–1942* (Washington: USGPO, 1955); the error-filled Barry Leach, *German Strategy against Russia, 1939–1941* (New York: Oxford, 1973); Trumbull Higgins, *Hitler and Russia: The Third Reich in a Two-Front War, 1937–1943* (New York: Macmillan, 1966); Albert Seaton, *The Battle for Moscow, 1941–1942* (New York: Stein & Day, 1971); and the popularized Werner Haupt, *Die Deutschen vor Moskau, 1941/42* (Dorheim: Podzun, 1972). Pertinent articles include A. Constantini, "La bataille de Smolensk (10 juillet–10 septembre 1941)," *Revue d'histoire de la deuxième guerre mondiale*, 15 (Jul 1965): 53–78; Jürgen Förster, "Hitler's War Aims against the Soviet Union and the German Military Leaders," *Militärhistorisk Tidskrift* (1979): 83–93;

idem, "The Wehrmacht and the War of Extermination against the Soviet Union," *Yad Vashem Studies* 14 (1981): 7–34; Hillgruber, "Die 'Endlösung' und das deutsche Ostimperium als Kernstück des rassenideologischen Programms des Nationalsozialismus," *Vierteljahrshefte für Zeitgeschichte*, 20 (Apr 1972): 133–153; Gerald R. Kleinfeld, "Hitler's Strike for Tikhvin," *Military Affairs*, 47 (Oct 1983): 122–128; Louis Rotundo, "The Creation of Soviet Reserves and the 1941 Campaign," *Military Affairs*, 50 (Jan 1986): 21–28; Amnon Sella, "'Barbarossa': Surprise Attack and Communication," *Journal of Contemporary History*, 134 (Jul 1978): 555–583; Russel H. S. Stolfi, "Barbarossa Revisited: A Critical Appraisal of the Opening Stages of the Russo-German Campaign (June–December 1941)," *Journal of Modern History*, 54 (Mar 1982): 27–46; Gerd Überschär, "Guerre de coalition ou guerre séparée; conception et structures de la stratégie germano-finlandaise dans la guerre contre l'URSS, 1941–1944," *Revue d'histoire de la deuxième guerre mondiale*, 30 (Apr 1980): 27–68; Martin van Creveld, "The German Attack on the USSR: The Destruction of a Legend," *European Studies Review*, 2 (Jan 1972): 69–86; and Alan Wilt, "Hitler's Late Summer Pause in 1941," *Military Affairs*, 45 (Dec 1981): 187–191.

3. Engel relates that after the meetings with Molotov in mid-November, Hitler told his adjutant, Schmundt, to begin constructing in haste battle headquarters in the east (Engel, *Heeresadjutant bei Hitler,* 91).

4. Hubatsch, hrsg. *Hitlers Weisungen,* 84–88.

5. Oberkommando des Heeres, GenStdH Op.Abt. (Ia) Nr. 050/41 g.Kdos.Chefs., "Aufmarschanweisung Barbarossa," 31. Januar 1941, T78/335/6291236, NA.

6. KTB/OKW, I, 361–362; and Millett and Murray, eds., *Military Effectiveness,* III, (Förster) 196.

7. Hinsley et al., *British Intelligence,* I, 476–479; and Gabriel Gorodetsky, "Was Stalin Planning to Attack Hitler in June 1941?" *Royal United Services Institution Journal,* 131 (Jun 1986): 70–71.

8. Bryan Fugate (*Strategy and Tactics on the Eastern Front, 1941* [Novato, CA: Presido, 1984]) has attempted to show that Stalin and his advisers were not totally unprepared. Among the many refutations, see Barry D. Watts and Williamson Murray, "Inventing History: Soviet Military Genius Revealed," *Air University Review,* 36 (March–April 1985): 102–112.

9. Überschär und Wette, hrsg., *"Unternehmen Barbarossa,"* (Überschär) 145–146; OKH, GenStdH/Gen Qu, Abt. H. Vers./Qu 1 Nr. I/0740/41 g.Kdos.Ch., 20. Juni 1941, T78/335/6291688, NA; and S. P. Ivanov, *The Initial Period of War: A Soviet View* (Washington: USGPO, 1986), 184.

10. Boog et al., *Das Deutsche Reich,* IV, 185.

11. OKH, 20. Juni 1941, T78/335/6291688; and General de Artillerie beim ObdH (Ia) Nr. 132/41 g.K.Chefs., "Geschutzzählen für Barbarossa," 20. Juni 1941, T78/335/6291685, NA.

12. Boog et al., *Das Deutsche Reich,* IV, 307–312.

13. Ibid., 301; and Murray, *Luftwaffe,* 59.

14. KTB/OKW, I, Anlagen, 21.6.41.

15. Boog et al., *Das Deutsche Reich,* IV, 307–312.

16. Besides in ibid., day-to-day combat and movements are covered in KTB/OKW, I.

17. Heeresgruppe Mitte Ia Nr T1/41 geh., "Morgenmeldung," 22.6.41, RH19 II/128, BA-MA.

18. The actual citation is in KTB/OKW, I, 418.

19. Ibid., 1036.

20. PzGr 2, "Kriegstagebuch," 24.8.1941, T313/86/7326511-7326512, NA; and PzGr 3, o Qu, "Kriegstagebuch," 15.8.41, T313/237/8504301, NA.

21. HGr Nord, "Kriegstagebuch," 15.8–29.9.41, T311/53/7066204–7066247, NA; and PzGr 3, O Qu, "Kriegstagebuch," 14.8–30.9.41, T313/237/8503423-8503581, NA.

22. HGr Nord, 24.9.1941, T311/51/7064953-7064155, NA.

23. PzGr 2, "Kriegstagebuch," 21.8.–22.9.41, T313/86/7326486–73267861, NA; and Kurt Zeitzler, "Die Operationen der 1. Panzerarmee," N63/50, BA-MA.

24. PzGr 2, O Qu, "Kriegstagebuch," 29.9.41, T313/80/7318144–7318146, NA; and PzGr 3, O Qu, "Kriegstagebuch." 1.10.41, T313/237/8503586, NA.

25. Erickson, *Road to Stalingrad*, 213–214.

26. Heeresgruppe Mitte, Ia Nr. T765/41 geh., "Zwischenmeldung," 2.10.41, RH 19II/132, BA-MA.

27. KTB/OKW, I, 695–707.

28. Halder Diary, III, 300; Pz AOK 2, "Meldung über die Panzer-Lage," 19.12.41, T313/96/7339053, NA; and Boog et al., *Das Deutsche Reich*, IV, 699.

29. Reinhardt, *Wende vor Moskau*, 100–101.

30. KTB/OKW, I, 1082.

31. Armeeoberkommando 2, Ia Nr. 695/41 g.Kdos., 21.12.41, T313/96/7339112–7339113, NA.

32. Kitchen, *British Policy towards the Soviet Union;* Churchill, *Grand Alliance,* 381–400; and Gilbert, VII, *Road to Victory,* 1209.

33. Überschär und Wette, hrsg., *"Unternehmen Barbarossa,"* (Überschär) 168.

34. Rotundo, "Creation of Soviet Reserves," 25–26.

35. Hillgruber, *Hitlers Strategie,* 551; Reinhardt, *Wende vor Moskau,* 293; and Hans Doerr, *Der Feldzug nach Stalingrad: Versuch eines operativen Überblicks* (Darmstadt: Mittler, 1955), 15.

36. OKH, GenStdH/Op. Abt.(III) Nr. 1617/41 g.Kdos., 10.11.41, T78/346/6304162; and OKH, GenStdH/Op. Abt. (III) Nr. 1614/41 g.Kdos.Chefs, 3.11.41, T78/346/6304172.

37. Ziemke, *Stalingrad to Berlin,* 15; and Basil H. Liddell Hart, *The German Generals Talk* (New York: W. Morrow, 1948), 195–199.

38. Hillgruber, *Zweite Weltkrieg,* 81; and Förster, "Wehrmacht and the War of Extermination," 33.

39. Halder Diary, III, 330.

40. Warlimont, *Inside Hitler's Headquarters,* 228; and Higgins, *Hitler and Russia,* 195.

41. Reinhardt, *Wende vor Moskau,* 263.

42. KTB/OKW, II, 1093–1098.

43. Halder Diary, III, 420–421.

44. Hubatsch, hrsg., *Hitlers Weisungen,* 183–191. A detailed, objective account of Germany's entire 1942 Russian campaign is Earl F. Ziemke and Magna E. Bauer, *Moscow to Stalingrad: Decision in the East* (Washington: USGPO, 1987). John Erickson's *The Road to Stalingrad* and volume two of the Soviet official history, previously mentioned, also contain valuable information on Blue/Brunswick. Specific aspects of the campaign are dealt with by one of the participants, Hans Doerr, in his *Feldzug nach Stalingrad;* by Carl Wagener in "Der Vorstoss der XXXX: Panzerkorps vom Charkov zum Kaukasus, Juli–August 1942," *Wehrwissenschaftliche Rundschau,* 5 (Sep 1955): 397–408, and (Oct 1955): 447–459; and by Earl Ziemke in "Operation Kreml: Deception, Strategy and the Fortunes of War," *Parameters,* 9 (Mar 1979): 72–83. Two popular works that relate in part are Peter Gosztony, *Hitlers Fremde Heere: Das Schicksal der nichtdeutschen Armeen im Ostfeldzug* (Düsseldorf: Econ, 1976); and Carl Wagener, *Heeresgruppe Süd: Der Kampf im Süden des Ostfront, 1941–1945* (Bad Nauheim: Podzun, 1967).

45. Doerr, "Sommerfeldzug 1942—Einzeldarstellungen 1941/43," N29/14, BA-

MA; Zeitzler, "Operationen der 1. Panzerarmee," N63/54; and Manfred Kehrig, *Stalingrad: Analyse und Dokumentation einer Schlacht* (Stuttgart: Deutsche Verlags-Anstalt, 1974), 25–26.

46. Erickson, *Road to Stalingrad*, 344–351; and Doerr, *Feldzug nach Stalingrad*, 16.

47. KTB/OKW, II, 386–396; and Zeitzler, "Operationen der 1. Panzerarmee," N63/54.

48. KTB/OKW, II, 1372–1377.

49. Ibid., 52.

50. Murray, *Luftwaffe*, 119; and Ziemke and Bauer, *Moscow to Stalingrad*, 294, 300–301.

51. Oberkommando der Wehrmacht Nr. 55435/42 g.K.Chefs., 30.6.42, MI14/298, IWM. The pertinent war diaries for Army Group South, Middle, and B are sketchy or no longer exist. Helpful, however, is Herresgruppe A, "Kriegstagebuch, Band 1, 11 Apr–31 Dec 1942," T311/151–152/7198951–7200380, NA.

52. Hubatsch, hrsg., *Hitlers Weisungen*, 196–200; and Ziemke, *Stalingrad to Berlin*, 18–20.

53. OKH/GenStdH/Op.Abt(III) Nr. 420743/42 g.K.Chefs., 21.9.42, AL 1570, IWM.

54. Zeitzler, "2. Jahre Chefs des Generalstabes," N63/18.

55. The best work on Stalingrad is Kehrig, *Stalingrad*. Geoffrey Jukes, *Hitler's Stalingrad Decisions* (Berkeley: University of California Press, 1985), has some helpful material on the command decisions. For concise treatments of the battle, see also Erickson, *Road to Berlin*; and Ziemke, *Stalingrad to Berlin*.

56. Der Führer, GenStdH/Op Abt (I) Nr. 420817/42 g.Kdos.Chefs., "Operationalsbefehl Nr. 1," 14 October 1942, T78/431/6402736, NA.

57. Erickson, *Road to Stalingrad*, 452–453.

58. Kitchen, *British Policy towards the Soviet Union*, 127–145.

59. Jodl, "Die strategische Lage," N68/18.

60. Reinhardt, *Wende vor Moskau*, 291.

61. Zeitzler, "Abwehrschlachten in Russland nach dem Wendepunkt im Kriege," N63/80, BA-MA; Ernst Klink, *Das Gezetz des handelns: Die Operation "Zitadelle" 1943* (Stuttgart: Deutsche Verlags-Anstalt, 1966), 57–58; and Heiber, hrsg., *Lagebesprechungen*, 191–193.

62. KTB/OKW, III, 1420–1421.

63. Ziemke, *Stalingrad to Berlin*, 124–128.

64. The outstanding account is Klink, *Das Gesetz des Handelns*. Citadel is also well covered in Ziemke, *Stalingrad to Berlin*, 118–173; and in Erickson, *Road to Berlin*, 97–129. For views of Red Army participants, see "The Kursk Battle—30 Years," *Soviet Military Review*, 9 (1973): 2–39. Other articles include Michael Parrish, "The Battle of Kursk," *Army Quarterly*, 49 (Oct 1969): 39–51; and Timothy P. Mulligan, "Spies, Ciphers and 'Zitadelle': Intelligence and the Battle of Kursk, 1943," *Journal of Contemporary History*, 22 (Apr 1987): 235–260.

65. KTB/OKW, III, 1425–1427.

66. KTB/OKW, III, 748–750; Guderian, *Panzer Leader*, 306–307; Manstein, *Lost Victories*, 447; Seaton, *Russo-German War*, 356; Clark, *Barbarossa*, 356–362; and Ziemke, *Stalingrad to Berlin*, 130–132.

67. Zeitzler, "Abwehrschlachten in Russland," N63/80; PzAOK4, "Kriegstagebuch II," 29.6.43, T313/365/8650569, NA; and AOK 9, "Kriegstagebuch Nr. 8," 12.6.43, T312/317/7886122, NA.

68. Ziemke, *Stalingrad to Berlin*, 130–132.

69. Klink, *Gesetz des Handelns*, 331–338; KTB/OKW, III, 731–736; and Ziemke, *Stalingrad to Berlin*, 133, 144.

70. For the two thrusts, see, PzAOK 4, "Kriegstagebuch II," 5.7.–18.7.43, T313/365/8650581–8650645; and AOK 9, "Kriegstagebuch Nr. 8," 1.7.–17.8.43, T312/317/7886139–7886232.

71. KTB/OKW, III, 754–755; and PzAOK 4, "Kriegstagebuch II," 7.7.43, T313/365/8650594.

72. Zeitzler, "Abwehrschlachten in Russland," N63/83.

73. Erickson, *Road to Berlin,* 110–111.

74. Ziemke, *Stalingrad to Berlin,* 136–138.

75. Ziemke, *Stalingrad to Berlin,* 112; and Seaton, *Russo-German War,* 367–368.

76. For chilling accounts of the Wehrmacht's treatment of Soviet military prisoners and the Russian population, see Christian Streit, *Keine Kameraden: Die Wehmacht und die sowjetischen kriegsgefangen, 1941–1945* (Stuttgart: Deutsche Verlags-Anstalt, 1978); and Omer Bartov, *The Eastern Front, 1941–45: German Troops and the Barbarisation of Warfare* (London: Macmillan, 1985).

77. Erickson, *Road to Berlin,* 84.

EIGHT. NORTH AFRICA AND SICILY, 1941–1943

1. OKH, Organisations-Abteilung(I) Nr. 908/43 g.K.Chefs., "Überschlägige Kräfteberechnung für das Jahr 1943 und ihre Auswirkung auf die Kampfkraft der Ostfront," 8.8.42, AL 1570, IWM.

2. Gwyer and Butler, *Grand Strategy,* III, 164–165.

3. MC(40)8, "Military Policy in the Middle East," 13 January 1940, CAB 83/4, PRO.

4. DCAS Harris to AMSO, 30.1.41, AIR 8/483, PRO. For a summary of the costly naval attempts to supply Malta, see Dora Alves, "The Resupply of Malta in World War II," *Naval War College Review,* 33 (Sep–Oct, 1980): 63–72.

5. COS(41)417, "Situation in the Middle East," 6.7.41, CAB 80/29, PRO; and JP(41)545, "Situation in the Middle East," 14 July 1941, CAB 84/32, PRO.

6. COS(41)395, "Tank Reinforcements for the Middle East," 22.6.41, CAB 80/28, PRO.

7. COS(41)138(O), "The Situation in the Middle East," 16.7.41, CAB 80/58, PRO.

8. COS(41) 250th Meeting, 17.7.41, CAB 79/12, PRO.

9. COS(41)150(o), "The Middle East," 24.7.41, CAB 80/58, PRO.

10. Gwyer and Butler, *Grand Strategy,* III, 182; COS(41)267th Meeting, 30.7.41, CAB 79/13;, PRO; and COS(41)24th Meeting (O), 30 July 1941, CAB 79/55, PRO.

11. COS(41)176(O), "The Western Desert, Appreciation," 22.8.41, CAB 80/59 PRO; and COS(41)27th Meeting (o), 25.8.41, CAB 79/55, PRO.

12. The most objective account of Crusader remains Ian S. O. Playfair, *The Mediterranean and the Middle East,* vol. 3, *British Fortunes Reach Their Lowest Ebb, Sep 1941–Sep 1942* (London: HMSO, 1960). Other excellent works primarily from an Allied perspective include Correlli Barnett, *The Desert Generals,* rev. ed. (Bloomington: Indiana University Press, 1982); Barrie Pitt, *The Crucible of War: Western Desert, 1941* (London: Jonathan Cape, 1980); and John A. I. Agar-Hamilton and Leonard C. F. Turner, *The Sidi Rezeq Battles, 1941* (London: Oxford University Press, 1957), the last being one of the South African official histories. Among Auchinleck's supporters are John Connell [pseud.], *Auchinleck* (London: Cassell, 1959); Roger Parkinson, *The Auk: Auchinleck, Victor at Alamein* (London: Granada, 1977); and Philip Warner, *Auchinleck: The Lonely Soldier* (London: Macmillan, 1981). For a favorable view of Neil Ritchie, see Michael Carver, *Dilemmas of the Desert War: A New Look at the Libyan Campaign, 1940–1942* (Bloomington: Indiana University Press, 1986). The use of special forces is dealt with in John W. Gordon, *The Other Desert War: British Special Forces in North Africa, 1940–1943* (Westport, CT: Greenwood, 1987).

For the Axis side, see Gerhard Schreiber et al., *Das Deutsche Reich und der Zweite Weltkrieg*, bd. 3, *Der Mittelmeerraum und Südosteuropa: Von der "non belligeranza" Italiens bis zum Kriegseintritt der Vereinigten Staaten* (Stuttgart: Deutsche Verlags-Anstalt, 1984); Rolf Georg Reuth, *Entscheidung im Mittlemeer . . . 1940–1942* (Koblenz: Bernard & Graefe, 1985); and Ronald Lewin, *The Life and Death of the Afrika Korps* (New York: Quadrangle, 1977).

13. Playfair, *Mediterranean and the Middle East*, III, 37–38.

14. Playfair, *Mediterranean and the Middle East*, III, 19; and ME/JP/89, "Middle East Joint Planning Staff Paper No. 66: Opposed Landings," 14 September 1941, WO 201/2355, PRO.

15. JP(41)856, "Possible Action in the Middle East and Mediterranean," 15 October 1941, CAB 84/36, PRO.

16. Kennedy, *Business of War,* 173.

17. Playfair, *Mediterranean and the Middle East*, III, 22–26.

18. Andrew B. Cunningham, *Sailor's Odyssey*, 420.

19. Ibid., 406; and Arthur Tedder, *With Prejudice: The War Memoirs of Marshal of the Royal Air Force, Lord Tedder* (London: Cassell, 1966), 139, 147–152, 175.

20. Playfair, *Mediterranean and the Middle East*, III, 27, 97, 100.

21. Ibid., 12, 15; HQ RAFME to Air Ministry, October 20, 1941, AIR 8/911; PRO; and ACAS(I), "Approximate Number of British and Axis A/C Serviceable in Eastern Mediterranean," 14 November 1941, WO 106/2174, PRO.

22. Playfair, *Mediterranean and the Middle East*, III, 409–410.

23. Hinsley et al., *British Intelligence*, II, 301.

24. Playfair, *Mediterranean and the Middle East*, III, 97; and Schreiber et al., *Das Deutsche Reich*, III, 658.

25. Gwyer and Butler, *Grand Strategy*, III, 230.

26. Schreiber et al., *Das Deutsche Reich*, III, 658.

27. Gordon, *The Other Desert War*, 77–84.

28. The action is well summarized in the personal dispatches from Auchinleck to Churchill, written between November 18 and January 12, and contained in WO 106/2097 and WO 106/2175.

29. Telegram, Private for P.M. from General Auchinleck, 26/11/41, WO 106/2174, PRO.

30. Telegram Private for PM from General Auchinleck, 30.11.41, WO 201/394, PRO.

31. Gilbert, VI, *Finest Hour*, 1252.

32. Telegram Personal P.M. from Gen. Auchinleck, 24/12/41, WO 106/2097, PRO.

33. Playfair, *Mediterranean and the Middle East*, III, 90–91.

34. Ibid., 97.

35. Terraine, *Time for Courage*, 361–362; and Playfair, *Mediterranean and the Middle East*, III, 98–100. Playfair's figures for air losses are slightly less.

36. Carver, *Dilemmas of the Desert War*, 50–54.

37. Schreiber et al., *Das Deutsche Reich*, III, 680.

38. Hinsley et al., *British Intelligence*, II, 283, 304–319. A good summary is contained in Barnett, *Desert Generals*, 119–120.

39. JP(41)1093, "Far East and Middle East," 25.12.41, CAB 79/16, PRO.

40. CAS, "Reinforcement of the Middle East," 4.2.42, AIR 8/509, PRO.

41. JP(42)14(S), "Notes for Meeting with Officers from the Middle East," 3 January 1942, CAB 84/40, PRO.

42. Martin Van Creveld, "Rommel's Supply Problems, 1941–42," *Royal United Services Institution Journal*, 119 (Sep 1974): 67.

43. KTB/OKW, II, 288; Panzerarmee Afrika Ia Nr. 2622/geheim, 14.4.42, RH19

VII/14, BA-MA; and Panzerarmee Afrika Nr. 3502/42 geh., "Tagesmeldung," 6.5.42, RH19 VIII/14, BA-MA.

44. Gundelach, *Die deutsche Luftwaffe im Mittlemeer,* I, 354; and Playfair, *Mediterranean and the Middle East,* III, 220.

45. Abt. für Afrikatransporte Nr. 1314/42 g.Kdos., 1. May 1942, RH 19 VIII/14, BA-MA.

46. Lewin, *Life and Death of Afrika Korps,* 126–127; and Playfair, *Mediterranean and Middle East,* III, 220.

47. Hinsley et al., *British Intelligence,* II, 341.

48. Barnett, *Desert Generals,* 139; and Deutscher General im Hq der ital. Wehrmacht, Ia Nr. 5036/42 g.K.Chefs., 24.3.42, RH 19 VIII/14, BA-MA.

49. KTB/OKW, II, 324; and Panzerarmee Afrika, "Kriegstagebuch Nr. 3," 24.4.–28.4.42, T313/426/8719135–8719139, NA.

50. ADAP, ser. E, II, 315–316; KTB/OKW, II, 101–102; and Oberkommando der Panzerarmee Afrika, Abt. Ia Nr. 31/42 g.Kdos.Chefs., 30.4.42, RH19 VIII/14, BA-MA.

51. Hugh Gibson, ed., *The Ciano Diaries, 1939–1943* (Garden City, NY: Doubleday, 1946), 478–479.

52. In addition to the accounts in Lewin *(Life and Death of Afrika Korps)* and Playfair *(Mediterranean and the Middle East,* III, 197–298), important insights into the Gazala campaign can be gleaned from Basil H. Liddell Hart, ed., *The Rommel Papers,* trans. Paul Findlay (London: Collins, 1953); H. C. Esebeck, *Afrikanische Schicksaljahre: Geschichte des Afrikakorps unter Rommel* (Wiesbaden: Limes, 1949); and Rommel's chief of staff, Alfred Gause, "Der Feldzug in Nordafrika im Jahre 1942," *Wehwissenschaftliche Rundschau,* 12 (Nov 1962): 652–680. Logistical aspects of the operation are covered in Van Creveld, "Rommel's Supply Problems"; and Walter Baum and Eberhard Weichold, *Der Krieg der "Achsenmächte" im Mittelmeerraum* (Göttingen: Musterschmidt, 1973), the latter being particularly good on sea communications. The air role is well described in Gundelach, *Die Deutsche Luftwaffe im Mittelmeer,* I, 366–398. For intelligence reports, see Hans-Otto Behrendt, *Rommels kenntnis vom Feind im Afrikafeldzug: Ein Bericht über die Feindnachrichtenarbeit, insbesondere die Funkaufklärung* (Freiburg: Rombach, 1980).

53. Obd Pz.Armee Afrika (FüAbt), "Kriegstagebuch Nr. 3," 6.5.42, RH 19 VII/13, BA-MA; Oberkommando der Panzerarmee Afrika, Abt Ia Nr. 42/42 g.Kdos.Chefs., "Armeebefehl für den Angriff," 11.5.42, RH 190 VIII/14, BA-MA; and ObdPz.Armee Afrika (Fü Abt), "Kriegstagebuch Nr. 3," 16.5.42, RH19 VIII/13, BA-MA.

54. KTB/OKW, II, 372–373.

55. Carver, *Dilemmas of the Desert War,* 61.

56. Panzerarmee Afrika Nr. 65/42 g.Kdos.Chefs., "Tagesmeldung," 25.5.42, RH19 VIII/14, BA-MA; and [Panzerarmee Afrika], "Kraftevergleich," 25.5.42, T313/426/8719764, NA.

57. Playfair, *Mediterranean and the Middle East,* III, 220; and Gundelach, *Die Deutsche Luftwaffe im Mittelmeer,* I, 377.

58. Lewin, *Life and Death of Afrika Korps,* 58.

59. Kahn, *Hitler's Spies,* 193–195; Barnett, *Desert Generals,* 175, 242–244; and Hinsley et al., *British Intelligence,* II, 383.

60. An excellent summary is in Arbeitsstab Afrika, "Schlachtbericht über die Kampfe der Panzerarmee Afrika," August 1943, RH 19 VIII/20, BA-MA. The battle is also well covered in Lewin, *Life and Death of Afrika Korps,* 126–139. On the Allied side, besides Playfair, see the South African official history, J. A. I. Agar-Hamilton and L. C. F. Turner, *Crisis in the Desert, May–July 1942* (Capetown: Geoffrey Cumberlege, 1952).

61. Panzerarmee Afrika Ia Nr. 65/42 g.Kdos.Chefs., "Tagesmeldung," 25.5.42, T313/426/8719790, NA.

62. *Rommel Papers*, 203, 224.

63. Playfair, *Mediterranean and the Middle East*, III, 275; and Terraine, *Time for Courage*, 375.

64. Barnett, *Desert Generals*, 168.

65. KTB/OKW, II, 440.

66. KTB/OKW, II, 107; and Baum and Weichold, *Krieg der "Achsenmächte,"* 236–237.

67. KTB/OKW, II, 515.

68. Carver, ed., *War Lords*, (Douglas-Home) 79; Van Creveld, "Rommel's Supply Problems," 72; Murray, *Luftwaffe*, 77; and Terraine, *Time for Courage*, 370.

69. Bryant, *Turn of the Tide*, 306, 362.

70. CinC Middle East for CIGS, 5 September 42, WO 106/2104, PRO; and CinC Middle East for CIGS, 1 September 42, WO 106/2104, PRO. See also Barnett, *Desert Generals*, 261–266.

71. Among the excellent books, see Playfair and C. J. C. Molony, *The Mediterranean and the Middle East*, vol. 4, *The Destruction of the Axis Forces in Africa* (London: HMSO, 1966), 1–101; Michael Carver, *El Alamein* (London: Batsford, 1962); Philip Warner, *Alamein* (London: William Kimber, 1979), based on interviews with participants; and Barrie Pitt, *The Crucible of War: Year of Alamein, 1942* (London: Jonathan Cape, 1982). See also portions of Nigel Hamilton, *Master of the Battlefield: Monty's War Years, 1942–1944* (New York: McGraw-Hill, 1984). For an interesting view from an Italian standpoint, see Paolo Caccia-Dominioni, *Alamein, 1933–1962; An Italian Story*, trans. Dennis Chamberlain (London: Allen & Unwin, 1966).

72. MA8A/107/G(P), "Appreciation and Plan: Operation 'Lightfoot,'" 19.8.42, WO 201/432, PRO.

73. Personal Telegram from Prime Minister to Deputy Prime Minister, 21.8.42, AIR 8/1040, PRO.

74. Telegram Most Secret and Personal to P.M. and CIGS from Gen. Alexander, 21.9.42, AIR 8/1039, PRO; and Telegram Personal from P.M. to CinC Middle East, [22.9.42], AIR 8/1039, PRO.

75. Hinsley et al., *British Intelligence*, II, 429–430; and Playfair and Molony, *Mediterranean and the Middle East*, IV, 6.

76. Leighton and Coakley, *Global Logistics and Strategy, 1940–43*, 290.

77. COS(42)160(o), "ME—Review by Commander-in-Chief," June 17, 1942, CAB 84/46, PRO; Playfair and Molony, *Mediterranean and the Middle East*, IV, 3; and Telegram and Personal for CAS from Tedder, 7.9.42AIR 9/1039, PRO.

78. Playfair and Molony, *Mediterranean and the Middle East*, IV, 6.

79. Ibid., 3–9, 30; Lewin, *Life and Death of Afrika Korps*, 163–164; Personal Telegram for CIGS from C-in-C, Middle East, 24 October 42, WO 106/2256, PRO; and H. S. K/1/8, "Diagrammatic Order of Battle—Middle East Forces," 8 October 42, WO 106/2218, PRO.

80. Lewin, *Life and Death of Afrika Korps*, 161–162; and Playfair and Molony, *Mediterranean and the Middle East*, IV, 35.

81. The day-to-day happenings are followed in telegrams from CinC Middle East to War Office, 23 October–7 November 1942, WO 106/2256, PRO. Weekly summaries are scattered among the Cabinet Memoranda, beginning with WP(42)493, 29.10.43, CAB 66/30, PRO, and ending with WP(42)562, 3.12.42, CAB 66/31, PRO. At corps level, see Brian Horrocks, *A Full Life* (London: Collins, 1960); and Rowland Ryder, *Oliver Leese* (London: Hamish Hamilton, 1987).

82. Eighth Army, "Operation 'Supercharge,'" 30 October 1942, WO 214/18, PRO.

83. Playfair and Molony, *Mediterranean and the Middle East*, IV, 477.

84. See especially Barnett, *Desert Generals*, 287–293.

85. Main HQ, Eighth Army, MEF, 19 November 1942, WO 214/18, PRO. Italics in the original.

86. C-in-C Middle East to CIGS, 7 November 42, WO 106/2256, PRO; and Playfair and Molony, *Mediterranean and the Middle East*, IV, 78.

87. Telegram CinC Middle East to War Office, 22 November 42, WO 106/2257, PRO; and Chef Heeresstab/OKW(II), 44/42 g.K.Chefs., 25. November 1942, T78/431/6402784, NA.

88. Tedder, *With Prejudice*, 360; and Telegram C-in-C, Middle East to War Office, 3 November 42, WO 106/2256, PRO.

89. Telegram CinC Middle East to War Office, 6 November 42, WO 106/2256; and Hinsley et al., *British Intelligence*, II, 435–437.

90. Playfair and Molony, *Mediterranean and the Middle East*, IV, 78.

91. Tedder, *With Prejudice*, 367, 357; and Playfair and Molony, *Mediterranean and the Middle East*, IV, 100–101.

92. Hinsley et al., *British Intelligence*, II, 454; Gilbert, *Road to Victory*, VII, 244–247; and Gordon, *Other Desert War*, 150–151.

93. Matloff, *Strategic Planning, 1943–1944*, 379; Albert N. Garland and Howard M. Smyth, *Sicily and the Surrender of Italy* (Washington: USGPO, 1965), 709; and Kennedy, *Business of War*, 276–277.

94. Bryant, ed., *Turn of the Tide*, 437.

95. COS(43)33(O), "Symbol," 28.1.43, CAB 80/67, PRO; and Bryant, *Turn of the Tide*, 458.

96. COS(40)53(O)(JP), "Occupation of Sicily," 24 December 1940, CAB 84/25, PRO.

97. JP(41)191, "Mediterranean Policy," 10 March 1941, CAB 84/28, PRO.

98. Nigel Nicolson, *Alex: The Life of Field Marshal Alexander of Tunis* (London: Pan, 1973), 154; and JP(41)860, "Operation Whipcord," 17 October 1941, AIR 8/911, PRO. The highest-level discussions are well covered in DO(41)64th Meeting, 15.10.41, CAB 69/2; DO(41)65th Meeting, 17.10.41, CAB 69/2 PRO; and DO(41), 69th Meeting, 21.10.41, CAB 69/8, PRO.

99. JP(42)264, "System of Command and Procedure in Planning," 11 March 42, CAB 84/43, PRO; and Cunningham, *Sailor's Odyssey*, 418.

100. JP(42)159th Meeting, 29 Sep 1942, CAB 84/49, PRO.

101. JP(42)886, "Mediterranean Strategy," October 20, 1942, CAB 84/49, PRO; and JP(43)18(Final), "'Brimstone' versus 'Husky,'" 9.1.43, CAB 79/59, PRO.

102. Kennedy, *Business of War*, 294; and COS(42)413(o), "Plans and Operations in the Mediterranean, Middle East and Near East," 24.11.42, CAB 80/66, PRO.

103. JP(43)7(Final), "Operation Husky," January 10, 1943, CAB 79/59, PRO.

104. Michael Howard, *Grand Strategy*, vol. 4, *August 1942–December 1943* (London: HMSO, 1972); and idem, *The Mediterranean Strategy in the Second World War* (New York: Praeger, 1968), 35.

105. The best works on the Sicily campaign remain C. J. C. Molony et al., *The Mediterranean and the Middle East*, vol. 4, *The Campaign in Sicily 1943 and the Campaign in Italy, 3rd September 1943 to 31st March 1944* (London: HMSO, 1973); and Garland and Smyth, *Sicily and the Surrender of Italy*. A controversial overall treatment, Carlo d'Este, *Bitter Victory: The Battle for Sicily 1943* (New York: Dutton, 1988), is particularly scathing on Alexander. Less extensive is S. W. C. Pack, *"Operation Husky": The Allied Invasion of Sicily* (New York: Hippocrene Books, 1977). The memoirs of the naval and air commanders (Cunningham, *Sailor's Odyssey*, and Tedder, *With Prejudice*) are helpful, but those of Lord Alexander of Tunis (*Memoirs 1939–45* [London: Cassell, 1962]) and Lord Montgomery of Alamein (*Memoirs* [London: Collins, 1948]), less so. The accounts of their biographers (Nigel Nicholson, *Alex*, and Hamilton, *Master of the Battlefield, 1942–44*) are of greater assistance. Michael Howard, *Grand Strategy*, IV, 459–467, provides an excellent summary of the planning stages. More

detailed is Alexander S. Cochran, Jr., *Spectre of Defeat: Anglo-American Planning for the Invasion of Italy in 1943*, Ph.D. diss., University of Kansas, 1985, especially valuable on American strategic thinking. The air portion is covered in Harry L. Coles, "Participation of the Ninth and Twelfth Air Forces in the Sicilian Campaign," 1945, USAFHRC 101-37. For insights into political developments in Italy, see Harold Macmillan, *War Diaries: The Mediterranean, 1943–1945* (New York: St. Martin's, 1984).

106. CCS 161/2, "Operation 'Husky,'" 22 March 1943, CAB 88/9, PRO; and CCS 161/5, "Operation 'Husky,'" 25 March 1943, CAB 88/9, PRO.

107. As cited in Howard, *Grand Strategy*, IV, 368–369.

108. Office of Commander-in-Chief Mediterranean, 28 April 1943, AIR 8/1346, PRO; Telegram from Tedder to CAS, 1 May 1943, AIR 8/1346, PRO; and Telegram, Eisenhower to Combined Chiefs, 3 May 43, AIR 8/1346, PRO.

109. Eighth Army, Montgomery to Alexander, 5.5.43, WO 214/21, PRO.

110. Matloff, *Strategic Planning, 1943–1944*, 146.

111. Twelfth Army, GP/202, "Operation Order No. 1," 31 May 43, WO 214/21, PRO.

112. Matloff, *Strategic Planning, 1943–1944*, 147; and Coakley and Leighton, *Global Logistics and Strategy, 1943–1945*, 49.

113. Edith C. Rogers, "The Reduction of Pantelleria and Adjacent Islands, 8 May–14 June 1943," 1945, USAFHRC 101-52.

114. Molony, *Mediterranean and the Middle East*, V, 67–75; and Tedder, *With Prejudice*, 445.

115. The figures are drawn from Molony, *Mediterranean and the Middle East*, V; and Garland and Smyth, *Sicily and the Surrender of Italy*, 91–96.

116. Hinsley et al., *British Intelligence*, 3, Pt 1, 71; and Molony, *Mediterranean and the Middle East*, V, 41–47.

117. Gundelach, *Die deutsche Luftwaffe im Mittelmeer*, II, 616, 621.

118. Daily operations can be followed in the telegrams sent by Field Marshal Alexander to Brooke in London, 10 July–18 August 1943, WO 106/3889, PRO. Excellent weekly summaries are located in the War Cabinet Memoranda, WP(43), 17.7–26.8.43, CAB 66/39 and CAB 66/40.

119. Telegram from General Browning to D.Air, 18 July 43, WO 106/3890, PRO; Telegram Personal for CAS from Tedder, 5 August 43, WO 106/3890, PRO; Field Marshal Alexander's Report to CIGS, "Future of Airborne Forces," 4 September 45, WO 214/21 PRO; and Tedder, *With Prejudice*, 449–450.

120. Hinsley et al., *British Intelligence*, III, pt. 1, 95.

121. Churchill, *Closing the Ring*, 36.

122. MAAF, "An Official Account of Air Operations in the Mediterranean Theater of War, Jan 1943 to May 1945," n.d., AIR 23/6337, PRO.

123. Martin Blumenson, *The Many Faces of George S. Patton, Jr.*, Harmon Memorial Lecture Number 14 (Colorado Springs: USAF Academy, 1972), 21.

124. Cochran, *Spectre of Defeat*, 231; Hinsley et al., *British Intelligence*, III, pt. 1, 69–100.

125. Telegram from Eisenhower to Combined Chiefs, 5 August 32, WO 214/22, PRO.

126. Cunningham, *Sailor's Odyssey*, 539.

127. Matloff, *Strategic Planning, 1943–1944*, 150.

NINE. THE BATTLE OF THE ATLANTIC

1. JP(41)444, "Future Strategy," 13 June 1941, CAB 84/31; and Roskill, *Churchill and the Admirals*, 94–96.

2. Salewski, *Die deutsche Seekriegsleitung*, II, 598–599; and Bird, *German Naval History*, 608–609.

3. Hinsley et al., *British Intelligence*, II, 549. Works on the Battle of the Atlantic abound. Those of Jürgen Rohwer and Sir Stephen Roskill stand out. Among Rohwer's many books and articles, see *The Critical Convoy Battle of 1943: The Battle for HX 229/SC 122* (London: Ian Allen, 1975); and "The U-Boat War against the Allied Supply Lines," in Jacobsen and Rohwer, eds., *Decisive Battles*, 259–312. Roskill's authoritative account is *The War at Sea*, 3 vols. (London: HMSO, 1956–1960). Other general studies include Dan Van der Vat, *The Atlantic Campaign: World War II's Great Struggle at Sea* (New York: Harper, 1988); Leonce Peillard, *La bataille de l'Atlantique*, 2 vols. (Paris: Éditions Robert Laffont, 1974); and the incisive article, Philippe Masson, "Les grandes étapes de la bataille de l'Atlantique," *Revue d'histoire de la deuxième guerre mondiale*, 18 (Jan 1968): 3–28. On the German side, see Jochen Brennecke, *Die Wende im U-boat-Krieg: Ursachen und Folgen, 1939–1943* (Herford: Koehlers Verlagsgesellschaft, 1984); Salewski, *Die Deutsche Seekriegsleitung*, 3 vols., for insights into strategy; and Eberhard Rössler, *The U-Boat: The Evolution and Technical History of German Submarines*, trans. Harold Erenberg (London: Armed and Armour Press, 1981), for technological aspects. Other specific topics are dealt with in Gerhard Hummelchen, *Die deutschen Seeflieger, 1935–1945* (München: Bernard & Graefe, 1976); and Wilhelm Meier-Dörnburg, *Die Ölversorgung der Kriegsmarine, 1935 bis 1945* (Freiburg: Rombach, 1973). The memoirs of Raeder *(My Life)* and Dönitz *(Memoirs)*, as discussed earlier, must be used with caution. Popular works include Cajus Bekker, *Hitler's Naval War*, trans. Frank Ziegler (Garden City, NY: Doubleday, 1974); and Franz Kurowski, *Krieg unter Wasser: U-Boote auf den sieben Meeren, 1939–1943* (Düsseldorf: Econ, 1979). On the British side, see W. S. Chalmers, *Max Horton and the Western Approaches: A Biography of Admiral Sir Max Kennedy Horton* (London: Hodder & Stoughton, 1954); and the various works of Peter Kemp and Brian Schofield, including Kemp, "La protection des convois britanniques," *Revue d'histoire de la deuxième guerre mondiale*, 18 (Jan 1968): 29–40, and Schofield, "The Defeat of the U-Boats during World War II," *Journal of Contemporary History*, 16 (Jan 1981): 119–129. American participation is well covered in Samuel Eliot Morison, *The Atlantic Battle Won, May 1943–May 1945* (Boston: Little, Brown, 1956); and Phillip K. Lundeberg, "La replique des Etats-Unis à la guerre sousmarine," *Revue d'histoire de la deuxième guerre mondiale*, 18 (Jan 1968): 67–96. Canada's contribution is highlighted in Marc Milner, *North Atlantic Run: The Royal Canadian Navy and the Battle for the Convoys* (Toronto: University of Toronto Press, 1985); idem, "Convoy Escorts: Tactics, Technology and Innovation in the Royal Canadian Navy, 1939–1943," *Military Affairs*, 48 (Jan 1984): 19–25; and W. A. B. Douglas, "Kanadas Marine und Luftwaffe in der Atlantik-Schlacht," *Marine Rundschau*, 77 (Mar 1980): 151–164.

4. Dönitz, *Memoirs*, 227–228.

5. BdU, "Kriegstagebuch," 1. September 1942, N236/2, BA-MA.

6. Roskill, *War at Sea*, II, 467–471, 475, 485–486.

7. As cited in Roskill, *Churchill and the Admirals*, 138.

8. COS(42) 187th Meeting (D), 23.11.42, CAB 79/58, PRO.

9. Roskill, *Churchill and the Admirals*, 229.

10. CCS 155/1, "Conduct of the War in 1943," January 19, 1943, CAB 80/67, PRO.

11. Salewski, *Die deutsche Seekriegsleitung*, II, 225–245; and Philip Joubert de la Ferté, *Birds and Fishes: The Story of Coastal Command* (London: Hutchinson, 1952), 183–184.

12. Rohwer, *Critical Convoy*, 112, 188.

13. Alexander to Sinclair, January 30, 1941, ADM 205/56, PRO.

14. Rohwer, *Critical Convoy*, 47. Rohwer's figures generally agree with those in BdU, "Kriegstagebuch," 15. March 1943, N236/2, BA-MA.

15. Carver, *War Lords* (Kemp), 476; and Morison, *Atlantic Battle Won*, 60.

16. Rohwer, *Critical Convoy*, 38.

17. Ibid., 27–36; Milner, *North Atlantic Run*, 66; and CCS 203, "Measures for Combatting the Submarine Force," April 24, 1943, CAB 88/11, PRO.

18. Hq, Coastal Command, 5/7001/4/ Air Tactics, "Coastal Command Tactical Memorandum No. 31," 10 May 1942, AIR 15/31, PRO; and 4038/Air, 27 May 1943, AIR 15/32, PRO.

19. Alexander to Prime Minister, 17 March 1943, ADM 205/27, PRO; AU(43) 84, "The Value of the Bay of Biscay's Patrols," 22 March 1943, CAB 86/3, PRO; and AU(43) 102, "The Bombing of the U-Boat Bases," 29 March 1943, CAB 86/4, PRO.

20. Besides in Rohwer and Roskill, the activities are outlined from the German side in Seekriegsleitung, "Kriegstagebuch, Teil A," (trans.), 1 December 1942–8 June 1943, Iowa State University Parks Library; and from the British side in WP(43), "Weekly Résumé," 1.1–10.6.43, CAB 66/27–37, PRO. A summary of the convoys and the U-boat groups are contained in "Battle of the Atlantic, Vol. II, U-Boat Operations," appendix A to pt. A, RG 457, SRH-008, NA; and Jürgen Rohwer, *Axis Submarine Successes* (Annapolis: US Naval Institute, 1983). British decryptions can be found in "German Navy-U-Boat Message Translations," 1 December 1942–31 May 1943, RG 457, SRGN 6628–SRGN 19198, NA. Specific convoy battles are related in Martin Middlebrook, *Convoy: The Battle for Convoys SC 122 and HX 229* (London: Alan Lane, 1976); and Sir Peter Gretton, *Crisis Convoy: The Story of HX 231* (London: Peter Davies, 1974).

21. "Battle of the Atlantic," II, SRH-008, 21–25.

22. First Sea Lord to Prime Minister, 9 February 1943, ADM 205/27, PRO.

23. COMSUBS to U-125, 14 December 1942, 1342/14/98/1828, SRGN 7313; COMSUBS to U-515, 31 December 1942, 1008/31/171, SRGN 8444; and COMSUBS to All Subs in Areas B-C-E-F, 31 December 1942, 1005/31/172/324/872/443, SRGN 8443.

24. COMSUBS to All Subs on Hubertus Circuit, 14 December 1942, 1128/14/812, SRGN 7306; Mansack to COMSUBS, 10 December 1942, 0747/10/5, SRGN 7176; COMSUBS to Raufbold Group, 16 December 1942, 2053/16/275, SRGN 7519; and COMSUBS to All Subs in Area A, 9 December 1942, 2234/9/96, SRGN 7159.

25. "Battle of the Atlantic," II, SRH-008, 33–46; Anti-Submarine Warfare Division, Naval Staff, "Analysis of U-Boat Operations in the Vicinity of SC 121, HX 228, SC 122, and HX 229, March 1943," 15 April 1943, ADM 199/2019, PRO; Seekriegsleitung, "Kriegstagebuch, Teil A," vol. 43, 4–24 March 1943; and Milner, *North Atlantic Run*, 234–235.

26. COMSUBS to All Subs in Series 8A, 19 March 1943, 1738/19/84, SRGN 13854.

27. Rohwer, *Critical Convoy*, 186–187.

28. COMSUBS to Boats of "Raubgraf" and "Sturmer" Groups, 21 March 1943, 1036/21/736/138/814, SRGN 14058.

29. Seekriegsleitung, "Kriegstagebuch, Teil A," vol. 43, 24 March 1943.

30. Roskill, *War at Sea*, II, 367–368.

31. Hinsley et al., *British Intelligence*, II, 561–562.

32. Staff Officer (Intelligence), St. John's [Newfoundland], "Submarine Appreciation Bulletin No. 33," 200/13/3/43, ADM 199/241, PRO; and Kahn, *Hitler's Spies*, 221–222.

33. Roskill, *War at Sea*, II, 371.

34. Seekriegsleitung, "Kriegstagebuch, Teil A," vol. 45, 8 May 1943.

35. "Battle of the Atlantic," II, SRH-008, 76–77.

36. Seekriegsleitung, "Kriegstagebuch, Teil A," vol. 45, 23 May 1943.

37. Hinsley et al., *British Intelligence*, II, 572; COS(43)281(O), "Trident (Part II)," 3 June 1943, CAB 80/70, PRO; AU(43)19th Meeting, 26 May 1943, CAB 86/2; and Pound to Cunningham, 30 May 1943, Cunningham Correspondence, MS 52561, BML.

38. Roskill, *War at Sea*, II, 485–486; and BdU, "Kriegstagebuch," 1. February–15. June 1943, N236/2.

39. CCS, 4th[?] Meeting, January 15, 1943, CAB 80/67, PRO; and CCS 160, "Minimum Escort Requirements to Maintain the Sea Communications of the United Nations," January 19, 1943, CAB 80/67, PRO.

40. AU(43)68, "Security of North Atlantic Convoys," March 8, 1943, CAB 86/3, PRO.

41. CCS, 4th[?] Meeting, January 15, 1943, CAB 80/67.

42. CCS 189/2, "VLR Aircraft for Anti-Submarine Duty," March 28, 1943, CAB 88/10, PRO; AU(43)107, "Anti-U-boat Warfare," 31 March 1943, CAB 86/4, PRO; and Roskill, *War at Sea*, II, 364.

43. CCS, 80th Meeting, April 16, 1943, CAB 88/2, PRO.

44. CPS 64/9, "Very Long Range Aircraft for Anti-Submarine Duty," May 5, 1943, CAB 88/55, PRO.

45. CPS, 64/13, "Very Long Range Aircraft for Anti-Submarine Duty," 2 June 1943, CAB 88/55, PRO.

46. Coastal Command, AMWR, "Weekly Statistical Analysis," 3–31 May 1943, AIR 22/164, PRO.

47. Morison, *Atlantic Battle Won*, 89; and Rohwer, *Critical Convoy*, 198–199.

48. Kahn, *Hitler's Spies*, 221–222; Cunningham, *Sailor's Odyssey*, 579; "Battle of the Atlantic, Vol. I, Allied Communications Intelligence, Dec 1942–May 1945," 24–30, RG 457, SRH-009, NA; and Rohwer, *Critical Convoy*, 37. See also Rohwer, "Ultra, XB-Dienst und Magic: Ein Vergleich ihrer Rolle für die Schlacht im Atlantik und den Krieg im Pazifik," *Marine Rundschau*, 76 (Oct 1979): 637–648; and idem, "La radiotelegraphie auxilliare du commandement dans la guerre sousmarine," *Revue d'histoire de la deuxième guerre mondiale*, 18 (Jan 1968): 41–66.

49. AU(42) 1st Meeting, 4 November 1942, CAB 86/2. The minutes of its meetings and appendices are located in CAB 86/2–7.

50. COS(43)33(O), "Symbol," 28.1.43, CAB 80/67, PRO.

51. "Atlantic Convoy Conference," 1–12 March 1943, AIR 8/1083, PRO; Morison, *Atlantic Battle Won*, 19–20; Roskill, *War at Sea*, II, 358; and Milner, *North Atlantic Run*, 230–234.

52. Salewski, *Die deutsche Seekriegsleitung*, II, 305; and Roskill, *War at Sea*, II, 377.

53. Roskill, *Churchill and the Admirals*, 263; and Roskill, *War at Sea*, III, 1, 364.

54. Beesly, *Very Special Intelligence*, 198, 202; Roskill, *War at Sea*, III, 1, 47, 375; and "Battle of the Atlantic," II, SRH-008, 112.

55. Terraine, *Time for Courage*, 244; and US Fleet Hdqrs., "Digest of Minutes: Conference on Anti-Submarine Warfare," August 10, 1943, ADM 1/12732, PRO.

56. Coakley and Leighton, *Global Logistics*, 838.

57. Roskill, *Churchill and the Admirals*, 135, 139.

58. Coakley and Leighton, *Global Logistics*, 842.

59. Jacobsen and Rohwer, *Decisive Battles*, (Rohwer) 312.

60. Roskill, *War at Sea*, II, 367; Beesly, *Very Special Intelligence*, 181; AU(43)90,

"Battle of the Atlantic," March 22, 1943, CAB 86/3, PRO; and Western Approaches Command, "General Survey of Events: 15th–31st March 1943," n.d., ADM 199/631, PRO.

TEN. STRATEGIC BOMBING VS. AIR DEFENSE

1. As on the Battle of the Atlantic, numerous works have been written on strategic bombing and air defense during the war. One cardinal difference, however, is that while archival materials are abundant on Britain's Bomber Command, and also on the United States' strategic air forces, those on the Luftwaffe are much more scattered and difficult to locate since the German Air Ministry destroyed its records just before the war ended. On the British side, the standard treatment is Webster and Frankland, *The Strategic Air Offensive*, 4 vols. An excellent summary of the British official history is contained in Noble Frankland, *The Bombing Offensive against Germany: Outline and Perspectives* (London: Faber & Faber, 1965). Three other noteworthy general studies are Max Hastings, *Bomber Command* (New York: Dial, 1979); Anthony Verrier, *The Bomber Offensive* (New York: Macmillan, 1969); and on a broader scale, John Terraine, *Time for Courage*. An outstanding statistical compilation, including some figures on damages to German cities, is Martin Middlebrook and Chris Everitt, *The Bomber Command War Diaries: An Operational Reference Book, 1939–1945* (New York: Viking, 1985). The American contribution is dealt with in Wesley F. Craven and James L. Cate, eds., *Europe: Torch to Pointblank, August 1942 to December 1943* (Chicago: University of Chicago Press, 1949); and that of Pathfinder's marking aircraft in Gordon Musgrove, *Pathfinder Force: A History of 8 Group* (London: MacDonald & Jane's, 1976); and D. C. T. Bennett, *Pathfinder* (London: Muller, 1958). An excellent article is Roger Beaumont, "The Bomber Offensives as a Second Front," *Journal of Contemporary History*, 22 (Jan 1987): 3–19. Two books on the controversial Bomber Command leader, Air Marshal Sir Arthur Harris, are Harris's own, *Bomber-Offensive* (London: Collins, 1947); and Dudley Saward, *'Bomber' Harris: The Story of Marshal of the Royal Air Force Sir Arthur Harris* . . . (London: Cassell/Buchan & Enright, 1984). On the German side, nothing rivals Webster and Frankland, but three excellent works which include portions of Germany's air defense effort are Horst Boog, *Die deutsche Luftwaffenführung*; Murray, *Luftwaffe*; and Overy, *Air War*. A short treatment is Karl-Heinz Volker, "Die deutsche Heimatluftverteidigung im Zweiten Weltkrieg," *Wehrwissenschaftliche Rundschau*, 16 (Feb 1966): 87–111. Edward Homze, *German Military Aviation: A Guide to the Literature* (New York: Garland, 1984), has references to air defense, and though dated, the 1948 British Air Ministry history, as pirated in works by W. H. Tantum IV and E. J. Hoffschmidt, eds. (*The Rise and Fall of the German Air Force (1933 to 1945)* [Old Greenwich, CT: WE, Inc., 1969]), and Harold Faber (*Luftwaffe: A History* [New York: Quadrangle, 1977]) contains useful information. Interesting, but of tangential value, are the USAF/GAF studies by Richard Suchenwirth (*Command and Leadership in the German Air Force* [Montgomery, AL: Air University, 1969]) and Andreas Nelson (*The German Air Force General Staff* [New York: Arno Press, 1959]). More pertinent is Richard J. Overy, "Hitler and Air Strategy," *Journal of Contemporary History*, 15 (Jul 1980): 405–422. On a more popular level are Franz Kurowski, *Der Luftkrieg über Deutschland* (Düsseldorf: Econ, 1977); and Alfred Price, *Battle over the Reich* (New York: Scribner's, 1977). Additional facts and figures are available in USSBS, *Effect of Strategic Bombing*; Wolfgang Dierich, *Die Verbände der Luftwaffe, 1935–1945: Gliederungen und Kurzchroniken—Eine Dokumentation* (Stuttgart: Motorbuch Verlag, 1976); and Olaf Groehler, "Starke, Verteilung und Verluste der deutschen Luftwaffe im Zweiten Weltkrieg," *Militärgeschichte*, 17 (1978): 316–336. Treatments of specific topics include Earl Beck, *Under the Bombs: The German Home Front, 1942–45* (Lexington: University

of Kentucky Press, 1986); Boog, "German Air Intelligence in World War II," *Aerospace Historian,* 33 (Jun 1986): 121–129; and Overy's seminal "The Luftwaffe and the European Economy, 1939–1945," *Militärgeschichte Mitteilungen,* 26, 2 (1979): 55–78. Two biographies of Göring which concentrate on his role in the air war are Overy, *Goering: The 'Iron Man'* (London: Routledge & Kegan Paul, 1984); and Asher Lee, *Goering—Air Leader* (London: Duckworth, 1972). For works on air production chief· Field Marshal Erhard Milch, see David Irving, *The Rise and Fall of the Luftwaffe: The Life of Field Marshal Erhard Milch* (Boston: Little, Brown, 1974), one of his best works but still subject to criticism in Theo Osterkamp, *Tragödie der Luftwaffe? Kritische Begnungs mit dem gleichmassigen Werk von Irving/Milch* (Neckargemünd: Vowinckel, 1971). On fighter operations, see Adolf Galland, *The First and the Last: German Fighter Forces in World War II,* trans. Mervyn Savill (London: Methuen, 1955). Among the many books on individual bombing campaigns, see Charles Messenger's brief *Cologne: The First 1000-Bomber Raid* (London: Ian Allen, 1982); and Martin Middlebrook, *The Battle of Hamburg: Allied Air Forces against a German City in 1943* (New York: Scribner's, 1980).

2. Butler, *Grand Strategy,* II, 410–411.

3. Middlebrook and Everitt, *Bomber Command War Diaries,* 122–229.

4. Murray, *Luftwaffe,* 130–131, 182; and Price, *Battle over the Reich,* 19.

5. Middlebrook and Everitt, *Bomber Command War Diaries,* 122–224; and Hastings, *Bomber Command,* 117–118.

6. Butler, *Grand Strategy,* II, 415; Gwyer and Butler, *Grand Strategy,* III, 523; and Middlebrook and Everitt, *Bomber Command War Diaries,* 122, 219.

7. Bomber Command, "Monthly Operational Summary," September 1940, AIR 14/934, PRO; and Bomber Command, "Monthly Operational Summary," September 1941, AIR 14/934, PRO.

8. Portal to Lord Beaverbrook, 5.7.41, AIR 8/339, PRO.

9. Prime Minister's Personal Minute, 27.9.41, AIR 8/258, PRO.

10. Quoted in Webster and Frankland, *Strategic Air Offensive,* I, 184–185.

11. DO(42)6, 22.1.42, CAB 69/4, PRO.

12. DO(42)14, "Bombing Policy," 9.2.42, CAB 69/4, PRO; and Webster and Frankland, *Strategic Air Offensive,* I, 323–324.

13. JIC(42)117(O) (Final), "Effect of Bombing Policy," 6.4.42, CAB 79/20, PRO; and DO(42)47, "The Bombing of Germany," 20.5.42, CAB 69/4, PRO.

14. Portal to Harris, 14 June 1942, AIR 8/407, PRO.

15. COS(42)71(O), "Future Strategy," 21.3.42, CAB 80/61, PRO; COS(42)171(O), "The Bombing of Germany," 16.6.42, CAB 80/63, PRO; COS(42)183(0), "The Bombing of Germany," 23.6.42, CAB 80/63, PRO; and Kennedy, *Business of War,* 246.

16. Harris to Churchill, 17 June 1942, AIR 8/405, PRO.

17. Verrier, *Bomber Offensive,* 160.

18. Murray, *Luftwaffe,* 182; Boog, *Die deutsche Luftwaffenführung,* 148; and Middlebrook and Everitt, *Bomber Command War Diaries,* 229–333.

19. Tantum and Hoffschmidt, eds., *Rise and Fall of the German Air Force,* 415–416.

20. Webster and Frankland, *Strategic Air Offensive,* I, 316–317; and Terraine, *Time for Courage,* 515–516.

21. Hastings, *Bomber Command,* 173–174, 416–424; and Middlebrook and Everitt, *Bomber Command War Diaries,* 240–241.

22. Webster and Frankland, *Strategic Air Offensive,* I, 419.

23. Hinsley et al., *British Intelligence,* II, 235–236, 244.

24. Hastings, *Bomber Command,* 425–427; and Price, *Battle over the Reich,* 201.

25. The raid is well covered in Webster and Frankland, *Strategic Air Offensive,*

I, 405–409; Middlebrook and Everitt, *Bomber Command War Diaries*, 272–273; and Terraine, *Time for Courage*, 483–488.

26. Harris to Air Vice Marshal W. A. Coryton, Hdqrs. No. 5 Group, 20 May 1942, AIR 14/2024, PRO.

27. No. 5 Group, "Amendment List No. 2 to 5 Group Operation Order No. B-758," 26 May 1942, AIR 14/2024, PRO.

28. Bomber Command, "Bombing Operation on 30/31st May 1942," n.d., AIR 14/929, PRO.

29. Webster and Frankland, *Strategic Air Offensive*, I, 340.

30. Webster and Frankland, *Strategic Air Offensive*, I, 410–417; Bomber Command, "Bombing Operation on 1/2 June 1942," n.d., AIR 14/929, PRO; and Bomber Command, "Bombing Operation on 25/26th June 1942," n.d., AIR 14/929, PRO.

31. Middlebrook and Everitt, *Bomber Command War Diaries*, 313–314.

32. Webster and Frankland, *Strategic Air Offensive*, I, 309, 315.

33. Middlebrook and Everitt, *Bomber Command War Diaries*, 229–340. Their figures do not deviate appreciably from those in Hastings, *Bomber Command*, 413.

34. Bomber Command, "Monthly Operational Summary," May, June, September 1942, AIR 14/934, PRO; and AMWR, "Weekly Statistical Analysis . . . ," 4.1–13.9.42, AIR 22/162, PRO.

35. Middlebrook and Everitt, *Bomber Command War Diaries*, 275.

36. Air Minister Sinclair to Churchill, n.d., AIR 8/405, PRO; and CAS to Prime Minister, 4.9.42, AIR 8/405, PRO.

37. Great Britain, *Statistical Digest*, 152–157.

38. Craven and Cate, eds., *Europe: Torch to Pointblank*, 841–843.

39. Murray, *Luftwaffe*, 182; Boog, *Die deutsche Luftwaffenführung*, 148; Volker, "Die deutsche Heimatluftverteidigung," 96–97; and Hinsley et al., *British Intelligence*, II, 521.

40. Frankland, *Bombing Offensive against Germany*, 101.

41. Webster and Frankland, *Strategic Air Offensive*, I, 343.

42. CCS 166, "The Bomber Offensive from the United Kingdom," January 20, 1943, CAB 88/9 PRO; and Terraine, *Time for Courage*, 441, 544–545.

43. Terraine, *Time for Courage*, 515–517; Hinsley et al., *British Intelligence*, III, 1, 294–296; Heiber, hrsg., *Hitlers Lagebesprechungen*, 295, 298; Galland, *First and the Last*, 160–165; KTB/OKW, III, 826–877; and Irving, *Rise and Fall of the Luftwaffe*, 246.

44. Terraine, *Time for Courage*, 515–517; Volker, "Die deutsche Heimatluftverteidigung," 101–103; Price, *Battle over the Reich*, 68–70, 100–103; Hastings, *Bomber Command*, 268–273; and Murray, *Luftwaffe*, 203–205.

45. Price, *Battle over the Reich*, 32–33; and Hinsley et al., *British Intelligence*, III, 1, 291–292.

46. Middlebrook and Everitt, *Bomber Command War Diaries*, 362–363, 390, 409.

47. Middlebrook and Everitt, *Bomber Command War Diaries*, 410–416; and Terraine, *Time for Courage*, 545–548.

48. Middlebrook and Everitt, *Bomber Command War Diaries*, 417–418, 445; and Craven and Cate, eds., *Europe: Torch to Pointblank*, 480–484.

49. Middlebrook and Everitt, *Bomber Command War Diaries*, 446, 456–457; and Murray, *Luftwaffe*, 202.

50. Middlebrook and Everitt, *Bomber Command War Diaries*, 340–462.

51. Bomber Command, September 1942, AIR 14/934; PRO; and Bomber Command, "Monthly Operational Summary," AIR 14/934, PRO.

52. Craven and Cate, eds., *Europe: Torch to Pointblank*, 843–852.

53. Bomber Command, "Monthly Operational Summary," September 1944, AIR 14/934, PRO.

54. Great Britain, *Statistical Digest*, 152–157.

55. USSBS, *Effects of Strategic Bombing*, 149; Boog, *Die deutsche Luftwaffenführung*, 140, 148; Terraine, *Time for Courage*, 543; Murray, *Luftwaffe*, 182; and Speer, *Inside the Third Reich*, 363.

56. Murray, *Luftwaffe*.

57. Ibid., 226–230.

58. Middlebrook and Everitt, *Bomber Command War Diaries*.

59. Boog, *Die deutsche Luftwaffenführung*, 90, 210; Gregor Janssen, *Das Ministerium Speer: Deutschlands Rüstung im Krieg* (Berlin: Ullstein, 1969), 336; and Overy, *Air War*, 150.

60. Great Britain, *Statistical Digest*, 152–157.

61. Volker, "Die deutsche Heimatluftverteidigung," 167.

62. Gwyer and Butler, *Grand Strategy*, III, 542; and Frankland, *Bombing Offensive against Germany*, 108.

63. Overy, *Air War*, 123.

64. Frankland, *Bombing Offensive against Germany*, 108.

65. *From Apes to Warlords: The Autobiography (1904–1946)* (London: Hamish Hamilton, 1978).

ELEVEN. BURMA AND WESTERN EUROPE, 1944–1945

1. The pertinent official history is S. Woodburn Kirby, *The War against Japan*, vol. 3, *The Decisive Battles* (London: HMSO, 1961). An excellent general account, especially helpful on Japanese actions, is Louis Allen, *Burma: The Longest War, 1941–45* (London: J. M. Dent, 1984); and Mountbatten's retrospective *Report to the Combined Chiefs of Staff: South-East Asia, 1943–1945* (London: HMSO, 1951), though overly laudatory, contains important information. For a strategic appraisal, see Raymond Callahan, *Burma, 1942–1945* (London: Davis-Poynter, 1978); parts of Thorne, *Allies of a Kind;* and Ehrman, *Grand Strategy*, V. Two shorter works are E. D. Smith, *Battle for Burma* (New York: Holmes & Meier, 1979); and M. G. Abhyankar, *The War in Burma, 1943–45*, 4th ed. (Dehra Dun: Natraj Publishers, 1974). The American viewpoint is told in Charles F. Romanus and Riley Sunderland, *Stilwell's Command Problems* (Washington: USGPO, 1956). The exploits of the legendary Fourteenth Army commander, Viscount Slim, are recounted in his own *Defeat into Victory* (London: Cassell, 1956); and in Ronald Lewin, *Slim the Standard-Bearer: The Official Biography of Field Marshal the Viscount Slim* (Hamdem, CT: Archon, 1976).

2. Kimball, *Churchill and Roosevelt*, II, 274.

3. Ismay, *Memoirs*, 309; Bryant, ed., *Turn of the Tide*, 567; and Roskill, *Churchill and the Admirals*, 250, 259–260. See also John J. Sbrega, "Anglo-American Relations and the Selection of Mountbatten as Supreme Allied Commander, South East Asia," *Military Affairs*, 46 (Oct 82): 139–145.

4. CCS 154, "Operations in Burma, 1943," 17 January 1943, CAB 88/9, PRO.

5. JP(43)148(S), "Alternative Operations Possible for Field Marshal Wavell to Carry out in 1943/44," 20 April 1943, CAB 84/53, PRO; and JP(43)165 (Final), "Operation 'Anakim,'—Possible Alternatives," April 27, 1943, CAB 84/53, PRO.

6. CCS, 84th Meeting (Revised), "Trident," May 14, 1943, CAB 88/2, PRO; and CCS 242/6, "Final Report to the President and Prime Minister," 25 May 1943, CAB 80/70, PRO.

7. COS(43)471(O), "Quadrant (Part I)," 17 August 1943, CAB 80/73, PRO; COS(Q)20, "The Burma Road," 13 August 1943, CAB 80/73, PRO; CCS 319/1, "Progress

Report to the President and Prime Minister," 21 August 1943, CAB 80/73, PRO; and COS(43)489(O), "Quadrant (Part V)," 31 August 1943, CAB 80/73, PRO.

8. JP(43)351 (Final), "Operations in South-East Asia in 1944," 6 October 1943, CAB 84/57, PRO.

9. CCS 327/1, "Operations from India," 28 September 1943, CAB 88/17, PRO.

10. Kirby, *War against Japan*, III, 455.

11. CCS 393, "Meeting between Generalissimo Chiang Kai-Shek and Admiral Mountbatten," 9 November 43, CAB 88/20, PRO.

12. CCS 26/1, "Report to the President and Prime Minister," 6 December 1943, CAB 80/77, PRO.

13. CCS 452/1, "Cancellation of Operation 'Pigstick,'" 6 January 1944, CAB 88/22, PRO.

14. COS(43)791(O), 25 February 44, CAB 80/77, PRO; and CCS 419, "Policy Decisions—South-East Asia Command," 4 December 1943, CAB 80/77, PRO.

15. JP(44)33(E)(T of R), "Operations in South-East Asia—Telegram SEACOS 85," 2 February 44, CAB 84/60, PRO; and Ehrman, *Grand Strategy*, V, 405–407.

16. CCS 300/2, "Estimate of Enemy Situation, 1944—Pacific and Far East," 18 November 43, CAB 80/77, PRO; Hq. South East Asia Command SAC (43) 96, "Alternative Plan to 'Tarzan,'" 1 December 1943, WO 203/1534, PRO; and Allen, *Burma*, 188.

17. MO 12, "Field Army—SEAC and India Commands," 8 November 43, 29 February 44, 19 April 44, WO 106/4589, PRO; MO 12, "Comparison of Forces—Burma," 25 April 44, WO 106/4589, PRO; and Allen, *Burma*, 662.

18. Mountbatten, *Report to the Combined Chiefs*, 19; Kirby, *War against Japan*, III, 387–390; and Allen, *Burma*, 337.

19. JP(44)50 (Final), "Transport Aircraft and Long-Range Penetration Groups in South East Asia Command," 20 February 1944, CAB 79/70, PRO.

20. Mountbatten, *Report to the Combined Chiefs*, 276.

21. Besides in the extended account in Allen, daily combat is summarized in a series of telegrams, mostly from Mountbatten to the chiefs of staff, and contained in Telegrams, 4th Feb–17th Mar 1944, WO 106/4654, PRO; 5th Feb–15th Jun 1944, WO 106/4531, PRO; and 17th May–17th Jul 1944, WO 106/4710, PRO. Two excellent studies of individual campaigns are Arthur Swinson, *Kohima* (London: Cassell, 1966); and Shelford Bidwell, *The Chindit War: Stilwell, Wingate, and the Campaign in Burma, 1944* (New York: Macmillan, 1979).

22. Allen, *Burma*, 638.

23. Supreme Allied Commander's Dispatch, Part II, "Operations in SEAC," n.d., 92, WO 203/5601, PRO.

24. Allen, *Burma*, 644; and Supreme Allied Commander's Dispatch, 140, WO 203/5601.

25. Haywood S. Hansell, Jr., *Strategic Air War against Japan* (Maxwell AFB, AL: Airpower Research Institute, 1980) 45–48.

26. Callahan, *Burma, 1942–1945*, 163.

27. COS(44)236th Meeting (o), 14 July 1944, CAB 79/77, PRO; and COS(44)262 Meeting (O), 7 August 1944, CAB 79/79, PRO.

28. Outstanding treatments of Overlord are Max Hasting's sobering *Overlord: D-Day, June 6, 1944* (New York: Simon & Schuster, 1984); and John Keegan's imaginative *Six Armies in Normandy: From D-Day to the Liberation of Paris, June 6th–August 25, 1944* (New York: Viking, 1982). The three most pertinent official histories—Lyle F. Ellis, *Victory in the West*, vol. 1, *The Battle of Normandy* (London: HMSO, 1962); Gordon A. Harrison, *Cross-Channel Attack* (Washington: USGPO, 1951); and Martin Blumenson, *Breakout and Pursuit* (Washington: USGPO, 1962)—have stood up well over time. Naval aspects of the campaign are detailed in Roskill, *War at Sea*, III;

Samuel Eliot Morison, *The Invasion of France and Germany, 1944–1945* (Boston: Little, Brown, 1957); and Brian B. Schofield, *Operation Neptune* (London: Ian Allen, 1974). Aerial aspects are covered in Wesley F. Craven and James L. Cate, eds., *The Army Air Forces in World War II*, vol. 3, *Europe: Argument to V-E Day, January 1944 to May 1945* (Chicago: University of Chicago Press, 1951); Walter Rostow, *Pre-Invasion Bombing Strategy* (Austin: University of Texas Press, 1981); and in a comparative article, Henry D. Lytton, "Bombing Policy in the Rome and Pre-Normandy Invasion Aerial Campaigns of World War II: Bridge-Bombing Strategy Vindicated—and Railyard Bombing Strategy Invalidated," *Military Affairs*, 47 (Apr 83): 53–58. Among the participants, see Sir Frederick E. Morgan, *Overture to Overlord* (New York: Doubleday, 1950); Dwight D. Eisenhower, *Crusade in Europe* (New York: Doubleday, 1948); Tedder, *With Prejudice;* and Viscount Montgomery of Alamein, *Normandy to the Baltic: A Personal Account of the Conquest of Germany* (London: Hutchinson, 1947), the last being the least valuable of the memoirs listed. Insightful on the Allied commanders is Weigley, *Eisenhower's Lieutenants*. Intelligence and deception activities are described in Hinsley et al., *British Intelligence*, III, pt. 2; Ralph Bennett, *Ultra in the West: The Normandy Campaign, 1944–45* (London: Hutchinson, 1979); idem, "Ultra and Some Command Decisions," *Journal of Contemporary History*, 16 (Jan 1981): 131–151; Charles Cruickshank, *Deception in World War II* (New York: Oxford University Press, 1979); and the popular account, Chenwynd J. D. Haswell, *The Intelligence and Deception of the D-Day Landings* (London: Batsford, 1979). The German side is discussed most thoroughly in Remy Desquesnes, *Atlantikwall et Südwall: Les défenses allemandes sur le littoral français (1941–1944)*, Ph.D. diss. Université de Caen, 1987. But see also Dieter Ose, *Entscheidung im Westen, 1944: Der Oberbefehlshaber West und die Abwehr der Allierten Invasion* (Stuttgart: Deutsche Verlags-Anstalt, 1982); Hans Wegmüller, *Die Abwehr der Invasion: Die Konzeption des Oberbefehlshaber West, 1940–1944* (Freiburg i.Br.: Rombach, 1979); and Alan Wilt, *The Atlantic Wall: Hitler's Defenses in the West, 1941–1944* (Ames: Iowa State University Press, 1975). The command controversy in the west is examined in Ose, "Rommel and Rundstedt: The 1944 Panzer Controversy," *Military Affairs*, 50 (Jan 1986): 7–11; and assessments by German commanders and staff officers in *The Rommel Papers;* Fredrich Ruge, *Rommel in Normandy* (San Rafael, CA: Presidio Press, 1978); Hans Speidel, *Invasion 1944*, trans. Theo Crevanna (New York: Paperback Library, 1968); and Siegfried Westphal, *The German Army in the West* (London: Cassell, 1951). General Günther Blumentritt's biography (*Von Rundstedt, The Soldier and the Man*, trans. Cuthbert Reavely [London: Odhams, 1952]) is also helpful. An attempt to put the invasion in a broader context is Wilt, "The Invasion of Europe: The Opening of the Western Front, 1943–44," in *Unesco Yearbook and Conflict Studies 1985* (Westport, CT: Greenwood, 1987), 153–174.

29. Ellis, *Victory in the West*, I, 14–16; Harrison, *Cross-Channel Attack*, 56–57; and Churchill, *Closing the Ring*, 61.

30. COS(42)288(O), "Future Strategy," 30.9.42, CAB 80/64, PRO; COS(942)293(O), "Planning for Offensive Operations in North-West Europe in 1943 and 1944," 4.10.42, CAB 80/64, PRO; and COS(42)421(O), "Future Strategy," 29.11.42, CAB 80/66, PRO.

31. Harrison, *Cross-Channel Attack*, 46.

32. Ellis, *Victory in the West*, I, 10–11.

33. COS(43)286(O), "Trident (Part III)," 7 June 1943, CAB 80/70, PRO.

34. Morgan, *Overture to Overlord*, 142.

35. COS(43)286(O), "Operation 'Overlord'—Report and Appreciation with Appendices," 30 July 1943, CAB 80/72, PRO; and COS(43)415(o), "Overlord—Digest of Plan," 30 July 1943, CAB 80/72, PRO.

36. COS(43)480(O), 23 August 1943, CAB 80/73, PRO; and Kennedy, *Business of War*, 298–299.

37. COS(43)791(O) (Part II), 25 February 1944, CAB 80/77, PRO.

38. COS(Sextant)14, "Anglo-American Operations in 1944," 28 November 1943, CAB 80/77, PRO.

39. CCS, 124th Meeting, 22 October 1943, CAB 88/3, PRO.

40. Prime Minister to First Sea Lord and Chief of Air Staff, 24.8.43, ADM 205/37, PRO.

41. Morgan Papers, WDM 2/2, IWM.

42. Ehrman, *Grand Strategy*, V, 232–236, 283–284.

43. Harrison, *Cross-Channel Attack*, 180–188. The detailed naval plan is contained in Military Branch II, "Operation Neptune's Naval Plan," 13 March 1944, ADM 1/16259, PRO.

44. Harrison, *Cross-Channel Attack*, 73–74; and Hastings, *Overlord*, 197.

45. Coakley and Leighton, *Global Logistics, 1943–45*, 350.

46. Cruickshank, *Deception in World War II*.

47. GenStdH, FHW, "Kraftverteilung Grossbrittannien/Nordirland," 31–12.43–1.8.44, T78/646/896–916, NA.

48. Hinsley et al., *British Intelligence*, III, pt. 2, 127; and Allied Naval C-in-C, Expeditionary Force War Diary, 6 June 1944, ADM 199/1397, PRO.

49. Hinsley et al., *British Intelligence*, III, pt. 2.

50. Among the many fine studies, see Henri Michel, *The Shadow War*, trans. Richard Berry (New York: Harper & Row, 1973); and Michael R. D. Foot, *SOE in France* (London: HMSO, 1966). For Normandy, see Marcel Baudot, *Libération de la Normandie* (Paris: Hachette, 1974).

51. Hdqrs., US Strategic Air Forces in Europe, Office of the Commanding General, 24 March 1944, AIR 8/1188, PRO; ATH/DO/4, 24 March [1944], AIR 8/188, PRO; DAC/MS.100, "Employment of Allied Air Forces in Support of Overlord," 24 March 1944, AIR 8/1188, PRO; and Tedder, *With Prejudice*, 513–517.

52. CCS 520/3 (Octagon), "Control of Strategic Bombing in Europe," 12 September 44, CAB 88/25, PRO; and Harrison, *Cross-Channel Attack*, 220.

53. DO(44), 5th–9th Meetings, 5.4.–3.5.44, CAB 69/6, PRO; Cunningham Correspondence, May 2, 1944, ADD MS 52577, BML; President Roosevelt to Prime Minister, 11.5.44, AIR 8/1190, PRO; and Harrison, *Cross-Channel Attack*, 223.

54. Tedder, *With Prejudice*, 534–537.

55. AEAF, "Daily Int-Ops Summary," 2–5 June 1944, AIR 37/59, PRO. These figures are almost identical to the American Cosintreps in RG 331, SHAEF 370.2–11, NA.

56. Terraine, *Time for Courage*, 627; and CAS from Tedder, "Overlord—Employment of Bomber Forces," 3 March 44, AIR 8/1188.

57. Wilt, *Atlantic Wall*.

58. KTB/OKW, I, 1262–1264; and Hubatsch, hrsg., *Hitlers Weisungen*, 176–181.

59. Oberfehlshaber West, Ia Nr. 1441/42 g.Kdos., "Grundlegender Befehl des Oberbefehlshaber West Nr. 7," 15.6.42, T78/317/6270726–6270727, NA.

60. Oberbefehlshaber West, Ia Nr. 4522/42 g.Kdos., "Lagebeurteilung durch Ob. West," 21.12.42, T78/311/6273036, NA; WFSt/O/(H), "Meldungen des W.Bfh. Norwegen und Ob. West über Küstenartillerie," 19.19.42, T77/424/605, NA; and KTB/OKW, II, 1398.

61. Ob West, Ia Nr. 236/44 g.Kdos., "Lagebeurteilung durch Ob. West," 10.1.44, T311/22/7025370–7025371, NA; Generaloberst Alfred Jodl, "Die strategische Lage am Anfang der 5. Kriegsjahre," 7.11.43, 11 November 1943, T77/1433/486, NA; and KTB/OKW, III, 1401.

62. Hubatsch, hrsg., *Hitlers Weisungen*, 233–237.

63. Ob West, Ia Nr. 4366/44 g.Kdos., "Lagebeurteilung durch Ob. West vom

29.5. bis 4.6.1944," 5.6.1944, T311/24/7029167–7029168, NA; Stoart AOK 15 Nr. 490/44 g.Kdos., "Artl. Gliederung der 15. Armee," 1 May 1944, T312/516/8115257–8115258, NA; AOK 1, Ia/Stoart Nr. 289/44 g.Kdos., "Artilleriegliederung der 1. Armee," 1.3.1944, T312/28/7535667–7535668, NA; Sonderstab Oehmichen, z.Zt. Armeeoberkommando 7, Ia/Stopak Nr. 67/44, g.Kdos., "Minenmeldung-Stand 30.5.1944," 3.6.44, T311/28/7034017, NA; and *Rommel Papers*, 458.

64. Ellis, *Victory in the West*, I, 116–117.

65. Wegmuller, *Abwehr der Invasion*, 257.

66. Wilt, *Atlantic Wall*, 105–115.

67. Ibid., 129.

68. Ob West, Ia Nr. 1409/44 g.Kdos., "Lagebeurteilung durch Ob West," 14.2.1944, T311/22/7026193, NA: Ob West, Ia Nr. 1609/44 g.Kdos., "Lagebeurteilung durch Ob. West," 21.2.1944, T311/22/7026336, NA; and Adjutant des Chefs der Generalstabes der Heeres Nr. 576/43 g.Kdos.Ch., 23. December 1943, T78/310/6262659–6262660, NA.

69. Ob West, Ia Nr. 4185/44 g.Kdos., "Lagebeurteilung durch Ob.West. von 22. bis 28.5.44," 29.5.44, T311/24/7028949–7028951, NA; Ob West, Ia Nr. 4366/44 g.Kdos., "Lagebeurteilung durch Ob. West von 29.5. bis 4.6.1944," T311/24/7029166, NA; HGr B, Ia Nr. 3060/44 g.Kdos., "Wochenmeldung 28.5.–3.6.44," 5. June 1944, T311/3/7022156, NA; KV 5751–6679, 30 May–6 June 1944, DEFE 3/163–166, PRO; and Hastings, *Overlord*, 76.

70. Ellis, *Victory in the West*, I, 116–121, 507–520; Hastings, *Overlord*, 348; Roskill, *War at Sea*, III, 2, 18–19; Craven and Cate, eds., *Europe: Argument to V-E Day*, 139; Alfred Jodl, "Die strategische Lage," 5.5.44, N69/17, BA-MA; and Karl Gundelach, "Drohende Gefahr West: Die deutsche Luftwaffe vor und während der Invasion, 1944," *Wehrwissenschaftliche Rundschau*, 8 (Jun 1959): 306.

71. KTB/OKW, IV, 308–309.

72. Murray, *Luftwaffe*, 265.

73. CCS 329/2, "Implementation of Assumed Basic Undertakings . . . 1943–1944," 26 August 1943, CAB 88/17, PRO.

74. AEAF, "Daily It/Ops," 6 June 44, AIR 37/59, PRO; and AI-536, "Cosintrep No. 11-PartIII-Air," 8 June 1944, RG 331, SHAEF 370.2–11, NA.

75. See, for example, his comments at a December 20, 1943, military conference (Heiber, hrsg., *Hitlers Lagebesprechungen*, 440–441). This is also one of the main themes in Hastings, *Overlord*; and from a broader perspective in Van Creveld, *Fighting Power*.

76. Daily happenings can be followed in ANCXF, "War Diary," 6–16 June, ADM 199/1397, PRO; 21st Army Group, 6.6.–2.8.44, WO 106/4355, PRO; ObdHGr B, 5.6.–31.7.44, T311/7002156–7002214, NA; and Ob West, 6.6.–30.6.44, T311/25/7029326–7029998, NA. The classic work on D-Day is Cornelius Ryan, *The Longest Day: June 6, 1944* (New York: Simon & Schuster, 1959). For the entire campaign, see, besides Hastings and Keegan, the controversial Carlo d'Este, *Decision in Normandy: The Unwritten Story of Montgomery and the Allied Campaign* (London: Grafton, 1983); and the more popularized Werner Haupt, *Rückzug im Westen 1944: Von der Invasion zur Ardennes-Offensive* (Stuttgart: Motorbuch Verlag, 1978). For the logistical buildup, see Roland G. Ruppenthal, *Logistical Support of the Armies*, I (Washington: USGPO, 1953); and portions of Martin Van Creveld, *Supplying War: Logistics from Wallenstein to Patton* (Cambridge: Cambridge University Press, 1978). The airborne portion is covered in Napier Crookenden, *Dropzone Normandy: The Story of the American and British Airborne Assaults on D Day 1944* (New York: Scribner's, 1976); and John C. Warren, *Airborne Operations in World War II, European Theater* (Manhattan, KS: MA/AH, 1956).

77. See, among others, Hastings, *Overlord;* and Terraine, *Time for Courage.*

78. KV 6589, 061002Z/6/44, DEFE 3/166, PRO; and KV 6549, 060219Z/6/44, DEFE, 3/166, PRO.

79. Bennett, "Ultra and Some Command Decisions," 140–142.

80. Tedder, *With Prejudice,* 553–556.

81. Panzergruppe West, Ia Nr. 2532/44 g.Kdos., "Verlaufe Eindrücke vom West-kampf," 13.6.44, T311/25/7029549, NA.

82. Hinsley et al., *British Intelligence,* III, pt. 2, 508.

83. Heiber, hrsg., *Hitlers Lagebesprechungen,* 593–594. The best book on Germany's holding on to the ports is Jacques Mordal [pseud.], *Les poches de l'Atlantique* (Paris: Presses de la Cité, 1965). Dunkirk, Lorient, St. Nazaire, and La Rochelle did not surrender until the end of the war.

84. *Unesco Yearbook,* (Wilt) 170–171.

85. The best book on the offensive is Charles B. MacDonald, *A Time for Trumpets: The Untold Story of the Battle of the Bulge* (New York: Morrow, 1985). Other excellent accounts are Hermann Jung, *Die Ardennen-Offensive 1944/45: Ein Beispiel für die Kriegführung Hitlers* (Göttingen: Musterschmidt, 1971); Hugh M. Cole, *The Ardennes: Battle of the Bulge* (Washington: USGPO, 1965); John S. D. Eisenhower, *The Bitter Woods* (New York: Putnam, 1969); and Michel Hérubel, *La bataille des Ardennes: décembre 1944–janvier 1945* (Paris: Presses de la Cité, 1979). A good synthesis is in Ellis, *Victory in the West,* vol. 2, *The Defeat of Germany* (London: HMSO, 1968), 175–197; and the version of one of the participants, General Hasso von Manteuffel, Fifth Panzer Army commander, is in Jacobsen and Rohwer, eds., *Decisive Battles,* 391–418. The air portion of the battle is dealt with in Craven and Cate, eds., *Europe: Argument to V-E Day,* 627–711. For the role of Allied intelligence, see Hinsley et al., *British Intelligence,* III pt. 2, 401–450; and Bennett, "Ultra and Some Command Decisions." An analytical article is Carl Wagener, "Strittige Fragen zur Ardennen-offensive," *Wehrwissenschaftliche Rundschau,* 11 (Jan 1961): 26–54.

86. Jung, *Ardennen-Offensive,* 101; and Hinsley et al., *British Intelligence,* III, pt. 2, 415–417.

87. The quote is taken from the November 10 order appended in Jung, *Ardennen-Offensive,* 306.

88. Heiber, hrsg., *Hitlers Lagebesprechungen,* 713–724; and Jacobsen and Roh-wer, eds., *Decisive Battles,* (Manteuffel) 401–402.

89. Hinsley, *British Intelligence,* III, pt. 2, 411–438.

90. Oberbefehlshaber West Ia Nr. 00218/44 g.Kdos.Chefs., "Gliederung der Heeresgruppe B für den beföhlenen Angriff," 16.12.44, RH 19 IV/84, BA-MA, OKH, "Iststarke Zumsammenstellung," 15.12.44, MI4/14/145, IWM; [Ob West], "Einsatz-bereite Panzer und Stürmgeschutze im Bereich Ob. West," 5.12.44, RW4/636, BA-MA; and Jung, *Ardennen-Offensive,* 343–350.

91. MacDonald, *Time for Trumpets,* 84.

92. Besides in MacDonald, the crucial stages of the battle can be followed in [Ob West], "Kriegstagebuch," 15.12.–31.12.44, RH19 IV/76, BA-MA; and Walter Model, "Zusammenfassender Bericht über die Kampfhandlungen der deutschen Heeresgruppen B von Mitte Oktober 1944 bis Mitte April 1945," N6/4, BA-MA. The section in Model's Nachlass is written by Colonel G. Reichhelm, Model's operations officer.

93. Ellis, *Victory in the West,* II, 188–195; and MacDonald, *Time for Trumpets,* 618.

94. Hinsley et al., *British Intelligence,* III, pt. 2, 445–451.

95. Among others, see Jung, *Ardennen-Offensive,* 199–201.

96. Maurice Matloff, "The 90-Division Gamble," in Kent Robert Greenfield, ed.,

Command Decisions (Washington: USGPO, 1960), 380; JP(44)262 (Final), "Planning Date for the End of the War with Germany," 29 October 1944, CAB 84/66, PRO; JP(45)11(S)(T of R), "Revised Planning Date for the End of the War with Germany," 9 January 1945, CAB 84/69, PRO: and COS(45)67(O), "Revised Planning Date for the End of the War with Germany," 22 January 1945, CAB 89/91, PRO.

97. JS(Octagon)(O) (Final), "Lines of Advance into Germany," 8 September 1944, CAB 80/88, PRO.

98. CCS 761/6 (Argonaut), 31 January 1945, CAB 80/92, PRO: Bryant, ed., *Triumph in the West*, 313; and Robert M. Hathaway, *Ambiguous Partnership: Britain and America, 1944–1947* (New York: Columbia University Press, 1981), 118–119.

99. 21 Army Group/oo/461/Ops(A), "Commander-in-Chiefs Meeting," 9 December 1944, WO 205/9, PRO; and MO 3, "Future Strategy in Western Europe," 13 December 1944, WO 106/4432, PRO.

100. The best account remains Ellis, *Victory in the West*, II, 250–277, although the Grenade offensive is more thoroughly covered in Charles B. MacDonald, *The Last Offensive* (Washington: USGPO, 1973), 135–184. An attempt to look at all of the February–March offensives is Peter Allen, *One More River: The Rhine Crossings of 1945* (New York: Scribner's, 1980), which is better on the British than on the American side of the operation. Canada's role is examined in Charles P. Stacey, *The Victory Campaign* (Ottawa: Queen's Printers, 1960); and that of XXX Corps is described by its commander, Brian Horrocks, in *A Full Life* (London: Collins, 1960). Diplomatic developments are discussed in Hathaway, *Ambiguous Partnership;* aerial aspects, though incompletely, in Craven and Cate, eds., *Europe: Argument to V-E Day*, 756–763; intelligence in Hinsley et al., *British Intelligence*, III, pt. 2, 670–678; and Allied command controversies in Weigley, *Eisenhower's Lieutenants*.

101. Hinsley et al., *British Intelligence*, III, pt. 2, 672–674.

102. Ellis, *Victory in the West*, II, 255–257; Allen, *One More River*, 29; and MacDonald, *Last Offensive*, 136–142.

103. The operations are covered on a daily basis in MO3, "Operations—Western Europe: CIGS Summaries," 9 February–12 March 1945, WO 106/4386 and WO 106/4387, PRO.

104. Hinsley et al., *British Intelligence*, III, pt. 2, 676; and Horrocks, *A Full Life*, 251.

105. 21 Army Gp, M563, 28 March 1945, WO 106/4358, PRO; and McDonald, *Last Offensive*, 183. Among the many controversies at the end of the European war, see, for example, Jean-Marie d'Hoop, "Eisenhower et la problème de Berlin en mars 1945," *Revue d'histoire de la deuxième guerre mondiale*, 22 (Oct 1972): 67–78.

106. Ellis, *Victory in the West* II, 277; and MacDonald, *Last Offensive*, 183.

107. Craven and Cate, eds., *Europe: Argument to V-E Day*, 758, 763.

CONCLUSION

1. Callahan, *Churchill: Retreat from Empire*, 79–80; and Charles Burdick, letter to author, November 6, 1988.

2. CCS 170/2, "Symbol: Final Report . . . ," January 23, 1943, *Wartime Conferences of the Combined Chiefs of Staff, 1941–1945*, reel 1 (Wilmington, DE: Scholarly Resources, 1982); and Feis, *Churchill, Roosevelt, Stalin*, 105–107.

Bibliography

The bibliography is divided into unpublished documents, published documents, books, dissertations, and articles. Additional bibliographic material is located in the notes.

DOCUMENTS: UNPUBLISHED

United States National Archives (NA)

T-77: 424, 777, 869, 1423	German Armed Forces High Command
T-78: 310, 311, 317, 335, 346, 430, 431, 521, 646, 821, 822	German Army High Command
T-311: 322, 24, 25, 27, 53, 140, 151, 152, 236	Germany Army Groups
T-312: 28, 317, 516, 977	German Armies
T-313: 80, 86, 92, 237	German Panzer Armies
T-517: 365, 426	"OKH Project #7"

Foreign Military Studies, T-111: "The German Army High Command"
Foreign Military Studies, T-101: "The German Army High Command"
RG 238, T-989: War Diaries and Correspondence of General Alfred Jodl
RG 319, ABC Decimal File
RG 457, SRGN 6628-SRGN 19198: German Navy/U-boat Message Translations
RG 457, SRH-008: Battle of the Atlantic, Vol. II
RG 457, SRH-009: Battle of the Atlantic, Vol. I
RG 457, SRH-024: Battle of the Atlantic, Vol. III
RG 457, SRH-025: Battle of the Atlantic, Vol. IV
RG 457, SRS-548: B-Berichte & X-B-Berichte, Dec 1942–Mai 1943
RG 59, M-679: General Records of the Department of State (Poole Mission)

Bundesarchiv-Militärarchiv (BA-MA)

RW 4/	Oberkommando der Wehrmacht/WFSt
RM 7/	Kriegsmarine
RL 2II/	Luftwaffe
RH 19 I–IV/	Heeresgruppen
RH 19 VIII/	Panzer Armeeoberkommando Afrika
N6	Nachlass Walter Model
N54	Nachlass Kurt Zeitzler
N69	Nachlass Alfred Jodl
N219	Nachlass Bernhard von Lossberg
N236	Nachlass Karl Dönitz

Public Record Office (PRO)

DEFE 3	Ultra Intelligence Signals
CAB 65	War Cabinet Minutes
CAB 66	War Cabinet Memoranda
CAB 69	Defence Committee (Operations)
CAB 70	Defence Committee (Supply)
CAB 79	Chiefs of Staff Committee Minutes
CAB 80	Chiefs of Staff Committee Memoranda
CAB 83	Military Co-ordination Committee

CAB 84	Joint Planning Committee
CAB 85	Anglo-French Committees
CAB 86	Committees on the Battle of the Atlantic and Anti-U-Boat Warfare
CAB 88	Combined Chiefs of Staff and Sub-Committees
CAB 99	Commonwealth and International Meetings
CAB 127	Private Collections: Ministers and Officials
PREM-1	Prime Minister Correspondence and Papers (to May 10, 1940)
PREM-3	Prime Minister Operational Papers (after May 10, 1940)
PREM 7	Private Collections
WO 106	Directorate of Military Operations and Intelligence Papers
WO 193	Directorate of Military Operations Collation Files
WO 197	Military Headquarters Papers, BEF
WO 201	Military Headquarters Papers, Middle East Forces
WO 203	Military Headquarters Papers, Far East
WO 204	Military Headquarters Papers, Allied Forces Headquarters
WO 205	Military Headquarters Papers, 21 Army Group
WO 212	Orders of Battle and Organisational Tables
WO 214	Lord Alexander of Tunis Papers
WO 216	Chief of the Imperial General Staff Papers
ADM 1	Admiralty and Secretariat Papers
ADM 116	Admiralty and Secretariat Cases
ADM 199	War History Cases
ADM 205	First Sea Lord Papers
AIR 8	Chief of the Air Staff
AIR 9	Director of Plans
AIR 14	Bomber Command
AIR 15	Coastal Command
AIR 16	Fighter Command
AIR 35	British Air Force in France
AIR 37	AEAF, 2nd TAF, and SHAEF
FO 837	Ministry of Economic Warfare

Imperial War Museum (IWM)

AL 1009	Heeresgruppe B
AL 1372	Heeresgruppe B
AL 1433	Heeresgruppe B
AL 1570	OKH/OpAbt

William D. Morgan Papers

British Museum Library (BML)
ADD 52557–525584   Lord Cunningham Correspondence

USAF Historical Research Center (USAFHRC)

K239.0512–838	General Elwood P. Quesade Interview
101–52	Edith C. Rogers, "The Reduction of Pantelleria and Adjacent Islands"
101–37	Harry L. Coles, "Participation of the Ninth and Twelfth Air Forces in the Sicilian Campaign"

DOCUMENTS: PUBLISHED

Akten zur deutschen Auswärtigen Politik, 1918–1945. Serie E: 1941–1945. Göttingen: Vandenhoeck & Ruprecht, 1969—.

Die Berichte des Oberkommandos der Wehrmacht 1939–1945. 2 vols. München: Verlag für Wehrwissenschaften, 1983.

Burdick, Charles B., and Donald Detwiler, eds. *World War II German Military Studies.* Vols. 4–6. Part III. New York: Garland, 1979.

Cabinet History Series. *Principal War Telegrams and Memoranda. 1940–1943.* 7 vols. Nendeln: KTO Press, 1976.

Documents on German Foreign Policy, 1918–1945. Series D: 1937–1941. 13 vols. Washington: USGPO, 1956–1966.

Domarus, Max, hrsg. *Hitler, Reden und Proklamationen, 1932–1945.* 2 vols. Würzburg: Verlags Schmidt Drückerei, 1962–1963.

Foreign Relations of the United States. *Conferences at Washington, 1941–1942, and Casablanca, 1943.* Washington: USGPO, 1968.

Foreign Relations of the United States. *The Conferences at Cairo and Teheran, 1943.* Washington: USGPO, 1961.

Foreign Relations of the United States. *Conferences at Malta and Yalta.* Washington: USGPO, 1955.

Fuehrer Conferences on Matters Dealing with the German Navy, 1939–1945. 7 vols. Washington: US Navy Department, 1947. (German edition, Gerhard Wagner, hrsg. *Lagevorträge des Oberbefehlshabers der Kriegsmarine von Hitler, 1939–1945.* München: J. F. Lehmanns Verlag, 1972.)

Genoud, François, ed. *The Testament of Adolf Hitler: The Hitler-Bormann Documents, February–April 1945.* Trans. R. H. Stevens. London: Cassell, 1961.

Heiber, Helmut, hrsg. *Hitlers Lagebesprechungen: Die Protokollfragmente seiner militarischen Konferenzen, 1942–1945.* Stuttgart: Deutsche Verlags-Anstalt, 1962. (Abridged English edition, Felix Gilbert, ed. *Hitler Directs His War: The Secret Records of His Daily Military Conferences.* New York: Oxford, 1950.)

Hubatsch, Walther, hrsg. *Hitlers Weisungen für die Kriegführung, 1939–1945.* Frankfurt a.M.: Bernard & Graefe, 1962. (English edition, Hugh R. Trevor-Roper, ed. *Hitler's War Directives, 1939–1945.* London: Sidwick & Jackson, 1964.)

Intelligence Reports on the War in the Atlantic, 1942–1945. Wilmington, DE: Michael Glazier, 1979.

Irving Collection. *Records and Documents Relating to the Third Reich. Group 5: German War Diaries.* Reels 18–25. East Ardsley, Yorkshire: EP Microforms, 1973.

James, Robert Rhodes, ed. *Winston S. Churchill: His Complete Speeches, 1897–1963.* 8 vols. New York: R. R. Bowker, 1974.

Jochmann, Werner, hrsg. *Adolf Hitler: Monologe im Führerhauptguartier, 1941–1944: Die Aufzeichnungen Heinrich Heims.* Hamburg: Albrecht Knaus, 1980. (English edition, Hugh R. Trevor-Roper, ed. *Hitler's Secret Conversations, 1941–1944.* Trans. Norman Camison and R. H. Stevens. New York: Farrar, Strauss, & Young, 1953.)

Kimball, Warren F., ed. *Churchill and Roosevelt: The Complete Correspondence.* 3 vols. Princeton: Princeton University Press, 1984.

Loewehheim, Francis L., et al. *Roosevelt and Churchill: Their Secret Wartime Correspondence.* New York: Saturday Review Press, 1975.

Nichols, H. G., ed. *Washington Dispatches, 1941–45; Weekly Reports from the British Embassy.* London: Weidenfeld & Nicolson, 1981.

Picker, Henry, hrsg. *Hitlers Tischgespräche im Führerhauptquartier, 1941–42.* Stuttgart: Seewald, 1963.

Schramm, Percy E., et al., hrsg. *Kriegstagebuch des Oberkommandos der Wehrmacht, 1940–1945.* 4 vols. in 7 parts. Frankfurt a.M.: Bernard & Graefe, 1961–65. Includes supplements.

Wartime Conferences of the Combined Chiefs of Staff, 1941–45. 3 reels. Wilmington, DE: Scholarly Resources, 1982.

BOOKS

Abhyankar, M. G. *The War in Burma, 1943–45.* 4th ed. Dehra Dun: Natraj Publishers, 1974.

Absolon, Rudolf, ed. *Rangliste: Der Generale der deutschen Luftwaffe nach dem Stand vom April 1945.* Friedburg: Podzun-Pallas, 1984.

Addington, Larry H. *The Blitzkrieg Era and the German Staff, 1865–1941.* New Brunswick, NJ: Rutgers University Press, 1971.

Agar-Hamilton, J. A. I., and L. C. F. Turner, *Crisis in the Desert, May–July 1942.* Capetown: Geoffrey Cumberlege, 1952.

———. *The Sidi Rezeq Battles, 1941.* London: Oxford University Press, 1957.

Lord Alexander of Tunis (Harold). *Memoirs, 1939–45.* London: Cassell, 1962.

Allen, Louis. *Burma: The Longest War, 1941–45.* London: J. M. Dent, 1984.

Allen, Peter. *One More River: The Rhine Crossings of 1945.* New York: Scribner's, 1980.

Andenaes, Johannes, et al. *Norway and the Second World War.* Oslo: Tanun, 1966.

Andrew, Christopher, and David Dilks, eds. *The Missing Dimension: Governments and Intelligence Communities in the Twentieth Century.* London: Macmillan, 1984.

Andrews, Allen. *The Air Marshals: The Air War in Western Europe.* New York: Morrow, 1970.

Ansel, Walter. *Hitler Confronts England.* Durham, NC: Duke University Press, 1960.

Aster, Sidney. *British Foreign Policy, 1918–1945: A Guide to Research and Research Materials.* Wilmington, DE: Scholarly Resources, 1984.

Bagnasco, Erminio. *Submarines of World War II.* London: Arms & Armour Press, 1977.

Barker, Elisabeth. *British Policy in South-East Europe in the Second World War.* London: Macmillan, 1976.

———. *Churchill and Eden at War.* London: Macmillan, 1978.

Barnard, Roy S. *The Era of World War II: Special Bibliography Series, No. 16.* Vol. 1. Carlisle Barracks, PA: USA Military History Research Center, 1978.

Barnett, Correlli. *The Audit of War: The Illusion and Reality of Britain as a Great Nation.* London: Macmillan, 1986.

———. *The Desert Generals.* Rev. ed. Bloomington: Indiana University Press, 1982.

Bartov, Omer. *The Eastern Front, 1941–45: German Troops and the Barbarisation of Warfare.* Oxford: Macmillan, 1985.

Baudot, Marcel. *Libération de la Normandie.* Paris: Hachette, 1974.

Baum, Walter, and Eberhard Weichold. *Der Krieg der "Achsenmächte" im Mittelmeerraum: Die Strategie der Diktatoren.* Göttingen: Musterschmidt, 1973.

Bayliss, Gwyn M. *Bibliographic Guide to the Two World Wars: An Annotated Survey of English Language Reference Materials.* New York: Bowker, 1977.

Beaulieu, Walter Charles de. *Generaloberst Erich Hoepner—Militärisches Porträt eines Panzerführers.* Neckargemünd: Vowinckel, 1969.

Beck, Earl R. *Under the Bombs: The German Home Front, 1942–45.* Lexington: University of Kentucky Press, 1986.

Bédarida, François. *La stratégie secrète de la drôle de guerre: Le conseil suprême inter-allie, septembre 1939–avril 1940.* Paris: Presses de la Foundation Nationale de la Sciences Politiques, 1979.

Beesly, Patrick. *Very Special Intelligence; The Story of the Admiralty's Operational Intelligence Centre, 1939–1945.* London: Hamish Hamilton, 1977.

Behrendt, Hans-Otto. *Rommels Kenntnis vom Feind im Afrikafeldzug: Ein Bericht über die Feindnachrichtenarbeit, Insbesondere die Funkaufklärung.* Freiburg i. Br.: Rombach, 1980.

Bekker, Cajus, pseud. *Hitler's Naval War.* Trans. Frank Ziegler. Garden City, NY: Doubleday, 1974.

———. *The Luftwaffe War Diaries.* Trans. Frank Ziegler. Garden City, NY: Doubleday, 1968.

Bell, P. H. M. *A Certain Eventuality: Britain and the Fall of France.* Lexington, MA: Saxon House, 1974.

Belot, R. de. *La Marine française pendant la campagne 1939–1940.* Paris: Plon, 1954.

Below, Nicholaus von. *Als Hitlers Adjutant, 1937–1945.* Mainz: Von Hase & Koehler, 1980.

Bennett, Ralph. *Ultra in the West: The Normandy Campaign, 1944–45.* London: Hutchinson, 1979.

Benz, Wolfgang, and Hermann Graml, hrsg. *Sommer 1939: Die Grossmächte und der Europäische Krieg.* Stuttgart: Deutsche Verlags-Anstalt, 1979.

Bethell, Nicholas. *The War Hitler Won: The Fall of Poland, September 1939.* New York: Holt, Rinehart & Winston, 1972.

Bezymenski, Lev. *The Death of Adolf Hitler: Unknown Documents from Soviet Archives.* New York: Harcourt, Brace & World, 1968.

Bidwell, Shelford. *The Chindit War: Stilwell, Wingate, and the Campaign in Burma, 1944.* New York: Macmillan, 1979.

———, and Dominick Graham. *Fire-Power: British Army Weapons and Theories of War, 1904–1945.* London: George Allen & Unwin, 1982.

Bird, Keith W. *German Naval History: A Guide to the Literature.* New York: Garland, 1985.

Blau, George E. *The German Campaign in Russia: Planning and Operations, 1940–1942.* Washington: USGPO, 1955.

———. *The German Campaigns in the Balkans (Spring 1941).* Washington: USGPO, 1953.

Blaxland, Gregory. *Destination Dunkirk: The Story of Gort's Army.* London: William Kimber, 1973.

Blumenson, Martin. *Breakout and Pursuit.* Washington: USGPO, 1962.

Blumentritt, Günther. *Von Rundstedt: The Soldier and the Man.* Trans. Cuthbert Reavely. London: Odhams, 1952.

Boelcke, Willi A., hrsg. *Deutschlands Rüstung im Zweiten Weltkrieg; Hitlers Konferenzen mit Albert Speer, 1942–1945.* Frankfurt, a. M.: Atheneum, 1969.

Boeninger, Hildegard R. *The Hoover Library Collection on Germany.* Stanford, CA: Stanford University Press, 1955.

Bond, Brian. *British Military Policy between the Two World Wars.* New York: Oxford University Press, 1980.

———. *France and Belgium, 1939–1940.* London: Davis-Poynter, 1975.

———, ed. *Chief of Staff: The Diaries of Lt.-Gen. Sir Henry Pownall.* 2 vols. London: Leo Cooper, 1973–75.

Boog, Horst. *Die deutsche Luftwaffenführung 1935–1945; Führungsprobleme-Spitzengliederung-Generalstabsausbildung.* Stuttgart: Deutsche Verlags-Anstalt, 1982.

———, et al. *Das Deutsche Reich und der Zweite Weltkrieg,* Bd. 4, *Der Angriff auf die Sowjetunion.* Stuttgart: Deutsche Verlags-Anstalt, 1982.

Boor, Wolfgang de. *Hitler: Mensch, Übermensch, Untermensch: Eine kriminalpsychologische Studie.* Frankfurt a. M.: R. G. Fischer, 1985.

Bor, Peter, hrsg. *Gespräche mit Halder.* Wiesbaden: Limes, 1950.

Boyd, Carl. *The Extraordinary Envoy: General Hiroshi Oshima and Diplomacy in the Third Reich, 1934–1939.* Washington: University Press of America, 1980.

Bracher, Karl Dietrich. *The German Dictatorship: The Origins, Structure, and Effects of National Socialism*. Trans. Jean Steinberg. New York: Praeger, 1970.

Bradley, Dermot, and Richard Schulze-Kossens, hrsg. *Tätigkeitsbericht des Chefs des Heerespersonalamtes General der Infanterie Rudolf Schmundt . . . 1.10.1942– 29.10.1944*. Osnabrück: Biblio, 1984.

Bryant, Arthur, ed. *Triumph in the West*. Garden City, NY: Doubleday, 1959.

———, ed. *The Turn of the Tide*. Garden City, NY: Doubleday, 1957.

Brennecke, Jochen. *Die Wende im U-Boot-Krieg: Ursachen und Folgen, 1939–1943*. Herford: Koehlers, 1984.

Buchheit, Gert. *Hitler der Feldherr: Die Zerstörung einer Legende*. Rastatt: Grote, 1958.

Buckley, Christopher. *Greece and Crete, 1941*. London: HMSO, 1952.

Buhite, Russell D. *Decisions at Yalta: An Appraisal of Summit Diplomacy*. Wilmington, DE: Scholarly Resources, 1986.

Bullock, Alan. *Hitler: A Study in Tyranny*. Rev. ed. New York: Harper, 1964.

Burns, James MacGregor. *Roosevelt: The Soldier of Freedom*. New York: Harcourt, Brace, Jovanovich, 1970.

Butler, J. R. M. *Grand Strategy*. Vol. II, *September 1939–June 1941*. London: HMSO, 1957.

Caccia-Dominioni, Paolo. *Alamein, 1933–1962: An Italian Story*. Trans. Dennis Chamberlain. London: Allen & Unwin, 1966.

Callahan, Raymond. *Burma, 1942–1945*. London: Davis-Poynter, 1978.

———. *Churchill: Retreat from Empire*. Wilmington, DE: Scholarly Resources, 1984.

Carlton, David. *Anthony Eden: A Biography*. London: Allen Lane, 1981.

Carr, William. *Hitler: A Study in Personality and Politics*. London: Edward Arnold, 1978.

Carroll, Berenice A. *Design for Total War: Arms and Economics in the Third Reich*. The Hague: Mouton, 1968.

Carver, Michael. *Dilemmas of the Desert War: A New Look at the Libyan Campaign, 1940–1942*. Bloomington: Indiana University Press, 1986.

———. *El Alamein*. London: Batsford, 1962.

———, ed. *The War Lords: Military Commanders of the Twentieth Century*. London: Weidenfeld & Nicolson, 1976.

Central Organisation for Defense. London: HMSO, 1946.

Chalfont, Alun. *Montgomery of Alamein*. London: Weidenfeld & Nicolson, 1976.

Chalmers, W. S. *Max Horton and the Western Approaches: A Biography of Admiral Sir Max Kennedy Horton*. London: Hodder & Stoughton, 1954.

Chapman, Guy. *Why France Fell*. London: Cassell, 1968.

Churchill, Winston S. *The Second World War*. 6 vols. Boston: Houghton Mifflin, 1948–54.

Clark, Alan. *Barbarossa: The Russian German Conflict, 1941–45*. New York: Morrow, 1965.

Coakley, Robert W., and Richard M. Leighton. *Global Logistics and Strategy, 1943– 1945*. Washington: USGPO, 1969.

Cole, Hugh M. *The Ardennes: Battle of the Bulge*. Washington: USGPO, 1965.

Collier, Basil. *The Defence of the United Kingdom*. London: HMSO, 1957.

Collier, Richard. *1940: The Avalanche*. New York: Dial, 1979.

Collins, John M. *Grand Strategy: Principles and Practices*. Annapolis: US Naval Institute, 1973.

Colville, John. *The Fringes of Power: Downing Street Diaries, 1939–1955*. London: Hodder & Stoughton, 1985.

———. *Man of Valour: Field Marshal Lord Gort*. London: Collins, 1972.

———. *Winston Churchill and His Inner Circle*. New York: Wyndham, 1981.

Comité d'Histoire de la 2ᵉ Guerre Mondiale. *La guerre en méditerranée, 1939–1945.* Paris: Editions du Centre Nationale de la Recherche Scientifique, 1972.

Connell, John [pseud.]. *Auchinleck.* London: Cassell, 1959.

Cooper, Matthew. *The German Air Force, 1933–1945: An Anatomy of Failure.* London: Jane's, 1981.

———. *The German Army, 1933–1945: Its Political and Military Failure.* New York: Stein & Day, 1978.

Craven, Wesley F., and James L. Cate, eds. *The Army Air Forces in World War II.* Vols. II–III. Chicago: University of Chicago Press, 1949–51.

Crookenden, Napier. *Dropzone Normandy: The Story of the American and British Airborne Assaults on D Day 1944.* New York: Scribner's, 1976.

Cruickshank, Charles. *Deceptions in World War II.* New York: Oxford University Press, 1979.

Lord Cunningham of Hyndhope (Andrew B.). *A Sailor's Odyssey.* London: Hutchinson, 1951.

Danchev, Alex. *Very Special Relationship: Field Marshal Sir John Dill and the Anglo-American Alliance, 1941–44.* London: Brassey's 1986.

Davidson, Eugene. *The Trial of the Germans.* New York: Collier, 1966.

Deakin, Frederick W. *The Brutal Friendship: Mussolini, Hitler and the Fall of Italian Fascism.* New York: Harper, 1963.

———, et al., eds. *British Political and Military Strategy in Central, Eastern and Southern Europe in 1944.* New York: St. Martin's, 1988.

Dean, Maurice. *The Royal Air Force and Two World Wars.* London: Cassell, 1979.

Deighton, Len. *Fighter: The True Story of the Battle of Britain.* New York: Knopf, 1978.

Deist, Wilhelm. *The Wehrmacht and German Rearmament.* London: Macmillan, 1981.

———, ed. *The German Military in the Age of Total War.* Leamington Spa: Berg, 1985.

———, et al. *Das Deutsche Reich und der Zweite Weltkrieg. Band 1: Ursachen und Voraussetzungen der deutschen Kriegspolitik.* Stuttgart: Deutsche Verlags-Anstalt, 1979.

Demeter, Karl. *Das deutsche Offizierkorps im Gesellschaft und Staat, 1650–1945.* Frankfurt a.M.: Bernard & Graefe, 1962.

Deutsch, Harold. *Hitler and His Generals.* Minneapolis: University of Minnesota Press, 1974.

Das Deutsche Heer, 1939: Gliederung, Standorte, Stellenbesetzung und Verzeichnis samtlicher Offiziere am 3.1.1939. Bad Nauheim: Podzun, 1953.

Dierich, Wolfgang, *Die Verbände der Luftwaffe, 1935–1945: Gliederungen und Kur-zchroniken—Eine Dokumentation.* Stuttgart: Motorbuch, 1976.

Dilks, David. *Neville Chamberlain.* Vol. I, *Pioneering and Reform, 1869–1929.* Cambridge: Cambridge University Press, 1984.

———, ed. *Retreat from Power: Studies in Britain's Foreign Policy of the Twentieth Century.* Vol. II, *After 1939.* London: Macmillan, 1981.

Divine, David. *The Nine Days of Dunkirk.* New York: Norton, 1959.

Dobson, Alan P. *US Wartime Aid to Britain, 1940–1946.* New York: St. Martin's, 1986.

Dönitz, Karl. *Memoirs: Ten Years and Twenty Days.* Trans. R. H. Stevens. Cleveland: World Publishing, 1959.

Doerr, Hans. *Der Feldzug nach Stalingrad: Versuch eines operativen Überblicks.* Darmstadt: Mittler, 1955.

Dupuy, Trevor N. *A Genius for War: The German Army and General Staff.* London: Macdonald and Jane's, 1977.

Ehrman, John. *Grand Strategy.* Vol. V, *August 1943–September 1944.* London: HMSO, 1956.

———. *Grand Strategy.* Vol. VI, *October 1944–August 1945.* London: HMSO, 1956.

Eisenhower, Dwight D. *Crusade in Europe.* New York: Doubleday, 1948.

Eisenhower, John S. D. *The Bitter Woods.* New York: Putnam, 1969.

Elble, Rolf. *Die Schlacht an der Bzura im September 1939 aus deutscher und polnishcher Sicht.* Freiburg i. Br.: Rombach, 1975.

Ellis, Lyle F. *Victory in the West.* 2 vols. London: HMSO, 1962–68.

———. *The War in France and Flanders, 1939–1940.* London: HMSO, 1953.

Engel, Gerhard. *Heeresadjutant bei Hitler, 1938–1943: Aufzeichnungen des Majors Engel.* Stuttgart: Deutsche Verlags-Anstalt, 1974.

Enser, A. G. S. *A Subject Bibliography of the Second World War: Books in English, 1939–1974.* London: Andre Deutsch, 1977.

———. *A Subject Bibliography of the Second World War: Books in English, 1975–1983.* London: Gower, 1985.

Erfurth, Waldemar. *Die Geschichte des deutschen Generalstabes von 1918–1945.* Göttingen: Musterschmidt, 1957.

Erickson, John. *The Road to Stalingrad: Stalin's War with Germany.* New York: Harper & Row, 1975.

———. *The Road to Berlin; Continuing the History of Stalin's War with Germany.* Boulder, CO: Westview, 1983.

Esebeck, H. G. von. *Afrikanische Schicksalsjahre: Geschichte des deutschen Afrikakorps unter Rommel.* Wiesbaden: Limes, 1949.

d'Este, Carlo. *Bitter Victory: The Battle for Sicily, 1943.* New York: Dutton, 1988.

———. *Decision in Normandy: The Unwritten Story of Montgomery and the Allied Campaign.* London: Grafton, 1983.

Eubank, Keith. *Summit at Teheran.* New York: Morrow, 1985.

Faber, Harold, ed. *Luftwaffe: A History.* New York: Quadrangle, 1977.

Feiling, Keith. *The Life of Neville Chamberlain.* London: Macmillan, 1946.

Joubert de la Ferté, Philip. *Birds and Fishes: The Story of Coastal Command.* London: Hutchinson, 1960.

Fest, Joachim C. *Hitler.* Trans. Richard and Clara Winston. New York: Vintage, 1975.

Fischer, Alexander, et al., hrsg. *Russland, Deutschland, Amerika: Festschrift zum 80. Geburtstag Fritz Epstein.* Wiesbaden: Steiner, 1978.

Foot, Michael R. D. *SOE in France.* London: HMSO, 1966.

Förster, Jürgen, *Stalingrad: Risse im Bundnis, 1942/43.* Freiburg i. Br.: Rombach, 1975.

Frankland, Noble. *The Bombing Offensive against Germany: Outline and Perspectives.* London: Faber & Faber, 1965.

Franks, Norman. *The Air Battle of Dunkirk.* London: William Kimber, 1983.

Fraser, David. *Alanbrooke,* New York: Atheneum, 1982.

———. *And We Shall Shock Them: The British Army in the Second World War.* North Pomfret, VT: Hodder & Stoughton, 1985.

Freiden, Seymour, and William Richardson, eds. *The Fatal Decisions.* Trans. Constantine Fitzgibbon. New York: W. Sloan Associates, 1956.

Fugate, Bryan, *Strategy and Tactics on the Eastern Front, 1941.* Novato, CA: Presidio, 1984.

Funk, Arthur L., comp. *The Second World War: A Select Bibliography of Books in English since 1975.* Claremont, CA: Regina Books, 1985.

Funke, Manfred, et al. *Demokratie und Diktatur: Geist und Gestalt politscher Herrschaft in Deutschland und Europa: Festschrift für Karl Dietrich Bracher.* Düsseldorf: Droste, 1987.

————, hrsg. *Hitler, Deutschland und die Mächte: Materialien zur Aussenpolitik des Dritten Reiches*. Düsseldorf: Droste, 1977.

Galante, Pierre. *Operation Valkyrie: The German Generals' Plot against Hitler*. Trans. Mark Howson and Gary Ryan. New York: Harper, 1981.

Galland, Adolf. *The First and the Last: German Fighter Forces in World War II*. Trans. Mervyn Savill. London: Methuen, 1955.

Garland, Albert N., and Howard M. Smyth. *Sicily and the Surrender of Italy*. Washington: USGPO, 1965.

Garlinski, Josef. *Poland in the Second World War*. London: Macmillan, 1985.

Gates, Eleanor M. *End of the Affair: The Collapse of the Anglo-French Alliance, 1939–1940*. Berkeley: University of California Press, 1981.

Gemzell, Carl-Axel. *Raeder, Hitler und Skandinavien: Der Kampf für einen maritimen Operationsplan*. Lund: C. W. K. Gleerups, 1965.

Gilbert, Martin. *Winston S. Churchill*. Vols. VI–VII. Boston: Houghton Mifflin, 1983–1986.

Glover, Michael. *The Fight for the Channel Ports: Calais to Brest, 1940*. Boulder, CO: Westview, 1985.

Gordon, John W. *The Other Desert War: British Special Forces in North Africa, 1940–1943*. Westport, CT: Greenwood, 1987.

Görlitz, Walter, hrsg. *Generalfeldmarschall Keitel: Verbrecher oder Offizier? Erinnerungen, Briefe, Dokumente des Chefs OKW*. Göttingen: Musterschmidt, 1961.

Gosztony, Peter. *Hitlers Fremde Heere: Das Schicksal der nichtdeutschen Armeen im Ostfeldzug*. Düsseldorf: Econ, 1976.

Goutard, Adolphe. *The Battle of France, 1940*. Trans. A. R. P. Burgess. New York: L. Washburn, 1959.

Graham, Dominick, and Shelford Bidwell. *Tug of War: The Battle for Italy, 1943–1945*. New York: St. Martin's, 1986.

Grant, Roderick. *51st Highland Division at War*. London: Ian Allen, 1977.

Great Britain. Central Statistical Office. *Statistical Digest of the War*. London: HMSO, 1975.

Greenfield, Kent Roberts, ed. *Command Decisions*. Washington: USGPO, 1960.

Greiner, Helmuth. *Die oberste Wehrmachtführung, 1939–1943*. Wiesbaden: Limes, 1951.

Gretschko, A. A. et al., hrsg. *Geschichte des Zweiten Weltkriegs*. 12 vols. Berlin: Militarverlag, 1975–.

Gretton, Peter. *Crisis Convoy: The Story of HX 231*. London: Peter Davies, 1974.

Gruchmann, Lothar. *Der Zweite Weltkrieg; Kriegsführung und Politik*. München: Deutscher Taschenbuch, 1967.

Guderian, Heinz. *Panzer Leader*. Trans. Constantine Fitzgibbon. New York: Dutton, 1952.

Gundelach, Karl. *Die deutsche Luftwaffe im Mittlemeer, 1940–1945*. 2 vols. Frankfurt a.M.: Peter Lang, 1981.

Gwyer, J. M. A., and J. R. M. Butler. *Grand Strategy*. Vol. III, *June 1941–August 1942*. London: HMSO, 1964.

Haase, Carl. *The Records of German History in German and Certain Other Record Offices. . . .* Boppard: Harald Boldt, 1975.

Haffner, Sebastian. *The Meaning of Hitler*. Trans. Ewald Osers. London: Weidenfeld & Nicholson, 1979.

Halder, Franz. *Hitler as War Lord*. Trans. Paul Finlay. London: Cassell, 1950.

Hamilton, Nigel. *Master of the Battlefield: Monty's War Years, 1942–1944*. New York: McGraw-Hill, 1984.

————. *Monty: The Field-Marshal, 1944–1976*. London: Hamish Hamilton, 1986.

Hancock, William K., and Margaret Gowing. *British War Economy*. London: HMSO, 1949.

Hansell, Haywood S., Jr. *Strategic Air War against Japan*. Maxwell AFB, AL: Airpower Research Institute, 1980.

Hardach, Karl. *The Political Economy of Germany in the Twentieth Century*. Berkeley: University of California Press, 1980.

Hardesty, Von. *Red Phoenix: The Rise of Soviet Air Power, 1941–1945*. Washington: Smithsonian, 1982.

Harris, Arthur. *Bomber Offensive*. London: Collins, 1947.

Harris, Kenneth. *Attlee*. New York: Norton, 1983.

Harrison, Gordon A. *Cross-Channel Attack*. Washington: USGPO, 1951.

Hastings, Max. *Bomber Command*. New York: Dial, 1979.

———. *Overlord: D-Day, June 6, 1944*. New York: Simon & Schuster, 1984.

Haswell, Chetwynd J. D. *The Intelligence and Deception of the D-Day Landings*. London: Batsford, 1979.

Hathaway, Robert M. *Ambiguous Partnership: Britain and America, 1944–1947*. New York: Columbia University Press, 1981.

Hauner, Milan. *Hitler: A Chronology of His Life and Time*. London: Macmillan, 1983.

———. *India in Axis Strategy; Germany, Japan, and Indian Nationalists in the Second World War*. Stuttgart: Klett-Cotta, 1980.

Haupt, Werner. *Die Deutschen vor Moskau, 1941/42*. Dorheim: Podzun, 1972.

———. *Rückzug im Westen 1944: Von der Invasion zur Ardennen-Offensive*. Stuttgart: Motorbuch, 1978.

———. *Heeresgruppe Nord, 1941–1945*. Bad Nauheim: Podzun, 1966.

Heiber, Helmut. *Adolf Hitler: Eine Biographie*. Berlin: Colloquium, 1960.

Heinz, Grete, and Agnes F. Peterson, eds. *NSDAP Hauptarchiv: Guide to the Hoover Institution Microfilm Collection*. Stanford, CA: Stanford University Press, 1965.

Herde, Peter. *Italien, Deutschland und der Weg in den Krieg im Pazifik 1941*. Wiesbaden: Steiner, 1983.

Hérubel, Michel. *La bataille des Ardennes: décembre 1944–janvier 1945*. Paris: Presses de la Cité, 1979.

Hiden, John, and John Farquharson. *Explaining Hitler's Germany: Historians and the Third Reich*. London: Batsford, 1983.

Higgins, Trumbull. *Soft Underbelly: The Anglo-American Controversy over the Italian Campaign, 1939–1945*. New York: Macmillan, 1969.

———. *Hitler and Russia: The Third Reich in a Two-Front War, 1937–1943*. New York: Macmillan, 1966.

Higham, Robin. *Air Power: A Concise History*. 2nd ed. Manhattan: Sunflower Press, 1984.

———. *Diary of a Disaster: British Aid to Greece, 1940–1941*. Lexington: University of Kentucky Press 1986.

———, ed. *A Guide to the Sources of British Military History*. Berkeley: University of California Press, 1971.

———, ed. *Official Histories: Essays and Bibliographies from Around the World*. Manhattan: Kansas State University Library, 1970.

Hildebrand, Klaus. *Deutsche Aussenpolitik, 1933–1945: Kalkul oder Dogma?* 4. Aufl. Stuttgart: W. Kohlhammer, 1980.

———, hrsg. *Deutsche Frage und europäisches Gleichgewicht: Festschrift für Andreas Hillgruber zum 60. Geburtstag*. Köln: Bohlau, 1985.

———. *Hitlers Strategie: Politik und Kriegführung, 1940–1941*. Frankfurt a.M.: Bernard & Graefe, 1965.

———, hrsg. *Probleme des Zweiten Weltkrieges*. Köln: Kiepenheuer & Witsch, 1967.

————. *Zweierlei Untergang: Die Zerschlagung des Deutschen Reiches und das Ende des europäischen Judentums.* Berlin: Siedler, 1986.

————. *Der zweite Weltkrieg, 1939–45: Kriegsziele und Strategie des grosen Mächte.* Stuttgart: Kohlhammer, 1983.

Hinsley, F. Harry. *Hitler's Strategy.* Cambridge: Cambridge University Press, 1951.

————, et al. *British Intelligence in the Second World War.* 3 vols. in 4 parts. New York: Cambridge University Press, 1979–88.

Hinze, Rolf. *Der Zusammenbruch der Heeresgruppe Mitte im Osten 1944.* Stuttgart: Motorbuch, 1980.

Hirschfeld, Gerald, and Lothar Kettenacker, hrsg. *Der "Führerstaat": Mythos und Realität: Studien zur Struktur und Politik des Dritten Reiches.* Stuttgart: Klett-Cotta, 1981.

Hoffmann, Peter. *The History of the German Resistance, 1933–1945.* Trans. Richard Barry. Cambridge, MA: MIT Press, 1977.

Hofmann, Hans Hubert, hrsg. *Das deutsche Offizierkorps, 1860–1960.* Boppard: Boldt, 1980.

Homer, F. X. J., and Larry D. Wilcox, eds. *Germany and Europe in the Era of Two World Wars.* Charlottesville: University of Virginia Press, 1986.

Homze, Edward L. *Arming the Luftwaffe.* Lincoln: University of Nebraska Press, 1976.

————. *German Military Aviation: A Guide to the Literature.* New York: Garland, 1984.

Horne, Alistair. *To Lose a Battle: France, 1940.* Boston: Little, Brown, 1969.

Horner, D. M. *High Command: Australia and Allied Strategy, 1939–1945.* Winchester, MA: Allen & Unwin, 1982.

Horrocks, Brian. *A Full Life.* London: Collins, 1960.

Hoth, Hermann. *Panzer-Operationen—Die Panzergruppe 3 und der operative Gedanke der deutschen Führung, Sommer 1941.* Neckargemünd: Vowinckel, 1956.

Hough, Richard. *The Greatest Crusade: Roosevelt, Churchill and the Naval Wars.* New York: Morrow, 1986.

Howard, Michael. *Grand Strategy.* Vol. IV, *August 1942–December 1943.* London: HMSO, 1972.

————. *The Continental Commitment.* London: Temple Smith, 1972.

————. *The Mediterranean Strategy in the Second World War.* New York: Praeger, 1968.

————. *Studies in War and Peace.* London: Temple Smith, 1970.

Hummelchen, Gerhard. *Die deutschen Seeflieger, 1933–1945.* München: Bernard & Graefe, 1976.

Illustrated Record of German Army Equipment, 1939–1945. 5 vols. in 6 parts. London: War Office, 1948.

Imperial War Museum. *Handbook.* London: HMSO, 1972.

Institut für Marxismus-Leninismus. *Geschichte der Grossen Vaterländischen Krieges der Sowjetunion.* Trans. 6 vols. Berlin: Deutscher Militärverlag, 1964.

International Commission for the Teaching of History. *The Two World Wars: Selective Bibliography.* New York: Pergamon Press, 1964.

Iriye, Akira. *Power and Culture: The Japanese-American War, 1941–1945.* Cambridge, MA: Harvard University Press, 1981.

Irving, David. *The Rise and Fall of the Luftwaffe: The Life of Field Marshal Erhard Milch.* Boston: Little, Brown, 1974.

Lord Ismay (Hastings). *The Memoirs of Lord Ismay.* London: Heinemann, 1960.

Ivanov, S. P. *The Initial Period of War: A Soviet View.* Washington: USGPO, 1986.

Jäckel, Eberhard. *Hitler in History.* Hanover, NH: University Press of New England, 1985.

Jackson, Robert. *Air War over France, May–June 1940.* London: Ian Allen, 1974.

Jacobsen, Hans-Adolf. *Dünkirchen: Ein Beitrag zur Geschichte des Westfeldzuges, 1940*. Neckargemünd: Vowinckel, 1958.

―――. *Fall Gelb: Der Kampf von den deutschen Operationsplan zur Westoffensive, 1940*. Wiesbaden: Steiner, 1957.

―――. *Zur Konzeption einer Geschichte des Zweiten Weltkrieges, 1939–1945*. Frankfurt a.M.: Bernard & Graefe, 1964.

―――, and Jürgen Rohwer, eds. *Decisive Battles of World War II*. Trans. Edward Fitzgerald. New York: Putnam, 1965.

―――, hrsg. *Dokumente zur Vorgeschichte des Westfeldzuges, 1939–1940*. Göttingen: Musterschmidt, 1956.

―――, hrsg. *Dokumente zum Westfeldzug, 1940*. Göttingen: Musterschmidt, 1960.

―――, hrsg. *Generaloberst Halder: Kriegstagebuch. . . .* 3 vols. Stuttgart: Kohlhammer, 1962–63. (English edition, *The Halder Diaries: The Private War Journals of Colonel General Franz Halder*. Boulder, CO: Westview, 1976, c. 1948.)

James, Robert Rhodes. *Anthony Eden*. London: Weidenfeld & Nicolson, 1986.

Janssen, Gregor. *Das Ministerium Speer: Deutschlands Rüstung im Krieg*. Berlin: Ullstein, 1969.

Jordan, Gerald, ed. *Naval Warfare in the Twentieth Century, 1900–1945*. London: Croom Helm, 1977.

Joslen, H. F. *Order of Battle: United Kingdom and Colonial Formations and Units in the Second World War, 1939–1945*. 2 vols. London: HMSO, 1960.

Jukes, Geoffrey. *Hitler's Stalingrad Decisions*. Berkeley: University of California Press, 1985.

Jung, Hermann. *Die Ardennen-Offensive, 1944–45: Ein Beispiel für die Kriegführung Hitlers*. Göttingen: Musterschmidt, 1971.

Kahn, David. *The Codebreakers: The Story of Secret Writing*. London: Weidenfeld & Nicolson, 1967.

―――. *Hitler's Spies: German Military Intelligence in World War II*. New York: Macmillan, 1978.

―――. *Kahn on Codes: Secrets of the New Cryptology*. New York: Macmillan, 1983.

Karslake, Basil. *1940: The Last Act: The Story of the British Forces in France after Dunkirk*. Hamden, CT: Archon, 1979.

Keegan, John. *The Mask of Command*. New York: Penguin, 1987.

―――. *Six Armies in Normandy: From D-Day to the Liberation of Paris, June 6th–August 25th, 1944*. New York: Viking, 1982.

Kehr, Helen, and Janet Langmaid, comps. *The Nazi Era, 1919–1945: A Select Bibliography of Published Works from the Early Roots to 1980*. London: Mansell, 1982.

Kehrig, Manfred. *Stalingrad: Analyse und Dokumentation einer Schlacht*. Stuttgart: Deutsche Verlags-Anstalt, 1974.

Keilig, Wolf, hrsg. *Rangliste der deutschen Heeres, 1944/45: Dienstalterslisten T und S der Generale und Stabsoffiziers des Heeres. . . .* Bad Nauheim: Podzun, 1955.

Kennedy, John N. *Business of War*. London: Hutchinson, 1957.

Kennedy, Robert M. *The German Conquest in Poland, 1939*. Washington: USGPO, 1956.

Kern, Erich, hrsg. *Adolf Hilter und der Krieg: Der Feldherr*. 2 Aull. Oldendorf: K. W. Schutz., 1973.

Kersaudy, François. *Churchill and De Gaulle*. London: Collins, 1981.

Kesselring, Albert. *Kesselring: A Soldier's Record*. Trans. Lynton Hudson. New York: Morrow, 1954.

Kieft, D. O. *Belgium's Return to Neutrality*. Oxford: Clarendon Press, 1972.

Kirby, S. Woodburn. *The War against Japan*. Vol. III, *The Decisive Battles*. London: HMSO, 1961.

Kitchen, Martin. *British Policy towards the Soviet Union during the Second World War*. New York: St. Martin's, 1986.

Klee, Karl. *Das Unternehmen "Seelöwe": Die geplante deutsche Landung in England, 1940.* Göttingen: Musterschmidt, 1958.

———, hrsg. *Dokumente zum Unternehmen "Seelöwe": Die geplante deutsche Landung in England, 1940.* Göttingen: Musterschmidt, 1958.

Klink, Ernst. *Das Gesetz des Handelns: Die Operation "Zitadelle," 1943.* Stuttgart: Deutsche Verlags-Anstalt, 1966.

Knipping, Franz, and Klaus-Jürgen Müller, hrsg. *Machtbewusstsein in Deutschland am Vorabend des Zweiten Weltkriegs.* Padenborn: Schöningh, 1984.

Knox, MacGregor. *Mussolini Unleashed, 1939–1941.* New York: Cambridge University Press, 1982.

Koch, H. W., ed. *Aspects of the Third Reich.* London: Macmillan, 1985.

Koller, Karl. *Die letzte Monat: Die Tagebuchaufzeichnungen des ehemaligen Chefs des Generalstabes der deutschen Luftwaffe von 14 April bis 27 Mai 1945.* Mannheim: Norbert Wohlgemuth, 1949.

Krausnick, Helmut, et al. *Anatomy of the SS State.* Trans. Richard Barry, Marian Jackson, and Dorothy Lang. New York: Walker, 1972.

Kurowski, Franz. *Deutsche Offizier im Staat, Wirtschaft und Wissenschaft.* Herford: Maximilian, 1967.

———. *Grenadiere, Generale, Kameraden. . . .* Rastatt: Pabel, 1968.

———. *Krieg unter Wasser: U-Boote auf den sieben Meeren, 1939–1945.* Düsseldorf: Econ, 1979.

———. *Der Luftkrieg über Deutschland.* Düsseldorf: Econ, 1977.

Langhorne, Richard, ed. *Diplomacy and Intelligence during the Second World War: Essays in Honour of F. H. Hinsley.* Cambridge: Cambridge University Press, 1985.

Leach, Barry. *German Strategy against Russia, 1939–1941.* New York: Oxford University Press, 1973.

Leasor, James. *War at the Top: Based on the Experience of General Sir Leslie Hollis.* London: Michael Joseph, 1959.

Lee, Asher. *The German Air Force.* New York: Harper, 1946.

———. *Goering—Air Leader.* London: Duckworth, 1972.

Lee, John Michael. *The Churchill Coalition, 1940–1945.* Hamden, CT: Archon, 1980.

Leeb, Werner von. *Tagebuchaufzeichnungen und Lagebeurteilung aus zwei Weltkrieg.* Stuttgart: Deutsche Verlags-Anstalt, 1976.

Leighton, Richard M., and Robert W. Coakley. *Global Logistics and Strategy, 1940–1943.* Washington: USGPO, 1955.

Lenz, Wilhelm, hrsg. *Archivalische Quellen zur deutschen Geschichte seit 1500 in Grossbritannien.* Boppard: Boldt, 1975.

Lewin, Ronald. *The Chief: Field Marshal Lord Wavell, Commander-in-Chief and Viceroy, 1939–1947.* New York: Farrar, Strauss, Giroux, 1980.

———. *Churchill as Warlord.* New York: Stein & Day, 1973.

———. *Hitler's Mistakes.* New York: Morrow, 1984.

———. *The Life and Death of the Afrika Korps.* New York: Quadrangle, 1977.

———. *Rommel as Military Commander.* London: Batsford, 1968.

———. *Slim the Standard-Bearer: The Official Biography of Field Marshal the Viscount Slim.* Hamden, CT: Archon, 1976.

———. *Ultra Goes to War.* London: Hutchinson, 1978.

Lewis, Samuel J. *Forgotten Legions: German Army Infantry Policy, 1918–1941.* New York: Praeger, 1985.

Liddell Hart, Basil H. *The German Generals Talk.* New York: Morrow, 1948.

———, ed. *The Rommel Papers.* Trans. Paul Findlay. London: Collins, 1953.

Lohmann, Walter, and H. H. Hildebrand, hrsg. *Die deutsche Kriegsmarine, 1939–1945; Gliederung, Einsatz, Stellenbesetzung.* 3 Banden. Bad Nauheim: Podzun, 1952.

Lossberg, Bernard von. *Im Wehrmachtführungsstab: Bericht eines Generalstabsoffizier.* Hamburg: Nolke, 1949.

Love, Robert W., Jr., ed. *Changing Interpretations and New Sources in Naval History: Papers from the Third United States Naval Academy History Symposium.* New York: Garland, 1980.

Ludwig, Karl-Heinz. *Technik und Ingenieure im Dritten Reich.* Düsseldorf: Droste, 1974.

MacDonald, Charles B. *The Last Offensive.* Washington: USGPO, 1973.

―――. *A Time for Trumpets: The Untold Story of the Battle of the Bulge.* New York: Morrow, 1985.

Macksey, Kenneth. *Guderian—Panzer General.* London: Macdonald & Jane's, 1975.

Macleod, Roderick, and Denis Kelly, eds. *The Ironside Diaries, 1937–1849.* London: Constable, 1962.

Macmillan, Harold. *War Diaries: The Mediterranean, 1943–1945.* New York: St. Martin's, 1984.

Maier, Klaus A., et al. *Das Deutsche Reich und der Zweite Weltkrieg.* Bd. 2, *Die Errichtung der Hegemonie auf dem europäischen Kontinent.* Stuttgart: Deutsche Verlags-Anstalt, 1979.

Maisky, Ivan. *Memoirs of a Soviet Ambassador: The War, 1939–43.* Trans. Andrew Rothstein. New York: Scribner's, 1967.

Manstein, Erich von. *Lost Victories.* Trans. Anthony G. Lowell. London: Methuen, 1958.

Manstein, Rudiger von, and Theodor Fuchs. *Manstein: Soldat im 20. Jahrhundert: Militärisch-politische Nachlese.* München: Bernard & Graefe, 1981.

Manvell, Roger, and Heinrich Fraenkel. *Hermann Göring.* London: Heinemann, 1962.

Martienssen, Anthony K. *Hitler and His Admirals.* New York: Dutton, 1949.

Maser, Werner. *Hitler: Legend, Myth and Reality.* Trans. Peter and Betty Ross. London: Allen Lane, 1973.

Mason, Francis K. *Battle over Britain: A History of the German Air Assaults on Great Britain, 1917–1918 and July–December 1940, and of the Development of Britain's Air Defences between the World Wars.* London: McWhirter, 1969.

Mason, Timothy W. *Arbeiterklässe und Volksgemeinschaft: Dokumente und Materialen zur deutschen Arbeiterpolitik von 1936 bis 1939.* Opladen: Westdeutscher Verlag, 1975.

Matloff, Maurice. *Mr. Roosevelt's Three Wars: FDR as War Leader.* Colorado Springs: USAF Academy, 1964.

―――. *Strategic Planning for Coalition Warfare, 1943–1944.* Washington: USGPO, 1959.

―――, and Edwin M. Snell. *Strategic Planning for Coalition Warfare, 1941–1942.* Washington: USGPO, 1953.

Mayer, S. L., and W. J. Koenig. *The Two World Wars: A Guide to Manuscript Collections in the United Kingdom.* New York: Bowker, 1976.

Mearsheimer, John J. *Conventional Deterrence.* Ithaca, NY: Cornell University Press, 1983.

Medlicott, William N. *The Economic Blockade.* 2 vols. London: HMSO, 1952–59.

Meier-Dörnberg, Wilhelm. *Die Ölversorgung der Kriegsmarine, 1935 bis 1945.* Freiburg i.Br.: Rombach, 1973.

Mellenthin, F. W. von. *German Generals of World War II as I Saw Them.* Norman: University of Oklahoma Press, 1977.

Mennel, Rainir. *Die Schlussphase des Zweiten Weltkriegs im Westen (1944/45): Eine Studie zur politischen Geographie.* Osnabrück: Biblio, 1981.

Meskill, Johanna M. *Hitler and Japan: The Hollow Alliance.* New York: Atherton, 1966.

Messenger, Charles. *Cologne: The First 1000-Bomber Raid.* London: Ian Allen, 1972.

Meyer, Brun, hrsg. *Dienstalterliste der Waffen-SS: SS-Obergruppenführer bis SS-Hauptsturmführer, Stand vom 1. Juli 1944.* Osnabrück: Biblio, 1987.

Michalka, Wolfgang. *Ribbentrop und die deutsche Weltpolitik, 1933–1940: Aussenpolitische Konzeptionen und Entscheidungsprozesse im Dritten Reich.* München: W. Fink, 1980.

Michel, Henri. *La défaite de la France (Septembre 1939–Juin 1940).* Paris: Presses Universitaires de France, 1980.

———. *The Second World War.* 2 vols. Trans. Douglas Parmee. New York: Praeger, 1975.

———. *The Shadow War.* Trans. Richard Barry. New York: Harper, 1973.

Middlebrook, Martin. *The Battle of Hamburg: Allied Air Forces against a German City in 1943.* New York: Scribner's, 1980.

———. *Convoy: The Battle for Convoys SC. 122 and HX. 229.* London: Allen Lane, 1976.

———, and Christ Everitt. *The Bomber Command War Diaries: An Operational Reference Book, 1939–1945.* New York: Viking, 1985.

Millett, Allan R., and Williamson Murray, eds. *Military Effectiveness.* Vol. III. Winchester, MA: Allen & Unwin, 1988.

Milner, Marc. *North Atlantic Run: The Royal Canadian Navy and the Battle for the Convoys.* Toronto: University of Toronto Press, 1985.

Milward, Alan S. *War, Economy, and Society, 1939–1945.* Berkeley: University of California Press, 1977.

———. *The German Economy at War.* London: Athlone, 1965.

Moll, Otto E. *Die deutsche Generalfeldmarschalle.* Rastatt: Pabel, 1961.

Molony, C. J. C. *The Mediterranean and the Middle East.* Vol. V, *The Campaign in Sicily, 1943, and the Campaign in Italy, 3rd September 1943 to 31st March 1944.* London: HMSO, 1973.

Mommsen, Wolfgang, A., hrsg. *Die Nachlässe in den deutschen Archiven (mit Ergängzungen aus anderen Bestanden).* 2 vols. Boppard: Harald Boldt, 1977–83.

Montagu, Ewen. *Beyond Top Secret Ultra.* New York: Coward, McCann, 1978.

Lord Montgomery of Alamein (Bernard). *Memoirs.* London: Collins, 1948.

———. *Normandy to the Baltic: A Personal Account of the Conquest of Germany.* London: Hutchinson, 1947.

Mordal, Jacques [pseud]. *Dunkerque.* Paris: Editions France-Empire, 1960.

———. *La guerre commence en Pologne.* Paris: Presses de la Cité, 1968.

———. *Les poches de l'Atlantique.* Paris: Presses de la Cité, 1965.

Morgan, Frederick E. *Overture to Overlord.* New York: Doubleday, 1950.

Morison, Samuel Eliot. *The Atlantic Battle Won, May 1943–May 1945.* Boston: Little, Brown, 1956.

———. *The Invasion of France and Germany, 1944–1945.* Boston: Little, Brown, 1957.

Mountbatten, Lord Louis. *Report to the Combined Chiefs of Staff: Southwest Asia, 1933–1945.* London: HMSO, 1951.

Mrazek, James E. *The Fall of Eben Emael: Prelude to Dunkerque.* Washington: Luce, 1970.

Müller, Klaus-Jürgen. *The Army, Politics, and Society, 1933–1946: Studies in the Army's Relationship to Nazism.* Manchester: Manchester University Press, 1987.

———. *Das Heer und Hitler: Armee und nationalsozialistisches Regime, 1933–1940.* Stuttgart: Deutsche Verlags-Anstalt, 1969.

Murawski, Erich. *Der deutsche Wehrmachtbericht, 1939–1945.* 2. Aufl. Boppard: Harald Boldt, 1962.

Murphy, W. E. *The Relief of Tobruk.* Auckland: Whitcombe & Tombs, 1961.

Murray, Williamson. *The Change in the European Balance of Power, 1938–1939: The Path to Ruin*. Princeton: Princeton University Press, 1984.

———. *Luftwaffe*. Annapolis: Nautical & Aviation, 1985.

Musgrove, Gordon. *Pathfinder Force: A History of 8 Group*. London: Macdonald & Jane's, 1976.

Nelson, Andreas. *The German Air Force General Staff*. New York: Arno, 1959.

Neuberger, Otto. *Official Publications of Present-Day Germany*. Washington: USGPO, 1942.

Nicholson, Nigel. *Alex: The Life of Field Marshal Alexander of Tunis*. London: Pan, 1973.

O'Neill, James E., and Robert W. Krauskopf, eds. *World War II: An Account of Its Documents*. Washington: Howard University Press, 1976.

Ose, Dieter. *Entscheidung im Westen, 1944: Der Oberbefehlshaber West und die Abwehr der allierten Invasion*. Stuttgart: Deutsche Verlags-Anstalt, 1982.

Osterkamp, Theo. *Tragödie der Luftwaffe? Kritische Begnungs mit dem gleichmassigen Werk von Irwing/Milch*. Neckargemünd: Vowinckel, 1971.

Overy, Richard J. *The Air War, 1939–1944*. London: Europa, 1980.

———. *Goering: The 'Iron Man.'* London: Routledge & Kegan Paul, 1984.

Pack, Stanley W. C. *Cunningham: The Commander*. London: Batsford, 1974.

———. *Operation "Husky": The Allied Invasion of Sicily*. New York: Hippocrene, 1977.

Padfield, Peter. *Dönitz: The Last Führer: Portrait of a Nazi War Leader*. London: Victor Gollancz, 1984.

Paret, Peter, ed. *Makers of Modern Strategy from Machiavelli to the Nuclear Age*. Princeton: Princeton University Press, 1986.

Parkinson, Roger. *The Auk: Auchinleck, Victor at Alamein*. London: Granada, 1977.

Parotkin, Ivan, ed. *The Battle of Kursk*. Trans. G. P. Ivanov-Mumjiev. Moscow: Progress Publishers, 1974.

Pawle, Gerald. *The War and Colonel Warden: Based on the Recollections of Commander C. R. Thompson, Personal Assistant to the Prime Minister, 1940–1945*. New York: Knopf, 1963.

Peillard, Leonce. *La bataille de l'Atlantique*. 2 vols. Paris: Robert Laffont, 1974.

Pelling, Henry. *Winston Churchill*. New York: Dutton, 1974.

Peterson, Agnes F. *Western Europe: A Survey of Holdings at the Hoover Institution of War, Revolution and Peace*. Stanford, CA: Hoover Institution, 1970.

Peterson, Edward N. *The Limits of Hitler's Power*. Princeton: Princeton University Press, 1969.

Petrow, Richard. *The Bitter Years; The Invasion and Occupation of Denmark and Norway, April 1940–May 1945*. New York: Morrow, 1974.

Pitt, Barrie. *The Crucible of War: Western Desert, 1941*. London: Jonathan Cape, 1980.

———. *Crucible of War: Year of Alamein, 1942*. London: Jonathan Cape, 1982.

Playfair, Ian S. O. *The Mediterranean and the Middle East*. Vol. II, *The Germans Come to the Help of Their Ally (1941)*. London: HMSO, 1957.

———. *The Mediterranean and the Middle East*. Vol. III, *British Fortunes Reach Their Lowest Ebb (Sep 1941–Sep 1942)*. London: HMSO, 1960.

———, and C. J. C. Molony. *The Mediterranean and the Middle East*. Vol. IV, *The Destruction of the Axis Forces in Africa*. London: HMSO, 1966.

Pogue, Forrest C. *George C. Marshall*. Vol. III, *Organizer of Victory, 1943–1945*. New York: Viking, 1973.

———. *The Supreme Command*. Washington: USGPO, 1954.

Poirer, Robert G., and Albert Conner. *The Red Army Order of Battle in the Great Patriotic War*. Novato, CA: Presidio Press, 1985.

Postan, M. M. *British War Production*. London: HMSO, 1952.

Price, Alfred. *Battle over the Reich*. New York: Scribner's, 1974.

——. *Luftwaffe Handbook, 1939–1945*. New York: Scribner's, 1977.

Public Record Office. *The Second World War: A Guide to Documents in the Public Record Office*. London: HMSO, 1972.

Puttkamer, Karl Jesko von. *Die Unheimliche See: Hitler und die Kriegsmarine*. Wien: K. Kuhne, 1952.

Raeder, Erich. *My Life*. Trans. Henry W. Drexel. Annapolis: US Naval Institute Press, 1960.

Regling, Volkmar, *Amiens 1940: Der deutsche Durchbruch südlich vom Amiens, 5. bis 8. Juni 1940*. Freiburg i.Br.: Rombach, 1968.

Reinhardt, Klaus. *Die Wende vor Moskau: Das Scheitern dem Strategie Hitlers im Winter 1941/42*. Stuttgart: Deutsche Verlags-Anstalt, 1972.

Les relations militaires Franco-Belges, mars 1936–10 mai 1940. Paris: Centre de la Recherche Scientifique, 1968.

Reuth, Ralf Georg. *Entscheidung im Mittelmeer: Die südliche Peripherie in der deutschen Strategie des Zweiten Weltkrieges, 1940–1942*. Koblenz: Bernard & Graefe, 1985.

Reynolds, David. *The Creation of the Anglo-American Alliance, 1937–1941: A Study in Competitive Cooperation*. Chapel Hill: University of North Carolina Press, 1982.

Rich, Norman. *Hitler's War Aims: Ideology, the Nazi State, and the Course of Expansion*. New York: Norton, 1973.

——. *Hitler's War Aims: The Establishment of the New Order*. New York: Norton, 1974.

Richards, Denis. *Portal of Hungerford: The Life of Marshal of the Royal Air Force Viscount Portal of Hungerford*. New York: Holmes & Meier, 1977.

Roberts, Henry L., et al., eds., *Foreign Affairs Bibliography, 1942–1972*. 3 vols. New York: Bowker, 1955–1976.

Rohde, Horst. *Das Deutsche Wehrmachttransportwesen im Zweiten Weltkrieg*. Stuttgart: Deutsche Verlags-Anstalt, 1971.

Rohwer, Jürgen. *Axis Submarine Successes, 1939–1945*. Trans. John Broadwin. Annapolis: US Naval Institute Press, 1983.

——. *The Critical Convoy Battles of 1943: The Battle for HX 229/SC 122*. London: Ian Allen, 1975.

——, and Gerhard Hummelchen. *Chronology of the War at Sea, 1939–1945*. 2 vols. Trans. Derek Martens. London: Ian Allen, 1974.

——, and Eberhard Jäckel, hrsg. *Kriegswende, Dezember 1941*. Koblenz: Bernard & Graefe, 1984.

Romanus, Charles F., and Riley Sunderland. *Stilwell's Command Problems*. Washington, USGPO, 1956.

Rose, Kenneth. *The Later Cecils*. New York: Harper, 1975.

Roskill, Stephen. *Churchill and the Admirals*. London: Collins, 1977.

——. *The War at Sea, 1939–1945*. 3 vols. London: HMSO, 1956–1960.

Rossler, Eberhard. *The U-Boat: The Evolution and Technical History of German Submarines*. Trans. Harold Erenberg. London: Arms & Armour Press, 1981.

Rothfeder, Herbert P., ed. *Checklist of Select German Pamphlets and Booklets of the Weimar and Nazi Period in the University of Michigan Library*. Ann Arbor: University of Michigan Library, 1961.

Rothwell, Victor. *Britain and the Cold War, 1941–1947*. London: Jonathan Cape, 1982.

Ruge, Friedrich. *Rommel in Normandy*. San Rafael, CA: Presidio Press, 1978.

Ruppenthal, Roland G. *Logistical Support of the Armies*. 2 vols. Washington: USGPO, 1953–1959.

Ryan, Cornelius. *The Longest Day: June 6, 1944*. New York: Simon & Schuster, 1959.

Ryder, Rowland. *Oliver Leese*. London: Hamish Hamilton, 1987.

Sainsbury, Keith. *The North Africa Landings, 1942: A Strategic Survey*. London: Davis-Poynter, 1976.

―――. *The Turning Point: Roosevelt, Stalin, Churchill, and Chiang Kai-shek, 1943: The Moscow, Cairo, and Teheran Conferences*. New York: Oxford University Press, 1985.

Salewski, Michael. *Die deutsche Seekriegsleitung, 1935–1945*. 3 vols. Frankfurt a.M.: Bernard & Graefe, 1970–75.

Saward, Dudley. *'Bomber' Harris: The Story of Marshal of the Royal Air Force Sir Arthur Harris*. . . . London: Cassell/Buchan & Enright, 1984.

Schall-Riaucour, Heidemarie Grafin. *Aufstand und Gehorsam: Offiziertum und Generalstab im Umbruch: Leben und Wirken von Generaloberst Franz Halder Generalstabschef, 1938–1942*. Wiesbaden: Limes, 1972.

Schmeller, Helmut J. *Hitler and Keitel: An Investigation of the Influence of Party Ideology on the Command of the Armed Forces in Germany between 1938–1945*. Fort Hays, KS: Fort Hays State College Press, 1970.

Schmidt, Matthias. *Albert Speer: The End of a Myth*. Trans. Joachim Neugroschel. New York: St. Martin's, 1984.

Schofield, Brian B. *Operation Neptune*. London: Ian Allen, 1974.

Schramm, Percy E. *Hitler: The Man and the Military Leader*. Trans. Donald S. Detwiler. Chicago: Quadrangle, 1971.

Schreiber, Gerhard, et al. *Das Deutsche Reich und der Zweite Weltkrieg*. Bd. 3, *Der Mittermeerraum und Südosteuropa: Von der "non belligeranza" Italiens bis zum Kriegseintritt der Vereinigten Staaten*. Stuttgart: Deutsche Verlags-Anstalt, 1984.

―――. *Hitler Interpretationen, 1923–1983: Ergebnisse, Methoden und Probleme der Forschung*. Darmstadt: Wissenschaftliche Buchgesellschaft, 1984.

―――. *Revisionismus und Weltmachtstreben: Marineführung und deutsch-italienische Beziehungen, 1919–1944*. Stuttgart: Deutsche Verlags-Anstalt, 1978.

Schroeder, Christa. *Er war mein Chef: Aus dem Nachlass der Sekretärin von Adolf Hitler*. Hrsg. Anton Joachimsthaler. München: Langen Müller, 1985.

Schumann, Wolfgang, hrsg. *Deutschland im Zweiten Weltkrieg*. 5 vols. Berlin: Akademie der Wissenschaften der DDR, 1974–1984.

Schustereit, Hartmut. *Vabanque: Hitlers Angriff auf die Sowjetunion 1941 als. Versuch durch den Sieg im Osten den Wester zu bezwingen*. Herford: Mittler, 1988.

Seaton, Albert. *The Battle for Moscow, 1941–1942*. New York: Stein & Day, 1971.

―――. *The German Army, 1933–45*. New York: St. Martin's, 1982.

―――. *The Russo-German War, 1941–1945*. New York: Praeger, 1971.

Seidler, Franz W. *Fritz Todt: Baumeister des Dritten Reiches*. München: F. A. Herbig, 1986.

Senger und Etterlin, Ferdinand M. Von. *German Tanks of World War II: The Complete Illustrated History of German Armored Vehicles, 1926–1945*. Trans. James Lucas. Harrisburg, PA: Stackpole, 1969.

Siegler, Fritz Freiheer von, hrsg. *Die höheren Dienststellen der deutschen Wehrmacht, 1933–1945*. München: Institut für Zeitgeschichte, 1953.

Siewert, Kurt. *Schuldig? Die Generale unter Hitler: Stellung und Einfluss der höhen militärischen Führer im nationalsozialistischen Staat*. Bad Nauheim: Podzun, 1968.

Slessor, John C. *The Central Blue: Recollections and Reflections*. London: Cassell, 1956.

Lord Slim (William). *Defeat into Victory*. London: Cassell, 1956.

Smith, Bradley F. *Adolf Hitler: His Family, Childhood and Youth*. Stanford, CA: Stanford University Press, 1968.

Smith, E. D. *Battle for Burma*. New York: Holmes & Meier, 1979.

Smith, Myron J., Jr. *World War II: The European and Mediterranean Theaters: An Annotated Bibliography*. New York: Garland, 1984.

Smith, Tommy J. *Ultra in the Battle of Britain: The Real Key to Success*. Alexandria, VA: Defense Technical Information Center, 1980.

Sorge, Martin K. *The Other Price of Hitler's War: German Military and Civilian Losses Resulting from World War II*. Westport, CT: Greenwood, 1986.

Spears, Edward L. *Assignment to Catastrophe*. 2 vols. London: Heinemann, 1954–55.

Speer, Albert. *Infiltration*. Trans. Joachim Neugroschel. New York: Macmillan, 1981.

———. *Inside the Third Reich*. Trans. Richard and Clara Winston. New York: Macmillan, 1970.

———. *Spandau: The Secret Diaries*. London: Collins, 1976.

Spiedel, Hans. *Invasion 1944*. Trans. Theo Crevanna. New York: Paperback Library, 1968, c. 1950.

Stacey, Charles P. *Six Years of War: The Army in Canada, Britain, and the Pacific*. Ottawa: Queen's Printer, 1955.

———. *The Victory Campaign: The Operations in North-West Europe, 1944–45*. Ottawa: Queen's Printer, 1960.

Staudinger, Hans. *The Inner Nazi: A Critical Analysis of Hitler's* Mein Kampf. Baton Rouge: Louisiana State University Press, 1981.

Stein, George H. *The Waffen SS: Hitler's Elite Guard at War, 1939–1945*. Ithaca, NY: Cornell University Press, 1966.

Stierlin, Helm. *Adolf Hitler, Familienperspektiven*. Frankfurt a.M: Suhrkamp, 1975.

Stoler, Mark A. *The Politics of the Second Front: American Military Planning and Diplomacy in Coalition Warfare, 1941–1943*. Westport, CT: Greenwood, 1977.

Strawson, John. *Hitler as Military Commander*. London: Batsford, 1971.

Streit, Christian. *Keine Kameraden: Die Wehrmacht und die sowietischen Kriegsgefangenen, 1941–1945*. Stuttgart: Deutsche Verlags-Anstalt, 1978.

Stumpf, Reinhard. *Die Wehrmacht Elite: Rang- und Herkunfts-Struktur der deutscher Generale und Admirale, 1933–1945*. Boppard: Boldt, 1982.

Suchenwirth, Richard. *Command and Leadership in the German Air Force*. Montgomery, AL: Aerospace Studies Institute, 1969.

Sweetman, John, ed. *Sword and Mace: 20th Century History of Civil and Military Relations in Britain*. London: Brassey's, 1986.

Sweets, John F. *Choices in Vichy France: The French under German Occupation*. New York: Oxford University Press, 1986.

Swinson, Arthur. *Kohima*. London: Cassell, 1966.

Tantum, W. H., IV, and E. J. Hoffschmidt, eds. *The Rise and Fall of the German Air Force (1933 to 1945)*. Old Greenwich, CT: WE, Inc., 1969.

Taylor, Alan J. P., et al. *Churchill Revised: A Critical Assessment*. New York: Dial, 1969.

Taylor, Telford. *The March of Conquest: The German Victories in Western Europe, 1940*. New York: Simon & Schuster, 1958.

———. *Sword and Swastika*. New York: Simon & Schuster, 1952.

Taysen, Adalbert von. *Tobruk 1941: Der Kampf in Nordafrika*. Freiburg i. Br.: Rombach, 1976.

Lord Tedder (Arthur). *With Prejudice: The War Memoirs of Marshal of the Royal Air Force, Lord Tedder*. London: Cassell, 1966.

Terraine, John. *A Time for Courage: The Royal Air Force in World War II*. New York: Macmillan, 1985.

Teske, Hermann. *Bewegungskrieg: Führungsprobleme einer Infanterie-Division im Westfeldzug, 1940.* Heidelberg: Vowinckel, 1955.

Tessin, Georg. *Verbande und Truppen der deutschen Wehrmacht und Waffen-SS im zweiten Weltkrieg, 1939–1945.* 14 vols. Frankfurt a.M.: Mittler, 1966–1977.

Thies, Jochen. *Architekt der Weltherrschaft: Die "Endziele" Hitlers.* Düsseldorf: Droste, 1976.

Thomas, Georg. *Geschichte der deutschen Wehr- und Rüstungswirtschaft (1918–1943/45).* Boppard: Boldt, 1966.

Thompson, R. W. *Churchill and Morton.* London: Hodder & Stoughton, 1976.

Thomson, David. *The Proposal for Anglo-French Union in 1940.* Oxford: Clarendon Press, 1966.

Thorne, Christopher. *Allies of a Kind: The United States, Britain, and the War against Japan, 1941–1945.* New York: Oxford University Press, 1978.

———. *The Approach of War, 1938–1939.* New York: St. Martin's, 1968.

Trevor-Roper, Hugh R. *The Last Days of Hitler.* London: Macmillan, 1950.

Tuker, Francis I. S. *Approach to Battle.* London: Cassell, 1963.

Turnbull, Patrick. *Dunkirk: Anatomy of a Disaster.* New York: Holmes & Meier, 1978.

Turner, Henry Ashby, Jr. *Hitler—Memoirs of a Confidant.* Trans. Ruth Hein. New Haven, CT: Yale University Press, 1985.

Überschär, Gerd R., and Wolfram Wette, hrsg. *"Unternehmen Barbarossa": Der deutsche überfall auf die Sowjetunion, 1941: Berichte, Analysen, Dokumente.* Paderborn: Schöningh, 1984.

Uhle-Wetter, Franz. *Höhe- und Wendepunkte: Deutscher Militärgeschichte.* Mainz: von Hase & Koehler, 1984.

Unesco Yearbook on Peace and Conflict Studies, 1985. Westport, CT: Greenwood, 1987.

United States Strategic Bombing Survey. *The Effects of Strategic Bombing on the German War Economy.* Washington: Overall Economic Effects Division, 1945.

van Creveld, Martin. *Fighting Power: German and US Army Performance, 1939–1945.* Westport, CT: Greenwood, 1982.

———. *Hitler's Strategy, 1940–1941: The Balkan Clue.* London: Cambridge University Press, 1973.

———. *Supplying War: Logistics from Wallenstein to Patton.* Cambridge: Cambridge University Press, 1978.

Van der Vat, Dan. *The Atlantic Campaign: World War II's Great Struggle at Sea.* New York: Harper & Row, 1988.

Van Ishoven, Armand. *Luftwaffe in the Battle of Britain.* New York: Scribner's, 1980.

Verrier, Anthony. *The Bomber Offensive.* New York: Macmillan, 1969.

Volker, Karl-Heinz. *Die Deutsche Luftwaffe, 1933–1939: Aufbau, Führung und Rüstung der Luftwaffe sowie die Entwicklung der deutschen Luftkriegstheorie.* Stuttgart: Deutsche Verlags-Anstalt, 1967.

———. *Dokumente und Dokumentarfotos zur Geschichte der Deutschen Luftwaffe: Aus Geheimakten des Reichswehrministeriums, 1919–1933, und des Reichsluftfahrtministeriums, 1933–1939.* Stuttgart: Deutsche Verlags-Anstalt, 1968.

Volkmann, Udo. *Die Britische Luftverteidigung und die Abwehr der deutschen Luftangriff während der 'Luftschlacht um England' bis zum Juni 1941.* Osnabrück: Biblio, 1982.

Vormann, Nikolaus von. *Der Feldzug 1939 in Polen: Die Operationen des Heeres.* Weissenburg: Prinz-Eugen Verlag, 1958.

Wagener, Carl. *Heeresgruppe Süd: Der Kampf im Suden der Ostfront, 1941–1945.* Bad Nauheim: Podzun, 1967.

Waite, Robert G. L. *The Psychopathic God: Adolf Hitler*. New York: Signet, 1977.

Warlimont, Walter. *Inside Hitler's Headquarters*. Trans. R. H. Barry. New York: Praeger, 1964.

Warner, Geoffrey. *Iraq and Syria, 1941*. London: Davis-Poynter, 1974.

Warner, Philip. *Alamein*. London: William Kimber, 1979.

———. *Auchinleck: The Lonely Soldier*. London: Macmillan, 1981.

Warren, John C. *Airborne Operations in World War II, European Theater*. Manhattan, KS: MA/AH, 1956.

Webster, Charles, and Noble Frankland. *The Strategic Air Offensive against Germany, 1939–1945*. 4 vols. London: HMSO, 1961.

Weeks, Ronald M. *Organisation and Equipment for War*. New York: Cambridge University Press, 1950.

Wegmuller, Hans. *Die Abwehr der Invaison: Die Konzeption des Oberbefehlshabers West, 1940–1944*. Freiburg i.Br.: Rombach, 1979.

Wegner, Bernd. *Hitlers politische Soldaten: Die Waffen-SS, 1933–1945*. Paderborn: Schöningh, 1982.

Weigley, Russell F. *Eisenhower's Lieutenants: The Campaigns of France and Germany, 1944–1945*. Bloomington: Indiana University Press, 1981.

Weinberg, Gerhard L. *The Foreign Policy of Hitler's Germany: Starting World War II, 1937–1939*. Chicago: University of Chicago Press, 1980.

———. *Germany and the Soviet Union, 1939–1941*. Leiden: E. J. Brill, 1954.

———. *World in the Balance: Behind the Scenes of World War II*. Hanover, NH: University Press of New England, 1981.

Werth, Alexander. *Russia at War, 1941–1945*. New York: Dutton, 1964.

Westphal, Siegfried. *Der deutsche Generalstab auf der Anklagebank Nürnberg, 1945–1948*. Mainz: Von Hase & Koehler, 1977.

———. *Erinnerungen*. Mainz: Von Hase & Koehler, 1975.

———. *The German Army in the West*. Abridged ed. London: Cassell, 1951.

Wheatley, Ronald. *Operation Sea Lion: German Plans for the Invasion of England, 1939–1942*. Oxford: Clarendon, 1958.

Wheeler-Bennett, John W. *The Nemesis of Power: The German Army in Politics, 1918–1945*. 2nd ed. New York: Macmillan, 1964.

Lord Wilson (Maitland). *Eight Years Overseas, 1939–1947*. London: Hutchinson, 1948.

Wilson, S. S. *The Cabinet Office to 1945*. London: HMSO, 1975.

Wilt, Alan F. *The Atlantic Wall: Hitler's Defenses in the West, 1941–1944*. Ames: Iowa State University Press, 1975.

———. *The French Riviera Campaign of August 1944*. Carbondale: Southern Illinois University Press, 1981.

Wistrich, Robert. *Who's Who in Nazi Germany*. New York: Macmillan, 1982.

Wolfe, Robert, ed. *Captured German and Related Records: A National Archives Conference*. Athens: Ohio University Press, 1974.

Wood, Derek. *Attack Warning Red: The Royal Observer Corps and the Defence of Britain, 1925–1975*. London: Macdonald & Jane's, 1976.

———, and Derek Dempster. *The Narrow Margin*. London: Hutchinson, 1961.

Woodward, Llewllyn. *British Foreign Policy in the Second World War*. 5 vols. London: HMSO, 1970–76.

Wright, Gordon. *The Ordeal of Total War, 1939–1945*. New York: Harper, 1968.

Wykeham, Peter. *Fighter Command: A Study of Air Defense, 1914–1960*. London: Putnam, 1960.

Zentner, Christian, and Friedemann Bedurftig, hrsg. *Das Grosse Lexikon der Drittes Reiches*. München: Südwest Verlag, 1985.

Ziegler, Janet. *World War II: Books in English, 1945–1965*. Stanford, CA: Hoover Institution, 1970.

Ziemke, Earl F. *The German Northern Theater of Operations, 1940–1945.* Washington: USGPO, 1959.

———. *Stalingrad to Berlin: The German Defeat in the East.* Washington: USGPO, 1968.

———, and Magna E. Bauer. *Moscow to Stalingrad: Decision in the East.* Washington: USGPO, 1987.

Zins, Alfred. *Die Operation Zitadelle: Die militärgeschichtliche Diskussion und ihr Niederschlag im öffentlichen Bewusstsein als didaktisches Problem.* Frankfurt a. M.: Peter Lang, 1986.

Lord Zuckerman (Solly). *From Apes to Warlords: The Autobiography.* London: Hamish Hamilton, 1978.

DISSERTATIONS

Cochran, Alexander S., Jr. *Spectre of Defeat: Anglo-American Planning for the Invasion of Italy in 1943.* Ph.D., University of Kansas, 1985.

Desquesnes, Remy. *Atlantikwall et Südwall: Les défenses allemandes sur le littoral français (1941–1944).* Ph.D., Université de Caen, 1987.

Gormley, Daniel J. *From 'Arcadia' to 'Casablanca': The Formation of Military-Political Policy, December 1941–January 1943.* Ph.D., Georgetown University, 1978.

Mierzejewski, Alfred C. *Wheels Must Roll for Victory: Allied Air Power and the German War Economy, 1941–1945.* Ph.D., University of North Carolina, 1985.

Schwedes, Jeffrey T. *Winston Churchill's War Aims in Europe, 1940–1945.* Ph.D., University of Minnesota, 1977.

ARTICLES

Alexander, Don W. "Repercussions of the Breda Variant." *French Historical Studies,* 8 (Spr 1974): 459–488.

Alexander, Martin S. "Prophet Without Honour? The French High Command and Pierre Tal Hinger's Report on the Ardennes Defences, March 1940." *War and Society,* 4 (May 1986): 52–77.

Alves, Dora. "The Resupply of Malta in World War II." *Naval War College Review,* 33 (Sep–Oct 1980): 63–72.

Assmann, Heinz. "Some Personal Recollections of Adolf Hitler." Trans. Roland Krause. *US Naval Institute Proceedings,* 79 (Dec 1953): 1288–1295.

"La bataille de l'Atlantique (Bibliographie)." *Revue d'histoire de la deuxième guerre mondiale,* 18 (Jan 1969): 113–126.

Baum, Walter. "Der Zusammenbruch der obersten deutschen Militärischenführung 1945." *Wehrwissenschaftliche Rundschau,* 10 (1960): 237–266.

Baumgart, Winfried. "Zur Ansprache Hitlers von der Führern der Wehrmacht am 22. August 1939." *Vierteljahrshefte für Zeitgeschichte,* 16 (Jan 1968): 120–149.

Beaumont, Roger. "The Bomber Offensive as a Second Front." *Journal of Contemporary History,* 22 (Jan 1987): 3–19.

Beck, Earl R. "The Allied Bombing of Germany, 1942–1945, and the German Response: Dilemmas of Judgment." *German Studies Review,* 5 (Oct 1982): 325–337.

Bédarida, François. "France, Britain and the Nordic Countries." *Scandinavian Journal of History,* 21 (1977): 2–27.

Bennett, Ralph. "Ultra and Some Command Decisions." *Journal of Contemporary History,* 16 (Jan 1981): 131–151.

Boehm, Hermann. "Zur Ansprache Hitlers vor den Führern der Wehrmacht am 22. August 1939." *Vierteljahrshefte für Zeitgeschichte,* 19 (July 1971): 294–304.

Bond, Brian. "Dunkirk: Myths and Lessons." *RUSI Journal,* 127 (Sep 1982): 3–8.

Boog, Horst. "German Air Intelligence in World War II." *Aerospace Historian,* 33 (Jun 1986): 121–129.

————. "Higher Command Leadership in the German Luftwaffe, 1935–1945." *Proceedings of the Eighth Military History Symposium,* US Air Force Academy, Oct 1978, 128–158.

————. "The Organization of the German Air Force High Command, 1935–1945." *Revue internationale d'histoire militaire,* 47 (1980): 95–106.

Buck, Gerhard. "Das Führerhauptquartier, Seine Darstellung in der deutschen Literatur." *Jahresbibliographie,* 38 (1966): 549–566.

————. "Der Wehrmachtführungsstab im Oberkommando der Wehrmacht." *Jahresbibliographie,* 45 (1973): 407–454.

Burdick, Charles B. "Die Unterlagen über Einheiten des deutschen Heeres im Zweiten Weltkrieg." *Wehrwissenschaftliche Rundschau,* 16 (1966): 55–58, 112–116, 172–176.

Butler, J. R. M. "L'organisation du Haut-Commandement du Royaume-Uni et son impact sur la strategie alliée." *Revue d'histoire de la deuxième guerre mondiale,* 25 (Oct 1975): 27–42.

"La campagne de France (mai–juin 1940)." *Revue d'histoire de la deuxieme guerre mondiale,* 2 (Jul 1953).

Cochran, Alexander S., Jr. "Magic, Ultra, and the Second World War: Literature, Sources, and Outlook." *Military Affairs,* 46 (Apr 1982): 88–92.

Cole, Robert. "The Other 'Phoney War': British Propaganda in Neutral Europe, September–December 1939." *Journal of Contemporary History,* 22 (Jul 1987): 455–479.

Constantini, A. "La bataille de Smolensk (10 juillet–10 septembre 1941)." *Revue d'histoire de la deuxième guerre mondiale,* 15 (Jul 1965): 53–78.

Danchev, Alex. "Dilly-Dally, or Having the Last Word: Field Marshal Sir John Dill and Prime Minister Winston Churchill." *Journal of Contemporary History,* 22 (Jan 1987): 21–44.

De Jong, C. T. "La préparation de l'attaque allemandes sur la Hollande en 1940." *Revue d'histoire de la deuxième guerre mondiale,* 4 (Oct 1955): 1–16.

Deutsch, Harold C. "The Influence of Ultra in World War II." *Parameters,* 4 (Dec 1978): 2–15.

Dilks, David. "Great Britain and Scandinavia in the 'Phoney War.'" *Scandinavian Journal of History,* 2 (1977): 29–51.

————. "The Twilight War and the Fall of France: Chamberlain and Churchill in 1940." *Transactions of the Royal Historical Society,* 28 (1978): 61–86.

DiNardo, R. L., and Austin Bay. "Horse-Drawn Transport in the German Army." *Journal of Contemporary History,* 23 (Jan 1988): 129–142.

Douglas, W. A. B. "Kanadas Marine und Luftwaffe in der Atlantik-Schlacht." *Marine Rundschau,* 77 (Mar 1980): 151–164.

Dupuy, Trevor N. "Mythos of Verity? The Quantified Judgment Model and German Combat Effectiveness." *Military Affairs,* 50 (Oct 1986): 204–210.

Edmonds, Robin. "Yalta and Potsdam: Forty Years Afterwards." *International Affairs,* 62 (Spr 1986): 214–228.

Emerson, William. "Franklin Roosevelt as Commander-in-Chief in World War II." *Military Affairs,* 22 (Wtr 1958): 181–207.

Förster, Jürgen. "Hitler's War Aims against the Soviet Union and the German Military Leaders." *Militärhistorisk Tidskrift* (1979): 83–93.

————. "The Wehrmacht and the War of Extermination against the Soviet Union." *Yad Vashem Studies,* 14 (1981): 7–34.

Funk, Arthur L. "Churchill, Eisenhower and the French Resistance." *Military Affairs,* 45 (Feb 1981): 29–33.

Gabel, Christopher R. "Books on Overlord: A Select Bibliography and Research Agenda on the Normandy Campaign, 1944." *Military Affairs*, 48 (Jul 1984): 144–148.

Gause, Alfred. "Der Feldzug in Nordafrika im Jahre 1942." *Wehrwissenschaftliche Rundschau*, 12 (Nov 1962): 652–680.

Gersdorff, Ursula von. "Das Erlebnis des Zweiten Weltkrieges in der deutschen Literatur." *Jahresbibliographie*, 32 (1960): 411–426.

———. "Das Militärgeschichtliche Forschungsamt." *Jahresbibliographie*, 40 (1968): 321–335.

Gorodetsky, Gabriel. "Churchill's Warning to Stalin: A Reappraisal." *Historical Journal*, 29 (Dec 1986): 979–990.

———. "Was Stalin Planning to Attack Hitler in June 1941?" *RUSI Journal*, 131 (Jun 1986): 69–72.

Groehler, Olaf. "Stärke, Verteilung und Verluste der deutschen Luftwaffe im zweiten Weltkrieg." *Militärgeschichte*, 17 (1978): 316–336.

Gundelach, Karl. "Drohende Gefahr West: Die deutsche Luftwaffe vor und während der Invasion 1944." *Wehrwissenschaftliche Rundschau*, 8 (Jun 1959): 306–320.

Gunsburg, Jeffrey A. "Coupable ou non? Le rôle du général Gamelin dans la défaite de 1940." *Revue historique des armeés*, 4 (1979): 146–163.

Günzenhauser, Max. "Die Bibliographien zur Geschichte des zweiten Weltkrieges." *Jahresbibliographie*, 33 (1961): 511–565.

Hauner, Milan. "Did Hitler Want a World Dominion?" *Journal of Contemporary History*, 13 (Jan 1978): 15–32.

Hildebrand, Klaus. "Le programme de Hitler et sa réalisation, 1939–1942." *Revue d'histoire de la deuxième guerre mondiale*, 21 (Oct 1971): 7–36.

Hillgruber, Andreas. "Die 'Endlösung' und das deutsche Ostimperium als Kernstück des rassenideologischen Programms des Nationalsozialismus." *Vierteljahrshefte für Zeitgeschichte*, 20 (Apr 1972): 133–153.

———. "England's Place in Hitler's Plan for World Domination." *Journal of Contemporary History*, 9 (Jan 1974): 5–22.

———. "La recherche sur l'histoire de la deuxième guerre mondiale en Allemagne federale." *Revue d'histoire de la deuxième guerre mondiale*, 21 (Oct 1971): 1–5.

———, and Jürgen Förster. "Zwei neue Aufzeichnungen über 'Führer' Besprechungen aus dem Jahre 1942." *Mitlitärgeschichtliche Mitteilungen*, 1 (1972): 109–126.

Hofer, Walther. "Fifty Years On: Historians and the Third Reich." *Journal of Contemporary History*, 21 (Apr 1986): 225–251.

d'Hoop, Jean-Marie. "Eisenhower et la problème de Berlin en mars 1945." *Revue d'histoire de la deuxième guerre mondiale*, 22 (Oct 1972): 67–78.

Howard, Michael. "The High Command in Britain during the Second World War." *Revue internationale d'historie militaire*, 47 (1980): 60–71.

Jacobsen, Hans-Adolf. "Der deutsche Luftangriff auf Rotterdam, 14 mai 1940: Versuch einer Klärung." *Wehrwissenschaftliche Rundschau*, 7 (May 1958): 257–285.

———. "L'Erreur du command allemand devant Dunkerque." *Revue historique de l'armée* (1958): 63–74.

Janssen, Gregor. "Todt et Speer." *Revue d'histoire de la deuxième guerre mondiale*, 21 (Oct 1971): 37–53.

Jarausch, Konrad. "Removing the Nazi Stain? The Quarrel of the German Historians." *German Studies Review*, 11 (May 1988): 285–301.

Kemp, Paul K. "La protection des convois britanniques." *Revue d'histoire de la deuxième guerre mondiale*, 19 (Jan 1968): 29–40.

Kirkland, Faris R. "The French Air Force in 1940: Was It Defeated by the Luftwaffe or by Politics?" *Air University Review*, 36 (Sep–Oct 1985): 101–118.

Kleinfeld, Gerald R. "Hitler's Strike for Tikhvin." *Military Affairs,* 47 (Oct 1983): 122–128.

Klink, Ernst, "The Organisation of the German Military High Command in World War II." *Revue internationale d'histoire militaire,* 47 (1980): 129–157.

Krause, Roland E. "The German Navy under Joint Command in World War II." *US Naval Institute Proceedings,* 73 (Sep 1947): 1029–1043.

Krieger, Leonard. "Nazism: Highway or Byway?" *Central European History,* 11 (Mar 1978): 3–22.

"The Kursk Battle—30 Years." *Soviet Military Review* (1973): 2–39.

Liddell Hart, Basil H. "Western War Strategy: A Critical Analysis of the Alanbrooke Diaries." *Journal of the Royal United Services Institution,* 105 (Feb 1960): 52–61.

Loock, Hans-Dietrich. "Weserübung—A Step Towards the Greater German Reich." *Scandinavian Journal of History,* 2 (1977): 67–88.

Lundeberg, Phillip K. "La réplique des États-Unis à la guerre sousmarine." *Revue d'histoire de la deuxième guerre mondiale,* 18 (Jan 1968): 67–96.

Lytton, Henry D. "Bombing Policy in the Rome and Pre-Normandy Invasion Aerial Campaigns of World War II. . . ." *Military Affairs,* 47 (Apr 1983): 53–58.

Marshall-Cornwall, James. "A Proposed Refuge in Brittany—June 1940." *RUSI Journal,* 121 (Jun 1976): 78–82.

Masson, Philippe. "La grandes étapes de la bataille de l'Atlantique." *Revue d'histoire de la deuxième guerre mondiale,* 18 (Jan 1968): 3–28.

Mead, P. W. "The Chindit Operations of 1944." *Journal of the Royal United Services Institution,* 100 (May 1955): 250–262.

Meier-Welcker, Hans. "Der Entschluss zum Anhalten der deutschen Panzer-Truppen im Flandern 1940." *Vierteljahrshefte für Zeitgeschichte,* 2 (1954): 274–290.

Messerschmidt, Manfred. "La stratégie allemand (1939–1945): Conception, objectif, commandement, réussite." *Revue d'histoire de la deuxième guerre mondiale,* 25 (Oct 1975): 1–26.

Milner, Marc. "Convoy Escorts: Tactics, Technology, and Innovation in the Royal Canadian Navy, 1939–1943." *Military Affairs,* 48 (Jan 1984): 19–25.

Müller, Klaus-Jürgen. "The Army in the Third Reich: An Historical Interpretation." *Journal of Strategic Studies,* 2 (Sep 1979): 123–152.

———. "Dünkirchen 1940: Ein Beitrag zur Vorgeschichte der britischen und franzosischen Evakuierung." *Marine Rundschau,* 57 (1960): 133–168.

Mulligan, Timothy P. "Spies, Ciphers and 'Zitadelle': Intelligence and the Battle of Kursk, 1943." *Journal of Contemporary History,* 22 (Apr 1987): 235–260.

Murray, Williamson. "The German Response to Victory in Poland: A Case Study in Professionalism." *Armed Forces and Society,* 22 (Wtr 1981): 285–298.

———. "The Strategy of the 'Phoney War': A Reevaluation." *Military Affairs,* 45 (Mar 1981): 13–17.

———. "Ultra: Some Thoughts on Its Impact on the Second World War." *Air University Review,* 35 (Jul–Aug 1984): 52–64.

Noel, Leon. "La project d'Union Franco-Britannique de juin 1940." *Revue d'histoire de la deuxième guerre mondiale,* 6 (Jan 1956): 22–37.

Ose, Dieter. "Rommel and Rundstedt: The 1944 Panzer Controversy." *Military Affairs,* 50 (Jan 1986): 7–11.

Overy, Richard J. "Hitler and Air Strategy." *Journal of Contemporary History,* 15 (Jul 1980): 405–422.

———. "Hitler's War and the German Economy: A Reinterpretation." *Economic History Review,* 33 (May 1982): 272–291.

———. "The Luftwaffe and the European Economy, 1939–1945." *Militärgeschichtliche Mitteilungen,* 26 (1979): 55–78.

Paret, Peter. "Between Strategy and Mass Murder: The Third Reich at War." *German Studies Review*, 8 (May 1985): 311–317.

Parrish, Michael. "The Battle of Kursk." *Army Quarterly* (Oct 1969): 39–51.

Peszke, Michael A. "Poland's Preparation for World War II." *Military Affairs*, 43 (Feb 1979): 18–24.

Plehwe, Friedrich-Karl von. "Operation Sealion 1940." *RUSI Journal*, 118 (Mar 1973): 47–53.

Resis, Albert. "Spheres of Influence in Soviet Wartime Diplomacy." *Journal of Modern History*, 53 (Sep 1981): 417–439.

Rohwer, Jürgen. "Der Einfluss der allierten Funkaufklärung auf den Verlauf des Zweiten Weltkrieges." *Vierteljahrshefte für Zeitgeschichte*, 27 (Jul 1979): 325-369.

———. "La radiotelegraphie auxiliare du commandement dans la guerre sousmarine." *Revue d'histoire de la deuxième guerre mondiale*, 18 (Jan 1968): 41–66.

———. "'Ultra,' XB-Dienst und 'Magic': Ein Vergleich ihrer Rolle für die Schlacht im Atlantik und den Krieg im Pazifik." *Marine Rundschau*, 76 (Oct 1979): 637–648.

Roos, Hans. "Der Feldzug im Polen vom September 1939." *Wehrwissenschaftliche Rundschau*, 9 (Sep 1959): 491–512.

———. "Die militärpolitische Lage und Planung Polens gegenüber Deutschland vor 1939." *Wehrwissenschaftliche Rundschau*, 7 (1957): 181–202.

Roskill, Stephen W. "Marder, Churchill and the Admiralty, 1939–42." *RUSI Journal*, 117 *Dec 1972): 49–53.

Ross, Graham. "Allied Diplomacy in the Second World War." *British Journal of International Studies*, 1 (Oct 1975): 243–292.

Rotundo, Louis. "The Creation of Soviet Reserves and the 1941 Campaign." *Military Affairs*, 50 (Jan 1986): 21–28.

Rozkuszka, W. David. "British Cabinet Office Records on the Second World War." *Albion*, 8 (Fall 1976): 296–299.

Sainsbury, Keith. "Second Front in 1942: Anglo-American Differences over Strategy." *British Journal of International Studies*, 4 (Apr 1978): 47–58.

Salewski, Michael. "Von Raeder zu Dönitz: Der Wechsel in Oberbefehl der Kriegsmarine, 1943." *Militärgeschichtliche Mitteilungen*, 7 (1973): 101–146.

Salmon, Patrick. "British Plans for Economic Warfare against Germany, 1937–1939: The Problem of Swedish Iron Ore." *Journal of Contemporary History*, 16 (Jan 1981): 53–72.

Sbrega, John J. "Anglo-American Relations and the Selection of Mountbatten as Supreme Allied Commander, South East Asia." *Military Affairs*, 46 (Oct 1982): 139–145.

Schofield, Brian B. "The Defeat of the U-Boat during World War II." *Journal of Contemporary History*, 16 (Jan 1981): 119–129.

Schrieber, Gerhard. "Der Mittelmeerraum in Hitlers Strategie, 1940: 'Programm' und militärische Planung." *Militärgeschichtliche Mitteilungen*, 28 (1980): 69–99.

———. "Les structures strategiques de la conduite de la guerre italo-allemande au cours de la deuxième guerre mondiale," *Revue d'histoire de la deuxième guerre mondiale*, 39 (Oct 1980): 1–32.

———. "Zur Kontinuität des Gross- und Weltmachtstrebens der deutschen Marineführung." *Militärgeschichtliche Mitteilungen*, 26 (1979): 101–171.

Schröder, Joseph. "L'Allemagne et ses allies." *Revue d'histoire de la deuxième guerre mondiale*, 22 (Oct 1972): 45–65.

Schröder, Klaus. "Die Gedanken des Oberbefehlshabers der Kriegsmarine zum Kampf gegen England im Atlantik und im Mittelmeer, 1939–1940." *Marine Rundschau*, 67 (1970): 257-272.

Sella, Amnon. "'Barbarossa': Surprise Attack and Communication." *Journal of Contemporary History*, 13 (Jul 1978): 555–583.

Sevostyanav, P. "On the Eve of the Great Battle: September 1939–June 1941." *International Affairs* (USSR), 4 (1978): 105–117; 6 (1978): 97–108.

Sexton, Donal J. "Phantoms of the North: British Deceptions in Scandinavia, 1941–1944." *Military Affairs*, 47 (Oct 1983): 109-114.

Spiller, Roger J. "Assessing ULTRA." *Military Review*, 59 (Aug 1979): 13–23.

Stegemann, Bernd. "Hitlers Ziele im ersten Kriegsjahr, 1939/40: Ein Beitrag zur Quellenkritik." *Militärgeschichtliche Mitteilungen*, 27/1 (1980): 93–105.

Stich, Karl. "Die sowjetische Luftblockade Stalingrads." *Militärgeschichte*, 22 (May 1983): 538–551.

Stolfi, Russell H. S. "Barbarossa Revisited: A Critical Appraisal of the Opening Stages of the Russo-German Campaign (June–December 1941)." *Journal of Modern History*, 54 (Mar 1982): 27–46.

———. "Equipment for Victory in France in 1940." *History*, 52 (Feb 1970): 1–20.

Suvorov, Victor. "Yes, Stalin Was Planning to Attack Hitler in June 1941." *RUSI Journal*, 131 (Jun 1986): 73–74.

Thomas, David. "Foreign Armies East and German Military Intelligence in Russia, 1941–1945." *Journal of Contemporary History*, 22 (Apr 1987): 261–301.

Trevor-Roper, Hugh R. "Hitlers Kriegsziele." *Vierteljahrshefte für Zeitgeschichte*, 8 (Apr 1960): 121–133.

Trythall, A. J. "The Downfall of Leslie Hore-Belisha." *Journal of Contemporary History*, 16 (Jul 1981): 391-411.

Überschär, Gerd R. "Guerre de coaliton ou guerre séparée: conception et structures de la stratégie germano-finlandaise dan la guerre contre l'URSS, 1941–1944." *Revue d'histoire de la deuxième guerre mondiale*, 30 (Apr 1980): 27–68.

Uhlich, Werner. "Decknamen deutscher Unternehmen und Vorhaben im Zweiten Weltkrieg." *Jahresbibliographie*, 44 (1972): 490–534.

van Creveld, Martin. "The German Attack on the USSR: The Destruction of a Legend." *European Studies Review*, 2 (Jan 1972): 69–86.

———. "Rommel's Supply Problems, 1941–42." *RUSI Journal*, 119 (Sep 1974): 67–73.

———. "War Lord Hitler: Some Points Reconsidered." *European Studies Review*, 4 (Jan 1974): 57–79.

Volker, Karl-Heinz. "Die deutsche Heimatluftverteidigung im Zweiten Weltkrieg." *Wehrwissenschaftliche Rundschau*, 16 (Feb 1966): 87–111; 6 (Mar 1966): 158–171.

Wagener, Carl. "Strittigen Fragen zur Ardennenoffensive." *Wehrwissenschaftliche Rundschau*, 11 (Jan 1961): 26–54.

———. "Der Vorstoss der XXXX: Panzerkorps vom Charkov zum Kaukasus, Juli–August 1942: Ein Beispiel für weitreichende Operationen mit schnellen Truppen." *Wehrwissenschaftliche Rundschau*, 5 (Sep 1955): 397–408; 5 (Oct 1955): 447–459.

Wanty, Émile. "La defense des Ardennes en 1940." *Revue d'histoire de la deuxième guerre mondiale*, 11 (Apr 1961): 1–16.

Watts, Barry D., and Williamson Murray. "Inventing History: Soviet Military Genius Revealed." *Air University Review*, 36 (Mar–Apr 1985): 102–112.

Weinberg, Gerhard L. "Reflections on Running a War: Hitler, Churchill, Stalin, Roosevelt, Tojo." *Phi Alpha Theater Lecture*, State University of New York at Albany, 1986.

Wilhelm, Hans-Heinrich, hrsg. "Hitlers Ansprache von Generalen und Offizieren am 26. Mai 1944." *Militärgeschichtliche Mitteilungen*, 20 (1976): 123–170.

Wilt, Alan F. "Hitler's Late Summer Pause in 1941." *Military Affairs*, 45 (Dec 1981): 187–191.

———. "The Summer of 1944: A Comparison of Overlord and Anvil/Dragoon." *Journal of Strategic Studies*, 4 (Jun 1981): 187-195.

Woodward, Ernest L. "Some Reflections on British Policy, 1939–1945." *International Affairs*, 31 (1955): 273–290.

Zebel, Sydney H. "Churchill, Macmillan, and the Reactiation of 'Force X.'" *Albion*, 11 (Wtr 1979): 360–374.

Ziegler, Janet. "Répertoire internationale des bibliographies publiées de 1945 à 1965 sur la seconde guerre mondiale." *Revue d'histoire de la deuxième guerre mondiale*, 16 (1966): 69–80.

Ziemke, Earl F. "Germany and World War II: The Official History." *Central European History*, 16 (Dec 1983): 398–407.

———. "Operation Kreml: Deception, Strategy and the Fortunes of War." *Parameters*, 9 (Mar 1979): 72–83.

Index

Aachen, 114, 274; air raid (Oct 1942), 234
Abbeville, 138
ABDA (American-British-Dutch-Australian) Command, 81
Absolute contraband, 125–127, 129
Admiralty, British, 224
Advanced Air Striking Force, 133
Aegean fiasco, 17
Afghanistan, 77
Afrika Korps, 78, 178, 187, 189–192, 195–196. *See also* Rommel, Erwin
Air Component, British, 133
Air defense: British, 68, 70, 72, 83, 147–151; German, 31–32, 59, 95, 101, 104, 113, 226–227, 230–234, 236–237, 241–242, 244–245, 263, 289, 292
Air Fleets, German: One, 121, 158; Two, 148, 158, 162; Three, 137, 148, 242, 267, 270; Four, 121, 158, 173; Five, 148, 149–150, 158; Six, 173; Reich, 243
Air forces, United States: Eighth, 234, 236, 239, 240, 241, 262, 281; Fifteenth, 262
Air Groups, British: Five, 32; Ten, 151; Eleven, 151–152; Twelve, 151–152; 201 Group, 181; 221 Group, 253
Aircraft, Allied: B-17 Fortresses, 111, 212, 220; B-24 Liberators, 111, 212, 220; C-46, 252; C-47, 252; P-51 Mustangs, 105
Aircraft, British: B-17, 214, 219; B-24, 214, 219–220, 224; Battle, 133; Blenheim, 133, 182; Halifaxes, 212, 219, 221, 231–234, 238–240, 243; Hampdens, 231, 233, 235; Hudsons, 219; Hurricanes, 133, 136, 149, 182; Lancasters, 231–235, 238–240, 243; Lysanders, 133; Manchesters, 231, 233, 235; Mosquitoes, 232, 234, 238–240; Spitfire, 149; Stirlings, 231–234, 238, 239–240, 243; Swordfish, 219; Wellingtons, 182, 212, 219, 224, 233–234, 238–239; Whitleys, 212, 231, 233, 235, 238
Aircraft, German: Messerschmitt Bf 109, 136, 149, 182, 227, 232; Bf 110, 150, 227, 232, 237; Focke Wulf 190, 182, 232; JU-88, 232, 237
Aircraft, United States: B-17, 243; B-24, 243; P-38, 243; P-47, 243, 269; P-51, 238, 243
Akyab, 248, 250
Alam Halfa battle, 93, 100, 192
Albert Canal, 132, 274
Alexander, Field Marshal Sir Harold, 38, 42, 112, 141, 192, 195, 200, 202, 204, 259
Algeria, 93, 195, 202
Algiers meeting (May 1943), 201

Ali, General Rashid, 78
Alsace, 116, 277
Amphibious trucks (DUKW), 205, 282
Andaman Islands, 112, 249–250. *See also* Buccaneer operation
Anti-Semitism, 12, 16, 23, 33, 98, 164, 286
Anti U-Boat Committee, 218, 221–222
Antwerp, 114–115, 132, 139, 274–275, 276, 278
Anvil operation. *See* French Riviera campaign
Anzio 110, 112
Arab Legion, 78
Arakan 249, 250, 252, 253
Arcadia conference (Dec 1941), 39, 44, 90–91, 118, 228
Archangel, 155–156
Ardennes campaign (Dec 1944), 15, 17, 54, 100, 115–116, 197, 246, 276–278, 280, 284, 289; preparations, 274–276
Ardennes Forest, 67, 275, 289
Ardennes operation (May 1940), 15, 70
Ardennes sector, 135, 137, 139
Argentia Bay conference (Aug 1941), 82, 179
Argentina, 129–130
Argonaut conference (Jun 1942), 91
Arlon, 137
Armed Force Command Netherlands, 276
Armed forces: British, 102; Commonwealth, 102; German, 102; United States, 102
Armed Forces High Command. *See* Oberkommando der Wehrmacht/OKW.
Armeeabteilung Kempf, 171, 173
Armies, British: Second, 259, 269–270, 279, 281, 284; Eighth, 179–185, 189, 192–193, 201, 203; Fourteenth, 116, 252, 255
Armies, Canadian: First, 279–283
Armies, French: First, 139; Sixth, 139; Seventh, 132; Ninth, 139
Armies, German: Second, 141, 162, 166, 173; Third, 121, 123; Fourth, 121–123, 137, 158; Sixth, 93, 141, 147, 166, 168, 174; Seventh, 266, 274, 276–277; Eighth, 121, 124; Ninth, 54, 141, 158, 172–173; Tenth, 121, 123; Eleventh, 92, 166–167; Twelfth, 137, 141, 156; Fourteenth, 106; Fifteenth, 261, 266, 271, 275–276, 281; Sixteenth, 137, 141; Seventeenth, 110, 166; Eighteenth, 138–139
Armies, German Panzer: First, 166–167, 171; Second, 162, 174; Fourth, 166–169, 171, 173–174; Fifth, 274, 276–277; Sixth, 173, 274–276, 277
Armies, Japanese: Fifteenth, 253
Armies, Romanian: Third, 169; Fourth, 169
Armies, United States: First, 259, 277, 281;

Third, 271, 277, 283; Seventh, 100, 203, 204, 205; Ninth, 280–282

Army Cooperative Command, 230, 234

Army Groups, British: 21st, 280, 283, 284

Army Groups, German: A, 70, 92, 135, 137, 139–140, 141, 166–168; B, 92, 135, 137–141, 167, 264, 269, 274, 276, 281; C, 135, 137, 142; Center, 112, 158, 160, 162, 171; Courland, 53; Don, 169; G, 265; H, 275; North, 121–122, 158, 161–162; South, 121, 122, 158, 162, 166, 170, 171

Army Groups, United States: 12th, 270, 279

Army High Command. *See Oberkommando des Heeres*/OKH

Army Personnel Office, German, 27, 28

Arnhem operation, 114

Arno River, 113

Arnold, General Henry H., 220

Arras, 138, 139–140

Artemovsk, 165

Astrakhan, 156, 167

Athens, 182

Atlantic Convoy conference (Mar 1943), 222

"Atlantic Empire," 74, 288

Atlantic Wall, 110, 114, 263–266, 273; significance, 272

Attlee, Clement, 23

Auchinleck, General Sir Claude, 18, 47, 80, 178–183, 185–187, 189, 191, 193

Augusta, 201

Australian forces, 78, 180–181

Austria, 64, 118, 240

Azore Islands, 74, 212

B-Dienst (German naval intelligence), 98, 216, 220

Baal, 282

"Baby blitz," 105

Bad Nauheim, 275

Badoglio, Field Marshal Pietro, 204

Bagration operation (Jun 1944), 112, 273, 285

Baku, 167

Balance of power, 13, 63, 286

Balkan campaign (Apr 1941), 17, 22, 28, 66, 82, 156–157; importance of, 76; myth, 97

Balkans, 68, 69, 75–76, 95, 99, 109, 133, 156, 204, 260, 285, 288–290; British planning, 66; resistance groups, 103–104

Baltic states, 127. *See also* individual states

Barbarossa campaign (1941), 5, 15, 17, 22, 28, 31, 65, 75, 76–78, 79, 88, 154, 158–162, 175, 177, 263, 288, 292; intelligence warnings, 99; preparations, 155–158

Bastogne, 137, 277

Battle Group Peiper, 277, 278

Battle of Britain (Aug 1940), 5, 21, 67, 69, 71–73, 74, 82, 120, 134, 149–152, 207, 288; preparations, 145–149

Battle of France (May 1940), 5, 15, 17, 19, 21, 22, 28, 31, 36, 44, 64, 67–70, 74, 82, 83, 120, 130, 137–145, 147, 152, 158, 255, 288; preparations, 125, 131–137

Battle of the Atlantic, 17, 56, 78, 87, 90, 93, 95, 103, 108, 118–119, 207–225, 245, 272, 289, 290, 292; role of intelligence, 98, 100

Battle of the Bulge. *See* Ardennes campaign (Dec 1944)

"Battle of the Rhine," 283

Battleaxe operation (June 1941), 78, 83, 178

Bay of Bengal, 247, 249

Bay of Biscay, 109, 208, 213, 219, 221, 223, 256, 264, 265, 271

Bayeux, 257, 261

Beaverbrook, Lord, 9

Beck, General Ludwig, 4, 51

Beda Littoria, 182

Beesley, Patrick, 225

Belgian forces, 132, 135, 136, 138, 181, 202

Belgium, 64, 65, 67, 68–69, 72, 113, 127, 131–135, 142, 202; capitulation, 70, 137–138; war trade agreement, 127

Belgorod, 175

Benghazi, 179, 185, 187, 195

Bennett, Ralph, 270

Berchtesgaden. *See* Berghof

Berghof, 5, 122, 146, 148, 155, 187, 271

Berlin, 5, 6, 70, 75, 117, 152, 246; air raids (Nov 1943–44), 240–244

Bermuda, 212

Bessarabia, 121

"Big Week" air offensive (Feb 1944), 243

Bir Hacheim, 190

Bismarck, 208

Black List Committee, 126

Black Sea, 167

Blackett, Professor Pat, 222

Blaskowitz, General Johannes, 122, 265

Bletchley Park, 99

Blitz, 149

Blitzkrieg, 31, 52, 124, 164; assessment, 64–65

Blockade, British. *See* Economic warfare, British

Blockbuster operation, 282

Blomberg, Field Marshal Werner, 1, 30, 50, 55

Blue/Brunswick operation (1942), 89–90, 92–93, 154, 166–170, 175, 272; preparations, 164–166

Blumenson, Martin, 205

Bock, Field Marshal Fedor von, 52, 89, 122, 137, 158, 164, 166–167

Bolero buildup, 256–257, 290

Bologna, 114

Bomber Command, British, 49, 89, 104, 152, 213, 221, 226–230, 233–235, 236–241, 242–

245, 281
Bombing priorities, Allied, 236
Bond, Brian, 70
Bordeaux, 142
Bormann, Martin, 6
Bose, Subhas Chandra, 253
Boston, 222
Boulogne, 139, 271
Bracken, Brendan, 9
Bradley, General Omar, 204, 270, 284
Brandenberger, General Erich, 274
Brauchitsch, General Walther von, 27–29, 30,
   75, 146, 155, 160, 163, 164; as C-in-C, 50–
   51; retirement, 89
Braun, Eva, 7
Brazil, 129–130
Breda, 132
Bremen air raid (June 1942), 90, 232–234
Brest, 114, 215
Brest-Litovsk, 123, 124
Bridges, Sir Edward, 11
Brigades, British: infantry, 181, 203; tank, 181
Brighton, 147
British army, 38, 43–46, 133. *See also* individual
   units
British Commonwealth and Empire, 8, 63, 65,
   81, 153, 235, 287, 289, 291
British Expeditionary Force, 35, 43, 132, 139–
   142
British Staff Mission, 40, 44, 47, 115
Brittany, 257, 259, 271
Broad front strategy, 115, 279
Broadhurst, Air Vice Marshal Harry, 202
Brooke, Field Marshal Sir Alan (Lord Alan-
   brooke), 10, 17, 21, 37–38, 50, 52, 104–106,
   115, 117, 142, 148, 192, 198–199, 230, 250,
   254, 258; character, 44–46
Brussels, 274
Bryansk, 174
Bryant, Sir Arthur, 46
Buccaneer operation, 108. *See also* Andaman
   Islands
Buchheim, Hans, 34
Budapest, 116
Buffalo amphibious vehicles, 284
Buhle, General Walter, 54
Bulgaria, 113
Burdick, Charles, 287
Burgdorf, General Wilhelm, 28, 58
Burma, 118, 290
Burma campaigns (1944), 48, 95, 97, 103, 112,
   116, 246–255, 284
Burma Road, 248, 254, 290
Burmese forces, 284
Busch, General Ernst, 158
Busse, General Theodor, 54
Butler, R. A., 10

Butt, D. M., 227

Cabinet for Defense of the Reich, 30
Caen, 112, 256, 257, 269, 285
Cairo conferences (Nov–Dec 1943), 40, 106–
   109, 250, 258
Calais, 114, 139
Canada, 78, 176, 222
Canadian forces, 119, 201, 220, 253, 266, 268,
   284
Canadian Northwest Atlantic Command, 211
Cape of Good Hope, 80, 178, 193
Cape Verde Islands, 74
Carentan, 270
Carls, Admiral Rolf, 57
Carver, General Sir Michael, 185
Casablanca, 126
Casablanca conference (Jan 1943), 94, 96, 97,
   118, 197–199, 200, 210, 219–222, 256, 290
Casualties, 102; Ardennes campaign, 278; Bar-
   barossa, 163–164; Battle of Britain, 152; Bat-
   tle of France, 144; Burma (1944), 254;
   Crusader, 185; El Alamein, 196; Kursk, 176;
   Overlord, 263, 271; Polish campaign, 124;
   Sicily, 205; Stalingrad, 170; Veritable-
   Grenade, 283
Catania, 199, 201, 204–205
Caucasian oil fields, 164
Caucasus, 53, 55, 77, 88–89, 165, 167–168, 170,
   193
Cecil, Lady Robert, 10
Ceylon, 88
Chamberlain, Neville, 7, 10, 36, 63, 70, 132,
   286; character, 19–20; problems, 20–21; rela-
   tion with Chiefs of Staff, 35
Chengtu, bombing from, 254
Chequers, 12
Cherbourg, 111, 257, 259, 266, 269
Chiefs of Staff, British, 24–26, 35–41, 42–43,
   43–50, 60–61, 63, 74, 78, 81, 90, 115, 117,
   132, 198–199, 200, 210, 287–289
Chief of Staff, Supreme Allied Command
   (COSSAC), 257, 260
Chief of the Imperial General Staff, 43–46
China, 40, 81, 86, 95, 97, 106–108, 118, 246,
   248, 253, 255, 290
China-Burma-India theater, 246
Chindits, 252, 254
Chindwin River, 248, 250
Chinese forces, 112, 248, 250, 252, 254, 284
Churchill, Winston S., 1, 2, 20, 23–24, 42–
   50, 60–61, 63, 70, 74, 78, 79–80, 84–85,
   87, 89, 93, 94–95, 97, 106–109, 112–115,
   116–118, 139, 141–143, 145–146, 163, 170,
   178–183, 190, 193, 197, 199, 200–201, 210,
   218, 228, 230, 232, 236, 241, 249, 255, 256–
   259, 262, 263, 286–289, 293; at Arcadia, 81–

90; attitudes, 9–11; becomes prime minister, 21; character, 7–8; early life, 7; ideas, 12–14, 18; relation with chiefs of staff, 36–41; routine, 11–12, 19; view of allies, 18; view of Hitler, 22–23; views, 14–18

Ciano, Count Galeazzo, 188

Citadel operation. *See* Kursk operation

Clausewitz, Carl von, 62

Cleves, 282

Coastal Command, British, 152, 211, 213, 220–221, 224, 230–231, 233–235, 245

Cologne, 275, 281

Colville, Sir John, 8, 9–10, 19

Combined bomber offensive. *See* Strategic bombing campaign

Combined Chiefs of Staff, 40–41, 81, 256

Combined Economic Boards, Anglo-US, 40

Combined Operations, British, 247

Commanders Council, British, 256

Commonwealth forces, 83, 86, 90, 91, 93, 178, 188, 252, 284, 289

Conditional contraband, 125–127, 129

Coningham, Air Vice Marshal Arthur, 181, 270, 280

Conservative Party, 7, 10, 14, 19

"Continental bloc," 4

Contraband Control Committee, 126, 129, 130

Convoys, 212, 213, 214, 215–216, 217, 222

Cooper, Matthew, 58

Coral Sea Battle, 83

Corps, British: IV, 250, 252, 253; X, 194–195; XIII, 179, 181, 183, 194, 204; XV, 250, 252, 253; XXX, 179, 181, 183, 194–195, 204, 277, 282; XXXIII, 252, 254

Corps, Canadian: II, 282

Corps, German: XXI, 66; XXXIX, 161

Corps, German Panzer: II SS, 175; XXIV, 161

Corps, United States: II, 204

Corsica, 103, 198

Coryton, Air Vice Marshal W. A., 232

Cotentin Peninsula, 257, 259

Crerar, General Henry, 281

Crete, 17, 76, 78, 156, 178, 182, 198

Crimea, 110, 163, 165–166, 169

Cripps, Sir Stafford, 10, 143

Croatian forces, 157, 169

Crocodile tanks, 284

Crusader operation (Nov 1941), 80, 82, 183–186, 198, 206; preparations, 178–181

Cudgel operation. *See* Arakan

Culverin operation, 112

Cunningham, General Sir Alan, 179–180, 183

Cunningham, Admiral Sir Andrew, 8, 21, 37, 200, 202, 206, 220; character, 42–43, 47–48

Curzon line, 108

Cyrenaica, 86, 88, 99, 178–180, 183, 185, 193, 196, 197

Czechoslovakia, 20, 51, 52, 64, 120

Dakar, 125

Daladier, Eduard, 132, 136

Danube River, 129

Danzig, 121

Declaration by United Nations, 81

Declaration of Union, Anglo-French, 70, 142–143

Defence Committee, British, 36, 37, 262

De Gaulle, General Charles, 95

Demjansk, 170

Dempsey, General Sir Miles, 281

Denmark, 29, 109, 261; war trade agreement, 127

Denmark operation, 28, 66–67, 134–135, 152, 288

Devon exercise, 266

Diadem operation, 112

Dieppe raid, 90, 256

Dietrich, Otto, 6

Dietrich, SS General Sepp, 274

Dilks, David, 19

Dill, General Sir John, 10, 37, 142, 178, 179; as CIGS, 43–44

Dimapur, 253

Dinant, 135, 137, 274, 277

Divisions: British Airborne, 259; British Armored, 181, 193; British Infantry, 193, 202, 203, 259; Canadian, 203, 259; German Infantry, 161, 174; German Light, 182, 189; German Motorized, 161; German Mountain, 135; German Panzer, 161, 175, 182, 189, 269, 270, 277; German Panzer Grenadier, 203, 266, 282; Indian, 181, 253; Italian, 189; New Zealand, 181, 195; South African, 181; United States Airborne, 259; United States Armored, 116; United States Infantry, 203, 259, 268

Dnieper River, 104

Dodecanese Islands, 104

Don River, 92, 165–167

Donetz River, 156, 160, 171

Dönitz, Grand Admiral Karl, 4, 31, 48, 56, 61, 95, 117, 209, 210, 214–217, 218, 224; as C-in-C Navy, 57–58

Dorman-Smith, General Eric, 192

Dortmund air raid (May 1943), 238

Douglas, Air Chief Marshal Sir Sholto, 247

Douhet, Guilio, 244

Dowding, Air Chief Marshal Sir Hugh, 151–152

Dragoon operation. *See* French Riviera campaign

Dunkirk, 44, 70, 79, 125, 139, 140–141, 144

Düsseldorf, 278–280, 283

Dyle River line, 68, 132, 138

Dynamo operation. *See* Dunkirk

Eagle Day, 148–149

Eagles' Nest headquarters, 5–6

East Africa, 76, 78, 82, 288
East Prussia, 5, 108, 121, 123–124, 155
Eben-Emael fortifications, German attack on, 16, 138
Economic warfare, British, 65–66, 79, 82–83, 120, 125–131, 256, 289
Edelweiss operation. *See* Caucasus
Eden, Sir Anthony, 10; mission to Moscow, 81
Egypt, 74, 78, 88, 92–93, 178, 187, 198, 202, 290
Eisenborn Ridge, 277
Eisenhower, General Dwight D., 108, 110–111, 115, 117, 198–199, 206, 277–279; as Mediterranean commander, 200–202, 204–205; as Overlord commander, 259, 261–262, 266
El Agheila, 80, 183, 185, 195
El Alamein, 190, 192; first battle, 92, 192; preparations, second battle, 192–195; second battle, 93, 195–198, 206
Enemy Exports Committee, 127
Enigma. *See* Ultra intelligence
Erickson, John, 154
Escort carriers, 209, 220, 222
Essen air raid (Jun 1942), 90, 232–234
Estonia, 71, 121
Eureka conference. *See* Tehran conference
European Advisory Commission, 108
Everitt, Chris, 234–235

Falaise battle, 271
Falke operation, 109
Falkenhorst, General Nikolaus von, 28, 66
Falmouth, 129
Fascist Grand Council, 204
Feiling, Sir Keith, 19
Fellers, Colonel Bonner, 99
Ferdinand deception, 261
Fest, Joachim, 7
Fighter Command, British, 72–73, 150–151
Fighter Training Command, 152
Finland, 68, 75, 92, 108, 113, 133, 157
Finnish forces, 156, 161
First Quebec conference. *See* Quadrant conference
First Washington conference. *See* Arcadia conference
Flanders, 140
Floating airfields (*Habbakuk*), 16
Flying Training Command, British, 147
Focke Wulf aircraft factory, 234
Foggia air fields, 104
Folkestone, 147
Forbes, Admiral Sir Charles, 10, 47
Force H, British, 182
Force K, British, 182
Foreign Armies East, German, 99
Foreshore obstacles, 265
Forstner, Baron von, 214

Fortitude North deception, 261
Fortress Europe, 105
Foster, Air Marshal, 220
France, 18, 39, 41, 64–66, 72, 90, 94, 104, 109, 111, 113, 114, 120, 121, 124, 125, 127, 135, 150, 234, 256, 257, 259, 263, 267–268, 270, 271, 273; armistice, 70, 142–143; bombing raids, 99; British commando raids, 16; rearmament, 20
Franco, Francisco, 74
Franke, Captain, 214
Frankland, Noble, 93, 233, 236
Fraser, Sir David, 48
Frederick Barbarossa, 1
Frederick the Great (II), 1
Free French forces, 78, 91, 93, 95, 104, 181, 190, 204, 266
Freeman, Air Chief Marshal Sir Wilfrid, 49
French navy, 143–144
French Resistance, 260–262
French Riviera campaign (Aug 1944), 103, 107–108, 111–113, 114, 250, 258, 265, 271, 273, 285, 290–292; postponement, 260; role of intelligence, 100
Freya radar, 227
Fritsch, General Werner von, 1, 50, 55
Fritz operation, 75. *See also* Barbarossa operation
Fromm, General Friedrich, 27
"Frontier Security East" plan, 121
Führer Directives: No. 16, 145; No. 17, 147; No. 21, 75, 155–156; No. 40, 263; No. 41, 165; No. 45, 92, 167; No. 51, 264
Führerprinzip, 26
Functionalists, 13

Gabr Saleh, 179–180, 183, 185
Gamelin, General Maurice, 132, 136
Gandhi, Mahatma, 2, 253, 293
Gazala operation (May 1947), 88, 91, 182, 183, 185, 186, 189–192, 206; preparations, 186–189
Geheimschreiber intelligence (Fish), 99
Gehlen, General Reinhard, 99
Geilenkirchen, 279
Geldern, 280, 283
George VI, 7
Georges, General Alphonse, 136
Gerbini airfields, 201
German air force, 13, 31–33, 66, 73, 78, 135, 141, 144, 146–152, 155, 157–158. *See also* individual units
German army, 1–2, 15, 26, 27, 33, 34, 167, 261. *See also* individual units
German navy, 15, 26, 31, 33, 66-67, 95, 98, 155, 158, 223. *See also* individual units
Gertrude operation, 109
Geyr von Schweppenburg, General Baron Leo, 161, 265, 270

Gibraltar, 74, 125, 180, 182
Giffard, General Sir George, 247
Gilbert, Martin, 12, 16
Gisevius, Bernd, 52
Givet, 132
Gleiwitz incident, 122
Goch, 280, 282
Godt, Rear Admiral Eberhardt, 211
Goebbels, Josef, 6
Göring, Reichsmarschall Hermann, 4, 31–32, 42, 50, 52, 61, 105, 141, 148, 150–151, 155, 226, 276; character, 58–60
Gort, Field Marshal Lord, 43, 132, 137, 139
Gott, General W. H. E., 192
Grand strategy, definition, 62–63
Grandcamp, 257
Greece, 74, 76, 78, 82, 156, 177–178, 182, 198; war trade agreement, 127
Greek forces, 181, 202
Greenland, 212, 217
Greim, General Robert von, 59, 61
Grenade operation (Feb 1945), 116, 282–284; preparations, 279–281
Gripfast operation. *See* Imphal
Group von Manteuffel, 276
Groups, German Panzer, 158, 160, 160–161
Grozny, 167
Guderian, General Heinz, 4, 28, 30, 42, 50, 77, 89, 115, 122, 123, 158, 160–162, 172, 278; as chief of staff, 54
Gulf of Bothnia, 128
Guzzoni, General Alfredo, 203
Gyldenfeldt, General Heinz von, 29
Gymnast operation, 81, 90, 91. *See also* Torch operation

Haffner, Sebastian, 2
Haifa, 125
Halder, General Franz, 27–28, 30, 42, 50, 54, 73, 75, 76, 88–89, 117, 122, 135, 137, 140, 155–156, 160, 164, 165–166, 168; character, 51–52; replaced, 92
Halifax, Lord, 21, 222
Hall, Commander Richard, 211
Hamburg air raids (Jul 1943), 226, 233, 237, 238–240
Hanna operation, 109
Harris, Air Marshal Sir Arthur, 230, 232–233, 234, 236, 240, 243, 262
Hassell, Ulrich von, 52
Hausser, SS General Paul, 34
Hawk operation, 171–172
Hecker commando group, 189
Height-finding, direction-finding (HF/DF) equipment, 209–210, 218–219, 222
Hepp, General Leo, 101
Hercules air engines, 240
Heron operation. *See* Stalingrad

Heusinger, General Adolf, 53
Hewitt, Admiral H. Kent, 202
Heydte, Colonel Friedrich von der, 277
High Command, German, 24–34, 35, 41, 42, 50–61, 63, 287–288
Hillgruber, Andreas, 73, 93
Himmelbett air defenses, 227
Himmler, Heinrich, 6, 28, 33
Hinsley, Sir F. Harry, 99
Hipper, 146
Hitler, Adolf, 1, 9, 12, 21–23, 24, 63–64, 70–71, 73–78, 84–85, 87–89, 92–93, 95–96, 104–105, 109–110, 113–118, 120–124, 134–136, 139–141, 143–149, 151, 154–157, 160–164, 165–175, 187, 191, 195, 204, 215, 216, 226, 237, 263–266, 269, 271, 273–279, 286–288, 293; attitude, 3–4, 26; character, 2–3, 5; death, 117; health, 22; ideas, 12–14, 18; relations with high command, 25–34, 50–61; routine, 5–7; view of allies, 18; view of Churchill, 22–23; views, 14–18
Hoepner, General Erich, 89, 122, 158
"Hold back" guarantee, 126, 130
"Holding" strategy, 93, 95, 103–104, 170–171, 272, 289
Hollis, General Sir Leslie, 12, 17, 36
Home Forces, British, 43–44
Homze, Edward, 59
Hong Kong, 81
Hopkins, Harry, 1, 91
Horrocks, General Brian, 282
Horton, Admiral Sir Max, 211, 221
Hoth, General Hermann, 122, 158, 160–161, 166–167, 171, 173–174
House, General Edwin, 202
Howard, Sir Michael, 199
Hungarian forces, 92, 157, 165–166, 173
Hungary, 75, 110
Husky operation. *See* Sicily campaign

Iceland, 211
Ijmuiden, 264
Imphal battle (Apr 1944), 246, 248, 250–254, 284
India, 77, 186, 235, 246, 248, 251, 253, 254, 255, 284, 289
Indian forces, 112, 252–253, 284
Indian National Army, 253
Indochina, 80
Influx operation, 198–199
Intelligence: Allied, 71, 261, 275–276; British, 68, 93, 98–101, 111, 127, 197, 205, 292; French, 137; German, 98–99, 101, 111, 150, 189, 232, 261, 265–266, 275–276, 292; Soviet, 175. *See also* Dienst intelligence; Ultra intelligence
Intentionalists, 13
Inter-Allied Anti-Submarine Survey Board, 221

Invergordon, 129
Iran, 77, 80, 89, 93, 116, 163, 186
Iraq, 77–78, 82, 89, 177–178, 187
Ireland, 83, 215
Ironside, General Sir Edmund, 36, 44, 72, 139, 142; as CIGS, 43
Isjum, 166
Isle of Wight, 145
Ismay, General Sir Hastings, 11, 17, 35–36, 42, 46, 118; contribution, 49–50
Italian army, 78, 80, 82–83, 88, 92, 156, 157, 165–166, 170, 177–178, 182, 187, 190–191, 194, 198, 202, 203, 205
Italian campaign, 106–107, 197, 237, 264, 273, 284, 290
Italian Supreme Command, 88
Italy, 18, 20, 29, 57, 65, 69, 74–75, 86–88, 95, 99, 104, 109–111, 113–114, 117–118, 127, 129, 131, 152, 177, 202–205, 228, 257, 265, 284, 287–288; enters war, 71–72, 130, 141, 178; invasion of, 103; surrender, 17, 204

Jackel, Eberhard, 3, 13
Japan, 17–18, 65, 71, 80, 83, 86–89, 93, 100, 103, 106–107, 112–113, 116, 117, 246, 284, 288–289
Japanese forces, 247, 250–255, 284, 289
Jarabub, 180
Jazz Music cannons, German, 237
Jeschonnek, General Hans, 59, 146, 155, 172
Jiang Jie-shi (Chiang Kai-shek), 106, 108, 246, 249, 254
Jodl, General Alfred, 6, 25, 29–30, 42, 50, 53, 73, 78, 114, 117, 145–146, 160, 168, 172, 179–180, 188, 269, 274; character, 55–56
Johnson, General Dudley, 44
Joint Chiefs of Staff, United States, 25, 40, 81, 115, 117, 198, 279
Joubert de la Ferté, Air Chief Marshal Sir Philip, 211
Julich, 282
July 20 assassination attempt, 53–54, 113, 273
Jupiter plans, 80

Kahn, David, 98–99
Kalemyo, 250
Kalinin, 162
Kammhuber, General Josef, 227, 230
Kangaroo personnel carriers, 284
Keitel, Field Marshal Wilhelm, 6, 27, 28–30, 42, 50, 54, 120, 134, 146, 160, 168, 172, 188; character, 54–55
Keller, General Alfred, 158
Kemp, Peter, 57
Kennedy, General Sir John, 38, 45, 107, 180
Kerch Peninsula, 165–166, 169
Kesselring, General Albert, 122, 148, 158, 187, 203, 205

Keyes, Admiral Sir Roger, 11
Kharkov, 91, 165–166, 169, 171, 175
Kiev, 77, 155, 160, 162, 175
King, Admiral Ernest J., 41, 114, 222
Kirby, S. Woodburn, 252
Kirkwall, 125, 129
Kleist, Field Marshal Ewald von, 137, 168
Klessheim Castle, 6, 187
Kluge, Field Marshal Günther von, 51, 122, 158, 160, 171–172, 174–175, 271, 274
Knowles, Captain Kenneth, 211
Kohima battle (Feb 1944), 246, 252–254, 284
Koller, General Karl, 60
Konev, Marshal Ivan, 117
Königsberg, 108
Korten, General Günther, 59–60
Krebs, General Hans, 54
Kreipe, General Werner, 5, 60
Kriegsmarine. See German navy
Kronstadt, 156
Krupp weapons factory, 234
Küchler, General George von, 158
Kupyansk, 171
Kursk battle (Jul 1943), 96, 103, 154, 174–176, 289; preparations, 171–174

Labor Party, 10, 14, 36
Labrador, 212, 222
Lake Ilmen, 161, 170
Lampedusa, capture of, 202
Landing craft problem, 97, 108, 111–112, 256, 260
Latvia, 71, 121
Le Havre, 111, 114, 125, 271
Lebensraum, 12–13, 23, 63, 64, 286
Ledo, 248, 252, 254
Leeb, Field Marshal Wilhelm von, 89, 137, 158, 161, 164
Leigh-Mallory, Air Vice Marshal Sir Trafford, 152, 259
Leith-Ross, Sir Frederick, 125
Leningrad, 75, 77, 89, 92, 93, 110, 155, 160–161, 167, 169, 171, 175
Lewin, Ronald, 17, 36, 43, 97
Ley, Robert, 6
Liberal Party, 7
Libya, 76, 78, 90, 178–181, 198
Licata, 201, 203
Lichtenstein radar, 232, 237
Liddell Hart, Captain Sir Basil, 53
Liège, 274, 276, 278
Lightfoot operation. *See* El Alamein
Lindemann, Sir Frederick (Lord Cherwell), 9, 262
List, Field Marshal Wilhelm, 92, 122, 166, 168
Lithuania, 71, 121, 124
Little, Admiral Sir Charles, 259
Lloyd George, David, 1

Local Defence Volunteers, British, 147–148
Lohr, General Alexander, 122, 158
Loire River, 109, 266
Long-range aircraft, 209–210, 212, 217–220, 222
Lord Halifax, 143
Lossberg, Lt. Col. Bernhard von, 155
Louvain, 132
Low Countries, 66, 68–69, 120, 152, 263, 288. *See also* Belgium; Netherlands
Lübeck air raid (Mar 1942), 229, 232
Luftwaffe. See German air force; individual units
Lulea, 128
Lütterade, 234
Lüttich, 274
Luxemburg, 67, 72, 137, 274
Lvov, 160
Lyme Bay, 146–147
Lyme Regis, 146

Madeira Islands, 74
Magic intelligence, 100–101, 261
Maginot Line, 124, 142
Maikop, 167
Maisky, Ivan, 21
Malaya, 81
Malmedy, 137
Malta, 80, 88, 92, 129, 178, 180, 182, 187–188, 191, 198, 202, 228, 279
Mandalay, 116, 255
Manila, 81
Manipur, 253
Manseck, submarine commander, 215
Manstein, General Erich von, 4, 30, 42, 51, 92, 122, 135, 167, 169, 171–172, 174–175
Manteuffel, General Hasso von, 277
Marcks, General Erich, 155
Marder 1 operation, 109
Marder 2 operation, 108
Marseilles, 125
Marshall, General George C., 44, 91, 115, 198, 258
Mason, Timothy, 13
Mayu Mountains, 250
Mediterranean strategy, 40–41, 90–91, 94, 96–97, 103–104, 106, 118, 197–199, 256–257, 290–291
Mein Kampf, 3, 12
Meisel, Admiral Wilhelm, 211
Merrill, Colonel Frank, 254
Mers-el-Kebir, 144
Messervy, General Frank, 253
Messina, 202, 204–205
Meuse River, 70, 115, 132, 135, 137, 139, 274, 277, 279, 281
Mewcerts, 126
Middle Eastern Air Command, 230

Middlebrook, Martin, 234–235
Midway battle, 88, 100
Milch, Field Marshal Erhard, 59, 237
Military Attack Command on Special Assignment, 276
Military strategy, definition, 62–63
"Milk" cows, 211–212
Millenium operation. *See* Cologne air raid
Ministerial Committee on Military Coordination, British, 35–36
Ministry for Armaments and War Production, German, 32–33
Ministry of Economic Warfare, British, 125–131
Minsk, 155, 160
Mitchell, General William, 244
Mius River, 174–175
Model, General Walter, 4, 172, 174, 274
Molotov, Vyacheslav, 75
Montgomery, General Sir Bernard, 42, 44, 100, 115, 192–196, 201–202, 259, 260, 270, 277, 279, 281, 283–284
Moore, Admiral Sir Henry, 218
Morgan, General Frederick, 106, 257–258
Morocco, 93, 195
Mortain counteroffensive, German, 100
Morton, Desmond, 9, 44
Moscow, 75, 77, 83, 155–156, 160–161, 163–164, 186; counteroffensive, 16, 162–165; meeting (Oct 1943), 105, 107, 258
Mt. Etna, 204
Mountbatten, Admiral Lord Louis, 37, 43, 247, 249–250
Morell, Theo, 6
Mulberry harbors, 260, 270
Müller, Klaus-Jürgen, 52
München-Gladbach, 282
Murmansk convoy, 57
Murray, Williamson, 66, 240, 242
Mussolini, Benito, 57, 71, 74, 85, 88, 135, 187–189, 191, 258, 287, 293; removed, 103, 204
Mustang aircraft, 238, 243
Myitkyina, 250, 254–255, 285

Naguma, Admiral Chuichi, 88
Nantes, 257
Naples, 104
Narvik, 67–69, 128
Naval Auxiliary Patrols, British, 147
Naval High Command, German. *See Oberkommando der Kriegsmarine*/OKM
Naval support groups, Allied, 209, 218–220
Navicerts, 126
Navy Group West, German, 267
Nazi-Soviet pact (Aug 1939(, 64, 122
Netherlands, 64–65, 67–69, 72, 127, 131–133, 135, 256, 264, 266, 275, 281; capitulation, 70, 138–139; war trade agreement, 121

Netherlands forces, 132, 135, 136, 202, 252
Neurath, Konstantin von, 4
Neuss, 282
New York, 222
Newall, Air Chief Marshal Sir Cyril, 37, 48
Newfoundland, 212, 222
Nijmegen, 279–283
Ninth Bombardment Command, United States, 281
Noble, Admiral Sir Percy, 47, 221
Normandy campaign. *See* Overlord campaign
Norrie, General Willoughby, 180
North Africa, 8, 17, 29, 66, 74, 76–78, 81, 82–83, 87–88, 90–91, 93–95, 99, 133, 142, 156, 170, 177–186, 187, 191–192, 195–200, 205–206, 230, 240, 288, 290, 292. *See also* individual states
North Sea battles, 207
Northern Finland, 29
Northern Italy, 116
Northern Lights operation. *See* Leningrad
Norway, 29, 109, 113, 148–149, 177–178, 198, 208, 261; British commando raids, 16; British plans, 15; war trade agreement, 127
Norwegian campaign, 15, 28, 56, 66–68, 82, 128, 134, 135, 146, 152, 207, 288; role of intelligence, 98
Norwegian forces, 202
Nugent, General Richard, 280
Nuremberg air raid (Mar 1944), 110, 240, 243
Nuremberg Trials, 55–59, 117
Nye, General Sir Archibald, 44, 45–46

Oberbefehlshaber West. *See* Army Groups, German, B
Oberkommando der Kriegsmarine / OKM, 30–31, 56–58, 210
Oberkommando der Luftwaffe/OKL, 31–32, 56
Oberkommando der Wehrmacht/OKW, 6, 25, 27–30, 54–56, 60, 67, 75–76, 88, 109, 120–121, 155, 156, 164–165, 168, 173, 263, 269, 275; plans for Norway, 66; tank reserve, 265
Oberkommando des Heeres/OKH, 16, 25, 27–30, 50–54, 56, 60, 64, 67, 75, 77, 88, 92, 115, 121, 122–124, 134–135, 139, 155–156, 158, 164–165, 168, 171–172
Octagon conference (Sep 1943), 113–114, 279
Oder River, 116
Odessa, 110
Oise-Aisne Canal, 141
Oklhovatka, 174
Omaha Beach, 268–269
Operation Orders, German: No. 5, 171; No. 6, 172
Oppenheim, 116, 283
Oran, 126
Orel, 162, 165, 174
Organisation Todt, 264

Orkney Islands, 125
Oshima, Baron Hiroshi, 100
Osoy, 283
Ostrov, 160
Ottawa, 81
Ourthe River, 137, 277
Overlord campaign (Jun 1944), 16, 41, 96, 97, 103–105, 107–108, 110, 112, 154, 198, 200, 245–246, 250, 255, 267–273, 284, 290–291, 292; adjustments, 111; background, 255–256; preparations, 224, 236, 243, 256–267; role of intelligence, 100
Overy, Richard, 71
Oxelosund, 128
Ozymandias, 286

Pachino, 203
Pacific strategy, 40–41, 95, 97, 103, 108, 109, 116, 247, 255, 289, 290–291
Padfield, Peter, 57
Paget, General Sir Bernard, 256
Palermo, 201, 204
Pantelleria, capture of, 202
Panther operation, 171–172
Panzer Group West, 270
"Parallel war," 71
Paris, 70; liberation, 271
Park, Air Vice Marshal Keith, 152
Pas de Calais, 257, 261, 266, 271, 273
Patch, General Alexander, Jr., 100
Pathfinder force, 231–232, 238–240
Patton, General George, 202, 205, 260, 271, 277, 283
Paulus, General Friedrich, 155, 168–170
Pearl Harbor, 80
Peirse, Air Chief Marshal Sir Richard, 247
Persian corridor, 170
Pétain, Marshal Philippe, 143
Phony War, 132
Pigstick operation. *See* Akyab
Pisa-Rimini line, 258
Pitt, William (Elder), 1
Pitt, William (Younger), 1
Ploesti oil fields, 76, 129, 240
Plunder operation, 283
Po River, 114, 246
Pointblank operation. *See* Strategic bombing campaign
Poland, 65, 108, 116, 121, 121–122, 124, 131, 155
Policy making, definition, 62–63
Polish campaign, 5, 15, 28, 30–31, 64, 65–66, 82, 83, 124–125, 132, 152, 288; preparations, 120–123
Polish forces, 121–124, 180, 181, 183, 202, 266
Pomerania, 121
Port-en-Bessin, 269
Port Said, 125

Portal, Air Chief Marshal Sir Charles, 10, 17, 37, 42–43, 50, 94, 117, 194, 228, 230, 232, 236, 262; character, 48–49
Portugal, 74, 109, 265
Pound, First Sea Lord Sir Dudley, 10, 17, 37, 38, 42–43, 45, 50, 61, 90, 144, 210, 211, 214, 225, 230; character, 46–47
Pownall, General Sir Henry, 21, 139, 247
PQ 17 convoy, 43, 47
Prince of Wales, 47, 81
Pripet Marshes, 155, 160
Prize Court, 126
Production: Allied, 101; British, 84, 101–102, 207, 235, 241, 244, 291; German, 64, 84, 95, 101–102, 208–209, 223, 236, 242–243, 244, 291; United States, 235, 241, 244
Prokhorovka, 174

Quadrant conference (Aug 1943), 97, 103–104, 118, 249, 257–258, 260
Queen Elizabeth, 219
Queen Mary, 219
Quesada, General Elwood, 100

Radar, 16, 65, 149, 209, 212, 220, 222, 227, 229–231, 232, 234; Gee, 229, 233; H2S (H2X), 230–231, 238, 239; Oboe, 230–231, 238
Radtke, Seaman First Class, 215
Raeder, Grand Admiral Erich, 4, 31, 50, 58, 61, 87, 95, 146; character, 56–57
Ragusa, 201
Ramree Island, 248
Ramsay, Admiral Sir Bertram, 202, 259
Ramsgate, 125, 129, 145, 146
Rangoon, 116, 246, 254–255
Rankin plan, 94
Rathenau, Walter, 33
Red Army, 77, 79, 87, 89, 92, 101, 103, 110, 116–117, 156, 158, 160–163, 165, 166–169, 172–176, 275, 288, 290; enters Poland, 124
Red operation. *See* Battle of France
Rees, 280, 283
Regiments, German, 161
Reichenau, General Walter von, 123, 158
Reichstag, 146
Reichswald, 280, 282
Remagen, 116, 283
Rennes, 266
Replacement army, German, 27–28
Repulse, 47, 81
Rest and Refitting Staff, 16, 276
Reynaud, Paul, 70, 132, 136, 139, 141–143
Rhine River, 115–116, 144, 246, 275, 278, 279–281, 283
Rhineland, 229
Rhodes, 104, 108

Ribbentrop, Joachim von, 4, 71, 75, 121
Richards, Sir Denis, 48
Richards, Colonel Hugh, 253
Riefenstal, Leni, 3
Riga, 160
Rintelen, General Enno von, 191
Ritchie, General Neil, 183, 189
Road Watch operation, 197
Roer River, 279–282
Rohwer, Jürgen, 208
Romania, 69, 71, 75, 113, 129, 156–157
Romanian forces, 92, 156, 165–166, 173
Rommel, General Erwin, 4, 42, 80, 82, 86, 88, 91, 99, 100, 206, 264–266, 271; command in western Europe, 110
Rommel Asparagus, 265
Roosevelt, President Franklin D., 1, 39, 40, 49, 79–81, 91, 94–95, 106–109, 113–114, 116, 200–201, 210, 249, 258–259, 293
Roskill, Sir Stephen, 17, 47, 224
Rostock air raid, 229, 232
Rostov, 155, 167
Roundup plan, 91, 256–257
Royal Air Force, 38, 76, 124, 131, 133, 144, 147–152. *See also* individual units
Royal Navy, 38, 46–48, 72. *See also* individual units
Ruhr area, 67, 115, 226, 229, 237, 283; air raids, 238
Rundstedt, Field Marshal Gerd von, 53, 89, 105, 110, 122, 137, 139–140, 158, 164, 168, 204, 265–266, 271, 274, 275
Russo-Finnish War, 68, 86, 128, 161
Rzhev salient, 51, 170

St. Lô, 271, 273
St. Paul's School briefing, 259
St. Tropez, 113
St. Vith, 276–278
Salmuth, General Hans von, 122
San Stefano, 205
Sardinia, 95, 103, 198–199, 203; possible assault, 97
Scapa Flow, 16
Schall-Riaucour, Countess Heidemarie, 51
Scheldt River, 139
Schlieffen plan, 67, 134
Schmidt, General Rudolf, 161
Schmundt, General Rudolf, 28
Schoppmann-Ketting, Radioman Third Class, 215
Schreiber, Gerhard, 76
Schweinfurt air raid (Oct 1943), 104, 237, 240
Schweitzer, Albert, 2
Sciacca, 200
Scoglitti, 203
Scoones, General Sir Geoffrey, 253
Scotland, 260

Sea Lion operation. *See* Battle of Britain
Seaton, Albert, 172
Second Argonaut conference. *See* Yalta conference
Second Quebec conference. *See* Octagon conference
Second Washington conference. *See* Argonaut conference (Jun 1942)
Sedan, 135, 137, 139
Seine River, 266
Semmering, 195
Senior Officer of Escort (SOE), 213
Sevastopol, 92, 166
Sextant conference. *See* Cairo conferences
Shaw, George Bernard, 143
Shuttle bombing, 106
Sichelschnitt operation, 136
Sicily, 76, 103, 185
Sicily campaign, 94–95, 97, 154, 177, 198, 203–206, 256–257, 273, 289–290, 292; preparations, 198–203
Sidi Rezegh, 180, 183
Silesia, 121
Simpson, General William, 280–284
Singleton, Justice John E., 229–230
Siracusa, 201, 203
Skorzeny, Lt. Col. Otto, 277
Sledgehammer plan, 90, 256, 273
Slim, General Sir William, 42, 116, 255
Slovak forces, 92, 157, 166
Slovakia, 75, 113
Smith, General Walter Bedell, 201, 259
Smolensk, 76, 104, 155, 160, 175
Snorkel, 223
Soissons, 271
Somerville, Admiral Sir James, 247
Somme River, 137, 141
Southeast Asia Command, 103, 249, 252. *See also* Mountbattan, Admiral Lord Louis
Southern France, 204. *See also* French Riviera campaign
Soviet air force, 156
Soviet-Japanese neutrality pact (Apr 1941), 156
Soviet offensive (Jan 1945), 278
Soviet Union, 4, 15, 17, 21, 40, 50, 52, 65, 68, 71–77, 79–80, 83–84, 96–90, 93, 94–97, 99, 103, 105–110, 112–114, 117–118, 121, 127, 129–130, 146, 153–157, 163–165, 175, 186, 204, 229, 258, 263, 287–292
Spaatz, General Carl, 262
Spain, 74, 77, 87, 264; possible Allied operation, 95
Spanish Blue division, 166, 173
Spanish Morocco, 74
Spears, General Edward, 142–143
Special Liaison Unit, British, 100
Speer, Albert, 2, 16, 32–33, 59, 172, 242

Sperrle, Field Marshal Hugo, 148
Spitzbergen expedition, 163
Stalin, Josef, 79, 90, 93–94, 105–108, 115–117, 157, 170, 176, 192, 201, 256, 258, 293
Stalingrad, 7, 53, 59, 92–93, 95, 165, 167–171, 290
"Static" divisions, German, 265
Statutory List, 126
Stilwell, General Joseph, 248, 250, 254
Strang, Sir William, 10, 62
Strategic bombing campaign, 17, 31, 59, 65, 79, 82–83, 90, 93–94, 102–103, 106, 108, 110–111, 113, 116, 118–119, 197, 207, 226–245, 256, 289, 290, 292
Strauss, General Adolf, 158
Stumpff, General Hans-Jürgen, 148
Submarine tracking room, 211
Suez Canal, 88
Sumatra, 112, 249
Supercharge operation. *See* El Alamein
Supreme Commander, Allied Expeditionary Force (SCAEF), 106
Supreme Commander, Mediterranean (SACMED), 106
Supreme War Council, Anglo-French, 39, 132, 143
Sweden, 128; war trade agreement, 127
Swedish iron ore, 66, 128, 129
Symbol conference. *See* Casablanca conference (Jan 1943)
Syria, 78, 82, 177, 178

Tactical air commands, United States, 100, 280–283
Tactical air forces, 205, 262
Tactical Air Forces, British, 270, 280, 282, 283
Taganrog, 163
Taiwan, 254
Takoradi air route, 80, 178, 193
Tame Boar tactic, 237–238
Tanks: British, 144, 181–182, 190, 194; French, 136, 144; German, 123, 127, 134, 136, 144, 157, 172–174, 181–182, 189, 194, 203, 266, 276; Soviet, 176
Tedder, Air Chief Marshal Sir Arthur, 111, 181–182, 194, 200–202, 259, 262
Tehran conference (Nov–Dec 1943) 105–109, 118, 258, 291
Ten Downing Street, 11
Terraine, John, 48, 192
Theseus operation. *See* Gazala operation
Third Washington conference (May 1943). *See* Trident conference
Tobruk, 78, 88, 91, 178–181, 183, 185, 187–189, 190–191, 198
Todt, Fritz, 32–33, 71
Torch operation (Nov 1942), 92, 93, 170, 195–

199, 205, 256, 280, 291–292
Tours, 142
Transportation plan, 262
Trenchard, Air Marshal Sir Hugh, 244
Trident conference (May 1943), 96–97, 218, 222, 248–249, 257
Triona, 205
Tripartite Pact (Sep 1940), 75, 81
Tripoli, 228
Tripolitania, 186
Triton naval code, German, 100
Trondheim, 69
Tunisia, 196–197, 200–202, 228, 289
Turkey, 77, 94, 106–108
Typhoon operation (Sep 1941), 77, 154, 158, 161–163

U-Boat Command, 211–212, 214, 217
U-boats, 31, 57–58, 64, 86, 116, 127, 208–210, 211–220, 222–223, 225; types, 211, 223
Ukraine, 5, 77, 110, 160, 161–162, 168
Ultra intelligence, 18, 73, 90, 98–101, 144, 149, 182, 185–186, 189, 197, 205–206, 208, 209–210, 212, 214–216, 218, 220–222, 232, 261, 266, 270, 278, 281, 282. *See also* Intelligence, British
Umbreit, Hans, 124
Unconditional surrender, 95, 275
Union of Soviet Socialist Republics (USSR). *See* Soviet Union
"United Chiefs of Staff" idea, 40
United Nations, 116
United States, 4, 20–21, 48–50, 65, 71, 72, 74–75, 78–84, 86, 89–91, 93, 96–97, 104–110, 112, 114–116, 118, 129, 153, 163–164, 170, 176, 186, 190, 197–198, 202, 206, 215, 222, 246–248, 255, 272, 287–288, 291–292; as British ally, 39–40; supplies from, 193
United States forces, 204–205, 211, 221, 236, 252, 254, 258, 266, 267, 270, 272, 274–276, 278, 284
United States Strategic Air Forces in Europe, 262
Urdingen, 283
Uruguay, 129–130

V-E Day, 117
V-1 flying bombs, 105, 112, 237, 271, 276
V-2 rockets, 32, 105, 112–113, 237, 276
V-weapons, 26
Van Creveld, Martin, 5, 15, 76
Venezia operation. *See* Gazala operation
Venlo, 281
Veritable operation (Feb 1945), 116, 246, 281–284; preparations, 279–281
Vest, Captain, 224
Via Balbia, 197

Vichy France, 71, 74, 78
Vinnitsa, 168
Vistula River, 124
Volchansk, 166
Volga River, 156, 167–168
Voronezh, 165–167
Vosges Mountains, 114
Vyasma, 162, 170

W-4 plan, 131
Waffen-SS, 32–33, 34
Waite, Robert, 5
War Cabinet, British, 35–37, 61, 68, 75, 132, 193, 262
War Department, United States, 256
War Office, British, 43, 45, 127
War Office, German, 30
Warlimont, General Walter, 25, 29, 55, 60
Warsaw, 121, 123–124
Watch on the Rhine operation. *See* Ardennes campaign (Dec 1944)
Wavell, Field Marshal Sir Archibald, 10, 18, 80, 178, 248
Wavre, 132
Webster, Sir Charles K., 93, 233
Weeks, General Ronald, 45
Wehrmacht Office, 30, 55
Weichs, Field Marshal Maximilian von, 92, 158, 161, 167
Weinberg, Gerhard, 19
Werewolf headquarters, 5
West Wall, 280
Western Approaches Command, British, 211, 221, 225
Western Desert Air Force, British, 196
Western Pacific, 81
Westphal, General Siegfried, 275
Weygand, General Maxime, 140, 142
Weymouth, 125, 129
Wheatley, Ronald, 73
Whipcord operation, 198–199
White operation. *See* Polish campaign
Wild Boar tactic, 237–238
Window antiradar strips, 237–238, 239
Wingate, Lt. Col. Orde, 249, 254
Winn, Captain Rodger, 211, 220–221
Winter War. *See* Russo-Finnish War
Witzleben, Field Marshal Erwin von, 264
Wolff, SS General Karl, 34
Wolfpacks, 212, 214, 215–216, 217
Wolf's Lair headquarters, 5
Würzburg radar, 227

Xanten, 116, 280, 283, 285

Yalta conference (Feb 1945), 116, 118, 279

Yellow operation. *See* Battle of France
Yugoslavia, 76, 78, 82, 104, 107, 156
Yunnan, 248, 254

Z-plan, 64
Zeitzler, General Kurt, 25, 28, 30, 50, 54, 60,
    117, 168, 172–173; as chief of staff, 52–54;

named chief of staff, 92
Zeppelin deception, 260–261
Zhukov, Marshal Georgi, 117
Ziemke, Earl, 167
Zitomir, 160
Zuckerman, Lord, 245